Programming with Microsoft® Visual Basic® 6.0:
An Object-Oriented Approach–Comprehensive

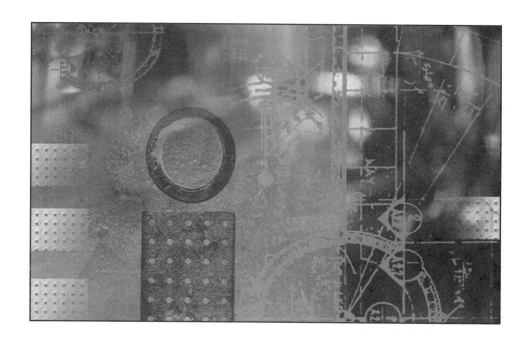

Michael V. Ekedahl

William A. Newman

COURSE
TECHNOLOGY

ONE MAIN STREET, CAMBRIDGE, MA 02142

an International Thomson Publishing company I T P®

Cambridge • Albany • Bonn • Boston • Cincinnati • London • Madrid • Melbourne • Mexico City
New York • Paris • San Francisco • Singapore • Tokyo • Toronto • Washington

Programming with Microsoft Visual Basic 6.0: An Object-Oriented Approach—Comprehensive is published by Course Technology.

Associate Publisher	Kristen Duerr
Product Managers	Cheryl Ouellette
	Margarita Donovan
Production Editor	Catherine G. DiMassa
Developmental Editors	Jill Batistick
	Kate Habib
Text Designer	Kim Munsell
Cover Designer	Efrat Reis

© 1999 by Course Technology— I⟨T⟩P®

For more information contact:

Course Technology, Inc.
One Main Street
Cambridge, MA 02142

International Thomson Editores
Seneca, 53
Colonia Polanco
11560 Mexico D.F. Mexico

ITP Europe
Berkshire House 168-173
High Holborn
London WCIV 7AA
England

ITP GmbH
Königswinterer Strasse 418
53227 Bonn
Germany

Nelson ITP, Australia
102 Dodds Street
South Melbourne, 3205
Victoria, Australia

ITP Asia
60 Albert Street, #15-01
Albert Complex
Singapore 189969

ITP Nelson Canada
1120 Birchmount Road
Scarborough, Ontario
Canada M1K 5G4

ITP Japan
Hirakawacho Kyowa Building, 3F
2-2-1 Hirakawacho
Chiyoda-ku, Tokyo 102
Japan

All rights reserved. This publication is protected by federal copyright law. No part of this publication may be reproduced, stored in a retrieval system, or transmitted in any form or by any means, electronic, mechanical, photocopying, recording, or otherwise, or be used to make a derivative work (such as translation or adaptation), without prior permission in writing from Course Technology.

Trademarks
Course Technology and the Open Book logo are registered trademarks and CourseKits is a trademark of Course Technology. Custom Editions and the ITP logo are registered trademarks of International Thomson Publishing Inc.

I⟨T⟩P® The ITP logo is a registered trademark of International Thomson Publishing.

Microsoft, Visual Basic, and Windows are registered trademarks of Microsoft Corporation.

Some of the product names and company names used in this book have been used for identification purposes only and may be trademarks or registered trademarks of their respective manufacturers and sellers.

Disclaimer
Course Technology reserves the right to revise this publication and make changes from time to time in its content without notice.

ISBN 0-7600-1076-5

Printed in the United States of America

6 7 8 9 10 BAW 02 01

Preface

Programming with Microsoft Visual Basic 6.0: An Object-Oriented Approach—Comprehensive is designed to provide the beginning Visual Basic programmer with the tools to create Visual Basic applications that conform to well-adopted Windows standards. This textbook assumes that students have little or no programming experience. It assumes familiarity with basic Windows 95 or Windows 98 concepts.

Organization and Coverage

Programming with Microsoft Visual Basic 6.0: An Object-Oriented Approach—Comprehensive begins by discussing how to get started using Visual Basic. No previous experience with Visual Basic is required, although any experience with Basic will be helpful.

Once the reader understands how to maneuver in Visual Basic, *Programming with Microsoft Visual Basic 6.0: An Object-Oriented Approach—Comprehensive* presents:

- Code and understanding variables, including examples related to creating expressions and calling functions.
- Objects and the events they generate, including a simple event model.
- Creating a program to manage data, including how to create a database.
- ActiveX database controls and an introduction to SQL.
- Windows Common Controls including the toolbar and status bar controls.
- MDI and class module programming.

Programming with Microsoft Visual Basic 6.0: An Object-Oriented Approach—Comprehensive also includes three appendices on the following topics: debugging, wizards, and creating databases using Microsoft Access.

Features

Programming with Microsoft Visual Basic 6.0: An Object-Oriented Approach—Comprehensive is a superior textbook because it also includes the following features:

- **"Read This Before You Begin" Page** This page is consistent with Course Technology's unequaled commitment to helping instructors introduce technology into the classroom. Technical considerations and assumptions about hardware, software, and default settings are listed in one place to help instructors save time.
- **Case Approach** Each chapter addresses programming-related problems that students could reasonably expect to encounter in business. Each case is followed by a demonstration of an application that could be used to solve the problem. Showing students the completed application before they learn how to create it is motivational and instructionally sound. When students see the type of application they will create in the chapter, they learn more effectively because they can see how the programming concepts in the chapter can be used and, therefore, why the concepts are important.

- **Step-by-Step Methodology** The unique Course Technology methodology keeps students on track. They write program code always within the context of solving the problems posed in the chapter. The text constantly guides students and lets them know where they are in the process of solving the problem. The numerous illustrations guide students to create useful, working programs.

- **Help** These paragraphs anticipate the problems students are likely to encounter and help them resolve these problems on their own. This feature facilitates independent learning and frees the instructor to focus on substantive issues rather than on common procedural errors.

- **Tips** These notes provide additional information on Graphical User Interface (GUI) design, programming, and computer performance—for example, an alternative method of performing a procedure, background information on a technique, or a commonly-made error to watch out for.

- **Questions** Each section concludes with meaningful, conceptual review questions that test students' understanding of what they learned in the chapter. These questions are divided into two types: multiple choice questions and short answer questions that require the student to write small code segments.

- **Summaries** Following each chapter is a Summary that recaps the programming concepts and commands covered in each section.

- **Exercises** Each chapter concludes with programming Exercises that give students additional practice with the skills and concepts they learned in the lesson. These exercises increase in difficulty and are designed to allow the student to explore the language and programming environment independently.

The Visual Basic Environment

This book was written using Microsoft's Visual Basic Release 6.0—Professional Edition installed on a Windows 95 personal computer. The Enterprise Edition of Visual Basic 6.0 will produce the same results. Specific instructions for installing Visual Basic are provided in the Instructor's Manual.

Teaching Tools

All of the teaching tools for this text are found in the Instructor's Resource Kit CD-ROM, which is also available on Course Technology's Web site. Additional teaching tools, including standardized naming conventions, can also be found on the same Web site.

- **Instructor's Manual** The Instructor's Manual was written by the author and thoroughly quality assurance tested. It is available through the Course Technology Faculty Online Companion on the World Wide Web at *www.course.com*. (Call your customer service representative for the specific URL and your password.) The Instructor's Manual contains the following items:
  - Answers to all of the Review Questions and solutions to all of the Exercises in the book.
  - Teaching notes to help introduce and clarify the material presented in the chapters.
  - Technical notes that include troubleshooting tips.

- **Course Test Manager Version 1.2 Engine and Test Bank** Course Test Manager (CTM) is a cutting-edge Windows-based testing software program, developed exclusively for Course Technology, that helps instructors design and administer examinations and practice tests. This full-featured program allows students to generate practice tests randomly that provide immediate on-screen feedback and detailed study guides for incorrectly answered questions. Instructors can also use Course Test Manager to create printed and online tests over a network. You can create, preview, and administer a test on any or all chapters of this textbook entirely over a local area network. Course Test Manager can automatically grade the tests students take at the computer and generate statistical information on individual as well as group performance. A CTM test bank has been written to accompany this textbook and is included on the Instructor's Resource Kit CD-ROM. The test bank includes multiple-choice, true/false, short answer, and essay questions.
- **Solutions Files** Solutions Files contain a possible solution to every program students are asked to create or modify in the chapters and cases. (Due to the nature of programming, students' solutions might differ from these solutions and still be correct.)
- **Student Files** Student Files, containing all of the data that students will use for the chapters and exercises in this textbook, are provided through Course Technology's Online Companion and on the Instructor's Resource Kit CD-ROM. A Help file includes technical tips for lab management. See the inside covers of this textbook and the "Read This Before You Begin" page before Chapter 1 for more information on Student Files.

Acknowledgments

Our appreciation goes to each of the reviewers whose suggestions and comments help to create this book. We would like to especially thank Michael Walton for his work as a reviewer. We would like to thank all the members of the Course Technology team who helped guide the book's development and production, and the staff at GEX for their fine work.

Special thanks to Kate Habib and Jill Batistick for their valuable suggestions and efforts as developmental editors, and to Cindy Johnson for her efforts. We would also like to thank Brian Munroe for his help.

Michael V. Ekedahl would like to thank his dog Rio for his constant companionship and amusing distraction. William A. Newman thanks his wife Anthea and mother-in-law Annette Karnas for their encouragement and support, and dedicates this book to his late father and mother, Mr. Robert H. Newman and Mrs. Irene Newman.

Michael V. Ekedahl
William A. Newman

Brief Contents

chapter 1

GETTING STARTED WITH VISUAL BASIC *1*

chapter 2

UNDERSTANDING CODE AND VARIABLES *59*

chapter 3

DECISION MAKING *117*

chapter 4

OBJECTS AND THE EVENTS THEY GENERATE *165*

chapter 5

CREATING A PROGRAM TO MANAGE DATA *205*

chapter 6

REPETITION AND MULTIPLE FORMS *265*

chapter 7

READING AND WRITING TEXT FILES INTO LIST BOXES AND ARRAYS *311*

extra case 1

UTILITY SOLUTIONS *365*

extra case 2

INDUSTRIAL PAPER *368*

extra case 3

COMPUTRONICS *372*

chapter 8

EXAMINING DATABASE OBJECTS AND THE STRUCTURED QUERY LANGUAGE (SQL) *377*

chapter 9

USING CUSTOM CONTROLS TO OPEN FILES AND TO INTERACT WITH A DATABASE *437*

chapter 10

WINDOWS COMMON CONTROLS *495*

chapter 11

CREATING A MULTIPLE-DOCUMENT APPLICATION *549*

chapter 12

PROGRAMMING WITH CLASS *613*

chapter 13

COMPILING AND DISTRIBUTING PROGRAMS *665*

extra case 4

MONARCH ROOFING *705*

extra case 5

LYONS BANK *715*

appendix A

DEBUGGING *A-1*

appendix B

VISUAL BASIC WIZARDS *A-17*

appendix C

DATABASE DESIGN *A-28*

index *I-1*

Contents

PREFACE *iii*
READ THIS BEFORE YOU BEGIN *xxiii*

chapter 1

GETTING STARTED WITH VISUAL BASIC *1*
Creating a New Program for Southern Properties Group *1*

Section A: Understanding the Parts of the Visual Basic User Interface *2*
    Understanding Visual Basic and Its Role in the Computer Industry *2*
    Learning the Logic Structure of Visual Basic *3*
    Starting Visual Basic *6*
        The Menu Bar and Toolbar *8*
    Planning a Program *9*
    Opening an Existing Project *10*
    Exploring Operating Modes *11*
        Running a Program *12*
        Stopping a Program *13*
    Identifying the Components of the Visual Basic Environment *13*
        Project Explorer *14*
        The Form Window *16*
        Properties Window *16*
        Toolbox *17*
    Accessing the Visual Basic Help Library *17*
        Using the Index Tab *18*
        Using the Table of Contents *21*
    Exiting Visual Basic *22*
    Questions *23*

Section B: Creating a New Program *25*
    Creating a New Project *25*
        Setting the Caption and Name Properties for a Form *27*

Saving the Project *29*
   Setting the Size and Position of a Form *31*
Creating Control Instances on a Form *32*
   Adding a Label Control Instance *33*
      Setting a Label's Properties *34*
      Moving a Label Object *35*
      Resizing an Object *36*
      Deleting an Object *37*
   The TextBox Control *38*
   The CommandButton Control *39*
   The Image Control *40*
Using the Code Window *42*
   Entering the Code for the Command Button *42*
Running the Completed Program *46*
Compiling a Program *48*
Summary *48*
Questions *52*
Exercises *53*

chapter 2

UNDERSTANDING CODE AND VARIABLES *59*

Designing and Writing a Financial Calculator Progam for the Island
Financial Company *59*

   Previewing the Calculator Program *60*

Section A: Designing and Modifying a Program *62*
  Designing a Computer Progam *62*
    Program Design Methodologies *62*
    Designing the User Interface *63*
  Expanding Your Knowledge of Controls *65*
    The Label Control *65*
    Changing Multiple Control Instances with the Property Window *66*
    The CommandButton Control *69*
    Changing Multiple Control Instances with the Format Menu Commands *71*
    The TextBox Control *72*

Setting the Tab Order *73*

Improving the User Interface with Graphical Controls *75*

The Shape Control *75*

The Line Control *77*

Questions *78*

Section B: Statements and Expressions *80*

Creating Well-Written Comments *80*

Text Box Events *81*

Looking Up Intrinsic Constants with the Object Browser *83*

Variables *87*

Declaring a Variable *89*

Declaring Module-Level Variables *91*

Using Expressions and Operators to Manipulate Variables *92*

Type Conversion Functions *95*

Formatting a Numeric Value with the Format Function *96*

Using the Future Value Function *99*

Explicitly Setting the Focus *102*

Solving Programming Errors *103*

Fixing Syntax Errors *104*

Fixing Run-Time Errors *104*

Printing a Program *105*

Summary *107*

Questions *109*

Exercises *110*

c h a p t e r   3

DECISION MAKING   *117*

Validating Input Data *117*

Previewing the Input Validation Program *118*

Section A: Validating User Input *120*

Input Validation *120*

Using Boolean Data *120*

Classification Functions *121*

Decision Making *122*

   Using Comparison Operators and the If Statement *123*

   Nested If Statements *126*

The Select Case Statement *129*

   Logical Operators *132*

   String Data *134*

   Date Data *140*

Questions *143*

Section B: Message Boxes and General Procedures *145*

The MsgBox Function *145*

Procedures *148*

Sub Procedures *153*

   Understanding Call by Value and Call by Reference *155*

Summary *156*

Questions *159*

Exercises *160*

chapter 4

OBJECTS AND THE EVENTS THEY GENERATE *165*

Developing an Event-Driven Cash Register Program for Master Burger *165*

Previewing the Cash Register Program *166*

Section A: Controls That Use Mouse Input *168*

Expanding the Visual Basic Event Model *168*

The CheckBox Object *168*

Adding Scroll Bars to the Form *171*

Choosing the Right Control *174*

Creating a Frame *174*

Creating Option Buttons *176*

Creating a Control Array *177*

Understanding the Change Event *181*

Creating User-Defined Constants *185*

Questions *188*

Section B: Working with Events *190*

Writing Code for Control Arrays *190*

Form Events *191*

Computing the Total *192*

Printing a Form Image *196*

Summary *197*

Questions *198*

Exercises *199*

chapter 5

CREATING A PROGRAM TO MANAGE DATA *205*

Developing a Contact Management System for Atlantic Marketing *205*

Previewing the Completed Program *206*

Section A: Creating a Menu System *208*

Adding Menus to a Program *208*

Creating the Menu Titles for the Contact Management System *209*

Creating Menu Items *211*

Creating Submenus with Separator Bars and Shortcut Keys *213*

Creating an Event Procedure for a Menu Item *216*

Questions *217*

Section B: Working with a Database *219*

Understanding How Visual Basic Uses a Database *219*

Using the Data Control to Open a Database *220*

The Recordset Object *223*

Objects and Their Methods *225*

Using Bound Controls *225*

Understanding the Beginning of File and the End of File *233*

Adding, Updating, and Deleting Database Records *236*

Adding New Database Records *236*

Updating Existing Database Records *237*

Deleting Database Records *241*

Questions *242*

Section C: Locating Database Records *243*

    Searching for Records *243*

        Locating a Record Using an Input Box *243*

    Verifying the Correctness of Data with the Validate Event *247*

    Developing an Either Handler *251*

    Trapping Errors Resulting from an Update Statement *252*

    Summary *255*

    Questions *257*

    Exercises *258*

chapter 6

REPETITION AND MULTIPLE FORMS *265*

Creating a Statistical Analysis System for Pacific Bank *265*

    Previewing the Loan Amortization Program *266*

Section A: Working with Multiple Forms *268*

    Adding an Existing Form to the Program *268*

    The Startup Object *270*

    Displaying and Unloading Forms *272*

    The Timer Control *273*

    Hiding a Form *275*

    Repetition Statements *276*

        The Do Statement *276*

        The For Statement *279*

    Refreshing Forms and Controls *283*

    Public Variables *283*

    Questions *286*

Section B: Printing Reports *287*

    Designing a Report *287*

    Implementing the Report Design *288*

    Printing a Report with the Printer Object *288*

        The Print Method and Printer Buffer *290*

Formatting the Page and Column Titles *292*

Printing the Amortization Schedule (Detail Lines) *297*

Printing the Detail Lines *299*

Printing a New Page *302*

Printing Graphical Objects *303*

Summary *305*

Questions *306*

Exercises *307*

chapter 7

READING AND WRITING TEXT FILES INTO LIST BOXES AND ARRAYS *311*

Creating a Quotation System for Star Plant Supply *311*

Previewing the Quotation System *312*

Section A: Working with Lists of Data *314*

The ComboBox Control *314*

The ListBox Control *317*

Processing Text Files *319*

Opening a Text File *319*

Reading a Text File *320*

The AddItem Method *323*

Closing a Text File *324*

Creating an Array to Store Information *326*

Storing Information in an Array *328*

Looping Through the Items in a List Box *335*

Questions *339*

Section B: Doing More with List Boxes and Arrays *340*

Modifying the Program *340*

Clearing the Contents of a List Box *340*

Removing a Specific Item from a List Box *342*

Creating a Two-Dimensional Array *345*

Adding Pictures to a Form *349*

Arrays of Variant Data *349*

Writing to a Text File *352*
Summary *356*
Questions *358*
Exercises *359*

e x t r a   c a s e   1

UTILITY SOLUTIONS *365*
Creating a Calculator *365*

e x t r a   c a s e   2

INDUSTRIAL PAPER *368*
Creating an Inventory Management System *368*

e x t r a   c a s e   3

COMPUTRONICS *372*
Creating a Customer Service Survey *372*

c h a p t e r   8

EXAMINING DATABASE OBJECTS AND THE STRUCTURED QUERY LANGUAGE (SQL) *377*
Creating a Payroll Program for Paymaster *377*
Previewing the Completed Payroll Application *378*

Section A: Creating and Using Recordsets Programmatically *380*
Preparing to Use Data Access Objects *380*
The DAO Hierarchy *381*
Default Methods and Properties *383*

Opening a Database Programmatically 385

Programming the Recordset Object 387

Referencing the Fields in the Recordset Object 390

Calling the Methods of the Recordset Object 393

Questions 395

Section B: Writing SQL Statements 397

Writing SQL Statements 397

Inserting Database Records with the INSERT Statement 398

Updating Database Records with the UPDATE Statement 404

Removing Database Records with the DELETE Statement 410

Questions 412

Section C: Selecting Data with the SELECT Statement 413

The SELECT Statement 413

Using the WHERE Clause with a SELECT Statement 424

Creating an ORDER BY Clause to Sort Records 426

Selecting Specific Fields from a Table or Query 427

Summary 429

Questions 430

Exercises 431

chapter 9

USING CUSTOM CONTROLS TO OPEN FILES AND TO INTERACT WITH A DATABASE 437

Creating an Event Registration System for Starlight Events 437

Previewing the Event Registration Program 438

Section A: An Introduction to ActiveX Controls 441

Types of Controls 441

Making an ActiveX Control Available to a Project 441

Displaying Multiple Records with the DBCombo and DBList Controls 444

Using the DBGrid Control to Display Multiple Rows and Columns 448

Changing the Behavior of the Tab Key in the DBGrid Control 451

Locating Records Programmatically *452*

Formatting Columns in the DBGrid Control *453*

Questions *462*

Section B: Programming the DBGrid and CommonDialog Controls *464*

Modifying Data with the DBGrid Control *464*

DBGrid Events and Objects *465*

Validating Data with the DBGrid Control *467*

Deleting Records with the DBGrid Control *472*

Creating an Open Dialog Using the CommonDialog Control *474*

Displaying the Open Dialog on the Screen *477*

Using the Controls Collection *480*

Understanding Screen and Printer Fonts *483*

Using the With Statement *485*

Summary *487*

Questions *488*

Exercises *489*

c h a p t e r   1 0

WINDOWS COMMON CONTROLS *495*

Creating a Part-Management System for Power Parts *495*

Previewing the Completed Application *496*

Section A: Using the Windows Common Controls *497*

Introduction to the Windows Common Controls *497*

Using the Status Bar Control *498*

Creating a Toolbar with the ImageList and Toolbar Controls *503*

Using the ImageList Control *504*

Using the Toolbar Control *508*

Using the RichTextBox Control *515*

Questions *517*

Section B: Programming the Windows Common Controls 519

Printing an RTF File 519

Opening and Saving Rich Text Files 521

Resizing a Form 528

Formatting a Rich Text Box 528

Programming a Toolbar 538

Summary 541

Questions 542

Exercises 543

chapter 11

CREATING A MULTIPLE-DOCUMENT APPLICATION 549

Creating the User Interface for ABC Concrete 549

Previewing the Completed Application 550

Section A: Multiple-Document Interface Programming 552

Creating a Multiple-Document Application (MDI) 552

Characteristics of MDI Parent Forms 553

Characteristics of MDI Child Forms 556

Understanding Object References 558

Explicitly Creating Objects 561

Hidden Variables 562

Changing the Lower Bound of an Array 564

Creating Form Properties 568

The Enum Statement 570

Questions 580

Section B: Programming Multiple Form Instances 582

Creating Multiple Instances of a Form 582

Arranging MDI Child Forms 586

Closing MDI Child Forms 587

Creating a User-Defined Type *589*

    Nesting User-Defined Types *593*

Closing an MDI Program *602*

Summary *605*

Questions *606*

Exercises *607*

chapter 12

PROGRAMMING WITH CLASS *613*

Creating an Airport Management System for Airsoft *613*

    Previewing the Completed Application *614*

Section A: Collections and Classes *616*

    Introduction to Class Modules *616*

    Creating the Properties of a Class *618*

        Using the Object Browser to Look at the Class *620*

    Creating a Collection *622*

        Adding Items to a Collection *623*

        Removing Items from a Collection *627*

        Finding an Item in a Collection *630*

    Hiding Data in a Class Module *631*

    Class Initialization *632*

    Creating Property Procedures *633*

        Creating a Read-Only Property *635*

    Questions *637*

Section B: Property Procedures and Methods *639*

    Creating Read-Write Properties *639*

        Generating a Run-Time Error *642*

        Setting the Default Property *646*

        Creating a Write-Once Property *648*

Creating a Method *649*

  Sub Methods *650*

  Function Methods *652*

Terminating a Class Instance *655*

Summary *657*

Questions *659*

Exercises *660*

chapter 13

COMPILING AND DISTRIBUTING PROGRAMS *665*

Creating a Distributable Program for MathTek *665*

  Previewing the Completed Application *666*

Section A: Program Settings and Interprogram Communication *669*

  Using the App Object *669*

  Executing Other Programs from Visual Basic *672*

  Creating an Executable Program *673*

    Advanced Optimizations *677*

  Optimizing Programs *680*

    Control Selection and Use *680*

    Data Type Selection *681*

    Array Management *681*

    Module Organization *681*

    Storing Data in Programs *681*

    Avoiding Dead Code *682*

  Questions *682*

Section B: Creating Programs for Distribution *684*

  Deploying Applications *684*

  Deploying a Package *695*

  Summary *699*

  Questions *700*

  Exercises *701*

e x t r a   c a s e   4

MONARCH ROOFING *705*
Creating an Order Entry System *705*

e x t r a   c a s e   5

LYONS BANK *715*
Creating a Customer Service Program *715*

a p p e n d i x   A

DEBUGGING *A-1*
Techniques for Resolving Errors in a Visual Basic Program *A-1*
The Visual Basic Debugging Environment *A-2*
Locating and Fixing Run-time Errors *A-4*
Tracing Program Execution *A-7*
Setting Breakpoints *A-9*
Using the Immediate Window *A-10*
Adding Watch Expressions *A-11*
Tracing Cascading Events in a Program *A-14*
The Locals Window *A-15*
Summary *A-16*

a p p e n d i x   B

VISUAL BASIC WIZARDS *A-17*
The Application Wizard *A-18*
The Data Form Wizard *A-24*
Templates *A-26*
Summary *A-27*

appendix C

DATABASE DESIGN *A-28*

The Purpose of a Database *A-28*

Designing a Database *A-29*

Creating a Database *A-31*

Creating a Table *A-31*

Creating a Relationship *A-35*

Creating a Query *A-38*

Summary *A-40*

index *I-1*

Read This Before You Begin

To the Student

Student Files

To complete the chapters and exercises in this book, you will need to download the Student Files from *www.course.com* or obtain the files from your instructor.

    If you are asked to make your own Student Files, you will need three blank, formatted high-density disks. You will need to copy a set of folders from a file server or standalone computer onto your disks. Your instructor or lab assistant will tell you which computer, drive letter, and folders contain the files you need. The following table shows you which folders go on each of your disks. If you follow these guidelines, you will have enough disk space to complete all the chapters and exercises:

Student Disk	Write this on the disk label	Put these folders on the disk
1	Chapters 1-4	Chapter.01, Chapter.02, Chapter.03, and Chapter.04
2	Chapter 5	Chapter.05
3	Chapters 6 and 7, Appendix A, Extra Cases	Chapter.06, Chapter.07, Appendix.A, ExtraCases
4	Chapter 8	Chapter.08
5	Chapters 9-10	Chapter.09 and Chapter.10
6	Chapters 11-13 and Extra Cases	Chapter.11, Chapter.12, Chapter.13 and ExtraCases

    When you begin each chapter, make sure that you are using the correct Student Files. See the Preface of this book for more information on Student Files, or ask your instructor or technical support person for assistance.

Using Your Own Computer

You can use your own computer to complete the hands-on steps in the chapters and end-of-chapter Exercises in this book. To use your own computer, you will need the following:

- **Software** Visual Basic Release 6.0—Professional or Enterprise Edition.
- **Hardware** A computer running Windows 95, Windows 98, or Windows NT 4.0 (or later).
- **Student Files** You can get the Student Files from your instructor or download them from *www.course.com*. You will not be able to complete all of the chapters and Exercises in this book using your own computer until you have the Student Files.

Visit Our World Wide Web Site

Additional materials designed especially for you might be available for your course on the World Wide Web. Go to **www.course.com**. Search for this book title periodically on the Course Technology Web site for more details.

To the Instructor

To complete all of the exercises and chapters in this book, your students must use a set of Student Files. These files are included in the Instructor's Resource Kit, as well as at *www.course.com*. Follow the instructions in the Help file to copy the Student Files to your server or standalone computer. You can view the Help file using a text editor, such as WordPad or Notepad.

    Once the files are copied, you can make Student Files for the students yourself, or tell students where to find the files so they can make their own. Make sure the files get copied correctly onto the student disks by following the instructions in the Student Files section. This will ensure that students have enough disk space to complete all of the chapters and exercises in this book.

Course Technology Student Files

You are granted a license to copy the Student Files to any computer or computer network used by students who have purchased this book.

Getting Started with Visual Basic

Creating a New Program for Southern Properties Group

case ► Southern Properties Group (SPG) leases and sells commercial real estate. The company is evaluating whether Visual Basic will be suitable as a programming language for its business applications. The development environment SPG uses must:

- Be Windows-compatible. SPG already uses many other Windows programs, and programs created with Visual Basic can include the buttons, menus, and other Windows features to which users are already accustomed.

- Have an integrated development environment (IDE). Programmers must be able to write and test programs in the same windows that the end-user will see when running the program.

- Work effectively with business data. SPG needs all new applications to interact with Microsoft Access and other databases.

To test the development environment, you will create a program that displays some of the properties SPG has for sale.

SECTION A
objectives

In this section you will:

- Understand Visual Basic and its role in the computer industry
- Learn the Visual Basic logic structure
- Start Visual Basic
- Plan a program
- Open an existing project
- Explore operating modes
- Access the Visual Basic Help library
- Exit Visual Basic

Understanding the Parts of the Visual Basic User Interface

Understanding Visual Basic and Its Role in the Computer Industry

Visual Basic is a computer programming language. A **programming language** uses words with a specific meaning, connected together in a specific order, to form a statement. A **statement** is much like a sentence in English. That is, both a statement and an English-language sentence must adhere to certain rules. The rules for English are somewhat flexible; the rules for a statement are absolute. Statements must be exactly correct and adhere to the programming rules known as **syntax**. When you assemble several statements together to accomplish a task, you create a program. A **program** is a set of statements written in a computer language in order to accomplish a specific task. Tasks can be as simple as adding a list of numbers together, or they can be as complex as navigating a satellite. In this chapter, you will use Visual Basic to create a program that will display different graphical images on the screen.

Operating systems, computers, and programming languages (such as Visual Basic) are related. Large mainframe computers typically use a proprietary operating system that is supplied by the vendor of the computer hardware itself. For example, MVS (an acronym for Multiple Virtual System) is an operating system often used on IBM mainframes. Such computers typically use the COBOL programming language as well. In contrast, minicomputers commonly use the UNIX operating system and the C programming language. Personal computers generally use **Microsoft Windows** as an operating system, in addition to the C and C++ programming languages.

Windows (whether Windows 95, Windows 98, or Windows NT) is the dominant operating system used on personal computers today. At one time, the limitations of personal computers prevented them from being accepted readily into the business community. Recent advancements in technology, however, have transformed the personal computer into a powerful tool able to solve today's business problems. Although a number of generic programs, such as Microsoft Word or Excel, can be used in the business environment, a particular company often needs to solve problems that are more specific in nature. Solving a problem specific to one business (or industry) generally involves writing a computer program.

When using a personal computer, you have several programming languages from which to choose. The C++ programming language can solve almost any problem. Its syntax, however, is difficult to learn. To overcome this problem, other languages have been created that simplify program development. One of these languages is Visual Basic, which has been continually evolving since its introduction in 1991. Visual Basic simplifies the development of Windows programs—for example, it allows the programmer to access different types of databases on a local computer or over a network. Visual Basic also supports the development of programs that operate with the Internet. Many of the tools introduced with Visual Basic 5 and Visual Basic 6 have made it possible for this programming language to solve the computational problems of small and large businesses alike. Because of its ease of use and its capabilities, Visual Basic is the most popular programming language used in the Windows environment today.

Learning the Logic Structure of Visual Basic

As noted earlier, Visual Basic simplifies the development of programs that can be used with the Windows operating system. Programs created with Visual Basic have the same characteristics as other Windows programs. Thus, the user of Visual Basic and other Windows programs interacts with the computer by clicking buttons, entering text into boxes, and so on. Each button and text box is considered a **window**. Buttons and text boxes appear inside other windows, which are called **forms** in Visual Basic. The collection of windows (buttons, text boxes, and forms) constitutes the user interface for the program. The **user interface** defines what a user of the program sees on the screen and how the user interacts with the program.

In writing a computer program in Visual Basic, you use various tools to design the end-user interface, or windows, for the program that you are creating. Microsoft Word has its own user interface, as does Excel. Visual Basic itself has a user interface, which is called an integrated development environment. An **integrated development environment (IDE)** includes all of the tools necessary to create and test a program. These tools operate in a single user interface rather than in separate programs. In other words, you can create the windows for a program, write the necessary statements, and test the program while remaining inside the same IDE.

Visual Basic is an event-driven programming language. **Event-driven** means that different windows on the screen can respond to events. An **event** is an action that occurs as a result of some user activity. For example, one event is generated when the end-user clicks a button, and a different event is generated when the end-user types characters in a text box. Such events cause the program's statements to execute.

Visual Basic is also an object-oriented programming language. **Object-oriented** means that the programmer creates objects that the end-user will use to perform tasks. An object can, for example, be a button that the user clicks or a box that will contain text, or one of many other objects. A programming object is similar to a real-world object, such as a telephone. That is, a programming object has a predefined set of behaviors or settings called **properties**, just as a telephone has many properties—hung-up, not hung-up, blue in color, and push-button or rotary. A programming object can perform a predefined set of actions called **methods**. Similarly, a telephone has its own methods—providing a dial tone when the receiver is picked up and sending audible tones to the phone system when numbers are dialed.

As a programmer, you use different tools to create objects. In Visual Basic, these tools are called **controls**. Each type of control has different characteristics (properties), responds to events that are discrete for each type of control, and performs a unique set of actions (methods). In this chapter, you will learn how to use four different controls:

- The **Label** control is used to create a box that can display text to describe the purpose of another control. The box can display output but cannot receive input.
- The **TextBox** also displays text. In addition to displaying output, however, it can receive input from the end-user of the program.
- The **Image** control is used to create a box that can display pictures saved in certain graphic formats.
- The **CommandButton** control allows the end-user to click a command button to perform a specific action.

To add a control to a form, you draw a copy of the control on the form. Each copy of the control placed on a form in this way is considered an object and is called a **control instance**. Figure 1-1 shows various Visual Basic control instances, drawn on a form, and their purposes.

display descriptive text for another object, such as a TextBox control

enter letters and numbers in a TextBox control

display a graphical image in an Image control

click a command button to cause some action to occur

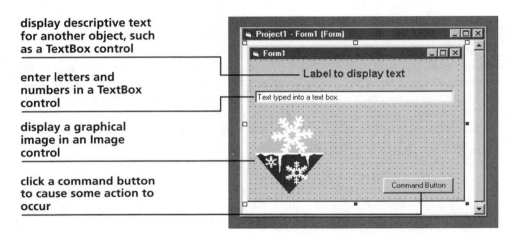

Figure 1-1: Sample of Visual Basic controls

In Visual Basic, a control is considered a class. A **class** is a template for an object, defining the object's supported properties, methods, and events. In other words, a class defines what an object does and how it behaves. When you create a control instance on a form, you are creating an instance of a class.

Every program you create in Visual Basic has a well-defined structure. Each form in the program is stored as a separate file, known as a form module. A **form module** contains information about the control instances that are drawn on the form. In addition, it contains the statements that are executed when the user interacts with the form's control instances—for example, by clicking a button. In this book, a group of statements is referred to as **code**.

Many programs contain multiple forms. In such a case, the program contains one form module (file) for each form. Visual Basic also supports a **standard module**, which contains statements that several forms can use. Each module contains specific statements written to perform some specific action. In Visual Basic, a **project file** lists each form and standard module (file) used in the program as well as information about the different types of controls used in each module. Each program has a single project file, regardless of the number of modules. The project that you will create in this chapter will contain one form module. Figure 1-2 depicts the relationships among a project file, its form modules, and its standard modules.

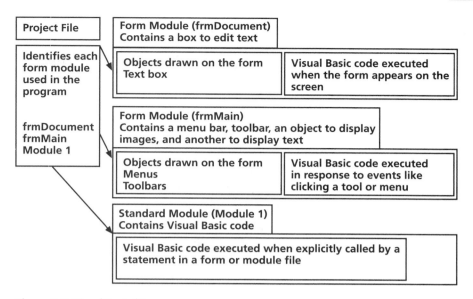

Figure 1-2: Visual Basic files

To create a program with Visual Basic, a programmer uses a three-step process. First, the programmer creates the interface that the end-user will see. Second, the programmer writes statements to perform each task required by the program. The third step is a loop in which the programmer tests the program, corrects any errors, then tests the program again. Figure 1-3 shows the steps involved in writing a program.

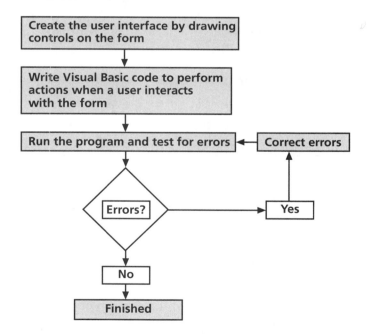

Figure 1-3: Steps for writing a program

As you write your computer programs, two tips may prove helpful. First, save your work frequently. If you later make a mistake from which you cannot recover, you can open the project containing your saved work and continue from that point. Second, test the code you write frequently to make sure it works as intended. If you perform such testing before you progress too far, it will save you time and frustration.

Starting Visual Basic

In this section, you will view the completed program created for Southern Properties Group. First, you need to start Visual Basic by using the Start button on the taskbar or by clicking an icon on the Windows desktop (if an icon has been defined for Visual Basic on your computer). Your instructor or computer lab staff will explain how to start Visual Basic in your particular environment.

To start Visual Basic:

1   Make sure your computer is on and the Windows desktop is displayed.

2   Locate the **Start** button 🏁Start at the bottom-left corner of the screen on the taskbar.

3   Click the **Start** button 🏁Start to display the Start menu, then point to the **Programs** command.

When the Programs command is highlighted, a submenu appears listing the programs available on your computer.

4   Move the mouse pointer to the item labeled **Microsoft Visual Basic 6.0**.

Another submenu appears, as shown in Figure 1-4, listing the Visual Basic components installed on your computer. Your list may vary, depending on the software installed on your computer.

Microsoft Visual Basic 6.0 command

Windows Start button

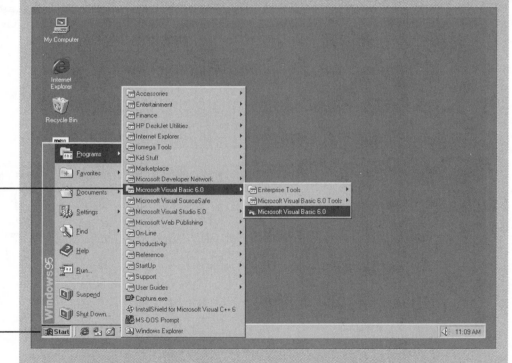

Figure 1-4: Starting Visual Basic

5 Move the mouse pointer to **Microsoft Visual Basic 6.0**, then click the mouse button to start Visual Basic.

The introductory Visual Basic screen, commonly known as a **splash screen**, appears while the rest of the Visual Basic system is loading into the computer's memory. The splash screen provides a visual clue to the user that the desired program is being loaded. When you start Visual Basic, make sure its splash screen contains the text "Visual Basic Professional Edition 6.0" or "Visual Basic Enterprise Edition 6.0." Several operating differences distinguish version 6.0 from the older versions of this programming language. You must be using version 6.0 of Visual Basic to complete these chapters.

6 Once Visual Basic is loaded, the New Project dialog will appear, as shown in Figure 1-5.

help

> If the Programs submenu does not list the Microsoft Visual Basic 6.0 option, check whether an icon for Visual Basic appears on the desktop. If so, double-click this icon to start Visual Basic. It also is possible that Visual Basic is not installed in the default location. In this case, it may appear in a different location on the Start menu. If Visual Basic is not found in the default location, consult your instructor or computer lab staff for assistance.

click Open button

click check box so
New Project dialog
will not open each time
you start Visual Basic

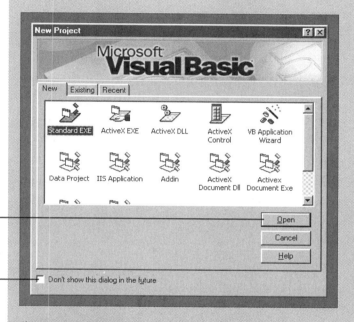

Figure 1-5: New Project dialog

7 Click the **Don't show this dialog in the future** check box to prevent the New Project dialog from opening every time Visual Basic is started.

8 Make sure **Standard EXE** is highlighted in the New Project dialog. Click the **Open** button. Your screen should resemble Figure 1-6.

help

> If the New Project dialog does not match that shown in Figure 1-5, your computer may be configured differently. Depending on the setup of your computer, some windows might be opened or closed initially, or they might be a different size. In such a case, you can skip Step 7.

menu bar

toolbar

Project window

toolbox

Form window

Properties window

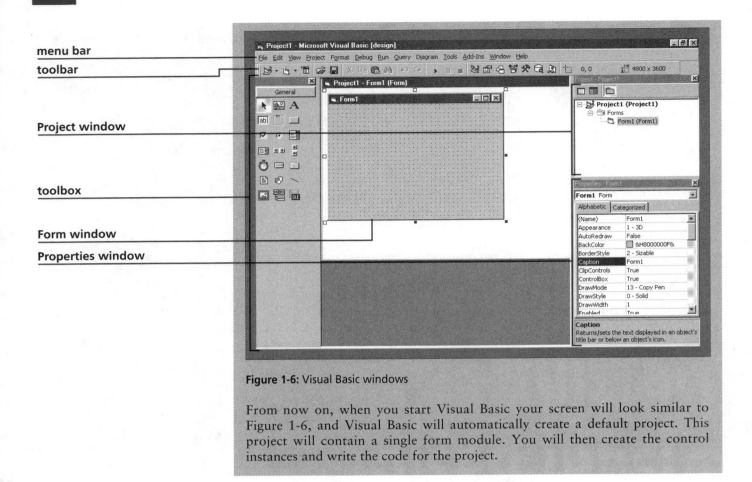

Figure 1-6: Visual Basic windows

From now on, when you start Visual Basic your screen will look similar to Figure 1-6, and Visual Basic will automatically create a default project. This project will contain a single form module. You will then create the control instances and write the code for the project.

When you start Visual Basic and open different project files, the sizes and locations of the windows on the screen will vary. You can change the sizes and positions of most Visual Basic windows to suit your own preferences, just as you can resize or move other windows. Some of the windows shown in Figure 1-6 may not be visible on your screen, depending on the Visual Basic settings on your computer.

The Visual Basic IDE contains several components common to many other Windows programs. For example, it has a menu bar and a toolbar. It also has a toolbox that allows you to create the buttons and other visual objects that make up the interface that the end-user will see.

The Menu Bar and Toolbar

The menu bar provides the commands used to create and run Visual Basic programs. It works like the menu bar in any other Windows program. The toolbar buttons duplicate many of the commands found on the menu bar. Thus clicking a toolbar button offers another way to execute a command on the menu bar. As in other Windows applications, you can display a ToolTip for a button on the Visual Basic toolbar by positioning and holding the mouse pointer over the button for a few seconds. The ToolTip that appears shows the name of that particular button.

To display a ToolTip for a toolbar button:

1 Position the mouse pointer over the **Add Standard EXE Project** button 🖼 at the far left end of the toolbar.

After a few seconds, the ToolTip appears and displays the purpose of the button, Add Standard EXE Project.

2 Move the mouse pointer away from the button.

The ToolTip disappears.

To customize the Visual Basic toolbars, you can add or remove different groups of tools from the toolbar. At this point, you will work only with the Standard toolbar, so you will now close any other toolbars that are open.

To configure the toolbars:

1 Click **View** on the menu bar, point to **Toolbars**, then click **Customize**.

The Customize dialog appears on your screen.

2 Click the **Toolbars** tab, if necessary.

3 Make sure the **Menu Bar** and **Standard** check boxes are checked, and clear any other check boxes. You cannot disable the Menu Bar check box. Figure 1-7 shows the Customize dialog.

Toolbars tab is active

Menu Bar check box
cannot be deactivated

displays the Standard
toolbar when checked

Customize dialog

click Close to accept the
toolbar settings

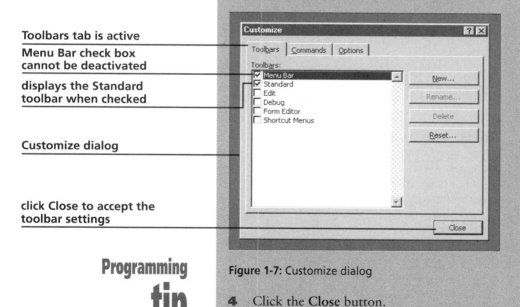

Figure 1-7: Customize dialog

4 Click the **Close** button.

Programming

tip

• • • • • • • • • • • • • • •

In addition to using the Customize dialog, you can display and hide toolbars by right-clicking the mouse over the Visual Basic toolbar. This action will activate a pop-up menu. On this pop-up menu, you can then click the particular toolbar you want to display or hide.

Planning a Program

Before you begin writing the program, always carefully consider the problem that you are trying to solve, the best solution for the problem, and the placement and purpose of the buttons, boxes, and other components that will be seen by the end-user of your program. Evaluate the layout and the organization of the different visual elements, as well as the specific tasks they will perform, before sitting down and creating the program on the computer. This approach will make the programming process easier and less vulnerable to errors. The main form's screen layout has already been created, as shown in the form design depicted in Figure 1-8. It lists and displays the locations of the control instances on the form.

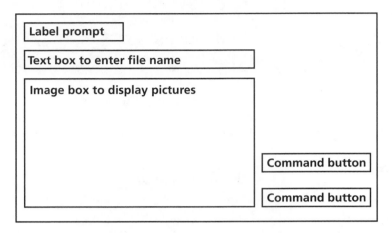

```
Label prompt

Text box to enter file name

Image box to display pictures




                                        Command button

                                        Command button

```

Figure 1-8: Form design for image viewer

As shown in Figure 1-8, a label describes the purpose of the text box. The text box will receive and display textual input (file name) from the user. The image box will display the picture that corresponds to the file name entered by the user in the text box. Clicking one command button will cause the image to be displayed; clicking the other will exit the program.

Opening an Existing Project

As you work through the chapters in this book, you will create new programs and modify existing ones. To examine the elements of the Visual Basic IDE, you will now open a completed version of the same project that you will create later in this chapter. All of the chapters in this book will take the same approach. That is, each chapter contains a completed example for you to review as well as instructions for creating a new application from scratch or from a partially completed application.

Before you open this project, a few words are in order about the data files corresponding to this book. Your instructor has all of the data files needed to complete the chapter and the material at the end of the chapter. For this chapter, the relevant files are found in the folder named Chapter.01. (Files for Chapter 2 appear in the folder named Chapter.02, and so on.) The Chapter.01 folder includes the Complete folder, which contains the completed exercise that accompanies the chapter. Some chapter folders have a partially completed program that you will finish as you work through the chapter. In those chapters, the program appears in a folder named Startup. At the end of each chapter, you will find a number of exercises designed to allow you to apply the material presented in the chapter. The files necessary to complete these exercises are found in the folder named Exercise. Your instructor will indicate the location to which you should copy these folders.

When we mention file names in this book, we will not explicitly reference the hard disk or the floppy disk. Rather, files will be identified relative to the current chapter. Thus, to open the completed project for this chapter, you will open the file **Chapter.01\Complete\SPG_C.vbp**. You will, however, need to specify the drive designator depending on the location of your files.

To open an existing project:

1 Click the **Open Project** button 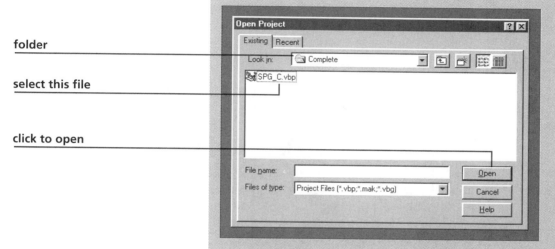on the toolbar to display the Open Project dialog.

2 From the list box, select the drive designator, as necessary, depending on where you copied the chapter files.

3 Double-click the **Chapter.01** folder in the List area, then double-click the **Complete** folder. The Open Project dialog will resemble Figure 1-9. Depending on the configuration of your computer, the file extensions may or may not appear.

folder

select this file

click to open

Figure 1-9: Open Project dialog

4 Click the file named **SPG_C.vbp**, then click the **Open** button.

The file name has a suffix of _C. Throughout this book, this nomenclature is used to indicate that the project contains the completed example. Startup files you complete in the chapter have a suffix of _S.

Now that you have started Visual Basic and loaded an existing project (program), you can run it to see how the program will appear to the end-user. First, a discussion of operating modes is warranted.

Exploring Operating Modes

Visual Basic operates in one of three modes: run mode, design mode, or break mode. The title bar at the top of the Visual Basic menu bar indicates the current mode. When you are running a program, the Visual Basic title bar contains the text "[run]", which means that the program is being executed and is in run mode. In design mode, you perform activities like creating and saving projects, designing forms, setting properties, and writing code. In this case, "[design]" appears on the Visual Basic title bar. Break mode is similar to run mode, but your program is suspended temporarily, allowing you to examine the program statements as they execute. When you are in break mode, "[break]" appears on the Visual Basic title bar. You will learn more about the design and run modes in Section B, when you create a program to display graphical images. You will learn more about break mode in later chapters.

When you create a Visual Basic program, you assume two roles. As the programmer, you write the code and create the user interface for the program. In addition, you must test the program (acting as an end-user) and correct any errors. Visual Basic allows you to perform both of these tasks using the same interface. In run mode, you assume the role of the end-user. In design mode, you assume the role of the programmer.

Running a Program

When you run a program, Visual Basic loads the startup (first) form and displays all of the objects drawn on the form. The program then waits for you to interact with it. When you click a button on the form, you generate an event; Visual Basic executes the code written in response to the event.

Below you will test the completed program to see how an executing Visual Basic program will appear to the end-user.

To run a project:

1   Click the **Start** button ▶ on the toolbar. The Visual Basic title bar displays "[run]".

2   In the text box, enter the file name **Chapter.01\Complete\Item1.bmp**, as shown in Figure 1-10.

Remember to change the drive designator as necessary. Thus, if you were running the program from the A drive, the full path name would be **A:\Chapter.01\Complete\Item1.bmp**.

3   Click the **Display Image** command button.

The image appears. See Figure 1-10.

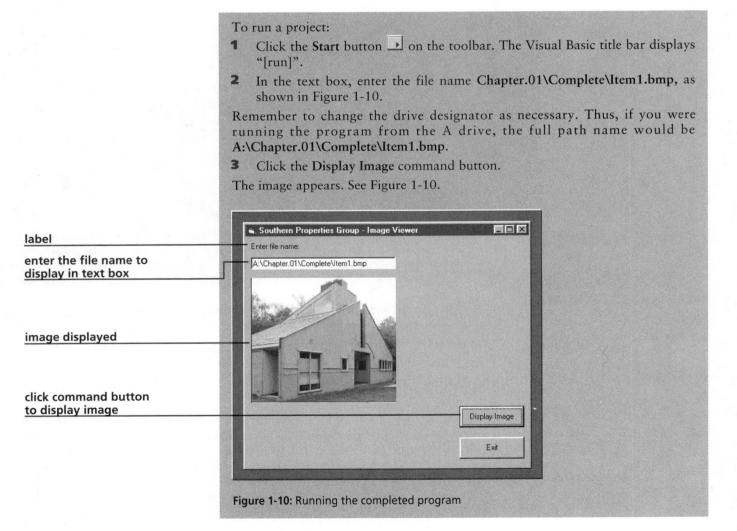

label

enter the file name to display in text box

image displayed

click command button to display image

Figure 1-10: Running the completed program

The necessary statements to display the graphical image have already been created. You will see how to create this code yourself later in this chapter.

Stopping a Program

You have finished looking at the completed program that Southern Properties Group will use. You can now stop running it. When you stop a program from running, you change the operating mode from run mode to design mode. You have two ways to achieve this goal: the End button on the toolbar and the End command on the Run menu.

To end a program:

1 Click the **End** button ▣ on the toolbar. Visual Basic stops running the program and returns to design mode. The form displays neither the file name in the text box nor the image. The title bar displays the text "[design]".

Now that you have experienced the different Visual Basic operating modes, you will learn about the different windows of the Visual Basic IDE.

Identifying the Components of the Visual Basic Environment

The visual interface for the Visual Basic IDE can appear in one of two environments:

- In the single document interface (SDI) environment, the windows used by Visual Basic can appear anywhere on the screen.
- In the multiple document interface (MDI) environment, the region of each Visual Basic window appears inside another window called an **MDI parent window**. This environment is much like working with multiple documents in Microsoft Word or multiple spreadsheets and charts in Microsoft Excel. Each Word document or Excel spreadsheet appears inside the region of another window.

You can select the environment by clicking Tools on the menu bar, then Options, to open the Options dialog. The Advanced tab contains a check box named SDI Development Environment. If this box is checked, Visual Basic operates in the SDI environment. Otherwise, it operates in the MDI environment. The choice of which environment to use is a matter of personal preference. In this book, the figures appear in an SDI environment unless otherwise indicated. Thus they illustrate a particular window of the IDE rather than the entire Visual Basic desktop.

Another feature of the Visual Basic IDE is called **docking**. When docking is turned on, different windows are displayed and moved relative to the other windows and the edge of the MDI parent window. When this feature is turned off, windows are positioned anywhere inside the MDI parent window. In this chapter you will not use docking. Thus you will verify that Visual Basic is running in the MDI environment and that docking is turned off.

To set the visual interface environment and docking options, you use the Options dialog.

To configure the Visual Basic environment:

1 Click **Tools** on the menu bar, then **Options,** to open the Options dialog.

2 Click the **Advanced** tab in the Options dialog. Make sure that the SDI Development Environment is not checked.

3 Click the **Docking** tab in the Options dialog.

4 Make sure that none of the options is checked.

5 Click **OK** to close the Options dialog.

As you develop the programs found throughout this book, open, close, and resize the windows as you see fit. There is neither a "right" number of windows to keep open nor a proper size for those windows. Furthermore, it is a matter of personal preference whether to use MDI or SDI environments and whether to enable docking. Explore the various options until you find the configuration that is most intuitive to you. You will now review the different windows that make up the IDE before you begin developing your own program.

Project Explorer

The **Project Explorer** lists the name of the current project and each component (module) that makes up the project. You use the Project Explorer to manage the individual module files of the completed program or project. In Visual Basic, the terms "project" and "program" are synonymous. A project usually consists of at least one form, known as a form module. It can use other types of modules as well, including standard modules, class modules, and modules used to create documents that work on the World Wide Web (the Web). Although Visual Basic can work with several projects at a time, the program developed in this chapter contains only a single form module.

To activate the Project Explorer:

1 Click the **Project Explorer** button ⊞ on the toolbar, if necessary, to activate the Project Explorer, as shown in Figure 1-11. This window already may be open.

Toggle Folders button

View Code button

View Object button

Forms folder open

Project Explorer

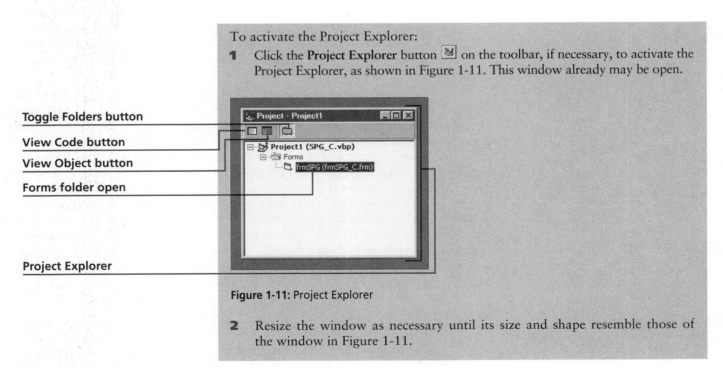

Figure 1-11: Project Explorer

2 Resize the window as necessary until its size and shape resemble those of the window in Figure 1-11.

The Project Explorer displays a hierarchical list of all forms and modules used in a project. Each type of module appears in a different folder, much in the same way that files do in the Windows Explorer program. Each line in the Project Explorer includes the following items:

- A box containing a plus or a minus sign. Clicking the plus sign will open the folder and display its contents. Clicking the minus sign will close the folder so that its contents will not be displayed.
- An icon listing the type of module.
- The name of the module as it is used inside the Visual Basic project.
- The file name of the module saved on the disk.

The Project Explorer also contains three buttons:

- The **View Code** button opens a window to display the Visual Basic statements that apply to the selected module.
- The **View Object** button displays a visual representation of a form or other object in a window called a **visual designer** window.
- The **Toggle Folders** button is used to hide and show the module folders.

To practice reviewing the different modules that make up a Visual Basic program, you will open each folder representing the module types.

To identify the modules that make up a project and activate the Form window:

1 If the Forms folder is closed, click the **plus sign** ⊞ next to the closed folder in the Project Explorer to open the folder.

2 Click the form named **frmSPG (frmSPG_C.frm)**.

3 Click the **View Object** button ⊞ in the Project Explorer to display the Form window. Resize the Form window as necessary until it resembles Figure 1-12.

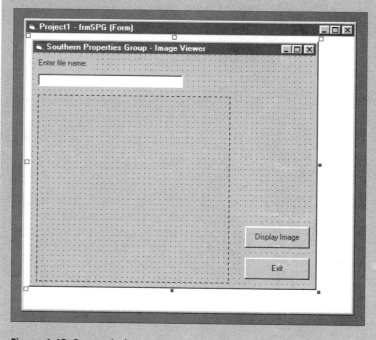

help

The Form window shown in Figure 1-12 may differ slightly from the one that appears on your desktop. The form in Figure 1-12 was captured in MDI mode. In SDI mode, small boxes do not surround the form. These small boxes, called **sizing handles**, identify the active object. This difference will not cause a problem as you complete the steps in this chapter.

Figure 1-12: Form window

The Form Window

The **Form window** is the window in which you design the user interface for the program. As mentioned earlier, it is also called a visual designer. This name stems from the fact that you design the interface for the form in a visual way by clicking and drawing directly on the form. When the end-user runs the program, he or she communicates with the program by clicking buttons or typing characters in the objects on the form. As depicted in Figure 1-12, the Form window shows the completed form.

Properties Window

The **Properties window** provides options to manage the appearance of each object (control instance) created on a form. A **property** is a characteristic of an object, such as its color, caption, screen location, or size.

To activate the Properties window for the form:

1   Click the **Properties Window** button 🔲 on the toolbar to activate the Properties window, if necessary. Resize the window as necessary until it resembles Figure 1-13.

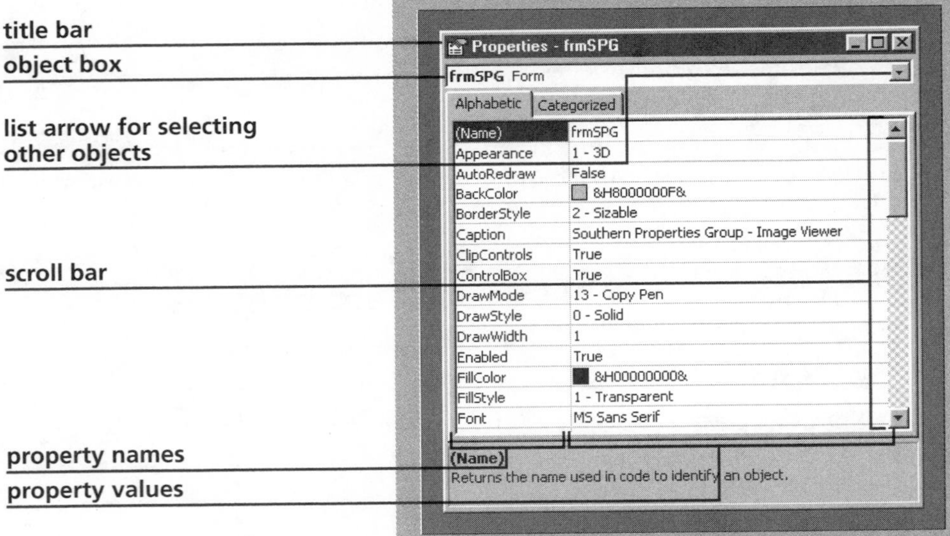

title bar

object box

list arrow for selecting other objects

scroll bar

property names

property values

Figure 1-13: Properties window components

As shown in Figure 1-13, the Properties window contains two tabs: Alphabetic and Categorized. When the Alphabetic tab is active, the properties appear sorted in alphabetic order. When the Categorized tab is active, the properties are organized based on the purpose of the property. The tab that you use is a matter of preference.

2 Click the **Alphabetic** tab in the Properties window, if necessary, to view the properties applicable to the form presented in alphabetic order.

3 Click the **Categorized** tab in the Properties window to view the properties applicable to a form grouped by category.

The Properties window contains two columns. The Name column lists the name of each property. The Value column lists the current value of each property. You can use the scroll bar at the right-hand side of the window to scroll through the list of properties if the entire list will not fit within the window. You will use the Properties window when you create the program to display graphical images.

Toolbox

The **toolbox** contains all of the visual tools necessary to create the user interface for a form. You use the icons on the toolbox to create control instances on a form. As noted earlier, a control (such as a box, button, or label) is also a class. When you draw an instance of a control onto a form, you have created an object from the class. You can create objects to permit user interaction and enhance your program's visual appeal.

All of the objects (control instances) already have been created for the completed program given in this chapter. These objects were created with the various controls on the toolbox. To help you identify the different controls on the toolbox, you can display a ToolTip as previously described.

Accessing the Visual Basic Help Library

Visual Basic has an extensive Help library that provides information about Visual Basic components, features, and commands. For example, you can look up how to write Visual Basic statements or study the financial and mathematical functions built into Visual Basic. The Help library used by Visual Basic has a different appearance than that included with many other Windows applications, such as Word and Excel. The purpose, however, is the same. The Help library relies on **hypertext**, which means that you can navigate through the Help library by looking at definitions of terms you do not understand or related topics without actually searching for the information. Most of the Help screens contain examples that you can copy and paste into actual Visual Basic code.

You can get help at any time by pressing the F1 key or by selecting an option on the Help menu. Figure 1-14 describes the options available on the Help menu. Depending on whether you are running the Visual Basic Professional or Enterprise Edition, your options might differ from those shown in Figure 1-14.

Contents	Displays a Help window that lists available Help topics on the Contents tab or searches for a particular topic from the Index tab
Index	Displays an alphabetical list of Help topics
Search	Searches for a particular Help topic by keyword
Technical Support	Displays the Contents tab of the Help window, where you can search for different ways to get support for Visual Basic
Microsoft on the Web	Allows you to access the Internet, if your computer is set up correctly, for information about Visual Basic
About Microsoft Visual Basic	Displays a screen indicating which version of Visual Basic you are using

Figure 1-14: Help menu options

The Visual Basic Help library contains not only information directly related to Visual Basic, but also Help information pertaining to other Microsoft programming products. You can restrict the help information displayed by selecting the Active Subset. This option may or may not be available, depending upon the configuration of Visual Basic on your computer.

In addition to the Help resources listed in Figure 1-14, numerous Web sites are devoted to Visual Basic. One particularly popular Web site is "Carl and Gary's Visual Basic," which is located at http://www.cgvb.com/.

Using the Index Tab

The Index tab of the Help library displays an alphabetical list of topics, much like an index found at the back of a book. You either can scroll through this list and select a topic, or type a topic to find information about it.

You now will use the Index tab to find Help information about projects.

To use the Index tab for Visual Basic help:

1   Click **Help** on the menu bar, then click **Index**.
2   In the Active Subset list box, click **Visual Basic Documentation**. Note that the subsets may vary based upon the Visual Studio software installed on your computer.
3   Make sure the Index tab is selected in the Help window, as shown in Figure 1-15.

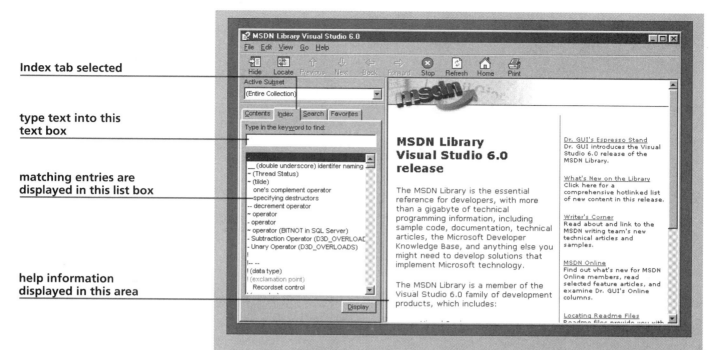

Index tab selected

**type text into this
text box**

**matching entries are
displayed in this list box**

**help information
displayed in this area**

Figure 1-15: Help library – Index tab

As shown in Figure 1-15, the Help window is divided into two sections. The section on the left-hand side of the window is used to locate and select information. The section on the right-hand side of the window is used to display that information.

4   In the text box, type **Project Explorer**. As you type, the box listing available Help topics changes to match your text. Press **Enter** to display the Topics Found dialog.

5   In the list box, make sure the topic **Project Explorer Window** (with subentries) is highlighted, then click the **Display** button. The Topics Found dialog opens, as shown in Figure 1-16. This dialog appears only if the index search finds multiple Help topics.

help

A flashing insertion point should appear in the text box of the Index tab. Click in the text box if the insertion point does not appear. In the text box, you can type the word or words for which you want information.

select this topic

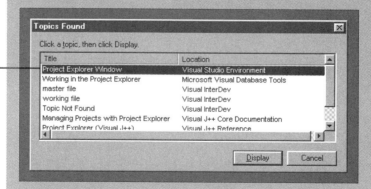

help

Note: The topics found shown in Figure 1-16 may vary based upon the Visual Studio components installed on your computer and the selected Active Subset. Also, depending on your Visual Basic installation, you may need to insert the appropriate MSDN CD.

Figure 1-16: Topics Found dialog

6 Click the topic **Project Explorer**, then click the **Display** button.

The Help library displays information about the Project Explorer, as shown in Figure 1-17.

scroll up arrow

related topics

scroll down arrow

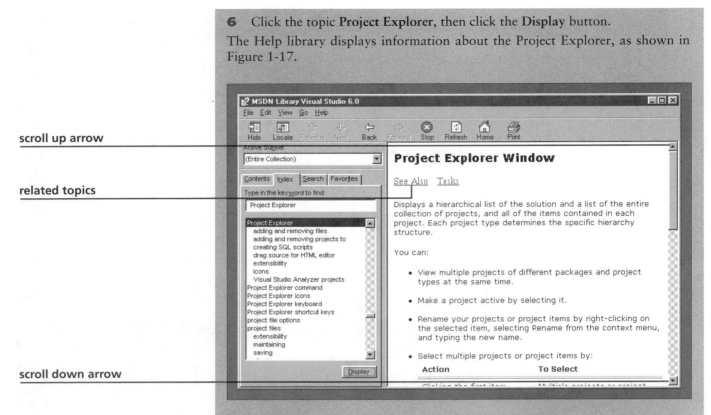

Figure 1-17: Help information about the Project Explorer window

Depending on your system's settings, the size and shape of the Help window might differ from the window shown in Figure 1-17. Just as with most windows, you can move and resize the window by dragging its border with the mouse pointer.

7 Read the displayed information, using the scroll arrows or the scroll box to move through the screen.

8 When you have finished reading the information, scroll to the top of the screen. Some terms appear in a different color and are underlined. You can click these terms to display additional Help information.

9 Click **See Also**, look at the displayed list of related topics, then click the **Cancel** button on the Topics Found window to close it.

Visual Basic is part of a larger group of software components called Visual Studio. The topics available in the Help library may differ depending on which Visual Studio components are installed on your computer.

In addition to searching for information with the index, you can locate information by using a table of contents.

Using the Table of Contents

The Contents tab of the Help library displays a set of books, each of which contains a particular category of information. You click a book icon to open it and display the topics in that category. Then you can choose a particular topic to review. Below you will use the Contents tab to view information about the Image control, a control that you will use in the program developed later in this chapter.

To use the Contents tab for Visual Basic Help:

1 Click the **Contents** tab in the Help window.

2 Click the **plus sign** ⊞ next to the book labeled **MSDN Library Visual Studio 6.0.**

3 Click the **plus sign** ⊞ next to the topic **Visual Basic Documentation.** Your screen will resemble Figure 1-18.

Contents tab selected

open book icon

closed book icon

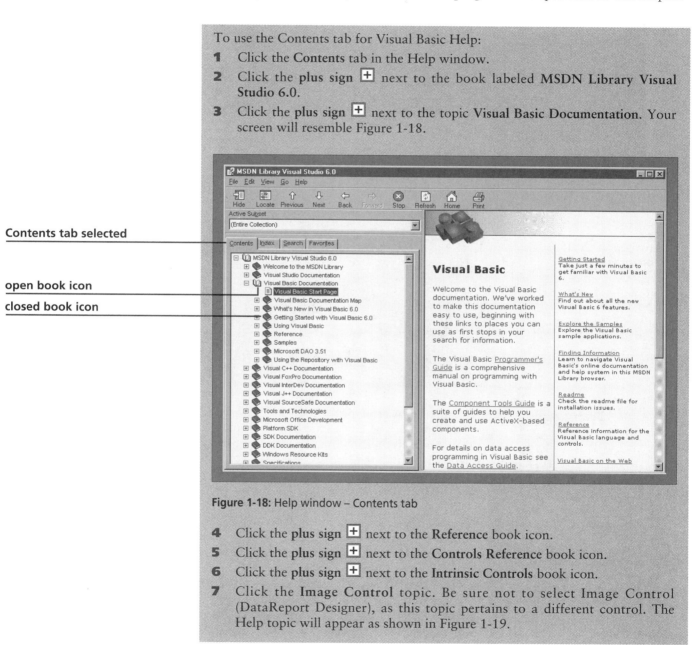

Figure 1-18: Help window – Contents tab

4 Click the **plus sign** ⊞ next to the **Reference** book icon.

5 Click the **plus sign** ⊞ next to the **Controls Reference** book icon.

6 Click the **plus sign** ⊞ next to the **Intrinsic Controls** book icon.

7 Click the **Image Control** topic. Be sure not to select Image Control (DataReport Designer), as this topic pertains to a different control. The Help topic will appear as shown in Figure 1-19.

Close button

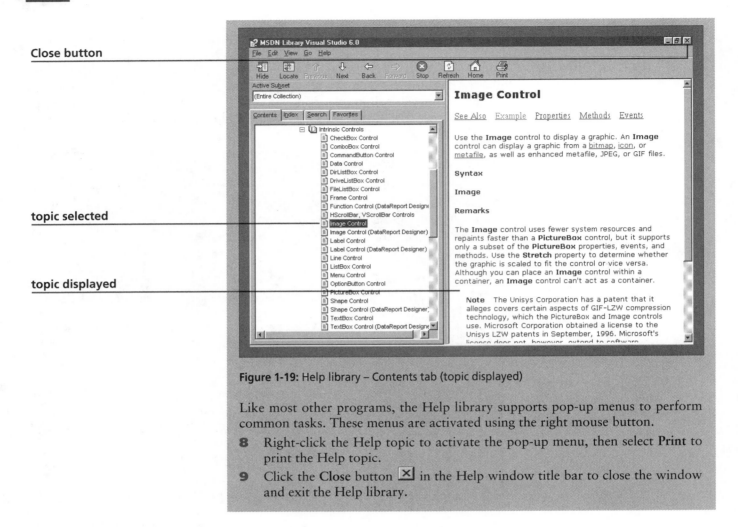

topic selected

topic displayed

Figure 1-19: Help library – Contents tab (topic displayed)

Like most other programs, the Help library supports pop-up menus to perform common tasks. These menus are activated using the right mouse button.

8 Right-click the Help topic to activate the pop-up menu, then select **Print** to print the Help topic.

9 Click the **Close** button ☒ in the Help window title bar to close the window and exit the Help library.

Programming

tip

● ● ● ● ● ● ● ● ● ● ● ● ●

▶ You can use the Help library to learn more about the specific controls that you will add to the form. The fastest way to find such information is to activate the control on the toolbox by clicking it, then press the F1 key to display the Help library.

Another way to locate information in the Help library is to use the Search tab. With this tab, you can locate help topics that contain a particular keyword. This feature is useful for finding all references pertaining to a specific topic.

Exiting Visual Basic

Now that you have examined the completed program, you can exit Visual Basic. Because you have not changed the program, you do not need to save it before exiting.

You can exit Visual Basic in either of two ways: clicking the Close button on the Visual Basic title bar or choosing the Exit command on the File menu. When you exit Visual Basic, it checks for unsaved project modules and unsaved changes in the project itself. If it identifies any such changes, Visual Basic displays a message asking if you want to save the files that were changed. Before exiting, Visual Basic closes all open forms and the project file.

To exit Visual Basic:

1   Click the **Close** button ⊠ on the Visual Basic title bar.

2   If you resized the form or made any other changes to it, Visual Basic will ask if you want to save the changes to the files that have been modified. Click the **No** button.

Visual Basic closes any open forms, the project file, and, finally, itself.

You have completed the programming for this section. In the next section, you will use the Visual Basic windows to create the program you viewed in this first section.

Q U E S T I O N S

1. A(n) _____ is an action that occurs as a result of some user activity.
   a. procedure
   b. event
   c. window
   d. form
   e. object

2. _____ are valid types of modules in Visual Basic.
   a. Form and Standard
   b. Project, Form, and Standard
   c. Visual and Standard
   d. Visual and Object
   e. None of the above.

3. A _____ file lists all of the modules in a program.
   a. Form
   b. Project
   c. Standard
   d. Module
   e. None of the above.

4. Which of the following are the Visual Basic operating modes?
   a. Start, Suspend, End
   b. Run, Suspend, Design
   c. Start, End
   d. Run, Break, Design
   e. None of the above.

5. The _____ window lists each component that makes up a Visual Basic program.
   a. Properties
   b. Form
   c. Module
   d. List
   e. Project Explorer

6. The _____ window is used to design the visual interface for a program.
    a. Properties
    b. Code
    c. Toolbox
    d. Form
    e. Standard

7. The _____ window is used to change the appearance of an object drawn on a form.
    a. Properties
    b. Code
    c. Toolbox
    d. Form
    e. Standard

8. Which of the following are valid tabs in the Help library?
    a. Contents
    b. Index
    c. Search
    d. All of the above.
    e. None of the above.

9. Which of the following are valid controls supported by Visual Basic?
    a. Label
    b. TextBox
    c. Image
    d. CommandButton
    e. All of the above.

10. Which of the following statements are true about Visual Basic?
    a. It is an integrated development environment.
    b. Programs are developed and tested using the same program.
    c. Visual Basic can be run in MDI or SDI mode.
    d. None of the above.
    e. All of the above.

In this section you will:

- Create a new project
- Save a project
- Create control instances on a form
- Use the Code window
- Run a completed program
- Compile a program

Creating a New Program

Creating a New Project

To create a new Visual Basic program, you begin by creating a new project with a single form. This form initially contains no visible control instances or statements. Alternatively, you can create a project using a wizard. A wizard can help you create a template for the different parts of the project, which you can then expand upon to make the program perform the desired tasks. For more information about using wizards, refer to "Appendix B: Wizards."

In Section A, you examined a completed program so as to identify the components of the Visual Basic user interface and see how to run a Visual Basic program. Here you will learn how to create a new project, developing its user interface and code so the program will display graphical images. When you start Visual Basic, it will automatically create a new project for you. The new project will contain a single form module but no control instances or code.

To create a new project:

1 Start Visual Basic.

Visual Basic creates a new project with a single form for you, as shown in Figure 1-20.

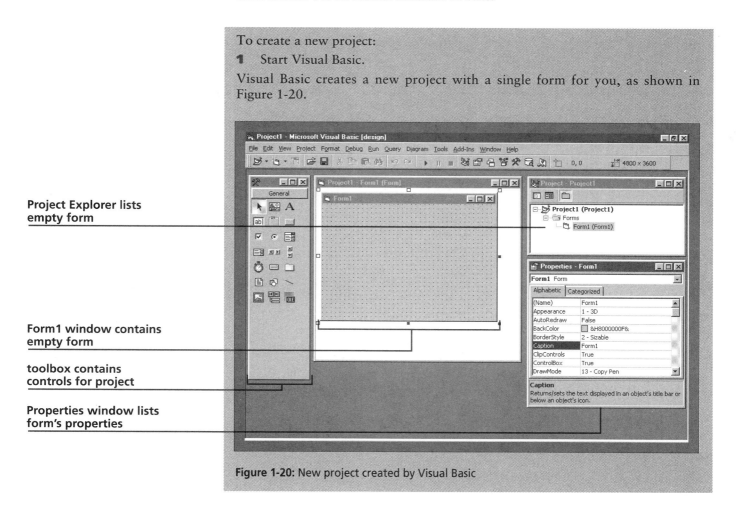

Project Explorer lists empty form

Form1 window contains empty form

toolbox contains controls for project

Properties window lists form's properties

Figure 1-20: New project created by Visual Basic

Figure 1-20 shows the Visual Basic IDE in MDI mode with the Form window, Project Explorer, Properties window, and toolbox open. You will use these windows in this section to complete the program.

2   Open, move, or resize the windows as necessary until your screen resembles Figure 1-20.

As shown in Figure 1-20, the new project contains a single form named Form1. Also, the toolbox contains the different controls with which you can create objects on the form. Finally, both the Properties window and the Project Explorer contain information about the current object and the current project, respectively.

You will create the following five objects on the form:

- An image that will display the pictures that Southern Properties Group has stored on the computer.
- A text box in which the user can type a file name to open.
- A label that will describe the purpose of the text box.
- One command button that, when clicked, will cause the image to appear.
- One command button that, when clicked, will end the program.

Because starting Visual Basic automatically created a new project with a single form, you now are ready to modify the form to make it useful for Southern Properties Group. In this case, you need to change the name of the main form so that it will be meaningful to other programmers. You will also set the form's Caption property to display a more meaningful title on the form's title bar.

To set or change any property, you first need to display the Properties window for the selected object (in this case, the form).

To display the Properties window for a form:

1   If necessary, open the Project Explorer by clicking the **Project Explorer** button ⬚. If the form is not displayed in the Forms folder, click the **plus sign** ⊞ to display it.

2   Click **Form1 (Form 1)** in the Project Explorer.

3   Click the **View Object** button ⬚ at the top of the Project Explorer.

The Form1 window becomes the active window.

4   Right-click the Form window with the caption Form1 to activate the pop-up menu.

5   Click **Properties** on the pop-up menu to activate the Properties window, then click the **Categorized** tab, if necessary. See Figure 1-21. Note that you can use the scroll bars to locate the different categories.

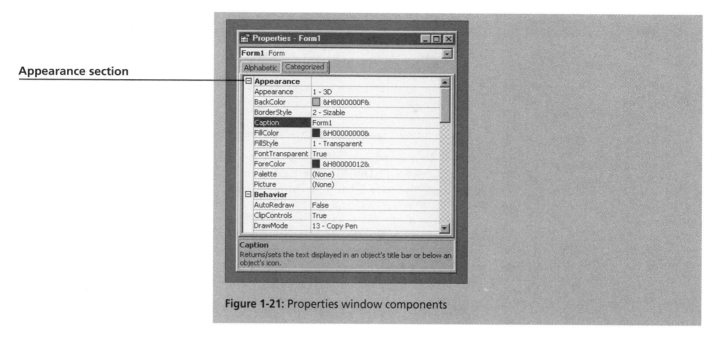

Appearance section

Figure 1-21: Properties window components

The Properties window title bar identifies the current object—in this case Form1—which is the value of the Name property assigned to the form. When Visual Basic creates a form or any other object, it assigns a default name to that object. The default name of the form in your project is Form1. The object box identifies the selected object (also Form1), followed by the type of the object (a Form object). You can use the list arrow at the right-hand side of the object box to select another object and display its properties. The left-hand column in the Properties window lists the properties available for the selected object, and the right-hand column lists the current value of each property. If all of the properties will not fit in the window, you can use the scroll bar to scroll through the Properties window and view the rest of the properties.

Next, you will use the Properties window to set the form's properties.

Setting the Caption and Name Properties for a Form

Like any window, a Visual Basic form contains text in the title bar that identifies its purpose. To specify this text, you set the form's Caption property. A caption can include spaces and punctuation characters. Although it can contain any number of characters, the caption should fit in the title bar of the form.

In this chapter, you will follow the convention of setting the caption of the form to the company name, followed by text indicating the purpose of the program. Thus a suitable caption for your form is "Southern Properties Group - Image Viewer." This text will communicate the purpose of the form to the user.

Each object you create has an associated name, which is stored in the Name property of the object. To improve the readability of the program, you will assign a more meaningful name to the form. In particular, you will set the Name property for most objects so they are easier to recognize in the code. This strategy will make your programs easier to understand.

Programming

tip

One exception to this naming rule involves descriptive labels. If you manually set the Caption property of a descriptive label that you will never access with code, you should leave the label's name set to the default value.

The following rules apply to naming objects:

- The first character of the name must be a letter.
- The subsequent characters of the name can be letters, numbers, or the underscore character.
- The name must be fewer than 255 characters in length.
- A name cannot include any special characters other than the underscore character.
- A name begins with a standard prefix describing the type of the object.

You set the name of the form so the name describes its purpose. Because the standard prefix of the form is "frm" and the program is an image viewer for Southern Properties Group, a suitable name to use is "frmSPG". Thus, in this example, the first letters of each word are used to build the form's name. Although you can create much longer descriptive names for a form, typing in long names as you write code can quickly become tedious. As you work through this book, therefore, you will use short names that convey the purpose of an object while minimizing typing.

To set the Caption and Name properties for the form:

1   Make sure the **Caption** property in the Appearance section in the Properties window is selected, then highlight its property value, **Form1**.

2   Type **Southern Properties Group - Image Viewer**. The caption in the form's title bar changes to the new value as you type, as shown in Figure 1-22.

Figure 1-22 appears in MDI mode, so the Form window includes sizing handles around the form. In SDI mode, these sizing handles do not appear.

caption in form's title bar

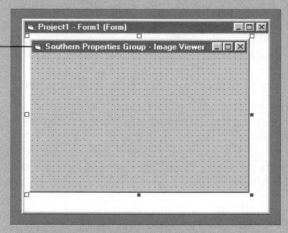

Figure 1-22: Setting the form's caption

3   Select the **Alphabetic** tab in the Properties window. Note that the (Name) property appears first. Highlight its property value, **Form1**.

4   Enter the name **frmSPG**.

The Name property for a form may differ from the file name stored on the disk. In this example, however, the name chosen will be the same.

Before creating other objects on the form, save both the form and the project. Continue to save your work periodically as you complete major steps in the program. If you later make a mistake, you will be able to open the already-saved files and continue from the saved program.

Saving the Project

Visual Basic does not automatically save the changes you make to the various modules that constitute a program. Thus, if the computer fails for any reason (such as a power outage), changes made since the program was last saved will be lost. In this section, you will see how to use the Save File As and Save Project As dialogs to save the different modules (files) that make up the project. When a project is saved for the first time, each module file is saved first, then the project file is saved. Although the modules and the project are stored in separate files, you can save them using one Visual Basic command—the Save Project command on the File menu.

Visual Basic creates default names for each module and project. The default name for the project is "Project1.vbp" and the default name for the first form in a project is "Form1.frm". The project has the three-character file extension ".vbp"; forms have a default file extension of ".frm". You will save your project with a descriptive name, "SPG_S.vbp". The "SPG" in this name denotes Southern Properties Group, and the "S" indicates the Startup folder. You also will save the form file using the appropriate name of "frmSPG_S.frm".

In this chapter, you will set the Name property of the form to "frmSPG", yet the file name of the form is "frmSPG_S". Visual Basic uses the Name property of the form to set properties and write code that will reference the form. In contrast, the file name "frmSPG_S.frm" is used to store the file on the disk. Thus the Name property and the file name need not be identical.

Programming

tip

• • • • • • • • • • • • • • • •

Do not change the three-character file extensions used by Visual Basic. These file extensions have critical implications in both Visual Basic and Windows.

To save a project for the first time:

1   If you intend to save your program on a floppy disk, place your Student Disk in drive A. If you plan to save information on the computer's hard disk, substitute the appropriate name drive designator as necessary.

2   Click **File** on the menu bar, then **Save Project** to activate the Save File As dialog. Because you have not yet saved any of the files associated with this project, Visual Basic first asks you to save each of the files that make up the project and only then save the project file itself.

3   Click the **Save in** list arrow, select the drive designator as necessary, then double-click the folder named **Chapter.01**.

The subfolders will appear in this dialog.

To ensure that you do not overwrite the completed example program, you will save your work in the Startup folder. Remember that the completed example was stored in the Complete folder. (This organization of files will be used throughout this book.)

4 Double-click the folder named **Startup**.

5 In the File name text box, enter **frmSPG_S.frm** (as shown in Figure 1-23), then click **Save**.

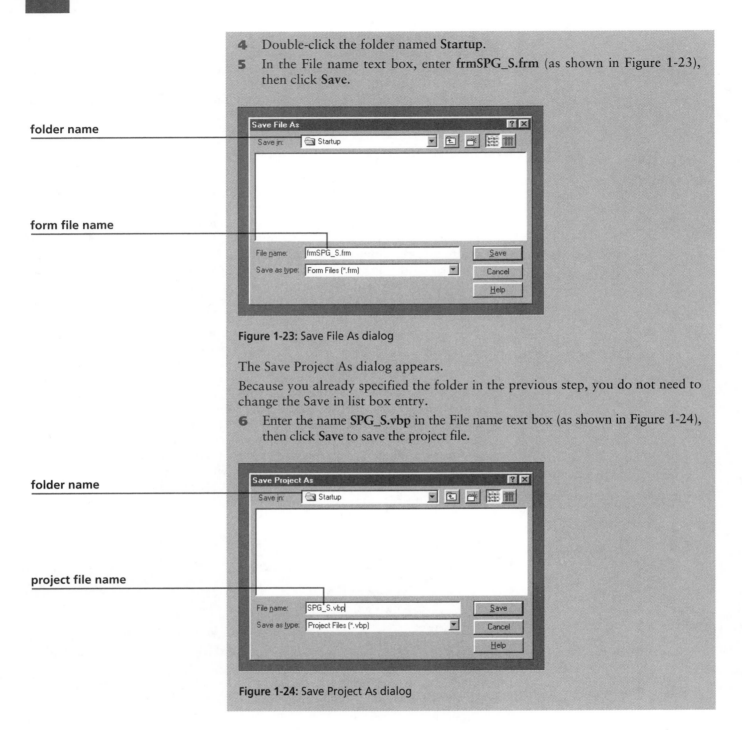

folder name

form file name

Figure 1-23: Save File As dialog

The Save Project As dialog appears.

Because you already specified the folder in the previous step, you do not need to change the Save in list box entry.

6 Enter the name **SPG_S.vbp** in the File name text box (as shown in Figure 1-24), then click **Save** to save the project file.

folder name

project file name

Figure 1-24: Save Project As dialog

Once the project has been saved, you can open it at any time using the Open Project command on the File menu. The project file then will locate all of the relevant forms and other Visual Basic components and load them.

Programming

tip

• • • • • • • • • • • • •

▶ The Open Project dialog contains a Recent tab. Visual Basic keeps track of the most projects that you loaded. If you are loading a project on which you have recently worked, click the Recent tab and locate the desired project.

You now have saved the form and project files on the disk. If you make a mistake from this point forward, you can reload the "SPG_S.vbp" project file and begin again from the point at which the project was last saved. By saving your work frequently, you will be able to return to that point and then continue your work.

You now set the remaining properties that pertain to the form.

Setting the Size and Position of a Form

The needs of the particular program dictate the size of the form. The program you are developing will display a 3-by-3-inch or smaller picture. In addition, you will be adding a label to the form that will display the name of the currently loaded file. This information will occupy the top 1 inch of the form. In addition, command buttons will appear to the right of the picture. These buttons require about 1½ inches of horizontal space. Thus the form is roughly 4 inches tall and 4½ inches wide.

To set the dimensions of a form, you use the Height and Width properties. All Visual Basic dimensions are measured in twips. **Twip** is a term for a unit of screen measurement. It is an acronym for twentieth of a point. A point is 1/72 of an inch. As 72×20 is about 1440, there are approximately 1440 twips per inch. Thus, to create a 4-by-4½-inch form, you would set the Height and Width properties to 5760 and 6480 twips, respectively. The size indicator on the far right of the toolbar indicates the height and width in twips of the current object (form or control instance).

You also can specify where on the screen the form will appear by setting the Left and Top properties. If you set both of these properties to zero (0), the form will appear in the upper-left corner of the screen. The position indicator on the right of the toolbar indicates the position of the active object. If the object is a form, then its position is given relative to the upper-left corner of the screen. If the object is a control instance you drew on the form, then its position is given relative to the upper-left corner of the form. To change the size and location of the form relative to the screen, therefore, you need to change four properties: Height, Width, Left, and Top.

Here you will create a 4-by-4½-inch form, located about 1 inch from the upper-left corner of the screen. Because 1 inch equals approximately 1440 twips, the height of the form will be 5760, the width of the form will be 6480, and the left and top dimensions will be 1440 each.

To set the size and position of the form:

1 Make sure the Properties window is active and set to the form named **frmSPG**. Click the **Categorized** tab, if necessary.

2 Scroll down the Properties window to locate the **Position** section of the list.

3 Locate the **Height** property, then highlight its default property value.

4 Type **5760**.

5 Press the **Enter** key.

The form changes size on your screen.

6 Locate the **Width** property, highlight the property value, then type **6480**.

7 Locate the **Left** property, highlight the property value, then type **1440**.

help

• • • • • • • • • • • • •

▶ If the Form window is not large enough to accommodate the new form size, resize the Form window by clicking and dragging the border.

> The size and location of the form change as you enter each value and either press the Enter key or select another property.
>
> **8** Locate the **Top** property, highlight the property value, then type **1440**.

When you saved the form module or project for the first time, Visual Basic asked you to specify the name of each file. When you subsequently save a form or project, however, Visual Basic assumes (without issuing any prompts to you) that it should use the same file name and save any modules in the project that have changed. You will now save the changes you just made to the form's properties.

Programming

tip

• • • • • • • • • • • • • • • •

▶ To change the name of a form or project, you can use the Save Form As and Save Project As commands, respectively, on the File menu.

> To save an existing project:
>
> **1** Click the **Save Project** button 🖫 on the toolbar.
>
> Visual Basic will save the form and project file without prompting you for any file names.

Now that you have set the properties for the form and saved the project, you are ready to create instances of the necessary controls on the form. You can then set the properties for each control instance.

Creating Control Instances on a Form

When you draw a control on a form, you are creating an instance of the control. A control instance is also known as an object. Likewise, the form itself is an object. You can have multiple occurrences or instances of the same type of control on a form. For example, you can include three command buttons on the same form that perform different actions. The controls available on the toolbox depend on two factors: your particular version of Visual Basic and whether any third-party add-in controls have been added to the toolbox. By default, Visual Basic displays a standard set of controls called **intrinsic controls**. A **third-party add-in control** is one created by another vendor and sold for use with the standard Visual Basic controls. Such add-in controls can provide greater functionality, such as spell-checking, or they can simply provide ways to make your programs more visually appealing.

In this section, you will use four types of intrinsic controls to create the program shown in Figure 1-25—a text box in which the user can type the name of a file, a label to describe the purpose of the text box, an image to display the picture stored in the file, and two command buttons. Note that Figure 1-25 is shown in SDI mode without sizing handles. The Display Image command button, when clicked, will cause the picture to appear on the screen. The Exit button will toggle Visual Basic from run mode to design mode. In other words, it will cause the program to exit.

label

text box

image

command buttons

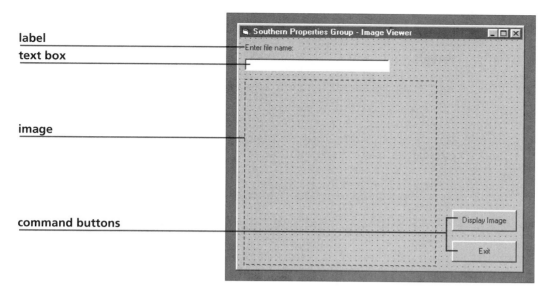

Figure 1-25: Form elements

To begin, you will add a Label control that will describe to the user the purpose of the text box in which the user will enter a file name. Next, you will create the text box to hold this file name. To add objects to a form, you use the controls on the toolbox. After you place a control instance (object) on the form, you can manipulate the object; for example, you can reposition, resize, or delete any object you create.

Adding a Label Control Instance

The Label control allows you to display text on a form. For example, you might want a label to include text that identifies another object. Alternatively, the label might display the results of some computation. For example, your program might add sales numbers and then show a number representing total sales. You can display such a value in a label. Labels are used for display (output) purposes only; a user cannot input information directly into a label.

Like a form, a label has properties. In addition to its Caption, Height, Left, Top, and Width properties, a label has properties that describe the font and the color of the foreground and background.

In this case, the label you will add to the form will display a prompt that describes the purpose of the TextBox control it identifies. This prompt will not change while the program is running.

To create an instance of the Label control:

1 Click the **Label** control ⒜ on the toolbox.

Move the pointer to the left-hand side of the Form window, where the upper-left corner of the Label object should appear. (See Figure 1-26 for the location of the control instance.) The pointer changes to +.

2 Click and hold the mouse button, then drag the pointer down and to the right to create an outline of the Label object.

When you are working in design mode, the form includes a grid of dots. By default, when you draw objects on the form, the object becomes aligned with the dots on the grid. Clicking Tools, Options, on the menu bar to activate the Options dialog can change this behavior. The General tab on this dialog includes an option named Align Controls to Grid. If this box is not checked, the control instances will not be aligned to the grid.

3   When the size of the object matches the size of the Label object shown in Figure 1-26, release the mouse button. The object then appears on the form. Note that Figure 1-26 is shown in SDI mode.

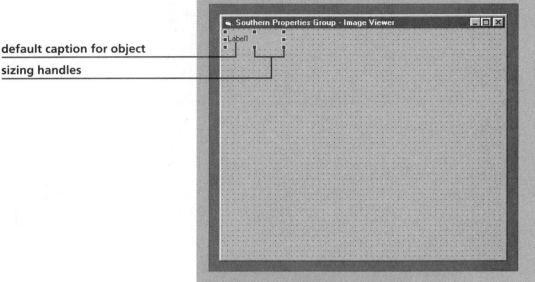

default caption for object

sizing handles

Figure 1-26: Creating a label

Do not worry if the Label object on your screen is not in exactly the same location or is not the same size as the object shown in Figure 1-26. You will reposition and resize the label later in this chapter.

Visual Basic automatically assigns a name to the instance of the Label control—in this case, Label1. Each object (control instance) on a form must have a unique name. Therefore, if you place a second instance of the Label control on the form without changing the name of the first label, Visual Basic would assign the name Label2 to this second Label object. Also, eight small, colored boxes (called sizing handles) appear around the border of the label. You can use the sizing handles to resize the object, as you will learn later in this section.

Because the label is the active object, the Properties window shows the properties for this object. You will not set these properties.

Setting a Label's Properties   Just as a form has properties, so, too, does each control instance created on a form have properties. These properties can determine the object's appearance (for example, its color), the font of the object's text (if any), the object's position on the screen, and its visibility on the screen. Some properties, such as color and screen location, are common to most types of objects. Other properties are unique, defining the specific attributes of a particular object type. As an analogy, consider two objects—an automobile and an airplane. Both an automobile and an airplane have similar properties, such as color, weight, and engine size. This does not necessarily mean that they have the same color, just that each has a color. Some properties, however, are meaningful only to the airplane; for example, only the airplane has a wing size. Similarly, both a label and an image have Left and Top properties that determine where the Visual Basic object appears on the form. Because the label is used to display text, however, it has a Caption property to describe text; the image, on the other hand, has a Picture property to indicate which picture should appear.

You will now set the properties for the Label object. You can set and change an object's properties at any time while Visual Basic remains in design mode. It is best to set them immediately after creating the object, however, to ensure that you do not forget this step. In this section, you will not change the value of the Name property, but you will change the value of the Caption property.

The initial name of the Label object you created is Label1, just as the initial name of the form object was Form1. Because you will not write any code that will reference the label, you will not change the Name of the label. In this book, we will follow the convention of setting the Name property only for those objects that are referenced with Visual Basic statements.

To set the Caption property of the Label object:
1 Make sure the Label object is selected (that is, that sizing handles surround the object).
2 Click the **Alphabetic** tab in the Properties window, if necessary, then highlight the **Caption** property default value, which is **Label1**.
3 Enter **Enter file name:** as the caption.

Moving a Label Object When you create an object on a form, you may need to change its location—perhaps because a design specification has changed or because the objects on the form are not visually balanced. You can move any object on a form by first clicking the object to select it, then using the mouse to drag the object to a new location. You will now practice moving the Label object on the form.

To move a control instance (object) using the mouse:
1 Make sure the Label object is selected.
2 Place the pointer anywhere within the Label object, but not on a sizing handle.
3 Click and hold the mouse button, then drag the object to a different location. An outline of the label appears on the form, moving to show the new object position as you move the mouse, as shown in Figure 1-27.

outline of object

position indicator ToolTip

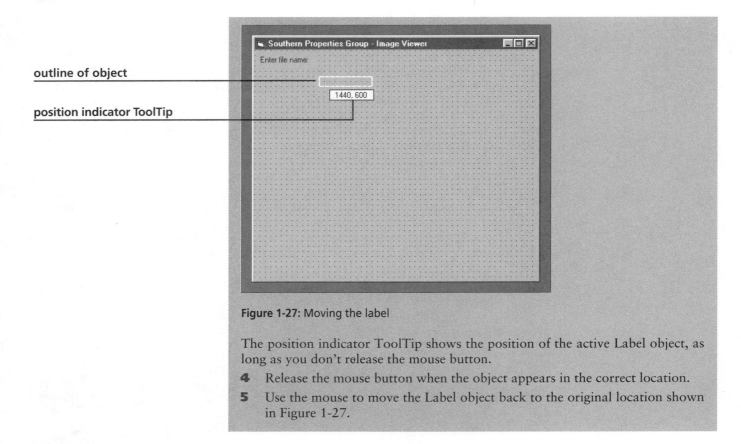

Figure 1-27: Moving the label

The position indicator ToolTip shows the position of the active Label object, as long as you don't release the mouse button.

4   Release the mouse button when the object appears in the correct location.

5   Use the mouse to move the Label object back to the original location shown in Figure 1-27.

Resizing an Object   In addition to moving an object, you can change an object's size by modifying its height or width. Again, this step might be necessary because of changes in design specifications or the need to improve or correct the appearance of objects on the form. For example, if you created a Label object that is too small to hold the label's Caption property value, you would need to increase the object's size.

To resize an object using the mouse:

1   Click the Label object on the form to select it.

2   Position the pointer on the sizing handle in the lower-right corner of the object. The pointer changes to ↘. When you use one of the four corner sizing handles to resize an object, the object will be resized both horizontally and vertically. When you use one of the center sizing handles, the object will be resized in one direction only, depending on which sizing handle you manipulate.

3   Click and hold the mouse button, then move the pointer down and to the right to increase the object's size, as shown in Figure 1-28.

help

• • • • • • • • • • • • • • • • •

▶ **If you accidentally double-click the object, Visual Basic will activate the Code window. (You will learn more about the Code window later in this section.) Click the Close button ☒ on the Code window title bar to close the window, then repeat Step 1.**

outline shows the
resized object

ToolTip shows
new width
and height

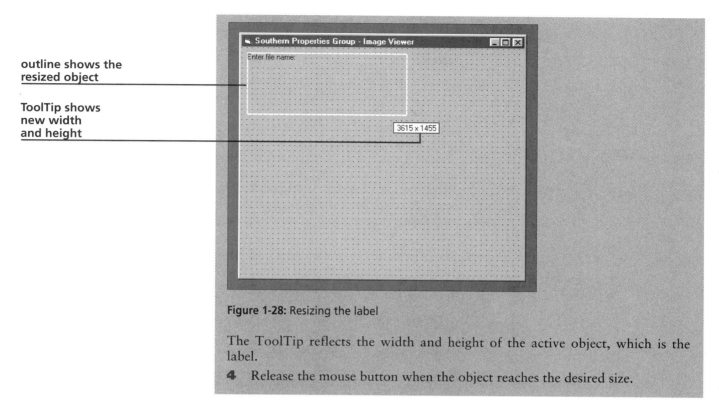

Figure 1-28: Resizing the label

The ToolTip reflects the width and height of the active object, which is the label.

4   Release the mouse button when the object reaches the desired size.

In the previous steps, you set the size of the control instance and its position on the form visually by dragging the object or its border. In the same way that you set the size and position of the form by setting the Height, Left, Top, and Width properties of the form, you can also set the properties of a control instance. The only difference is that the Left and Top properties of an object are relative to the form, not the entire screen.

To set the size and position of an object using the Properties window:

1   Make sure the Label object is selected.

2   Set the following properties for the Label object in the Properties window: Height = 255; Left = 120; Top = 120; Width = 1215.

Deleting an Object   Occasionally, you may need to delete an object from a form—perhaps because you created the object by mistake or because the program no longer uses the object. To delete an object, click the object, then press the Delete key. Because you will use the Label object created here in your program, you need not delete it.

Now that you have created the label and set its properties, you can create the next control instance on the form—the text box.

The TextBox Control

The TextBox control also works with text. In addition to simply displaying textual information, however, the user can enter text directly into a text box. In other words, the Label control can be used only for output but the TextBox control can accommodate both input and output. Like the Label control, the TextBox control has a Name property and properties that describe its position on the form. The Text property specifies the information displayed in a text box.

Unlike the label, you will write code for the TextBox control instance. Thus you will set the Name property for the text box to a more meaningful name. The standard three-character prefix for a text box is "txt". Because your text box will be used to get the file name of a picture from the user, a suitable name for it is "txtFileName". In addition, because the user will enter the text into this object when the program is running, the Text property will be blank when the program starts.

To create the text box and set its initial properties:

1 Click the **TextBox** control [ab] on the toolbox.

2 Move the pointer to the left-hand side of the Form window just below the label you created previously, where the upper-left corner of the TextBox object should appear. (See Figure 1-29 for the location and size of the TextBox control.)

3 Click and hold the mouse button, then drag the pointer down and to the right to create an outline of the TextBox object.

When Visual Basic is in design mode, the form includes a grid of dots. When you draw objects on the form, the object becomes aligned with the dots on the grid.

4 Set the Name property to **txtFileName**.

5 Remove the default value **Text1** from the Text property.

6 Set the following properties for the TextBox object in the Properties window: Height = **285**; Left = **120**; Top = **480**; Width = **3255**. Your screen should now resemble Figure 1-29.

new TextBox object

Figure 1-29: Creating the text box

The CommandButton Control

After the user enters the file name containing a picture into the text box, the program needs to use this file name to display the picture in an image control instance. You also need a way for the user to end the program. The CommandButton control, when clicked, will perform some type of action, such as displaying a picture, ending the program, or any other task. You have used command buttons before, such as when you clicked an OK or Cancel button in a dialog in Visual Basic or other Windows programs. When you customized your Visual Basic settings, for example, the Options dialog had three command buttons across the bottom of the form with the captions OK, Cancel, and Help. Here, you will create a command button that, when clicked, will display a picture in an Image object as well as a second command button to exit the program.

Like the Label and TextBox objects you just created, the CommandButton control uses the Top, Left, Height, and Width properties to define the size of the button and its position on the form. Inside a command button, you usually include a descriptive prompt that describes the button's purpose. The prompt, like the prompt in a label, is stored in the Caption property.

As with the other objects you have created to this point, you set the name of a command button by using a standard prefix followed by a name that describes the button's purpose. The standard prefix for a command button is "cmd". Your first command button, which will be used to display an image, will be named "cmdDisplayImage". The second, which will be used to exit the program, will be named "cmdExit".

You now will create the command buttons and set the necessary properties.

To create command buttons:

1 Click the **CommandButton** control ⬚ on the toolbox.

2 Draw a command button on the form.

3 In the Properties window, highlight the default value **Command1** for the Name property.

4 Enter the name **cmdDisplayImage**.

5 Highlight the default value **Command1** for the Caption property.

You may need to use the scroll bars to locate the property.

6 Enter the caption **Display Image**.

As you edit the value of the Caption property, the caption in the command button that appears on the form changes.

7 Set the following properties for the CommandButton object in the Properties window: Height = **495**; Left = **4800**; Top = **3960**; Width = **1455**.

8 Draw a second command button on the form, just below the first button.

9 Set the following properties for this second CommandButton object in the Properties window: Name = **cmdExit**; Caption = **Exit**; Height = **495**; Left = **4800**; Top = **4680**; Width = **1455**.

When complete, your form should resemble Figure 1-30.

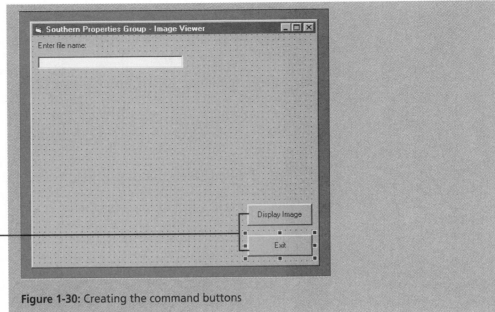

Figure 1-30: Creating the command buttons

command buttons

You have now created two instances of the same control (two command buttons). You can create as many instances of a particular control on a form as you need.

The Image Control

GUI tip

Consider the dialogs you have used in other Windows programs. Typically, the buttons on a form appear either across the bottom of the form or on the right-hand side. Also, the buttons usually have the same size and are spaced evenly apart.

The program you are creating for Southern Properties Group must display different graphical images as selected by the end-user. You also can include graphical images or pictures on a form to add visual interest to your program. Graphical images are stored in many different formats. In this case, Southern Properties Group uses Windows bitmap files to store the images. Bitmap files typically have the extension ".bmp".

The Image control can display graphical images inside the region of the control. By default, the picture inserted in an Image object has a fixed size. Because its size is determined by the size of the bitmap itself, this picture may differ from the size and shape of the Image object. So, if you create a 1-by-1-inch Image object on a form and then insert a 2-by-2-inch picture into that object, the picture will appear cropped. Furthermore, if you stretch a 1-by-2-inch picture into a 2-by-2-inch control, the picture will appear distorted. Setting the Image object's Stretch property to True resizes the picture to fit in the region of the image. Whether the Stretch property should be to True depends on the particular picture placed on the form. For example, if the shape of the picture differs significantly from the shape of the Image object and the Stretch property is set to True, the picture will scale to fill the Image object and will appear distorted.

Like the TextBox and CommandButton controls, the Image control has a standard prefix for the Name property, allowing you to identify the type of object easily as you write and read Visual Basic code. The standard prefix for an Image object is "img".

Here you will create the Image object and set its properties so that it can display different images when the program is running. Because all images will be the same size, you do not need to set the Stretch property to True. Remember that the program requirements specified a common 3-by-3-inch picture size. Given that 1 inch is equivalent to 1440 twips, the size of the image will be 4320 by 4320.

To create the Image object and set its initial properties:

1   Click the **Image** control [icon] on the toolbox.

2   Position the pointer in the upper-left region of the form.

3   Hold the mouse button and drag the mouse down and to the right.

An outline of the Image object appears on the form.

4   Set the following properties for the Image object in the Properties window:
Name = **imgCurrent**; Height = **4230**; Left = **120**; Top = **960**; Width = **4320**.

The form should now resemble Figure 1-31. Note that Figure 1-31 is shown in SDI mode, so that sizing handles do not appear around the form. Also, because the Image control instance is the active object, handles surround the image.

Image object

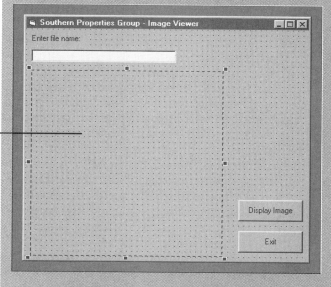

Figure 1-31: Creating the Image object

You have now created the necessary objects to display the file name and an image. In the next step in the program's development, you will write the necessary statements to display the image and exit the program.

Using the Code Window

To create the Visual Basic code that will display a graphical image and its corresponding file name, you must define the actions taken when the event (clicking a command button) occurs. You must therefore write Visual Basic code contained in event procedures. An **event procedure** is a set of Visual Basic statements that execute when a user performs an action on an object, such as clicking a command button. An object can have several different event procedures. For example, an object may execute one series of statements when the user clicks it and another series of statements when the user double-clicks it. These actions are two different events, and an object can execute different event procedures in response to different events.

You will write all Visual Basic statements using the Code window. The **Code window** is an intelligent text editor specifically designed to edit the code pertaining to a Visual Basic program. After you type a line of code and press the Enter key, Visual Basic will format the line and check the syntax of the statement to ensure that it is correct. If you enter a statement that Visual Basic cannot understand, a dialog describing the error will appear.

The code that you will write at this time will perform one task. That is, it will load a picture in the Image object you created. This code needs to execute when the user clicks the command button on the form.

Entering the Code for the Command Button

To create the code for a command button, you will open the Code window, create the desired object and event procedure, and enter the necessary statement(s). Before you can write the code for the cmdDisplayImage object's Click event procedure, however, you need to understand how to use the Code window to select an object and the appropriate event procedure.

The Code window contains two list boxes. The Object list box shows all objects pertaining to the open module (form). The form itself and the different control instances you have drawn on the form are referenced in this list box by their respective Name properties. The Procedure list box lists the different events to which the object can respond. Each object can respond to events such as the clicking of a command button. The events shown in the Procedure list box depend on the type of object selected, because different objects respond to different events.

Two ways exist to locate a specific event procedure for an object. If you double-click an object like a command button, the Code window will open to the most frequently used event for the object. In the case of the command button, this event is the Click event. Alternatively, you can select an event procedure manually by opening the Code window from the pop-up menu, selecting the desired object using the Object list arrow, then selecting the desired event procedure using the Procedure list arrow.

To select the object and event procedure in the Code window:

1 Make sure the Form window is the active window.

2 Right-click the form to activate the pop-up menu.

3 Click **View Code** on the pop-up menu. The Code window opens.

4 Click the Object list arrow (the list arrow that accompanies the list box on the left side of the window), then click **cmdDisplayImage**, as shown in Figure 1-32.

Object list box

Object list arrow

Procedure list box

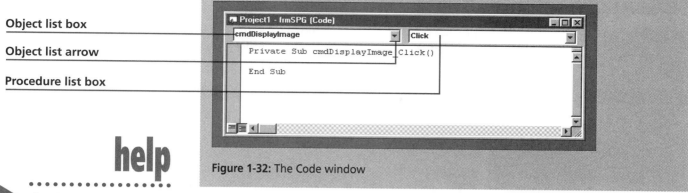

Figure 1-32: The Code window

help

· · · · · · · · · · · · · ·

▶ The size and shape of your Code window might differ from the window shown in Figure 1-32. If you like, you can resize the Code window to suit your preferences. The initial entries in the Object and Procedure list boxes might also differ from those in the figure, depending on the object selected when the Code window opened.

Now you need to write the code to display the file in the Image object using the file name in the TextBox object. Once you have selected the object and the event procedure, you can complete the code necessary to open a graphical image and display it in an Image object.

You need to type the statements shown in bold:

```
Private Sub cmdDisplayImage_Click( )
    ' Load the image using the file name stored in
    ' the TextBox control.
    imgCurrent.Picture = LoadPicture(txtFileName.Text)
End Sub
```

Before you enter the code in the Code window, take a moment to examine each statement separately to understand what it does.

Visual Basic created both the Private Sub and End Sub statements automatically.

```
Private Sub cmdDisplayImage_Click( )
```

This line begins with the keywords Private Sub. These keywords tell Visual Basic that this line is the beginning of a procedure that can contain Visual Basic code. A **keyword** is a word that has a special meaning to Visual Basic. The word Private tells Visual Basic that this event procedure can be used only inside this form. The word Sub indicates that the procedure will not send information back to other procedures. In addition, cmdDisplayImage is the name of the object, and Click is the name of the object's event procedure. An object and its event procedure are linked together with an underscore character to create a single identifier: the cmdDisplayImage_Click event procedure.

```
End Sub
```

The End Sub statement tells Visual Basic where the procedure ends. When the program reaches this statement, the event procedure stops executing and the program waits for the user to do something that causes another event to occur.

The cmdDisplayImage_Click( ) procedure will execute when a user clicks the Display Image command button. If you accidentally change the name of this procedure, Visual Basic cannot locate the event procedure or execute the code it contains in response to clicking the Display Image command button.

```
' Load the image using the file name stored in
' the TextBox control.
```

These two statements are known as program comments. **Program comments** explain the purpose of the program or procedure and describe what it accomplishes. A program comment always begins with the apostrophe character ('). Visual Basic ignores all program comments and does not execute them. Their purpose is to help programmers understand the functioning of the procedure.

In the code shown earlier, both the program comments and the following statement are indented in the procedure. Statements between the Private Sub and End Sub statements are usually indented to enable the programmer to more easily recognize the start and the end of a procedure. Indenting statements is done solely for the benefit of the programmer. Visual Basic ignores all leading spaces and tab characters that you use to indent statements.

```
imgCurrent.Picture = LoadPicture(txtFileName.Text)
```

This line in the program contains a statement that Visual Basic executes. This statement consists of two parts: a left-hand side and a right-hand side separated by an equal sign (=). This is called an **assignment statement**. In other words, the task on the right-hand side is performed and assigned to the left-hand side. The right-hand side contains a function named LoadPicture. A **function** is one way of executing a set of statements that perform a common task. Visual Basic supplies several **intrinsic functions** that perform mathematical tasks, such as computing the square root of a number, or tasks such as loading a graphical image into an Image control. To send information to a function, you provide arguments. **Arguments** contain information such as numbers, in the case of the function to compute a square root, or a string of characters representing a file name, in the case of the LoadPicture function. To use a function in a Visual Basic statement, you call the function. When you **call** a function, the code in that function executes using the supplied arguments. After the code has executed, intrinsic functions return a value, such as the square root of a number, or an object, such as a graphical image.

This assignment statement also sets a property at run time. Until now, you have set an object's properties by changing values in the Properties window at design time. You can, however, write Visual Basic statements that allow you to view and change properties while a program is running. You can perform many tasks—changing the font of text in a text box for emphasis, for example, while a user is entering text.

The best time to set properties depends on the needs of your program. Properties that do not change and initial values for properties, such as a label's caption, are generally set at design time using the Properties window. When the appearance of an object needs to change while the program is running, you must change the property by writing Visual Basic code. In fact, you cannot use the Properties window while the program is running. Thus you might set the initial font and type style of a text box using the Properties window. Then, when the object becomes active while the program is running, you might change the font to emphasize the object to the user.

To set the properties of an object while the program is running, you use the following general syntax of the assignment statement:

Syntax	***ObjectName.PropertyName = value***
Dissection	■ *ObjectName* is the name you assigned to the object's Name property when you created it. Remember, Visual Basic always assigns a name to an object. You can change the Name property to better explain the object's purpose in the program.
	■ *PropertyName* is the name of the object's property to be changed while the program is running.
	■ The *value* is the new value for the property. Be careful to assign only valid values to properties. For example, properties such as Caption can contain any text value, whereas properties such as Picture, which you use to control the graphical image displayed in an Image object, can contain only pictures.
Code Example	`imgCurrent.Picture = LoadPicture("A:\Chapter.01\Item1.bmp")`
Code Dissection	This assignment statement contains a right-hand side and left-hand side, just like any assignment statement. On the right-hand side, the LoadPicture function is called with one argument—the file named "A:\Chapter.01\Item1.bmp". When this statement executes, this picture will be loaded and stored in the Picture property of the Image object named imgCurrent.

The **LoadPicture** function loads a graphical image into the Picture property of an Image object at run time. It accepts one argument—a string of characters containing the name of the desired picture file—and returns the picture to be stored in the Picture property of an Image object.

Now that you understand the code you need to write, you are ready to enter the statements in the Code window. First, however, you should be aware of **IntelliSense technology**, such as ToolTips, that will guide you through the process of writing Visual Basic statements. As you write code, Visual Basic will list the possible options for completing a statement. For example, consider the statement you are prepared to write.

```
imgCurrent.Picture = LoadPicture(txtFileName.Text)
```

After you type the object name (imgCurrent) and the period (.), Visual Basic will display a list box containing the properties and methods supported by the Image control. This list appears because Visual Basic recognized that imgCurrent is an instance of the Image control. As with any list box, you can use scroll bars to select an item from this list.

IntelliSense technology also guides you through the process of completing the function arguments—in this case, the LoadPicture function. After you enter the name of the function (LoadPicture), Visual Basic will display a ToolTip that lists the arguments pertaining to the function.

To write the code for an event procedure:

1   Enter the code shown in Figure 1-33.

comments

IntelliSense list box

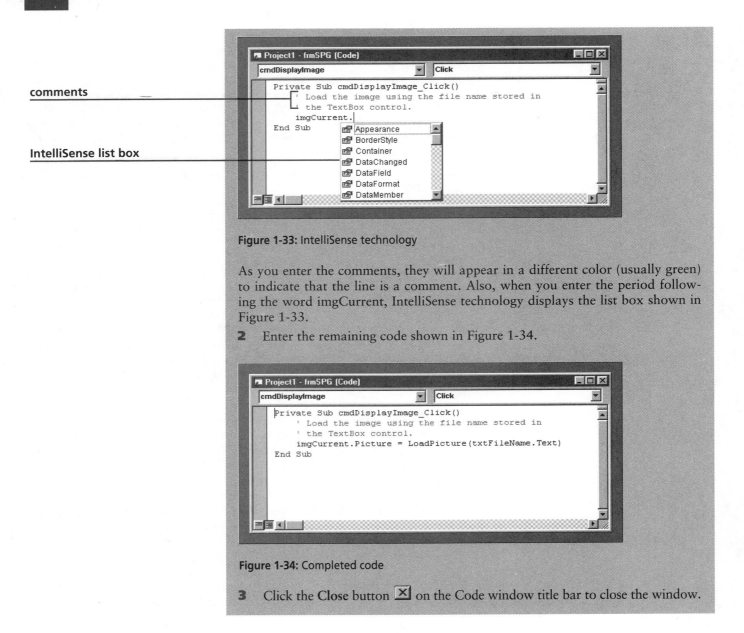

Figure 1-33: IntelliSense technology

As you enter the comments, they will appear in a different color (usually green) to indicate that the line is a comment. Also, when you enter the period following the word imgCurrent, IntelliSense technology displays the list box shown in Figure 1-33.

2   Enter the remaining code shown in Figure 1-34.

Figure 1-34: Completed code

3   Click the **Close** button ⊠ on the Code window title bar to close the window.

You have reached another milestone in the program. Now, you will save your program and test it to ensure that it works correctly.

Running the Completed Program

To run a program, click the Start button on the toolbar (just as you did in the first section). Remember, whenever you run a program, Visual Basic switches from design mode to run mode, activates the startup form, and waits for user input. You can stop a program at any time by clicking the End button on the Visual Basic toolbar.

To test a program:

1 Click the **Save Project** button 🔲 on the toolbar to save your work.

2 Click the **Start** button ▶ on the toolbar.

The form appears on the screen—Visual Basic has loaded all of the form's objects and their associated code.

3 Test the program by entering the file named **A:\Chapter.01\Startup\Item1.bmp** in the text box. Change the drive designator as necessary.

4 Click the **Display Image** command button to load the image stored in the file named Item1.bmp.

The graphical image appears on the form.

5 Click the **End** button ■ on the toolbar.

Although you, as the programmer, can click the End button on the toolbar to end the program and switch Visual Basic from run mode to design mode, the end-user of your program will not execute the program from the Visual Basic IDE. Rather, the end-user will likely run the executable program just as you would run any other executable program. Thus you need to provide the user with a way to end the program. The most common strategy for unloading a program is to put an **Unload** statement in an event procedure for a command button.

Syntax	Unload *formname*
Dissection	■ The **Unload** statement unloads a form, ending the program. ■ *formname* contains the name of the form to be unloaded. If the unloaded form is the only one loaded, the program ends.
Code Example	`Unload frmSPG`
Code Dissection	This statement unloads the form named frmSPG. Because it is the only form loaded, the program will end.

Now you can write the code for the command button that the end-user will use to exit the program.

To program the Exit button:

1 Open the Code window.

2 In the Object list box, select the command button named **cmdExit**. In the Procedure list box, make sure that the **Click** event procedure is selected.

3 Enter the following statement between the line containing the words Private Sub cmdExit_Click() and the line containing the words End Sub.

```
Unload frmSPG
```

4 Close the Code window.

5 Test the program. Click the **Start** button ▶ on the toolbar, then click the **Exit** command button. Visual Basic will switch from run mode to design mode.

Compiling a Program

You have now completed the program for this chapter. As mentioned earlier, however, the user likely will not run the program from Visual Basic. Instead, the program will be run from the Windows Start menu, independently of Visual Basic. As a consequence, you must translate the Visual Basic form and statements on that form into a type of file understood by the computer. This process is called **compilation** (compiling a program). Compiling a program translates the source-language statements—in this case, Visual Basic—into statements that the computer can execute directly. Visual Basic makes it very easy to compile a program. Simply click the Make SPG_S.exe option on the File menu and complete the dialogs.

To compile a program:

1 Save the project.
2 Click **File**, then click **Make SPG_S.exe**.
The Make Project dialog appears.
3 In the File name text box, select the default option **SPG_S.exe**, then click the **OK** button.
Visual Basic will check the program for errors and create the SPG_S.exe file.
4 Test the program and then exit Visual Basic. Using the Windows Explorer, locate the folder **Chapter.01\Startup** on the appropriate drive, click the **SPG_S.exe** file, then press the **Enter** key.
The program now runs just as it did inside the Visual Basic IDE.
5 Enter the file name **Chapter.01\Startup\Item1.bmp**, then click the **Display Image** command button. Set the drive designator for the file as necessary.
6 The image appears. End the program by clicking the Exit button.

If you were compiling a program for distribution, you might want to make the name of the file more intuitive. For the purposes of learning the steps to compile a program, however, it is sufficient to accept the default.exe file name.

S U M M A R Y

To start Visual Basic:

■ Click the Start button on the taskbar, then point to Programs, Microsoft Visual Basic 6.0, then click Microsoft Visual Basic 6.0.
or
Double-click the Microsoft Visual Basic 6.0 icon on the Windows desktop.

To display a ToolTip for a toolbar button:

■ Hold the insertion point over a button on the toolbar or toolbox until the ToolTip appears.

To configure the toolbars:

■ Click View, then Toolbars, then Customize. Use the Toolbars tab in the Customize dialog to select the check boxes next to the toolbars that should appear.
or
Right-click the toolbar, then click any toolbar name to display or hide the desired toolbar.

To open an existing project file:

■ Click File, click Open Project, then specify the drive, folder, and file name to open an existing project.
or
Click the Open Project button on the toolbar, then specify the drive, folder, and file name to open an existing project.

To run a project:

■ Click the Start button on the toolbar.

To end a program:

■ Click the End button on the toolbar.

To configure the Visual Basic environment:

■ Click Tools, click Options, then use the Options dialog to choose the desired environment settings.

To activate the Project Explorer:

■ Click the Project Explorer button on the toolbar, if necessary, to activate the Project Explorer.
or
Click View, then click Project Explorer to activate the Project Explorer.

To identify the modules that make up a project:

■ If any folder is closed in the Project Explorer, click the plus sign next to the closed folder in the Project Explorer to open the folder.

To activate the Form window:

■ Click the form in the Project Explorer, then click the View Object button in the Project Explorer to display the Form window.

To activate the Properties window:

■ Click the Properties Window button on the toolbar to activate the Properties window.
or
Right-click the control instance, then click Properties on the pop-up menu to activate the Properties window.
or
Click View on the menu bar, then click Properties window to activate the Properties window.

To use the Index tab for Visual Basic Help:

■ Click Help on the menu bar, then click Index. In the text box, type the word or phrase for which you want to access the Help library. In the list box, highlight the topic, then click the Display button. If the Topics Found dialog opens, click the appropriate topic, then click the Display button.

To use the Contents tab for Visual Basic Help:

■ Click Help, then Contents. Click the plus sign next to the appropriate listing as many times as needed to reach the desired topic in the Help library. A book icon appears when you have accessed a topic.

To print the Help topic:

■ Right-click the Help topic to activate the pop-up menu, then select Print.

To exit Visual Basic:

■ Click the Close button on the Visual Basic title bar.
or
Click File on the menu bar, then click Exit.

To create a new project file:

■ Start Visual Basic. A new project file is created automatically.
or
After Visual Basic is started, click File, then click New Project.

To display the Properties window:

■ Click the Project Explorer button, then click the View Object button.
■ Right-click the Form1 window, then click Properties on the pop-up menu.
■ Click the Categorized tab, if necessary.

To set the properties for the form:

■ Make sure the appropriate property in the Properties window is selected, then highlight its property value. Type or select the new value.

To save a project for the first time:

■ Click File on the menu bar, then click Save Project to activate the Save File As dialog.
or
Click the Save Project button on the toolbar to activate the Save File As dialog.
■ Click the Save in list arrow, select the drive designator as necessary, then double-click the desired folder name(s). In the File name text box, enter the desired name for the module file(s). Click Save.
■ The Save Project As dialog appears. Because you already specified the folder, you do not need to change the Save in list box entry. Enter the desired name for the project in the File name text box. Click Save.

To set the size and position of the form:

■ Activate the Properties window and select the object. Click the Categorized tab, then scroll down the Properties window to locate the Position section. Locate the Height property, highlight its default property value, and set it to the desired value. Locate the Width property, highlight the initial property value, and set it to the desired value. Locate the Left property, highlight the initial property value, and set it to the desired value. Locate the Top property, highlight the initial property value, and set it to the desired value.
or

■ Resize and reposition the object using the mouse. To resize the object, click the object, then position the pointer on one of the sizing handles to resize the object. Release the mouse button when the object has reached the desired size. To reposition the object, place the pointer anywhere within the object, but not on a sizing handle. Click and hold the mouse button, then drag the object to a different location. Release the mouse button when the object appears in the desired location.

To save an existing project:

■ Click the Save Project button on the toolbar. Visual Basic will save the form and project file without prompting you for any file names.

To create a control instance on a form:

■ Click the desired control on the toolbox, then click and drag to draw the control on the form. Use the Properties window to set the characteristics of the control instance.

To delete a control instance:

■ Click the object, then press the Delete key.
or
Click the object, click Edit on the menu bar, then click Delete.
or
Click the object, then click the Delete key on the toolbar.

To select the object and event procedure in the Code window:

■ In the Form window, right-click the form to activate the pop-up menu. Click View Code on the pop-up menu. When the Code window opens, click the Object list arrow, then click the appropriate object name. Click the Procedure list arrow, then click the appropriate event procedure name.

To write the code for an event procedure:

■ Select the object and event procedure in the Code window. Write the appropriate statements and program comments between the Private Sub and End Sub statements in the event procedures.

To assign a value to an object's property with code:

■ Use an assignment statement:

ObjectName.PropertyName = value

To end a program:

- In the Visual Basic IDE, click the End button on the toolbar.
  or
  Create a command button and, in its Click event procedure, include a statement to unload the form:

    Unload [*formname*]

  Click the command button to end the program.
  or
  Click the Close button on the form.

To test a program:

- Save your project. Click the Start button on the toolbar. The form appears on the screen—Visual Basic has loaded the form's objects and their associated code. Enter any necessary data and click any necessary command buttons. End the program.

To compile a program:

- Click File on the menu bar, then click Make *Project1*.exe (where *Project1* is the name of the current project).

Q U E S T I O N S

1. The _____ properties define the size and position of a form and the objects created on a form.
   a. LeftMargin, RightMargin, TopMargin, and LeftMargin
   b. Position and Size
   c. Position
   d. Height, Width, Top, and Left
   e. None of the above.

2. Which of the following are true regarding object names?
   a. The first character must be a letter.
   b. Names can contain spaces.
   c. Names must be less than 255 characters long.
   d. Both a and c.
   e. All of the above.

3. Which of the following statements are true regarding a label?
   a. It only displays output.
   b. It accepts input and displays output.
   c. It supports the Caption property.
   d. Both a and c.
   e. All of the above.

4. Which of the following statements are true regarding a text box?
   a. It only displays output.
   b. It accepts input and displays output.
   c. It supports the Caption property.
   d. Both a and c.
   e. All of the above.

5. Which of the following statements are true regarding a command button?
   a. It supports the Caption property.
   b. It supports the Text property.
   c. It responds to an event when clicked.
   d. Both a and b.
   e. Both a and c.

6. An event procedure begins with the words _____ and ends with the words
   _____ .
   a. Begin Sub, End Sub
   b. Begin Sub, Exit Sub
   c. Start Sub, End Sub
   d. Private Sub, End Sub
   e. Private Sub, Exit Sub

7. A comment begins with the _____ character.
   a. #
   b. &
   c. "
   d. comment
   e. '

8. What is the name of the statement that can be used to unload a form?
   a. Quit
   b. Stop
   c. Terminate
   d. Unload
   e. None of the above.

9. Write a statement that stores the Text property of the text box named txtOne in the Caption property of Label1.

10. Write a statement that loads the picture named **A:\Pic1.bmp** into the picture box named **picOne**.

11. Write a statement that loads a picture into the picture box named **picOne**, assuming that the name is stored in the text box named **txtOne**.

E X E R C I S E S

1. The staff at Southern Properties Group reviewed the program you created that displayed graphical images. They would like you to create another program that simulates the effect of a stoplight. Consider a stoplight as an object that can be green, yellow, or red. To accomplish this task, you will need to create an instance of the Image control and call the LoadPicture function to display three similar pictures. Each picture shares a common characteristic—they all look like a stoplight. Each picture, however, has a slightly different appearance. That is, each displays the same stoplight but illuminates a different light. To demonstrate the effect of the stoplight, you will create three command buttons (Stop, Caution, and Go) that, when clicked, display the correct image. Each control instance should have an appropriate name and caption. When a particular command button is clicked, the image corresponding to that button should appear. In addition to using the Text property of a text box as an argument in the LoadPicture function, you can specify a file name explicitly by enclosing it in quotes. When you have finished creating the program, you will run and test it. Figure 1-35 shows the completed form for the program.

Figure 1-35: Exercise 1

a. Run the executable file named **Chapter.01\Exercise\Sample\Ex1.exe**. Set the drive designator as necessary. Click each command button, noting how the icon changes as each button is clicked. End the program. (For the program to work properly, the icon files must reside in the same folder as the executable application.)

b. Start Visual Basic.

c. Set the appropriate property so that the title bar of the form contains the text **Southern Properties Group - Stop Light**.

d. Set the Name property of the form to **frmEx1**.

e. Resize the form until it resembles Figure 1-35.

f. Draw an Image control on the form. Refer to Figure 1-35 for placement and sizing.

g. Set the name of the image to **imgStopSign**.

h. Set the Stretch property so that the picture will fill in the region of the Image object.

i. Create three command buttons on the form. Set the Caption properties of the buttons to **Stop**, **Caution**, and **Go**, respectively.

j. Create a fourth command button and set its Caption property to **Exit**. Write the necessary code to exit the program when the user clicks this button.

k. Set the Name property for each command button using the correct prefix. Make sure the name conveys the purpose of each control instance.

l. Display the image named **Chapter.01\Exercise\Stop.ico** in the object named **imgStopSign**, using the following statement. (Although this statement appears on two lines here, when entering the statement into the Visual Basic Code window it appears on a single line.)

```
imgStopSign.Picture =
    LoadPicture("A:\Chapter.01\Exercise\Stop.ico")
```

m. Write the necessary statements in the **Click** event procedure for the Caution and Go command buttons to display the corresponding bitmap file in the Image object. The relevant images are stored in the files **Chapter.01\Exercise\Caution.ico** and **Chapter.01\Exercise\Go.ico**.

n. Add a program comment to each event procedure to describe its purpose.

o. Save the form and project with the names **Chapter.01\Exercise\frmEx1.frm** and **Chapter.01\Exercise\Ex1.vbp**, respectively.

p. Test the program. Click each command button to make sure a sign appears with the green, yellow, and red light visible.

q. Correct any mistakes and save your work again, if necessary.

2. Advanced Computer Graphics uses many graphic images in its Visual Basic programs. The owners of this company also know that Windows contains a large number of bitmap (.bmp) and other graphics files. They would like to use the Image control to display both their original images and Windows graphic images. Because all of the images may not be the same size, they would like to see the effect of setting the Stretch property on the various images. You will create a program with a text box in which the user enters the name of a graphical image as well as a command button that, when clicked, displays the selected graphics in two Image objects. One Image object will have the Stretch property set to True, and the other will have the Stretch property set to False.

This program will illustrate to the owners of Advanced Computer Graphics how the Stretch property controls the size of the loaded images. When your program is complete, your screen should resemble Figure 1-36.

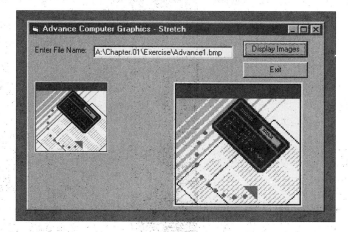

Figure 1-36: Exercise 2

a. Run the executable file named **Chapter.01\Exercise\Sample\Ex2.exe**. Set the drive designator as necessary. Enter the file name **Chapter.01\Exercise\Advance1.bmp** (include the appropriate drive designator) and click the Display Images button. The picture will appear in each Image control's instance created on the form, as shown in Figure 1-36. End the program.

b. Start Visual Basic.

c. Resize the form to match that shown in Figure 1-36.

d. Set the form name to **frmEx2**.

e. Set the title bar on the form to contain the text **Advanced Computer Graphics - Stretch**.

f. Draw a text box on the form and set the Name property using the correct prefix.

g. Remove the initial text from the text box.

h. Draw a label that describes the purpose of the text box as **Enter File Name:**.

i. Draw two Image objects on the form, one on the right-hand side and one on the left-hand side. Make both objects fairly large, but leave room for the CommandButton object. Set the Name property for each Image object appropriately.

j. Change the Stretch property of the right-hand Image object to True, so that the bitmap will fill in the region of the object.

k. Create a command button and set the caption as shown in Figure 1-36. Set the Name of the command button to **cmdDisplayImages**.

l. Write two statements that will execute when the user clicks the button: one to display the selected image files in the first Image object, and a second to load the selected image file in the other image.

m. Create a second command button with a caption of **Exit**. When clicked, this button should end the program. Save the form and project with the names **Chapter.01\Exercise\frmEx2.frm** and **Chapter.01\Exercise\Ex2.vbp**, respectively.

n. Test the program. Use the bitmap images named **Chapter.01\Exercise\Advance1.bmp** and **Chapter.01\Exercise\Advance2.wmf**, respectively.

o. Correct any mistakes and save your work again, if necessary.

3. Atlantic Beverages is a supplier of soft drinks to the hotel industry. It needs a program to produce a list that will be used by the company's drivers. This program will move a variety of standard text items to different parts of a completed shipping document. You will create a sample form to demonstrate how text can be moved to different control instances created on the form. You need to create a form that includes three labels, three text boxes, and three command buttons. Figure 1-37 shows the completed form.

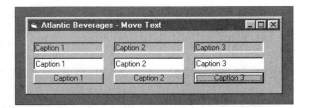

Figure 1-37: Exercise 3

a. Run the executable file named **Chapter.01\Exercise\Sample\Ex3.exe**. The form contains three labels, three text boxes, and three command buttons. Click each command button. When clicked, the command button's caption is copied to the label and text box that appears above the button, as shown in Figure 1-37. End the program.

b. Start Visual Basic.

c. Set the name of the form to **frmEx3**.

d. Resize the form to match that shown in Figure 1-37.

e. Set the title bar of the form so it contains the text shown in Figure 1-37.

f. Draw three Label objects of approximately the same size in the upper-top half of the form. Set the Name properties of the objects to **lbl1, lbl2**, and **lbl3**, respectively. Change the BorderStyle property to 1-Fixed Single.

g. Remove the initial text from each label.

h. Draw three text boxes of approximately the same size just below the labels. Set the Name property of each text box appropriately.

i. Remove the initial text from each text box.

j. Draw three CommandButton objects of approximately the same size in the lower-bottom half of the form. Set the captions of the command buttons to **Caption 1, Caption 2**, and **Caption 3**, respectively, and set the Name properties of each appropriately.

k. Open the Code window for the first command button's **Click** event.

l. Write two statements that will display the command button's caption in the corresponding label and text box.

m. Repeat the previous step for the second and third command buttons.

n. Save the form and project with the names **Chapter.01\Exercise\frmEx3.frm** and **Chapter.01\Exercise\Ex3.vbp**, respectively.

o. Test the program. Click each command button. The caption of the command button should appear in the corresponding label and text box as shown in Figure 1-37.

p. Correct any mistakes and save your work again, if necessary.

4. Mountaintop College is a small, private, two-year college. The chairperson of the computer department, Mary Gorden, would like an organization chart of the department, but she does not have a computer application specifically designed to draw organization charts. You will use Visual Basic to create the organization chart. The top-level box of the chart should contain the name of the department chairperson (Mary Gorden). Two middle-level boxes will contain the names of the two computer instructors, Judie Kindschi and Tom Galvez. One bottom-level box will contain your name. You will use labels as boxes to hold the names. After you have created the form for the organization chart, it should resemble Figure 1-38. You will then run the program to test it.

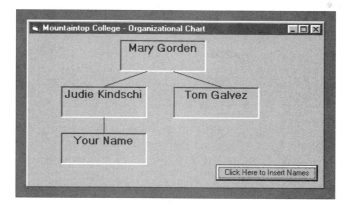

Figure 1-38: Exercise 4

a. Run the executable file named **Chapter.01\Exercise\Sample\Ex4.exe**. The form contains the labels and lines depicted in Figure 1-38. Click the Click Here to Insert Names command button to display the names in the labels, as shown in Figure 1-38. End the program.

b. Start Visual Basic.

c. Starting from the top and working down, draw four labels that resemble the boxes shown in Figure 1-38.

discovery ▶
discovery ▶

d. Change the BorderStyle property of all four labels to **1 - Fixed Single**.

e. Look up "Line control" in the Help library and read the Help information about this topic. Then, using the Line control, draw lines showing the departmental relationship between the labels.

f. Draw a CommandButton object on the bottom-right side of the form.

g. Specify the caption **Click Here To Insert Names** for the CommandButton object. If the entire caption does not fit in the command button, increase the size of the button.

h. Open the Code window for the CommandButton object and type the following program comment between the Private Sub and End Sub statements:

```
' This code will place each department member's name in the
' appropriate label.
```

i. Type the following lines of Visual Basic code between the Private Sub and End Sub lines. Substitute your name for the reference *Your Name*.

```
lbl1.Caption = "Mary Gorden"
lbl2.Caption = "Judie Kindschi"
lbl3.Caption = "Tom Galvez"
lbl4.Caption = "Your Name"
```

j. Test the program, clicking the command button to insert the names. Your screen should resemble Figure 1-38. If any names do not fit correctly in the appropriate label, click the **End** button on the toolbar and resize the label. Repeat this step as necessary until all names are fully displayed in the labels.

k. Save the form and project with the names **Chapter.01\Exercise\frmEx4.frm** and **Chapter.01\Exercise\Ex4.vbp**, respectively.

l. Correct any mistakes and save your work again, if necessary.

Understanding Code and Variables

Designing and Writing a Financial Calculator Program for the Island Financial Company

case▶ The Island Financial Company is an investment management firm. As part of their everyday business practices, the company's analysts forecast their clients' investment growth over time. The analysts use this information to estimate cash flow and income. They need a calculator program to compute the future value of an investment.

Previewing the Calculator Program

The user of the calculator program will supply three input values. The first input value represents the initial value of an annuity. The second input value represents the term of the annuity expressed in years. The third and final input value represents the interest rate of the annuity, also expressed as a percentage.

The program contains three command buttons as well. One command button has the caption Compute Future Value. When clicked, it will use the input values to process and display the future value of the annuity and the gain on the investment. Another command button will clear the input and output values. The third command button will exit the program. The completed form for the calculator program will look like Figure 2-1.

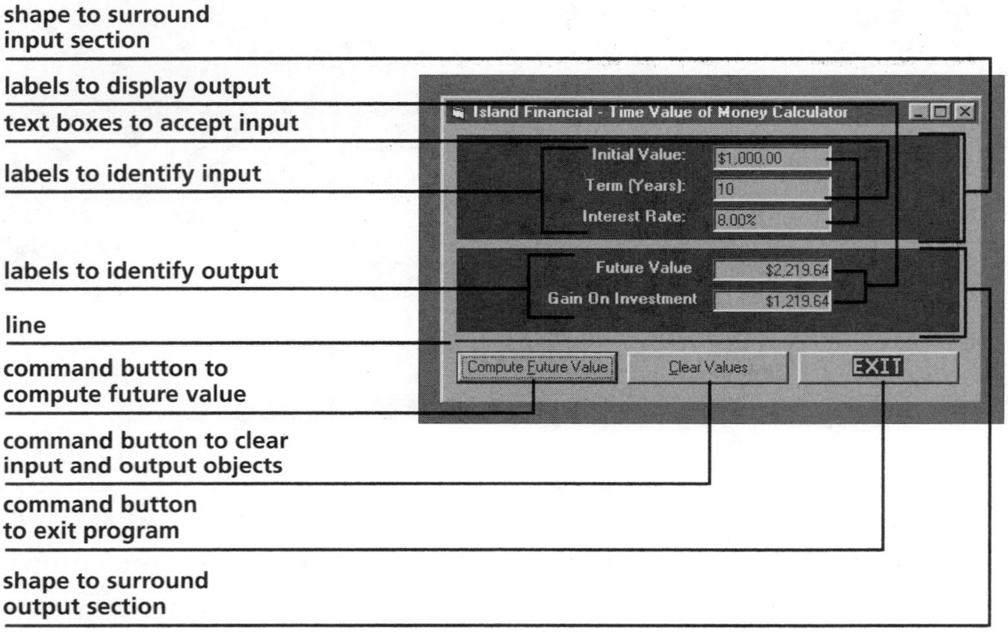

shape to surround input section

labels to display output

text boxes to accept input

labels to identify input

labels to identify output

line

command button to compute future value

command button to clear input and output objects

command button to exit program

shape to surround output section

Figure 2-1: Completed calculator form

As shown in Figure 2-1, the form is divided into two visual sections. The upper section contains the control instances in which the user will enter input values. The lower section displays the output from the program. In Figure 2-1, the input values of $1000.00, 10 years, and 8.00% were used to compute the future value of the investment. The results appear in the output section of the form.

You will begin this chapter by opening the project file that contains the completed calculator form and reviewing the tasks that it performs.

To preview the completed application:

1 Start Visual Basic, then open the project file named **Chapter.02\Complete\ IF_C.vbp**. Note that, depending upon your computer's system settings, the file extension may not appear. Set the drive designator, as necessary, to reflect whether you copied the files to the hard or floppy disk.

2 Run the program by clicking the Start button ▶ on the toolbar. Enter 1000.00 as the initial value, press the **Tab** key, enter **10** as the term of the investment, press the **Tab** key, enter **8.00** as the interest rate, then click the **Compute Future Value** command.

As you enter input, the characters in the current control instance will appear in a blue bold font to emphasize the current object to the user. Also, as you press the Tab key to move from one control instance to another, the previous control instance becomes formatted as a dollar amount with two decimal places or as a percentage with two decimal places. After clicking the Compute Future Value command button, the output values are displayed as shown in Figure 2-1.

3 Click the **Clear Values** command button.

The input and output fields are cleared.

4 Click the **EXIT** command button.

Visual Basic switches from run mode to design mode.

5 Exit Visual Basic.

In the previous chapter, you reviewed a completed program, then created that program from scratch. That is, you created a new project. As a programmer, you will sometimes create new programs from scratch, but more often you will modify existing ones. In fact, most programmers spend far more time on the latter task than on the former one.

In this chapter, you will modify and add to an existing project. First, however, you will learn the logic and methodology used to create good computer programs.

In this section you will:

- Become familiar with the elements of program design
- Understand the fundamentals of Visual Basic project files
- Create and use multiple instances of labels, text boxes, and command buttons
- Use Visual Basic's formatting tools to align multiple control instances
- Improve a program's user interface with shapes and lines

Designing and Modifying a Program

Designing a Computer Program

Before creating a program, you should spend time ensuring that it will meet the intended users' needs. Creating programs involves much more than simply sitting down at a computer, developing a user interface, and writing the code. In fact, to ensure a high-quality product, most companies require programmers to understand a problem and its best solution before actually writing the program. This planning stage can prevent many hours of **debugging**, which is the process of locating and fixing errors that cause a program to run incorrectly. For more information about how to debug a program, refer to "Appendix A: Debugging."

Well-written computer programs complement other programs already in use by an organization. To accomplish this synergy, many companies follow a standard set of steps, known as a **methodology**, for designing programs. A strong methodology requires the completion of one step before the programmer attempts the next step. The basic methodology in designing a computer program is as follows:

1. Completely understand the problem and the data needed to solve it.
2. Analyze and break down the problem into English sentences that use simple, nontechnical terms. The English sentences that describe the solution to the problem are often referred to as **pseudocode**.
3. Sketch a picture of the user interface design for each form in the program.
4. Identify the tasks to be performed and their location in the program.

Whenever an industry has a standard methodology, industry participants will improve upon it. We discuss such improvements next.

Program Design Methodologies

Over the past 30 years, programmers have used many tools to plan and document programs and complete applications. One of the first development and design tools was NCR's Accurately Defined Systems (ADS), which was developed in the late 1960s. Programmers also have other modern and nonproprietary tools at their disposal: program flowcharts, data flow diagrams, Gantt charts, Critical Path Method (CPM), Program Evaluation and Review Technique (PERT), structure charts, decision trees, structured walkthroughs, data modeling, query analysis, Computer Aided Software Engineering (CASE), and prototyping. In addition to these nonproprietary tools, programmers can choose from among hundreds of proprietary products and methodologies that are sold by vendors. All of these tools help the programmer write programs that are:

- Accurate—A program that does not accomplish what its originators intended it to do is worthless.

- Easy to understand—A program that is understood only by the original programmer does not serve the long-term needs of a large business. In a large business, the original programmer is rarely available to maintain the program.
- Easy to change—A program that can be understood but that is impossible or difficult to modify is useless. Visual object-oriented languages and the end-user interfaces that they produce are easily modified.
- Improvements to programmer efficiency—The language used to construct the program must be powerful enough to eliminate many of the **microtasks**, or smaller tasks, that formerly concerned the programmer. Before the advent of object-oriented languages, the programmer had to reinvent the wheel with almost every program. Today, however, the programmer is made vastly more productive and efficient by his or her ability to reuse code and to take advantage of prewritten, named code blocks that are simple to understand and use, but in reality may be quite complex.
- Efficiently executed—Even though the typical end-user has tremendous computing power on his or her desktop, new operating systems that run many programs simultaneously require vast amounts of computing horse-power. Today's programs must coexist easily, and they must not slow down the user's machine.

(Adapted from Philippakis, A. S., and Leonard J. Kazmier. *Program Design Concepts*. New York: McGraw Hill, 1983.)

Designing the User Interface

Designing a user interface requires an artistic eye and adherence to several design principles. Figure 2-2 describes the principles that will help you create a good user interface.

Control	The user always should control the program, rather than the other way around.
User-friendliness	The interface should help the user accomplish tasks and not call attention to itself. Too many different fonts, lines, or images tend to distract the user from the task at hand.
Intuitiveness	The interface should follow a direct style that proceeds logically. Thus, if a user needs to complete different steps to accomplish an activity, the steps should be grouped together.
Consistency	The interface should be conceptually, linguistically, visually, and functionally consistent. Also, the font style used should be consistent throughout the interface. Avoid using more than two or three fonts on a form. Too many fonts can cause the user interface to appear cluttered and unbalanced.
Clarity	Visual elements should be readily comprehensible.
Feedback	The interface should provide immediate and clear feedback to the user. For example, if a user adds a record to a file, the interface should inform the user that the record was added. Likewise, if a user makes an error when entering data, the interface should communicate the cause of the error and possible solutions to the user.

Figure 2-2: Principles of a good user interface

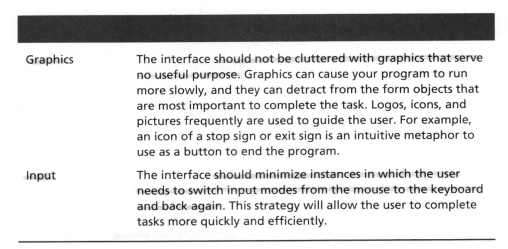

Graphics	The interface should not be cluttered with graphics that serve no useful purpose. Graphics can cause your program to run more slowly, and they can detract from the form objects that are most important to complete the task. Logos, icons, and pictures frequently are used to guide the user. For example, an icon of a stop sign or exit sign is an intuitive metaphor to use as a button to end the program.
Input	The interface should minimize instances in which the user needs to switch input modes from the mouse to the keyboard and back again. This strategy will allow the user to complete tasks more quickly and efficiently.

Figure 2-2: Principles of a good user interface (continued)

In following the principles described in Figure 2-2, a programmer would sketch a user interface on a piece of paper before creating it on the computer. Figure 2-3 shows the user interface design for the calculator program.

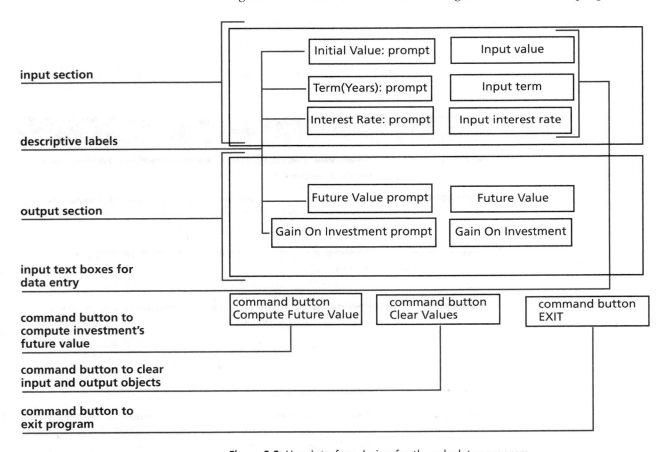

Figure 2-3: User interface design for the calculator program

As shown in Figure 2-3, this interface provides three text boxes for the user to input the initial value of an investment, its term, and its interest rate. The design includes descriptive labels (prompts) to the left of the three text boxes, alerting the user about which data should be entered into which text box. The interface also contains labels to describe the output values. As noted at the beginning of the chapter, the form will also include three command buttons—one to calculate the future value and gain on an investment, another to clear both the input and output values in preparation for another calculation, and the third to exit the program.

In this chapter, you will work on a partially completed program. The parts of the program that have already been completed cover topics presented in Chapter 1. For example, this chapter's program includes labels and text boxes; you created labels and text boxes in the previous chapter. This strategy allows you to focus on the new concepts of the chapter without performing repetitive tasks with which you are already familiar.

The form in this chapter's program contains five labels, three of which describe input values—Initial Value:, Term(Years):, and Interest Rate:. The text boxes to the right of the labels will hold the actual input values. The other two labels describe the program's output: Future Value and Gain On Investment. The form's caption is "Island Financial - Time Value of Money Calculator," which appears in the title bar of the form.

Now that you understand the purpose of this chapter's program, you will use it as a base on which to build your knowledge of controls and formatting menu items.

Expanding Your Knowledge of Controls

As you learned in Chapter 1, you add control instances to a form and set their properties using the Properties window. In that chapter, you used the Label, TextBox, Image, and CommandButton controls to create the program's user interface. Many more properties pertain to each of these controls than were explained in Chapter 1. In this chapter, you will learn about these additional properties.

The Label Control

Properties relating to the label (and most visible controls for that matter) are used to determine the foreground and background color of the control instance and the text it contains. In addition, other properties are used to determine the font and the alignment of the text.

Syntax	**Label**
Definition	The **Label** control is used to display textual output. The standard prefix for this control is "lbl".
Properties	■ The **Alignment** property determines how the textual characters are aligned in the region of the label. Text can be left-, right-, or center-aligned.
	■ The **Appearance** property, if set to 1 - 3D, causes the label to appear recessed. If set to 0 - Flat, the label does not appear recessed. For the label to appear recessed, the BorderStyle property must also be set to 1 - Fixed Single.
	■ The **BackStyle** property works in conjunction with the BackColor property. If the BackStyle is set to 0 - Transparent, the background color of the form or image behind the control is visible. If it is set to 1 - Opaque, then the background color is defined by the BackColor property.

- The **BackColor** and **ForeColor** properties are used to specify the background and foreground colors, respectively, for the label. The visible region of the label appears in the background color, and the characters appear in the foreground color.

- The **Caption** property identifies the text that appears in the label.

- The **Font** property defines the typeface and the size of the text.

- The **Name** property defines the name by which you will call the label in the code. In this book, the Name property will be set only when code is written to reference the label.

The Label control instances in this program and other programs identify the contents of other control instances and display the output resulting from computations. The user will not change the text in the labels or interact with them in any way. In this chapter, you will modify the properties of the various labels so as to see the visual effects. First, however, you will learn about several Visual Basic tools available to help you align and format the control instances on a form.

Changing Multiple Control Instances with the Property Window

As you create the user interface for a program, you should pay attention to the user interface principles discussed in Figure 2-2. Adhering to these principles will make the program easier to understand and more readily acceptable to the user. For example, control instances on a form should adhere to the following principles:

- Alignment—Control instances appearing in a column should be aligned vertically.
- Balance—Control instances should be distributed evenly about the form. That is, they should not all appear on the left-hand side or right-hand side of the form.
- Appropriate color—Although color can improve a user interface greatly, it can also be abused. Use soft colors like blue, green, or gray for most forms, and avoid including too many colors on a single form. Bright colors like red and orange should be used only for emphasis. Be sure to maintain sufficient contrast between the foreground and the background colors used on a form.
- Function grouping—Control instances that share a similar purpose should be grouped together visually. For example, the program in this chapter divides the controls between input and output sections.
- Consistent sizing—Control instances should be consistent in size. For example, when a form has multiple command buttons, they should be the same size.

To help you apply these principles, Visual Basic supports several formatting tools. These tools allow you to align multiple control instances with one another and space the instances evenly on a form. To use the formatting tools, you must learn how to select multiple control instances.

Visual Basic allows you to select multiple control instances at the same time. In such a case, one control instance will be the **active control** and will appear with dark blue sizing handles. The sizing handles for the other selected control instances will appear with a border, but the border will not be filled in.

You can use two techniques to select multiple control instances. Using the first technique, you can hold down the Shift or Control key, click on the first control instance, then click on all subsequent control instances without releasing the Shift or Control key. The other technique takes advantage of the Pointer tool on the toolbox. To select a group of controls, click the Pointer tool, then drag the mouse to define a rectangular region around the control instances. When the mouse button is released, the control instances that appear inside the drawn rectangle will be selected. Even if only part of a control's visible region lies in the rectangle, the control instance will be selected. When you select multiple control instances, you can set specific properties for all of them simultaneously, rather than on an individual basis.

As you perform the following steps, save your work frequently. If you later make an error that you cannot correct, you can load the most recently saved copies of the form and project file and continue your work from that point.

To set the properties of multiple control instances:

1. Start Visual Basic, then open the partially completed project file named **Chapter.02\Startup\IF_S.vbp**. Set the drive designator as necessary.

2. Open the Project Explorer, if necessary, open the **Forms** folder, click the form named **frmIslandCalculator**, then click the **View Object** button 🖼 to display the form.

3. The Form window opens and displays the partially completed form, as shown in Figure 2-4.

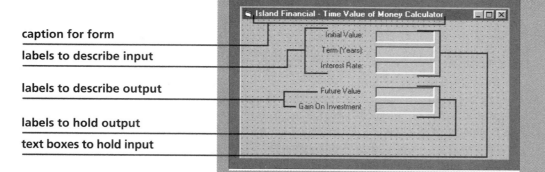

caption for form

labels to describe input

labels to describe output

labels to hold output

text boxes to hold input

Figure 2-4: Calculator form with initial objects created

This form contains the text boxes and labels that are used in the final program. Many of their properties have not been set, however. You will set those properties here. In addition, you will create the missing command buttons and graphical shapes as you complete the steps in the chapter.

4. To select multiple objects, click the **Pointer tool** on the toolbox, then draw a rectangle around the Label objects shown in Figure 2-5 to activate them. Remember to select only the labels that contain text. Do not select labels or text boxes used to hold output or input. In Figure 2-5, the active selected control appears with shaded sizing handles. Note that the active selected control shown in the figure may differ from the one on your form depending upon how you draw the rectangle around the control instances.

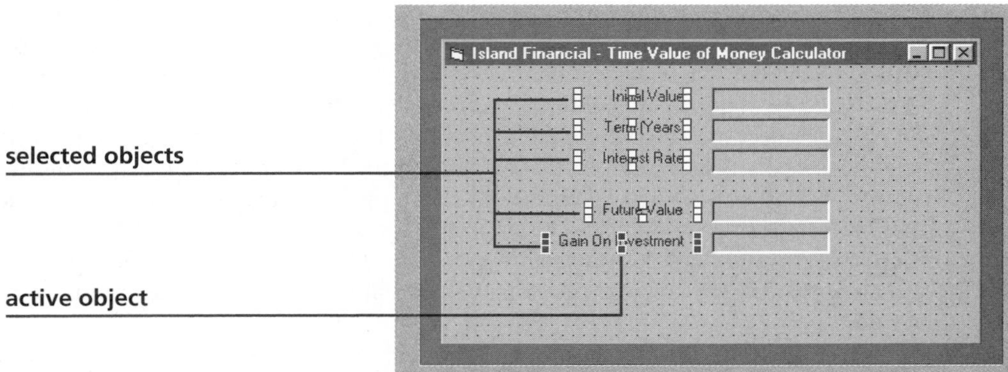

selected objects

active object

Figure 2-5: Selecting multiple objects

5   If it is not already open, open the Properties window by clicking the **Properties Window** button 🖳 on the toolbar.

6   Make sure that the **Categorized tab** is active and that its **Appearance** section is visible, as shown in Figure 2-6.

no object listed

Figure 2-6: Properties window with multiple objects selected

In Figure 2-6, nothing appears in the Object list box because multiple controls are selected, and you are setting properties for all of the selected controls simultaneously. Also, the title bar in the Properties window is misleading. It displays the name of one of the objects selected.

7   Click the **ForeColor** property, click its **Value column**, click the **Properties** button 🔽, click the **Palette tab**, if necessary, to open the color palette, then click **light blue**.

The text color of the label changes.

8   In the Font section of the Categorized tab, click the **Value column** for the **Font** property to display the Properties button, then click the **Properties** button 🔳. The Font dialog opens.

9   Click **Bold** in the Font style list box, as shown in Figure 2-7, then click the **OK** button.

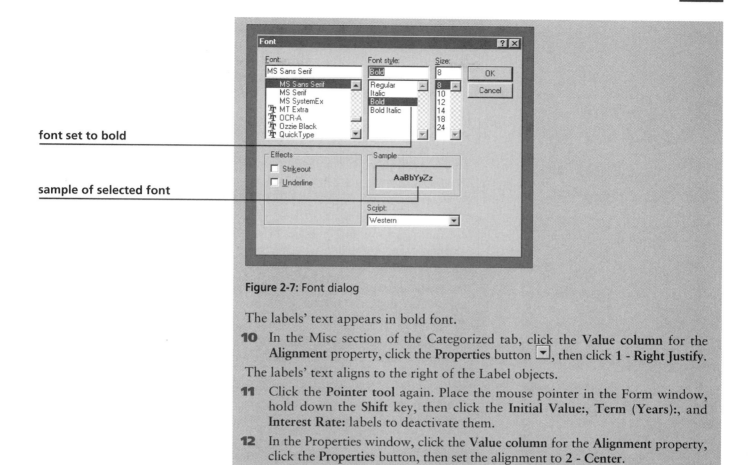

font set to bold

sample of selected font

Figure 2-7: Font dialog

The labels' text appears in bold font.

10 In the Misc section of the Categorized tab, click the **Value column** for the **Alignment** property, click the **Properties** button ⬇, then click **1 - Right Justify**.

The labels' text aligns to the right of the Label objects.

11 Click the **Pointer tool** again. Place the mouse pointer in the Form window, hold down the **Shift** key, then click the **Initial Value:**, **Term (Years):**, and **Interest Rate:** labels to deactivate them.

12 In the Properties window, click the **Value column** for the **Alignment** property, click the **Properties** button, then set the alignment to **2 - Center**.

At this point, the descriptive labels and the background color of the form have inadequate contrast. Later in this chapter, you will solve this problem by creating graphical shapes on the form to group the controls into input and output sections. Right now, you turn your attention to the CommandButton control.

The CommandButton Control

As you saw in Chapter 1, the CommandButton control on the toolbox allows you to create a button that a user clicks to carry out an action. In most forms, a command button appears as a three-dimensional raised object. Inside the visible region of the command button, you can place text to describe the button's function or display a picture to represent the button's purpose visually. In this section, you will display text on two command buttons and a graphical image on a third command button.

Like a label, a command button has both a Caption property and a Name property. In addition, it has other properties to control its appearance. As with other types of objects, you should use a standard prefix to name the command button.

Syntax	**CommandButton**
Definition	The **CommandButton** control is used to create a button that the end-user clicks. When clicked, the button responds to the Click event, causing the corresponding Click event procedure to be executed. The standard prefix for the command button is "cmd".

Properties	■ The **Caption** property contains the text that should appear on the button. You also can create a hot key for a command button by inserting an ampersand character (&) in the Caption property just before the character that should act as the hot key. A **hot key** is a set of keystrokes, such as Alt+C, that, when typed, will produce the same result as clicking the command button. Each hot key on a form must be unique.
	■ The **Default** property, when set to True, allows a user to press the Enter key as an alternative to clicking the button to activate the button's Click event procedure. Only one CommandButton object on a form can serve as the default object—that is, have its Default property set to True. It would not make sense to have two default objects attempt to respond to the Enter key being pressed.
	■ You can create your own ToolTips by setting the **ToolTipText** property. Whenever the mouse pointer is positioned over the button for about one second, the message stored in this property will appear just below the button.
	■ The **Enabled** property can be either True or False. If True, the button will respond when clicked. If False, the caption will appear shaded and the button will not respond to events.
	■ The **Picture** property contains a picture that will appear on the command button instead of a caption. To display a different picture indicating that the button is disabled or that the event procedure is currently running, you can set the **DisabledPicture** and **DownPicture** properties, respectively. If the Caption property receives a value as well, the caption will appear on the button along with the picture.
	■ The **Style** property can be set to 0 - Standard, which causes the caption to appear on the button. When set to 1- Graphical, both a caption (if one exists) and a picture will appear on the button.
Events	■ The **Click** event occurs whenever the user clicks the button. If the command button is the default button, then the Click event will occur when the user presses the Enter key.

Setting the Default property of a command button can improve the form's user interface by allowing the user to press the Enter key to execute the most commonly used button rather than forcing the user to move from the keyboard to the mouse and back again. Good programmers minimize user transitions between the keyboard and mouse whenever possible. Using hot keys gives the user an even quicker way to execute a command.

To set the properties for the command buttons:
1   Create the **Compute Future Value** command button on the form. Remember, to create a control instance, you click the control in the toolbar. You then move the mouse to the form, hold down the mouse button, and draw the region of the control instance.

2   Set the Name property to **cmdComputeFutureValue**, then the Caption property to **Compute &Future Value**. When you type "&" next to "F", "F" becomes the hot key for the button. You do not need to write any code or set any other properties to define the hot key. Set the Default property to **True**. Set the ToolTipText property (found in the Misc section of the Categorized tab) to **Click to compute the investment's future value.**

3   As you create the buttons, position and size them to match the buttons shown in Figure 2-8. Later, you will use the alignment tools to align the buttons visually on the form.

4   Create the **Clear Values** command button on the form, as shown in Figure 2-8. Set the Caption property to **&Clear Values**, then set the Name property to **cmdClearValues**. The character "C" becomes the hot key for the button. Set the ToolTipText property to **Reset the calculator.**

5   Create the **Exit** command button on the form, then set the Name property to **cmdExit**.

6   Click the **Value column** for the Picture property (found in the Appearance section), then click the **Properties** button ⊡ for the Picture property. The Load Picture dialog appears, allowing you to select the file to load. Click the file named **Chapter.02\Startup\Exit.bmp**, then click the **Open** button. Set the drive designator as necessary.

7   Remove the caption **command1** from the command button's Caption property.

8   Set the Style property to **1 - Graphical**. Set the ToolTipText property to **Stop running the program.**

9   Test the program by moving the mouse pointer over each of the command buttons to make sure the ToolTips appear.

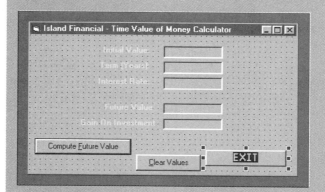

Figure 2-8: Command button controls

Now that your form contains multiple command buttons, you will learn about the menu commands that help you change the size and alignment of control instances such as command buttons.

Changing Multiple Control Instances with the Format Menu Commands

The Format menu contains a number of menu items that are used to align multiple control instances. The following list summarizes the different options:

- The **Align** command aligns the borders of multiple controls with one another. For example, you can align the left, right, top, or bottom margins of the selected controls. In all cases, the selected controls align to the active selected control.

- The **Make Same Size** command, as its name implies, makes all of the selected controls the same size. This size is determined by the active selected control.
- The **Horizontal Spacing** command sets the amount of space (horizontally) between each of the selected controls to ensure that the space between each control is the same.
- The **Vertical Spacing** command sets the amount of space (vertically) between each of the selected controls to ensure that the space between each control is the same.
- The **Center in Form** command centers the selected controls between either the top and bottom margins of the form or the left and right margins.

Each of these commands works the same way, and each uses the active selected control instance to determine the size and/or alignment of the other control instances.

Your form already includes multiple command buttons. Now you can use the formatting tools to make these control instances the same size and to align them on the form.

To size and align multiple control instances:

1   While holding down the Shift key, select the three command buttons at the bottom of the form by clicking the left mouse button on each control instance. Make sure that you select the **EXIT** command button last. The **EXIT** command button becomes the active control instance.

2   Click **Format** on the menu bar, point to **Make Same Size**, then click **Both**.

The command buttons all become the same size.

3   Click **Format**, point to **Align**, then click **Tops** to align the control instances vertically.

4   Click **Format**, point to **Horizontal Spacing**, then click **Make Equal**.

The distances between the three command buttons become identical.

5   Click **Format**, point to **Center in Form**, then click **Horizontally**.

The three command buttons become centered between the left and right margins of the form.

As you can see, formatting commands significantly simplify the process of aligning various control instances on a form. Formatting commands can be used on other types of control instances as necessary.

The TextBox Control

As you learned in Chapter 1, a TextBox object displays textual information and allows a user to type in values to be used in the program. That is, a text box is used for both input and output.

Like a label, the TextBox control supports properties, such as Alignment and Font, that you can set. The text displayed in a label is set through the Caption property, whereas the text that appears in a text box is determined by the Text property. The text box has some properties that allow it to behave differently than a label. For example, sometimes text may not fit in the region of the text box. In such a case, if you want the text to appear on multiple lines, you can set the

Use the Label control for text that will not change, such as prompts, or when it will display only output. Use the TextBox control when the object must both receive input and display output.

MultiLine property to True. You can then set the ScrollBars property to True, which allows the user to scroll through text box contents that are not visible in the region of the text box initially shown on the screen.

Syntax	TextBox
Definition	The **TextBox** control accepts textual input and displays textual output. The standard prefix for this control is "txt".
Properties	■ The **Appearance, BackColor, BorderStyle, ForeColor, Font**, and **Name** properties are identical to the Label control properties of the same name.
	■ The **Alignment** property is used to left-, right-, or center-align text in a text box. The alignment of the text, however, is changed only if the MultiLine property is set to True when Windows 95 is being used. When the operating system is Windows NT, this case does not apply.
	■ The **MultiLine** property can be either True or False. If True, text will appear on multiple lines. If False, text will appear on a single line.
	■ The **ScrollBars** property can be either True or False. If True, scroll bars will appear.
	■ The **TabIndex** property determines the order in which the object receives the focus when the user presses the Tab key.
	■ The **Text** property contains the text that appears in the text box.
Events	■ The **Change** event occurs each time the contents of a text box change. This event is useful for verifying that the user is entering valid information.
	■ The **Click** event occurs when the user clicks the mouse pointer in the text box.
	■ The **GotFocus** event occurs when the text box becomes the active object.
	■ The **LostFocus** event occurs when another object on the form (other than the active text box) becomes active.
	■ Each time a user types a character in a text box, the **KeyPress** event is generated. It allows you to find out exactly what key the user typed in the box.
Methods	■ The **SetFocus** method is used to set the input focus to a particular text box or other object that can receive input focus.

In the program in this chapter, the user will type the initial value, term, and interest rate into the text boxes on the form. The text boxes appear to the right of the labels. As you may recall, the text boxes already have meaningful names. The first text box, which accepts the initial value for the investment, has the name txtInitialValue. The second box's name is txtTermYears, and the third box's name is txtInterestRate. We changed the names because you will write code to reference the text boxes with code.

Setting the Tab Order

Every form has only one active control instance at any given time. When you type text in a TextBox object, for example, that text box is the active object. The active object has the **focus** or **input focus**. When running a program, the user generally changes the focus between one object and another by pressing the Tab key or clicking an object.

The TabIndex property determines the order in which objects receive the focus when a user presses the Tab key. This **tab order** is determined initially by the order in which the objects were created on the form. To change the tab order, you modify the value of the TabIndex property. When you alter the TabIndex property of one object, the TabIndex properties of the other objects on the form are adjusted accordingly. The TabIndex property begins by counting from 0 and incrementing each object by 1. Thus the object that first receives focus on a form has a TabIndex property of 0, the second has a TabIndex property of 1, the third has a TabIndex property of 2, and so on. You do not have to set the tab order for objects, such as labels, that never receive focus.

The analysts at Island Financial will type information into the three text boxes on the form, then click the Compute Future Value command button. The TextBox objects are arranged in a column, so the tab order moves from the top text box to the middle text box to the bottom text box, then to the Compute Future Value command button. The EXIT command button is the last item to receive focus in this program.

As noted earlier, the default tab order corresponds to the order in which objects were created on the form. You will now change that order so that the first text box in the column (txtInitialValue) receives the focus first, then the next text box, and so on. Thus the txtInitialValue text box needs a TabIndex property setting of 0, the txtTermYears text box needs a TabIndex property setting of 1, the txtInterestRate text box needs a TabIndex property setting of 2, the Compute Future Value command button needs a setting of 3, the Clear Values command button needs a TabIndex property setting of 4, and the EXIT command button needs a TabIndex property of 5.

GUI

tip

• • • • • • • • • • • • • •

▶ Setting the tab order logically for the objects on the form is important; the tab order should be arranged so that as the user presses the Tab key, the objects receive focus in a vertical or horizontal sequence. That is, when a user types information into the objects on a form, the information is completed from top to bottom or left to right, depending on the way the form's objects are positioned.

To set the tab order of objects:

1   Click the **txtInitialValue** object to the right of the Initial Value: label to select it.

2   Verify that the TabIndex property value for the text box is 0.

3   Click the **txtTermYears** object to the right of the Term (Years): label, then verify that its TabIndex property is 1.

4   Click the **txtInterestRate** object to the right of the Interest Rate: label, then verify that its TabIndex property is 2.

5   Click the **Compute Future Value** command button, then set its TabIndex property to 3.

6   Click the **Clear Values** command button, then set its TabIndex property to 4.

7   Click the **EXIT** command button, then set its TabIndex property to 5.

8   Test the program. The first object to receive focus should be the Initial Value text box at the top of the form. Continue pressing the **Tab** key to change the focus from object to object to ensure the tab order is correct. Exit the program.

Once the tab order is correct, you need to add the form's visual objects—a line to separate the command button and two dark blue areas to identify the input and output sections.

Improving the User Interface with Graphical Controls

When a form contains multiple objects, a consistent presentation or logical grouping of those objects will improve the user interface. For example, the calculator program includes three logical groupings: a section for input, a section to display the output, and a section containing the buttons that perform the processing. To communicate this structure to the user, you can separate each of these sections visually by using the Shape control or the Line control.

Whether you use these two controls in isolation or in tandem, color will influence their effectiveness. When selecting colors for a form and the control instances created on the form, keep them simple and consistent. Although different applications may have different color requirements, the following guidelines will help you with color selection:

- Use bright colors such as red, orange, and yellow only to attract the user's attention to something important or extraordinary.
- For objects with which the user interacts regularly, choose neutral or soft colors. For instance, make a form background light gray instead of bright purple.
- Similar objects should have similar colors. That is, all labels on a form describing text boxes should have the same background and font colors.
- Provide adequate contrast between foreground and background colors. Text boxes, for example, should have a white or light gray background and a dark-colored or black text foreground.

The Shape Control The Shape control visually groups related objects. In this program, you will place the input items into one group and the output items into another group. This arrangement can be accomplished by enclosing each group in a dark blue region.

Syntax	Shape
Definition	With the **Shape** control, you can draw rectangles and circles on a form and fill the shapes with different colors and patterns. The standard prefix for an instance of the Shape control is "shp".
Properties	■ The **BackColor** and **BackStyle** properties work together to define the shape's background. When the BackStyle property is set to its default, 0 - Transparent, the BackColor setting is ignored.
	■ The **BorderColor** property defines the color of the border surrounding the shape.
	■ The **BorderStyle** property defines the appearance of the border surrounding the shape. This property can assume any of the values listed in the Properties window for that shape.
	■ The thickness of the shape's border is set via the **BorderWidth** property. A BorderWidth setting of 0 indicates that no border will surround the shape.
	■ The **FillColor** property works with the **FillStyle** property to set the color of the region inside the border. When the FillStyle property is set to its default, 1 - Transparent, the FillColor setting is ignored.
	■ The **FillStyle** property lets you draw a pattern on the shape's background. You can identify the valid values for the different patterns in the Properties window for that shape.

■ The appearance of the Shape control is set via the **Shape** property. The valid values for the Shape property are Rectangle, Square, Oval, Circle, Rounded Rectangle, and Rounded Square.

■ The **Visible** property of a shape can be set to either True or False. A shape will be visible at run time only when its Visible property is set to True.

The calculator program needs a rectangular shape drawn around the input section and another rectangular shape drawn around the output section. You will make both shapes dark blue with a solid black border. Because you will not write any code to reference properties of the shapes, you do not need to change the Name property.

To add the Shape objects to the calculator program:

1   Click the **Shape** control [icon] on the toolbox.

2   Move the pointer to the form and draw a shape similar to the one shown in Figure 2-9. By default, the Shape control draws a rectangle.

rectangular shape to
group input section

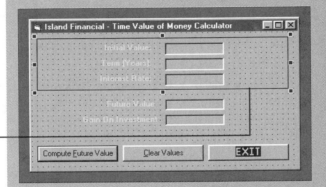

Figure 2-9: Creating the Shape object

3   Activate the **Properties** window for the Shape object, if necessary.

4   Click the **Value column** for the **BorderColor** property, then click the **Properties** button [icon] to activate the color palette.

5   Click the **Palette** tab to display the color palette, if necessary.

6   Select **black** for the BorderColor property to emphasize the shape's region against the background of the form.

7   Set the FillColor property to **dark blue**.

8   Set the FillStyle property to 0 - **Solid**.

The shape has obscured the Label objects. You need to place this object behind the Label objects.

9   Make sure the shape is the active object. Position the insertion point over the shape, right-click to activate the pop-up menu, then click **Send to Back**.

10   Repeat Steps 1 through 9 to create a second shape. The resulting form should resemble Figure 2-10.

shaded shape surrounding input section

shaded shape surrounding output section

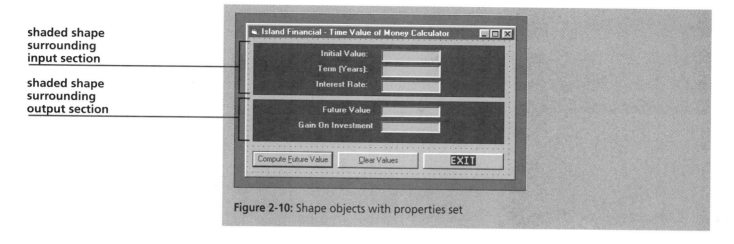

Figure 2-10: Shape objects with properties set

The Line Control Lines identify different sections of a form or draw attention to a particular form. You can draw lines in any direction, choosing different thicknesses and colors for them via the Line control on the toolbox.

Syntax	Line
Definition	The **Line** control is used to draw a line on the form. Lines can have different widths and patterns. The standard prefix for a Line object is "lin".
Properties	■ Setting the **BorderColor** property changes the line's color. ■ You can create dashed and dotted lines by setting the **BorderStyle** property. ■ The line thickness is set via the **BorderWidth** property.

In the calculator program, you will draw a horizontal line to separate the input and output sections from the buttons.

To create a horizontal line on the form:

1 Click the **Line** control ⬍ on the toolbox, then use the mouse to draw a horizontal line between the output section (labels and text boxes) and the processing section (command buttons). Release the mouse button when the line is the same width as the shape above it, as shown in Figure 2-11.

line begins here

line ends here

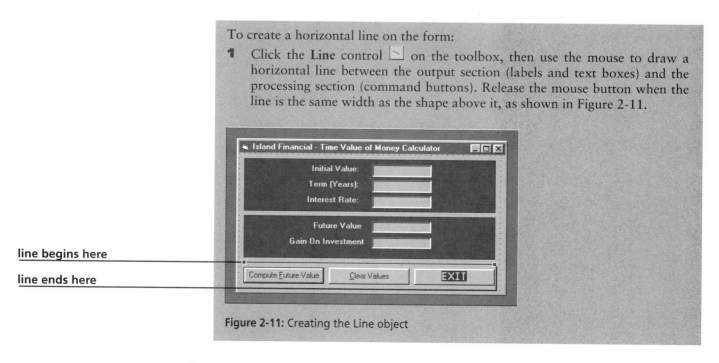

Figure 2-11: Creating the Line object

2 Set the BorderWidth property of the line to **2**.

3 Click the **Value column** of the **BorderColor** property.

4 Click the **Properties** button to open the color palette. Make sure the Palette tab is active, then set the BorderColor property to **dark blue**.

The line looks like the one shown in Figure 2-12. The form now contains all of the necessary objects.

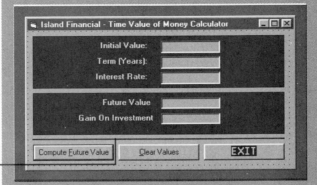

Line object with thickness and color set

Figure 2-12: Setting the line's color and thickness

5 Save the project.

help
. . . .

> If the line is in the wrong place or is not horizontal, click the object to select it. Use the mouse to reposition the line, or apply the mouse to one of the sizing handles to resize the line as necessary.

You did not name the Line object because you will not reference it in code.

You have completed the user interface for Island Financial Company's program. The form contains all of the necessary visual elements.

Q U E S T I O N S

1. Which of the following statements is true of the Visual Basic alignment tools?
    a. Controls can be aligned horizontally and vertically.
    b. The horizontal and vertical space between controls can be made the same.
    c. Only two controls can be aligned at the same time.
    d. Both a and b.
    e. All of the above.

2. Which of the following statements is true of selecting multiple control instances on a form?
    a. The Shift key and left mouse button can be used to select multiple control instances.
    b. The pointer tool can be used to select multiple control instances.
    c. You can select as many control instances as desired.
    d. Only one control instance can be the active selected control.
    e. All of the above.

3. Which of the following statements is true of the CommandButton control?
    a. A command button can display a ToolTip.
    b. A command button can display text but not a picture.
    c. A command button can respond to a Click event.
    d. Both a and b.
    e. Both a and c.

4. What is the difference between a label and a text box?
   a. A label supports the Caption property while a text box supports the Text property.
   b. A label is used for output while a text box is used for both input and output.
   c. A text box is used for output while a label is used for both input and output.
   d. Both a and b.
   e. Both b and c.

5. The _____ and _____ properties are used to set the background and foreground colors for a control, such as a label or text box.
   a. BackGround, ForeGround
   b. BackGroundColor, ForeGroundColor
   c. Back, Fore
   d. BackColor, ForeColor
   e. None of the above.

6. Which of the following statements is true of a program's user interface?
   a. The size and position of control instances drawn on a form are immaterial.
   b. Bright colors should be used only for emphasis.
   c. The sizes of related control instances should be consistent.
   d. Both a and c.
   e. Both b and c.

7. To execute a command button's Click event procedure when the user presses the Enter key, the _____ property should be set to True.
   a. Default
   b. Enter
   c. Click
   d. Return
   e. TabOrder

8. Which of the following properties do both the Shape and Line controls support?
   a. Color, Style, and Width
   b. LineStyle
   c. LineColor, LineStyle, and LineWidth
   d. BorderColor, BorderStyle, and BorderWidth
   e. Style

9. What is the name of the property used to set the order in which objects receive focus?
   a. TabIndex
   b. Tab
   c. TabOrder
   d. Order
   e. Focus

10. Which of the following objects can receive input focus?
    a. TextBox
    b. Shape
    c. Line
    d. Both a and b.
    e. Both a and c.

SECTION B
objectives

In this section you will:

- Create program comments
- Look up intrinsic constants
- Use the Val, Format, and Future Value functions
- Explicitly set the focus
- Solve programming errors
- Print the program

Statements and Expressions

Creating Well-Written Comments

In Chapter 1, you saw how to create a program comment to describe the purpose of a particular statement or procedure. Although a few small programs may be self-explanatory, most larger programs are not. Comprehensive and standardized comments will help you and other programmers understand what your program is doing and how. Comments should be written as you develop a program. As you modify the program, the comments should be changed to reflect its new behavior. All of your procedures should begin with a comment block if the procedure is not self-explanatory. This comment block should contain the following elements:

- The purpose of the procedure.
- Information that the procedure needs (inputs) to operate properly. This information usually includes variables that are declared outside the procedure or variables in other forms.
- A description of what the procedure produces (outputs).

These guidelines provide a foundation for good comments. As you develop more and larger programs, however, you may find it useful to add more information, such as a history of revisions. This type of information is especially important when multiple programmers develop and modify a program. Comments in many programs may account for 50 percent or more of the program's statements. Increasing the number of comments will not affect the speed of your program because all of the comments are removed when you create an executable file from your program. Only programmers will use these statements as they examine the code.

You must understand the following syntax rules when writing comments:

- Any line beginning with an apostrophe (') is considered a comment line and is ignored by Visual Basic.
- Any characters following an apostrophe after a statement on one line are considered a comment and are ignored by Visual Basic.

If you have used programs written in older versions of Visual Basic, you may have used the REM statement to denote a comment. Although Visual Basic still supports this convention, we will not use the REM statement in this book.

The following code segment illustrates two different comments:

```
'This line is a comment.
txtDemo.Text = "100"   ' Store the string 100 in the text box.
```

The first line contains only a comment. The second line contains an assignment statement followed by a comment.

We have reviewed comments here for a particular reason. As you write the code for the program developed in this chapter, you will also create comments pertaining to that code. These comments will help you and other programmers better understand the purpose and function of your new code.

Text Box Events

The TextBox object supports many types of events, including the GotFocus and LostFocus events. As you have seen in this book, objects can respond to events such as being clicked. Different objects respond to different events; a TextBox object, for example, can respond to events like receiving and losing focus. The GotFocus event occurs when a text box receives focus. The LostFocus event occurs when a text box loses focus. In this section, you will continue to work on Island Financial's program by selecting the first text box, txtInitialValue, and its GotFocus event, then writing the code for the event so that text typed in the object will appear bold and dark blue as the user types it. The FontBold property, when set to True, causes the text to appear in bold type. Remember, Visual Basic's IntelliSense technology will assist you in completing the statements you write.

You begin by opening the Code window to the first object you need to program—txtInitialValue.

To change the font when the txtInitialValue receives focus:

1   Make sure the form **frmIslandCalculator** is displayed.

2   Double-click the object named **txtInitialValue** to open the Code window, as shown in Figure 2-13.

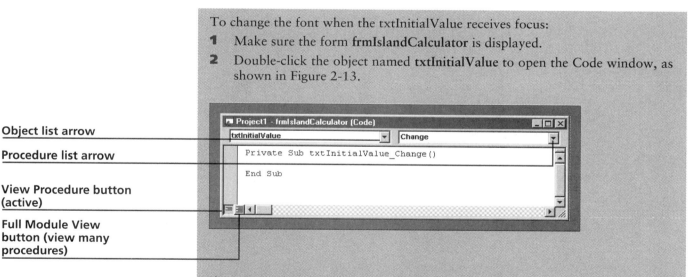

Object list arrow

Procedure list arrow

View Procedure button (active)

Full Module View button (view many procedures)

Figure 2-13: Selecting an object in the Code window

3   Click the **Procedure View** button ▤, if necessary, which is located at the lower-left corner of the Code window, to view a single procedure.

The size and shape of your Code window might differ from the window depicted in Figure 2-13. You can resize the Code window to suit your preferences.

4   Click the **Procedure** list arrow, then click **GotFocus,** as shown in Figure 2-14.

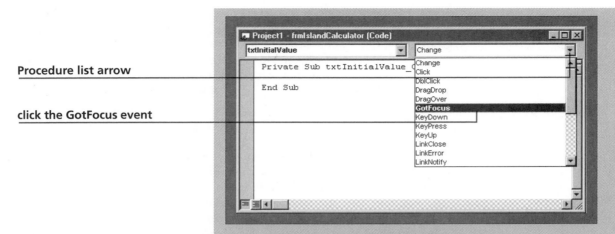

Procedure list arrow

click the GotFocus event

Figure 2-14: Selecting an object and event procedure

Your new code for the event will execute when the TextBox object receives focus. If the desired object or event procedure does not appear in the list box, use the scroll bars to search for it.

5 Enter the comment lines shown in Figure 2-15. Note that these procedure comments appear outside the procedure. That is, they do not appear between the Private Sub and End Sub statements. Comments can exist both inside and outside a procedure.

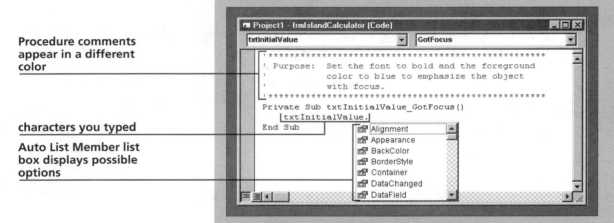

Procedure comments appear in a different color

characters you typed

Auto List Member list box displays possible options

Figure 2-15: Writing a statement

6 In the blank line between the beginning and ending lines of code, enter the code (including the period) shown in Figure 2-15. When the period (.) is typed, Visual Basic lists the applicable properties that you can set.

7 Use the scroll bars to locate the FontBold property. Click the **FontBold** property to highlight it, then press the **spacebar**. The text that you just selected appears on the line you are typing.

8 Type an **equal sign** (=). Another list box appears, listing the possible values for the property, as shown in Figure 2-16. In this case, the FontBold property can have the values True or False.

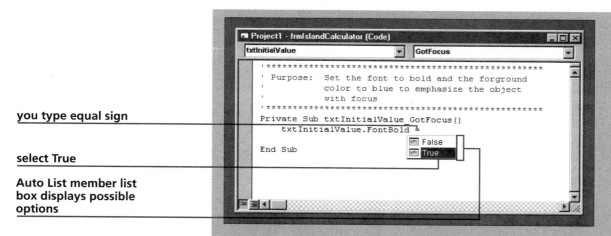

you type equal sign

select True

Auto List member list box displays possible options

Figure 2-16: Completing a statement

9 Click the value **True,** then press the **Enter** key to finish entering the line. Move to the next line.

Visual Basic automatically inserts a space between the equal sign and the word True.

Now you need to write code to change the color of the text when the TextBox object of the text receives focus. As with other properties, the color of an object can be set at design time by using the Properties window or at run time by using Visual Basic code. The easiest way to specify a color at run time is to include a constant in your code.

Looking Up Intrinsic Constants with the Object Browser

Constants store values that do not change while the program is running. Visual Basic supports two types of constants: intrinsic constants and user-defined constants. **Intrinsic constants** are defined by Visual Basic itself. In contrast, the programmer defines **user-defined constants** by means of Visual Basic statements. You will learn about user-defined constants in later chapters.

Using a Visual Basic tool called the Object Browser, you will see how to express color values as intrinsic constants. The **Object Browser** allows you to examine the intrinsic constants defined by Visual Basic. These constants relate to the properties of the objects you create as well as to the modules and procedures you define for your project. They are listed in the Help library.

To render your program more readable, you will use intrinsic constants to change the color of the foreground text in each text box when the text box has focus. Before you can use these constants, however, you must discover their names. You can look up the names of intrinsic constants via the Object Browser. The names of all Visual Basic intrinsic constants begin with the prefix "vb".

To use the Object Browser to examine intrinsic constants:

1 Click the **Object Browser** button 📷 on the toolbar.

The Object Browser opens.

2 Click **ColorConstants** in the Classes section of the Object Browser.

Use the scroll bars, if necessary, to locate the desired list item. The Members section of the Object Browser contains the different color constants, as shown in Figure 2-17.

Visual Basic color constants

vbBlack will return color to its original setting

Click vbBlue to view its value

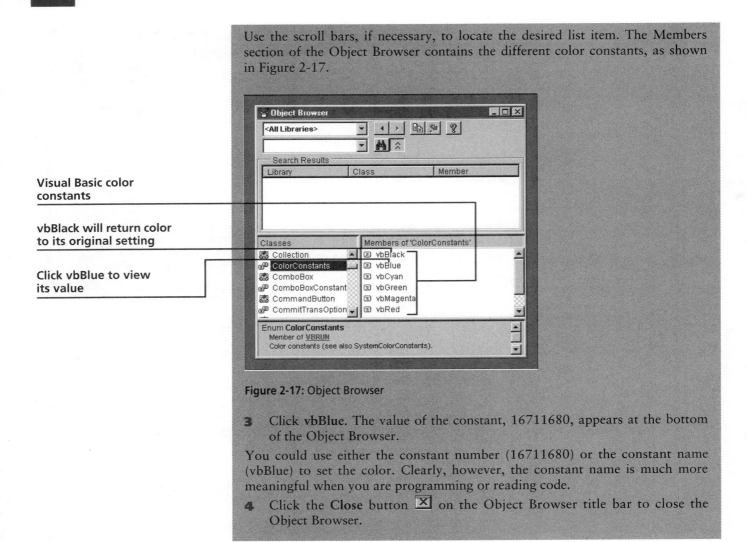

Figure 2-17: Object Browser

3   Click **vbBlue**. The value of the constant, 16711680, appears at the bottom of the Object Browser.

You could use either the constant number (16711680) or the constant name (vbBlue) to set the color. Clearly, however, the constant name is much more meaningful when you are programming or reading code.

4   Click the **Close** button ☒ on the Object Browser title bar to close the Object Browser.

When you use intrinsic constant names in a program, Visual Basic converts the names into their respective values when the program is run. This approach makes the program more readable and reliable. For example, if you needed to set the ForeColor property to blue, each of the following two statements would accomplish this task; the statement containing the constant, however, makes it easier for the programmer to understand that the foreground color is set to blue:

```
txtInitialValue.ForeColor = 16711680
txtInitialValue.ForeColor = vbBlue
```

You will now use intrinsic constants to write code that changes the foreground color of the text in the text box to blue.

To change the color of the text:

1   Make sure that the Code window is open and that the **txtInitialValue_GotFocus** event procedure is active.

2 Enter the line of code shown in Figure 2-18 on the line following the statement that sets the FontBold property.

enter this statement to set foreground color to blue

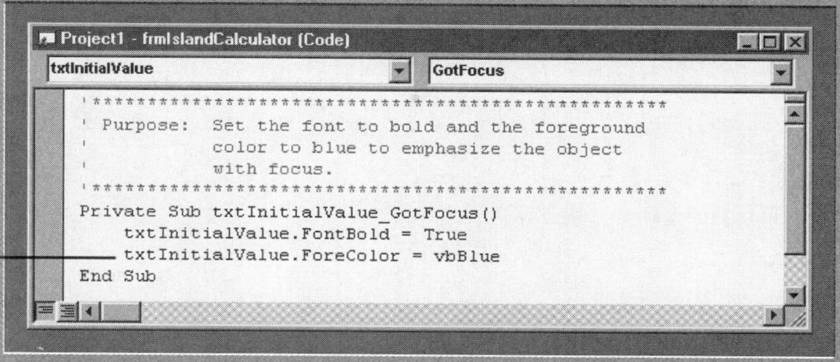

Figure 2-18: Setting the foreground color with code

Now that you have written the code for the object's GotFocus event, you can change the font to normal and the color to black when the text box loses focus.

To return the text box to its initial settings:

1 Click the **Procedure** list arrow, then click **LostFocus**. When you select the new event procedure, the Code window displays the beginning and ending lines of code for this procedure. The code you wrote for the previous event procedure no longer appears in the Code window.

Earlier, the figures showed the complete Code window to illustrate the IntelliSense technology and to help you use this window. As the procedures you write become larger, however, the code may not fit in the visible region of the Code window. Thus, from this point forward, the code you should enter will appear in a bold Courier font.

2 Enter the following code (displayed in bold) for the **txtInitialValue_LostFocus** event procedure:

```
'***************************************************
' Purpose:  Set the font to normal and the foreground
'               color to black when the object loses
'               focus.
'***************************************************'
Private Sub txtInitialValue_LostFocus( )
    txtInitialValue.FontBold = False
    txtInitialValue.ForeColor = vbBlack
End Sub
```

The constant vbBlack is used for the color black. This constant can also be determined using the Object Browser.

The code you entered for the Initial Value text box will change the text to normal when the text box is no longer active—that is, when the LostFocus event occurs for the object. You now need to enter the same code for the other two text boxes. First, you select the txtTermYears object using the Object list arrow in the Code window. Next, you write the code for the object's GotFocus and LostFocus events.

To write the code for the other two TextBox objects:

1 Click the **Object** list arrow, then click **txtTermYears**.

2 Click the **Procedure** list arrow, then click **GotFocus**.

3 Enter the following code (shown in bold) for the **txtTermYears_GotFocus** event procedure:

```
'*****************************************************
' Purpose:   Set the font to bold and the foreground
'            color to blue to emphasize the object
'            with focus.
'*****************************************************
Private Sub txtTermYears_GotFocus( )
    txtTermYears.FontBold = True
    txtTermYears.ForeColor = vbBlue
End Sub
```

4 Select the **LostFocus** event procedure, then enter the following code for the **txtTermYears_LostFocus** event procedure:

```
'*****************************************************
' Purpose:   Set the font to normal and the foreground
'            color to black when the object loses
'            focus.
'*****************************************************'
Private Sub txtTermYears_LostFocus( )
    txtTermYears.FontBold = False
    txtTermYears.ForeColor = vbBlack
End Sub
```

5 Repeat steps 1 through 4 for the **txtInterestRate** object, changing "txtTermYears" in each statement to "txtInterestRate".

help

▶ If the text in any of the text boxes did not appear bold when you typed it in, open the Code window and select the GotFocus event procedure for the appropriate text box. Check your code against the code created in Steps 1 through 5. If the text does not return to a normal type style when you leave the object, check the code for the appropriate LostFocus event. Make any necessary corrections, then repeat step 6.

Programming tip

▶ In the previous set of steps, you wrote very similar code for each event procedure. Like Microsoft Word and many other programs, Visual Basic supports copy and paste features. Thus you can select a statement or multiple statements, click Edit on the menu bar, click Copy, click the insertion point where you want to paste the text, click Edit, then click Paste.

As you develop programs, it is a good idea to test your work frequently. This approach will help you discover and correct mistakes as you make them. Before testing, you should save your work in case you make an error, the computer crashes, or the power fails.

6   Test the program. The insertion point will appear as a flashing vertical line in the text box to the right of the Initial Value: label. Type any number in each of the three text boxes, pressing the **Tab** key to move from one text box to the next. Verify that the text you type appears in a blue, bold font when a text box has focus and in regular black font when it loses focus. When you press **Tab** after entering text in the last text box, the Compute Future Value command button will receive focus. Nothing will happen if you click this button or press Enter, however, because you have not written any code to perform the computations.

7   Click the **End** button on the toolbar to stop running the program.

Variables

In addition to receiving user input through text boxes and displaying information with labels, a program generally needs to perform computations on the input to produce the desired output. Island Financial's calculator program should compute the future value of an investment based on the three input values. It should also compute the gain on investment. To store the results of these calculations while the program is running, you will use variables. A **variable** is a programming element used to store a value in the program while the program is running. As was the case with objects, every variable you create has a name. A variable is analogous to a box in which you can store information and then retrieve the same information while the program is running. Consider the memory in a calculator. You can store a value into the calculator's memory for future use. When the value is needed later, you can retrieve the value from the memory. Conceptually, this operation is the same as that involved with a variable.

Unlike an object, a variable does not have properties or respond to events. Instead, it simply stores information while the program is running. Every variable has a data type that determines the kind of information it can store. Some types of variables can store only numbers. Furthermore, Visual Basic distinguishes between different types of numbers. Some numeric data types store whole numbers and numbers containing decimal points. Others store date and time information or values like True or False.

Every variable consumes physical space in the computer's memory. Variables of different data types consume different amounts of memory and store different kinds of values. Like the objects you have created, each variable should have a prefix that identifies its data type. Figure 2-19 lists selected Visual Basic data types, their storage sizes in bytes, standard prefixes, and some possible values for each data type. You will learn about other Visual Basic data types in subsequent chapters.

Data Type	Storage Size	Prefix	Possible Values
Date	8 bytes	dat	Dates between 1/1/100 and 12/31/9999.
Integer	2 bytes	int	Positive and negative whole numbers between -32,768 and 32,767. A number such as 84 or -1,715 can be stored as an integer.
Long Integer	4 bytes	lng	Positive and negative whole numbers between -2,147,483,648 and 2,147,483,647.
Single	4 bytes	sng	A number with a decimal point, such as 3.14, -10,034.388, or 0.113. The Single data type can store at most six digits to the right of a decimal point.
Double	8 bytes	dbl	A number with a decimal point. The Double data type can store at most 14 digits to the right of a decimal point.
String	1 byte per character	str	You can store up to about 2 billion characters for variable-length strings. Text entries such as "John Doe" or "Pacific Ocean" are stored as strings.

Figure 2-19: Partial list of Visual Basic's data types

Choosing the correct data type for a variable is important. For example, if a variable will contain only whole numbers (numbers without a decimal point), you should choose the Integer or Long Integer data type instead of the Single data type. Furthermore, if the value of a whole number will always be between −32,768 and 32,767, then you should use an Integer instead of a Long Integer to conserve memory. Although you will not declare any String variables in Island Financial's program, Visual Basic always considers the information stored in the Text property of a TextBox object to be a String. To perform a numeric calculation on a String, you must convert it explicitly to a number. The Date data type is used to store date and time information. Note that Windows does not suffer from the year 2000 (Y2K) problem; its largest year is 9999.

Just like object names, variable names must adhere to certain standards. Figure 2-20 presents some basic requirements and recommendations for naming variables. When you create a variable, you should assign it a name that follows these naming conventions.

Variable names **must**	Variable names **should**
begin with a letter.	begin with a four-character prefix indicating the scope and type of data stored in the variable, followed by a descriptive name.
not contain periods, dashes, or spaces.	always use a capital letter as the first character of each word in the descriptive portion of the name.
not exceed 255 characters in length.	
be unique.	

Figure 2-20: Variable naming conventions

In addition to the three-character prefix that denotes a variable's data type, you should include a fourth character that denotes a variable's scope. The **scope** of a variable indicates which procedures can use it. A variable that can be used only by a single procedure carries a prefix of "p" for procedure, and a variable that can be used by all procedures in a module has a prefix of "m" for module. In contrast, a variable that can be used by all modules in a program bears a prefix of "g" for global. Figure 2-21 contains examples of valid and invalid variable names.

Valid Variable Names	Invalid Variable Names
pstrValidStringName	1InvalidStringName
mintValid_Integer	intInvalid.Integer
plngValid_LongInteger	int Invalid Long Integer
psngValidSingle	sng Invalid-Variable

Figure 2-21: Variable names

In this chapter, you will create only **module-level** variables. Thus the prefix of each will be "m". Global and procedure-level variables will be discussed in later chapters.

Declaring a Variable

The process of creating a variable is known as declaring a variable. To declare a variable, you can use the Visual Basic **Private** statement, the **Public** statement, or the **Dim** statement.

Syntax	[Private|Public|Dim] *Varname* **As** *Type*
Definition	■ The **Private**, **Public**, and **Dim** statements are used to declare a program variable. A vertical bar (	) separates the Private, Public, and Dim keywords. It indicates that one of the three keywords is used in a statement. We will use this nomenclature when presenting syntax to indicate that any of several keywords can be used. ■ The **Private** keyword declares a variable, meaning that the memory for the variable is allocated. When declared with the Private keyword, the variable can be used only in the module (form) in which it is declared and by the procedures in that module. ■ The **Public** keyword creates a variable that can be used by multiple modules. This keyword is discussed more fully in later chapters that use multiple modules. ■ The **Dim** keyword, depending on where it is used, creates a variable that can be used by the procedure in which it is declared and by other procedures. ■ *Varname* is the name by which the variable is known. ■ *Type* is the data type of the variable.
| **Code Example** | ```
Private msngInterestRate As Single
Private mintCounter As Integer
``` |
| **Code Dissect** | The first statement declares a module-level variable with the name of msngInterestRate. It can store a floating-point number, which is a variable containing a decimal point. The second statement declares a variable named mintCounter. This variable can store whole numbers between –32,768 and 32,767. |

When you use a Private, Public, or Dim statement to declare a variable, you *explicitly* declare the variable. On the other hand, if you use a variable name in any Visual Basic statement without first explicitly declaring it with the Private, Public, or Dim statement, Visual Basic will create the variable automatically in a process known as **implicit declaration**. For example, if you intended to use a variable named msngInterestRate in a statement, but you made a typographical error, Visual Basic would assume that you wanted to create a new variable. Although the program would run, the variable would not contain the correct information. Thus the program would produce erroneous results when you use the variable in a computation. In this way, implicit declaration may lead to hard-to-find programming errors.

You can prohibit Visual Basic from implicitly creating variables by using the Option Explicit statement.

Syntax	Option Explicit
Definition	The **Option Explicit** statement forces you to declare all variables explicitly with the Private, Public, or Dim keyword in the module where the Option Explicit statement appears. The Option Explicit statement must be the first statement in the general declarations section of the module.
```

Programming

tip

• • • • • • • • • • • • • • • •

▶ To automatically include the Option Explicit statement in all of your programs, click Tools on the menu bar, then click Options. Make sure the Require Variable Declarations check box on the Editor tab is checked. Any new project or module will then include the Option Explicit statement.

If you try to use a variable that was not declared with a Private, Public, or Dim statement, and Visual Basic displays a dialog indicating that the variable has not been defined, you can thank the Option Explicit statement for catching your mistake. This statement also helps identify incorrectly spelled variables that would create logic errors. Such mistakes are more difficult to detect because Visual Basic will not display a dialog specifying the exact cause of the error. All of the programs you create in this book will contain the Option Explicit statement.

Declaring Module-Level Variables

Now that you know *how* to declare variables, you need to know *where* to declare them. If you declare a variable outside a procedure using the Private statement, then the variable can be used by all of the different procedures in the module (form). This type of variable is called a module-level variable, meaning that the variable and its value exist whenever the module is loaded. Module-level variables are declared in the **general declarations section** of the module. This part of the module appears before the procedures. Figure 2-22 illustrates module-level variables declared in a form module.

general declarations section

event procedure

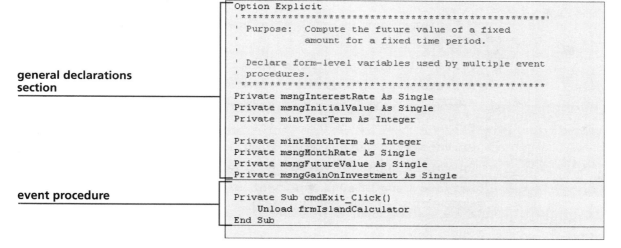

```
Option Explicit
'***********************************************************'
' Purpose:   Compute the future value of a fixed
'            amount for a fixed time period.
'
' Declare form-level variables used by multiple event
' procedures.
'***********************************************************
Private msngInterestRate As Single
Private msngInitialValue As Single
Private mintYearTerm As Integer

Private mintMonthTerm As Integer
Private msngMonthRate As Single
Private msngFutureValue As Single
Private msngGainOnInvestment As Single

Private Sub cmdExit_Click()
    Unload frmIslandCalculator
End Sub
```

Figure 2-22: Declaring module-level variables

As shown in Figure 2-22, the general declarations section of the module contains the declarations of the module-level variables. The Object list box indicates General and the Procedure list box indicates Declarations. These variables—and their values—exist whenever the form is loaded.

As noted earlier, you will declare only module-level variables in this chapter; thus the variables can be used by all of the procedures in the module. As shown in Figure 2-22, each of the variable declarations begins with the Private statement. Furthermore, each variable carries a prefix that indicates its scope and its data type. These variables will be used to store the interest rate, initial investment amount, term, future value, and gain on the investment.

To declare module-level variables:

1 Click the **View Code** button in the Project Explorer to open the Code window.

2 Click the **Object** list arrow, then click (**General**).

3 Click the **Procedure** list arrow, then click (**Declarations**), if necessary.

In the general declarations section of the form, you will include a comment block containing a brief description of the form's purpose.

4 Enter the following comments and variable declarations in the general declarations section of the Code window.

```
Option Explicit
'
' Purpose:   Compute the future value of a fixed
'                amount of many different interest
'                rates for a fixed time period.
'
' Declare module-level variables used by multiple event
' procedures.
Private msngInterestRate As Single
Private msngInitialValue As Single
Private mintYearTerm As Integer
Private mintMonthTerm As Integer
Private msngMonthRate As Single
Private msngFutureValue As Single
Private msngGainOnInvestment As Single
```

Programming

tip

● ● ● ● ● ● ● ● ● ● ● ● ● ● ●

▶ You can include blank lines between comments or statements. Visual Basic ignores this whitespace. Inserting whitespace in your code between the declarations of groups of related variables or between other related statements, however, can improve the readability of the code. Including the comment character (apostrophe) on a blank line is optional.

The Option Explicit statement tells Visual Basic that all of the variables in the module must be declared before they are used. The lines following this statement are comment lines, so each must start with an apostrophe (').

The remaining lines declare the module-level variables that will store data as the program computes the future value and the gain on investment. The module-level variables of the Single data type have names that begin with the prefix "msng"; the module-level variables of the Integer data type have names that begin with the prefix "mint".

When you type the statements in the Code window, Visual Basic automatically capitalizes the first character of all reserved words, even if you enter lowercase letters. **Reserved words** are part of the Visual Basic language—for example, Option Explicit, Public, Private, Dim, As, and Single are all reserved words.

Using Expressions and Operators to Manipulate Variables

After you have declared all necessary variables for your program, you can store information in these variables and use them to perform computations and to display the results of those computations. For example, you can take an annual interest rate entered by the user and divide it by 12 to obtain the monthly interest rate. The result of this computation will be stored in the module-level variable, msngMonthRate, which you declared earlier.

In Chapter 1, you created an assignment statement that stored a graphical image in an instance of the Image control. Although this simple assignment statement did not perform any calculations, many other assignment statements perform computations like multiplying or adding numbers together. Consider the following example:

```
mintResult = 3 * 2
```

When an assignment statement performs a calculation, its right-hand side contains an expression. An **expression** consists of variables, constants, values, and operators (+, −, and so on) that perform calculations. In the previous code segment, 3 * 2 is an expression. When this statement is executed, it multiples the two numbers together and stores the result (6) in the variable mintResult. An **operator**, as the name implies, performs some mathematical or other type of computation. In the previous example, the * operator multiplied the numbers 3 and 2 together.

When you write expressions using operators and variables, you need to understand the concept of precedence. **Precedence** dictates the order in which the arithmetic operations in a statement are performed. For example, multiplication and division take place before addition and subtraction. When a computer executes an expression, it scans an expression from left to right, looking for the highest-level operation (exponentiation). If it fails to find any operations at that level, it returns to the beginning of the expression and looks for the next-level operations (multiplication and division). When the computer finds an operation at the current level, it executes that operation. This pattern of "search and execution" continues until all operations have been completed. If the computer finds more than one operator of the same precedence, it carries out the left-hand operation first.

Figure 2-23 lists the Visual Basic operators that work with numeric data, describes them, and provides sample expressions of their use.

Operators in Order of Precedence	Description	Example
^	Raises a number to the power of an exponent	2 ^ 3 is equal to 8
*, /	Multiplication and division	2 * 3 is equal to 6 8 / 4 is equal to 2
\	Integer division	10 \ 3 is equal to 3 5 \ 2 is equal to 2
Mod	Modulus arithmetic; returns the integer remainder of a division operation	10 mod 3 is equal to 1
+, -	Addition and subtraction	2 + 3 is equal to 5 2 - 3 is equal to -1

Figure 2-23: Arithmetic operators

In many cases, you may need to change the standard order of operations to ensure that operators are applied in a specific sequence. You can accomplish this goal by using one or more matched pairs of parentheses. Enclosing an operation within parentheses ensures that the operation takes precedence over all of the levels in the standard order of precedence. For example, in the formula $(Var1 + Var2)^{Var3}$, the addition would take place before the exponentiation because the addition operator is enclosed in parentheses. In the formula $((Var1 + Var2) - (Var3 + Var4))^{Var5}$, the parentheses are **nested**, which means that the innermost and left-hand operation $(Var1 + Var2)$ would occur first, $(Var3 + Var4)$ would occur second, the result of each addition would be subtracted third $((Var1 + Var2) - (Var3 + Var4))$, and finally, the result would be raised to the power $Var5$.

$$\left(\frac{Var1 + Var2}{Var3 + Var4}\right) \times Var5^{Var6}$$

Figure 2-24: Algebraic formula

Consider the formula shown in Figure 2-24. Here the order of operations is clearly shown through the way the formula is presented. If you transformed this formula directly into a computer-readable expression, it would look like the formula given in Figure 2-25.

$$Var1 + Var2 / Var3 - Var4 \times Var5^{Var6}$$

Figure 2-25: Computer-readable expression

Without using parentheses, the order of execution of the operators would follow the standard order of precedence. The parentheses change the results. Figure 2-26 shows the order of precedence with and without the parentheses.

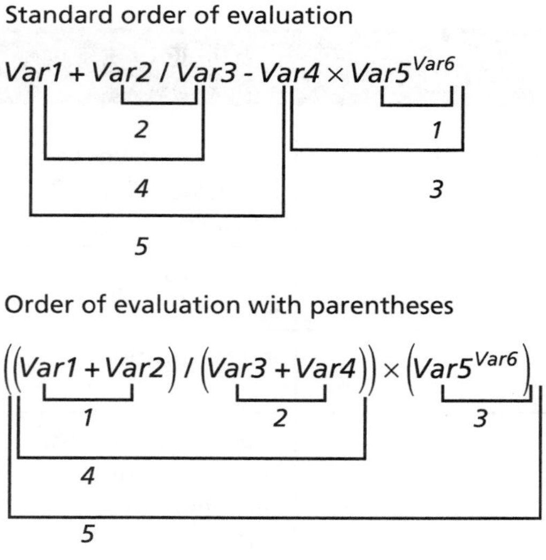

Standard order of evaluation

Order of evaluation with parentheses

Figure 2-26: Evaluating expressions

Additional parentheses can greatly improve the readability of a program, so you should use them liberally. For example, including parentheses around the subexpression (*Var5*^{*Var6*}) in Figure 2-26 does not change the order of evaluation, but it does enhance readability by clarifying the order in which the computer should evaluate the expression.

In addition to writing expressions containing arithmetic operators, you can write expressions that use operators to perform comparisons. Comparisons are useful to evaluate such situations as whether two numbers are equal or two text strings are the same. Furthermore, you can use logical operators to connect expressions together. You will learn about comparison and logical operators in later chapters.

Type Conversion Functions

As noted earlier, Visual Basic includes **intrinsic functions**, procedures that were written by the language's designers and built into the programming language. Intrinsic functions differ from event procedures in that you must explicitly write a Visual Basic statement to call them. Intrinsic financial and mathematical functions return a value—such as a number, a string, or other data type—that you can store in a variable or compatible object property. In Island Financial's program, you will use several intrinsic function procedures, including the Val function, the Format function, and the Future Value (FV) function.

The Val function is a type conversion function. Such functions can be used to check the correctness of user input. Consider your program for a moment. Although the values entered by the user in the three TextBox objects will contain only digits (0–9) and, in some cases, a decimal point, dollar sign, or percent sign, Visual Basic nevertheless stores each of these values in a text box as a string of characters rather than as a number. That is, the data can be envisioned as being of the String data type. Visual Basic does not know how you intend to use the information stored in a TextBox object, so it always stores the value as a string of characters. When the program tries to perform an arithmetic operation on the text in the text box, Visual Basic attempts to convert the value from a string of characters to a number. If the user entered a letter instead of a number in one of the TextBox objects, however, Visual Basic cannot properly convert the value into a number, and a run-time error will occur. You will learn about run-time errors later in this section.

A **type conversion function** prevents this undesirable outcome. The **Val** function, for example, automatically converts a string of characters (a value assigned the String data type) to a number; you must use a number if the data are to be used in a calculation. If the string contains letters, the Val function stops scanning the string and returns the value of the digits scanned to that point. When you use a function such as Val, you provide information to it using an **argument**. Arguments can consist of variables in your program, constants, or literal values.

In addition to the Val function, Visual Basic provides similar functions to convert strings to other data types such as Integer, Long Integer, and Single.

Syntax

result = **Val**(*string*)
result = **CInt**(*string*)
result = **CLng**(*string*)
result = **CSng**(*string*)

Definition

- The **Val** function accepts one argument, a string, and, if possible, converts it to a number.

- The **CInt** function accepts one argument, a string, and, if possible, converts it to an Integer.

- The **CLng** function accepts one argument, a string, and, if possible, converts it to a Long Integer.

- The **CSng** function accepts one argument, a string, and, if possible, converts it to Single precision number.

- The *string* contains the input value that will be converted to a number.

- The converted string is stored in the *result*.

Code Example	
| | ```
pintResult = Val("123AA")    ' 123
pintResult = Val("0")        ' 0
pintResult = CInt("123AA")   ' Error
``` |

Code Dissection	In the first statement, the characters are converted until the function reaches the letter "A". Thus the value stored in pintResult equals 123. In the second example, the value 0 is stored in pintResult. The final statement will cause an error because CInt requires that the entire string represent a valid number.

Formatting a Numeric Value with the Format Function

Recall from Chapter 1 that you displayed text in a label by setting its Caption property. Here, you will once again use the Caption property to display information. This time, however, you will display numbers instead of text. Numbers should be formatted so they appear in a form most understandable to the user. For example, currency data should usually be formatted with two digits to the right of the decimal place. Additionally, a dollar sign ($) should be displayed. You can change the way numbers are displayed with the Format function.

Syntax	**Format**(*expression*[,*format*])
Definition	- The **Format** function formats numeric values and dates, allowing them to appear in a form most meaningful to the user. - It reads the numeric value contained in *expression* and converts it to a string. - The Format function enables you to control the appearance of the string by placing information in the *format* argument. - You can specify an optional *format* argument in one of two ways: (1) you can select from a list of predefined formats, or (2) you can use special symbols to control, in more detail, the appearance of the text. Formats already defined for you are called **named formats**. One of the more common, the **Fixed** format, displays information with two decimal places and a leading zero (0) if the value is less than one (1). Another named format, **Currency**, displays information with a leading dollar sign and two decimal places. The **Percent** format displays information as a percentage with two decimal places followed by the percent sign (%). Review the Help library's information on the Format function to see all of the options for named formats.
| Code Example | ```
lblCurrency.Caption = Format(psngFutureValue,"Currency")
lblFixed.Caption = Format(psngFutureValue,"Fixed")
``` |
| Code Dissection | The first statement formats the Single precision value stored in psngFutureValue as Currency and stores the result in the Caption property of lblCurrency. The second statement formats the same value as Fixed (two decimal places) and stores the result in the Caption property of lblFixed. The words Currency and Fixed are considered named formats and appear in quotation marks. |

When you use the Format function or write other, more complicated statements, each statement might not fit on a single line in the Code window. You can break a statement into multiple lines by using the underscore character (_) at the end of a line to tell Visual Basic that the next line continues the statement on the current line. When used in this way, the underscore character is called a **continuation character**. Several rules apply to the use of continuation characters:

- You must always precede the continuation character with a space.
- You cannot put a trailing comment at the end of a line containing a continuation character.
- You can insert a continuation character only between words; you cannot break up a word.

If a statement still will not fit within the displayed region of the Code window, you can include the continuation character at the end of multiple lines. Generally you indent **continuation lines**—lines that follow the continuation character in a statement—to ensure that they stand out.

In Island Financial's program, the user will enter three input values representing the initial value of an investment, the term of the investment (expressed in years), and the annual interest rate (also expressed in years). In the steps that follow, you will perform two groups of operations on these input values. First, you will convert the textual information into a numeric value using the Val function. Second, you will format the input values to ensure that they appear in a form generally accepted by the user. For example, you will format the initial investment amount as a currency value with a leading dollar sign and the interest rate as a percentage. Your code will perform these tasks when each text box loses focus.

To format the initial investment amount and store the value in a numeric variable:

1 Click the **View Code** button 🔲 in the Project Explorer to open the Code window, if necessary.

2 Click the **Object** list arrow, then click **txtInitialValue**.

3 Click the **Procedure** list arrow, then click **LostFocus**.

4 Enter the following statements (shown in bold) in the **txtInitialValue_LostFocus** event procedure:

```
txtInitialValue.ForeColor = vbBlack
msngInitialValue = Val(txtInitialValue.Text)
txtInitialValue.Text = Format(msngInitialValue, _
    "Currency")
End Sub
```

5 Test the program. Enter a number in the Initial Value: text box, then press the Tab key so the object loses focus. When this event occurs, the number becomes formatted with a leading dollar sign and two decimal places.

The first of the two statements that you just entered converts the initial investment amount, stored in the Text property of the txtInitialValue text box, to a Single precision number and stores the result in the variable named msngInitialValue. The next statement uses that variable to format the value and again stores the result back in the text box. The continuation character appears because the statement spans two lines.

Your next job is to enter statements that format the interest rate. In addition, the program needs to account for the fact that the value entered by the user is expressed in years but the future value of the investment is computed with values expressed in months. Your program must also accommodate the fact that the user enters an interest of 8.5 percent as "8.5" rather than "0.085"; thus it must divide the number entered by the user by 100 to obtain the actual monthly interest rate. Again, all of these tasks must be performed when the Interest Rate text box loses focus during the running of the program.

To calculate the monthly interest rate and format the value:

1   Enter the following statements (shown in bold) in the **txtInterestRate_LostFocus** event procedure:

```
txtInterestRate.ForeColor = vbBlack
    msngInterestRate = Val(txtInterestRate.Text) / 100
    msngMonthRate = msngInterestRate / 12
    txtInterestRate.Text = Format(msngInterestRate, _
        "Percent")
End Sub
```

These statements are very similar to the statements you wrote in the txtInitialValue_LostFocus event procedure.

```
msngInterestRate = Val(txtInterestRate.Text) / 100
```

The preceding statement converts the interest rate entered by the user to a number and divides the intermediate result by 100. Thus, if the user entered a value of 8.5, msngInterestRate would contain the value 0.085.

```
msngMonthRate = msngInterestRate / 12
```

This statement uses the annual interest rate to compute the monthly interest rate. It divides the annual interest rate by 12 and stores the result in the variable msngInterestRate.

```
txtInterestRate.Text = Format(msngInterestRate, _
    "Percent")
```

The final statement formats the annual interest rate as a percentage to ensure that the value appears in the most intuitive way to the user. Again, the continuation character is used to break up the statement over two lines.

Your next job is to convert the term of the investment from years to months using the same technique you used to convert the interest rate. In other words, the number must be converted to a Single precision number and that Single precision number must be multiplied by 12.

To express the interest rate in months:

1 Enter the following statements (shown in bold) in the **txtTermYears_LostFocus** event procedure:

```
    txtTermYears.ForeColor = vbBlack
    mintYearTerm = Val(txtTermYears.Text)
    mintMonthTerm = mintYearTerm * 12
End Sub
```

These statements are similar to the statements you wrote for the other two LostFocus event procedures. They convert the value stored in the text box to a number and then convert that value, which is expressed in years, to a value expressed in months. This goal is accomplished by multiplying the value by 12. No formatting is needed because the term in years can be expressed as an Integer.

Next, you need to write the code for the CommandButton object. This code will compute the future value of the initial investment at different interest rates.

Using the Future Value Function

The **Future Value (FV)** function returns the future value of a fixed amount of money based on a constant interest rate.

Syntax	**FV**(*rate,periods,payment*[,*presentvalue*][,*type*])
Definition	■ The **FV** function computes the future value of an annuity (investment).
	■ The *rate* represents the monthly interest rate per period.
	■ The *periods* represents the number of time periods in months.
	■ If regular payments are made, they are identified by *payment*. Thus, if you are computing the future value of a fixed amount, which does not involve regular payments, the value of *payment* would be 0. You can think of a regular payment as equivalent to making a deposit into an investment account during each period.
	■ The next two arguments are optional and, therefore, are enclosed in brackets. When computing the future value of an amount, you list the *presentvalue* (or current value) of the sum. When the present value represents a payment to an account, which is analogous to a deposit, the number will be negative.
	■ The optional *type* argument describes when payments are made. If they take place at the end of the period, *type* has a value of 0. If they are made at the beginning of a period, *type* has a value of 1.

| **Code Example** | ```
psngResult = FV(.01,12,0,-1000)
psngResult = FV(msngMonthRate1, psngMonthTerm, 0, _
     -psngInitialValue
``` |
| **Code Dissection** | The first call to the Future Value function computes the future value of $1000.00 for 12 periods at a rate of 1 percent. The second call uses variables to compute the result. |

Your program will use the FV function to compute the three future values of an investment made by an Island Financial client. Because the statements containing the FV function are too long to fit on one line, you will use the continuation character to spread the statement across two lines.

To compute the future value of an investment using the FV function:

1   In the Code window, click the **cmdComputeFutureValue** object, then click the **Click** event procedure if necessary.

2   Enter the following code (shown in bold) in the **cmdComputeFutureValue_Click** event procedure:

```
'
'*****************************************************
' Purpose:   From the information contained in the module-
'            level variables, compute the future values
'            and gain on investment.
'*****************************************************
Private Sub cmdComputeFutureValue_Click( )
    msngFutureValue = FV(msngMonthRate, mintMonthTerm, _
        0, -msngInitialValue)
    lblFutureValue.Caption = Format(msngFutureValue, _
        "Currency")
    msngGainOnInvestment = msngFutureValue - msngInitialValue
    lblGainOnInvestment.Caption = _
        Format(msngGainOnInvestment, "Currency")
End Sub
```

The first statement uses the module-level variables from the previous steps to compute the future value of the investment.
```

```
msngFutureValue = FV(msngMonthRate, mintMonthTerm, _
     0, -msngInitialValue)
```

The variable msngMonthRate holds the interest rate expressed in months. The variable mintMonthTerm contains the term of the investment expressed in months, and the variable msngInitialValue stores the initial value of the investment. The minus sign preceding the msngInitialValue variable causes the future value of the investment to be a positive number. For each argument, a negative number represents an amount paid. The minus sign preceding msngInitialValue converts this value to a negative number, which causes the future value to be a positive number.

```
lblFutureValue.Caption = Format(msngFutureValue, _
     "Currency")
```

This statement formats the future value as Currency. Again, this transformation causes the value to appear with a leading dollar sign and two decimal places.

```
msngGainOnInvestment = msngFutureValue - msngInitialValue
lblGainOnInvestment.Caption = _
     Format(msngGainOnInvestment, "Currency")
```

These final statements compute the gain on the investment by using the module-level variables. The resulting value is then formatted appropriately.

You have now completed all of the code needed to compute the future values of the investment, format the future values with a leading dollar sign, and display the output in the appropriate labels. Next, you must test your program. You will use an initial investment amount of $1500.00, an interest rate of 5 percent, and a term of 10 years.

To run the program and enter the test values:

1 Test the program. Enter **1500.00** as the initial value, **10** as the term, and **5.00** as the interest rate, pressing the **Tab** key to move from one text box to the next.

2 Press the **Tab** key to move to the Compute Future Value button, then press the **Enter** key.

Because you set the Default property of the command button to True, you could have just pressed the Enter key to activate the command button and execute its Click event procedure. The program calculates the results for the future values and gain on investment, as shown in Figure 2-27.

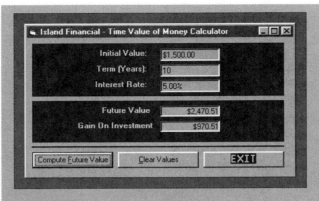

Figure 2-27: Testing the calulator program

If your results differ from those shown in Figure 2-27, your code probably contains an error either in the cmdComputeFutureValue object's Click event procedure or the txtInterestRate object's LostFocus event procedure. Stop the program, and check the event procedures in your program against the code shown in this chapter. Make any necessary corrections, then repeat steps 1 and 2.

3 Click the **END** button on the toolbar to stop running the program.

Pressing the Enter key to activate the Click event for the Compute Future Value command button causes your program to call the FV function to compute the future value. You did not have to worry about how Visual Basic computed the future value—the intrinsic function handled this task for you. The output was then displayed according to the settings specified by the Format function.

You will now write code that programs the Clear Values command button. When clicked, this button should clear the values from the text boxes used for input and the labels used to hold the output. It must also make the Initial Value: text box receive focus.

Explicitly Setting the Focus

You can explicitly set the focus for an object by calling the **SetFocus** method. Methods are essentially procedures that are built into an object. The following statement sets the focus to the object named txtInitialValue.

```
txtInitialValue.SetFocus
```

Throughout this chapter, you have set properties for objects by using the assignment statement you learned in Chapter 1. Although the previous statement has very similar syntax to an assignment statement, you are not setting a property. Instead, you are calling a function supported by the text box. This function is similar conceptually to an intrinsic function, but it pertains to the TextBox object only. Functions that relate to a specific object are called **methods**.

You can now write the code for the Clear Values command button. Remember that text boxes and labels store their contents as strings. In addition, be aware that the null string—represented by the constant vbNullString—is an empty string. An empty string contains no characters. (You can look up the null string constant in the Object Browser if you like.) In the following code, you will include code that halts the running program via the EXIT command button.

To set all of the objects to their default settings and explicitly set the focus:

1   Activate the Code window to the **Click** event procedure for the object named **cmdClearValues**.

2   Enter the following statements in the Code window for the **cmdClearValues_Click** event procedure:

```
txtInitialValue.Text = vbNullString
txtTermYears.Text = vbNullString
txtInterestRate.Text = vbNullString
lblFutureValue.Caption = vbNullString
lblGainOnInvestment.Caption = vbNullString
txtInitialValue.SetFocus
```

These statements clear the text from the object on the form and set the focus to the text box named txtIntialValue. You now will test the code for the Clear Values and the Exit buttons.

To test the Clear Values command button:

1   Open the Code window, then use the **Object** list arrow to select the **cmdExit** object. Make sure the **Click** event is selected.

2   Enter the following statement in the **cmdExit_Click** event procedure:

```
Unload frmIslandCalculator
```

3   Test the program. Enter the values shown in the first three text boxes of Figure 2-27, click the **Compute Future Value** button, then click the **Clear Values** button. The output values in the text boxes—output future values and gain on investment—should be blank and the insertion point should appear in the Initial Value: text box. Finally, test the **EXIT** command button. When clicked, Visual Basic returns to design mode.

At this juncture, you have written all of the code for Island Financial's calculator program. If you made mistakes writing statements or entered invalid data in any of the text boxes, you may have received an error message. Several types and causes of errors exist.

Solving Programming Errors

Errors are classified as one of three types: syntax errors, run-time errors, and logic errors. **Syntax errors** occur when a statement violates the rules of the Visual Basic language. Typographical errors, mismatched parentheses, and the omission of the comment character as the first character on a comment line are all examples of syntax errors. Visual Basic identifies some syntax errors while you are writing code in the Code window. After you type each line, Visual Basic scans it for correctness.

Many errors are not discovered until you run a program, however. Such **run-time errors** occur when you enter a valid statement that is impossible to execute for some reason.

Logic errors occur when your program contains a design problem that causes the program to produce incorrect results. For example, you may have added two variables together instead of multiplying them. Visual Basic cannot find logic errors; instead, the programmer must identify and correct them. For more information on correcting logic errors, refer to "Appendix A: Debugging."

Fixing Syntax Errors

When a syntax error occurs, Visual Basic displays a message box like the one shown in Figure 2-28.

Figure 2-28: Syntax error message box

To correct a syntax error, click the OK button in the message box. Visual Basic will activate the Code window and highlight the statement containing the error. You can then analyze the statement and make the necessary corrections. To continue running the program, click the Start button on the toolbar.

Fixing Run-Time Errors

One common run-time error occurs when the program tries to store too large a number in a variable. This problem is called **numeric overflow**. For example, if you try to enter too large a number in the calculator program's text boxes, a numeric overflow error will occur. Run-time errors also occur when you try to store the wrong kind of information in a variable or when you try to perform arithmetic operations, such as multiplication, on variables that do not contain numbers. The latter problem is called a **type mismatch** error, because Visual Basic expects the variables used in an arithmetic operation to contain numbers, not text.

To illustrate a run-time error, you will enter values that will cause numeric overflow.

To purposely generate a run-time error:

1   Enter the value **1000000** for the Term Years Value. Press the **Tab** key to execute the LostFocus event procedure for the text box. Visual Basic will display a run-time error message box indicating numeric overflow. See Figure 2-29.

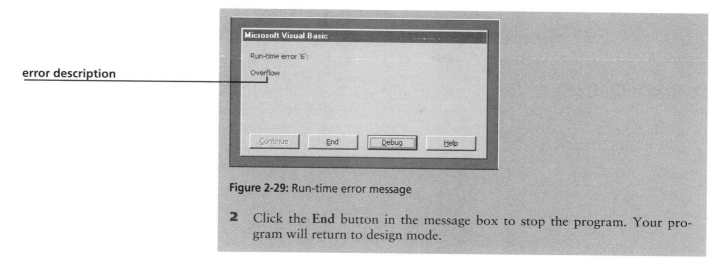

Figure 2-29: Run-time error message

error description

2 Click the **End** button in the message box to stop the program. Your program will return to design mode.

In subsequent chapters, you will write code to prevent and fix run-time errors. Locating and correcting errors in your program are important steps in the programming process. For more information about locating and correcting errors, refer to "Appendix A: Debugging."

After you have corrected any errors, you will print the calculator program code.

Printing a Program

As you develop a program, you may find it helpful to print the code you have written, the object properties you have changed using the Properties window, and an image of the form itself. Furthermore, as your programs become larger and more complex, a printed copy of your code serves as a handy reference. Now that your calculator program is complete, you will print the contents of all files that make up the program.

To print the elements of a program:

1 Click **File** on the menu bar, then click **Print**. The Print dialog opens, as shown in Figure 2-30.

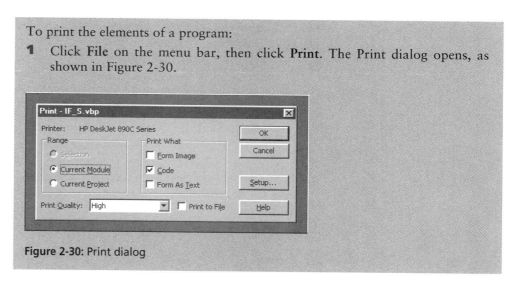

Figure 2-30: Print dialog

2 Click the **Current Module** option, if necessary, in the Range section of the Print dialog (your program contains only one module).

3 Select the **Form Image**, **Code**, and **Form As Text** options in the Print What section of the dialog, then click the **OK** button.

Visual Basic will print the code for your Island Calculator project first, the Form As Text next, and finally the Form Image.

4 Save the project.

5 Exit Visual Basic.

The Code option prints the contents of the general declarations section and then each of the procedures that apply to the form. The Form As Text option prints all of the objects you created on the form and the properties you changed. For each object, it displays the properties you set using the Properties window. If you did not change a property, it will not be printed. The Form Image option prints an image of the form as it appears on the screen.

Now examine the information you just printed. The output contains all of the code in your program. The statements in the general declarations section are printed first, followed by each of the event procedures printed in alphabetical order according to the object's name.

Next, look at the selected output from the Form As Text section.

```
VERSION 6.00
```

The first line lists the version of Visual Basic.

```
Begin VB.Form frmIslandCalculator
BackColor   = &H00C0C0C0&
Caption     = "Island Financial - Time Value of Money Calculator"
ClientHeight    = 3840
ClientLeft      = 3330
ClientTop   = 2970
...
```

These lines define the form itself by identifying its name and properties, including all of the nondefault values on the form, such as the background color. Remember that the Caption property was set for you already. The ClientHeight, ClientLeft, and ClientTop properties specify the form's position on the screen. You did not set these properties explicitly—Visual Basic set them when you created the form. Depending on the location of the form on your particular computer's screen, these property values might differ from those in your printout.

```
Begin VB.CommandButton cmdComputeFutureValue
    Caption     = "Compute Future Value"
    Default     = -1  'True
    Height      = 375
    Left        = 2760
    TabIndex    = 3
    ToolTipText     = "Click to compute the investment's future value."
    Top         = 3360
    Width       = 1935
End
```

These lines identify the properties you set for the CommandButton object. As with the form, the Caption and the position of the object are defined, but two new properties—Default and TabIndex—are listed as well. You set the Default property to ensure that the Click event occurs when a user presses the Enter key. You also set the TabIndex property, which determines the order in which objects are selected when a user presses the Tab key. Finally, the End statement terminates the definition. The calculator program is now complete.

SUMMARY

To select multiple objects:

- Click the **Pointer tool** on the toolbox. Draw a rectangle around the objects to activate them. The active control appears with its sizing handles shaded.

To align multiple controls:

- Select the multiple objects.
- Click **Format, Make Same Size, Both** to make the objects match in size.
- Click **Format, Align, Tops** to align the tops of controls.
- Click **Format, Horizontal Spacing, Make Equal** to make the distance between the objects the same.
- Click **Format, Center in Form, Horizontally** to center the objects between the left and right margins of the form.

To set the tab order of objects:

- Select the object that should receive the initial focus of the form, set its **TabIndex** property to 0, then set the TabIndex property of each subsequent property in order.

To add a Shape object to a form:

- Click the **Shape** control on the toolbox. Move the pointer to the form and draw an outline of the shape. By default, the Shape control draws a rectangle. Set additional properties as necessary.

To create a Line object on a form:

■   Click the **Line** control on the toolbox. Move the pointer to the form and draw a horizontal line on the form. Release the mouse button when the line reaches the desired width or length. Set additional properties as necessary.

To change the font when the text box receives focus:

■   Open the Code window to the text box's **GotFocus** event. The code you will enter for the event will execute when the TextBox object receives the focus. For example,

   TextBox.**FontBold = True**

will make the text in the text box bold when it receives focus.

To change the font when the text box loses focus:

■   Open the Code window to the text box's **LostFocus** event. The code you will enter for the event will execute when the TextBox object loses the focus.

To use the Object Browser to examine intrinsic constants:

■   Click the **Object Browser** button on the toolbar. The Object Browser opens. Click any entry in the Classes section of the Object Browser. The Members section of the Object Browser contains the different members of the selected class. Click the **Close** button on the Object Browser title bar to close the Object Browser.

To declare module-level variables:

■   In the general declarations section of the form, include the following syntax:

   [**Private|Public|Dim**] *Varname* **As** *Type*

To format the contents of a text box:

■   Use the following statement:

   Format(*expression*[,*format*])

To store the contents of a text box as a numeric variable:

■   Use one of the following statements:

   result = **Val**(*string*)

 or

   result = **CInt**(*string*)

 or

   result = **CLng**(*string*)

 or

   result = **CSng**(*string*)

To compute the future value of an investment:

■ Use the FV function:

FV(*rate*,*periods*,*payment*[*,presentvalue*][*,type*])

To set objects to their default settings:

■ Set the object to an empty string:

LabelOrCaption.**Text**|**Caption = vbNullString**

To set the focus explicitly:

■ Call the SetFocus method:

Object.SetFocus

To print the elements of a program:

■ Click **File** on the menu bar, then click **Print**. In the Print dialog, select the Range section, click the **Form Image, Code,** and **Form As Text** options in the Print What section of the dialog, then click the **OK** button.

Q U E S T I O N S

1. Which of the following is a valid Visual Basic data type?
   a. Integer
   b. Long
   c. Single
   d. Date
   e. All of the above.

2. Which of the following are valid keywords to declare a variable?
   a. Priv and Dim
   b. Private and Dim
   c. Private and Dimension
   d. Create, Private, and Dimension
   e. None of the above.

3. Which of the following statements is true of a variable declaration?
   a. Local variables can be used only in the procedure in which they are declared.
   b. Module-level variables can be used by all of the procedures in a module.
   c. There is no difference between module-level and local variables.
   d. Both a and b.
   e. None of the above.

4. Which of the following lists operators in their correct precedence order?
   a. + - , * /, ^
   b. ^, + -, * /
   c. ^, * /, + -
   d. * +, / -, ^
   e. None of the above.

5. Which of the following are valid type conversion functions?
   a. Val, CInt, CLng, and CSng
   b. CVal, CInt, CLng, and CSng
   c. Val, Int, Lng, and Sng
   d. Value, Integer, Long, and Single
   e. None of the above.

6. Which character is used to denote a continuation line?
   a. &
   b. +
   c. -
   d. _
   e. #

7. Which of the following is a type of programming error?
   a. syntax
   b. logic
   c. run-time
   d. None of the above.
   e. All of the above.

8. Declare two module-level variables named mintCounter and msngTotal. The first is the Integer data type and the second is the Single data type.

9. Write the statement(s) to add the numbers 1, 2, and 3 together, multiply the intermediate result by 4, then raise that intermediate result to the power of 2 (squared). Store the result in a variable named mintResult.

10. Write the statement(s) to convert the string "123.44" to a Single precision number. Do not use the Val function.

11. Write the statement(s) to format the numeric value stored in the variable msngOutput with two decimal places and a leading dollar sign. Store the result in a variable named mstrOutput.

12. Write the statement(s) to compute the future value of an investment having an initial value of $2500.00 and an interest rate of 10 percent per year for 30 years. Store the result in a variable named msngFV. Make sure to compound the interest monthly rather than annually.

13. Write the statement(s) to set the focus to a text box named txtName.

E X E R C I S E S

① In addition to investment services, the Island Financial Company provides tax preparation services for its clients. In this exercise, you will create a program that computes the straight-line depreciation of an asset for a period. The program should provide an interface through which the user inputs the initial cost of the asset, the value of the asset at the end of its useful life, and the life of the asset. Because the program has a similar function to that of the future value calculator you created earlier in this chapter, it should employ a similar user interface. To create the program, you will use the SLN function, which is an intrinsic financial function like the FV function. When complete, the user interface will look like Figure 2-31.

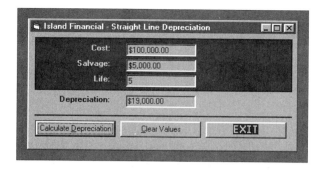

Figure 2-31: Exercise 1 – completed form

a. Run the executable file named **Chapter.02\Exercise\Sample\Ex1.exe**. Set the drive designator as necessary. Enter a cost of 100000, a salvage of 1500, and a life of 5, then click the **Calculate Depreciation** command button. End the program.

b. Start Visual Basic and create a new project, if necessary.

c. Change the Caption property of the form to **Island Financial - Straight Line Depreciation**.

d. Change the Name property to **frmEx1**.

e. Save the form and project using the names **Chapter.02\Exercise\frmEx1.frm** and **Chapter.02\Exercise\Ex1.vbp**, respectively.

f. Draw four Label objects in a column on the form.

g. Change the Caption property of these labels to **Cost:**, **Salvage:**, **Life:**, and **Depreciation:**, respectively, starting from the top label.

 h. Check the Font and Alignment property values for the Island Calculator project. Change the Font and Alignment properties of the labels in the new form to use the same settings as the Island Calculator.

i. Draw four TextBox objects next to the labels. Change the Name properties of the text boxes to **txtCost**, **txtSalvage**, **txtLife**, and **txtDepreciation**, starting from the top text box. Change the Text property for each text box to blank.

j. Create a label to hold the output named **lblDepreciation**. Set the properties so that the contents are left-aligned and have a similar appearance to the text boxes.

k. Draw a Shape object behind the Cost:, Salvage:, and Life: labels and text boxes. This shape should be a **dark blue** rectangle that resembles the shapes in the Island Calculator project.

l. Create three CommandButton objects on the bottom of the form.

m. Change the Name property of the left-hand button to **cmdCalculateDepreciation**; change its Caption property to **Calculate Depreciation**. Set it as the default button and use the character **D** as the hot key. Adjust the width of the command button to accommodate its caption, as necessary. Create an appropriate ToolTip for the command button.

n. Change the Name property of the center button to **cmdClearValues**; change its Caption property to **Clear Values**. Use the character **C** as the hot key. Create an appropriate ToolTip for the command button.

o. Change the Name property of the right-hand button to **cmdExit**. Set the necessary properties so that the image **Chapter.02\Exercise\exit.bmp** will appear in the button.

p. Draw a Line object between the Depreciation: label and text box and the command buttons. This line should be **dark blue** so as to resemble the line in the Island Calculator project.

q. Open the Code window for the **cmdExit** object's **Click** event procedure, then enter the code that will end the running program when this button is clicked. Remember to include comments explaining what the procedure does in all of your code.

discovery ▶

r. For each of the three text boxes, write the necessary code to set the label to a blue, bold font when the text box receives focus and not a blue, bold font when the text box loses focus.

discovery ▶

s. In the LostFocus event procedure for each of the three text boxes, store the value of the text box in a module-level variable. You will need to declare the variables in the general declarations section of the Code window. In addition, format the Cost: and Salvage: text boxes as Currency when these text boxes lose focus.

discovery ▶

t. Use the Index tab in the Help library to consult Visual Basic's online Help for information on financial functions. Open the Help window for the SLN function. Print the Help topic to guide you through the creation of the rest of this program.

discovery ▶

u. Open the Code window for the **cmdCalculateDepreciation** object's **Click** event procedure. Type the code that will compute the straight-line depreciation and store the result in the output label named **lblDepreciation**. Format the output as a Currency value.

discovery ▶

v. Open the Code window for the **cmdClearValues** object's **Click** event procedure and enter code that will set to blank the Text property of the three TextBox objects and output depreciation label. Set the focus to the text box named **txtCost.**

w. Test your program by entering **100000** as the asset cost, **5000** as the salvage value, and **5** as the asset life in years. Click the **Calculate Depreciation** command button to execute the depreciation function. The result should be $19,000.00 as the depreciation amount for each year. Test the **Clear Values** and **EXIT** command buttons.

x. Correct any mistakes and save your work again, if necessary.

2. Perfect Printing needs a program that creates a charge for a printing order. The cost of the order should be based on the paper size and the number of pages printed. The finished form should resemble Figure 2-32.

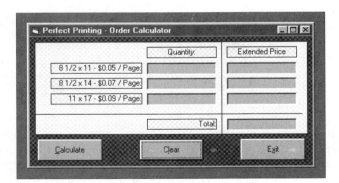

Figure 2-32: Exercise 2 – completed form

As shown in Figure 2-32, the form includes numerous control instances. Part of the task is to align these controls and create a visually appealing user interface. A yellow color theme was chosen in the sample solution for this exercise. Use your artistic eye to develop a different color scheme, if you like.

a. Run the executable file named **Chapter.02\Exercise\Sample\Ex2.exe** on the Student Disk to view the user interface. Exit the program.

b. Start Visual Basic and create a new project, if necessary.

c. Change the Name property of the form to **frmEx2**. Change the Caption property of the form to **Perfect Printing – Order Calculator**.

d. Save the form and project using the names **Chapter.02\Exercise\frmEx2.frm** and **Chapter.02\Exercise\Ex2.vbp**, respectively.

e. Create the descriptive labels for the rows and columns, as shown in Figure 2-32. Also, create the label for the Total: description. These labels all have similar formatting characteristics, so you can set the color and border for all of them simultaneously.

f. Create three text boxes to store a quantity-ordered value for each of the different paper sizes, and set the visual properties as you desire. Because you will write code to multiply the quantity ordered for a particular paper size, you should set the Name property to meaningful names that describe the purpose of each text box.

g. Create three labels to the right of the text boxes you created in the previous step. Also, create another label to store the order total. Because all of these objects serve a similar function, you should set the visual properties so that each label shares the same characteristics.

h. Create the shapes and lines necessary to define the regions of the form, as shown in Figure 2-32.

i. Create three command buttons on the form that calculate the extended price and order total, clear the input and output fields, and exit the program.

j. Write the necessary code to calculate the extended price for each paper size. The extended price can be computed by multiplying the quantity by the price per page. (*Hint*: Use module-level variables to store the numeric representation of each input value and the extended price.) The output displayed in the labels should be formatted with a leading dollar sign and two decimal places.

k. In the same event procedure, write statements to add the extended prices of the individual items together, format the result, and display it in the total label.

l. In the event procedure for the Clear command button, write statements to remove the contents from the input and output fields.

m. In the event procedure for the Exit command button, end the running program.

n. Test the program to verify that the extended price and total are computed correctly. Also, make sure you have applied the user interface principles (discussed earlier in this chapter) so as to present a pleasing user interface.

o. Correct any mistakes and save your work again, if necessary.

3. Timberline, Ltd., is an engineering firm that constructs planning models in Visual Basic of various ecosystems around the world. Because so much of its work relies on using proper formulas in their calculations, Timberline requires that the model formulas be correct. You will work on one of these models to test your ability to convert algebraic formulas to their proper computational forms. Specifically, you will build a program to convert and test the formulas shown in Figure 2-33.

$$1 \quad \frac{\left(mintVar1 + mintVar2\right)}{\left(mintVar3\right)}$$

$$2 \quad \frac{\left(mintVar1\right)^{mintVar5}}{\left(mintVar2\right)\left(mintVar4\right)}$$

$$3 \quad \frac{\left(mintVar1 - mintVar2\right)^{mintVar3}}{\left(mintVar4\right)}$$

$$4 \quad \frac{\left(mintVar4 - mintVar2\right)\left(\left(mintVar3\right)\right)}{\left(mintVar5\right)^{mintVar2}}$$

$$5 \quad \left(\frac{\dfrac{mintVar2}{mintVar1}}{\dfrac{mintVar4}{mintVar5}}\right)^{mintVar2}$$

$$6 \quad \frac{\left(\dfrac{mintVar1}{mintVar2}\right)\left(\dfrac{mintVar3}{mintVar4}\right)}{\left(mintVar5\right)^{mintVar1}}$$

Figure 2-33

When complete, the form should resemble Figure 2-34.

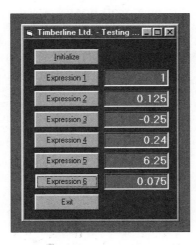

Figure 2-34: Exercise 3 – completed form

a. Make sure that your Student Disk is in the appropriate disk drive. Run the executable file named **Chapter.02\Exercise\Sample\Ex3.exe**. Click the command buttons on the form to display the result of each formula.

b. Start Visual Basic and create a new project, if necessary.

c. Change the Name property of the form to **frmEx3**. Change the Caption property of the form, as shown in Figure 2-34.

d. Save the form and project using the names **Chapter.02\Exercise\frmEx3.frm** and **Chapter.02\Exercise\Ex3.vbp**, respectively.

discovery ▶

e. The user interface contains command buttons and corresponding labels that display the output from the formulas shown in Figure 2-33. In addition, a command button initializes the values for the various variables and another exits the program. Create these labels and command buttons. Set the name and caption properties as shown, align them, and set the other visual properties. Use your artistic eye, along with Figure 2-34 as a template.

f. Open the general declarations section in the Code window and type the statements to declare five integer variables with the following names: **mintVar1, mintVar2, mintVar3, mintVar4,** and **mintVar5**.

discovery ▶

g. In the Code window for the **Initialize** command button's **Click** event procedure, assign numerical values to each of the variables as follows: **mintVar1 = 1, mintVar2 = 2, mintVar3 = 3, mintVar4 = 4,** and **mintVar5 = 5**.

h. For the **Exit** command button, set the Name property as necessary and write a statement to unload the form.

discovery ▶

i. Open the Code window for the **Expression 1** command button object's **Click** event procedure, then enter the expression that will set the caption of lblAnswer1 to the converted algebraic form of formula 1 in Figure 2-33.

discovery ▶

j. For the remaining five command buttons, enter the proper formula conversions for the formulas 2 through 6 in Figure 2-33.

discovery ▶

k. Test the program by testing each label. The following answers should be displayed in the labels:

lblExpression1.Caption = 1
lblExpression2.Caption = 0.125
lblExpression3.Caption = –0.25
lblExpression4.Caption = 0.24
lblExpression5.Caption = 6.25
lblExpression6.Caption = 0.075

If any of your answers do not match these answers, you have made a mistake in converting a formula. Click the **Exit** button. Fix each incorrect expression by changing the code in the Code window for the appropriate label. Repeat this step until your answers are correct. Test the **Exit** button.

l. Correct any mistakes and save your work again, if necessary.

4. Mile High Surveying performs various types of land surveys. The company needs a calculator to convert measurements between U.S. and metric values. In other words, it needs to perform tasks like converting feet to meters. When complete, the final form should resemble Figure 2-35. To perform these conversions, you need to know that there are 2.54 centimeters per inch and 100 centimeters per meter. From this knowledge, you can calculate that there are 0.394 inch per centimeter.

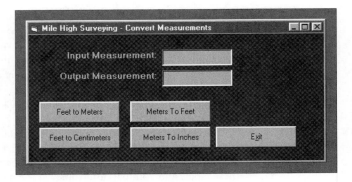

Figure 2-35: Exercise 4 – completed form

a. Run the executable file named **Chapter.02\Exercise\Sample\Ex4.exe**. Set the drive designator as necessary. Type in a valve in the Input Measurement textbox and click the command buttons on the form to display the result of each conversion.

b. Start Visual Basic and create a new project, if necessary.

c. Change the Name property of the form to **frmEx4**. Change the Caption property of the form as shown in Figure 2-35.

d. Save the form and project using the names **Chapter.02\Exercise\frmEx4.frm** and **Chapter.02\Exercise\Ex4.vbp**, respectively.

e. Create two descriptive labels, as shown in Figure 2-35.

f. Adjacent to the descriptive labels you created in the previous figure, create a text box so that the user can enter an input measurement. Also, create a label that will display the converted output measurement. Because you will write code to reference both of these objects, set the Name properties appropriately.

discovery ▶

discovery ▶

g. Create the command buttons shown in Figure 2-35, and set the Caption and Name properties appropriately.

h. In the Click event procedure for the four conversion command buttons, write statements to convert the input value to the output value. That is, write code to convert feet to meters, meters to feet, and so on. Remember that there are 2.54 centimeters per inch and 100 centimeters per meter. You will need to declare module-level variables to store temporary information.

i. Test the program. To validate the computations, approximate that there are roughly 3 feet per meter. From this information, you will be able to derive the number of units per inch.

j. Correct any mistakes and save your work again, if necessary.

Decision Making

Validating Input Data

case▶ DataTronics, a software development company, has been hired to create a computer program that will issue building permits. A building permit must be issued before a homeowner or contractor begins a construction project. Several pieces of information are needed to obtain a building permit, including the name of the applicant, the date construction is expected to start, the square footage of the project, and the height of the building. A central office issues building permits for four counties in the region. The computer program's requirements must carefully validate that the user input is as accurate as possible. For example, the construction start date must be a valid future date. The county must be the name of a regional county. Also, restrictions are placed on the length of a string, such as a person's name. In this chapter, you will create a set of procedures that will help validate input data to ensure its accuracy.

Previewing the Input Validation Program

The processing in this program consists of two parts. The first part will validate the input as the user enters it. The second part will compute the cost of the building permit. This cost is based on the square footage of the building and the county in which the building is being constructed. The following list describes the input requirements for the program:

- Every person's name must have a prefix beginning with Mr., Mrs., or Ms.
- A person's first name must be less than or equal to 15 characters.
- A person's last name must be less than or equal to 25 characters.
- The start date for construction must be a valid date and its value must be greater than the current date; that is, the value must be some future date.
- The county must be one of four regional counties serviced by the building permit office: Amil, Barker, Cascade, or Delphi.
- The square footage of the project must be a number that is greater than zero (0).
- The height of the building must be between 8 and 200 feet.

The program can validate user input at different points. For example, it might validate the input as the user enters it. Using this technique, you can validate each field as it loses focus. Alternatively, the program might validate all of the fields at once. Using this technique, you can validate the input only after the user has entered values in all of the input fields and pressed the Calculate button. In this chapter, we will use the second technique.

help

▶
••••••••••••••••
The date in Figure 3-1 appears with a four-digit year. If your screen does not match this figure, you can change the Short date style on the Date tab in the Regional Settings Properties dialog available from the

date

To preview the completed program:

1 Start Visual Basic, then open the project named **Chapter.03\Complete\DT_C.vbp**. Set the drive designator as necessary.

2 Start the program.

Figure 3-1 shows the completed form during run time. The current date appears in the lower-right corner of the form.

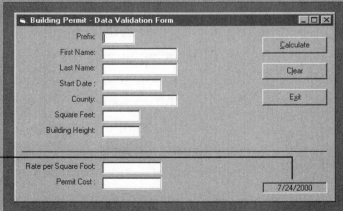

Figure 3-1: Completed form

3 Enter an invalid prefix of **John**, then press the **Tab** key to move the cursor to the next field. Click the **Calculate** button to validate the input.

Whenever invalid input, including a blank field, is detected, a type of form called a **dialog** appears to advise the user that an error occurred. Figure 3-2 shows the Error dialog. This form will be discussed in detail later in this chapter.

Figure 3-2: Error dialog

4   Click the **OK** button to close the Error dialog and return to the main form. A label appears to the right of the prefix, indicating that the value is invalid. Also, other labels appear to the right of the Start Date, County, Square Feet, and Building Height fields because information was not entered for those fields. Each input field works in the same way. If an invalid value is entered in any field, or if any field is left blank when the user clicks the Calculate button, a label appears to the right of the text box to indicate the error.

5   Enter the information shown in the top section of Figure 3-3, then click the **Calculate** button to calculate the cost of the building permit.

current date

calculated output

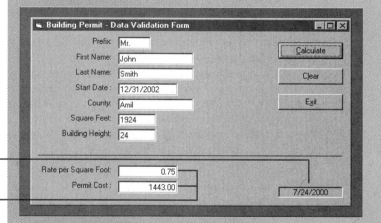

Figure 3-3: Completed form at run time

6   End the program, then exit Visual Basic.

The first section of this chapter presents a great deal of interrelated material that you must understand before you can begin to program the user interface. Although Section A includes some hands-on steps, most of the programming of the user interface is left to Section B of this chapter.

SECTION A

In this section you will:

- Validate input
- Use Boolean data
- Use a Select Case statement to make decisions
- Manipulate strings

Validating User Input

Input Validation

When the user makes a mistake while entering information into a program, the program should advise the user of the error and help correct it. This concept is called **input validation**. Many types of input can be validated.

- When data must be a date, any value that cannot be converted to a date is invalid.
- When data must be numeric—for example, when entering a salary or hours worked—the value must be numeric or else it is invalid. Furthermore, the value for a field like hours worked must be greater than zero (0).
- Data must often fall within some valid range. For example, a valid date of birth cannot be a future date, and a valid square footage of a building must be a number that is greater than zero. A well-designed program should warn the user when the input entered exceeds some reasonable value; this approach is called **range checking**. For example, the value of 15,000 for the square footage of a house—although possible—is unlikely.
- Sometimes data must have a particular format. For example, telephone numbers in the United States begin with a three-character area code, followed by a three-character exchange number, followed by a four-digit number. The value contained in a telephone number field can be validated to make sure it has the required characteristics.
- In some cases, character strings should not exceed a maximum length.

To create the best possible user interface, input data should be validated for correctness. The programmer needs to be aware, however, that not all input can be validated. For example, a person's name may be spelled incorrectly, but the program cannot detect the incorrect spelling.

Using Boolean Data

To create fully functional programs, you often must use data types other than the numeric data types. In the previous chapter, you stored textual data in the Text property of the textbox. You then converted textual data to numeric data and then performed computations on that numeric data. When data is not numeric and instead represents a status or a situation, such as True or False, it comprises Boolean data.

Boolean data operates like an on/off switch; that is, the keyword True signifies on and the keyword False signifies off. Variables can be declared as the Boolean data type. Furthermore, as you saw in Chapters 1 and 2, many properties store and some functions return Boolean values.

When you assign a numeric value to a Boolean variable, the value will be converted to True or False. If the value is 0, it is converted to False. All other values are converted to True. For example, if you store a value like 3.14 or 7 in a Boolean variable, the result will be True. If you try to store a string in a Boolean variable, an error will occur.

Two keywords represent the two possible values for the Boolean data type: True and False. The following statements declare a variable and set it first to True, then to False:

```
Dim pblnDemo As Boolean
pblnDemo = True      ' True
pblnDemo = False     ' False
```

The first statement declares a Boolean variable named pblnDemo. This variable can store the values True and False. The three-character prefix for a Boolean variable is "bln". The "p" indicates a procedure-level variable. The next two assignment statements store a value in the Boolean variable. The first uses the keyword True; the next statement stores the value False in the Boolean variable.

Visual Basic will convert numeric data to Boolean data in assignment statements. Attempting to convert textual (string) data to a Boolean data type will cause an error. The following statements set a Boolean variable using numeric data:

```
pblnDemo = 0         ' False
pblnDemo = 1         ' True
pblnDemo = 328       ' True
pblnDemo = "Error"   ' Run-time error occurs
```

These statements are less intuitive than those given in the earlier example. In the first statement, the numeric value zero (0) is converted from a numeric value into a Boolean data type; that is, the numeric value zero is converted to False. In each of the next two assignment statements, the numeric value on the right-hand side of the equals sign is converted to a Boolean value. The result of both conversion operations is True because all numeric values except zero (0) are converted to True. The final statement will produce a run-time error because a string cannot be converted into a Boolean value.

In addition to variables, many properties have Boolean values. Two common Boolean properties are as follows:

- An object's **Visible** property determines whether the object appears on the screen when the program is running. If the value is True, the object is visible. If the value is False, it is invisible.
- An object's **Enabled** property determines whether the object will respond to events. For example, if you set the Enabled property for a command button to False, it will appear grayed and will not respond to a Click event. If you set the Enabled property for a text box to False, it neither receives focus nor responds to events. As a result, a user cannot edit the contents of a disabled text box.

Programs often use Boolean data to evaluate a condition and then execute different statements based on whether the condition is True or False.

Classification Functions

In the previous chapter, you learned how to use type conversion functions to convert information from one data type to another. For example, you used the Val function to convert a string to a number before using it in an arithmetic expression. The input validation program in this chapter validates input data to ensure that it is correct or at least plausible. **Classification functions**, which form a subset of intrinsic functions, determine whether a string of characters has specific characteristics. For example, you can use classification functions to determine whether a string can be converted into a date or a number.

Syntax	**IsDate**(*expression*) **IsNumeric**(*expression*)
Dissection	■ The **IsDate** and **IsNumeric** classification functions determine whether a value can be successfully converted to a date or a number, respectively. Note, however, that these functions do not actually convert the data. They merely determine whether the data can be converted. ■ The *expression* contains the string value that will be tested. If the expression can be converted to a date or number, the intrinsic classification function returns a value of True; otherwise, it returns a value of False.
Code Example	``` Dim pstrCurrent As String Dim pblnResult As Boolean pstrCurrent = "123.45" pblnResult = IsNumeric(pstrCurrent) pblnResult = IsDate(pstrCurrent) ```
Code Dissection	The preceding statements first declare the variables pstrCurrent and pblnResult, then store the value 123.45 in the String variable named pstrCurrent. When the IsNumeric function is called, it tests the string to determine whether the string contains a number. It does, so the function returns a value of True, which is stored in pblnResult. When the IsDate function is called, however, the value returned is False because pstrCurrent does not represent a valid date value. Thus the value stored in pblnResult is False.

In many cases, classification functions are combined with other statements. That is, it is not sufficient that the program knows that a variable contains a number. It must also inform the user when data is invalid and process correct user input.

Decision Making

The programs that you developed in Chapters 1 and 2 sequentially executed statements in the order that they appeared in the procedure, continuing in this fashion until the procedure reached the End Sub statement. This approach is fine for simple tasks, but most programs need the capability to execute one series of statements in certain circumstances and another series of statements in different circumstances. Visual Basic allows you to write statements to address such different conditions. For example, you can write the following sentences in English: "If an input value is not a valid Integer, then alert the user that the input is invalid. Otherwise continue." A general form of this sentence can be expressed as pseudocode:

```
If some expression is True Then
    Execute one group of statements.
Otherwise
    Execute a different group of statements.
End of If statement.
```

Using Comparison Operators and the If Statement

When you understand that the English word "if" represents a decision, then the transition to decision-making code is easy. To determine which series of statements to execute and when, you use a conditional statement. A **conditional statement** executes one group of statements when the condition is True and another group of statements when the condition is False. When writing a conditional statement, you use **comparison operators** on two or more values or expressions. Visual Basic uses the following comparison operators: equal to (=), not equal to (<>), less than (<), greater than (>), less than or equal to (<=), greater than or equal to (>=), and contains the string (Like).

A conditional operation always produces a Boolean value as its result: True or False. Comparison operators all have the same precedence. When they are used in conjunction with arithmetic operators, however, the arithmetic operations are performed first, before the comparison operations. You can use parentheses to override this default precedence.

Comparison operators are seldom used alone. Rather, they are included as part of another statement, such as an If statement. The simplest form of an If statement will execute a group of statements if a specific condition is True. If the condition is not True, those statements will not be executed.

Syntax	**If** condition **Then**
	    statements
	End If

Dissection	■ The **If** statement tests the value of some condition. If the condition is True, then the statements between the If and End If statements are executed, and the procedure continues with the statement following the End If. If the condition is False, these statements are not executed, and the procedure continues with the statement following the End If statement. ■ The condition part of an If statement must evaluate to a Boolean value. If the value is a numeric value like an Integer or a Single, it will be converted to a Boolean value. ■ The statements can include any valid Visual Basic statement or statements that will execute when the condition is True. ■ If the condition is False, the statements between the **If** and the **End If** will not be executed, and execution of the program continues at the statement following the End If.
| Code Example | ```
Dim pblnValid As Boolean
Dim pintSquareFeet As Integer
If IsNumeric(txtSquareFeet.Text) = True Then
    pintSquareFeet = Val(txtSquareFeet.Text)
    pblnValid = True
End If
``` |
| Code Dissection | These statements first declare the variables pblnValid and pintSquareFeet. The If statement is then used to determine whether the text box named txtSquareFeet contains a valid number. If it does, the statements between the If and End If are executed. These statements assign the value of the text box to the variable pintSquareFeet and set the variable pblnValid to True. If the text box does not contain a number, these statements are not executed and execution of the procedure continues at the statement following the End If. |
```

The syntax of the previous If statement begins by evaluating IsNumeric(txtSquareFeet.Text):

```
If IsNumeric(txtSquareFeet.Text) = True Then
```

Assuming that the value of IsNumeric(txtSquareFeet.Text) contains a number, the result of the intermediate operation (True) is compared with True. These two values match, so the result of the If statement is True.

We can also abbreviate this If statement. The following variation of the preceding If statement produces the same effect as the original code:

```
If IsNumeric(txtSquareFeet.Text) Then
```

The condition (If IsNumeric(txtSquareFeet.Text)) is True—the same result produced by the previous statement. Thus, in many cases, you can write the same If statement in many different ways.

Although the simple form of the If statement is useful, it does not help the programmer when a different activity should be executed if a condition is False. Fortunately, we can expand the previous code to set the variable pblnValid to False if the square footage is less than or equal to zero (0). This type of If statement is called an If...Then...Else statement.

Syntax	**If** *condition* **Then**
	    statements(True)
	Else
	    statements(False)
	End If

Dissection	■ The **If...Then...Else** statement is similar to the previously given form of an If statement. It differs in that it includes a group of statements to be executed when the *condition* is False. ■ If the *condition* is True, then the *statements(***True***)* between the If and Else statements execute, and the procedure execution continues at the statement following the End If statement. ■ If the *condition* is False, then the *statements(***False***)* between the Else and End If statements are executed, and the procedure execution continues at the statement following the End If statement.

Code Example	```Dim pblnValid As Boolean
	Dim pintSquareFeet As Integer
	If IsNumeric(txtSquareFeet.Text) Then
	    pintSquareFeet = Val(txtSquareFeet.Text)
	    pblnValid = True
	Else
	    pblnValid = False
	End If```

Code Dissection

This form of the If statement illustrates a **two-way decision**, which provides two possible outcomes for the If statement. That is, if the text box named txtSquareFeet contains a number, the variable pblnValid is set to True; otherwise, it is set to False.

Just as you can write several versions of a simple If statement, you can also write an If...Then...Else statement in different ways. Both of the following If statements determine whether a square footage value is valid (greater than zero (0)) and both set the value of the Boolean variable pblnValid accordingly:

```
Dim pblnValid As Boolean
Dim pintSquareFeet As Integer
If pintSquareFeet > 0 Then
    pblnValid = True
Else
    pblnValid = False
End If


If pintSquareFeet <= 0 Then
    pblnValid = False
Else
    pblnValid = True
End If
```

Programming

tip

● ● ● ● ● ● ● ● ● ● ● ● ● ●

▶ **You can often write an If statement in several ways to produce the same result. In such a case, you should choose the most readable and intuitive statement.**

Both If statements give equivalent results. Each If statement, however, uses a different condition. One tests whether pintSquareFeet is greater than zero (0). The other tests whether pintSquareFeet is less than or equal to zero (0). Because the conditions are essentially reversed, the settings of pblnValid are reversed as well.

As you can see, we have indented the statements between the If and Else statements, the statements between the Else and End If statements, and the statements between the If and End If statements. This convention makes the program more readable because it is readily apparent which statements are executed when the condition is True and which statements are executed when the condition is False. Furthermore, the words If, Else, and End If are aligned vertically in the same column, which helps to identify the beginning and the end of the If statement.

Consider once again DataTronics' desired program. With the above form of the If statement, you can validate user input to ensure that the square footage entered by the user is a number greater than zero (0). To accomplish this validation, you can use the Val function discussed in Chapter 2 to convert the text to an Integer data type. Then you can include an If statement to determine whether that number is greater than zero (0). If it is not, you will make a label visible to alert the user about the error condition. This label will appear next to the corresponding text box. If the number is greater than zero (0), you will make the label invisible.

The logic required by your program, however, requires more than an If... Then... Else statement. For example, the actions to be carried out may depend on certain circumstances, which may in turn depend on other circumstances. In such a case, If statements may be nested inside one another.

Nested If Statements

Although the previous examples illustrated simple uses of the If statement, they did not fully exploit its capabilities. If statements can be nested; that is, one If statement can appear inside of another If statement:

```
If IsNumeric(txtSquareFeet.Text) Then
    msngSquareFeet = txtSquareFeet.Text
    If msngSquareFeet <= 0 Then
        lblSquareFeet.Visible = True
    Else
        lblSquareFeet.Visible = False
    End If
Else
  lblSquareFeet.Visible = True
End If
```

The preceding statements illustrate the use of a nested If statement. The first If statement tests whether txtSquareFeet.Text contains a valid number. If it does, the character string in the text box is converted to a number and stored in the variable msngSquareFeet. The inner If statement is then executed to determine whether the value of the variable is less than or equal to zero (0). If this result is True, then lblSquareFeet becomes visible. Otherwise, this text box remains invisible.

Again, we have indented the inner If statement; the statements inside the inner If statement are indented as well. This formatting improves the program's readability.

In addition to validating the square footage, you can validate the construction start date entered by the user. The expected construction start date must be both a date and a value in the future. As mentioned, your program will validate all of the form fields simultaneously when the user clicks the Calculate button. All of the following code needs to be written in the cmdCalculate_Click event procedure.

The code in this event procedure must validate each input text box. If the contents of a text box are invalid, a label should appear to the right of the text box, indicating that the user has entered invalid data. If one or more text boxes contain invalid data, you must also display a dialog indicating this fact. (You will learn to display a dialog later in this chapter.) To keep track of whether the fields contain invalid data, you can use a Boolean variable.

To create a nested If statement:

1 Start Visual Basic, then open the project named **Chapter.03\Startup\ DT_S.vbp**. Set the drive designator as necessary. The form looks the same as the completed form you observed in the completed program at the beginning of the chapter. The code to validate the input data, however, is missing.

2 Make sure the Code window for the **cmdCalculate_Click** event procedure is active, then enter the following statements (shown in bold). The local variables used in the procedure and the module-level variables have already been declared.

```
          mblnValid = True
      If IsDate(txtStartDate.Text) Then
          mdatStartDate = CDate(txtStartDate.Text)
          If mdatStartDate > Date Then
              lblStartDate.Visible = False
          Else
              lblStartDate.Visible = True
              mblnValid = False
          End If
      Else
          lblStartDate.Visible = True
          mblnValid = False
      End If
      If IsNumeric(txtSquareFeet.Text) Then
          msngSquareFeet = txtSquareFeet.Text
          If msngSquareFeet <= 0 Then
              lblSquareFeet.Visible = True
              mblnValid = False
          Else
              lblSquareFeet.Visible = False
          End If
      Else
          lblSquareFeet.Visible = True
          mblnValid = False
      End If
End Sub
```

3 Test the program. Enter the values shown in Figure 3-4, then click the **Calculate** button. The error labels should appear next to the invalid fields, as shown in Figure 3-4.

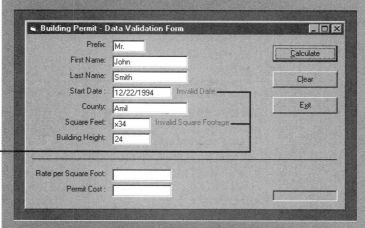

invalid data

Figure 3-4: Input errors

> **4**   Correct the data by entering a valid date (one that is greater than the current date) and a square footage that is greater than zero (0). Click the **Calculate** command button again. The error labels should become invisible. The output fields listing the Rate per Square Foot and the Permit Cost contain no data because you have not written code to compute the output.

The final variation on the If statement is the **multiway If statement**. This form provides for three or more possible outcomes.

Syntax	If *condition* **Then**
	    [*statements*]
	[**ElseIf** *condition-n* **Then**
	    [*elseifstatements*]]...
	[**Else**
	    [*elsestatements*]]
	End If

Dissection	■ The **multiway If statement** is used to make decisions that have three or more possible outcomes. ■ If the *condition* is **True**, then the *statements* between the If and the first ElseIf execute. Program execution subsequently continues at the statement following the End If statement. If the *condition* is not **True**, then the *condition-n* is tested. If that *condition-n* is **True**, then the statements following the **ElseIf** execute, the multiway If statement exits, and program execution subsequently continues following the **End If** statement. If *condition-n* is not True, then the program tests the conditions of subsequent **ElseIf** statements in order. ■ If no *condition* is **True**, then the statements between the optional **Else** and **End If** statements execute, and program execution continues following the **End If** statement. If the optional **Else** statement is omitted, then program execution continues at the statement following the **End If** statement.

Code Example	<pre>If pstrCounty = "Amil" Then
	    msngRate = 0.75
	ElseIf pstrCounty = "Barker" Then
	    msngRate = 0.76
	ElseIf pstrCounty = "Cascade" Then
	    msngRate = 0.8
	ElseIf pstrCounty = "Delphi" Then
	    msngRate = 0.82
	Else
	    lblCounty.Visible = True
	    mblnValid = False
	End If</pre>

Code Dissection	This If statement determines whether the user has entered a valid county. There are four possible values for the county: Amil, Barker, Cascade, and Delphi. If the county is valid, then the variable msngRate is set to a value. This value represents the cost per square foot of the new building. (You will use this value later in the chapter to compute the amount of the building permit.) If the county is not valid, then the label indicating the error becomes visible and the Boolean variable mblnValid is set to False, indicating the error.

Figure 3-5 illustrates the execution sequence of the preceding If statement.

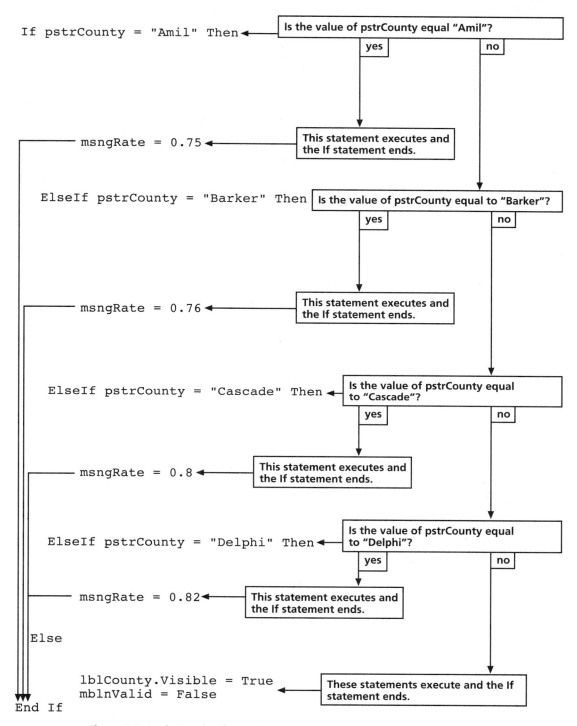

Figure 3-5: Analyzing the If statement

The Select Case Statement

You have seen how an If statement is used to test conditions and execute different statements based on those conditions. In circumstances where an ElseIf condition in an If statement uses the same expression in each condition and compares it with a different value, the Select Case decision structure can both simplify program logic and make a program more readable. Select Case statements resemble If statements, but instead of testing multiple expressions, they test only one expression and execute different statements based on the results of that test.

Syntax	**Select Case** *testexpression*
	  Case *expressionlist-1*
	    statement-block1
	  Case *expressionlist-2*
	    statement-block2
	  Case *expressionlist-n*
	    statement-blockn
	  [**Case Else**
	    [*statements*]]
	End Select

Dissection

- Visual Basic executes the **Select Case** statement by evaluating the *testexpression* once when the Select Case statement first starts. It then compares the *expressionlist-1* with the *testexpression*. If they match, the statements in *statement-block1* are executed, and the entire Select Case statement exits. If they differ, the *expressionlist-2* is compared with the *testexpression*. This process repeats until no more expressions remain to be tested. Program execution then continues with the statement following the End Select statement.

- If no expression matches the *testexpression*, the statements in the optional **Case Else** clause are executed. If no expression matched the *testexpression* and the code does not include a Case Else statement, then no statement block will be executed, and program execution continues with the statement following the End Select statement.

- If more than one *expressionlist* matches the *testexpression*, only the statements in the first matching Case statement are executed. Program execution then continues with the statement following the End Select statement.

- The *expressionlist* can consist of a list of values—such as 6,7,8—separated by commas. It also can comprise a range of values separated by the word To, as in "5 To 10". Refer to the Visual Basic Help library for a complete discussion of the ways to use the Select Case statement.

Code Example

```
Select Case pstrCounty
    Case "Amil"
        msngRate = 0.75
    Case "Barker"
        msngRate = 0.76
    Case "Cascade"
        msngRate = 0.8
    Case "Delphi"
        msngRate = 0.82
    Case Else
        lblCounty.Visible = True
        mblnValid = False
End Select
```

Code Dissection

This Select Case statement has the same effect as the If statement given earlier. The condition of the Select Case statement is the variable pstrCounty. If the variable contains the value "Amil", then the variable msngRate is set to 0.75. If the value is "Barker", then the value of msngRate is set to 0.76, and so on. If the county is not valid, then the Case Else block executes, which causes the corresponding label to become visible.

Figure 3-6 shows the If statement from Figure 3-5 written in the form of a Select Case statement.

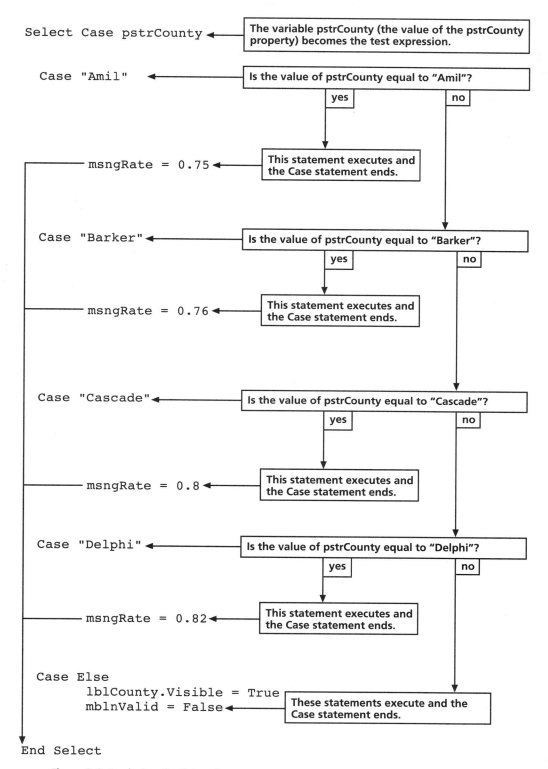

Figure 3-6: Analyzing the Select Case statement

Performance
tip

• • • • • • • • • • • • • • • • •

The code in Figure 3-6 will execute more quickly than the code in Figure 3-5 because Visual Basic needs to check the condition only once in the first line of the Select Case statement, rather than many times in each If and ElseIf statement. In addition, this Select Case statement will make your program easier to read than does the longer If statement.

You are now ready to write the code that will validate the county using a Select Case statement. As before, the input is validated when the Calculate command button is clicked.

To create a Select Case statement:

1 Make sure the Code window for the **cmdCalculate_Click** event procedure is active, then enter the following statements at the end of the procedure:

```
    End If
    pstrCounty = StrConv(txtCounty.Text, vbProperCase)
    lblCounty.Visible = False
    Select Case pstrCounty
          Case "Amil"
                msngRate = 0.75
          Case "Barker"
                msngRate = 0.76
          Case "Cascade"
                msngRate = 0.8
          Case "Delphi"
                msngRate = 0.82
          Case Else
                lblCounty.Visible = True
                mblnValid = False
       End Select
End Sub
```

2 Test the program. Enter the value **abcdef** in the county field, then click the **Calculate** button. The message "Invalid County" should appear next to the text box. Note that other messages also appear next to other text boxes. Enter the value **Amil** into the County text box, then click the **Calculate** button. Because this input is a valid value, the label becomes invisible.

Logical Operators

Use of another type of operator, called the logical operator, can further enhance the If statement. Logical operators consist of words like And and Or. Their meaning in Visual Basic is similar to their meaning in English. Logical operators allow the programmer to concatenate multiple expressions into a single If statement.

A **logical operator** performs the same role as a **conjunction** (and) or a **disjunction** (or) in English. In the sentence "If the value is a valid date and the value is greater than the current date, then the date is valid," the word "and" is used as a conjunction. If the phrases to the left and right of the conjunction are both True, then the entire sentence is True. Figure 3-7 lists the more common logical operators.

Logical operator	Example	Result
Not	```If Not 1 > 2, Then statements End If If Not 2 > 1, Then statements End If```	True False
And	```If 2 > 1 And 3 > 1, Then statements End If If 1 > 2 And 3 > 1, Then statements End If```	True False
Or	```If 2 > 1 Or 3 > 1, Then statements End If If 1 > 2 Or 3 > 1, Then statements End If If 1 > 2 Or 1 > 3, Then statements End If```	True True False
Xor	```If 2 > 1 Xor 3 > 1, Then statements End If If 1 > 2 Xor 3 > 1, Then statements End If If 1 > 2 Xor 1 > 3, Then statements End If```	False True False

Figure 3-7: Logical operators

In this program, you will use logical operators with If statements to validate String data. For example, the valid prefixes for a person's name are Mr., Mrs., and Ms. Thus the Or operator could be used to test whether the input prefix is one of these three options.

Like arithmetic operators, logical operators have an order of precedence. All operations involving arithmetic operators and comparison operators are performed first. The logical operations are performed next, in the following order: Not, And,

Or, Xor. The And operator can be used to perform range checking to determine whether a value is between two other values. For example, in a payroll application, you may want to validate the hours worked by an employee to verify that the value is between 1 and 40:

```
If pintHoursWorked >= 1 And pintHoursWorked <= 40 Then
    ' Valid
Else
    ' Invalid
End If
```

The Or operator can also be used for input validation, especially in a situation where the user must enter either Yes or No in the text box named txtOK:

```
If txtOK.Text = "Yes" Or txtOK.Text = "No"
    ' Valid
Else
    ' Invalid
End If
```

String Data

Many properties store data as a series of consecutive characters called a **string**. In Chapter 2, you used strings when you converted information stored in the Text property of a text box to a number. You can also declare variables of type String, store values in them, and perform operations on them.

In DataTronics' program, you can validate the name prefix to ensure that it contains one of the following strings: Mr., Mrs., or Ms. Although you could write three separate If statements to carry out this task, using the Or logical operator simplifies the process. The following statements determine whether the prefix input is valid:

```
If txtPrefix.Text = "Mr." Or _
    txtPrefix.Text = "Mrs." Or _
    txtPrefix.Text = "Ms." Then
    lblPrefix.Visible = False
Else
    lblPrefix.Visible = True
    mblnValid = False
End If
```

The preceding If statement uses the logical Or operator to concatenate three conditions. If none of the conditions is True, the label named lblPrefix becomes visible, causing the error message to appear.

To write an If statement with a logical operator:

1 Make sure the Code window for the **cmdCalculate_Click** event procedure is active, then enter the following statements (shown in bold) at the end of the procedure:

```
        End Select
        If txtPrefix.Text = "Mr." Or _
            txtPrefix.Text = "Mrs." Or _
            txtPrefix.Text = "Ms." Then
            lblPrefix.Visible = False
        Else
            lblPrefix.Visible = True
            mblnValid = False
        End If
End Sub
```

2 Test the program. Enter an invalid value in the Prefix text box, then click the **Calculate** button. The label adjacent to the text box should appear. Again, labels should appear next to the other text boxes. Enter a valid value in the Prefix text box, then click the **Calculate** button. The label should become invisible.

Just as you can perform operations such as addition and subtraction on numbers, so, too, can you perform operations on strings. The most common operation on a string is concatenation. Strings are concatenated, or appended together, using the & operator. The following statements concatenate a string:

```
Dim pstr1 As String
Dim pstr2 As String
Dim pstrResult As String
pstr1 = "First"
pstr2 = "Last"
pstrResult = pstr1 & " " & pstr2
```

These statements illustrate the use of the String data type and string concatenation. Three variables—pstr1, pstr2, and pstrResult—are declared as having a String data type. The next two statements store the strings "First" and "Last" in the String variables pstr1 and pstr2, respectively. These literal String values are enclosed in double quotation marks.

The last statement concatenates two string variables and a literal value. After this statement executes, the string pstrResult contains the String value "First Last". A space separates "First" and "Last". In this statement, three strings are linked together. The first string contains "First", the second string contains a space character, and the third string contains the text "Last".

In addition to string concatenation, other intrinsic functions work with strings. One function, for example, measures the length of a string. It is useful when you want to store data in a database or other file where a fixed number of characters has been allocated to hold the data. An error arises when the data to be stored is too long for this space—for example, when your name or address becomes truncated on a mailing label. To determine the length of a string, you use the Len function.

Syntax	**Len**(*string*)
Dissection	■ The **Len** function returns the number of characters (bytes) necessary to store a string. ■ The *string* argument contains the string to be evaluated.

Code Example	`Dim pintLen As Integer`
	`Dim pstrDemo As String`
	`pstrDemo = "ABC"`
	`pintLen = Len(pstrDemo)`

Code Dissection	These statements determine the length of the string named pstrDemo. The string contains three characters, so pintLen is set to 3.

Earlier in this chapter, we noted that DataTronics' program requires that the first name be less than or equal to 15 characters and that the last name be less than or equal to 25 characters. To ensure that the input meets these criteria, you can write an If statement and use the Len function.

To determine the length of a string:

1 Activate the Code window for the **cmdCalculate_Click** event procedure, then enter the following statements (shown in bold) at the end of the procedure:

```
    End If
    If Len(txtFirstName) > 15 Then
        lblFirstName.Visible = True
        mblnValid = False
    Else
        lblFirstName.Visible = False
    End If
    If Len(txtLastName.Text) > 25 Then
        lblLastName.Visible = True
        mblnValid = False
    Else
        lblLastName.Visible = False
    End If
End Sub
```

2 Test the program. Enter a name longer than 25 characters in each of the two fields, then click **Calculate**. The error labels next to the First Name and Last Name text boxes should appear. Now enter correct data, and click **Calculate**. The labels should disappear.

You can use several intrinsic constants with strings. These constants can represent special characters, such as the tab character or a carriage return. The following list summarizes a few of the commonly used constants:

- **vbTab** represents the Tab character.
- **vbNullString** stores an empty string.
- **vbCrLf** represents a carriage return, line feed sequence.

The following statements concatenate a string using intrinsic constants:

```
Dim pstr1 As String
pstr1 = "One" & vbTab & "Two"
pstr1 = vbNullString
pstr1 = "One" & vbCrLf & "Two"
```

The first assignment statement embeds a Tab character between the two strings. The second creates an empty string, and the third creates a string that will appear on two lines. The characters "One" will appear on the first line, and the characters "Two" will appear on the second line.

The following code has already been written in the cmdClear_Click event procedure to clear the contents of the text boxes on the form:

```
txtPrefix = vbNullString
txtFirstName = vbNullString
txtLastName = vbNullString
. . .
```

Another group of string functions converts a string to a standard form. For example, you may want to make all of the characters in a string uppercase or lowercase.

Syntax

StrConv(*string, conversion*)

Dissection

- The **StrConv** function converts a string into different formats depending on the *conversion* argument. It returns the converted string.

- The *string* argument contains the string to be converted.

- The *conversion* argument contains a constant that defines how the string is converted. If vbUpperCase is used, the characters in the string are converted to uppercase characters. If vbLowerCase is used, the characters are converted to lowercase characters. If vbProperCase is used, the first character of each word is capitalized and the other characters are converted to lowercase. You can use both the Visual Basic Help library and the Object Browser to look up the values of these constants.

Code Example	`txtName.Text = StrConv(txtName.Text, vbProperCase)`
Code Dissection	This statement assumes that txtName is an existing text box object. The contents of the text box are converted to **proper case**; that is, the first character of each word is capitalized. After conversion of the data, the result is stored in the same text box.

To illustrate the use of the StrConv function, you will convert to proper case the text boxes used to store the first name and the last name when either text box loses focus.

> To convert a string to proper case:
>
> **1** Make sure that the Code window for the **txtFirstName_LostFocus** event procedure is active, then enter the following statement:
>
> ```
> txtFirstName.Text = StrConv(txtFirstName.Text,vbProperCase)
> ```
>
> **2** Make sure the Code window for the **txtLastName_LostFocus** event procedure is active, then enter the following statement:
>
> ```
> txtLastName.Text = StrConv(txtLastName.Text,vbProperCase)
> ```
>
> **3** Test the program. In the **First Name** text box, enter the name **michael** in all lowercase characters, then press the **Tab** key to move to the next field. When the text box loses focus, the string should be converted to **Michael**. Enter the name **VAN BUREN** in the **Last Name** text box, then press the **Tab** key. When the text box loses focus, the string should be converted to **Van Buren**.

Another category of intrinsic functions that are used with strings either determines whether a string contains a specific pattern or extracts a specific group of characters from a string. These functions are named InStr (In string) and Mid (Middle), respectively.

Syntax	**InStr**([*start,*]*string1, string2*[*, compare*]) **Mid**(*string, start*[*, length*])
Dissection	■ The **InStr** function searches a string to determine whether it contains a specific pattern. If it finds the pattern, InStr returns the position within the string where the pattern appears. If it does not find the pattern, InStr returns zero (0). InStr examines *string1* to see whether it contains the pattern stored in *string2*. ■ The **Mid** function returns a selected number of characters from a string. For example, it allows you to select a specific word or phrase from a string. In the Mid function, *length* defines the number of characters that are copied from *string*.

- Both the InStr function and the Mid function use the optional *start* argument. In the case of InStr, *start* defines the character position in *string1* where the search begins. In the case of Mid, *start* defines the character position of the first character selected in the string.

- The optional *compare* argument is used by the InStr function to determine how to compare the strings. The internal representation of the characters is used when the *compare* argument is set to zero (0). If it is set to one (1), the characters are compared using the textual sort order of the underlying language. Different languages have different characters that make up the language, and the manner in which these characters are sorted varies from language to language.

Code Example	``` Dim pintFound As Integer Dim pstrResult As String pintFound = InStr(1, "Characters", "act") ' 5 pstrResult = Mid("First Last", 7, 4) ' "Last" ```
Code Dissection	The call to the InStr function searches the string "Characters" for the pattern "act". The search begins at the first character in the string. The call to the Mid function returns four characters from the string "First Last", starting at position 7.

In addition to working with strings, functions can operate on individual characters. Every character in a string can be represented by a number between 0 and 255 or by a Visual Basic constant. The first 128 characters conform to a standard set of characters known as ASCII and represent all of the standard characters on a keyboard. The other 128 characters include special characters and symbols. For example, a space is represented by the number 32; it is also represented by the constant vbKeySpace. The KeycodeConstants class in the Object Browser lists all of the Visual Basic constants.

To convert an ASCII character to its corresponding numeric value, you use the Asc function. To convert the numeric value back to a character, you use the Chr function.

Syntax	**Asc**(*string*) **Chr**(*charcode*)
Dissection	- The **Asc** function accepts one argument—a string containing a character. It returns a number corresponding to the ASCII character. - The **Chr** function accepts one argument—a numeric character code. It returns a string containing the character.
Code Example	``` Dim pstrChar As String Dim pintChar As Integer pstrChar = "A" pintChar = Asc(pstrChar) ' 65 pstrChar = Chr(pintChar) ' A ```
Code Dissection	The character code for an uppercase A is 65. Thus the call to the Asc function returns 65. Calling the Chr function with the argument value of 65 returns the letter "A".

These functions, for example, can be used to validate input. When a text box should contain an integer, you can prevent the user from entering characters other than the digits 0 through 9 by using the KeyPress event. Each time the user types a character into a control instance, such as a text box, the KeyPress event occurs. This event procedure supplies one argument, which is the numeric representation of the typed character. The following KeyPress event procedure for the text box named txtInteger begins by evaluating the range of the key that was pressed by the user:

```
Private Sub txtInteger_KeyPress(KeyAscii As Integer)
    If KeyAscii >= 48 And KeyAscii <= 57 Then
        Exit Sub
    Else
        KeyAscii = 0
    End If
End Sub
```

The character code representing the character that was typed at the keyboard is passed as an argument to the KeyPress event procedure. The keycodes for the numbers 0 through 9 are 48 through 57. Thus the preceding If statement tests whether the keycode lies between 48 and 57 by using the logical conjunction And in an If statement. If the character is between 48 and 57, the event procedure exits. Otherwise, KeyAscii is set to zero (0). This statement is significant because, when the KeyAscii argument is set to zero (0) in the KeyPress event procedure, it causes the character to be ignored. Thus the character will not appear in the text box.

Date Data

In addition to String and Boolean data, many business applications perform operations on dates. For example, you may want to examine information that was collected between a range of dates, or you may need to determine the number of elapsed days, months, or years between two dates. To help process information containing dates, Visual Basic supports the Date data type and offers several intrinsic functions that operate on dates. Three intrinsic functions are available to retrieve the current date and time from the system, each of which returns a value having the Date data type.

Syntax	**Date** **Time** **Now**
Dissection	■ The **Date** function returns the current date. ■ The **Time** function returns the current time. ■ The **Now** function returns the current date and time combined. ■ These functions take no arguments, and each returns a Date data type.

Code Example	``Dim datCurrent As Date``
	``datCurrent = Date    ' Current date.``
	``datCurrent = Time    ' Current time.``
	``datCurrent = Now     ' Current date and time combined.``

Code Dissection	The first statement declares a variable of Date type named datCurrent. The three-character prefix for a Date variable is "dat". The subsequent statements store the current date, current time, and the combined current date and time.

In DataTronics' program, you will use the Date function to display the current date on the form as the form loads. An event procedure called the Form_Load event procedure will execute each time the form is loaded into the computer's memory. Although form events will be discussed in more detail in Chapter 4, here you will see how to display the current date on the form when the form is loaded.

To call the Date function:

1   Enter the following statement in the **Form_Load** event procedure:

```
lblDate.Caption = Date
```

2   Test the program. When you run the program, the current date should appear in the label at the bottom of the form.

The previous statement stored the current date in the label named lblDate when the form loaded. A label was used instead of a text box, as the user will never enter data into this control instance.

Certain arithmetic operators can be used with dates. For example, you can add and subtract integers from both date and time values. The following statements perform mathematical operations on Date variables:

```
Dim datCurrent As Date
Dim datNew As Date
datCurrent = "3/4/2002"
datNew = datCurrent + 30     ' 4/3/2002
datNew = datCurrent - 365    ' 3/4/2001
```

The first two assignment statements add and subtract integers from a date value. These operations add or subtract the number of days from the date. The power of the Date data type derives from the intrinsic functions that operate on dates. For example, you can compute the elapsed amount of time between two dates with the DateDiff function.

Syntax	**DateDiff**(*interval, date1, date2*[, *firstdayofweek*[, *firstweekofyear*]])
Dissection	■ The **DateDiff** function computes the number of time intervals between two dates and returns a Long integer.
	■ The required *interval* argument contains a string that defines the time interval. For example, "m" = month and "yyyy" = years. Refer to the Visual Basic Help library for a complete listing of the date intervals.

- The required *date1* and *date2* arguments define the two dates used in the calculation. If *date1* is later than *date2*, then the result is negative.

- The optional *firstdayofweek* argument is used to determine which day Visual Basic considers the first day of the week. The default is Sunday.

- The optional *firstweekofyear* argument allows you to change what Visual Basic considers the first week of the year. By default, the first week of the year is the week containing January 1.

Code Example	```Dim pdatStart As Date
Dim pdatEnd As Date
Dim plngElapsed As Long
pdatStart = "12/1/2001"
pdatEnd = "12/15/2002"
plngElapsed = DateDiff("m", pdatStart, pdatEnd)   ' 12
plngElapsed = DateDiff("yyyy", pdatStart, pdatEnd) ' 1```
Code Dissection	These statements declare two Date variables, pdatStart and pdatEnd, and then store Date values in those variables. The variable plngElapsed stores a Long Integer value representing elapsed time. The DateDiff function is called to determine the number of elapsed months and years between the two dates. The result is a Long Integer that is stored in plngElapsed.

To illustrate the use of the DateDiff function, consider the following statements, which display the number of months that have elapsed from the current date and a date in the future:

```
Dim datFuture As Date
If IsDate(txtFuture.Text) Then
    datFuture = CDate(txtFuture.Text)
    If datFuture > Date Then
        lblMonths.Caption = DateDiff("m", Date, datFuture)
    End If
End If
```

Using an If statement, we convert the contents of the text box named txtFuture to a date only if the text box contains a valid date. Another If statement tests whether the date entered is greater than the current date. In other words, datFuture should be a later date than the current date. If it is, the DateDiff function is called and the number of elapsed months is stored in lblMonths.Caption.

In addition to these functions, Visual Basic supports several other functions to manage dates, as shown in Figure 3-8.

Day(*date*)	Returns an integer between 1 and 31 representing the day of the month.	`pintVar = Day(Now())`
Month(*date*)	Returns an integer between 1 and 12 representing the month of the year.	`pintVar = Month(Now())`
Year(*date*)	Returns a four-digit integer representing the year.	`pintVar = Year(Now())`
Hour(*date*)	Returns an integer between 0 and 23 representing the hour of the day.	`pintVar = Hour(Now())`
Minute(*date*)	Returns an integer between 0 and 59 representing the minute of the hour.	`pintVar = Minute(Now())`
Second(*date*)	Returns an integer between 0 and 59 representing the second of the minute.	`pintVar = Second(Now())`

Figure 3-8: Date functions

You have completed the programming for this section of the chapter. You have seen various ways to validate input data and advise the user if the data is incorrect.

QUESTIONS

1. Which of the following statements regarding Boolean data is true?
   a. The valid values are True and False.
   b. Numbers can be converted to the Boolean data type.
   c. Strings can be converted to the Numeric data type.
   d. Both a and b.
   e. All of the above.

2. Which of the following Visual Basic comparison operators are valid?
   a. > , < , = , !>, >=, <=
   b. > , < , = , <>, >=, <=
   c. > , < , = , <>, =>, =<
   d. + , − , = , <>, >=, <=
   e. +, − , = , <>, =>, =<

3. Which of the following statements regarding If statements is true?
   a. They must evaluate to a Boolean data type.
   b. There can be only one condition in an If statement.
   c. The Exit If statement marks the end of the If statement.
   d. All of the above.
   e. None of the above.

4. Which of the following string functions are valid?
   a. StrConv, Len, Mid, InStr
   b. Convert, Len, Mid, InStr
   c. Convert, Length, Mid, InStr
   d. Convert, Length, Middle, InStr
   e. None of the above.

5. Which of the following functions can be used to obtain the date and the time from a system?
   a. Date
   b. Time
   c. Now
   d. None of the above.
   e. All of the above.

6. Write an If statement that determines whether the variable pintBalance is greater than 1000.01. If it is, multiply pintBalance by 1.005.

7. Write the statement(s) that convert all of the characters in the string named pstrName to uppercase and store the result in the string pstrUpper.

8. Write the statement(s) that determine whether the string pstrMessage contains the pattern "Error". If it does, store the Boolean value True in the variable pblnResult. Otherwise, store the Boolean value False in the variable.

9. Write an If statement that determines whether the text box named txtTotal contains a valid number. If it does, format the contents to two decimal places. Otherwise, clear the contents of the text box.

10. Write an If statement that determines whether the string named pstrOffice contains one of the following strings: "Dallas", "Atlanta", "Seattle", or "Phoenix". If the string contains "Dallas" or "Atlanta", set the string named pstrRegion to "Central". Otherwise, set it to "Western".

In this section you will:

■ Display a message box
■ Create general procedures that are called from event procedures
■ Understand the different types of general procedures
■ Call a general procedure

Message Boxes and General Procedures

The code that you have written thus far validates user input. In all cases, when the input is invalid, a label becomes visible to alert the user of the erroneous data. You can use a different mechanism to inform the user of an error or to provide an informative message. In this section, you will display a message when the user inputs invalid data. When the user clicks the Exit command button, you will also display a message to verify that he or she really wants to exit the program.

The MsgBox Function

To prevent the user from exiting the program if the Exit command button is clicked accidentally, you can display a dialog and request confirmation from the user. This dialog should include a Yes button for exiting the program and a No button to continue running it. Visual Basic supports a standard dialog called a **message box** that will display a message, an icon to identify the importance or purpose of the message, and a set of buttons that contain captions like Yes, No, or OK. You cannot define either your own buttons or your own icons. Thus a message box is nothing more than a standardized form that appears when your program calls the MsgBox function. This function returns a value to indicate which button was clicked. You generally use this value to determine the appropriate course of action.

Syntax	MsgBox(*prompt*[, *attributes*][, *title*])
Dissection	■ The **MsgBox** function displays a message box. The user cannot interact with other forms in the program until he or she closes the message box.
	■ The required *prompt* is a string expression that controls the text displayed in the message box. The MsgBox function receives this text as an argument. The maximum number of characters allowed in a *prompt* is 1024. You can create the arguments for the text using String variables.
	■ The *attributes* argument is an expression containing intrinsic constants that define the behavior of the message box. The vbMsgBoxStyle class in the Object Browser lists each constant.

■ You can include a *title* for the message box, which appears on the message box's title bar in the same way as the form's Caption property.

| **Code Example** | ```
Dim pintResult As Integer
pintResult = MsgBox("Exit?", vbYesNo + vbQuestion, "Respond")
If pintResult = vbYes Then
    Unload frmDT
End If
``` |
| **Code Dissection** | These statements call the MsgBox function with the necessary arguments to display the prompt "Exit?", the two buttons with the captions "Yes" and "No", and the question mark icon. The title "Respond" appears on the message box's title bar. |

The difficult part of displaying a message box relates to choosing the correct attributes. The attributes are divided into six groups of constants. The first group of constants, those with the values 0 through 5, determines which buttons appear in the message box. The constant to display a message box with Yes and No buttons can be represented either by the constant vbYesNo or by the value 4.

Inside the message box, you can include one of several different icons to communicate the importance of the message. The second group of constants, those with the values 16 through 64, identifies the corresponding icons. For example, the constant vbQuestion displays a question mark icon.

You can use one of four constants from the third group to define which button is the default. These constants—vbDefaultButton1, vbDefaultButton2, vbDefaultButton3, and vbDefaultButton4—correspond to the first, second, third, and fourth buttons in the message box. Pressing the Enter key as an alternative to clicking a captioned button will activate the default button. Assigning a default button is optional; if a default button does not make sense in your program, do not assign one.

One constant from each group can be added together in an expression to make up the attributes argument. If you do not want to select an item from a group, simply omit the constant. Refer to the MsgBox function Help topic for a complete list of the constants supported by the MsgBox.

You are now ready to display a message box to confirm that the user wants to exit the program. In addition, you can write the code to display a message box if the user enters any invalid data. If all of the data is valid, you can compute the rate per square foot and the cost of the building permit and display that information. The control instances used for output are text boxes rather than labels. The Locked property has been set to True, thereby preventing the user from changing the contents of the control instance. From the user's perspective, using a label and using a text box as an output-only control are equivalent. The main difference is that the user can select the contents of a text box and copy its contents to the Windows Clipboard; this option does not work with the Label control.

GUI

tip

● ● ● ● ● ● ● ● ● ● ● ● ● ● ●

Carefully consider which icon to display in a message box. If you are asking a question, display a Warning Query icon using the vbQuestion constant. You should reserve the Critical Message icon (vbCritical) for indicating only very serious problems or consequences. Use the Warning Message icon (vbExclamation) for less critical problems. The Information Message icon (vbInformation) is a good choice when you are explaining something.

Performance

tip

● ● ● ● ● ● ● ● ● ● ● ● ● ● ●

It takes fewer resources for Windows to manage a Label control instance than a TextBox control instance. Thus, if a form must include several controls, consider using Label controls to identify output.
```

To display a message box:

1 Open the Code window for the **cmdExit_Click** event procedure, then enter the following statements:

```
Dim pintResult As Integer
pintResult = MsgBox("Do you want to exit?", _
    vbQuestion + vbYesNo, "Exit?")
If pintResult = vbYes Then
    Unload frmDT
End If
```

2 Open the Code window for the **cmdCalculate_Click** event procedure, then enter the following statements (shown in bold) at the end of the procedure:

```
    End If
    If mblnValid = False Then
        Call MsgBox("Invalid input", _
            vbInformation + vbOKOnly, "Error")
    Else
        txtRate = Format(msngRate, "Fixed")
        psngCost = Val(txtRate.Text) * _
            Val(txtSquareFeet.Text)
        txtCost.Text = Format(psngCost, "Fixed")
    End If
End Sub
```

3 Test the program. Enter invalid information into each text box, click the **Calculate** command button, then click **OK** to close the Error dialog. Next, enter valid information into each text box, then click the **Calculate** button. The correct output should appear in the output text boxes. Click the **Exit** command button to exit the program. The message box will appear, as shown in Figure 3-9.

title
icon
prompt
buttons

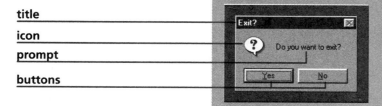

Figure 3-9: Message box

4 Click **No** to continue running the program, click the **Exit** command button again, then click **Yes** to exit the program.

Procedures

One of the computer's greatest assets is its capability to perform repetitive tasks quickly. As your programs become more complex, you will find that you carry out many simple tasks over and over again. Some of these problems involve validating input entered by the user, as you saw in the previous section.

Although you could rewrite the same code in several event procedures to check that a value is an Integer, Visual Basic and most other programming languages allow you to create a a general procedure that can be used by other procedures. A **general procedure** resembles an event procedure, except that you must explicitly call a general procedure because it does not respond to events. One strategy for writing successful programs is to divide tasks into logical components, such as general procedures, which then can be reused within the same program or in one or more different programs.

Two types of general procedures exist: **Function procedures** (functions) and **Sub procedures** (subroutines). These procedures differ in how they communicate their results to the procedure from which they were called. Function procedures return a result of a specific data type that you generally assign to a variable or appropriate property. Sub procedures do not return a value.

Syntax

[**Public|Private**] **Function** *name* [(*argumentlist*)] [**As** *type*]
  [*statements*]
  [*name = expression*]
  [**Exit Function**]
  [*statements*]
  [*name = expression*]
End Function

Dissection

- The **Function** keyword creates a Function procedure that returns a value to the procedure that called it.

- The optional **Public** keyword indicates that the other modules in the program can use this function.

- The optional **Private** keyword indicates that this function is accessible only to the procedures in the module where it is declared.

- The required *name* argument contains the procedure name and must be unique.

- The optional *argumentlist* describes the argument names and the data types passed to the function.

- The optional **As** *type* clause defines the data type of the value returned by the function.

- By assigning the *name* of the function to an *expression*, you define the return value of the function. Thus, if you declared a function named ValidDate and then assigned a value to ValidDate, that value would be returned by the function.

- The optional **Exit Function** statement causes the function to exit immediately. Execution continues at the statement following the one that called the **Function** procedure. A function can contain any number of Exit Function statements, including none at all.

- The **End Function** statement defines the end of the Function procedure.

An important part of using functions is to understand how the arguments work. An **argument** is the mechanism by which you communicate information to a procedure. The *argumentlist* contains the arguments for a procedure.

Syntax	**[ByRef|ByVal]** *variablename*[( )] **[As** *type*] [= *defaultvalue*]
Dissection	■ The optional **ByRef** keyword (the default) indicates that the argument is passed by reference. ■ The optional **ByVal** keyword indicates that the argument is passed by value. ■ The required *variablename* contains the name of the variable representing the argument. ■ The optional **As** *type* indicates the data type of the argument passed to the procedure. ■ The optional *defaultvalue* can be any constant or constant expression and is valid for optional parameters only. If the type is an **Object**, **Nothing** is the only valid default value.
| **Code Example** | ```
Public Function ValidDate(pstrValue As String, _
    pdatMin As Date, pdatMax As Date) _
    As Boolean
    Dim pblnValue As Boolean
    ' Code to validate the pstrValue and set the value of
    ' pblnValue
    ValidDate = pblnValue
End Function
``` |
| **Code Dissection** | This code declares a function named ValidDate that accepts one required String argument named pstrValue. Two other required arguments, pdatMin and pdatMax, specify the minimum and maximum valid dates, respectively. The function, although incomplete at this point, will set the value of the variable pblnValue to True or False depending on whether pstrValue contains a valid date. The Function procedure returns the result by assigning it to the function name. The other arguments allow the user to specify a minimum or maximum value. The function returns a Boolean value. |

To illustrate the use of a function, you will create a function that determines whether a string represents a valid number, and whether that number is within a range of numbers. It should accept three arguments—the string to be tested and two numbers that define the lower and upper bounds of valid numbers. If the value is a number between the lower and upper bounds, the function returns True. Otherwise, it returns False.

Two ways to create Function and Sub procedures exist. First, you can type the declaration into the Code window. Second, you can use the Add Procedure dialog shown in Figure 3-10.
```

Name text box

Type section

Scope section

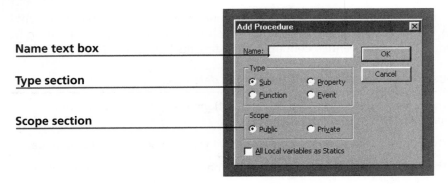

Figure 3-10: Add Procedure dialog

The Add Procedure dialog includes three sections—Name, Type, and Scope.

- In the **Name** text box, you type a name for the general procedure. The requirements for procedure names are the same as for variable names.
- The **Type** section identifies whether the procedure is a Sub procedure, a Function procedure, a Property procedure, or an event procedure. **Sub procedures** communicate information to other parts of the program by setting form-level variables, but they do not return values to the procedures from which they were called. **Function procedures** return values to the procedures from which they were called. **Property procedures** are used in class modules to create properties for the objects in those modules. **Event procedures** create user-defined events; they are also used when you create your own controls. (The topic of creating your own controls is not discussed in this book.)
- The Public and Private keywords describe the **Scope** of the procedure. If a procedure is **Private,** it can be called only from the form in which it is declared. If it is **Public,** the procedure can be called from any module in the program. Public procedures are useful only when a program contains multiple modules.

The Add Procedure dialog has some limitations. For example, you cannot use it to declare arguments for a Function or a Sub procedure, and you cannot explicitly specify the return type of a Function procedure. Furthermore, the Add Procedure dialog cannot add the ByVal and ByRef keywords. Consequently, you may prefer to create a procedure by typing the declaration in the Code window.

When you use the Add Procedure dialog to enter a Function or Sub declaration, Visual Basic automatically inserts the appropriate End Function or End Sub statement.

Regardless of which method you use, when you create a general procedure, you must specify the procedure name, type, and scope. For the input validation program, Visual Basic will help you create a template for the procedure using the information you supply in the Add Procedure dialog.

To add a procedure using the Add Procedure dialog:

1   Make sure that the Code window is active. It does not matter which object and event procedure combination is active; when you create the new procedure, the Code window will automatically display the new procedure.

2   Click **Tools,** then click **Add Procedure** to activate the Add Procedure dialog.

3   Enter the name **ValidNumber** in the Name text box.

4 Click the type **Function** to create a Function procedure.

5 Set the Scope to **Private**.

6 Click **OK** to close the Add Procedure dialog. The new procedure is created in the module, as shown in Figure 3-11.

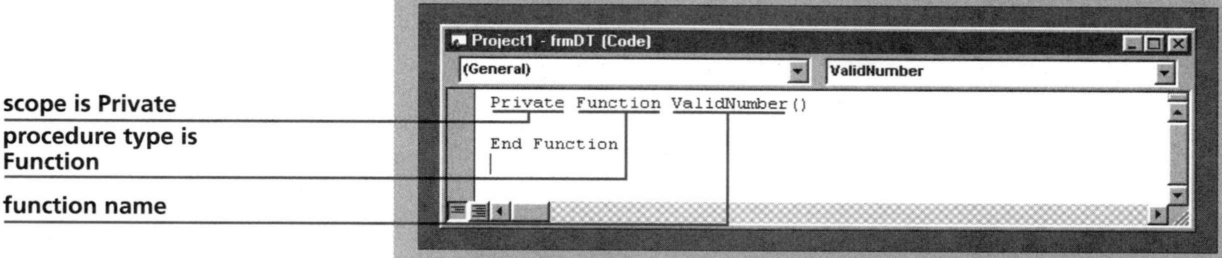

scope is Private

procedure type is
Function

function name

```
Project1 - frmDT (Code)
(General)                          ValidNumber

    Private Function ValidNumber()

    End Function
    |
```

Figure 3-11: New procedure

7 Enter the following code (shown in bold) into the procedure:

```
Private Function ValidNumber(pstrInput As String, _
    psngMin As Single, _
    psngMax As Single) As Boolean
    Dim psngInput As Single
    If IsNumeric(pstrInput) Then
        psngInput = Val(pstrInput)
        If psngInput >= psngMin And _
            psngMax >= psngInput Then
            ValidNumber = True
        Else
            ValidNumber = False
        End If
    Else
        ValidNumber = False
    End If
End Function
```

These statements require careful analysis because they demonstrate several important concepts presented in this chapter. The function accepts three arguments—one String and two Single data types. It returns a Boolean value. The first If statement uses the IsNumeric classification function to determine whether the variable pstrInput contains a valid number. If it does not, the Else part of the outer If statement executes, ValidNumber is set to False, and the function exits. If the number is valid, however, the input is converted to a number and tested to see whether it falls between the values psngMin and psngMax. This procedure demonstrates the use of nested If statements.

Once you have created a function, it must be called explicitly. General Function and Sub procedures do not execute in response to events. Rather, you must write a statement to call them explicitly. The statement to call a general procedure—the Call statement—can be included in an event procedure or in another general procedure.

Syntax	[**Call**] *procedurename*(*argumentlist*)
Dissection	■ The **Call** statement will call a Sub or Function procedure. The **Call** keyword is optional. ■ The required *procedurename* indicates which procedure is being called. ■ The optional *argumentlist* contains the arguments that are communicated to the procedure.
Code Example	``` Dim pblnValid As Boolean pblnValid = ValidNumber(txtHeight.Text,8,200) ```
Code Dissection	This code segment calls the ValidNumber function. The function is called with three arguments: the string containing the value to be tested, a minimum value of 8, and a maximum value of 200. If the number is valid and within that range, ValidNumber will return True.

Continuing with DataTronics' program, you now can write the code to call the ValidNumber procedure from the Form module. You will validate the text box named txtHeight, which indicates the building height. Restrictions in the area prevent a building from being less than 8 feet and greater than 200 feet in height. Because the value must contain a valid Single precision number, we can use the ValidNumber function. This value will be validated in the cmdCalculate event procedure along with all the other text boxes.

To call a Function procedure:

1 Locate the **cmdCalculate_Click** event procedure, then enter the following statements (shown in bold) just before the If statement that tests the value of the variable mblnValid and calls the MsgBox function:

```
End If
If ValidNumber(txtHeight.Text,8,200) Then
    lblInvalidHeight.Visible = False
Else
     lblInvalidHeight.Visible = True
     mblnValid = False
End If
If mblnValid = False Then
     . . .
```

2 Test the program. In the Building Height text box, enter invalid information; that is, enter a value that contains letter characters or a value that is not between 8 and 200. Click **Calculate**. Where the values are invalid, error labels should appear adjacent to the text boxes. Enter correct information, then click **Calculate**. The error labels should disappear.

In addition to Function procedures, you can work with Sub procedures, which do not return a value.

Sub Procedures

Other than not returning a value, Sub procedures are identical to Function procedures. Like Function procedures, Sub procedures can be Public or Private and accept zero or more arguments. A Sub procedure, however, cannot be used on the right-hand side of an expression, unlike a Function procedure, because it does not return a value.

Syntax	**[Private|Public] Sub** *name* [*(argumentlist)*] [*statements*] **[Exit Sub]** [*statements*] End Sub
Dissection	■ The optional **Public** keyword indicates that the Sub procedure can be used by the other modules in the program. ■ The optional **Private** keyword indicates that the Sub procedure is accessible only to the procedure in which it is declared. ■ The required *name* argument contains the name of the procedure, must be unique, and must adhere to the standard variable naming conventions. ■ The optional *argumentlist* describes the names and data types of the arguments passed to the Sub procedure. A comma separates each variable. The *argumentlist* has the same syntax as is used for Function procedures. ■ The optional *statements* include any statements to be executed within the Sub procedure. ■ The **Exit Sub** statement causes the Sub procedure to exit immediately. Execution continues at the statement following the one that called the Sub procedure. A Sub procedure can contain any number of Exit Sub statements, including none.
Code Example	``` Private Sub FormatTextBox(txtInput As TextBox) ' Code to format the text box. End Sub ```
Code Dissection	The procedure in this example, named FormatTextBox, takes one argument—a reference to a TextBox object. The argument type is the TextBox class. The procedure uses the argument to format the given text box.

Once you have declared a Sub or Function procedure, you must call it explicitly. Two ways to call a procedure exist. One technique uses the Call statement; the other does not. The following statements call the Sub procedure named FormatTextBox:

```
Call FormatTextBox(txtFirstName, "Focus")
FormatTextBox txtFirstName, "Focus"
```

When using either technique, you separate the arguments with a comma. When you use a Call statement, you enclose the arguments in parentheses. When you do not use a Call statement, you omit the parentheses. In developing your programs, use whichever method is most intuitive for you.

Suppose that you want to format the text boxes on the form so that they appear emphasized when they receive focus, and return to normal when they lose focus. This type of task is repetitive—that is, you need to perform the same task when a text box receives focus regardless of which text box is involved. To create a procedure without using the Add Procedure dialog, you will type the entire procedure directly into the Code window.

To create a Sub procedure:

1   Activate the Code window for the Form module. Locate the end of the module by pressing **Ctrl+End**, then enter the following Sub procedure:

```
Private Sub FormatTextBox(txtInput As TextBox, _
    pstrFormat As String)
    If pstrFormat = "Focus" Then
        txtInput.FontBold = True
        txtInput.ForeColor = vbBlue
    ElseIf pstrFormat = "LostFocus" Then
        txtInput.FontBold = False
        txtInput.ForeColor = vbBlack
    End If
End Sub
```

2   In the **LostFocus** event procedure for each text box (txtCounty, txtFirstName, txtHeight, txtLastName, txtPrefix, txtSquareFeet, and txtStartDate), enter the following statement:

```
FormatTextBox txtCounty, "LostFocus"
```

Make sure to replace the first argument—in this case, **txtCounty**—with the name of each respective text box.

3 In the **GotFocus** event procedure for each text box listed in Step 2, enter the following statement:

```
FormatTextBox txtCounty, "Focus"
```

Make sure to replace the first argument—in this case, **txtCounty**—with the name of each respective text box.

4 Test the program. Enter valid information in each text box, then press the **Tab** key to move from one text box to the next. As a text box receives focus, its font should become bold and blue. When focus is lost, its font and color should return to normal.

This general procedure illustrates several important concepts. First, instead of writing the same code repeatedly as you did in Chapter 1, you call the code as needed with the Sub Procedure. In the first argument to the Sub Procedure, the data type of the argument is TextBox. Just as you can pass intrinsic data types as arguments to a procedure, so, too, can you pass objects. When an object is passed as an argument, it is of the Object data type. For example, if you were passing a label, the data type would be Label instead of TextBox.

Understanding Call by Value and Call by Reference

Procedure arguments are passed by reference or by value. When an argument is passed by reference (the default), the variable's address in memory is passed as the argument. Thus the called procedure can change the actual value of the argument. When an argument is passed by value, the current value of the variable is determined and a copy of the variable is passed to the procedure. If the procedure changes the variable's value, only the copy is changed. That is, the value of the original variable remains unchanged.

The following functions and subroutines illustrate two different approaches to computing the square of a number:

```
Public Sub SquareSub(ByRef pintResult As Long, _
    pintArg As Integer)
    pintResult = pintArg * pintArg
End Sub
Public Function SquareFn(pintArg As Integer) As Long
    SquareFn = pintArg * pintArg
End Function
```

Using the Sub procedure, the result is passed as an argument. In this approach, the result is declared by reference to enable the result to be communicated back to the calling procedure. Thus the function returns the result. When a procedure returns a single value, a Function procedure is generally preferable because the code is more intuitive. If a procedure must return multiple values, however, it must be implemented as a Sub Procedure. Each value to be returned must be a ByRef argument. The following statements could be used to call the two procedures:

```
SquareSub txtOutput, txtInput
Call SquareSub(txtOutput,txtInput)
txtOutput = SquareFn(txtInput)
```

The statements assume that txtInput and txtOutput are text boxes and that txtInput contains a valid integer number.

S U M M A R Y

To validate a string or number that can be converted into a date:

■ **IsDate**(*expression*)

To validate a string that can be converted into a number:

■ **IsNumeric**(*expression*)

To create an If statement:

■ **If** *condition* **Then**
    statement(*s*)
End If

To create a two-way If statement:

■ **If** *condition* **Then**
    statements(*True*)
Else
    statements(*False*)
End If

To create a multiway If statement:

■ **If** *condition* **Then**
    [*statements*]
[**ElseIf** *condition* **Then**
    [*elseifstatements*]] ...
[**Else**
    [*elsestatements*]]
End If

To create a nested If statement:

■ **If** *outercondition* **Then**
    outerstatements(True)
    If *innercondition* **Then**
       innerstatements(True)
    Else
     innerstatements(False)
    End If   ' End of inner If statement
Else
    outerstatements(False)
End If   ' End of outer If statement

To create a Select Case statement:

■ **Select Case** *testexpression*
    Case *expressionlist-1*
      statement-block1
    Case *expressionlist-2*
      statement-block2
    Case *expressionlist-n*
      statement-blockn
    [**Case Else**
      [*statements*]]
    End Select

To write an If statement with a logical operator:

■ **If** *condition1 logicaloperator* _
    condition2 logicaloperator _
    condition **Then**
    statement-block1
    Else
    statement-block2
    End If

To determine the length of a string:

■ **Len**(*string*)

To convert a string:

■ **StrConv**(*string, conversion*)

To determine if a string includes certain characters:

■ **InStr**([*start,*]*string1, string2*[*, compare*])
   or
  Mid(*string, start*[*, length*])

To determine the keycode of a character:

■ **Asc**(*string*)
   or
  Chr(*charcode*)

To call the Date function:

■ **Date**
or
Time
or
Now

To determine the difference between two dates:

■ **DateDiff**(*interval, date1, date2*[, *firstdayofweek*[, *firstweekofyear*]])

To display a message box:

■ **MsgBox**(*prompt*[, *attributes*][, *title*])

To add a Function procedure:

■ Make sure the Code window is active. Click **Tools,** then click **Add Procedure** to activate the Add Procedure dialog. Set the type to **Function.** Enter the name and scope. Click **OK** to close the Add Procedure dialog. Enter the following code into the procedure:
  [Public|Private] Function *name* [(*argumentlist*)] **[As type]**
    [*statements*]
    [*Name = expression*]
  [Exit Function]
    [*statements*]
    [*Name = expression*]
  End Function
  or
■ Make sure the Code window is active. Press **Ctrl+End** to go to the end of the module. Enter the following code directly into the procedure:
[Public|Private] Function *name* **[ByRef|ByVal]** *variablename*[( )] **[As** type] [= *defaultvalue*] **[As** *type*]
    [*statements*]
    [*Name = expression*]
[Exit Function]
    [*statements*]
    [*Name = expression*]
End Function

To add a Sub procedure:

■ Make sure the Code window is active. Click **Tools,** then click **Add Procedure** to activate the Add Procedure dialog. Set the type to **Sub.** Enter the name and scope. Click **OK** to close the Add Procedure dialog. Enter the following code into the procedure:
  [Private|Public] Sub *name* [(*argumentlist*)]
    [*statements*]
  [Exit Sub]
    [*statements*]
  End Sub
  or

- Make sure the Code window is active. Press **Ctrl+End** to go to the end of the module. Enter the following code directly into the procedure:

  [Private|Public] Sub *name* [(*argumentlist*)]
      [*statements*]
  [Exit Sub]
      [*statements*]
  End Sub

To call a procedure:

- **[Call]** *procedurename*(*argumentlist*)

Q U E S T I O N S

1. Which of the following statements is true about the MsgBox function?
   a. The title bar always contains the name of the program.
   b. You specify how many buttons are displayed using the values 1, 2, or 3 for the Button argument.
   c. You set the Picture property to display an icon.
   d. Both a and b.
   e. All of the above.

2. Which of the following statements is true about general procedures?
   a. You must call a general procedure explicitly.
   b. A general procedure is called by Visual Basic in the same way as an event procedure.
   c. A general procedure and an event procedure are identical.
   d. Visual Basic does not support general procedures.
   e. None of the above.

3. Function procedures _____.
   a. have a name
   b. return a value
   c. can accept arguments
   d. Both a and c.
   e. All of the above.

4. Sub procedures _____.
   a. have a name
   b. return a value
   c. can accept arguments
   d. Both a and c.
   e. All of the above.

5. Write a Select Case statement that tests the value of the integer pintCategory. If the category is 100, set the String variable named pstrDescription to "Asset" and set the String variable as follows for the other categories: 200 = "Liability", 300 = "Capital", 600 = "Income", 700 = "Expense".

6. Write the statement(s) that display a message box with the title "Error", an exclamation point icon, and an OK button.

7. Write the statement(s) that create a function named Area that determines the area of a rectangle (length * width) and then returns this value.

8. Write the statement(s) that create a Boolean function named BeforeNow that accepts one argument (a date) and returns True if the date stored in the argument is earlier than the current date and False otherwise.

9. Write the statement(s) that create a subroutine named Active that enables and makes Visible a text box supplied to the procedure as an argument.

10. Write the statement(s) that create a subroutine named Cat, with four String arguments, that concatenates the first three arguments and stores the result in the fourth argument.

E X E R C I S E S

1. Create a program that computes the volume of a cube. To calculate the volume of a cube, you multiply its length by its width by its height. Because many different programs could use a similar formula, you will develop a function that computes the volume of the cube based on the input values. You will also create another function that validates each of the input numbers. Figure 3-12 shows the completed form for the program.

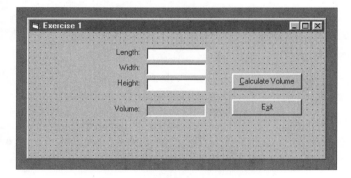

Figure 3-12: Exercise 1 – completed form

a. Run the executable file named **Chapter.03\Exercise\Sample\Ex1.exe**. Set the drive designator as necessary. Enter values in the Length, Width, and Height text boxes, then click the **Calculate Volume** command button. If you enter invalid data, you are advised of the invalid input. If the input is correct, the program calculates the volume of the cube. Exit the program.

b. Start Visual Basic and create a new project, if necessary. Change the Caption property of the form to **Exercise 1**. Change the Name property to **frmEx1**. Save the form and project using the names **Chapter.03\Exercise\ frmEx1.frm** and **Chapter.03\Exercise\Ex1.vbp**, respectively. Set the drive designator as necessary.

c. Create three text boxes on the form to store the following input values: **Length, Width,** and **Height**. Create a label to store the volume of the cube. Modify the name of each object as appropriate.

d. Create four labels to describe the three input values and the output value.

discovery ▶

e. Create a Private function named **Volume**. This function should accept three arguments—Length, Width, and Height. It should multiply these input values and then return the result—the volume of the cube. The data type of each argument and the data type of the return value are both Single.

discovery ▶

f. Create a function named **ValidNumber** that takes a string as its argument and returns a Boolean value. If the value of the argument is greater than zero (0), the function should return True; otherwise, it should return False.

g. Create a command button with the caption **Calculate Volume**. The **Click** event procedure should call the **ValidNumber** function for each input value. If the input is valid, it should compute the volume of the cube by calling the **Volume** function. Otherwise, a message box should advise the user that the input was invalid.

h. Create an **Exit** command button. Write the code necessary to display a message box that asks the user to confirm that he or she wants to exit the program.

i. Test the program by entering both valid and invalid data.

j. Correct any mistakes and save your work again, if necessary.

discovery ▶ 2. Develop a program that computes the average of three test scores and displays a letter grade. Arguments to the program should include the name of a student and the student's three test scores for the term. Figure 3-13 shows the completed form for this program.

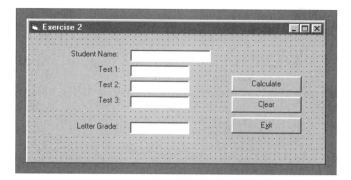

Figure 3-13: Exercise 2 – completed form

a. Run the executable file named **Chapter.03\Exercise\Sample\Ex2.exe**. Set the drive designator as necessary. Enter the test scores as numbers. The program will calculate the average score and assign a letter grade based on the following ranges: A >= 90, B = 79 to 89, C = 69 to 78, D = 59 to 68, F < 59.

b. Create a function named **ValidGrade** that checks that a specific grade entered is a number between 0 and 100.

c. Create the program using a Select Case statement that assigns a letter grade based on the average. It should display the result in a text box in response to the Click event for a **Calculate** command button. Also, include a **Clear** button to clear the text and captions of all objects before the user inputs data for another student.

d. Write the code for an **Exit** button that displays a message box asking the user if he or she wants to exit the program. Verify that your input objects have the correct tab order.

e. Test the program. Print the Form Image and Code.

f. Save the form and project as **Chapter.03\Exercise\frmEx2.frm** and **Chapter.03\Exercise\Ex2.vbp**, respectively. Set the drive designator as necessary.

g. Correct any mistakes and save your work again, if necessary.

3. Mail Order Sales accepts orders for products over the telephone. Its input form, which contains numerous control instances, is shown in Figure 3-14.

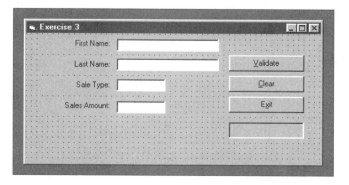

Figure 3-14: Exercise 3 – completed form

a. Run the executable file named **Chapter.03\Exercise\Sample\Ex3.exe** to see the user interface. Set the drive designator as necessary. Exit the program.

b. Start Visual Basic and create a new project, if necessary. Change the Name property of the form to **frmEx3**. Change the Caption property of the form to **Exercise 3**. Save the form and project using the names **Chapter.03\Exercise\frmEx3.frm** and **Chapter.03\Exercise\Ex3.vbp**, respectively. Set the drive designator as necessary.

discovery ▶ c. Create objects and write code so that, when the form loads, it displays the current date.

discovery ▶ d. All input should be validated when the user clicks the **Validate** command button. If an input field is not valid, the foreground color of the text in the field should change to Red. First, validate the First Name and Last Name text boxes to ensure that the first name is less than or equal to 20 characters in length and the last name is less than or equal to 25 characters in length. Also, write the code to ensure that the user does not leave the fields blank.

discovery ▶ e. Sales can be either Cash or Credit. Validate the contents of the **Sale Type:** text box, which can contain any of three values to indicate a Cash sale (CA, Cash, 1). Likewise, the user can input any of three values to indicate a Credit sale (CR, Credit, 0). When the Validate button is clicked, the program should validate the input. If it is valid, display the value "Cash" or "Credit" in the text box. Otherwise, display in red the value entered by the user.

f. The sales amount must be a number greater than zero (0). Verify that the content of the field is valid. If it is, the foreground of the text should appear in black. Otherwise, it should appear in red.

g. Create a **Clear** command button that will remove the contents from each of the text boxes.

h. Create an **Exit** command button that, when clicked, will display a message box to obtain confirmation from the user.

i. Test the program.

j. Correct any mistakes and save your work again, if necessary.

4. Gen, Inc., is a multinational distribution company. Each month, it must pay its salesforce based on a known formula that uses each employee's monthly sales, number of years with the company, and title. The formula is as follows. For sales amounts between $100,000 and $200,000, the sales commission is 1 percent. For sales amounts between $200,001 and $300,000, the sales commission is 1.5 percent. This 1.5 percent sales commission applies to the entire sales amount, not just the incremental amount. For sales amounts between $300,001 and $400,000, the sales commission is 1.75 percent. For sales amounts greater than $400,000, the sales commission is 2 percent. Each salesperson also receives a 1/10 of 1 percent incentive for each year with the company, up to 1 percent at 10 years. Thus a salesperson working for 5 years would receive a ½ percent incentive. Finally, apprentice salespeople do not receive a title incentive, associate salespeople receive a 0.1 percent title incentive, and senior salespeople receive a 0.2 percent title incentive. When your form is complete, it should resemble the form shown in Figure 3-15.

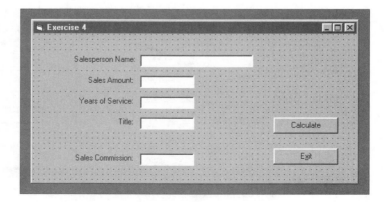

Figure 3-15: Exercise 4 – completed form

a. Run the executable file named **Chapter.03\Exercise\Sample\Ex4.exe** to test the user interface. Set the drive designator as necessary. Exit the program.

b. Start Visual Basic and create a new project. Save the form and project using the names **Chapter.03\Exercise\frmEx4.frm** and **Chapter.03\Exercise\Ex4.vbp**, respectively. Set the drive designator as necessary.

discovery ▶

c. Create a function named **Validate** that checks each of the input fields for correctness. Validate the sales amount to make sure it is a positive number. Verify that the years of service is also a positive number. In addition, confirm that the title is valid. Valid titles are **Apprentice**, **Associate**, and **Senior**. The function should return the Boolean value True if all of the input is valid and False otherwise.

discovery ▶

d. The **Calculate** button should call the Validate function you just wrote. If all of the input is valid, calculate the sales commission. If not, display a message box to the user.

discovery ▶

e. Write another function that calculates the sales commission. Call this function from the **Calculate** command button. The function should return a Single indicating the amount of the sales commission.

f. Test the program.

g. Correct any mistakes and save your work again, if necessary.

Objects and the Events They Generate

Developing an Event-Driven Cash Register Program for Master Burger

case ▶ Master Burger is a fast-food business. In this chapter, you will develop a prototype for a cash register to be used in the Master Burger restaurant. The mouse will be the only input device for the cash register, so the program must use only Visual Basic controls that do not require keyboard input. The restaurant's menu consists of three items: burgers, french fries, and soft drinks. When the clerk selects an item or the quantity ordered for an item changes, the program must compute the extended price of the item, the sales tax for the order, any delivery charges, and the total. The restaurant charges for delivery based on the distance of the customer's address from the restaurant. The delivery area has been divided into three zones; each zone is associated with a different delivery charge.

Previewing the Cash Register Program

The completed program in this chapter is a prototype for the cash register that will be ultimately implemented. The following list identifies some of the significant design criteria for the program:

- The clerk must be able to select menu items and specify the quantity ordered for each menu item using only the mouse as the input device. No keyboard input will be used.
- The program must update the extended prices for each item, the sales tax, and the total charged when the quantity ordered for a particular item changes. When the clerk selects a different delivery area, the program must recompute the delivery charge and order total.

The user interface visually separates the input and output regions of the form with a vertical line. The Shape control groups together elements in the input region. The interface contains command buttons to print the current order, reset the cash register in preparation for the next order, and exit the program. The output section contains labels to display different unit prices, quantities ordered, extended prices of ordered items, any delivery charges, the taxable amount, and the order total.

To preview the completed application:

1   Start Visual Basic, then open the project file named **Chapter.04\ Complete\MB_C.vbp**. Figure 4-1 shows the completed form.

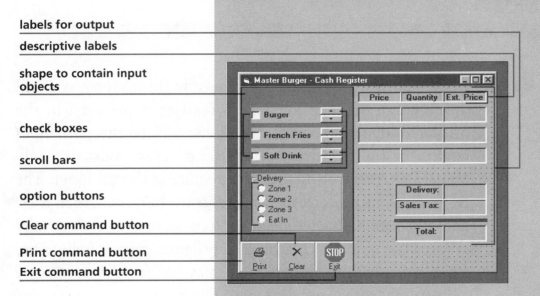

labels for output

descriptive labels

shape to contain input objects

check boxes

scroll bars

option buttons

Clear command button

Print command button

Exit command button

Figure 4-1: Initial cash register form

2   Run the program. Click the check boxes with the captions of Burger, French Fries, and Soft Drink. As you indicate that each item is ordered, scroll bars become visible that allow you to specify the quantity ordered. Labels also become visible that show the price of an item, the default quantity ordered (which is 1), and the item's extended price. Also, the sales tax and order total are computed instantaneously without clicking another command button to compute the total. Figure 4-2 depicts the running program while an order is in progress.

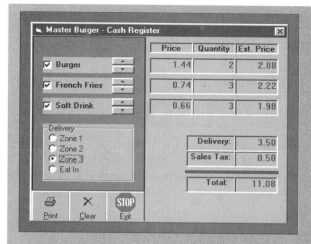

Figure 4-2: Initial cash register form (run time)

3   Click each **scroll bar**.

As you click the up arrow, the quantity ordered increases by one (1). As you click the down arrow, the value decreases by one (1). Whenever the clerk changes any input value, the program recomputes all of the output values (extended price, delivery, sales tax, and total).

4   Click each **option button**.

As you click each option button, the program recomputes the delivery charge and order total.

5   Click the **Print** command button.

An image of the form prints. Note that depending on the fonts supported by your printer, the numeric values may be formatted incorrectly.

6   Click the **Clear** command button.

The input values are reset in preparation for a new order.

7   Click the **Exit** command button on the form to exit the program. A message box appears, asking whether you want to exit the program. Click **Yes**. Visual Basic returns to design mode.

8   Exit Visual Basic.

GUI

tip

● ● ● ● ● ● ● ● ● ● ● ● ● ● ● ●

▶ When you select the controls that make up the user interface, you should choose the control that is best suited to a particular task. For example, use textual controls, such as a label or a text box, only when entering or displaying text. When the user can select a value from a list, other controls will be better suited for the task.

This program differs from the programs you created in the previous chapters in two important ways. First, the input validation requirements differ significantly. In Chapters 2 and 3, the user entered textual information. Because the user could potentially enter invalid characters into a text box, the program had to test the validity of the input. In this program, the objects themselves manage the validity of the input data. For example, the clerk can specify different quantities ordered for an item only by clicking the scroll bars; it is impossible for the clerk to specify an invalid input value. Consequently, there is no need to validate the input.

The other significant difference between the program in this chapter and the program in previous chapters relates to the manner in which output values are computed. In Chapters 2 and 3, the user clicked a command button to compute the program output. For the cash register program in this chapter, the output is recomputed immediately whenever any input value changes.

Controls That Use Mouse Input

Expanding the Visual Basic Event Model

In the previous chapters, you learned how to use some of the many events supported by Visual Basic controls. For example, you created event procedures that executed when a text box lost focus, when a text box received focus, and when a command button was clicked. In this chapter, you will learn how to use additional controls. You will also learn about the Change event, which occurs when the content of a control instance changes. To understand how this program uses the Change event, consider what happens when you knock over a row of dominos. One domino falls on another, which falls on another, and so on. In this program, the Change event "knocks over" tasks in much the same way. Changing the quantity ordered recomputes the extended price, which in turn recomputes the sales tax and the order total. Here, the important concept is that one event can cause another event to occur.

The CheckBox Object

The cash register program uses three objects that represent three menu items: burgers, french fries, and soft drinks. The clerk selects an item to indicate that it is ordered. To receive the clerk's input, you could use a text box; that choice, however, would require input from the keyboard, which would violate the design specifications. In designing your program, consider the kind of input that is being supplied by the clerk, who either wants to order an item or not. That is, the clerk is making a yes/no decision. Visual Basic supports the CheckBox control, which is designed for situations in which yes/no or on/off are the only choices.

Syntax	CheckBox
Definition	The **CheckBox** control creates a box that can be checked or unchecked. It contains two visible regions—a box that indicates whether the box is checked and a descriptive prompt. The standard prefix for a check box is "chk".
Properties	■ The value of the **Caption** property appears in the visible region of the control to describe its purpose.

- The **Value** property indicates the current state of the check box. Using the Properties window, it can be set to 0 - Unchecked, 1 - Checked, or 2 - Grayed. These values can also be set with code by using the intrinsic constant values vbUnchecked, vbChecked, and vbGrayed. If you click a dimmed check box once, it becomes unchecked; if you click it twice, it becomes checked. A dimmed check box informs the user that the box is neither checked nor unchecked and that input needs to be provided.

Events

Like a command button, the CheckBox control responds to the **Click** event when the box is clicked. This event resets the Value property.

The CheckBox control commonly executes some function when the control itself is clicked. In our program, whenever the clerk clicks a check box, a Click event occurs and the Value property of the check box is set to one of three values. Assuming that the program includes a check box named chkBurger, the following Select Case statement in the check box's Click event procedure could be used to process the three possible values:

```
Private Sub chkBurger_Click( )
    Select Case chkBurger.Value
        Case vbUnchecked
            ' Placeholder for statements executed
            ' when not checked.
        Case vbChecked
            ' Placeholder for statements executed when checked.
        Case vbGrayed
            ' Placeholder for statements executed when grayed.
    End Select
End Sub
```

We could also rewrite this Select Case statement as an If statement. In the cash register, check boxes will indicate whether a clerk entered a burger, french fries, and/or a soft drink.

To create the CheckBox objects:

1 Start Visual Basic, then open the project file named **Chapter.04\Startup\MB_S.vbp**.

2 View the form named **frmMB_S**; it looks like Figure 4-3.

labels for output

shape to hold
input objects

command buttons

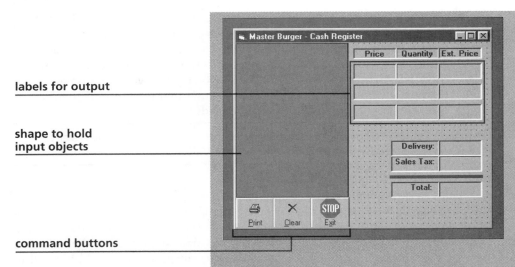

Figure 4-3: Partially completed cash register form

The shape to hold the input objects, the command buttons to print an order, clear input values, and exit the program, and the labels for output have already been created.

3 Click the **CheckBox** control on the toolbox.

4 Draw a check box inside the Shape object, as shown in Figure 4-4. Set the Caption property for the check box to **Burger** and the Name property to **chkBurger**.

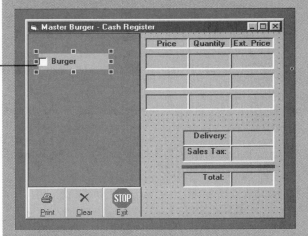

new check box

Figure 4-4: Creating a CheckBox object

5 Create a second check box of the same size and position it directly below the first check box.

6 Set the Caption property for the second check box to **French Fries** and the Name property to **chkFrenchFries**.

7 Repeat Step 5, setting the Caption property to **Soft Drink** and the Name property to **chkSoftDrink**. The form should now resemble Figure 4-5.

help
∙ ∙ ∙ ∙ ∙ ∙ ∙ ∙ ∙ ∙ ∙ ∙ ∙ ∙ ∙ ∙ ∙

Depending on the number of colors supported on your computer, the cross-hair pointer may disappear against the dark background of the Shape object. You can, however, create the control instance and use the sizing handles to position it.

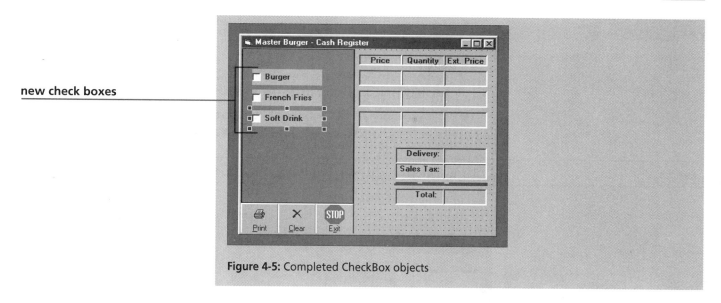

new check boxes

Figure 4-5: Completed CheckBox objects

Now you can create the ScrollBar objects that will allow the clerk to specify the quantity ordered for a specific item.

Adding Scroll Bars to the Form

The user interface for the cash register must permit a clerk to use only a mouse to enter the quantity ordered for a particular item. For example, if a customer orders three burgers, the clerk will click the Burger check box to indicate that the item has been ordered, but the clerk also must be able to indicate that a customer ordered more than one burger. Because the mouse is the only means of input, the clerk cannot type in the number of burgers ordered using a control such as a text box.

For each type of item ordered, you could create two command buttons—one that would contain the code to increment a variable representing the quantity ordered and one that would contain the code to decrement this variable. Although this approach would work, you would have to write several lines of code, so it is not the most efficient or easiest solution. Luckily, Visual Basic supports a **ScrollBar** control that will increment and decrement a number without requiring you to write any code at all.

Visual Basic supports vertical and horizontal scroll bars, both of which work the same way as the scroll bars in most Windows programs. The two types of scroll bars share the same properties, so the choice of which one to use depends on the requirements of the user interface.

Syntax	**HScrollBar VScrollBar**
Definition	Both the **HScrollBar** control and the **VScrollBar** control store a number that represents a value within a specified range. The range can describe the current position within a document or the distance traveled between two cities. The prefix for a vertical scroll bar (VScrollBar) control is "vsb", and the prefix for a horizontal scroll bar (HScrollBar) control is "hsb".
Properties	■ The range of valid values is controlled by the **Max** and **Min** properties. Each property can have a value between –32,768 and 32,767.

- The **Value** property is an Integer data type containing the current value of the scroll bar.

- When the user clicks the arrows at either end of the scroll bar, the Value property increases or decreases by the value contained in the **SmallChange** property. The default value of the SmallChange property is 1.

- When the user clicks the region between the arrows, the Value property changes by the value of the **LargeChange** property. The default value of the LargeChange property is 1.

Events   The **Change** event occurs whenever the value of the scroll bar changes.

A scroll bar is divided into two regions, as shown in Figure 4-6.

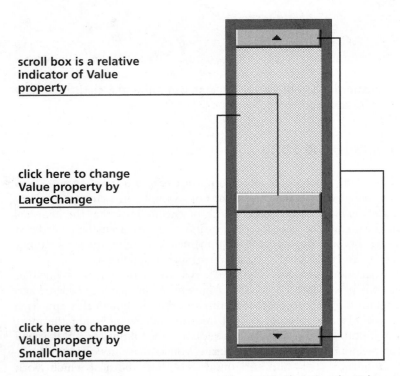

scroll box is a relative indicator of Value property

click here to change Value property by LargeChange

click here to change Value property by SmallChange

Figure 4-6: Changing the Value property of a vertical scroll bar

By default, the Value property of a vertical scroll bar increases as the bar moves downward, based upon the default settings of the Max and Min properties. If you used the default values from the Min property (0) and the Max property (32,767), clicking the up arrow would cause the value to decrease, and clicking the down arrow would cause the value to increase. You can think of the scroll bar as scrolling down through a page in a document; the down arrow moves you from line 1 of the page to the next line. The line number continues to increase as you move farther down the page, as illustrated in Figure 4-7.

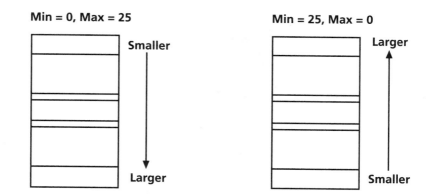

Figure 4-7: Setting the Max and Min properties

GUI

tip

● ● ● ● ● ● ● ● ● ● ● ● ● ● ● ● ●

Horizontal scroll bars are well suited for measures of distance, such as inches, because the metaphor of a ruler on a map tends to be a left-to-right sliding scale. Because an order quantity moves up and down, rather than left to right, the vertical scroll bar is a better choice for the cash register program. In circumstances where the type of scroll bar is irrelevant, consider using the one that will balance the layout of the screen.

For the cash register program, you will create three vertical scroll bars that specify the quantity ordered for each of the three food items. When the clerk clicks the vertical scroll bar's up arrow, the order quantity for the specific item must increase by 1. When the clerk clicks the scroll bar's down arrow, the order quantity must decrease by 1. To produce this result, you set the value of the Min property such that it is greater than the value of the Max property.

Setting the Max property to 0 and the Min property to the expected value of the largest order enables the value of a scroll bar to increase when its up arrow is clicked. The expected value of the largest possible order is 25, so you will set the Min property to 25.

To create vertical scroll bars:

1 Click the **VScrollBar** control 🗉 on the toolbox.

2 Draw a scroll bar to the right of the Burger check box. Refer to Figure 4-8 for the placement of this and subsequent scroll bars.

3 Set the Name property for the scroll bar to **vsbBurger**, the Max property to 0, and the Min property to **25**.

4 Create a second vertical scroll bar to the right of the French Fries check box. Set its Name property to **vsbFrenchFries**, its Max property to 0, and its Min property to **25**. If you choose to copy and paste the scroll bar from Step 2, the Max and Min properties of that scroll bar will be copied from the original as well.

5 Create the third vertical scroll bar to the right of the Soft Drink check box. Set its Name property to **vsbSoftDrink**, its Max property to 0, and its Min property to **25**. The completed form should match Figure 4-8.

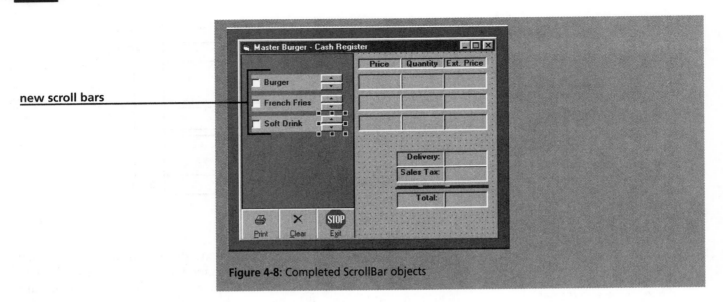

Figure 4-8: Completed ScrollBar objects

You have now completed setting the necessary properties for the scroll bars. You do not need to change the SmallChange or LargeChange properties from their default values of 1 because the quantity ordered should increase or decrease by 1 when the user clicks any part of the scroll bar. You are now ready to create the option buttons that the clerk will use to select the delivery zone.

Choosing the Right Control

You can group multiple instances of the same control to allow a clerk to select one of three delivery zones or to specify that an order will be eaten in the restaurant. The Master Burger restaurant breaks down the delivery area into three zones based on the distance from the restaurant to the customer's address. Although the clerk could use a check box to select a delivery area, the CheckBox control would not ensure that the clerk marked only one delivery area in the group (one check box from a group of check boxes). You could change the value of the other check boxes when one check box is selected, but this solution would require a significant amount of code. You could use a TextBox control, but this option violates the constraint that the mouse be the only means of input. An **OptionButton** control allows you to create a group of option buttons from which the clerk can select only one at a time. Option buttons often are called **radio buttons** because they are reminiscent of car radio buttons.

OptionButton objects are usually positioned and operated as a group from inside a **Frame** object. When you create an instance of a Frame control on a form and place option buttons inside it, the option buttons form an **option group**. Only one OptionButton object in an option group can be selected at a time. In addition to grouping controls such as option buttons together, a frame resembles a Shape control in that it can also be used to identify a group of items visually.

To implement the user interface, you will add a frame and four option buttons to the form. When the clerk clicks one of the four option buttons to specify whether an order is delivered and, if so, to which zone, the other three option buttons in the group will be unselected automatically.

Creating a Frame

When you create a frame that will be used to group controls such as option buttons, you must create an instance of the frame first, then create an instance of the other controls inside the frame. If you do not create the other control instances inside the

GUI tip

Option buttons consume a large amount of space on the screen. Use option buttons only when fewer than five choices exist. When the number of choices exceeds five, consider using a list box or a combo box. These types of controls are discussed in subsequent chapters.

new scroll bars

frame, the option buttons will not belong to the same option group. Thus it will be possible to click more than one option button. If you create an option button outside a frame and then try to move the object inside the frame, it may appear on top of the frame but the option button will not function as part of an option group. Finally, if you use the Clipboard to copy and paste option buttons, you must make the frame become the active object before pasting the option button.

The frame you draw must be large enough to hold all of the option buttons. Like other objects, a frame can be resized as needed. Typically, a Frame object's Caption property provides the user with a descriptive message about the purpose of the option buttons or other objects grouped inside it.

Syntax	Frame
Definition	The **Frame** control can be used to identify sections on the form visually. It is also used to group other control instances together. The standard prefix for a Frame object is "fra".
Properties	■ The **Caption** property contains the caption that appears along the top of the frame.
	■ If the **BorderStyle** property is set to 0 - None, no border appears around the frame. If it is set to 1 - Fixed Single, a border surrounds the frame.
	■ The **BackColor** and **ForeColor** properties control the foreground and background colors of the frame, respectively. These properties have the same effect as the properties of the same name for other controls you used in earlier chapters.

For the cash register program, you will create a Frame object named fraDelivery that will contain four option buttons indicating which delivery zone is specified or whether the order will be eaten in the restaurant.

To add the Frame object to the form:

1 Click the **Frame** control 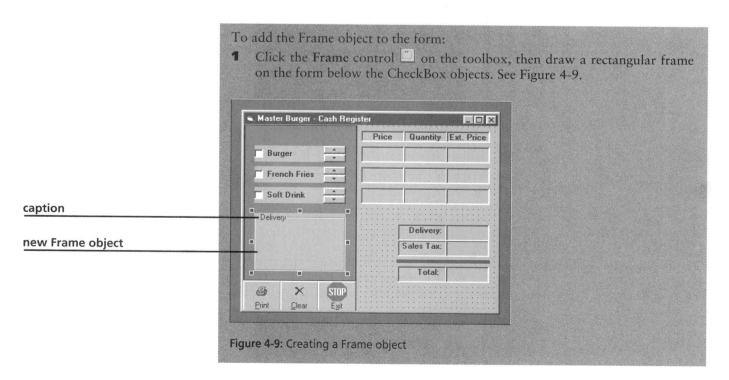 on the toolbox, then draw a rectangular frame on the form below the CheckBox objects. See Figure 4-9.

caption

new Frame object

Figure 4-9: Creating a Frame object

2 Set the Caption property of the frame to **Delivery**. Because you will not write any code for this object, you do not need to set the Name property.

A frame is rarely used by itself. Instead, it is generally used to group together other controls. The Frame control is a **container**; that is, it contains other control instances like option buttons.

Creating Option Buttons

When you create OptionButton objects, you are usually interested in finding out which button in a group of option buttons is currently selected. The OptionButton object has the standard naming prefix of "opt".

Syntax	**OptionButton**
Definition	The **OptionButton** control instances generally are used as a group. Within a group of option button instances, only one button can be selected at a time.
Properties	■ The **Caption** property contains the text that appears to the right of the option button.
	■ The **Value** property can be either True or False. When True, the option button is selected. When False, the option button is deselected. When an option button that is part of an option group is selected, Visual Basic automatically sets the Value properties for the other option buttons in that group to False.
	■ The **Index** property is an Integer data type that Visual Basic uses in conjunction with the Name property to identify each object uniquely in a control array. The Index property starts at zero (0) for the first object and is incremented by one (1) for each subsequent object in the control array.
Events	The **Click** event occurs when the user clicks the option button. It is similar to the Click event for the command button.

You will now create four option buttons inside the frame: one for each delivery zone and one for orders eaten in the restaurant. These option buttons will make up an option group. Visual Basic allows you to create multiple option groups by creating multiple frames and inserting option buttons into each frame. In the cash register program, an appropriate name for the option button is optDelivery because it indicates the delivery location of the order; its caption, however, will be Zone 1.

To create an option button:

1 Click the **OptionButton** control [●] on the toolbox.

2 Draw an option button inside the frame. Set the option button's Name property to **optDelivery** and its Caption property to **Zone 1**. The form should match Figure 4-10.

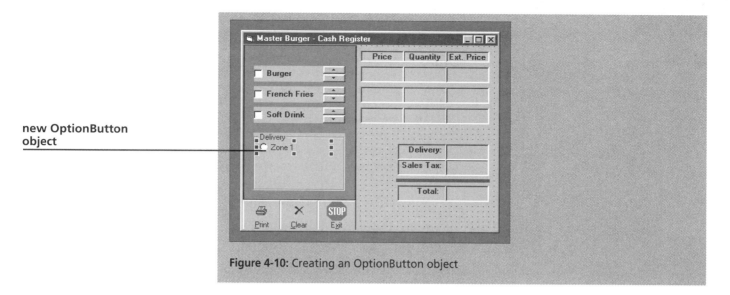

new OptionButton object

Figure 4-10: Creating an OptionButton object

You still need to create the remaining option buttons. First, however, you must learn how to create objects that respond to the same Click event procedure rather than unique Click event procedures. This approach ensures that the same Click event procedure will execute no matter which option button in the group is clicked.

Creating a Control Array

Until now, each object you have created on a form has had a unique name and responded to unique event procedures. That is, each command button executed its own distinct Click event procedure when clicked. It is also possible to group objects of the same type (such as option buttons) together into a **control array**, so they will all share the same name and event procedures.

To understand the concept of a control array, consider a person's street address. That address uniquely identifies the person's home. If an individual lives in an apartment building, however, all people in the same apartment building share the same street address. To identify the person uniquely, you must use both the street address and the apartment number. In Visual Basic, a control array is analogous to an apartment building. Multiple control instances have the same address (Name property), but each is uniquely identified by its apartment number (Index property).

Depending on which option button is clicked, the program must apply the correct delivery charge or no charge if the customer plans to eat in the restaurant. You will use a control array of option buttons so the buttons will work together as a group. Consequently, you will write only one event procedure.

When you create objects in a control array, each object shares the same name; that is, they have the same value for their Name properties. Visual Basic uses the **Index** property in conjunction with the Name property to identify each object uniquely in a control array. The first object in the control array has an Index property of zero (0). Event procedures for control arrays receive an Index argument that contains the value of the Index property for the selected control instance. The Index property determines which option button is selected from an option group.

The easiest way to create a control array is to copy and paste one object so as to create multiple instances of that object, as described below:

1. Create an instance of an option button in the frame and set its properties.
2. Activate the option button.
3. Copy the option button to the Windows Clipboard by pressing Ctrl+C.
4. Click the Frame object to activate it.
5. Paste the copied option button into the frame by pressing Ctrl+V.
6. Make sure the option button appears at the top of the frame and not at the top of the form.
7. Click the Yes button in the message box when it asks if you want to create a control array.
8. Move the new option button to the appropriate location.
9. Repeat Steps 4 through 8 to paste and move each option button to be added to the control array.

You will copy the first Delivery option button and paste it into the Delivery frame three times to create the option buttons for delivery to Zone 2, delivery to Zone 3, and Eat In.

To create the objects of a control array:

1   Click the **Zone 1** option button to activate it.

2   Press **Ctrl+C** to copy the OptionButton object to the Windows Clipboard.

3   Click the **Delivery** frame to select it. Sizing handles appear around the frame.

4   Press **Ctrl+V** to paste the copied option button into the frame.

A message box opens and asks if you want to create a control array.

5   Click the **Yes** button.

The copy of the option button appears in the upper-left corner of the frame.

6   Drag the new option button below the **Zone 1** option button, then set the Caption property of the new option button to **Zone 2**. The value of the Index property is 1, and the name has not changed from optDelivery.

7   Repeat Steps 3, 4, and 6 to create the third and fourth option buttons, and set their Caption properties to **Zone 3** and **Eat In**, respectively. Because the object you are pasting is now a member of a control array, you will not be asked again if you want to create a control array. Figure 4-11 shows the option buttons that you created inside the frame.

help

· · · · · · · · · · · · · · · ·

If the option button appears in the upper-left corner of the form rather than the frame, the option button resides on the form rather than on the frame. To ensure that the option buttons work correctly as an option group, you must delete the new option button, then repeat Steps 1 through 5.

option buttons in control array

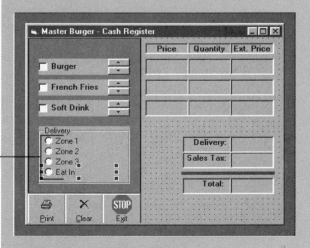

Figure 4-11: Creating a control array of option buttons

8 Test the program by clicking each option button. When one button is selected, the others should be deselected.

In the previous set of steps, you created a control array of option buttons. You also can create a control array of text boxes, labels, or any other control. The only restriction is that all controls in a control array must be of the same type; that is, a control array can consist of text boxes or labels, but not both. You can create as many control arrays on a form as necessary.

All of the visible form objects are now in place. Next, you need to write the Visual Basic code to compute and display the output in the labels drawn on the form.

To help a clerk visually confirm that an item has been ordered, each scroll bar, its corresponding quantity ordered, unit price, and extended price labels should be visible only when the item's check box has been clicked. The scroll bars and labels should remain invisible when an item's check box has not been clicked. You can accomplish this goal by setting the Visible property of the scroll bar and labels to True or False.

When the cash register program starts, no scroll bars or labels should appear on the form until a clerk clicks the corresponding check box.

To set the Visible property for the scroll bars and labels:

1 Activate the Form window. Press and hold down the **Shift** key as you click each scroll bar and each label for unit price, the quantity ordered, and the extended price. As you activate an object, it becomes marked with blue sizing handles and the other selected objects appear with dimmed sizing handles. See Figure 4-12.

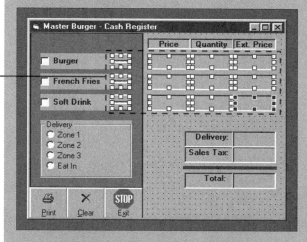

Figure 4-12: Selecting multiple objects

When you select multiple control instances, the Properties window works somewhat differently. As shown in Figure 4-13, it displays only those properties that are common to both a label and a vertical scroll bar. The object in the title bar may differ depending on the order in which you selected the objects.

help

If you can click more than one option button at a time, the buttons are not all members of the same option group. In that case, end the program. Click the frame and move it to another location on the form. The option button(s) that do not move with the frame are in a different option group. Delete these option button(s), then move the frame and option buttons back into position. Activate an option button that is inside the frame, then press Ctrl+C to copy it to the Clipboard. Click the frame to select it, then press Ctrl+V to paste the copied button into the frame. Repeat Step 8. In addition, you may need to reset the Index property of the option buttons as follows: Zone 1 = 0, Zone 2 = 1, Zone 3 = 2, Eat In = 3. You may also need to reset the Caption property.

marked objects
appear with handles

Performance tip

Control arrays improve a program's efficiency. When you add an object to a control array, the new object shares the event procedures of the other option buttons. This strategy conserves system memory. Control arrays also provide a way to overcome some programming limitations of Visual Basic. For example, you can specify up to 256 different control names on a form. This number can be limiting—even this small cash register program contains more than 30 instances of various controls. If you need more than 256 controls on a form, you can use control arrays. Each control array can contain a maximum of 32,767 objects.

no object name
displayed

only properties
common to a label
and vertical scroll
bar are displayed

set this property
to False

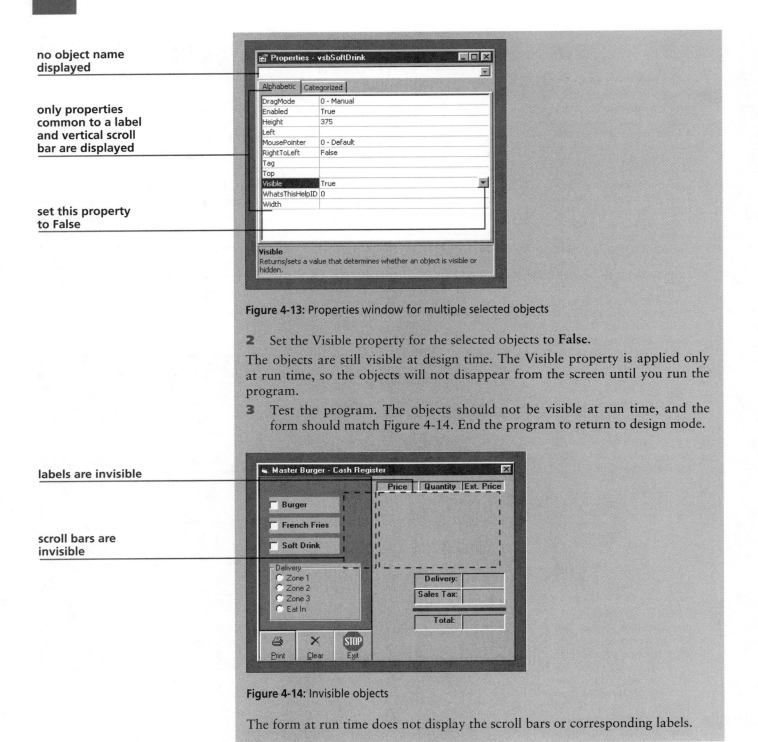

Figure 4-13: Properties window for multiple selected objects

2   Set the Visible property for the selected objects to **False**.

The objects are still visible at design time. The Visible property is applied only at run time, so the objects will not disappear from the screen until you run the program.

3   Test the program. The objects should not be visible at run time, and the form should match Figure 4-14. End the program to return to design mode.

labels are invisible

scroll bars are
invisible

Figure 4-14: Invisible objects

The form at run time does not display the scroll bars or corresponding labels.

You now need to write the statements to make the scroll bar, unit price, quantity ordered, and extended price labels visible when a clerk clicks the corresponding check box.

Understanding the Change Event

When the program begins, the scroll bars and labels are initially invisible because the Visible property for each scroll bar was set to False in the Properties window. You will write statements to make each object visible when its corresponding check box is checked. You want the scroll bars and labels to remain invisible, or to become invisible again, whenever the corresponding check box is not checked. Thus you will set the Visible property of each object to the Boolean values of True or False, as needed. You will write an If...Then...Else statement to make visible or invisible the scroll bar, unit price, quantity ordered, and extended price label for each menu item when its corresponding check box is checked. For example, when the chkBurger object is checked, the Visible property for the vsbBurger, lblPriceBurger, lblQtyBurger, and lblExtBurger output labels should be set to True; otherwise, they should be set to False. The initial value of the scroll bar should also be 1. As the opposite example, a customer may decide not to order a product that has already been ordered. The clerk will reverse the order by clicking a check box that already has been checked. When a check box is unchecked, the scroll bar and the labels for quantity ordered and extended price should be set to 0 and become invisible again.

Using the Object Browser, you will identify which intrinsic constant to use to express each valid check box value. As you saw in previous chapters, Visual Basic converts intrinsic constant names into their respective values when the program is run. This approach makes the program more readable and reliable. Here, you will use intrinsic constants to write the statements to make the scroll bars and labels that display the unit price, quantity ordered, and extended price visible or invisible when a clerk checks or unchecks a check box.

To set the Visible property for the scroll bars and labels based on the check box values:

1 Click **View**, then click **Object Browser** on the menu bar to activate the Object Browser. Look up the **CheckBoxConstants** values, as shown in Figure 4-15.

intrinsic constants supported by CheckBox object

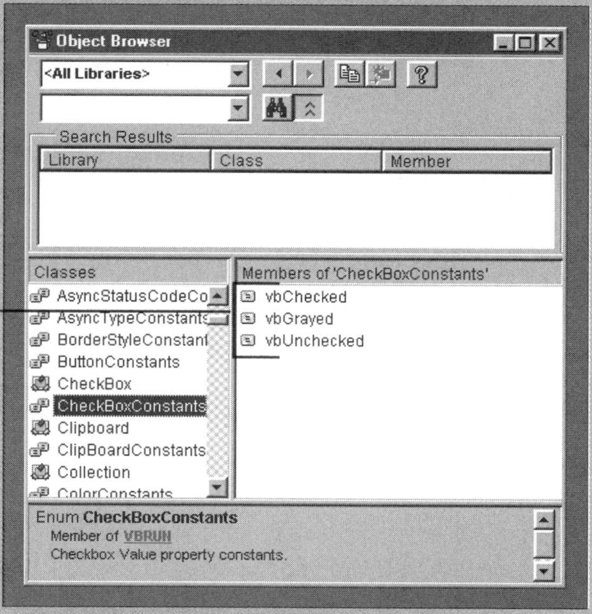

Figure 4-15: Object Browser dialog

2 Click **vbChecked**. The value of the constant is 1; it appears at the bottom of the dialog. Click **vbGrayed**, and note that the value of the constant is 2. Click **vbUnchecked**, and the value of the constant is shown as 0.

3 Open the Code window for the **chkBurger_Click** event procedure and enter the following statements:

```
If (chkBurger.Value = vbChecked) Then
    vsbBurger.Visible = True
    vsbBurger.Value = 1
    lblPriceBurger.Visible = True
    lblQtyBurger.Visible = True
    lblExtBurger.Visible = True
Else
    vsbBurger.Visible = False
    vsbBurger.Value = 0
    lblPriceBurger.Visible = False
    lblQtyBurger.Visible = False
    lblExtBurger.Visible = False
End If
```

4 Repeat Step 3 for the **chkFrenchFries_Click** event procedure, using the object names **vsbFrenchFries, lblPriceFrenchFries, lblQtyFrenchFries,** and **lblExtFrenchFries**. (You can select the statements you just wrote and use the copy and paste operations supported by Windows. Select the statements you want to copy and press Ctrl+C. Position the insertion point in the Code window at the point at which the statements should be pasted and press Ctrl+V, then search and replace the object names in the new text. If you use the search and replace technique, select the Current Procedure option button.)

5 Repeat Step 3 for the **chkSoftDrink_Click** event procedure, using the object names **vsbSoftDrink, lblPriceSoftDrink, lblQtySoftDrink,** and **lblExtSoftDrink**.

6 Test the program. Click the **Burger** check box. The corresponding scroll bar, vsbBurger, and the labels lblPriceBurger, lblQtyBurger, and lblExtBurger should become visible. Click the **Burger** check box again. The objects should become invisible again. Click the **French Fries** and **Soft Drink** check boxes to select them and clear them. End the program to return to design mode.

help

▶ **If an object's visibility does not change when you click the corresponding check box, end the program, open the Code window for the CheckBox object's Click event procedure, and verify that your code matches that shown in the previous steps. Make any necessary corrections, then repeat Step 6.**

The statements you wrote in the previous steps make the scroll bars and labels visible when the value of a corresponding check box is 1 (vbChecked) and set the Value property of the scroll bar to 1 when its box is first checked. These statements also will reset the Visible and Value properties to False and 0, respectively, when the check box Value property is 0 (vbUnchecked).

```
If (chkBurger.Value = vbChecked) Then
```

Although they are not required for correct evaluation of the preceding statement, the parentheses in this If statement can improve the readability of your program. They make it clear that chkBurger.Value is first compared with the constant vbChecked. If True, the statements before the Else are executed. If False, the statements after the Else are executed.

When it is run, the cash register program displays the corresponding scroll bars and quantity ordered fields when a check box is checked and makes those objects invisible when the corresponding check box is not checked. You are now ready to begin programming the scroll bar objects so that when the clerk moves a scroll bar, the program updates the corresponding quantity ordered label.

In this program, whenever the clerk clicks the check box representing a menu item, a Click event occurs for the check box. The code you wrote in the Click event procedure makes visible or invisible the corresponding labels. In addition, it explicitly sets the Value property of the scroll bar. You need to know when the numeric value of a scroll bar changes so that the program can update the quantity ordered and extended price of an item and display this information in the corresponding Label objects. Whenever a clerk clicks part of a scroll bar and changes its value, it generates a Change event. This event is also generated when you set the Value property of the scroll bar with code. You will use a Change event with the Value property of the scroll bar in a computation to update the captions of the necessary labels.

Figure 4-16 shows how each event causes the next event. Clicking a check box causes a Click event to occur. The code in the Click event procedure sets the Value property of the corresponding scroll bar, generating a Change event for the scroll bar.

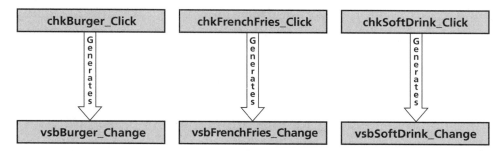

Figure 4-16: Relationship between events (1)

Now you need to write the statements to program the Change event that will update the caption in the quantity ordered label whenever the value of the scroll bar changes. You have several different ways to write the statements to accomplish this task. The following event procedure for the Burger scroll bar's Change event would validate the input and set the label's caption:

```
Private Sub vsbBurger_Change( )
    mintQtyBurger = Val(vsbBurger.Value)
    lblQtyBurger.Caption = mintQtyBurger
End Sub
```

In previous chapters, you have validated input and used conversion functions like Val to convert a string into a numeric value. These steps are unnecessary in the cash register program. Because the scroll bar's value will always contain an Integer number, you do not need to validate the value or perform the type conversion explicitly. Visual Basic will take care of these tasks automatically. Thus the event procedure becomes very simple, as shown in the following statement:

```
lblQtyBurger.Caption = vsbBurger.Value
```

You will use this technique with the scroll bars in this chapter.

To program the Change event for the scroll bars:

1   Open the Code window for the **vsbBurger_Change** event and enter the following statement:

```
lblQtyBurger.Caption = vsbBurger.Value
```

When the scroll bar for the burger changes, Visual Basic generates a Change event for the vsbBurger object. The code in this Change event procedure copies the Value property of vsbBurger to the Caption property of lblQtyBurger.

You now need to create the same code for the scroll bars for the French Fries and Soft Drink items.

2   Repeat Step 1 for the **vsbFrenchFries_Change** event procedure, using the names **lblQtyFrenchFries** and **vsbFrenchFries**.

3   Repeat Step 1 for the **vsbSoftDrink_Change** event procedure, using the names **lblQtySoftDrink** and **vsbSoftDrink**.

4   Test the program. Click the **Burger** check box; the corresponding label should display the value 1. Click the **Burger** scroll bar's up arrow; the corresponding label should display the value 2. Click the **Burger** scroll bar's down arrow; the label should display the value 1. Because you did not change the SmallChange property from its default value of 1, the value of the scroll bar changes by 1 each time you click its arrows. Test the **French Fries** and **Soft Drink** scroll bars and display labels. End the program to return to design mode.

help

If any quantity ordered label did not change correctly, end the program, and open the Code window for the corresponding scroll bar. Check the code and ensure that the Caption property is set for the correct Label object. If the value of an item incremented or decremented incorrectly, check the Min and Max properties of the corresponding scroll bar; Min should be 25 and Max should be 0. Make any necessary corrections, then repeat Step 4.

Whenever a clerk clicks a scroll bar, your code will display the quantity ordered for the item in the caption of the corresponding label. The value for the label's caption is determined by the value of the scroll bar, which means that a Change event is generated for the scroll bar. Figure 4-17 illustrates this process.

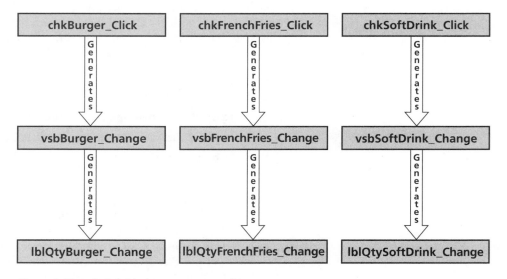

Figure 4-17: Relationship between events (2)

When the clerk clicks the chkBurger check box, it generates a Click event for the chkBurger object. The code in this event procedure sets the value of the corresponding scroll bar to its initial value of 1. Thus a Change event occurs for the vsbBurger scroll bar. The code in the Burger scroll bar's Change event procedure then sets the caption of the lblQtyBurger label, which generates a Change event for the lblQtyBurger. You have not yet written any code that will execute when the Change event occurs to the label.

Creating User-Defined Constants

You still must create the code to compute and display the labels for the extended prices. Before you can compute these extended prices, you must declare the price of each item in the program. You could declare variables for the prices and assign values to them, as you did in Chapters 2 and 3, or you could just use numbers in the computations. In this case, however, the price of an item will not change while the program is running, so a constant is a better choice for storing the prices. You have already used an intrinsic constant in the If statement you wrote to determine whether a check box is checked.

In addition to intrinsic constants, you can create user-defined constants. A **user-defined constant** works just like an intrinsic constant—it assigns a name to a value that does not change. Its purpose is to improve the readability of the program. A user-defined constant is declared using the Const (Constant) statement.

Syntax	[**Public**	**Private**] **Const** *constantname* [**As** *type*] = *expression*
Dissection	■ You can declare constants with the **Const** statement in the general declarations section of a module or inside a procedure.
	■ The **Public** keyword is used at the module level to declare constants that can be used by all procedures in all forms and other modules. Use the Public keyword only if the project includes more than one module. Public constants can be declared only in standard modules.
	■ The **Private** keyword is used at the module level to declare a constant that can be used only by procedures in the module where the constant is declared. If you omit the Public or Private keyword, the constant will be Private by default. You should explicitly use the Private keyword, however, to declare module-level constants and to improve the program's clarity.
	■ The *constantname* assigned to a user-defined constant should follow the naming conventions for variables. That is, the constant should begin with the letter "c" (indicating a constant), followed by a three-letter prefix describing its data type, followed by a descriptive name.
	■ Constants can be defined as any of the Visual Basic data types by using the optional **As** *type* clause. If you do not explicitly declare the constant type using the **As** *type* clause, the constant will have the data type that is most appropriate for the expression. Explicitly supplying the desired data type creates more readable code and will prevent type conversion errors.
	■ The required *expression* represents a valid Visual Basic expression that becomes the value of the constant. The *expression* often is a simple value, such as a price, but it also can consist of other constants and operators. (The Visual Basic Help library provides more information on the Const statement.) The value of the constant must be set when the constant is declared.

Code Example	```Private Const csngPI As Single = 3.14159``` ```Private Const cstrCompany As String = "Master Burger"```
Code Dissection	The first statement declares a Private constant named csngPI (the value of PI). The second statement declares a string constant that stores the company name "Master Burger". Both constants can be used only in the module in which they were declared because the declaration uses the Private keyword.

Because your program has only one form, the constants need to be visible only in the form in which they are declared. As a result, you will declare them as Private in the form module. You will declare each constant as a Single data type because the prices contain decimal points. You will then use the price constants in various expressions throughout the program to compute the extended prices of the items ordered.

Next, you will declare the prices and the sales tax rate as constants in the general declarations section of the form module, thereby making them available to all procedures in the form.

Programming

tip

Creating user-defined constants makes a program more readable. Constants also simplify the maintenance of a program, because when the value of a constant changes, you need to change the value only once in the statement where the constant is created, rather than searching for every occurrence of that value in the program.

To declare constants:

1   Open the Code window to the **general declarations** section of the form module.

2   Type the following statements (shown in bold):

```
Option Explicit
Private Const csngPriceBurger As Single = 1.44
Private Const csngPriceFrenchFries As Single = 0.74
Private Const csngPriceSoftDrink As Single = 0.66
Private Const csngPercentTax As Single = 0.07
```

These statements declare three constants for the item prices and another constant for the sales tax rate. They also explicitly set the data type and value for each constant to Single.

Next, you must create the code to calculate the extended price and place it in the caption of the corresponding extended price label. Consider carefully the appropriate event procedure to place the code. Whenever the quantity ordered for an item changes, the program should recompute the extended price. Remember the sequence of events that occurs when the clerk clicks a scroll bar. First, the Change event occurs for the scroll bar. You wrote code for this event procedure, which changes the caption of the corresponding quantity ordered label. This code generates a Change event for the label. Thus you can write code in the Change event for each quantity ordered label to update the corresponding extended price. You also can write the same code in the Change event procedure for the scroll bar.

Now that you have declared the necessary constants, you can use them in the code that will display the unit price for an item and calculate the extended prices. The unit price will not change when the cash register is running. Thus you will write the code to store the unit price constant for an item in the Form_Load event procedure.

To write the statements that will calculate and display the extended prices:

1 Activate the Code window for the **Form_Load** event procedure and enter the following statements:

```
lblPriceBurger = csngPriceBurger

lblPriceFrenchFries = csngPriceFrenchFries

lblPriceSoftDrink = csngPriceSoftDrink
```

2 Activate the Code window for the **vsbBurger_Change** event—make sure that you activate the Change event, not the Click event—and enter the following statements (shown in bold):

```
Private Sub vsbBurger_Change( )
    Dim psngExtBurger As Single
    lblQtyBurger.Caption = vsbBurger.Value
    psngExtBurger = lblQtyBurger.Caption * _
        csngPriceBurger
    lblExtBurger.Caption = Format(psngExtBurger, _
        "Fixed")
End Sub
```

3 Repeat Step 2 for the **vsbFrenchFries_Change** event procedure, substituting **lblQtyFrenchFries** for lblQtyBurger, **psngExtFrenchFries** for psngExtBurger, **csngPriceFrenchFries** for csngPriceBurger, and **lblExtFrenchFries** for lblExtBurger.

4 Repeat Step 2 for the **vsbSoftDrink_Change** event procedure, substituting **lblQtySoftDrink** for lblQtyBurger, **psngExtSoftDrink** for psngExtBurger, **csngPriceSoftDrink** for csngPriceBurger, and **lblExtSoftDrink** for lblExtBurger.

You now have written all of the code needed to update the extended price of each item when the quantity ordered changes. The Format statement sets the output format as Fixed (two decimal places). Data type conversion takes place as Visual Basic executes the following:

```
psngExtBurger = lblQtyBurger.Caption * _
    csngPriceBurger
```

In this statement, lblQtyBurger.Caption contains a string representing the quantity ordered. Visual Basic automatically converts this string to a number. In Chapter 3, you used classification functions to determine the data type of an input value and conversion functions to convert that value into a number. In this example, however, the clerk is not directly entering this value. As a result, the program does not need to validate it.

It also is possible to condense the statements in Step 2 into a single statement:

```
lblExtBurger.Caption = Format(lblQtyBurger.Caption * _
    csngPriceBurger, "Fixed")
```

This statement computes the extended price, formats the value, and stores the result in the Caption property of lblExtBurger. Thus it has the same effect as the previous statements you entered. Your choice of which one to use is a matter of style. Some programmers write very terse programs, and others write more verbose programs. Generally, terse programs are more difficult to read.

Now is a good time to test your program, correct any errors, and save the form and project files.

To test the extended prices:

1 Test the program. Click each check box. The extended prices should be computed, placed in the labels, and formatted. Click the scroll bars to change the quantities. The extended prices should be recomputed. End the program to return to design mode.

You have completed the cash register programming for this section. The clerk can select items and specify the corresponding quantity ordered. Whenever the quantity ordered changes, the program will recompute the extended price of the item. You took advantage of the Change event to determine when the extended price needs to be recomputed instead of forcing the clerk to click a command button to explicitly compute the extended price.

help

If an extended price is not computed correctly, end the program, and activate the Code window for the Change event procedure of the corresponding quantity ordered scroll bar object. Make sure that the code is identical to that shown in the previous set of steps. Make any necessary corrections, then repeat Step 1. If an extended price is not formatted as Fixed, verify that you wrote the correct Format statement for the correct corresponding extended price label. Repeat Step 1.

Q U E S T I O N S

1. Which constants represent valid values for a check box?
    a. vbChecked, vbUnchecked, vbGrayed
    b. vbMarked, vbUnmarked
    c. vbYes, vbNo
    d. Checked, Unchecked, Grayed
    e. None of the above.

2. Which properties control the range of a scroll bar?
    a. Start, End
    b. Begin, End
    c. Top, Bottom
    d. Max, Min
    e. Maximum, Minimum

3. Which properties control how much the value is changed when different regions of the scroll bar are clicked?
    a. ChangeLarge, ChangeSmall
    b. Change1, Change2
    c. Large, Small
    d. LargeChange, SmallChange
    e. None of the above.

4. Which of the following statements is true about option buttons?
   a. They work just like a check box.
   b. They typically are used in an option group.
   c. Only one option button in an option group can be selected at a time.
   d. Both b and c.
   e. None of the above.

5. What are the uses of a frame?
   a. To identify a group of controls visually
   b. To create option groups
   c. To draw a picture frame
   d. Both a and b.
   e. Both b and c.

6. Which of the following statements is true about a control array?
   a. All of the controls must be of the same type.
   b. All of the controls share the same name.
   c. A particular control is identified uniquely by its name and index.
   d. The controls in a control array share event procedures.
   e. All of the above.

7. Which of the following controls supports the Change event?
   a. Label
   b. ScrollBar
   c. CheckBox
   d. Both a and b.
   e. Both b and c.

8. What is the name of the statement to declare a user-defined constant?
   a. ConstantVariable
   b. Const
   c. User-Defined
   d. Dim
   e. None of the above.

9. Write the statement(s) to declare a module-level constant named **cintMax** having a data type of **Single** and a value of **35**.

10. Write the statement(s) to declare a module-level constant named **cstrCompany** having a data type of **String** and a value of **ABC Electronics**.

Working with Events

Writing Code for Control Arrays

In the cash register program, you need a way to check which Delivery option button is selected and a Select Case statement that will update the delivery charges accordingly. As noted earlier, in a control array, a specific control instance is identified by its Index property. When a control instance is a member of a control array, the event procedure contains an argument named Index. This argument consists of the index of the current element in the control array. Figure 4-18 shows the argument for the Delivery option buttons' Click event procedure.

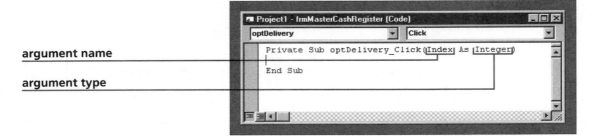

argument name

argument type

Figure 4-18: Argument in the event procedure

The syntax of this argument looks like any other declaration statement except that the keyword, Dim or Private, is omitted. The argument includes a variable name, Index, and an As clause containing the data type, which is Integer. Visual Basic stores the Index of the active option button as a local variable, enabling you to use it in the event procedure. If the form includes more than one control array, each control array will use a local variable with the name Index. Like other local variables, this variable exists only while the procedure is running. It allows your program to communicate information from one procedure to another or, in this situation, Visual Basic to communicate information to your event procedure. If the user clicks the Zone 1 option button, Visual Basic will set the Index property to 0; if he or she clicks the Zone 2 option button, Visual Basic will set the Index property to 1. Likewise, when the user clicks the Zone 3 option button, Visual Basic will set the Index property to 2; if the Eat In option button is clicked, Visual Basic will set the Index property to 3. In this way, Visual Basic tracks and shares code among the control array's objects.

You will use this information to determine the delivery charge, if any, by writing a Select Case statement in the Code window that defines the control array's Click event.

To write the Select Case statement for the control array:

1 Activate the Code window for the **optDelivery_Click** event procedure and enter the following statements:

```
Select Case Index
    Case 0     ' Zone 1
        lblDelivery.Caption = Format(1.5, "Fixed")
    Case 1     ' Zone 2
        lblDelivery.Caption = Format(2.5, "Fixed")
    Case 2     ' Zone 3
        lblDelivery.Caption = Format(3.5, "Fixed")
    Case 3     ' Eat In
        lblDelivery.Caption = Format(0, "Fixed")
End Select
```

2 Test the program by clicking each option button in the Delivery control array. The Delivery label should change with each option button clicked. End the program to return to design mode.

help

If the Delivery label does not reflect the changes when each option button is clicked, end the program. Verify that the statements in the option buttons' Click event procedure match the statements in the previous set of steps.

This event procedure is executed when the user clicks any of the four option buttons. To determine which option button has been clicked, you examine the value stored in the Index property. The Select Case statement first evaluates the value of Index, and then executes the statements for the corresponding case. The delivery charge is then formatted and displayed by setting the caption of lblDelivery. Because no other possibility exists, you did not include a Case Else statement.

The cash register program now computes a delivery charge. In the preceding statements, you wrote literal values that were used to indicate the amount of the delivery charge. You could also define constants for these values.

Form Events

You have seen that the control instances created on a form can respond to events. A form resembles a control instance in many respects. For example, you can set properties for a form using the Properties window, just as you set properties for a control instance. More importantly, a form responds to events in the same way that a control instance responds to events. Many of these events occur when the program is run and the form is loaded into the computer's memory. Other events occur when the program ends and the form is unloaded from memory. The following list describes several form events and notes when they occur:

- When a program is first run, the first form and its objects are initialized and the **Initialize** event occurs.
- After the Initialize event occurs, the **Load** event occurs.
- In programs with multiple forms, only one form can be active (have focus) at a time. When a form is activated, the **Activate** event occurs for the form.

■ When the program exits, the **Unload** event occurs just before the form is destroyed.

To improve the program's user interface, the most common delivery option—an order being eaten in the restaurant—should be selected when the program starts. You therefore need to set the value of the Eat In option button to True when the form loads. This option button has the Index value of 3 and the name of optDelivery.

You created four option buttons, each having the same name (optDelivery) and a unique Index value (ranging from 0 to 3). To reference a specific element in a control array, you use the name of the control instance, followed by the Index value of the desired element enclosed in parentheses.

To reference a control array element:

1 Open the Code window for the **Form_Load** event procedure and enter the following statement (shown in bold):

```
Private Sub Form_Load( )
    optDelivery(3).Value = True
    lblPriceBurger = csngPriceBurger
```

2 Test the program. The Eat In option button should be selected; the Delivery charge should equal 0.00. End the program to return to design mode.

As with other controls introduced in earlier chapters, you reference a specific property by typing the object's name and the desired property, separated by a period (.). The syntax is the same as that involved in using a control array, but the object's Index value in parentheses follows the object name. The Index value specifies which option button in the control array should be set.

Computing the Total

According to the program specifications, the cash register program must compute the sales tax and order total automatically whenever the extended price of a menu item changes. In case of such a change, the Change event occurs to the corresponding extended price label. Thus you can write statements for the extended price label's Change event procedure in the same way that you wrote code for other Change event procedures. This time, however, the same action will be carried out: You will compute the total by using all of the extended prices. Because the task is the same for all three events, a general procedure is suitable for it.

To write the general procedure to compute the sales tax and total:

1 Click **Tools**, then click **Add Procedure** to activate the Add Procedure dialog. Create a general procedure with the name **ComputeTotals**, the type **Sub**, and the scope **Private**. Click **OK** to close the dialog.

The Code window is active; "(General)" appears in the Object list box and "ComputeTotals" appears in the Procedure list box. They indicate that the ComputeTotals procedure does not execute when an event occurs to a specific object. Instead, it is general to the Form module and can be called explicitly by any event or general procedure. Because the procedure is Private, it can be called only from event or general procedures in this form.

2 Enter the following statements into the general procedure:

```
Dim psngSubtotal As Single
Dim psngSalesTax As Single
psngSubtotal = Val(lblExtBurger.Caption) + _
    Val(lblExtFrenchFries.Caption) + _
    Val(lblExtSoftDrink.Caption)
psngSalesTax = csngPercentTax * psngSubtotal
lblSalesTax.Caption = Format(psngSalesTax, "Fixed")
lblTotal.Caption = Format(psngSubtotal + psngSalesTax _
    + lblDelivery.Caption, "Fixed")
```

Now you can examine each statement in more detail.

```
Dim psngSubtotal As Single
Dim psngSalesTax As Single
```

The variables psngSubtotal and psngSalesTax are declared inside the ComputeTotals general procedure because you need these variables only when this procedure runs. These variables are considered local to the procedure, meaning that other event or general procedures cannot reference them. Furthermore, the memory for the variables exists only while the procedure continues executing. It is allocated only when the procedure is called; it is released when the procedure terminates.

```
psngSubtotal = Val(lblExtBurger.Caption) + _
    Val(lblExtFrenchFries.Caption) + _
    Val(lblExtSoftDrink.Caption)
```

This statement computes a subtotal by adding the extended prices for each item. These values are stored in the Caption property of each extended price label. They exist as text strings, which Visual Basic converts to numeric values using the Val function before performing the arithmetic. Again, because the clerk cannot possibly enter an invalid number, you do not need to validate these properties. Because the statement was too long to fit on a single line, you used the continuation character.

```
psngSalesTax = csngPercentTax * psngSubtotal
```

Using the subtotal from the previous statement and the form-level constant representing the sales tax rate, this statement computes the sales tax.

```
lblSalesTax.Caption = Format(psngSalesTax, "Fixed")
```

Because the form should display all results with two decimal places, this statement formats the sales tax and displays the formatted result in the label.

```
lblTotal.Caption = Format(psngSubtotal + psngSalesTax _
    + lblDelivery.Caption, "Fixed")
```

This statement computes the order total by using the local subtotal variable, the sales tax variable, and the current value of the delivery label. Rather than storing the total in a separate variable, the computation is performed inside the first argument of the Format statement. We used this approach because the value of lblTotal will never be used in another calculation and because Visual Basic lets you embed expressions inside arguments. First, psngSubtotal, psngSalesTax, and lblDelivery.Caption are added together. Next, the Format statement is called with the result and the second argument of Fixed.

The newly created general procedure should be called whenever the extended price of an item changes.

To call the general procedure to compute the sales tax and total:

1   Activate the Code window for the **lblExtBurger_Change** event procedure—make sure it is the **Change** event rather than the Click event—and enter the following statement:

```
ComputeTotals
```

Calling the ComputeTotals general procedure in the Change event for this extended price label ensures that when the extended price changes, the program updates the sales tax and total.

2   Repeat Step 1 for the **lblExtFrenchFries_Change** event procedure, selecting the object named **lblExtFrenchFries** instead of lblExtBurger and the **Change** event instead of the Click event.

3   Repeat Step 1 for the **lblExtSoftDrink_Change** event procedure, selecting the object named **lblExtSoftDrink** instead of lblExtBurger and the **Change** event instead of the Click event.

Now that you have written the code for the ComputeTotals general procedure and called this procedure whenever an extended price changes, you should examine the relationship between the events in the program. Figure 4-19 illustrates these relationships.

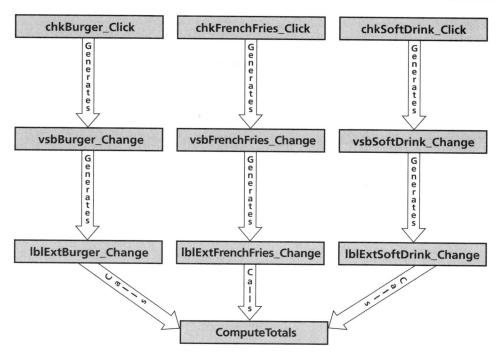

Figure 4-19: Event diagram for the cash register program

When a clerk clicks one of the check boxes, the code in the Click event procedure changes the value of the corresponding scroll bar by generating a Change event for the scroll bar. The code for the scroll bar's Change event then updates the quantity ordered, generating another Change event. The Change event for the quantity ordered, in turn, updates the extended price. The Change event for each extended price label calls the ComputeTotals general procedure, which updates the sales tax and total labels. Understanding the relationships between multiple objects and the different events that occur is critical to writing Visual Basic programs.

Now you will run the program and verify that the total is being computed correctly and recomputed when necessary.

help
· · · · · · · · · · · · · ·

▶ If the sales tax and total do not change, make sure that each Extended Price label's Change event is calling the ComputeTotals general procedure.

To test the general procedure to compute the sales tax and total:

1 Test the program. Enter an order and verify that the sales tax and total are computed correctly.

2 Click the **Zone 1** option button. Click the remaining option buttons. The total should not change because you have not written the code to add the delivery charges to the total. End the program to return to design mode.

According to the design specifications, the cash register program should update the total when the value of lblDelivery changes. Recall that the ComputeTotals general procedure sums the subtotal, sales tax, and delivery charges to get a total each time any extended price changes. To update the total when the delivery charge changes, the lblDelivery_Change event also must call the ComputeTotals general procedure.

To compute the total when the Delivery label changes:

1   Open the Code window for the **lblDelivery_Change** event procedure and enter the following statement:

```
ComputeTotals
```

2   Test the program. Enter an order, including a delivery zone. Verify that the total is updated when you click the appropriate Delivery option button. Test each option button. End the program to return to design mode.

help

. . . .

▶ If the program does not update the Total label correctly when you click one of the option buttons, end the program. Make sure you have called the ComputeTotals general procedure from the lblDelivery_Change event procedure. Repeat Step 2.

You can now program the Print and Clear command buttons.

Printing a Form Image

According to the design specifications, the cash register program should print each order to the default printer. To perform this task, you need to call the PrintForm method of the Form object.

Syntax	***formname*.PrintForm**
Dissection	■ The **PrintForm** method prints an image of a form, as it appears on the screen.
	■ If *formname* is omitted, the current form is printed. If *formname* is specified, that particular form is printed.
Code Example	`Form1.PrintForm`
Code Dissection	This PrintForm statement prints the form image of Form1 to the default printer.

To print the form image:

1   Open the Code window for the **cmdPrint_Click** event procedure, then enter the following statement in the Code window:

```
frmMasterCashRegister.PrintForm
```

2   Test the program. Enter an order in the cash register program, then click the **Print** command button. An image of the form should print to the default printer. Note that depending on the fonts supported by your printer, the numeric values may be formatted incorrectly. End the program to return to design mode.

The statement above prints the form Master Cash Register to the printer. Because this form is the current form, you also could have written this statement as follows:

```
PrintForm
```

In addition to the Print command button, another command button should reset the cash register for a new order. This command button, when clicked, must uncheck each check box, set the quantity ordered (stored in the Value property of each scroll bar) to zero (0), and set the option button corresponding to the Eat In delivery status to True so that it appears selected.

To reset the user interface:

1 Enter the following statements into the **cmdClear_Click** event procedure:

```
chkBurger.Value = vbUnchecked
chkFrenchFries.Value = vbUnchecked
chkSoftDrink.Value = vbUnchecked
optDelivery(3).Value = True
```

2 Test the program. Enter an order, then click the **Clear** command button. The delivery amount, sales tax, and total should be set to zero (0), the labels and scroll bars should become invisible, and the Eat In option button be selected. End the program to return to design mode.

The first three statements in Step 1 uncheck each of the check boxes. The statements you wrote for each check box's Click event change the value of the scroll bars and make the scroll bars and corresponding labels invisible. Because a Click event occurs whenever the value of a scroll bar changes or the user clicks the object, you do not have to clear the scroll bars explicitly. Instead, the code designed to respond to the different events performs all of the necessary tasks for you.

Because the option button corresponding to the Eat In delivery status has an Index value of 3, you set the Value property of this option button to True. This choice causes this option button to be selected. You have now completed programming the Clear command button.

S U M M A R Y

To create a check box:

- Click the **CheckBox** control on the toolbox and draw the check box. Set the appropriate properties.

To create vertical scroll bars:

- Click the **VScrollBar** control on the toolbox and draw the vertical scroll bar. Set the appropriate properties.

To create horizontal scroll bars:

- Click the **HScrollBar** control on the toolbox and draw the horizontal scroll bar. Set the appropriate properties.

To create a frame:

■ Click the **Frame** control on the toolbox and draw the frame. Set the appropriate properties.

To create an option button:

■ Click the **OptionButton** control on the toolbox and draw the option button. Set the appropriate properties.

To create a control array:

■ Click the first object in the control array. Press **Ctrl+C** to copy the OptionButton object to the Windows Clipboard. Click the container object to select it. Press **Ctrl+V** to paste the copied object into the container. Click the **Yes** button to indicate that you want to create a control array. Drag the new object to the desired location. Repeat these steps to create additional objects of the control array.

To create constants:

■ [**Public** | **Private**] **Const** *constantname* [**As** *type*] = *expression*

To reference a control array element:

■ *object*(*index*)

To print the form image:

■ *formname.***PrintForm**

Q U E S T I O N S

1. Which of the following events does the Form object support?
   a. Initialize
   b. Load
   c. Activate
   d. Unload
   e. All of the above.

2. What is the name of the method to print an image of the form?
   a. Print
   b. PrintForm
   c. FormPrint
   d. Form
   e. None of the above.

3. Write an If statement to set the Visible property of the label named **lblActive** to **True** if the check box named **chkActive** is checked; otherwise, set the Visible property to **False**.

4. Write the statement(s) to set the Value property of the check box named **ChkActive** so that the box appears checked.

5. Write the statement(s) to store the Value property of the scroll bar named **vsbCurrent** in the caption of the label named **lblCurrent**.

6. Write the statement(s) to store the value of a scroll bar's Min property in the Value property. Use the name **vsbCurrent** for the scroll bar.

7. Write the statement(s) to activate the last option button in the control array named **optCurrent** that has Index values ranging from 0 to 5.

8. Write a Select Case statement in the object's **Click** event procedure that sets the caption of the label named **lblStatus** to **Zero, One,** or **Two,** depending on which option button is selected in the **Opt3Way** control array that has Index values 0, 1, and 2.

9. Write the statement(s) to deselect the option button named **optThing(0).**

10. Write the statement(s) to select the option button named **optThing(1).**

E X E R C I S E S

1. Easy Carpet Emporium specializes in home carpeting. The company would like you to develop a carpet-selecting program that its customers can use to select the color, fabric, and pile of carpeting after looking through the samples in the store. This system will allow Easy Carpet to keep only one salesperson on the floor, who will process the order after the customer has entered the information into the computer.

   When a customer clicks the Select command button, the carpet selector program should clear any existing text from the text box, examine the option buttons that the customer has checked, and build a text string describing the carpet in a text box.

   When you finish creating a program, the program's user interface should resemble Figure 4-20.

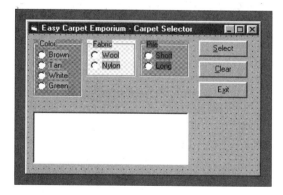

Figure 4-20: Exercise 1 – completed form

   a. Execute the program named **Chapter.04\Exercise\Sample\Ex1.exe** to review the user interface. Exit the program.
   b. Start Visual Basic, then create a new project, if necessary. Change the Name property of the form to **frmEx1.** Save the form and project using the names **Chapter.04\Exercise\frmEx1.frm** and **Chapter.04\Exercise\Ex1.vbp**, respectively.
   c. Set the Caption property as shown in Figure 4-20.
   d. Create a frame for the Color options, then set the caption to **Color** and the background color to **light blue.**

e. Create a control array of four option buttons in the Color frame. Name the option buttons **optColor**, change the background color to **light blue**, and set the Caption properties of the option buttons to **Brown, Tan, White,** and **Green,** respectively. Make sure you select the frame after you copy the first option button and before you paste each subsequent option button; otherwise, the option group will not work correctly.

f. Create a frame for the Fabric options, then set the caption to **Fabric** and the background color to **light yellow**.

g. Create a control array of two option buttons in the Fabric frame. Name the option buttons **optFabric**, change the background color to **light yellow**, and set the Caption properties of the option buttons to **Wool** and **Nylon,** respectively.

h. Create a frame for the Pile options, then set the caption to **Pile** and the background color to **orange**.

i. In the Pile frame, create a control array of two option buttons. Name the option buttons **optPile**, change the background color to **orange**, and set the Caption properties to **Short** and **Long,** respectively.

j. Create a text box to display the customer's selection, then set the name to **txtCarpet**. The text box should display multiple lines of text. Clear the initial text.

k. Create a command button at the right of the form named **cmdSelect** and set the caption as shown in Figure 4-20.

l. Create a **Clear** command button below the **Select** command button. Set the name of the object to **cmdClear** and set the caption as shown in Figure 4-20.

m. Create an **Exit** command button below the Select command button, then write the statements to exit the program.

n. In the general declarations section in the Form module, declare the variables **mintIndexColor, mintIndexFabric,** and **mintIndexPile.** They will preserve the local variable Index, which is passed to each of the option button's procedures for use in the text box. All variables should be declared before they are used in code.

discovery ▶
o. In the Code window for the **optColor_Click** event procedure, write a statement to assign the local optColor variable Index to the form-level variable mintIndexColor.

discovery ▶
p. Repeat the previous step for the other two option buttons' Click event procedures, using the appropriate variable names.

q. In the Code window for the **cmdSelect_Click** event procedure, write a statement to remove the contents of the text box.

r. Still in the cmdSelect_Click event procedure, write the following If statement to verify that one button from each button in the optColor option group is selected. When the program reaches the Exit Sub statement, the procedure should exit and no more statements in the procedure should execute.

```
If mintIndexColor = -1 Then
      MsgBox ("Select a color")
    Exit Sub
End If
```

discovery ▶
s. Write If statements to verify that selections were made for the other two option groups and to display applicable messages.

discovery ▶
t. Create a string in which you will store the carpet selection information, as shown in Figure 4-20. *Hint:* Remember to use the concatenation character to combine the statement by using option button captions and text strings that you have enclosed in quotation marks.

discovery ▶
u. Store the contents of the string (variable pstrOutput) in the text box.

discovery ▶

v. Write statements for the Clear command button that clear the option buttons by setting the index variables back to -1 (no option button selected). Also, clear the contents of the text box.

w. Test the program.

x. Correct any errors and save the project again, if necessary.

2. Nutrition Foods operates a national chain of health food stores. The company allows one group manager to be in charge of up to four franchises. Each group manager receives a commission based on the overall sales of the franchises to which he or she is assigned. Nutrition Foods would like you to develop a calculator program that computes automatically the commission for each group manager.

The calculator program should include labels to identify and display the sales for each region, the commission for that region, the total commission, and the total sales; scroll bars to enter the sales amounts in $100 increments; and a command button to exit the program.

The labels identifying and displaying the sales for each region should form a control array, as will the scroll bars for entering the sales amounts.

Each time a scroll bar's Change event occurs, the program should automatically recalculate the total commission and the total sales amounts in the appropriate labels. The manager's commission is paid at the following rates:

■ For Sales < $5000, Commission = 0
■ For Sales >= $5000 and <= $50,000, Commission = 1% of Sales
■ For Sales > $50,000 and < $250,000, Commission = 2% of Sales
■ For Sales >= $250,000, Commission = 3% of Sales

Figure 4-21 shows the completed user interface.

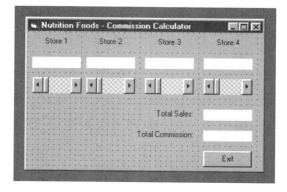

Figure 4-21: Exercise 2 – completed form

a. Execute the program named **Chapter.04\Exercise\Sample\Ex2.exe** to review the user interface. Exit the program.

b. Start Visual Basic, then create a new project, if necessary. Change the Name property of the form to **frmEx2**. Save the form and project using the names **Chapter.04\Exercise\frmEx2.frm** and **Chapter.04\Exercise\Ex2.vbp**, respectively.

c. Create four labels across the top of the form and set their captions to **Store 1, Store 2, Store 3**, and **Store 4**, respectively. Align the text in the center of the labels.

d. Create a control array of four labels below the store number labels. Set the name to **lblRegionSales**, set the background color to **white**, and remove the text from the caption.

e. Create a control array of four horizontal scroll bars below the Label control array such that the smallest value, 0, appears at the left of the scroll bar, and the largest value, 10,000, appears at the right. Name the object **hsbRegionSales**. (Sales will be entered in $100 increments; later, you will multiply the scroll bar value by 100.)

f. Create two identifying labels below the Store 3 column and set their captions to **Total Sales** and **Total Commission**, respectively.

g. Create two output labels below the Store 4 column, and set their Name properties to **lblTotalSales** and **lblTotalCommission**, respectively. Set the background color to **white**, and remove the text from their captions.

h. Create an **Exit** command button with the appropriate statements to end the program.

i. In the general declarations section of the form, create four module-level variables to store the subtotal of the sales for each region.

j. In the Code window for the **hsbRegionSales_Change** event procedure, declare a variable named **psngCommissionPercent** that will hold the percentage of sales that the group manager has earned as a commission.

k. In the Code window for the **hsbRegionSales_Change** event, type the statements that will set each **lblRegionSales** object's Caption property to the value of its corresponding scroll bar multiplied by 100 and format it as **Currency**. *Hint*: You need to use the Index argument to reference the correct label and scroll bar.

l. After you have set the caption of the lblRegionSales object, calculate **plngSubtotal** by adding the values of all scroll bars and multiplying this sum by 100. *Hint*: You need to use the Index value of each scroll bar in the control array and the Value property.

m. Write the necessary statements to calculate the commission. Using the variable plngSubtotal, test the amount against the sales amount to determine the commission rate. Store the commission rate in the variable **psngCommissionPercent**.

n. Write a statement to format **plngSubtotal** as **Currency** and place it in the Caption property of **lblTotalSales**.

o. Write a statement to calculate the commission and store the result in the Caption property of **lblTotalCommission**.

p. Test the program. Click each ScrollBar object and observe the results in the Total Commission and Total Sales labels. Verify with a calculator that the program applies the commission rules correctly. When you are satisfied that the program works correctly, click the Exit command button.

q. Correct any errors and save the project again, if necessary.

3. Williams Lumber Company sells a variety of lumber products to contractors. Most lumber, like 2 × 4's, 2 × 6's, and 2 × 8's, is sold in fixed lengths, such as 8', 10', 12', and 14', and is priced by the foot. The company would like you to create a program to determine the total feet and total cost for each type of lumber. The completed form should be divided into an input and output section using two shapes. The input area needs a label for the customer name and a corresponding text box. You should create three check boxes for the different types of lumber—2 × 4, 2 × 6, and 2 × 8. Each product is sold in four lengths—8', 10', 12', and 14'. You also need to create a check box for each length of each product. To simplify the programming process, you should use a control array for each procedure length. Thus you will have a control array of check boxes for the lengths of 2 × 4's, another for 2 × 6's, and another for 2 × 8's. Each check box will have a corresponding text box in which to specify quantity desired; these check boxes should also be created as control arrays. All of the orders are delivered to one of four areas. A delivery charge is calculated as follows, based on the number of feet delivered and the delivery zone:

■ 1 to 499 feet = $10.00
■ 500 to 999 feet = $20.00
■ 1000 to 2000 feet = $30.00
■ more than 2000 feet = $40.00

Your program should add to these feet-based charges $10.00 for Delivery Area 1, $20.00 for Delivery Area 2, $30.00 for Delivery Area 3, and $40.00 for Delivery Area 4.

In the output section of the form, you should create labels to hold the number of feet of each product and the total cost. You will need another label to hold the delivery total and the order total.

The charge for lumber is based on the number of feet ordered, as follows:

- 2 × 4 = $0.16/foot
- 2 × 6 = $0.22/foot
- 2 × 8 = $0.31/foot

You should use constants for these values.

Your program needs three command buttons: one to compute the order total based on the input, another to clear each of the input and output fields in preparation for a new order, and an Exit command button. Figure 4-22 shows the completed user interface for the program.

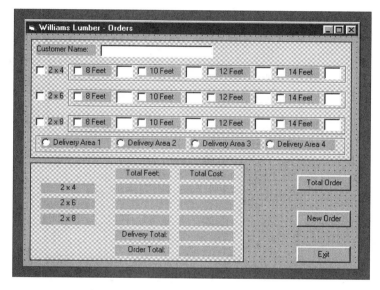

Figure 4-22: Exercise 3 – completed form

    a. Execute the program named **Chapter.04\Exercise\Sample\Ex3.exe** to review the user interface. Exit the program.

    b. Start Visual Basic, then create a new project, if necessary. Change the Name property of the form to **frmEx3**. Save the form and project using the names **Chapter.04\Exercise\frmEx3.frm** and **Chapter.04\Exercise\Ex3.vbp**, respectively.

    c. Create the objects on the form, as shown in Figure 4-22.

    d. Write the statements to store the value 0 (zero) in each of the text boxes when the form loads.

    e. Write statements for the **New Order** command button to uncheck all of the text boxes, unselect all the option buttons, set the text boxes to zero (0), and clear the output labels.

    f. Write statements for the **Total Order** command button. They should calculate the total feet of lumber ordered for each dimension (2 × 4, 2 × 6, 2 × 8); compute the total cost of each dimension; compute the delivery total based on the delivery area and the number of feet of lumber ordered; and calculate the order total.

    g. Save and test the program.

    h. Write the statements for the **Exit** command button that will end the program.

    i. Correct any errors and save the project again, if necessary.

discovery ▶ 4. As you have seen, color is an important part of a program's user interface. In previous chapters, you learned to set the foreground and background colors of various objects. There is much more to color than just setting the Foreground and Background colors of an object, however. Like a television set, a computer generates different colors based on three colors: Red, Green, and Blue. The result commonly is called RGB color. Each of the three colors can have a value between 0 and 255. The color you see on the screen consists of three values, one for each of the three RGB colors. Visual Basic supports a function called RGB that will convert RGB values into a Long Integer number representing the displayed color:

```
Dim plngColor As Long
plngColor = RGB(200,200,200)
```

In this exercise, you will create a program with scroll bars in which the user can select each of the primary colors. As the scroll bars change, the new color will be displayed in a Shape control. Figure 4-23 shows the completed form.

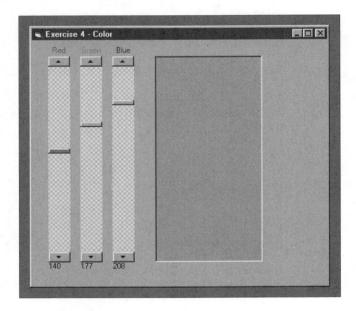

Figure 4-23: Exercise 4 – completed form

  a. Execute the program named **Chapter.04\Exercise\Sample\Ex4.exe** to review the user interface. Exit the program.
  b. Start Visual Basic, then create a new project, if necessary. Change the Name property of the form to **frmEx4**. Save the form and project using the names **Chapter.04\Exercise\frmEx4.frm** and **Chapter.04\Exercise\Ex4.vbp**, respectively.
  c. Create the scroll bars and PictureBox control on the form, as shown in Figure 4-23. Create three labels below the scroll bars to display the current value of the corresponding scroll bar.
  d. Set the properties of each scroll bar so that the values can range from 0 to 255.
  e. Create a function named **SetColor**. This function should call the RGB function. The arguments should consist of the value of each scroll bar, and the function should return a Long Integer color. This color should then be set to the **FillColor** property of the Shape control.
  f. When the value of any of the scroll bars changes, the program should call the function you just wrote to display the new color.
  g. Test the program. The number of colors supported on your computer will depend on the hardware installed and the configuration of that hardware. Some systems support 16 colors, some support 256 colors, and others support millions of colors. You can use the Display icon on the Control panel to view these settings.
  h. Correct any mistakes and save the project again, if necessary.

Creating a Program to Manage Data

Developing a Contact Management System for Atlantic Marketing

case ▶ Atlantic Marketing provides marketing services to industrial companies. Its sales staff uses a paper-based contact management system to keep track of client information. The current system consists of a paper form for each client. Each salesperson keeps these forms in a binder, sorted by the client's last name. Because Atlantic Marketing now has more than 1000 clients and approximately 2500 prospective clients, this paper-based system has become slow and burdensome.

In this chapter, you will develop a Visual Basic application together with a Microsoft Access database to manage the client information. A database simplifies the task of writing any program that needs to manage large quantities of data. Atlantic Marketing's new contact management system must be able to store each client's name, ID number, telephone number, the date added, estimated sales, and client notes—all sorted by the client's last name. The system must operate with an infinite number of clients and simplify client retrieval. A salesperson must be able to add, change, and remove clients from the database. The Access database, test data, and a form containing the necessary objects have already been created. In this chapter, you will complete the contact management system.

Previewing the Completed Program

The completed contact management system is based on the current paper form, which is shown in Figure 5-1. This form contains a client's name, ID number, telephone number, date added, and estimated annual sales revenue. A salesperson can record notes on extra lines provided on the form.

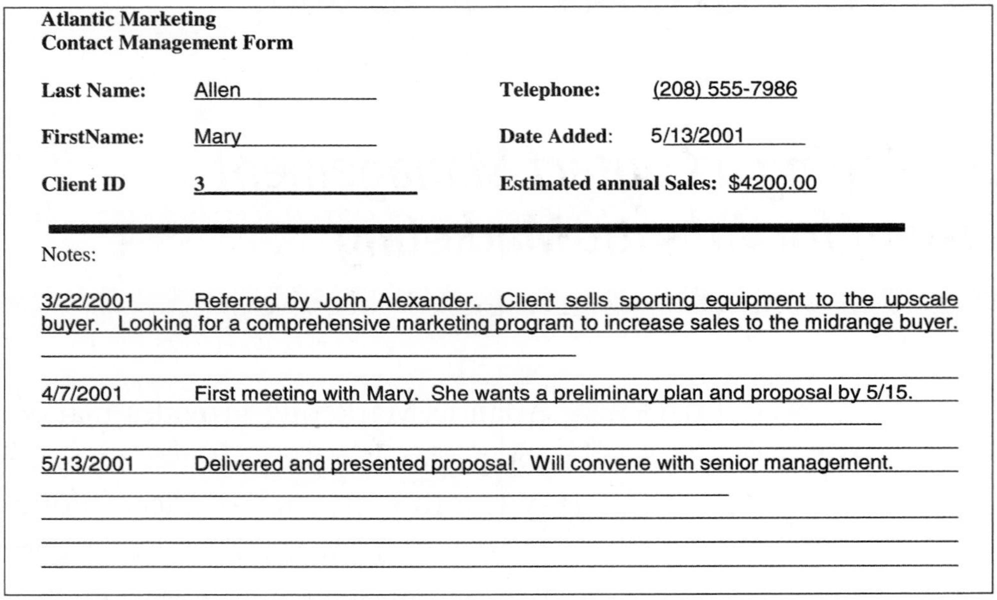

```
Atlantic Marketing
Contact Management Form

Last Name:     Allen                    Telephone:       (208) 555-7986

FirstName:     Mary                     Date Added:      5/13/2001

Client ID      3                        Estimated annual Sales: $4200.00


Notes:

3/22/2001      Referred by John Alexander.  Client sells sporting equipment to the upscale
buyer.  Looking for a comprehensive marketing program to increase sales to the midrange buyer.


4/7/2001       First meeting with Mary.  She wants a preliminary plan and proposal by 5/15.


5/13/2001      Delivered and presented proposal.  Will convene with senior management.
```

Figure 5-1: Contact management form

To preview the completed application:

1   Start Visual Basic, then open the project file named **Chapter.05\Complete\ AMCMS_C.vbp**. Set the drive designator as necessary.

2   Run the program. When the program is run, information is loaded into the text boxes on the form, as shown in Figure 5-2. Note that the program initially attempts to read the database file named A:\Chapter.05\ Complete\AMCMS.mdb. If you are using a different drive or path, you must change the DtabaseName property of the Data control to the correct drive and path.

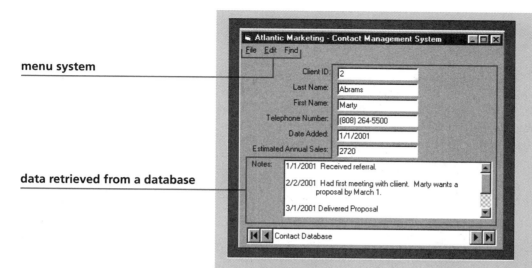

menu system

data retrieved from a database

Figure 5-2: Contact management form

The data is read into the Visual Basic program using a program called a **relational database management system,** designed to organize and present information to other programs. A database file stores this presented information. The data pertaining to a particular client appears sorted by the client's last name.

The form shown in Figure 5-2 also contains a menu. This menu works like the menu in any other Windows program.

3   Click the **File** menu and highlight the other menus. You can navigate through the menu system just as you can through the menu system of any other Windows program.

4   Click **Find,** highlight **Navigate,** then click **Last** to locate the information pertaining to the last client. When you click this menu item, the data pertaining to Mary Zorn appears.

5   End the program and exit Visual Basic.

Creating a Menu System

Adding Menus to a Program

Although the end user could use command buttons to perform program's tasks, such as printing the form, exiting the program, and adding, updating, deleting, and locating client information, this approach would require an excessive number of command buttons, causing the form to appear cluttered and disorganized. A menu system, on the other hand, offers an uncluttered and organized way to complete tasks by organizing those tasks into functional groups. For example, the Edit menu of this program includes menu items to add, change, and delete client information. All of these tasks pertain to editing. If each menu item was implemented as a separate command button, the user would need to search through numerous buttons to locate the correct one. With a menu system, the user does not have to hunt through a myriad of command buttons. Rather, the user can navigate through a menu organized by functional task.

A menu system created in Visual Basic works in the same way as the menu system in any Windows program. Each menu system consists of several parts. Figure 5-3 shows the anatomy of a menu.

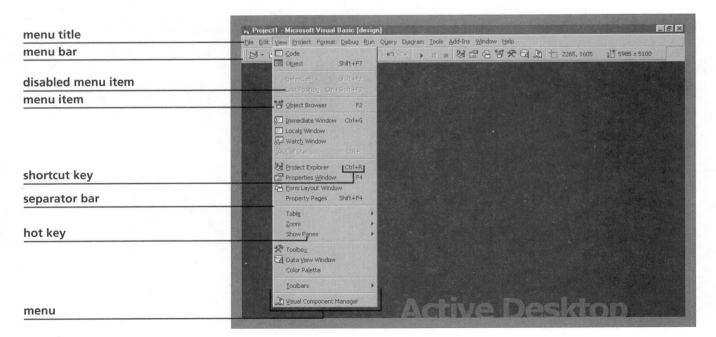

Figure 5-3: Anatomy of a menu

In Visual Basic, you use the **Menu Editor** to create a menu system that consists of a menu bar and menu items. Each menu item is similar to a command button. It has a name and a caption, and it can respond to a Click event. Both Windows and Visual Basic menus support shortcut keys and hot keys (or access keys). A **shortcut key** is a function key (such as F5) or a key combination (such as Ctrl+A or Ctrl+X) that executes a command; you can create a shortcut key for a menu item, but not for a menu title. A **hot key** is a key that you press while holding down the Alt key so as to open a menu or carry out a command. For example, Alt+F opens the File menu in most Windows applications.

Creating the Menu Titles for the Contact Management System

A menu system works much like a group of command buttons on a form. Each menu item has a Name property and a Caption property and responds to a Click event. Atlantic Marketing's program has a single form. Because a menu system is bound to a form, each form in your program can have a unique menu system associated with it.

Each item in the menu system is considered to be a distinct object. Thus each menu item is analogous to a command button. The initial step in developing a menu system is to create the menu titles that appear on the menu bar. The first letter of a menu caption should be capitalized. You can create a hot key for a menu title by inserting the ampersand character (&) in the caption immediately to the left of the character you want to use as the hot key. When the program is run, the character designated as the hot key appears underlined. The effect is the same as creating a hot key for a command button.

Menu items are objects. As such, they have the standard prefix "mnu", followed by a descriptive name for the Name property. The descriptive name should be identical to the menu item's caption, albeit with all spaces removed. Visual Basic provides the Menu Editor, a sophisticated programmer interface with which you create the menu system for a form. You use it to define the entire menu system for each form in a project. You then use the Code window to create the event procedure, just as you would create any other event procedure.

The order in which you create the menu system for a form is often a matter of personal choice. Some programmers prefer to create all of the menu titles first and then the menu items that correspond to those titles. Others may create a menu title and all of the menu items that appear beneath it before proceeding to the next menu title.

Just as a command button is drawn on a form, so too is a menu. In Visual Basic, each form can have a menu system. The menu system bound to a form is unique to that form. To create a menu system for a form, the Form window must be active to enable the Menu Editor to be activated.

Programming tip

Be careful not to specify the same hot key for two items on a menu. If you do, when the user presses the hot key, only one hot key will be recognized.

To create the menu titles:

1 Start Visual Basic, then open the project file named **Chapter.05\Startup\ AMCMS_S.vbp**. Set the drive designator as necessary.

2 Make sure that the form **frmAtlanticContact** is displayed on your screen and is active.

3 Click the **Menu Editor** button 🖹 on the toolbar to open the Menu Editor, as shown in Figure 5-4.

menu item properties

menu list box

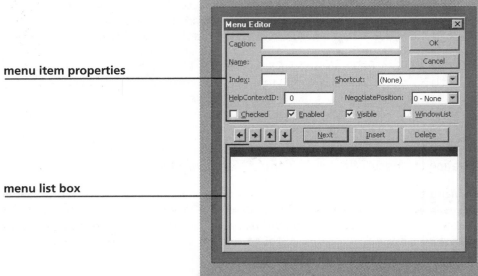

Figure 5-4: Menu Editor components

4   In the Caption text box, type **&File**. The & character to the left of the letter "F" identifies Alt+F as the hot key combination for the File menu.

5   In the Name text box, type **mnuFile**. The File menu title is added to the menu control list box. Your screen should resemble Figure 5-5.

menu title caption
menu title name

menu title appears in the menu control list box

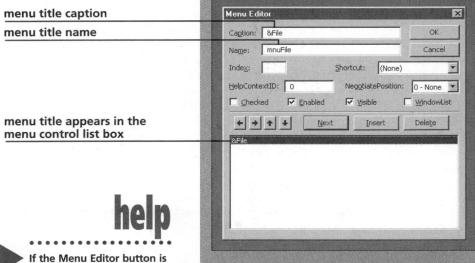

Figure 5-5: Creating the File menu title

6   Click the **Next** button.

7   To create the second menu title, type **&Edit** in the Caption text box, type **mnuEdit** in the Name text box, then click the **Next** button.

8   To create the third menu title, type **F&ind** in the Caption text box, type **mnuFind** in the Name text box. (We use Alt+I as the hot key because the File menu has already claimed Alt+F.)

help
● ● ● ● ● ● ● ● ● ● ● ● ● ● ● ● ●

If the Menu Editor button is disabled, make sure the form is the active window, then repeat Step 3. Because menus are bound to a form, the desired form must be active before you can open the Menu Editor, which is available only at design time. Make sure the Visual Basic title bar says [design].

You have created the three menu titles for the contact management program. Your next task is to add the menu items for each menu title.

Creating Menu Items

GUI tip

• • • • • • • • • • • • • • • •

▶ You should use accepted style guidelines to create a menu system that has the look and feel of menu systems used in other Windows programs. For instance, a menu item's caption should be short enough to appear on one line, but it can contain multiple words to clearly convey its purpose. When menu items contain multiple words, the first letter of each word should be capitalized and each word should be separated by a space. If a menu item displays a dialog or requires the user to complete other information, the item's name should be followed by an ellipsis (...).

Now you must create the menus and the menu items that appear when the user clicks a menu title. When clicked, each menu item generates a Click event and Visual Basic calls the corresponding Click event procedure. The effect is the same as clicking a command button to generate a Click event. Although the menu titles generate a Click event, you do not have to write any code to display the menu when the user clicks a menu title; Visual Basic performs this task for you.

You can create a hot key for a menu item by embedding the & character in the Caption property, as you did for the menu titles. The name of a menu item also begins with the prefix "mnu" and includes the title of the menu on which it appears. For example, the Print menu item on the File menu has the name "mnuFilePrint".

Now you will create the menu items for the File and Edit menus.

To create menu items:

1 In the menu control list box, click **&Edit** to select the Edit menu, then click the **Insert** button to insert a blank line before the Edit menu title.

2 Type **&Print** in the Caption text box. This action sets the hot key combination to Alt+P for the Print menu item. Type **mnuFilePrint** in the Name text box.

3 Click the **right arrow** button ⬛ to change the indent level of the menu item. The Print menu item appears on the File menu; the indented menu item appears with four leading dots, as shown in Figure 5-6.

Print menu item (indented)

Figure 5-6: Adding a menu item

4 Click the **Next** button, then click the **Insert** button to insert another new menu item before the Edit menu title.

5 Repeat Steps 2 and 3, using the caption **E&xit** and the name **mnuFileExit**. The hot key for the Exit menu item is Alt+X. Windows programs typically use the letter X rather than the letter E for an Exit menu item.

6 Indent the **Exit** menu item to the same level as the Print menu item. To indent the menu item, select it, then click the **right arrow**.

7 Click the **Next** button until the Find menu title becomes highlighted, then click the **Insert** button to insert a new menu item before the Find menu title.

8 Repeat Steps 2, 3, and 7 using the following captions and names. Make sure that the following menu items appear indented under the Edit menu.

Caption	Name
&Add	mnuEditAdd
&Edit Record	mnuEditRecord
&Update	mnuEditUpdate
&Delete	mnuEditDelete
&Refresh	mnuEditRefresh

The Menu Editor should look like Figure 5-7.

File menu completed

Edit menu completed

Figure 5-7: File and Edit menus completed

The name mnuEditRecord violates the rule of using the menu title caption followed by the menu item caption for the name. If you followed this rule, however, the name would be mnuEditEditRecord—a long and confusing choice. In cases where the menu's combined captions cause the name to appear misleading or too long, change the name or abbreviate it as necessary.

A menu can be initially enabled or disabled. To disable a menu item, you remove the check mark from the Enabled check box in the menu editor. In this program, the Update menu item on the Edit menu should be initially disabled.

To disable a menu item:
1   Verify that the Menu Editor is active.
2   Select the **Update** menu item.
3   Click the **Enabled** check box to initially disable the menu.

A menu system supports other characteristics that can improve its appearance and make it more efficient for the user. For example, you can draw separator bars and create shortcut keys.

Creating Submenus with Separator Bars and Shortcut Keys

You can visually group menu items using a separator bar. A **separator bar** is a horizontal line that visually separates menu items. Like all components of a menu, it must have a unique name or be a member of a control array. You create a separator bar by setting a menu item's Caption property to a hyphen (-).

Shortcut keys are particularly helpful when menu items themselves have submenus. A **submenu** is a menu that appears when the user selects a menu title or menu item. You can create a submenu by indenting the submenu items another level. The Find menu, for example, includes the Navigate menu item, which displays a submenu containing the menu items First, Last, Previous, and Next. The Find menu also contains a menu item that searches for a client's last name. A separator bar divides the Navigate menu items from the Last Name menu items because they have different purposes. The Last Name menu item includes a shortcut key definition, enabling users to choose the item by using either the keyboard or the mouse. A shortcut key is appropriate here, because searching for a last name will be a commonly executed command. Using a shortcut key eliminates the user's transition from the mouse to the keyboard. To specify the shortcut key for a menu item, you select it from the Shortcut list box in the Menu Editor. You cannot create shortcut keys that are not listed in the Shortcut list box.

GUI tip

You should create shortcut keys for the more frequently used menu items because they minimize the number of keystrokes needed to activate a menu item by using a hot key. By allowing both mouse and keyboard input for the menus, the interface will appeal to the broadest number of users. When selecting characters for a shortcut key, use the same characters as are used in other common programs for similar tasks; using the first character of the menu caption is also a common choice. For example, many programs employ Ctrl+P as the shortcut key for printing.

To create the menu item and submenu for the Find menu:
1   In the menu control list box, click the blank line below the Find menu title.
2   Type **&Navigate** in the Caption text box, then type **mnuFindNavigate** in the Name text box.
3   Click the **right arrow** button ➡ to indent the Navigate menu.
4   Click the **Next** button. The next line in the menu control list box is automatically indented, and the menu item appears on the Find menu.
5   Create the separator bar by setting the caption to a hyphen (-) and the name to **mnuFindSep**.
6   Click the **Next** button.
7   Type **&Last Name...** in the Caption text box, then type **mnuFindLastName**.
8   Click the **Shortcut** list arrow, then select **Ctrl+A**. The menu control list box for the Last Name item now contains the shortcut key for the last name.

The final step in developing the menu system is to create the menu items that appear on the screen when the user selects the Navigate submenu item. These items need to appear under the Navigate submenu item in the menu control list box. They appear indented with eight dots in the Menu Editor.

To create menu items on the submenu:

1   Enter the following menu items such that they appear below the **Navigate** menu item. Click the **right arrow** button ➡ to indent each item. These menu items should appear with eight leading dots.

Caption	Name	Shortcut
&First	mnuFindNavigateFirst	Ctrl+F
&Last	mnuFindNavigateLast	Ctrl+L
&Previous	mnuFindNavigatePrevious	Ctrl+P
&Next	mnuFindNavigateNext	Ctrl+N

Your screen should look like Figure 5-8.

Figure 5-8: Completed menu

The Find menu is complete. Later, you will write the code for the Click event procedure corresponding to each menu item. For now, you will check the accuracy of the menu system. If you forgot to indent a menu item, it might appear on the menu bar rather than within the menu. You should also verify that the hot keys and shortcut keys appear. You can view all of the menu items, hot keys, and shortcut keys at design time, so you do not have to run the program.

To view the menu system:

1   Click the **OK** button to close the Menu Editor.

shortcut keys

help

▶ If you receive an error message indicating that a menu item must have a name, you may have neglected to assign a menu name to a particular menu title or menu item. Click the OK button to close the message box. The menu item in question will be highlighted, and you can enter a valid name in the Name text box.

If you receive the error message "Menu control array must have an index," you have assigned the same name to two menu titles or menu items. Like other objects you created in previous chapters, menu items can be created as a control array, with each sharing the same event procedures. To create a control array of menu items, you create menu items with the same name and assign an index to each menu using the Index text box in the Menu Editor. Visual Basic does not create a control array of menu items automatically.

2 Save the project.

3 Click the **File** menu on the form. The menu items are displayed, as shown in Figure 5-9.

File menu ————————————

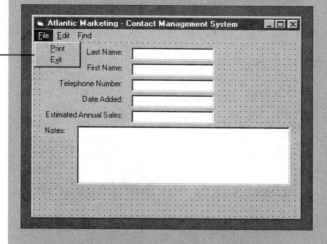

Figure 5-9: File menu displayed

4 Click or highlight the **Edit** menu on the form. The menu items are displayed, as shown in Figure 5-10. Note that the Update menu item is disabled.

Edit menu ————————————

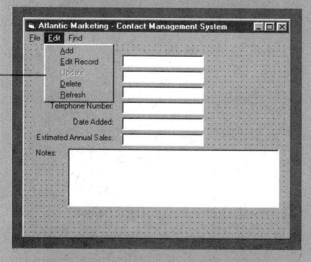

Figure 5-10: Edit menu displayed

5 Click or highlight the **Find** menu on the form, then click or highlight the **Navigate** submenu to display its menu items. The menu items are displayed, as shown in Figure 5-11.

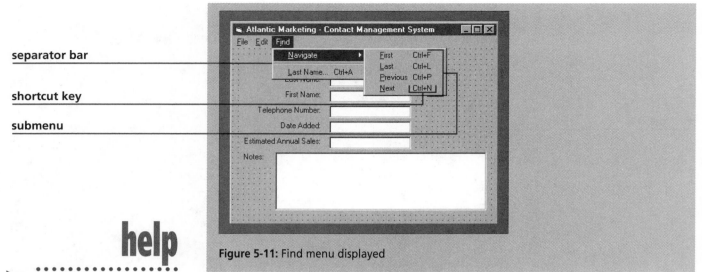

separator bar

shortcut key

submenu

Figure 5-11: Find menu displayed

help

. . . .

▶ If a menu title or menu item does not appear on the menu, open the Menu Editor and verify that the Visible check box for the item is checked. If a check mark appears to the left of a menu item, open the Menu Editor; if the Checked check box is selected, click it to remove the check mark. If a menu title or menu item is dimmed, open the Menu Editor and verify that the Enabled check box for the item is checked.

Programming

tip

. . . .

▶ You can quickly open the Code window to a menu item's Click event procedure by clicking the menu and then the desired menu item at design time, rather than locating the object and its Click event procedure in the Code window.

Although the menus for the program now exist, they will do nothing at this point—you have not yet written the code for each menu item's Click event procedure.

Creating an Event Procedure for a Menu Item

The first menu item you will program is the Exit menu item on the File menu. The mnuFileExit object's Click event ends the program. You write the code for an Exit menu item's Click event procedure in the same way you would for an Exit command button's Click event procedure. That is, you can locate the object and event procedure in the Code window and enter the statements that end the program.

To write the code for the Exit menu item:

1 Click the **File** menu title. The menu items appear.

2 Click the **Exit** menu item. The Code window automatically displays the **mnuFileExit_Click** event procedure.

3 Enter the following statement into the **mnuFileExit_Click** event procedure:

```
Unload frmAtlanticContact
```

The Exit menu item is operational. Now you can write the code to print the form using the PrintForm method, just as you did in Chapter 4.

To write the code for the Print menu item:

1 In the Code window, display the **mnuFilePrint_Click** event procedure, then enter the **PrintForm** statement into the event procedure:

```
PrintForm
```

2 Close the Code window.

3 Test the program. Click **File**, then click **Print** to print the form to the printer. Click **File**, then click **Exit** to end the program.

Again, such regular testing of your work will help you locate and correct errors more quickly.

The menu system and the code for each item on the File menu are complete. The menu system provides a better user interface than would the creation of 12 command buttons, which would make the screen confusing and cluttered. As you complete the different components of the program, you will add the necessary code to the Click event procedure that corresponds to each menu item.

Q U E S T I O N S

1. A hot key for a menu is created using the _____ character.
   a. –
   b. &
   c. *
   d. $
   e. @

2. Which of the following is true about menu captions?
   a. They can contain spaces.
   b. They cannot contain spaces.
   c. Each word of a menu caption is capitalized.
   d. Both a and c.
   e. Both b and c.

3. Which of the following is true about menu names?
   a. They cannot contain spaces.
   b. They can contain spaces.
   c. The & character specifies the hot key.
   d. Both a and b.
   e. Both a and c.

4. What character is used to create a separator bar?
   a. –
   b. &
   c. *
   d. !
   e. @

5. What is the standard prefix for a menu name?
   a. meu
   b. men
   c. menu
   d. mnu
   e. None of the above.

6. To create a submenu, you _____.
   a. use the SubMenu command.
   b. respond to the SubClick event procedure.
   c. indent the menu.
   d. All of the above.
   e. None of the above.

7. A menu item responds to the _____ event procedure.
   a. ItemClick
   b. Menu_Click
   c. DoubleClick
   d. Click
   e. None of the above.

8. Which of the following statements is true about menus and forms?
   a. A menu system is bound to a specific form.
   b. Two or more forms can share the same menu system.
   c. A project can have only one menu system.
   d. Both a and b.
   e. Both a and c.

9. If a menu item contains a submenu, the caption should contain _____.
   a. the characters ->
   b. an ellipsis (…)
   c. the keyword "More"
   d. Any of the above.
   e. None of the above.

10. To activate the Menu Editor, which of the following must be true?
    a. The Code window must be open.
    b. The Form window must be open.
    c. The Properties window for the form must be open.
    d. All of the above.
    e. None of the above.

Working with a Database

Understanding How Visual Basic Uses a Database

Before you can complete Atlantic Marketing's program, you need to understand what a database is and how Visual Basic objects interact with a database. If you have never created or used a database, refer to "Appendix C" of this book; it explains how to create a database using Microsoft Access.

A **database** is a set of information related to a particular topic or purpose. This information is stored inside a data structure called a table. Most databases contain several tables. A **table** consists of rows and columns. Each column defines a name for, and characteristics of, the stored information. The columns in a table are called **fields**. The Atlantic Marketing database includes seven fields in the tblContact table: Client ID, Last Name, First Name, Telephone Number, Date Added, Estimated Sales, and Notes.

The information is stored in the rows of the table, which are called **records**. So that you can test the program, six records are provided for use as test data. Figure 5-12 shows the six rows (records) and seven column names (fields) in the tblContact table. Field names have the prefix "fld".

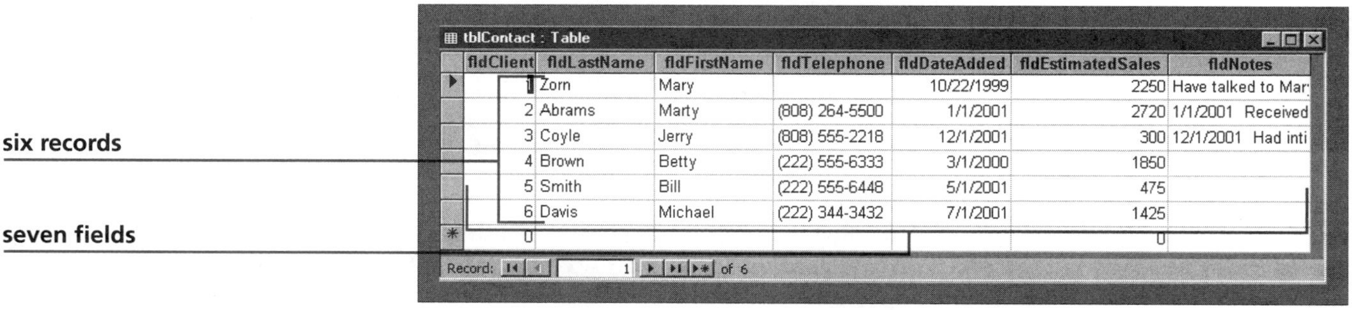

six records

seven fields

fldClient	fldLastName	fldFirstName	fldTelephone	fldDateAdded	fldEstimatedSales	fldNotes
1	Zorn	Mary		10/22/1999	2250	Have talked to Mar
2	Abrams	Marty	(808) 264-5500	1/1/2001	2720	1/1/2001 Received
3	Coyle	Jerry	(808) 555-2218	12/1/2001	300	12/1/2001 Had inti
4	Brown	Betty	(222) 555-6333	3/1/2000	1850	
5	Smith	Bill	(222) 555-6448	5/1/2001	475	
6	Davis	Michael	(222) 344-3432	7/1/2001	1425	

Record: 1 of 6

Figure 5-12: Database fields and records

In a modern database, or **database management system (DBMS)**, multiple users can access the information contained in a database simultaneously. If two users add records at the same time, the DBMS keeps track of each request without causing an error or losing either user's information. In Visual Basic and Windows, you use the **Microsoft Jet database engine** as the DBMS to retrieve data from, and store data to, an Access database. A database can organize and store information so that it can be viewed and retrieved based on the needs of a particular user. For example, the contact management system contains only part of the data that

Atlantic Marketing employees must manage. Another component of the company's data comprises its sales system. If the contact management system could access information about sales accounts, a salesperson could view an existing client's sales history before talking with him or her.

Most databases in use today are **relational**; that is, they can relate information contained in several tables in different ways. A **relational database management system** (**RDBMS**) allows you to define the relationships between the different pieces of information in these tables. For example, in Atlantic Marketing's database, information in the tblContact table is related to the information in the tblSales table by using a query. A **query** is an instruction to a database to return a set of records from one or more tables and to do so in a specific order. An RDBMS has become an increasingly popular option for managing large volumes of data as software technology has evolved and computer hardware has become fast enough to run this complex software effectively.

Using the Data Control to Open a Database

Before a Visual Basic program can communicate with a database, it must make a connection to the database. Two ways exist to connect a Visual Basic program to a database: writing Visual Basic statements to access a database, and using the Data control in the toolbox.

Syntax	Data
Definition	The Data control enables you to move from record to record and to display information inside other control instances created on a form. By setting the properties of the Data control, you can use its buttons to locate different records without writing any code. You cannot use the Data control to create new databases, only to connect to existing ones. You can create your own databases using Microsoft Access, as described in "Appendix C." The standard prefix for a Data control is "dat".
Properties	■ Like a label, the Data control supports the **Caption** property. This property defines the text displayed inside the Data control. ■ The **Connect** property provides information about the type of database that will be used. The Data control can work with Access, dBASE, FoxPro, and Paradox databases by using the Connect property. By default, the Connect property is set to Access. ■ The **DatabaseName** property identifies the name and location (folder) of the database file. Microsoft Access database files have the extension ".mdb". ■ As you add and edit records, you set a property that contains the status of the current record. The **EditMode** property is supported by the Recordset object and can assume one of three values. The constant dbEditNone indicates that no editing operation is in progress. The constant dbEditInProgress indicates that the Edit method has been called and that the current record occupies the copy buffer. The constant dbEditAdd indicates that the AddNew method has been called and that the current record in the copy buffer is a new record that has not been saved to the database table or query. ■ The **RecordSource** property identifies the table or query that you want to use in the database.

■ The **RecordsetType** property determines which operations can be performed on the table or query that you identified when you set the RecordSource property. By default, the RecordsetType property is set to 1 - Dynaset. A **dynaset** is a dynamic view of the information contained in a database table or query. You can create dynasets to view and change the contents of rows from one or more tables, depending on the needs of your program. The other RecordsetType property values are 0 - Table and 2 - Snapshot.

You need to create an instance of the Data control to establish a connection with the Atlantic Marketing database.

To create the Data control:

1   Click the **Data** control 🖳 on the toolbox and draw an instance of it across the bottom of the form, as shown in Figure 5-13.

2   Set the Name property of the Data control to **datContact** and the Caption property to **Contact Database**. The form should resemble Figure 5-13.

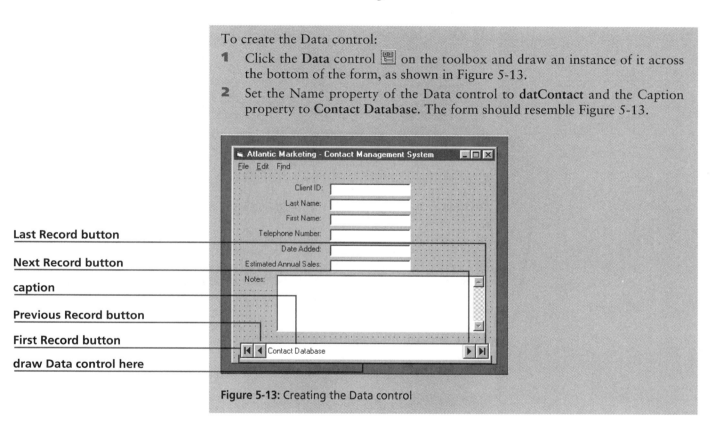

Last Record button

Next Record button

caption

Previous Record button

First Record button

draw Data control here

Figure 5-13: Creating the Data control

The database, which has already been created for you, contains the tables and other information needed to complete the program. Although the form now includes an instance of the Data control, it cannot store or display the information in the existing database until you set the necessary properties to connect the Data control to the database.

When you set these properties, the Data control creates the necessary objects to access a table or query in the database at run time. The order in which you set the Data control properties is important. You must select the database (set the DatabaseName property) before you select the table (set the RecordSource property). Then, when you set the RecordSource property, Visual Basic connects to the database and shows a list of its available tables. The file containing the contact management test database is named Chapter.05\Startup\AMCMS.mdb.

To connect the Data control to the Access database:

1   In the Properties window for the Data control you just created, make sure that the value of the Connect property is **Access**.

2   Click the Value column of the **DatabaseName** property.

3   Click the **Properties** button [...] and choose the file **Chapter.05\Startup\ AMCMS.mdb**. Change the drive designator as necessary.

The Properties window should look like Figure 5-14.

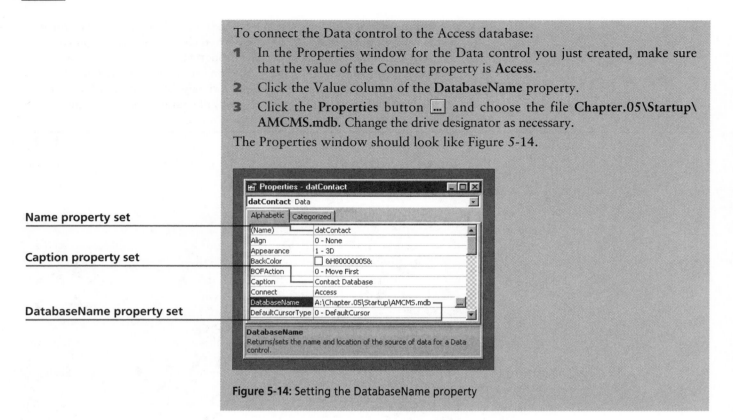

Name property set

Caption property set

DatabaseName property set

Figure 5-14: Setting the DatabaseName property

You have now identified the database that you want to use. The Data control can establish a connection with this database for the contact management system. Next, you need to identify which database table or query you want. To do so, you set the RecordSource property to a table or query that exists in the database. The Properties window displays a list of available tables or queries in the database from which you can select. The standard prefix for a table object is "tbl", and the standard prefix for a query is "qry". The query for the contact management system is named qryContact.

help

● ● ● ● ● ● ● ● ● ● ● ● ● ● ● ●

▶ If no information appears when you click the Properties button ▼ for the RecordSource property, then you have not selected the database correctly. Verify that the DatabaseName property is set to the proper path and file name, Chapter.05\ Startup\AMCMS.mdb, and that the file exists on your Student Disk. Then repeat Step 1.

To view the tables and queries in the database:

1   Click the Value column of the **RecordSource** property, then click the **Properties** button ▼ to display the list of tables and queries.

2   Click **qryContact** to select the query. Make sure that the RecordsetType property is set to **1 - Dynaset**, the default setting. The Properties window should look like Figure 5-15.

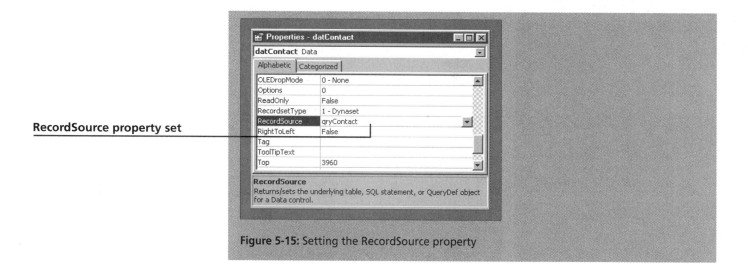

RecordSource property set

Figure 5-15: Setting the RecordSource property

The Recordset Object

When you set the properties of the Data control, the control uses that information to create a Recordset object. A reference to this object is stored in the Recordset property of the Data control when the program is run. Because the Data control sets the Recordset property only at run time, this property does not appear in the Properties window. You use the Recordset object at run time to locate different records and to add, change, and delete records.

A Recordset object provides a view of a table or query stored in the database. When you examine records stored in the Recordset object, only one record can be active at a time. The **current record pointer** indicates the active record in a Recordset object. You do not access the current record pointer explicitly. Rather, you move the current record pointer indirectly using the Recordset object's methods.

The Recordset object is not a visible object. That is, you do not create an instance of it with the toolbox. Instead, it is referenced by using code. Furthermore, the Recordset object supports a vast set of properties and methods but does not respond to any events.

Syntax	Recordset
Definition	A **Recordset** object provides a view of a table or query stored in the database. It does not respond to any events. The standard prefix for a Recordset object is "rst".
Properties	■ When the current record pointer is positioned just before the first record, the **BOF** property is True, and the recordset is at the beginning of the file. Otherwise, BOF is False.
	■ When the pointer is positioned immediately after the last record, the **EOF** property is True, and the recordset is at the end of the file. Otherwise, EOF is False.
	■ Whenever the program calls the FindFirst method, the method sets the **NoMatch** property of the Recordset object. If one or more records are found, the NoMatch property is set to False. If no record is found, then the NoMatch property is set to True.

Methods

- The **MoveFirst** method locates the first record in the Recordset object.

- The **MoveLast** method locates the last record in the Recordset object.

- The **MoveNext** method locates the next record in the Recordset object.

- The **MovePrevious** method locates the previous record in the Recordset object.

The buttons on the Data control call different procedures that act on the Recordset object. These procedures, which are considered methods, work the same way as the methods defined in the previous chapters. Figure 5-16 illustrates how the Data control creates a Recordset object and shows some of the object's properties and methods.

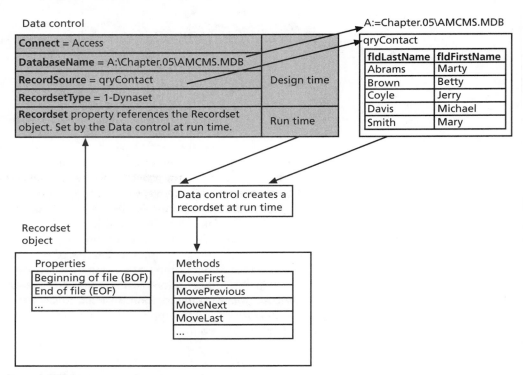

Figure 5-16: Recordset object

By setting the Connect, DatabaseName, RecordSource, and RecordsetType properties at design time, the Data control can retrieve information from the query named qryContact at run time. It performs this operation by creating an instance of the Recordset object and storing a reference to the object in the Recordset property of the Data control. Once the Data control has created the Recordset object, you can locate records and perform other operations.

Objects and Their Methods

An object is made up of properties, events, and methods. The methods of an object contain code that is built inside the object to accomplish a particular task. In this way, methods supply functionality to an object. Consider a television's remote control as an object. The remote control can carry out a specific set of methods, or actions, such as changing a channel or adjusting the volume. You could use the ChannelUp and ChannelDown methods to set the CurrentChannel property. Likewise, certain methods apply to the Recordset object.

The Data control simplifies the process of working with a Recordset object by providing buttons that navigate through the records in the Recordset object without explicitly calling methods. This control, however, has some limitations. For example, it does not support a method to remove a record from a Recordset object. To perform this operation, you need to call a method of the underlying Recordset object (stored in the Recordset property of the Data control).

To learn more about the methods applicable to the Recordset object, look at the Help library. Using the Index tab, review the information on recordsets, then Recordset Object, then Recordsets Collection Summary (DAO). Print the information for future reference.

A Recordset object is considered a Data Access Object. **Data Access Objects (DAO)** enable you to use a programming language to access and manipulate data in databases, as well as to manage databases, their objects, and their structures.

Using the Data control, you can click buttons located on a control instance to navigate through records without writing any code. In essence, the Data control calls the methods pertaining to the recordset for you. The user can therefore use the menu items you created earlier in this chapter to move forward and backward through the client list. This approach requires the fields to be bound to the text boxes.

Using Bound Controls

In Atlantic Marketing's program, each field in the recordset needs to be displayed in the corresponding TextBox object already created on the form. You do not need to write any code to accomplish the task. Instead, you simply set some additional properties for each TextBox object so that each object displays information from the database query.

The TextBox objects on the form are the same as those you created in previous chapters. The Text properties of these TextBox objects, however, are not explicitly set in the Properties window or by the code you write in event procedures. Rather, each TextBox control is bound to a specific field in a Recordset object via the Data control. A **bound control** (also known as a **data-aware control**) displays the changes in the current record of the Recordset object on the form. When a text box is bound to a Data control, changes in the current record of the Recordset object are reflected in the TextBox object. Each bound TextBox object corresponds to a field in the Recordset object. Many different controls that can hold text (such as Label and ListBox controls) and graphics (such as ImageBox and PictureBox controls) can be bound to a field in a Recordset object.

The process of binding a control, such a a text box, to an instance of the Data control requires you to set properties that you have not used as yet. These properties are common to all bound controls. When you create a bound control such as a text box, these properties are initially blank; you must set them explicitly.

- The **DataSource** property of a bound control is set to an instance of a Data control drawn on the same form. To see the list of available choices for this property, you click its Properties button. In the contact management program, this property is set to datContact (the name you assigned to the Data control). If a form interacts with multiple tables or queries, you can create multiple Data control instances, then select the desired Data control.
- The **DataField** property is set to a field in the table or query. When you select a field with the Properties button, Visual Basic looks in the database table or query (which you specified with the DataSource property) to see which fields are available.

Figure 5-17 shows the properties used to bind controls to interact with fields in a Recordset object.

Programming

tip

• • • • • • • • • • • • • • •

When you create instances of bound controls and set their properties at design time, you should set the properties of the Data control instance first. If the Data control instance does not reference an existing table or query in a database, the Properties windows of the bound TextBox objects will not display the table names and field names.

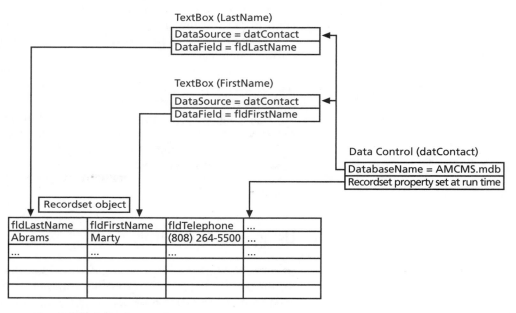

Figure 5-17: Bound controls

You will set the DataSource property for all TextBox objects on the form as a group because they all must be set to datContact, the only Data control on the form. You will then set the DataField property for each TextBox object to its corresponding field in the database table. At run time, each text box interacts with a field in the Recordset object that was created by the Data control.

To set the properties for the TextBox objects:

1 Press and hold down the **Shift** key, then click all seven **TextBox** objects to select them. The form should look like Figure 5-18.

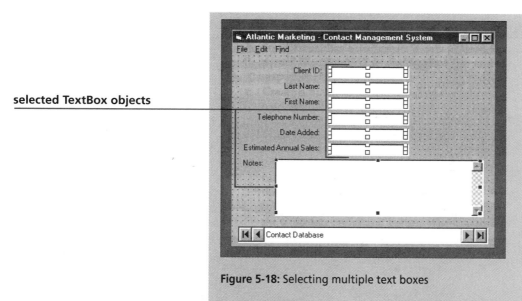

Figure 5-18: Selecting multiple text boxes

selected TextBox objects

2 In the Properties window, set the DataSource property to **datContact**, which is the name of the Data control. It is the only option available because the form includes only one Data control. The Properties window should look like Figure 5-19.

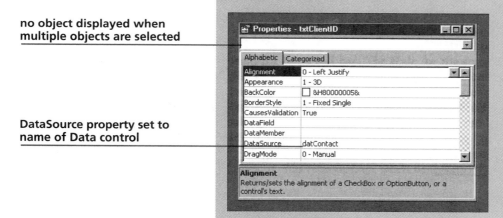

no object displayed when
multiple objects are selected

DataSource property set to
name of Data control

Figure 5-19: Setting the DataSource property

3 Click any blank area of the form to deactivate the selected objects.

4 Click the text box for **Client ID**.

5 Click the Value column for the DataField property, then click the **Properties** button ▼ for the DataField property. The Properties window should look like Figure 5-20.

click the Properties button to
see the fields in the table

click fldClientID

available fields shown
in list box

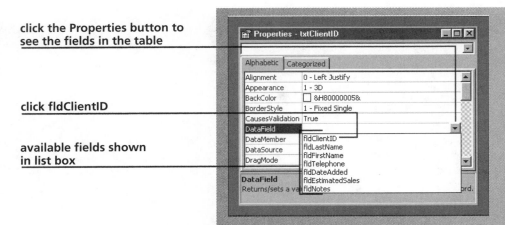

Figure 5-20: Setting the DataField property

help

● ● ● ● ● ● ● ● ● ● ● ● ● ● ● ●

If clicking the Properties
button does not display
the fields in the database
or you get an error mes-
sage, the DataSource
property has been set
incorrectly. It should be
set to datContact. In addition, you should verify
that the DatabaseName
property of the Data con-
trol is set to the file
AMCMS.mdb in the
Chapter.05\Startup folder
and that the database
exists in that folder.

6 In the displayed list of fields, click **fldClientID**.

The text box txtClientID is now bound to the field fldClientID in the query qryContact. When you run the program, the information contained in this record will appear in the text box.

7 Repeat Steps 4 through 6, setting the DataField property as follows:

Object	Property
txtLastName	fldLastName
txtFirstName	fldFirstName
txtTelephone	fldTelephone
txtDateAdded	fldDateAdded
txtEstimatedSales	fldEstimatedSales

The form contains a text box for notes and the table includes a Notes field, which holds notes that the salesperson writes about interactions with the client. You need to modify the properties for the txtNotes object so that it will display several lines of text from the Notes field of the database.

8 For the **txtNotes** object, set the MultiLine property to **True**, the ScrollBars property to **2 - Vertical**, and the DataField property to **fldNotes**.

The program now displays the appropriate information from a database record in the text boxes when you run it. You can move from record to record by using the buttons on the Data control. Now is a good time to save the project, verify that the program works correctly, and correct any errors. When the database and the table containing the clients were designed, the query was developed in such a manner that the records would appear sorted by last name. When you run the program, the records display alphabetically by last name.

To test the program:

1 Run the program. The first record in the Recordset object should be displayed, as shown in Figure 5-21.

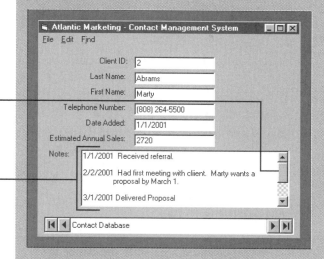

scroll bar displayed

**information from
Notes field displayed
in text box**

Figure 5-21: Form with multiline text box

![help]

▶ If you cannot scroll through the Notes field information, you probably neglected to set the MultiLine property to True. Stop the program, set the MultiLine property for the Notes text box to True, then repeat Steps 1 and 2.

The record for Marty Abrams appears on the screen because Abrams is the first surname alphabetically in the database. In Figure 5-21, the date shown is 1/1/2001. Depending upon the short date format setting on your computer, this date may appear as 1/1/01.

2 Drag the scroll box in the Notes text box to the bottom of the scroll bar. The rest of the information from the Notes field should appear.

3 Click the **Next Record** button ▶ in the Data control. The form should display the information for Betty Brown.

4 Click the **Previous Record** button ◀ in the Data control. The form should display the information for Marty Abrams again.

5 Click the **Last Record** button ▶| in the Data control. The form should display the information for Mary Zorn.

6 Click the **First Record** button |◀ in the Data control. The form should display the information for Marty Abrams again. End the program to return to design mode.

The text boxes now connect to the database query via the Data control and display the client ID, name, telephone number, date added, estimated annual sales information, and notes from the Recordset object in the text boxes.

In addition to using the buttons on the Data control, you can call the methods of the Recordset object explicitly. These methods operate on data in the database table or query. For example, you can use the MoveFirst, MoveLast, MoveNext, and MovePrevious methods to locate records in the table.

The Data control does not explicitly support these four methods. Rather, the Recordset object supports them. The Recordset property of the Data control stores a reference to the Recordset object at run time. When you call an object's methods, you place a period (.) between the object and method names. The following statement calls the MoveNext method of the Recordset object by using the Data control's Recordset property to locate the next record in the recordset:

```
datContact.Recordset.MoveNext
```

The first part of the statement (datContact.Recordset) refers to the Recordset property of the Data control. The final part of the statement refers to the MoveNext method pertaining to the Recordset object. Although this statement is valid, if you will refer to this Recordset object more than once in your program, you can save a considerable amount of typing by creating an object variable to store the reference. To create an object variable, you use the same declaration statements you have used in earlier chapters.

Syntax	[**Private** I **Dim**] *VariableName* **As** [**New**] *Object*
Dissection	■ *VariableName* specifies the name of the object variable and must follow the standard naming conventions for variables. The Private and Dim keywords are used in the same way as for ordinary variables. If you use the Dim keyword inside a procedure, then the variable remains local to the procedure. If you use the Private or Dim keyword in the general declarations section of a module, then the variable is available to the entire module. ■ You can use the optional **New** keyword to create new objects. ■ *Object* is a placeholder for the kind of object you want to reference.
Code Example	`Private mrstContact As Recordset`
Code Dissection	The previous statement declares an object variable that can be used to refer to an instance of a Recordset object.

In this section, you will use the object variable to reference an existing object, the Recordset object, so you will not need the New keyword. An object variable has different characteristics than an ordinary variable. When you declare a variable using the Visual Basic intrinsic data types (Integer, Long, and so on), Visual Basic allocates memory to store the data itself. That is, it allocates memory to store the actual information when the variable is declared.

When you declare an object variable, the variable itself does not store any data. Rather, the object variable in the following statements contains a memory address, which in turn holds the data:

```
Private mrstContact As Recordset
mrstContact.MoveFirst
```

These statements produce an error because the object variable named mrstContact does not yet refer to a valid Recordset object. After you declare an object variable, the variable must be set to point to an existing object or to create a new instance of an object. You accomplish this task with the Set statement.

Syntax	Set *VariableName* = [**New**] *ObjectExpression* | **Nothing**
Dissection	■ The *VariableName* can be any valid object variable name. ■ The optional **New** keyword creates a new instance of the object. ■ The optional *ObjectExpression* can consist of any instance of an object, such as a recordset, a form, or an instance of a control. When the New keyword is absent, the instance of the object must already exist. ■ The optional **Nothing** keyword disassociates an object variable from an actual object. When you assign Nothing to an object variable, the variable no longer refers to an actual object. If multiple object variables reference the same object, setting all of them to Nothing frees the memory and system resources used by the object.
Code Example	```Private mrstContact As Recordset``` ```Set mrstContact = datContact.Recordset```
Code Dissection	The previous statements assume that datContact is an existing instance of a Data control. The Set statement assigns a reference to the recordset stored in the Data control to the object variable mrstContact.

The Set statement is simply an assignment statement for object variables. Instead of assigning the data in the variable, it assigns a reference to an object that will set the data in the variable. Once you have used the Set statement, two references to the same object exist. The following statements reference the same recordset:

```
Private mrstContact As Recordset
Set mrstContact = datContact.Recordset
mrstContact.MoveFirst
datContact.Recordset.MoveFirst
```

In this code segment, both mrstContact and datContact.Recordset refer to the same Recordset object—that is, the same memory address. Thus the two can be used interchangeably.

You now can create an object variable and use it to reference the existing Recordset object. Because this variable will appear in many different event procedures, you declare it in the general declarations section of the form module as a module-level variable.

To declare an object variable:

1 Enter the following statement (shown in bold) in the general declarations section of the form module:

```
Option Explicit
Private mrstContact As Recordset
```

After you have created a variable to store a reference to the Recordset object, you must assign it to a valid recordset instance before using it. Normally, you assign such a value once when the form is loaded. Because of the order in which the events occur to the form and the timing of the Data control's initialization, however, the recordset does not exist when the form's Load event procedure occurs. In contrast, the Reposition event occurs each time you locate a different record in a recordset. You must write the code for this event procedure. This code will store a reference to the recordset created by the Data control, so you must assign the variable in this event procedure.

Although you could set the value of the object each time the recordset is repositioned, this operation needs to be done only once. Thus you can create a variable and an If statement to test the value of that variable to determine whether it marks the first occurrence of the Reposition event. You cannot use an ordinary local variable—its value is lost each time the procedure exits. Although a form-level variable would work, the best choice is a **static variable** that retains its value whenever the form is running.

Syntax	**Static** *VariableName* [**As** *Type*]
Dissection	■ The **Static** keyword works much like the Private and Dim keywords, but creates static variables. Like variables declared inside a procedure with the Dim statement, however, the variable created in this way can be referenced only by that procedure.
	■ *VariableName* can be any valid variable name.
	■ **Type** can be any valid data type or object type. If you omit the optional **As** type clause, the data type of the variable is Variant.
Code Example	`Static pblnFirst As Boolean`
Code Dissection	This statement, which must appear in a general or event procedure, declares a variable named pblnFirst. The variable's value persists from one procedure call to the next.

Programming

tip

· · · · · · · · · · · · · · ·

▶ **When only one procedure uses the variable and the variable's value must persist whenever a module is running, you should declare a Static variable inside the appropriate event or general procedure. As programs become larger, several procedures may use the module-level variables. It then becomes difficult to keep track of each procedure that is manipulating the variable, and logic errors easily can happen. If you use a Static variable, no other procedure can reference the variable and any undesirable side effects are eliminated.**

To set the object variable to a recordset instance:

1   Enter the following statements in the **datContact_Reposition** event procedure:

```
Static pblnFirst As Boolean
If pblnFirst = False Then
    Set mrstContact = datContact.Recordset
    pblnFirst = True
End If
```

In this code, the Static statement declares the variable pblnFirst as a Boolean variable. Although it is visible only from this general procedure, the value of the variable persists while the program is running. The first time the procedure executes, the value of the variable is False (Boolean variables are initialized to False by default), so the statements inside the If block execute. The next time the procedure executes, the value of the variable is True, so the statements in the If block do not execute.

Now that you have assigned the object variable to the active recordset, you can call the recordset's methods to locate different records from the menu item's event procedures. To accomplish this task, you must call the MoveFirst, MoveNext, MovePrevious, and MoveLast methods pertaining to the Recordset object.

Before writing this code, you should consider the possible errors that can occur. Remember that the current record pointer identifies the current record. Also, the data for this record appears in the bound text boxes.

Understanding the Beginning of File and the End of File

The Next and Previous items on the Navigate submenu are disabled when the BOF or EOF properties, respectively, are True. Any visible object, such as a command button, text box, or menu item, can be disabled at run time by setting its Enabled property to False. When disabled, a control instance cannot receive focus, even though it remains visible. That is, a command button or menu item does nothing (does not cause an event to occur) when clicked. The object also appears with a gray foreground. You will now write the necessary statements to enable and disable the menu items.

To accomplish this task, you need to know when the position of the current record pointer changes. You can write the statements in this event procedure to determine whether the BOF or EOF property of the recordset is True and disable the corresponding menu items. You reference these properties in the same way that you reference any other property.

If the first record is the current one, and the user can try to locate the previous record, a current record will no longer exist, and the BOF property will be True. The same problem will occur if the user tries to locate the next record when the last record of the table is the current record. To prevent the user from trying to perform such an impossible action, you can write the following statements to detect whether the current record pointer is at the beginning or at the end of the file and to respond accordingly:

```
mrstContact.MovePrevious
If mrstContact.BOF Then
    mrstContact.MoveFirst
    mnuFindNavigatePrevious.Enabled = False
    mnuFindNavigateNext.Enabled = True
End If
```

These statements first locate the previous record, which may cause the current record pointer to be at the beginning of the recordset (BOF = True). In this case, no current record exists. The If statement tests for BOF. If it is True, then the first record is located. Also, the menu item to locate the previous record is disabled because no previous record exists. The menu item to locate the next record is enabled because this operation is possible.

To use the navigational methods of the Recordset object:

1   Open the Code window for the **mnuFindNavigateFirst_Click** event procedure and enter the following statements:

```
mrstContact.MoveFirst
mnuFindNavigateFirst.Enabled = False
mnuFindNavigateLast.Enabled = True
mnuFindNavigatePrevious.Enabled = False
mnuFindNavigateNext.Enabled = True
```

2   Enter the following statements into the respective event procedures.

For the **mnuFindNavigateLast_Click** event procedure:

```
mrstContact.MoveLast
mnuFindNavigateFirst.Enabled = True
mnuFindNavigateLast.Enabled = False
mnuFindNavigatePrevious.Enabled = True
mnuFindNavigateNext.Enabled = False
```

For the **mnuFindNavigatePrevious_Click** event procedure:

```
mrstContact.MovePrevious
 If mrstContact.BOF Then
     mrstContact.MoveFirst
     mnuFindNavigateFirst.Enabled = False
     mnuFindNavigateLast.Enabled = True
     mnuFindNavigatePrevious.Enabled = False
     mnuFindNavigateNext.Enabled = True
 Else
     mnuFindNavigateFirst.Enabled = True
     mnuFindNavigateLast.Enabled = True
     mnuFindNavigatePrevious.Enabled = True
     mnuFindNavigateNext.Enabled = True
 End If
```

For the **mnuFindNavigateNext_Click** event procedure:

```
mrstContact.MoveNext
If mrstContact.EOF Then
     mrstContact.MoveLast
     mnuFindNavigateFirst.Enabled = True
     mnuFindNavigateLast.Enabled = False
     mnuFindNavigatePrevious.Enabled = True
     mnuFindNavigateNext.Enabled = False
Else
     mnuFindNavigateFirst.Enabled = True
     mnuFindNavigateLast.Enabled = True
     mnuFindNavigatePrevious.Enabled = True
     mnuFindNavigateNext.Enabled = True
End If
```

3 Set the Visible property of the Data control to **False**.

4 Test the program. Test the items on the Navigate submenu to verify that they can locate different records in the database. The menu items should be enabled and disabled as necessary to prohibit the user from attempting to perform an impossible action, and the Data control should remain invisible. End the program to return to design mode.

Although the buttons on the Data control allow the user to browse through the data in the database, an undesirable side effect can occur. If a user changes a record and then locates a different record using the Data control's buttons, those changes will be saved to the database table or query, regardless of the user's intentions. To allow the user to abandon changes to a record, you can make use of properties supported by the recordset. In such a case, only the commands on the menu bar should be used for database navigation and updating.

To prevent the user from interacting with the Data control and to force him or her to use the commands on the menu, you can disable the control so that it will not respond to user activity or you can make the control invisible. With the latter approach, the user cannot see the Data control, yet your program can continue to set properties and call methods at run time. The choice of making the Data control invisible or disabled is somewhat subjective. Because the user cannot click the Data control's buttons and the control provides no visual assistance to the user, it seems logical to make the control invisible.

Now that you have programmed the menu items to navigate through the database records, you can write the code to modify the contents of the database.

Adding, Updating, and Deleting Database Records

By creating objects on a form and setting the necessary properties, you have developed a Visual Basic program that will operate with a database. So far you can only navigate through the records in a Recordset object. Now that your program and its objects are able to communicate with the database, you can proceed to the next phase of the program's development: providing add, update, and delete capabilities to the user. You must therefore write Visual Basic statements for each menu item's Click event procedure to add, update, and delete records in the Recordset object.

When you add or change database records, the changes are not immediately recorded to the database. Instead, a temporary storage area called the **copy buffer** stores newly added records and records currently being edited. It holds the current record and any changes made to it before those changes are actually written to the underlying database table or query. By storing the changes in the copy buffer, you can choose not to update the database if you make an error.

You must also prevent the user from attempting an impossible action during these operations. For example, if the user adds a new record, that record is placed in the copy buffer. The new record must then be saved to the database or the record addition must be canceled. If the user tries to add another new record before this decision is made, a run-time error will occur. To prevent this type of error, you can enable and disable menu items as necessary.

Adding New Database Records

The Recordset object supports the AddNew method, which allows you to add records to a database. When the program calls the AddNew method, it creates a new blank record, which you then can edit. After entering the information for the new record, you need to call the Update method to store the new record in the database.

Syntax	*Object*.**AddNew**
Dissection	■ *Object* must be a valid instance of a recordset.
	■ The **AddNew** method acts on a Recordset object and creates an empty database record ready to be edited.

GUI tip

● ● ● ● ● ● ● ● ● ● ● ● ● ●

▶ As a general rule, if the visible object provides no information to the user, make it invisible; otherwise, disable it.

Code Example	`mrstContact.AddNew`
Code Dissection	This statement creates a new record in the copy buffer for the recordset named mrstContact.

The RecordsetType property of the Data control was previously set to 1 - Dynaset; therefore, all new records are inserted at the end of the Recordset object, even if the recordset was sorted earlier. You will write the code to add a new blank record to the database when the user clicks the Add menu item. During that activity, the user should be prevented from locating a different record or performing any record editing action other than updating the new record from the database.

To add new database records:

1 Open the Code window for the **mnuEditAdd_Click** event procedure and enter the following statements:

```
mrstContact.AddNew
mnuEditAdd.Enabled = False
mnuEditRecord.Enabled = False
mnuEditDelete.Enabled = False
mnuEditUpdate.Enabled = True
mnuEditRefresh.Enabled = False
mnuFind.Enabled = False
```

The AddNew method operates on the Recordset object. When the program calls the AddNew method, it creates a new blank record in the copy buffer. A user then can enter data into each of the bound text boxes to identify Atlantic Marketing's new client. The Find menu and all menu items on the Edit menu, except for the Update menu item, are disabled. Consequently, the user cannot attempt to perform an impossible action.

Updating Existing Database Records

To change information in an existing record, you must first make the current record available for editing by using the Edit method that pertains to the Recordset object. This process places the data from the current record into the copy buffer. After making changes, you can save them explicitly with the Recordset object's Update method. When you move from one record to another by calling the methods of the Recordset object, such as MovePrevious or MoveNext, or if you close the Recordset object without calling the Update method, the changes in the copy buffer are lost.

To put a new record in sorted order, you must also use the Requery method of the Recordset object. If you do not call this method, newly added records will always appear at the end of the Recordset object until the program is run again, which refreshes the Recordset object.

Syntax	*Object*.**Edit**
	Object.**Update**
	Object.**Requery**

Dissection

- *Object* must be a valid instance of a recordset.
- To enable editing on the record, the program must call the **Edit** method. After editing is complete, it must call the **Update** method.
- The **Update** method writes the contents of the copy buffer to the underlying recordset. This action saves a new record created by the AddNew method or an existing record edited with the Edit method.
- The **Requery** method reloads the contents of the underlying table or query into the recordset. When the program calls this method, the query is run again and the recordset reflects any changes made by you, or another user. To ensure that any bound text boxes will display information from the new recordset, you can call a method like MoveFirst after calling the Requery method.

Code Example

```
mrstContact.Edit
mrstContact.Update
mrstContact.Requery
```

Code Dissection

The first statement makes the current record available for editing by copying its contents to the copy buffer. The second statement writes the contents of the copy buffer back to the recordset. The final statement refreshes the recordset.

You now can write the code for the Edit Record, Update, and Refresh menu items. Once again, you must enable and disable the menu items as necessary. When a record is being edited, the user must update this record before attempting to locate another record or perform another operation.

To write the code to edit, update, and sort the database records:

1 Activate the Code window for the **mnuEditRecord_Click** event procedure and enter the following statements:

```
mrstContact.Edit
mnuEditAdd.Enabled = False
mnuEditRecord.Enabled = False
mnuEditDelete.Enabled = False
mnuEditUpdate.Enabled = True
mnuEditRefresh.Enabled = False
mnuFind.Enabled = False
```

2 Activate the Code window for the **mnuEditUpdate_Click** event procedure and enter the following statements:

```
mrstContact.Update
mnuEditAdd.Enabled = True
mnuEditRecord.Enabled = True
mnuEditDelete.Enabled = True
mnuEditUpdate.Enabled = False
mnuEditRefresh.Enabled = True
mnuFind.Enabled = True
```

3 Activate the Code window for the **mnuEditRefresh_Click** event procedure and enter the following statements:

```
mrstContact.Requery
mrstContact.MoveFirst
```

Examine the code you wrote to update the database any time a user adds or changes a record.

```
mrstContact.Edit
```

The Edit method operates on a Recordset object. When the program calls the Edit method, the copy buffer stores the current contents of the record; it reflects any changes made by the user to the record. The Update method saves the contents of the copy buffer to the disk. Again, the menu items are disabled such that the only possible editing action is to update the record.

```
mrstContact.Update
```

When the user clicks the Update menu item, the contents of the copy buffer are written to the Recordset object and therefore saved to the underlying table in the database. In other words, they become permanent. This menu item should be called after the user adds a new record or edits an existing record. Calling this method enables and disables the menu items such that the user can add, edit, delete, and locate records, but cannot update different records.

```
mrstContact.Requery
mrstContact.MoveFirst
```

The Requery method reinitializes the Recordset object so that it remains in sorted order. The MoveFirst method repositions the current record to the first record in the database, giving the user a visual clue that the recordset has been resorted. If you wanted to resort the recordset when the user added a name or added a new contact, you could have called the Requery and MoveFirst methods in the Update and Add menu item event procedures.

Next, you will use the Add, Edit Record, and Update menus to add a new record to the test database to verify that the program works correctly.

To use the Add and Update menu items on your form to add a record to the database:

1   Test the program. Click the **Edit** menu on your form, then click **Add** to create a new blank record. Enter the information shown in Figure 5-22. Note that when you click the Add button, both the Client ID and estimated sales values contain a zero (0) because the underlying database fields are numeric. This is a characteristic of bound control instances interacting with numeric data.

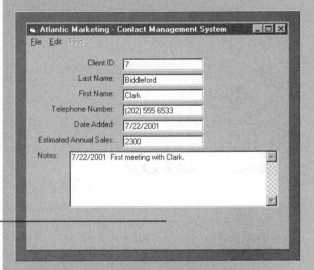

Data control is invisible

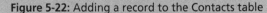

Figure 5-22: Adding a record to the Contacts table

2   Click **Update** on the **Edit** menu to save the new record to the database. The form displays the information for Marty Abrams again, and the record you just added is stored at the end of the recordset.

3   Type **Ctrl+L** to locate the last record. Because you have not run the Requery method, Clark Biddleford appears at the end of the recordset.

4   Click the **Edit** menu, then click **Refresh** to reload the recordset in sorted order.

5   Locate the record for **Clark Biddleford**.

The new record should have been added between the records for Marty Abrams and Betty Brown.

6   End the program to return to design mode.

help
. . . .

If you receive a run-time error, you probably tried to update the database without completing all of the fields. End the program, then repeat Steps 1 and 2.

When the program calls the Update method, it immediately stores the changes in the underlying table in the database. If the power goes out or the computer crashes, none of the changes made is lost. When you start the program again, Clark Biddleford's record will still be present.

You now are ready to program the Delete menu item that allows salespeople to remove obsolete records from the database.

Deleting Database Records

You need to write the necessary statement for the Delete menu item's Click event procedure so as to delete an existing record from the database. In this code, you will use the Delete method of the Recordset object.

Syntax	*Object*.**Delete**
Dissection	■ *Object* must be a valid instance of a recordset.
	■ The **Delete** method deletes the current record from a Recordset object, which in turn removes the corresponding row from the underlying database table. When the program calls the Delete method on a Recordset object, the information from the deleted record still appears in the bound text boxes on the form even though the data no longer exists in the database.

After the Delete method removes the current record, you should explicitly move the current record pointer to another record with the MoveNext or MoveFirst methods of the Recordset object. Now you will write the code for the Delete menu item's Click event procedure.

To write the code to delete database records:

1 Open the Code window for the **mnuEditDelete_Click** event procedure and enter the following statements:

```
mrstContact.Delete

mrstContact.MoveNext
```

The first statement calls the Delete method to delete the current record from the recordset. The second statement positions the current record pointer on the next record of the Recordset object and clears the deleted record from the screen.

2 Test the program. Click **Find**, highlight **Navigate**, then click **Next** to locate the record for Clark Biddleford. Click **Edit**, then click **Delete** to delete the record. After you have deleted this record, the form should display the record for Betty Brown, which is the next record in the Recordset object.

help
••••••••••••••••••
▶ If a run-time error occurs, you may have tried to delete a record when no record was displayed in the form. End the program, then repeat Step 1.

You now can manipulate information in the database with Visual Basic as well as navigating through the existing information. A user can add, update, and delete information with a simple click of a menu.

At this point, your program can locate, add, change, and delete records. These functions will appear in nearly every program you create to manage data in a database.

Q U E S T I O N S

1. Which of the following statements is true regarding a database?
    a. A table consists of rows and columns.
    b. The columns in a table are called fields.
    c. The rows in a table are called records.
    d. None of the above.
    e. All of the above.

2. Which of the following properties pertain to the Data control?
    a. Connection, DatabaseName, RecordSource, RecordsetType
    b. Connection, Database, RecordSource, RecordsetType
    c. Connection, Database, Record
    d. Connect, DatabaseName, RecordSource, RecordsetType
    e. None of the above.

3. What are the names of the properties used to indicate the beginning of file and the end of file for a Recordset object?
    a. Begin, End
    b. BOF, EOF
    c. BeginOfFile, EndOfFile
    d. BeginningOfFile, EndOfFile
    e. None of the above.

4. What two properties are set to transform a control into a bound control?
    a. DataField, DataSource
    b. Database, Table
    c. Table, Field
    d. DataControl, Field
    e. Row, Column

5. Write the statement(s) to locate the first record in the recordset named mrstCurrent.

6. Write the statement(s) to locate the last record in the recordset named mrstCurrent.

7. Write the statement(s) to determine if the recordset named mrstCurrent is at the end of file. If it is, set the Boolean variable named pblnEOF to True.

8. Write the statement(s) to add a new record to the recordset named mrstCurrent.

9. Write the statement(s) to delete the current record for the recordset named mrstCurrent.

10. Write the statement(s) to enable editing on the current record identified by the recordset named mrstCurrent.

SECTION C

objectives

In this section you will:

- Locate records in a database using a search string
- Validate user input
- Write Visual Basic code to detect errors that occur while a program is running

Locating Database Records

Searching for Records

Moving from record to record using the Navigate submenu is efficient only when working with a small number of records. The contact management system, however, will ultimately contain about 3500 client records. The salespeople need to locate a specific record quickly, without scrolling through 3500 records one at a time.

You can use the FindFirst method, which also pertains to a Recordset object, to locate a specific record easily.

Syntax	*Object*.**FindFirst** *Criteria*
Dissection	■ The *Object* can be any valid Recordset object.
	■ The **FindFirst** method locates the first record in a recordset that satisfies the criteria. The current record pointer is moved to that record.
	■ *Criteria* defines which record in the database is located. If several records match the criteria, then the first record found becomes the active record. The syntax of the FindFirst method varies slightly depending upon the data type of Criteria; you must enclose a string in single quotation marks to enable the FindFirst method to properly recognize it. In contrast, you must enclose a date value in pound signs.
	■ You can use the **FindNext** method after the FindFirst method to locate subsequent occurrences of records matching the criteria. The FindNext method has the same syntax as the FindFirst method. The Help library provides more information about the FindFirst and FindNext methods.

Code Example	`mrstContact.Findfirst "fldClientID = 3"`
	
	`mrstContact.FindFirst "fldLastName = 'Zorn'"`

Code Dissection	In these statements, the field fldClientID is assumed to be a number. The field fldLastName, however, is assumed to be a string. A string must be enclosed in single quotation marks to be properly recognized by the FindFirst method.

Locating a Record Using an Input Box

Atlantic Marketing's completed form should include a dialog in which the user can enter a last name. This dialog also contains a corresponding command button that, when clicked, locates and displays the record with the specified last name.

You can create this dialog as a window that appears only when called. This approach, which does not place other objects on the form, is consistent with the appearance of the Windows user interface.

When a user wants to locate a specific record, he or she clicks the Find menu item; a temporary window called an input box then appears. An **input box** is similar to a message box, but it sends a text string back to your program. Thus the user can enter a client's last name for which to search and click a button in the input box. The input box closes and then, using the string returned by the InputBox function, the FindFirst method is called and the client's record is displayed on the screen, if it exists. To display an input box, you call the InputBox function.

Syntax	*string* = **InputBox**(*prompt*[,*title*][,*default*])
Dissection	■ When the **InputBox** function is called, it displays a prompt, a text box to enter input, and two command buttons—OK and Cancel. The InputBox function always returns a string. If the user clicks the OK button, it returns the contents of the input box to the program and stores them in a variable. If the user clicks the Cancel button, the InputBox function returns an empty string. You can use an input box for any task that must prompt the user to enter a text string.
	■ The *prompt* argument contains descriptive text that appears inside the input box.
	■ The optional *title* argument appears in the title bar of the input box.
	■ If the optional *default* argument contains a value, that value is displayed in the input box's text box when the input box appears. When the user clicks the OK button, this value is returned to the program, unless the user changed the contents of the text box. When users will frequently make the same response to the prompt, a default can save them time.
| **Code Example** | ```
Dim pstrReturn As String

pstrReturn = InputBox("Enter the Last Name","Find")
``` |
| **Code Dissection** | The previous statement displays an input box with a title of "Find" in the title bar and a prompt of "Enter the Last Name". |

Figure 5-23 shows the parts of an input box.

input box title

descriptive text

user types text here

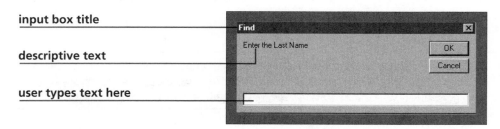

Figure 5-23: Parts of an input box
```

The InputBox function returns a string that contains a last name, which is stored in a String variable. The string containing the last name is only part of the criteria You must also define the name of the field you want to use. The criteria must include a string that contains the field name you want to search, followed by an operator like the equals sign (=), followed by the search text (in this case, a client's last name) enclosed in single quotation marks. To look for the name "Smith", the string containing the criteria would be formatted as follows:

```
fldLastName = 'Smith'
```

The word "Smith" is enclosed in single quotation marks, which signals the Microsoft Jet database engine that the contents of the field is a string. If you were searching for a number, you would not use any quotation marks. To create this criteria string, you use the string concatenation operator. Depending on the user's choice in the input box, your program should perform one of two actions. If the user clicked the Cancel button, the code should not attempt to find a record. If the user clicked the OK button, your code should call the FindFirst method to locate the record in the recordset. You can use an If statement to accomplish this task. Remember, if the user clicks the Cancel button, the InputBox function will return a zero-length string.

It is possible that the user may enter a name that is not in the database. In that case, the program will display an appropriate message box.

After calling the FindFirst method, you check the value of the NoMatch property. If it is True, the program should display a message box to the user.

Now you will use the FindFirst method of the Recordset object and the InputBox function to display the information for a specific record in the TextBox objects. The input box has the title "Find" and the prompt "Enter the Last Name". If the Jet database engine does not find a match for the last name, the user sees a message box that says "Cannot find (last name)". You need to declare a variable to determine whether the user clicked the OK or Cancel button and to hold the value returned by the InputBox function (the last name typed by the user). This variable, which is named pstrLastName, is used by this procedure only.

Programming tip

• • • • • • • • • • • • •

▶ A message box provides a visual clue to the user about the results of a request, such as indicating that the database engine could not find a specific record in the database. Otherwise, the user might think that the program did not look for the record. Whenever the program cannot perform a task as requested, it should advise the user about what happened and why. Also, if possible, it should suggest how the user might achieve the desired results.

To write the code to display an input box and locate a specific record:

1 Open the Code window for the **mnuFindLastName_Click** event procedure and enter the following statements:

```
Dim pstrLastName As String
pstrLastName = InputBox("Enter the Last Name", "Find")
If pstrLastName <> "" Then
    mrstContact.FindFirst "fldLastName = " & "'" & _
        pstrLastName & "'"
    If mrstContact.NoMatch = True Then
        MsgBox "Cannot find " & pstrLastName, _
            vbInformation, "Atlantic Marketing"
    End If
End If
```

Examine the statements you just wrote. The code executes in response to a Click event for the Find menu's Last Name item. The outer If statement tests whether the user entered a name; if it is True, the program calls the FindFirst method. The inner If statement checks whether a record was found; if it is False, the program displays a message box.

```
Dim pstrLastName As String
pstrLastName = InputBox("Enter the Last Name", "Find")
```

First, you declared a local variable named pstrLastName to hold the value returned by the InputBox function. Then you called the InputBox function using the prompt "Enter the Last Name" and the title "Find". A default value is not appropriate in this case, because each user will likely search for a different record each time.

```
If pstrLastName <> "" Then
```

This statement provides part of the error checking for the procedure. In this case, the program should try to locate the record only if the user supplied a last name, so it must test to make sure pstrLastName is not blank.

```
mrstContact.FindFirst "fldLastName = " & "'" & _
    pstrLastName & "'"
```

This statement provides the functionality for the FindFirst method. You need to tell the FindFirst method what to find by building a text string that the FindFirst method will process. You can perform the string concatenation in this example in several ways. Instead of concatenating the two strings, for instance, you could combine them into one string.

```
FindFirst fldLastName = 'Smith'
```

If the variable pstrLastName contained the text "Smith", the string would evaluate to the above statement.

```
If mrstContact.NoMatch = True Then
    MsgBox "Cannot find " & pstrLastName, _
        vbInformation, "Atlantic Marketing"
End If
```

After the program called the FindFirst method, it checked whether that client was found in the database. If no client exists with the specified name, the FindFirst method sets the recordset's NoMatch property to True. The If statement tests to see whether this activity happened and displays a message box if no record was found.

Now is a good time to test the Last Name menu item to see if it calls the InputBox function and FindFirst method correctly.

To test the code for the Last Name menu item:

1   Test the program by clicking the **Find** menu on your form, then clicking **Last Name**. The Find input box should appear. Enter the last name **Zorn** in the Find input box, as shown in Figure 5-24. Click the **OK** button. The form should now display the information for Mary Zorn.

enter name to search for

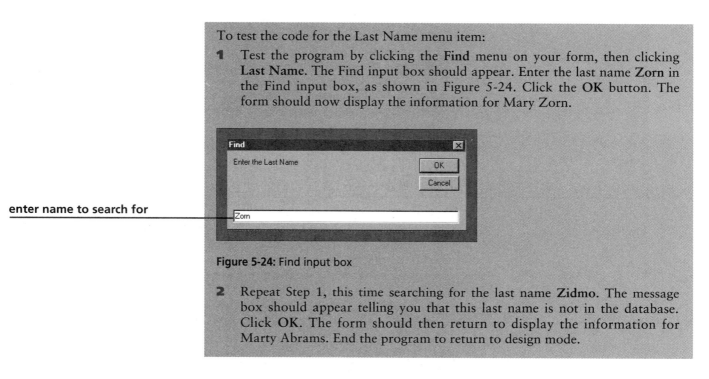

Figure 5-24: Find input box

2   Repeat Step 1, this time searching for the last name **Zidmo**. The message box should appear telling you that this last name is not in the database. Click **OK**. The form should then return to display the information for Marty Abrams. End the program to return to design mode.

Verifying the Correctness of Data with the Validate Event

In addition to notifying the user when the beginning and end of file have been reached, the program should prevent the user from entering invalid data. For example, before the database can accept a record, the record must contain a first and last name, a correctly formatted value for the date, and a valid number for the estimated annual sales. To validate this data, you use the same validation functions and techniques described in Chapter 3. Although you could place these If statements in the LostFocus events for each text box, the Data control supports an event called the Validate event that is better suited for this purpose.

Syntax   **Private Sub** *Object*_**Validate** (*[index* **As Integer,**] *action* **As Integer,** *save* **As Integer)**
                                  statements
                              End Sub

Dissection   ■ *Object* is any instance of a Data control.

■ Several different actions cause a **Validate** event to occur. Whenever the current record is repositioned, a record is updated, or a record is deleted, the argument is passed to the Validate event using an argument named *action*.

■ The optional *index* argument identifies the Data control if it is a member of a control array.

■ The *action* argument is an integer that indicates which of several operations caused the Validate event to occur. Each of these actions can be expressed as a constant. The statements in the Validate event procedure determine to which constant the action argument is set. Valid constants for the action argument include the following: vbDataActionCancel, vbDataActionMoveFirst, vbDataActionMovePrevious, vbDataActionMoveNext, vbDataActionMoveLast, vbDataActionAddNew, vbDataActionUpdate, vbDataActionDelete, vbDataActionFind, vbDataActionBookmark, vbDataActionClose, and vbDataActionUnload. Refer to the Help library to obtain more information about these constants.

■ The *save* argument is a Boolean expression specifying whether bound data has changed.

In the code for the Validate event, you need to cancel the current action, updating a record, whenever the program detects invalid data. If the input is valid, then the update proceeds. If it is invalid, you display a message box to the user describing the nature of the problem and then cancel the update. To accomplish this task, you set the action argument to the constant vbDataActionCancel when the program identifies invalid data. When the program reaches the end of the event procedure, the Update method that caused the Validate event is canceled.

The Validate event for the Data control is programmed to ensure that both the First Name and Last Name text boxes contain text, that the Date Added text box contains a valid date, and that the Estimated Annual Sales text box contains a valid number. You first declare variables that are used only within the Validate procedure: pstrMessage holds the message that the user sees in the case of invalid data and pintReturn holds the return value of the MsgBox function. Because these variables are used by this procedure only, you declare them as local variables.

To validate the user input and display a message if necessary:

1 Open the Code window for the **datContact_Validate** event procedure and enter the following statements:

```
Dim pstrMessage As String
Dim pintReturn As Integer
If Action = vbDataActionUpdate Then
    If txtLastName.Text = "" Or txtFirstName.Text = _
        "" Then
        pstrMessage = _
            "You must enter both a first and last name."
        Action = vbDataActionCancel
    End If
    If IsDate(txtDateAdded.Text) = False Then
        pstrMessage = pstrMessage & Chr(vbKeyReturn) & _
            "The date " & txtDateAdded.Text & _
            " is not a date."
        Action = vbDataActionCancel
    End If
    If IsNumeric(txtEstimatedSales.Text) = False Then
        pstrMessage = pstrMessage & Chr(vbKeyReturn) & _
            "The estimated sales " & _
            txtEstimatedSales.Text & " is not a number."
        Action = vbDataActionCancel
    End If
    If Action = vbDataActionCancel Then
        pintReturn = _
            MsgBox(pstrMessage, vbOKOnly, "Input error")
    End If
End If
```

These statements test the value of each input field. The MsgBox function is called only once. The program could have called the MsgBox function each time it detected invalid input, but that approach might confuse the user as several message boxes would appear one after another.

```
If Action = vbDataActionUpdate Then
```

The statement to test for valid input needs to execute only when the user attempts to update a record. If a record is repositioned or is being deleted, you do not need to verify these changes. In other words, when the program calls the Update method, the Action argument is set to vbDataActionUpdate and the Validate event occurs. Thus you check this argument to determine whether to validate the input.

```
If txtLastName.Text = "" Or txtFirstName.Text = _
    "" Then
    pstrMessage = _
        "You must enter both a first and last name."
    Action = vbDataActionCancel
End If
```

The If statement determines whether txtLastName or txtFirstName contains no text. If either of these conditions is True, then the string pstrMessage is changed accordingly. Setting the variable Action to the constant vbDataActionCancel cancels the Update method that causes this event when the event procedure ends.

```
If IsDate(txtDateAdded.Text) = False Then
    pstrMessage = pstrMessage & Chr(vbKeyReturn) & _
        "The date " & txtDateAdded.Text & _
        " is not a date."
    Action = vbDataActionCancel
End If
```

This If statement calls the IsDate function to determine whether the date added contains a valid date value. If it does not (that is, IsDate is False), then additional information becomes appended to the existing contents of the message, and the Update action is canceled. The next If statement behaves identically but uses the IsNumeric function to check whether the Estimated Annual Sales text box contains a valid number.

```
If Action = vbDataActionCancel Then
    pintReturn = _
        MsgBox(pstrMessage, vbOKOnly, "Input error")
End If
```

Finally, the program checks the contents of the argument Action to see whether the pending method that caused this Validate event should be canceled. If so, the message box appears. Next, you will test the code for the Validate event.

To test the code for the Validate event:

1   Save and test the program. Click **Edit**, then click **Add**. Enter **10** as the Client ID. Leave the First Name and Last Name blank. Enter **1/1/1/3** as the Date Added. Enter **22.3.3** as the Estimated Annual Sales. Click **Edit**, then click **Update** to attempt to save your changes. A message box should appear describing the input errors, as shown in Figure 5-25.

Figure 5-25: Input error message box

2   Click **OK** to close the Input error dialog and return to the data form, then end the program to return to design mode.

Developing an Error Handler

As currently written, this program still permits certain user actions that will produce a run-time error. For example, the database requires that each Client ID be unique. If the user tries to change the Client ID to an already existing value, a run-time error occurs.

A set of statements collectively referred to as an error handler can solve this problem. An **error handler** consists of statements placed inside a procedure that execute when a run-time error occurs. To enable an error handler in a procedure, you simply include it in that procedure. If a run-time error occurs in that procedure, the code in the error handler will execute instead of generating a run-time error. When a run-time error occurs, the error handler becomes active; that is, it begins to execute the statements that make up the error handler. Figure 5-26 illustrates the processing that takes place by a procedure's error handler.

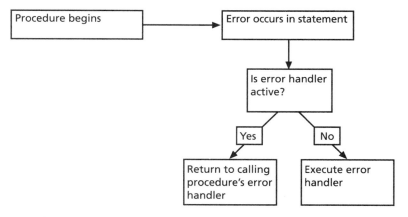

Figure 5-26: Control flow of an error handler

If the error handler is enabled but not active, then the statements in the calling procedure's error handler will execute. If another run-time error occurs while the error handler is executing, control returns to the calling procedure. This process continues until the program finds an enabled but inactive error handler.

The code in an error handler is not a separate Function or Sub procedure; rather, it is a set of statements placed inside a procedure. Depending on the cause and severity of the error, your error handler may display a message box describing the cause of the error or it may reset the variables. It can then continue executing the program.

Trapping Errors Resulting from an Update Statement

An end user creates problems when he or she tries to update a record when no current record exists. In addition, some tables are created such that every value of a field must be unique—for example, the database may require that no two records have the same value for a Client ID. Duplicating these values would produce a run-time error. Trying to update a record before making it available for editing also causes such an error.

You can use the On Error statement to identify errors and, optionally, the Resume Next statement to tell the program where to continue processing. The On Error statement creates an enabled error handler for the procedure. The Resume Next statement causes execution to continue at the statement following the one that caused the error. If you omit the Resume Next statement, then statements continue to execute until the program reaches an End Sub or Exit Sub statement.

Syntax	**On Error GoTo** *ErrorHandler*
	   statements
	Exit Sub
	ErrorHandler:
	   statements

Dissection

- The **On Error** statement tells Visual Basic that when a run-time error occurs in this procedure, the ErrorHandler should execute. You do not explicitly call the error handler. Rather, Visual Basic calls it when an error occurs. If an error occurs, Visual Basic uses the **GoTo** statement to determine which code to execute in response to the error.

- The name *ErrorHandler* is called a line label. A line label defines a location in your program by identifying a single line of code. Line labels must begin in the first column, start with a letter, and end with a colon (:). In this case, when the program calls the error handler, the next statement executed is the ErrorHandler statement.

- After the statements in the error handler have executed, the optional **Resume Next** statement tells Visual Basic to continue execution at the statement immediately following the one that caused the error. Otherwise, execution continues in the error handler until it reaches an End Sub or Exit Sub statement.

Usually, a procedure exits when it reaches its last line (End Sub), which means Visual Basic would continue execution of the procedure. Thus the statements in the error handler would execute even if no error occurred. The **Exit Sub** statement can appear anywhere in a Sub procedure; it does not have to be part of an error handler. When the Exit Sub statement is reached, the procedure exits. Because the error handler usually appears at the end of a procedure, the Exit Sub statement is necessary to exit a procedure when no error occurs. Otherwise, the error handler would execute every time the program called the procedure. The corresponding statement for Function procedures is the Exit Function statement.

When an error occurs in the contact management system, the program executes code in response to the error and displays a message box explaining the cause of the error to the user. A numeric code and description of the error are stored in a predefined object called the Err object.

Syntax	**Err**
Properties	The predefined **Err** object stores a numeric code and description of the error. A predefined object works just like other objects you have used in earlier chapters. You do not create an instance of the Err object; Visual Basic creates it for you.

- The **Description** property contains a short description of the error.

- The **Number** property holds a numeric value representing the error.

- The **Source** property contains the name of the object or program that originally generated the error.

Your error handler displays a general message for run-time errors that occur in the Update menu item's Click event procedure. This message informs the user of the number and the description of the error encountered.

To display a message when a run-time error occurs and to continue program execution:

1 Open the Code window for the **mnuEditUpdate_Click** event procedure and enter the following statements (shown in bold):

```
Private Sub mnuEditUpdate_Click()
    Dim pstrMessage As String
    On Error GoTo mnuEditUpdate_Error
    mrstContact.Update
    mnuEditAdd.Enabled = True
    mnuEditRecord.Enabled = True
    mnuEditDelete.Enabled = True
    mnuEditUpdate.Enabled = False
    mnuEditRefresh.Enabled = True
    mnuFind.Enabled = True
    Exit Sub
mnuEditUpdate_Error:
    pstrMessage = "Cannot perform operation" & _
        Chr(vbKeyReturn) & "Error #" & _
        Err.Number & ": " & Err.Description
    MsgBox pstrMessage, vbExclamation, _
        "Atlantic Contact - Database Error"
    mrstContact.CancelUpdate
End Sub
```

Examine the code you just wrote. This code executes whenever the user clicks an Update menu item and causes a run-time error—for example, when a user tries to update a record and no current record exists, when the program finds a duplicate Client ID, or when the record has not been made available for editing.

```
On Error GoTo mnuEditUpdate_Error
```

This line of code identifies the line label for the error handler (mnuEditUpdate_Error) in the procedure. When an error occurs, the statement following the line label named mnuEditUpdate_Error: is executed. Remember that run-time errors can still occur, but the program can now deal with these errors. This approach, known as error trapping, is a programming concept that you can exploit to prevent run-time errors from ending a program.

```
Exit Sub
```

The Exit Sub statement causes the procedure to exit and to return to the calling procedure or, in this case, to wait for more events. Without this statement, Visual Basic would continue execution of the procedure. Thus the statements in the error handler would be executed, even if no error occurred.

```
mnuEditUpdate_Error:
```

This statement is the line label for the error handler. A line label provides a reference for the GoTo statement. In this example, when an error occurs, Visual Basic goes to the line label, causing execution to continue at the statement following it. The line label appears in the first column and ends with a colon.

```
pstrMessage = "Cannot perform operation" & _
    Chr(vbKeyReturn) & "Error #" & _
    Err.Number & ": " & Err.Description
MsgBox pstrMessage, vbExclamation, _
    "Atlantic Contact - Database Error"
```

These statements are the essence of the error handler. You used another object provided by Visual Basic, the Err object, to describe the nature of the error to the user. In your program, the message box displays the Number property of the error and its corresponding Description property.

Now is a good time to see how the error handler works when the program is running. To test the error handler, you can make an intentional error. For instance, because you cannot update before clicking the Edit Record menu item, the Update menu item will generate a run-time error.

To test the error handler:

1 Test the program. Click the **Edit** menu, then click **Edit Record** to attempt to update the record for Marty Abrams.

2 Change the Client ID to 1 for that record. A Client ID of 1 already exists, and the database cannot include two records with the same Client ID. Click **Edit**, then click **Update**. The error handler should display a message box describing the error, as shown in Figure 5-27. End the program to return to design mode.

Cannot perform operation
Error #3200: The record cannot be deleted or changed because table 'tblSales' includes related records.

Figure 5-27: Message box displayed by the Update error handler

As you can see from Figure 5-27, you cannot perform an update that would violate the rules of the database.

The contact management system is now complete. The various objects on the form—the Data control, text boxes, and menu—make it easy for Atlantic Marketing's salespeople to enter, locate, and maintain information about clients. The error handlers help users correct errors while running the program. The contact management system represents a great improvement over the paper-based system, and it will be well received by the company's sales staff.

 # S U M M A R Y

To create menu titles:

■ Make sure that the form is active, then click the Menu Editor button. In the Caption text box, type the menu caption. Use the & character to the left of the character you want to identify as the hot key combination for the menu. In the Name text box, type the menu name, beginning with the standard prefix "mnu". Click the Next button to insert another new menu.

To create menu items:

■ In the menu control list box, click the menu caption to select the menu into which you want to add menu items. Click the Insert button to insert a blank line before the menu title. In the Caption text box, type the menu item caption. Use the & character to the left of the character you want to identify as the hot key combination for the menu item. In the Name text box, type the menu item name, beginning with the standard prefix "mnu" and the name of the menu. Set the shortcut key, if desired. Click the right arrow button to change the indent level of the menu item. An indented menu item will appear with four leading dots. Click the Next button, then click the Insert button to insert another new menu item before the next menu.

To create submenus:

■ In the menu control list box, click the menu caption to select the menu into which you want to add the submenu. Click the Insert button to insert a blank line before the menu title. In the Caption text box, type the submenu caption. Use the & character to the left of the character you want to identify as the hot key combination for the submenu. In the Name text box, type the submenu name, beginning with the standard prefix "mnu" and the name of the menu. Click the right arrow button to change the indent level of the menu item. Click the Next button, then click the Insert button to insert the submenu items before the next menu or menu item. In the Caption text box, type the submenu item caption. Use the & character to the left of the character you want to identify as the hot key combination for the submenu item. In the Name text box, type the submenu item name, beginning with the standard prefix "mnu", the name of the menu, and the name of the submenu. Set the shortcut key, if desired. Click the right arrow button to change the indent level of the submenu item. An indented submenu item will appear with an additional four leading dots. Click the Next button, then click the Insert button to insert another new submenu item before the next menu.

To view the menu system:

■ Click the menus while in design mode. You can view all menu items, hot keys, and shortcut keys at design time, so you do not need to run the program.

To create a Data control and connect it to an Access database:

■ Click the Data control on the toolbox and draw an instance of it on the form. In the Properties window, set the Name and the Caption properties as necessary. Make sure that the value of the Connect property is Access. Set the DatabaseName property to the name of the database to which you want to connect. Set the RecordSource property to a table or query that exists in this database. Make sure that the RecordsetType property is set to 1 - Dynaset, the default setting.

To set the properties for bound objects:

■ Select the object(s) you want to bind to the database. In the Properties window, set the DataSource property to the name of the Data control. Set the DataField property to the desired field in the database.

To declare an object variable:

■ **[Private|Dim]** *VariableName* **As [New]** *Object*
  Set *VariableName* = **[New]** *ObjectExpression*|**Nothing**

To set the object variable to a recordset instance:

■ **Static** *VariableName* **[As** *Type*]

To add new database records:

■ *Object.***AddNew**

To edit, update, and sort the database records:

■ *Object.***Edit**
  *Object.***Update**
  *Object.***Requery**

To delete database records:

■ *Object*.**Delete**

To display an input box and locate a specific record:

■ *Object*.**FindFirst** *Criteria*
  string = **InputBox**(*prompt*[, *title*][, *default*])

To validate the user input and display a message if necessary:

■ **Private Sub** *Object*_**Validate** ([*index* **As Integer**,] *action* **As Integer**, *save* **As Integer**)
    statements
  End Sub

To display a message when a run-time error occurs and continue program execution:

■ **On Error GoTo** *ErrorHandler*
    statements
    Exit Sub
  ErrorHandler:
    statements

QUESTIONS

1. What methods are used to find a specific record in a database?
  a. FindFirst, FindNext
  b. MoveFirst, MoveNext
  c. First, Next
  d. LocateFirst, LocateNext
  e. None of the above.

2. Which of the following statements is true of the InputBox function?
  a. It returns a string.
  b. It returns an integer.
  c. It displays an OK and Cancel button.
  d. Both a and b.
  e. Both a and c.

3. What is the name of the property used with the FindFirst and FindNext methods to indicate that a record was not found?
  a. BOF
  b. EOF
  c. NoMatch
  d. NotFound
  e. None of the above.

4. Which of the following statements is true of the Validate event?
  a. The cause of the event is stored in the Action argument.
  b. It pertains to the Recordset object.
  c. It occurs only when the user clicks the Data control.
  d. Both a and b.
  e. Both b and c.

5. Which of the following statements is used to create an error handler?
   a. On Error
   b. Resume Next
   c. Return Error
   d. Both a and b.
   e. All of the above.

6. Write the statement(s) to locate the first record in the recordset named mrstCurrent that has a client name (fldClient) of Betty Smith (string).

7. Write the statement(s) to locate the first record in the recordset named mrstCurrent that has a client ID (fldID) of 122 (integer).

8. Write the statement(s) to display an input box having a prompt of "Enter Name" and a title of "Atlantic Marketing".

9. Write the statement(s) to determine if the Action causing the datCurrent_Validate event is an Update action. If so, cancel the action.

10. Write the statement(s) to create the error handler in the event procedure named mnuEditDelete. If an error occurs, display a message box.

E X E R C I S E S

1. Atlantic Marketing has asked you to construct a program that can be used by each salesperson and the sales manager to look at the sales records of each client. Each client may have one or more sales records. The program must locate a specific client by using an input box. After it finds the client, the user needs to be able to review the multiple sales records for that client. You must create command buttons to accomplish this task. The first command button should display an input box in which the user will enter the client's name. Based upon that information, the program should search for the multiple sales records. The second command button should locate the next record given the user-input criteria. This information is stored in a query, named **qryContactSales**, based on the contact table and the sales table. Users locate records in the query using the command buttons, so the Data control should remain invisible. Figure 5-28 shows the completed form for the program.

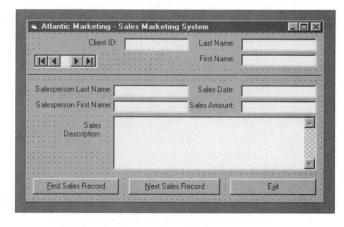

Figure 5-28: Exercise 1 - completed form

a. Run the executable file **Chapter.05\Exercise\Sample\Ex1.exe**.

b. Start Visual Basic. Create a new project and save the form and the project with the names **Chapter.05\Exercise\frmEx1.frm** and **Chapter.05\Exercise\Ex1.vbp**, respectively. Change the form caption to **Atlantic Marketing - Sales Management System**.

discovery ▶

c. Draw a **Data** control on the form. Set the Visible property so that the Data control will remain invisible when the program is run. Set the properties of the Data control so it connects to the table named **qryContactSales** in the Access database named **Chapter.05\Exercise\Ex1.mdb**. The Recordset object created should be a **Dynaset** type recordset. Name the Data control **datContactSales**.

Because the Data control remains invisible when the program runs, it does not matter where you draw this Data control; you simply use its functionality to connect to the database.

d. Draw eight text boxes and their corresponding labels so your form looks like Figure 5-28. The Sales Description text box must be able to display multiple lines and contain vertical scroll bars. Set the name for each text box as follows:

txtClientID
txtLastName
txtFirstName
txtSalesLastName
txtSalesFirstName
txtSalesDate
txtSalesAmount
txtSalesDescription

discovery ▶

e. Set the properties for each text box so that it can communicate with the Data control created in Step C. The corresponding field names in the table are as follows:

fldClientID
fldLastName
fldFirstName
fldSalesLastName
fldSalesFirstName
fldSalesDate
fldSalesAmount
fldSalesDescription

f. Create three command buttons on the form to find the first sales record for a client, find the next sales record for a client, and exit the program, as shown in Figure 5-28. Each command button should have a corresponding hot key; the command buttons are named **cmdFindClient, cmdNextSalesRecord**, and **cmdExit**.

discovery ▶

g. Declare a String variable named **mstrLastName** that can be used by all event procedures in the program. This variable is used to build a search string for record retrieval from the database. Require that all variables be declared explicitly.

h. For the **Exit** command button, write the statement to end the program.

i. For the **Find Sales Record** command button, write the statements to display an input box that asks the user which last name to find. The return value of the input box is the last name for which the user is searching. This last name will be stored in the string named mstrLastName. Include a descriptive prompt and title for the input box. In the same event procedure, write a statement to create the search string. Using that search string, call the FindFirst method of the recordset to locate the first sales record. If it finds a record, the program should display that record in the bound text boxes. If it does not find a record, it should display a message box indicating that result.

j. For the **Next Sales Record** command button, write a statement to locate the next record using the criteria you specified in the previous step. If it finds a record, the program should display that record. If it does not find a record, it should display a message box indicating that result.

k. Test the program. Click the **Find Sales Record** button and enter the name **Zorn**. Click the **Next Sales Record** button to locate the other records for the client Zorn. Also, test the buttons by finding sales records for the clients named **Abrams, Coyle,** and **Cantor**. No sales information exists for Cantor. Test the **Exit** command button.

l. Correct any mistakes and save the project again, if necessary. Exit Visual Basic.

2. Neptune Warehouse stores a variety of goods for the auto parts industry and is creating a system that manages inventory. The company has asked you to create a menu system for this program. The menu system should support features to add, change, delete, and locate records. The completed form for the program is shown in Figure 5-29.

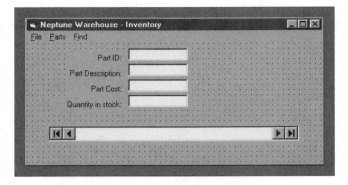

Figure 5-29: Exercise 2 - completed form

a. Run the executable file **Chapter.05\Exercise\Sample\Ex2.exe**.

b. Start Visual Basic and create a new project and change the form name to **frmEx2** and its caption to **Neptune Warehouse - Inventory**. Save the form and the project with the names **Chapter.05\Exercise\frmEx2.frm** and **Chapter.05\Exercise\Ex2.vpb**, respectively.

c. Create the menu system for the program. The **File** menu should have one menu item with which to exit the program. The **Parts** menus should have the following menus: **Add Part, Edit Part, Record,** and **Delete Part**. The **Find** menu should have the following items: **Previous, Next, First,** and **Last**.

d. Create an instance of the **Data** control on the form such that it will connect to the database named **datParts**. The Data control should connect to a table named **tblParts** in the database named **Chapter.05\Exercise\Ex2.mdb**.

e. Create the necessary labels and bound text boxes on the form, as shown in Figure 5-29.

f. For the **Exit** menu item, write the necessary code to end the program.

g. For the **Add Part** menu item, write the necessary code to add a new record.

h. For the **Edit Part** menu item, write the necessary code to enable editing of the current record.

i. For the **Update Record** menu item, write the necessary code to record the changes to an edited record or a newly added record.

j. For the **Delete Part** menu item, write the necessary code to delete the current record. After deleting the current record, the program should locate the first record in the recordset.

k. For the **Previous** menu item, locate the previous record in the recordset.

l. For the **Next** menu item, locate the next record in the recordset.

m. For the **First** menu item, locate the first record in the recordset.

n. Write statements to disable and enable menu items as necessary to prevent errors from occurring.

o. For the **Last** menu item, locate the last record in the recordset.

p. Test the program. Locate different records, and add, change, and delete records.

q. Correct any mistakes and save the project again, if necessary. Exit Visual Basic.

3. Galaxy Personnel is a payroll services company. Each day, it needs to enter hundreds of weekly time sheets into a database. Because the volume of data entry in payroll is so large, and accuracy is so important, the company needs a form that validates all user input before adding records. Also, to minimize the number of keystrokes or mouse clicks that the user must type to add a time sheet, the program should validate automatically all of the fields when the last data entry field loses focus. If the fields are correct, the program adds the record to the database, clears the text boxes of their contents in preparation for the next record, and sets the focus to the first data entry field. If the input contains any errors, the program displays a message box, cancels the update, and sets the focus back to the first input field. The program operates in two modes. While in Browse mode, the user can click the buttons on the Data control to locate different records but cannot change the contents of the text boxes. While in Add mode, the Data control is invisible and the text boxes are enabled, allowing the user to add records. When the program first starts, the form is in Browse mode. Figure 5-30 shows the names of the fields, their valid values, and a brief description of each field.

Field name	Description	Valid values
fldEmployeeID	Employee identification number	Between 100 and 1000
fldHoursWorked	Number of hours worked	Must be greater than 0 and less than 60
fldPayRate	Rate of employee pay	Between 4.25 and 32.5
fldPayDate	Date paid	Must be a valid date value

Figure 5-30: Field names and valid values

When complete, the form should look like Figure 5-31.

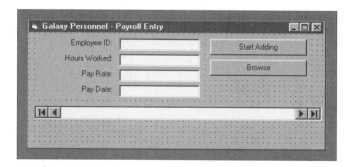

Figure 5-31: Exercise 3 – completed form

a. Run the executable file **Chapter.05\Exercise\Sample\Ex3.exe**.

b. Start Visual Basic. Create a new project and save the form and the project with the names **Chapter.05\Exercise\frmEx3.frm** and **Chapter.05\Exercise\Ex3.vbp**, respectively.

c. Create a Data control, four labels, and corresponding text boxes, as shown in Figure 5-31. Set the Name properties of the text boxes to **txtEmployeeID**, **txtHoursWorked**, **txtPayRate**, and **txtPayDate**, and set the name of the Data control to **datPayroll**. Connect the Data control to **tblPayroll** in the **Chapter.05\Exercise\Ex3.mdb** database on your Student Disk. Bind the text boxes to the corresponding fields.

d. Create two command buttons named **cmdStartAdding** and **cmdBrowse**, and set their captions.

discovery ▶

e. Write the statements for the **datPayroll_Validate** event procedure to validate the data in each of the input fields based on the requirements in Figure 5-30. The Validate event occurs before a new record becomes the current record and when the program calls the Update method on a recordset. The validation statements execute when the Update method triggers the Validate event. This information is stored in the Action argument. When the Update method triggers the event, the Action argument is set to the constant vbDataActionUpdate.

discovery ▶

f. The first field to validate is txtEmployeeID. Write an If statement to verify that the Employee ID number lies between 100 and 1000. Write the statement to cancel the action if it is not in this range, and append a message to the string describing the problem to the user.

g. Create an If statement to validate the hours worked. If the hours worked are not between 0 and 60, then the action should be canceled. Append a message to the String variable describing the problem to the user.

h. Create an If statement to validate that the pay rate lies between $4.25 and $32.50.

i. Create an If statement to validate the pay date using the IsDate classification function.

j. Create an If statement that tests whether the action was canceled. If it was, then display a message box to the user.

discovery ▶

k. Write the statements for the **cmdStartAdding_Click** event procedure to add a new record to the database. Because the first three fields hold numbers, Visual Basic automatically inserts a 0 (zero) in the text boxes. Write the statements to remove this text from the text boxes. Also, when the user is adding records, the Data control should remain invisible because the program is in Add mode rather than Browse mode.

[handwritten: rst Employee. AddNew]
[handwritten: rst Employee. Visible = False]

l. To make the user interface as fast as possible for the user, set the initial focus to the text box containing the Employee ID.

m. Create a statement for the **Browse** command button ensuring that when Browse mode is selected, the program tests whether the user is editing a record. If he or she is, then the program should cancel the update. Write an If statement to determine whether the EditMode property of the recordset is equal to the constant dbEditAdd. If it is, the program should cancel the update by calling the CancelUpdate method.

[handwritten: If rst Employee. Edit = True dbEditAdd Then Cancel]

n. Create a statement to locate the first record in the recordset and to make the Data control visible.

[handwritten: rst Employee. Move First dat Employee. Visible = True]

discovery ▶

o. Create a statement to save the new record that was added when the txtPayDate text box lost focus.

[handwritten: ① rst Employee. Update]
[handwritten: ① rst Employee. Edit]

discovery ▶

p. Create a statement such that, if the Validate event does not cancel the Update action, the EditMode property of the recordset remains dbEditAdd and the contents of the text boxes are cleared. Immediately following the Update action, enter a statement that determines whether the update succeeded; that is, write a statement to determine whether the EditMode property is still dbEditAdd.

q. Create a statement in the **txtPayDate_LostFocus** event that resets the focus to the Employee ID text box.

r. Test the program. Click the **Start Adding** button. Enter several records to verify that each text box is validated correctly; that is, enter numbers that are both valid and invalid for each field. Click the **Browse** command button. Check that the Data control becomes visible; use its navigation buttons to verify that the valid records you entered were actually added and that invalid records were ignored.

s. Correct any errors and save the project again, if necessary. Exit Visual Basic.

4. Perfect Printing makes photocopies and provides other printing services. The price of a copy depends on the size, color, weight, and quality of the paper. The price per copy also depends on the number of copies made. The price breaks are as follows:

1–100 copies

101–500 copies

more than 500 copies

The complete price break table is stored in a database named **Chapter.05\Exercise\Ex4.mdb**. This database includes the following table and indicated fields:

tblPrice

fldPaperSize

fldPaperColor

fldPaperWeight

fldPaperQuality

fldPrice1

fldPrice100

fldPrice500

You need to create a program that allows the user to select a type of paper, number of copies, and choice of single-sided or double-sided copies. When double-sided copies are made, instead of charging for two copies, Perfect Printing charges for 1.9 copies because only 1 piece of paper is used. Figure 5-32 shows the completed user interface.

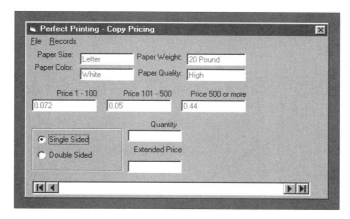

Figure 5-32: Exercise 4 – completed form

a. Run the executable file **Chapter.05\Exercise\Sample\Ex4.exe**.

b. Start Visual Basic and create a new project. Name the form **frmEx4** and give it an appropriate caption. Save the form and the project as **Chapter.05\Exercise\frmEx4.frm** and **Chapter.05\Exercise\Ex4.vbp**, respectively.

c. Create an instance of the Data control and set its properties to connect to the table named **tblPrice** in the database named **Chapter.05\Exercise\Ex4.mdb**.

d. Create the necessary text boxes, labels, and command buttons, as shown in Figure 5-32. Set the Caption and Name properties as necessary. Remember to use meaningful names for all objects.

e. Set the necessary properties of the text boxes so they are bound to the fields in **tblPrice**.

discovery ▶ f. Create a frame with two option buttons. The option buttons are members of a control array named **optSides**. Set their captions to **Single Sided** and **Double Sided**.

discovery ▶ g. In the **Form_Load** event procedure, set the value of the Single-sided option button to **True** so that it is checked when the program starts.

h. Create a menu system for the project. On the **File** menu, create an **Exit** menu item. On the **Records** menu, create the following menu items: **Add, Update, Refresh, Delete,** and **Compute**.

i. Write an If statement to determine the appropriate price based on the quantity ordered. Store the extended price in a local variable.

j. Write an If statement to determine which option button is selected. If the Double-sided button is selected, multiply the extended price by 1.9. Store the final result in the Quantity text box.

k. Write a statement in the **cmdExit_Click** event procedure to end the program.

discovery ▶

discovery ▶

discovery ▶

l. Create the code to add new records to the database.

m. Create the code to update existing records, and write the necessary error handler.

n. Create the code to refresh the recordset.

o. Create the code to delete records from the database. Be sure to write an error handler that traps errors if the user attempts to delete a record when no current record exists.

p. Test the program. Use the navigation buttons on the Data control to select different records and to specify quantities that test the three possible prices. Be sure to test both option buttons.

q. Correct any errors and save your work again, if necessary. Exit Visual Basic.

Repetition and Multiple Forms

Creating a Statistical Analysis System for Pacific Bank

case ▶ Pacific Bank extends loans to its customers. These loans require that the borrower make a monthly payment for a fixed time period. Part of each payment is applied to interest; the remainder is applied to the principal. The amount applied to the principal reduces the balance of the loan. Pacific Bank needs a program that will print an amortization schedule—a table containing the payment number, the loan balance, the interest, and principal for each payment made. For example, if the bank generated a one-year loan, 12 payments would be due and, therefore, 12 lines would appear on the report. The program must support loans having different initial values, terms, and interest rates.

Previewing the Loan Amortization Program

Until now, all of the programs you have created contained only one form. Most real-world programs are more complex, however, and a single form is rarely sufficient. Like most Windows programs, the completed program presented in this chapter displays a startup form, also known as a splash screen, when the program first begins. This splash screen identifies the program to the user and provides a visual clue that the program is starting; many large programs take some time to load, and the startup form informs the user that the application is working. After the splash screen appears on the screen, the program's main form appears, and the splash screen disappears.

The main form in this amortization program is a data entry form, which allows the user to input the values pertaining to a loan. The main form contains a button to print a report based upon the input values. When the user clicks this button, a dialog appears, allowing the user to set the print options. When the print options in this dialog are accepted, the dialog closes and the loan amortization schedule prints to the default printer.

To preview the loan amortization program:

1 Start Visual Basic, then load the project **Chapter.06\Complete\PB_C.vbp**. Set the drive designator as necessary.

2 Run the program. The first form to appear is the splash screen, as shown in Figure 6-1.

Figure 6-1: Completed splash screen

The splash screen is **animated**. That is, the logo for Pacific Bank moves from left to right across the form and ultimately appears to the right of the company name. After the splash screen is displayed, the main form appears, as shown in Figure 6-2.

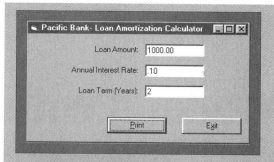

Figure 6-2: Completed main form

3 Enter the input values shown in Figure 6-2, then click the **Print** button. The Print Options dialog shown in Figure 6-3 then appears, allowing you to customize the margins on the page and the size of the page itself.

Unlike dialogs in previous chapters, while this dialog is open, the user cannot interact with other forms in the program.

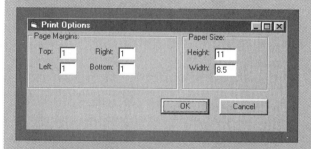

Figure 6-3: Completed print dialog

4 Click the main form. It cannot receive focus while the Print Options dialog remains open.

5 Do not change the default print options. Click the **OK** button in the Print Options dialog. The amortization schedule prints to your default printer. Keep a copy of this printout next to you as you complete the steps in this chapter. It will help you to verify that your output matches that from the completed program example.

6 End the program, then exit Visual Basic.

SECTION A
objectives

In this section you will:

■ Add multiple forms to a project

■ Display and hide forms

■ Use the Timer control

■ Execute statements repetitively

Working with Multiple Forms

Adding an Existing Form to the Program

All of the programs you created in earlier chapters of this book contained a single form. The program in this chapter, however, will contain three forms: the main form, the splash screen, and the Print Options dialog. All three forms have already been created, but the project file contains only the main form. You will begin by adding the splash screen and Print Options dialog to the project file. As you remember from Chapters 1 and 2, the project file contains a list of all forms in a program.

You can often simplify the programming process by adding an existing form to a project and then modifying it slightly, if necessary, to fit a particular purpose. In this case, the splash screen has already been built, but you must add it to the project. The splash screen contains the Pacific Bank name, its logo, and the name of the program, which is Loan Amortization Program.

You can use the Add Form dialog to add both new and existing forms to an existing project file. When adding a new form, you can either create a blank form or create a new form based upon a template. A **template** is an existing form for which several basic elements have already been created. Visual Basic supplies several templates that can be used, for example, to create splash screens, login forms, or about forms. A **login form** is used to authenticate a user by getting a user name and a password. An **about form** typically displays license and copyright information pertaining to the program.

To add an existing form, you select the Existing tab on the Add Form dialog to display the Open dialog. From this dialog, you locate and select the form to add. Your first step is to add the existing splash screen and Print Options dialog to the project in this chapter.

GUI

tip

● ● ● ● ● ● ● ● ● ● ● ●

▶ **Most programs begin by displaying a splash screen that identifies the program name, program purpose, and copyright information. To adhere to Windows standards, you should display a splash screen for each program you write.**

To add forms to a project:

1 Start Visual Basic, then open the project named **Chapter.06\Startup\PB_S.vbp.** Set the drive designator as necessary.

2 Click the **Project Explorer** button 🖼 on the toolbar to activate the Project Explorer. Click the **plus sign** ⊞ to the left of the Forms folder to open it, if necessary. The project contains only one form: frmMain.

3 Click **Project**, then click **Add Form** on the menu bar to add a new form to the project. The Add Form dialog appears, as shown in Figure 6-4.

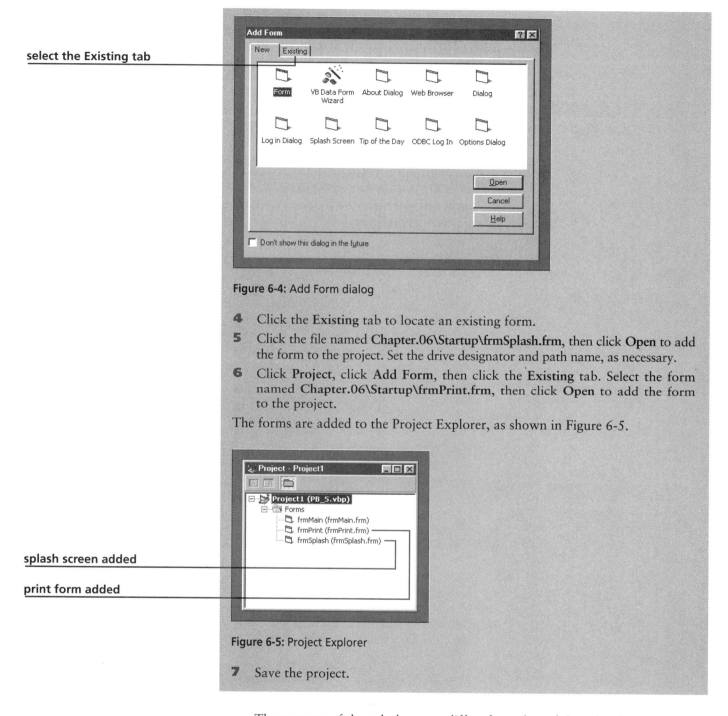

select the Existing tab

Figure 6-4: Add Form dialog

4   Click the **Existing** tab to locate an existing form.

5   Click the file named **Chapter.06\Startup\frmSplash.frm**, then click **Open** to add the form to the project. Set the drive designator and path name, as necessary.

6   Click **Project**, click **Add Form**, then click the **Existing** tab. Select the form named **Chapter.06\Startup\frmPrint.frm**, then click **Open** to add the form to the project.

The forms are added to the Project Explorer, as shown in Figure 6-5.

splash screen added

print form added

Figure 6-5: Project Explorer

7   Save the project.

The purpose of the splash screen differs from that of the other forms you have created. The splash screen merely provides a visual message to the user while the rest of the program loads; it then disappears without any input from the user. Thus the splash screen does not need many of the form elements you have used previously—a title bar, a border, or any input objects—because the user will not interact with the form.

Nevertheless, the splash screen still requires some work. As you learned in Chapter 2, a form's BorderStyle property can be set to 0 - None so that the form does not display a border or title bar at run time. The title bar and border are, however, visible at design time. In addition to changing the form's border, you can set the form's position on the screen. Although you could set the Left and Top properties of the form, the Form object supports the **StartUpPosition** property. One benefit of using the StartUpPosition property is that you can center a form on the screen without manually calculating the Left and Top properties to identify the desired position.

- When the StartUpPosition property is set to 0 - **Manual**, the form appears as defined by the Left and Top properties.
- When it is set to 2 - **CenterScreen**, the form is centered on the whole screen.
- When it is set to 3 - **WindowsDefault**, the form appears on the upper-left corner of the screen.

You will now set the splash screen's properties to ensure that it appears at run time in the center of the screen with no border. Because this project will include three forms, you must be careful to set the properties for the correct form. One Properties window displays the properties for all the forms and control instances that make up the project. It displays the properties for only one form and its control instances at a time. The Properties window sets the properties for the active form and the control instances created on that form. If you want to set the properties for a different form, you must make that particular form become the active form. You cannot use the Properties window to select different forms, however.

To remove the form's borders and set the startup position:

1 Activate the Properties window for the form named **frmSplash**. If the title bar of the Properties window does not display the text "frmSplash", you will set the properties for the wrong form.

2 Set the BorderStyle property to 0 - **None**. The border continues to appear at design time but will disappear at run time. The form has no caption. Because the title bar will not appear at run time, the caption is not relevant.

3 Set the StartUpPosition property to 2 - **CenterScreen**.

Although you have added the splash screen to the project, it will not appear on the screen when the program first begins. Rather, the project will load its default startup object, frmMain. You now need to define the startup object that appears when a program begins. When a program is started, Visual Basic can display any form in a project or call a Sub procedure with the name Main.

The Startup Object

When Visual Basic runs a program, it loads the startup object. The **startup object** can consist of a form or a general procedure that executes when the program runs. In the programs you have created so far, you have used only a single form, which, by default, has been the startup object. This chapter's program, however, includes three form modules: one for the main form, another for the splash screen, and another for the Print Options dialog. Because the splash screen that you just added should be displayed before the main form, you need to change the startup object to the splash screen.

To change the startup object:

1 Click **Project**, then click **Project1 Properties** on the menu bar to open the Project Properties dialog, as shown in Figure 6-6.

general tab is active

Startup Object list box

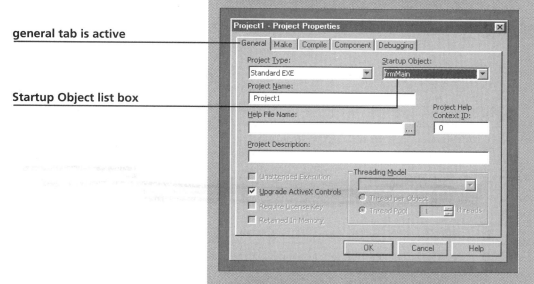

Figure 6-6: Project Properties dialog

2 Be sure that the **General** tab is active, then click the **Startup Object** list arrow.

The Startup Object list box includes three objects. Each object corresponds to a form module in the project. The list box also contains an option for the Sub Main procedure.

3 Select **frmSplash**, then click the OK button.

4 Test the program. The splash screen should appear instead of the main form. Note that the splash screen appears at run time with no border, as shown in Figure 6-7. End the program to return to design mode.

help

If the splash screen does not appear, you most likely set the startup object to the wrong form. End the program and check whether the startup object is frmSplash. In addition, if the splash screen did not appear in the center of the screen, you did not set the StartUpPosition property correctly.

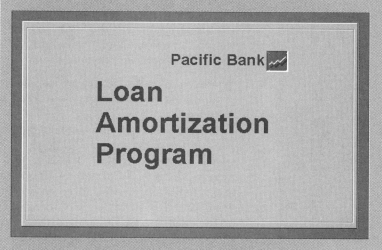

Figure 6-7: Splash screen

After the splash screen appears and the program loads, you want the main form to display and receive focus.

Displaying and Unloading Forms

Your program includes three forms, each having a unique set of event procedures. Visual Basic allows you to open one Code window for each module (form) in a project. As a result, you must ensure that you write code in the Code window pertaining to the correct module—because you could have all three Code windows open at once. Again, the number of Code windows you keep open at any given time is a matter of personal preference. Like the Properties window, each Code window displays a module (form) name in the title bar to help you verify that you are interacting with the correct module.

Because the splash screen is the startup object, you must explicitly write code to display the main form after the splash screen appears. The Form object supports a method called Show that displays a form. When the program calls the Show method, the specified form displays and receives focus.

Syntax	*object*.**Show** [*style*]
Dissection	■ The *object* can be any Form object.
	■ When the program calls the **Show** method, the specified form displays on the screen and becomes the active form (has focus).
	■ If you call the Show method with the intrinsic constant vbModal as the optional *style* argument, then the form is considered modal and must be unloaded or hidden before another form in the program can receive focus. A **modal form** must be closed before focus can switch to another form in the program. Modal forms, however, do not prevent the user from interacting with other applications, like Microsoft Word or Excel. A message box is an example of a modal form. Forms that allow a user to change focus from one form to another form are called **modeless forms**. If you call the Show method with no *style* argument, then the form is modeless by default.

When the program calls the Show method, several different events may occur, depending on the current state of the form. The following list describes what happens when a form loads initially and becomes the active object:

1. When Visual Basic creates an instance of the Form object at run time, the Initialize event occurs first. This event occurs only at the initial time that a form loads.
2. The Load event occurs next as Visual Basic begins to make the form become the active object. When the form is the startup object, this event occurs only when a program starts and the form loads. Loading the form merely places the form and its objects into the computer's memory; it does not actually display the form on the screen. Once a form loads, you can write Visual Basic statements to interact with the methods and properties of the form's objects. You can read and write a form's properties even though the form may not be visible. This ability is useful when you want to set properties before the form first displays on the screen.

3. The Activate event occurs for the form after the form loads. If the form is the startup object, the form is activated automatically. Each time the program calls the Show method or the form receives focus, the Activate event occurs.

4. Once activated, the form becomes the active object, and the GotFocus event occurs for the control instance having the TabIndex property of zero. A form can become active by user action, such as clicking the form, or by calling the Show or SetFocus methods in code.

In addition to explicitly displaying a form, it is sometimes useful to remove a form from memory. In previous chapters, you used the Unload statement to remove a form from the computer's memory. With the Unload statement, the form and its objects are no longer available to the program. You will use the Unload statement again in this chapter.

To display the main form, you will call the Show method from the splash screen. This task is performed in the form's Activate event. Because the splash screen will not be used again after the main form loads, it should be unloaded after the main form appears.

To display a form using the Show method:

1 Make sure that the Code window for the form named **frmSplash** is active.

2 Enter the following statements into the **Form_Activate** event procedure:

```
frmMain.Show
Unload frmSplash
```

3 Test the program. The splash screen should appear, but only momentarily, because this program is quite small and takes very little time to load. End the program to return to design mode.

help

If the main form does not appear, you most likely entered the statements given in Step 2 into the Code window for the wrong form. Verify that the Show method was called from the form named frmSplash and that the code matches that in Step 2, then repeat Step 3.

The current version of the program displays and removes the splash screen so quickly that the user will not have enough time to read the text. A timer is needed to delay the loading of the main form for a few seconds. The timer works like an alarm that is set for some time in the future. When the alarm goes off, an event occurs. You will write code for this event to load the main form.

The Timer Control

The Timer control generates events at regular time intervals. In this program, you will use the Timer control to generate an event that will display the splash screen for three seconds, then call the Show method to display the main form. Thus the main form will not appear until three seconds have elapsed.

Syntax	Timer
Definition	The **Timer** control is not visible at run time. It generates events that occur at regular time periods based upon the setting of the Interval property. The user does not interact with the control instance in any way. The standard prefix for the Timer control is "tmr".

Properties	■ The **Enabled** property can be True or False. If True, the Timer event occurs at regular intervals based upon the value of the Interval property. If False, the Timer event does not occur.
	■ The **Interval** property contains a number between 1 and 65,535. This number represents the number of milliseconds that elapse between Timer events. There are 1000 milliseconds in a second, so a value of 3000 represents three seconds.
Events	■ The **Timer** event occurs at regular time periods based upon the setting of the Interval property. It occurs only when the Timer is enabled (that is, the Enabled property is True).

In this program, you will delay the loading of the main form for three seconds (3000 milliseconds). By generating a Timer event three seconds after the splash screen has been loaded and then calling the Show method for the main form, you can solve the user interface problem. That is, the user will be able to clearly see and read the splash screen.

To create a timer:

1 Make sure that the form named **frmSplash** is active.

2 Click the **Timer** control ⏱ in the toolbox and create an instance of it on the form. It does not matter where you place the control instance because the Timer control will not be visible at run time.

3 Activate the Properties window for the Timer control, then set the Name property to **tmr1**.

4 Set the Interval property to **3000**.

5 Activate the Code window for the form named **frmSplash**. Select the object named **tmr1**. Because the Timer control supports only the Timer event, the Timer event procedure is selected automatically. Enter the following statements into the Timer event procedure:

```
frmMain.Show
Unload frmSplash
```

6 Remove the statements from the **Form_Activate** event procedure, as you have now moved these statements to the Timer event procedure. When the Timer event occurs, the code you added in Step 5 will execute, causing the main form to appear and the splash screen to unload.

7 Test the program. The startup form (splash screen) should appear for about three seconds. The Timer event then executes, causing the main form to appear and the splash screen to be unloaded. End the program to return to design mode.

Hiding a Form

In certain circumstances, unloading a form does not have the desired effect. In this program, for example, you will display the Print Options dialog as a modal form in which the user can specify various print options. When the user has finished specifying those options, however, the main form must use this information. That is, the main form needs to reference the contents of the text boxes and variables in the Print Options dialog. Thus the Print Options dialog should not be unloaded. The **Hide** method makes a form invisible but does not remove it from the computer's memory. Thus the form's objects and variables can still be referenced with code.

When the program calls the Hide method, the Visible property of the form is set to False, and the form is no longer visible on the screen. Thus the user cannot interact with the form or any objects drawn on it. Nevertheless, the form's objects still exist and can be referenced with Visual Basic code. Calling the Show method on a hidden form that has been loaded causes the Activate and GotFocus events to occur. Because the form has already been loaded, however, the Initialize and Load events do not occur again. The Hide method has the same syntax as the Show method. For example, the following statement would be used to hide the form named frmPrint:

```
frmPrint.Hide
```

The program must display the Print Options dialog when the user clicks the Print button on the main form. This dialog will be displayed as a modal form, with other forms subsequently using the values of the objects on the form. You must therefore write statements to display the Print Options dialog when the user clicks the Print button on the main form. You must also write statements to hide the Print Options dialog when the user has finished with it. The Print Options dialog will become hidden when the user clicks the OK or Cancel button on the Print Options dialog. The main form will use the information specified in this dialog. Thus, instead of unloading the Print Options dialog, the program must hide it.

Performance tip

When a program no longer needs to use a form, call the Unload statement to free the memory allocated to the form and its objects. This approach will improve the performance of the program and other programs running on the computer. When a program repeatedly needs to use a form but does not need it to remain visible all of the time, use the Hide and Show methods to make the form invisible and visible. It takes less time to show a hidden form than to load a previously unloaded form.

To display and hide a modal form:

1 Activate the Code window for the form named **frmMain**. (Make sure that the name frmMain appears in the title bar of the Code window.)

2 Enter the following statement (shown in bold) at the end of the variable declarations in the **cmdPrint_Click** event procedure:

```
. . .
Dim psngTotalInterest As Single
frmPrint.Show vbModal
```

The style is set to vbModal, which causes the form to appear as a modal dialog.

3   Close the Code window for the form named **frmMain**, then open the Code window for the form named **frmPrint**.

4   Enter the following statement in both the **cmdOK_Click** and **cmdCancel_Click** event procedures.

```
frmPrint.Hide
```

5   Test the program. When the main form appears, click the **Print** button to display the Print Options dialog. When the Print Options dialog appears, click the **OK** button to hide the dialog.

6   Repeat Step 5, but test the **Cancel** button this time. End the program to return to design mode.

In addition to hiding or referencing the current form by using its name, you can use another keyword to reference the current form or control instance—the **Me** keyword. The Me keyword allows you to reference the current form without retyping the form name over and over. If you wanted to call the Hide method on the current form, for example, you could write the following statement:

```
Me.Hide
```

As you saw earlier in this chapter, the completed program will contain an animated company logo. This logo should move from the left side of the window to the right, then down to the right side of the company name. To write the code that accomplishes this task, you must learn how to use another group of Visual Basic statements.

Repetition Statements

In Chapter 3, you used the If and Select Case statements to make decisions. These statements altered the sequential execution of statements by executing one group of statements if a condition was True and another group of statements if the condition was False. **Repetition** statements, also called **loops**, alter the sequential execution of statements by executing the same statements over and over again. Visual Basic supports two categories of repetition statements. A Do statement or Do loop executes statements repeatedly until some condition becomes True or False. A For statement or For loop can be used instead of a Do statement when you know in advance exactly how many times the loop should execute.

The Do Statement

A Do statement repeatedly executes a block of statements while a condition remains True or until a condition becomes True.

Syntax

Do [**While** | **Until**] *condition*
    statements
Loop

Dissection

- The **Do** statement evaluates the *condition* before executing any of the *statements*.

- If you use the **While** keyword, the *statements* execute while the *condition* remains True. The *condition* is then tested again and, if it is still True, the *statements* execute again. When the *condition* becomes False, the loop exits, and the statement after the **Loop** statement executes.

- If you use the **Until** keyword, the *statements* execute until the *condition* becomes True. Then the loop exits and the statement after the **Loop** statement executes.

You can write a Do statement in many ways to achieve the same results. To illustrate the use of a Do statement, we will begin with a very simple example that will loop ten times and print a list of numbers to the Immediate window using the Debug.Print statement. If you are unfamiliar with the Print method of the Debug object, refer to "Appendix A: Debugging."

```
Dim pintCounter As Integer
pintCounter = 1
Do Until pintCounter > 10
    Debug.Print pintCounter
    pintCounter = pintCounter + 1
Loop
```

The statements in this Do Until loop will execute 10 times. The first time the Do statement executes, pintCounter has a value of 1. Because 1 is less than 10, the statements inside the loop execute. The statements inside the loop print the value of pintCounter to the Immediate window and then add 1 to the value of the variable. The next time through the loop, the value of the variable will be 2, then 3, and so on, until the pintCounter is greater than 10. When this situation occurs, the statements in the loop will not execute; rather, the statement following the Loop statement executes.

In the previous loop, the variable pintCounter was incremented by one (1) each time the loop executed. This variable is known as a **counter**. A counter's value increases by a constant value (usually one) each time some activity occurs. In the preceding example, the activity executed the Do statement. In this chapter's program, a counter will count the number of payments required to pay off a loan. A counter takes the following general form:

MyCounter = MyCounter + 1

Closely related to the counter is the **accumulator**. Just like the value of a counter, the value of an accumulator changes each time some action occurs. The program increments the value of an accumulator based upon the contents of some other variable while the value of a counter is incremented by one (1). In this chapter, you will use an accumulator to tally the interest paid on a loan. For each payment, the interest is computed. This value will be added to an accumulator for each payment made. An accumulator takes the following general form:

MyAccumulator = MyAccumulator + *variable*

When writing a loop, you must be careful that some condition occurs at some point and that it causes the loop to exit. Consider what would happen if you wrote the following Do Until loop:

```
pintCounter = 1
Do Until pintCounter > 10
    Debug.Print pintCounter
Loop
```

Programming tip

▶ As you develop programs with loops, you may inadvertently create an infinite loop. In this case, Visual Basic will appear to be locked in run mode. The buttons on the form will not respond to events because the program executes the statements in the loop indefinitely. You can press the Ctrl+Break keys to suspend the program. Visual Basic will enter break mode and highlight the statement currently executing — typically a statement inside the loop that is executing.

This loop has a serious problem: No statement in the loop changes the value of the variable pintCounter. As a result, the loop will execute forever and never exit. Such an **infinite loop** is one of the most common problems in programming loops.

Now that you understand the mechanics of the Do Until loop, consider a variation of this type of loop. Instead of writing a loop with the Do Until statements, you can write the same loop with Do While statements:

```
Dim pintCounter As Integer
pintCounter = 1
Do While pintCounter <= 10
    Debug.Print pintCounter
    pintCounter = pintCounter + 1
Loop
```

This loop has exactly the same effect as the previous loop written with Do Until statements. The condition has been reversed, however, so that the loop executes while pintCounter is less than or equal to 10. Either variation of the Do statement will work, so the choice of which one to use is a matter of style and personal preference. In general, you should use the variation that seems most readable and intuitive to you.

In addition to the Do statement, the For statement is a type of repetition statement.

The For Statement

The For statement works like a counter. Each time the statements in the loop execute, a counter is incremented until the counter is the same as some value you assign. Such a For loop can always be written as a Do loop. Not every Do loop, however, can be written as a For loop. If possible, Do loops should be written as For loops because a For loop executes more quickly than an equivalent Do loop. For example, the following Do loop cannot be written as a For loop:

```
Dim pblnDone As Boolean
Do Until pblnDone = True
    If pblnDone = False And pintCounter = 3 Then
        pblnDone = True
    End If
Loop
```

Use the For statement when you know in advance how many times the statements in the loop need to execute. In this program, you will create a For loop that will move the Image containing Pacific Bank's logo across the screen.

Syntax	**For** *counter = start* **To** *end* [**Step** *increment*]
	    [*statement-block*]
	    [**Exit For**]
	    [*statement-block*]
	Next [*counter*]

Dissection	■ The **For** statement executes the *statement-block* a fixed number of times. ■ When the loop is initialized, *counter* is set to *start*. The statements in the loop execute until *counter* reaches *end*. ■ By default, *counter* is incremented by one each time through the For loop. You can change this value by using the **Step** *increment* clause. ■ The For loop can be terminated prematurely using the optional **Exit For** statement. The Exit For statement is typically placed inside a decision-making statement and executed in response to some abnormal condition.
| **Code Example** | ```
Dim pintCounter As Integer
For pintCounter = 1 To 10
    ' statements
Next
``` |
| **Code Dissection** | This For statement uses the variable named pintCounter as the counter for the loop. The statements in the loop will execute ten times. Each time through the loop, the variable pintCounter will be incremented by one. |

Consider the For statement as a structure that works with counters, as illustrated in Figure 6-8.
```

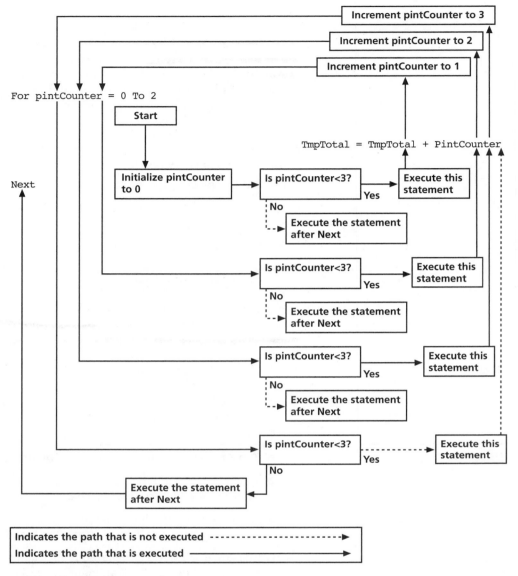

Figure 6-8: The For loop

When you execute a For statement, the following activities happen:

1. The first time the For statement executes, the *counter* is initialized to the value of *start*. The *counter* is a variable of the Integer or Long data type.
2. Every time through the loop, the value of the *counter* increases by the *increment*. If you do not specify the increment, the default value is one. You do not write code to set the value of the *counter*; the For statement performs this task automatically for you.
3. When the value of the *counter* is greater than *end*, the For statement exits and the *statement-block* in the loop is not executed again.
4. If the *counter* is less than *end*, the first *statement-block* executes.

5. If the program reaches an Exit For statement, usually enclosed in an If statement as the result of an abnormal condition, the For statement will exit. Otherwise, the next *statement-block* executes. A For loop does not require an Exit For statement.

6. When the program reaches the Next statement, the *counter* is incremented and the For statement is tested again.

In the programs you have created thus far, the positions of control instances were set at design time and never changed again. You can change the position and size of a control instance at run time, however, by changing the values of the Left and Top properties. These properties are the same ones you have used in the past to position a control instance at design time through the Properties window. You can also call a method to position or resize a control instance. Calling this method, known as the Move method, will reset the Top and Left properties.

Syntax	*object*.**Move** *left*, [*top*], [*width*], [*height*]
Dissection	■ The **Move** method changes the position or size of an object on the form. You can also use it to change the position and size of the form itself.
	■ The required *left* argument moves the object horizontally.
	■ The optional *top* argument moves the object vertically.
	■ The optional *width* argument changes the width of the object.
	■ The optional *height* argument changes the height of the object.
	■ By default, each argument is measured in twips.
Code Example	`picLogo.Move 50,50,500,500`
Code Dissection	This statement moves the picture box named picLogo so that it appears 50 twips from the left and top margins of the form. The size is set to 500 by 500. That is, the Height and Width properties will be set to 500 and 500, respectively.

To move the image horizontally across the form, you can either set the Left property or call the Move method. In this example, we will use the Move method, although our decision is somewhat arbitrary. Both a Do statement and a For statement will work to move the control instance across the form. Consider the following Do statement, which moves the control instance from left to right across the form:

```
Dim pintCounter As Integer
Dim pintLeft As Integer
pintLeft = picLogo.Left
Do While pintCounter <= pintLeft
    picLogo.Move pintCounter, 150
    pintCounter = pintCounter + 3
Next
```

This Do statement moves the picture box named PicLogo three twips at a time while pintCounter is less than or equal to pintLeft. Note that the value of pintLeft is set to the original Left position of the picture box. When pintCounter becomes greater than pintCounter, the loop exits. This loop can also be written as a For loop:

```
Dim pintCounter As Integer
Dim pintLeft As Integer
pintLeft = picLogo.Left
For pintCounter = 1 To pintLeft Step 3
    picLogo.Move pintCounter, 150
Next
```

The initial position of the control instance (picLogo) is stored in the variable pintLeft. The For statement increments pintCounter by three each time through the loop; thus pintCounter is initially set to 1. The second time through the loop pintCounter becomes 3, then 6, then 9 and so on, until it is greater than or equal to pintLeft. Each time through the loop, the control instance moves across the form from left to right.

To animate the control instance representing Pacific Bank's logo, you will move it both horizontally and vertically on the form. In this case, the For statement is considered preferable because you know the starting and ending conditions. The statement could also be written as a Do loop, if you like.

To create a For loop:

1   Activate the Code window for the module named **frmSplash**. Select the **Form_Activate** event procedure for the form and enter the following statements:

```
Dim pintCounter As Integer
Dim pintLeft As Integer
pintLeft = picLogo.Left
For pintCounter = 1 To pintLeft Step 3
    picLogo.Move pintCounter, 150
Next
For pintCounter = 150 To 600
    picLogo.Move pintLeft, pintCounter
Next
```

2   Test the program. The screen will not refresh as you might expect. That is, the logo for Pacific Bank does not appear to move across the form. Rather, it appears at its final destination. End the program to return to design mode.

To force a control or form instance to be redrawn at certain times, you must learn when and how Windows processes events.

Refreshing Forms and Controls

As you saw when you ran the program in the previous steps, the picture box was not redrawn on the form each time the control instance moved. Each time the program calls the Move method, Windows should redraw the control instance at the new position. Currently, this method is being called at a rate faster than Windows can redraw the control instance on the form. To solve this problem, you can call the Refresh method to repaint the form each time through the For loop.

The syntax of the Refresh method is very simple. You enter the name of the form or control to be refreshed, followed by a dot (.), followed by the keyword Refresh. To refresh the form named frmSplash, for example, you would use the following statement:

```
frmSplash.Refresh
```

To fix the repainting problem and call the Refresh method, you will modify the code you just wrote.

To force Windows to repaint the form as the control instance is moved:

1 Modify the **Form_Activate** event procedure for the splash screen by entering the following statements (shown in bold):

```
        picLogo.Move pintCounter, 150
            frmSplash.Refresh
Next
For pintCounter = 150 To 600
        picLogo.Move pintLeft, pintCounter
        frmSplash.Refresh
Next
```

2 Test the program. The logo for Pacific Bank should move smoothly across and down the form. End the program to return to design mode.

You now have completed the statements to display the splash screen and to load and display the main form. You have also created the statements to display and hide the Print Options dialog. You now need a way for the main form to obtain the information contained in the Print Options dialog.

Public Variables

In the past, your programs have had only one form. In this chapter's program, however, you need to communicate information between the Print Options form and the main form. You can accomplish this goal by using Public variables.

When more than one event or general procedure on a form uses a variable, you declare the variable in the general declarations section of the form module by using the Private keyword. Other modules (forms), however, cannot use variables declared with the Private keyword. To declare a variable that can be used by multiple forms, such as the main form and the Print Options dialog, you must use the Public keyword.

To declare a **Public variable**, you use the same syntax as is used to declare a Private variable, except that you replace the Private keyword with the Public keyword. To declare a Public variable named Response that has a data type of Integer, for example, you would use the following statement:

```
Public Response As Integer
```

The syntax to reference Public variables in a form module differs from the syntax to reference a Private variable. When you declare a Public variable in a form module, it is referenced just like the properties of an object. When you want to reference the Public variable named Response declared in the form module that is named frmPrint, for example, you would use the following statement:

```
frmPrint.Response
```

Because the Public variable is declared in a form module and treated as a property, you did not use the standard prefix for the variable. Rather, you used a name that resembles a property. Property names generally use complete words with the first letter of each word being capitalized.

One important element of any good user interface is its ability to allow the user to cancel an action. For example, suppose the user clicked the Print button on the main form to activate the Print Options dialog but decided not to print the amortization schedule. To allow the user to make this choice, the Print Options dialog has two buttons: an OK button and a Cancel button. To determine which button was clicked, you can use a Public variable declared in the Print Options dialog. This variable will store a value indicating which button was clicked. On the main form, you can test the value of this variable to decide whether to print the report.

To declare and use a Public variable:

1   Activate the Code window for the form named **frmPrint,** then enter the following statement in the **general declarations** section of the module:

```
Public Response As Integer
```

2   Enter the following statement (shown in bold) in the **cmdOK_Click** event procedure:

```
Response = vbOK
frmPrint.Hide
```

3   Enter the following statement (shown in bold) in the **cmdCancel_Click** event procedure:

```
Response = vbCancel
frmPrint.Hide
```

4   Activate the Code window for the form named **frmMain**, then enter the following statements (shown in bold) at the end of the **cmdPrint_Click** event procedure:

```
frmPrint.Show vbModal
If frmPrint.Response = vbCancel Then
    Exit Sub
End If
```

5   Test the program. In the main form, enter a loan amount of **1000.00**, an interest rate of **.10**, and a term of **1**. Click the **Print** command button to display the Print Options dialog. Click the **Cancel** button. The value of the variable Response should be checked by the If statement you wrote in Step 4, and the cmd_Click event procedure should exit. End the program to return to design mode.

These statements illustrate the ability to use variables to communicate information between forms. The variable Response is declared as Public in the Print Options dialog. As a result, the other forms in the project can use it. The form remains hidden instead of being unloaded. Had the Print Options dialog been unloaded, the form—and its variables—would no longer exist in memory.

Consider carefully the syntax of the If statement:

```
If frmPrint.Response = vbCancel Then
    Exit Sub
End If
```

This statement is written in the form named frmMain. On the other hand, the variable that is being tested is declared in the form named frmPrint. To reference the variable from frmMain, you must use the form name (frmPrint) to specify the form where the variable is declared.

Q U E S T I O N S

1. What are the valid values for a form's StartUpPosition property?
   a. 0 - Manual
   b. 2 - CenterScreen
   c. 3 - WindowsDefault
   d. None of the above.

2. Which of the following statements is true about the startup object?
   a. It is set using the Project Properties dialog.
   b. Only one form can be the startup object.
   c. Multiple forms can be the startup object.
   d. Both a and b.
   e. Both a and c.

3. The _____ method will load and display a form, and the _____ method will make a form invisible while keeping it in memory.
   a. Load, Unload
   b. Load, Hide
   c. Show, Unload
   d. Show, Hide
   e. Visible, Invisible

4. Which of the following statements is true about modal and modeless forms?
   a. Visual Basic forms are always modal.
   b. Visual Basic forms are always modeless.
   c. Modeless forms must be closed before the user can interact with other forms in the program.
   d. Both b and c.
   e. None of the above.

5. Which of the following statements is true about the Timer control?
   a. It is invisible at run time.
   b. It responds to the Timer event.
   c. The Interval property sets the frequency of the Timer event.
   d. The Timer event occurs at regular intervals.
   e. All of the above.

6. _____ statements are used to execute the same code repeatedly.
   a. Logical
   b. Decision-making
   c. Boolean
   d. Repetition
   e. None of the above.

7. Write the statement(s) that will increment the variable pintCounter from 1 to 100 by 1 and add the current value of the counter to the variable named pintTotal.

8. Write the statement(s) that will move the picture box named picCurrent to the upper-left corner of the form and set the size to 500 by 500.

9. Write the statement(s) to redraw the form named frmCurrent.

10. Write the statement(s) to make a global variable named Status visible to multiple forms as an Integer.

SECTION B
objectives

In this section you will:

■ Design a report

■ Print a report with the Printer object

■ Print titles on a report

■ Print detail lines on a report

■ Align information on a report

■ Print graphical objects on a report

Printing Reports

Designing a Report

In the previous section, you wrote the code necessary to define the interaction between the three forms in the program. That is, the splash screen appears first, waits for a three-second interval, then displays the main form. When the user clicks the Print button on the main form, the Print Options dialog appears, allowing the user to specify the paper size and page margins.

Before you actually write the code to print the report, you need to understand the fundamentals of report design. Just as a well-designed form makes the user interface of a program easy to use, a well-designed report makes it easy for the user to read and understand the output information. In general, a report should have a page title that describes its purpose. Reports often are organized into columns. Each column should have a title that describes the information contained in the column, and the columns should be spaced evenly on the page. That is, the left and right margins should be the same, the spacing between the columns should be uniform, and numeric data should be aligned such that the decimal points are aligned under one another. Many reports have subtotals and totals, which should appear under the respective columns and be aligned with those columns. Figure 6-9 illustrates the loan amortization report you will create in this section.

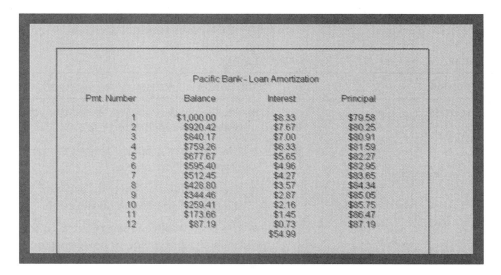

Pmt. Number	Balance	Interest	Principal
1	$1,000.00	$8.33	$79.58
2	$920.42	$7.67	$80.25
3	$840.17	$7.00	$80.91
4	$759.26	$6.33	$81.59
5	$677.67	$5.65	$82.27
6	$595.40	$4.96	$82.95
7	$512.45	$4.27	$83.65
8	$428.80	$3.57	$84.34
9	$344.46	$2.87	$85.05
10	$259.41	$2.16	$85.75
11	$173.66	$1.45	$86.47
12	$87.19	$0.73	$87.19
		$54.99	

Figure 6-9: Completed report

Implementing the Report Design

In the report design discussion, we identified page titles, column titles, detail lines, and report totals as parts of the report. The page title and column titles will be printed at the top of each page. Then, the detail lines are printed. When a page becomes full, a new page must be printed with titles and then the detail lines. After all detail lines print, the report totals are printed.

Although some reports are more complicated than the one you will create here, the same basic logic applies to nearly every report you print. Although you could write all of the code to print the report in a single event procedure, you will instead divide the code into different general procedures. This process of dividing a task into multiple subtasks is called **modularization**. Dividing programs into multiple procedures, also called **component modules**, simplifies the debugging process, because you can identify the procedure containing an error and focus on only those few lines of code. As your program grows, you can reuse component modules in other sections of the program or in other programs. This approach saves time in the development process. In this program, you will create a general procedure to print the page headers and other general procedures to format the components that make up each detail line.

Printing a Report with the Printer Object

Visual Basic offers several ways of printing text and graphics. In this section, you will print using the Printer object, which initially is set to the default system printer. The Printers collection stores the list of printers on the system. A **collection** is an object that contains similar objects and that groups like objects together. The Printers collection contains a reference to each printer defined on your system. Visual Basic sets the Printer object to the default printer on your system.

The Printer object supports different methods to control how your output appears on the printed page. It also contains properties containing information such as the current page number.

Syntax	Printer
Definition	The **Printer** object is used to send output to the default printer.
Properties	■ The **CurrentX** property defines the position on the *x*-axis where text or graphics will be printed.
	■ The **CurrentY** property defines the position on the *y*-axis where text or graphics will be printed.
	■ The **DrawStyle** property is used with the line-drawing methods and defines the type of line drawn on the page.
	■ The **DrawWidth** property is used with the line-drawing methods and defines the width of the line or box drawn on the page.
	■ The **FontName** property sets the font for the printer. Depending on the type of printer attached to your computer, different fonts may be available. You can use the Windows Control Panel to view the different fonts on your printer. Many fonts are **proportional**—that is, the space used by a character depends on the size of the character. With this type of font, the letter "I" will take up less space than the letter "W". Other fonts like Courier are **monospace**.

■ The **FontSize** property sets the size of the font. It is measured in points.

■ The **Page** property keeps track of the current page number. It is initially set to one. Each time the program calls the **NewPage** method, it increases the Printer object's Page property by one. Also, if a page becomes full and a new page begins, the Page property will be incremented by one.

■ The **ScaleMode** property determines the unit of measure for the CurrentX and CurrentY properties.

Methods

■ When the program calls the **EndDoc** method, it causes any unprinted text sent to the Printer object with the Print method to be printed. If you have printed only a partial page when the method is called, the partial page is printed. After calling the EndDoc method, the Page property of the Printer object is set to one again.

■ The **Line** method draws a line or box on the page.

■ The **NewPage** method advances the printer to the next page.

■ The **Print** method prints text at the current *x,y* position.

■ The **TextWidth** method determines the width of a text string as it appears on the printed page. The value returned is based upon the font and the current ScaleMode.

Before beginning to program the Printer object, a brief discussion about how the Printer object relates to a piece of paper is necessary. Remember that a piece of paper has a fixed size. Regardless of its size, it also has an *x*-axis, a *y*-axis, and a coordinate system. All are usually measured in inches. The upper-left corner of a piece of paper has an *x,y* position of 0,0. That is, if you draw a point at the upper-left corner of a piece of paper, its *x* and *y* values will both be 0. As you increase the value of the *y* coordinate, the point moves down on the piece of paper—that is, the point moves down the *y*-axis. As you increase the value of the *x* coordinate, you move the point to the right along the *x*-axis. Figure 6-10 illustrates the *x*-axis and *y*-axis on a page.

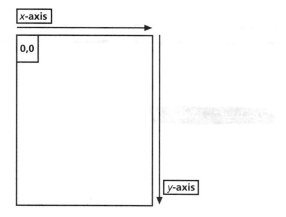

Figure 6-10: Printing coordinates

The *x*-axis defines the horizontal position on the page, and the *y*-axis defines the vertical position on the page. In printing data on a page, you set the print position to the desired *x,y* coordinates, then print text or graphical objects as desired. For example, if you wanted to print a title one inch from the left edge of the page and one inch from the top of the page, you would set the current *x,y* position to 1 on the *x*-axis and 1 on the *y*-axis, then print the text.

In the previous paragraph, we assumed that the coordinate system for the printed page was measured in inches. Visual Basic also supports other units of measure. For example, coordinates can be expressed in inches, centimeters, twips, or many other units of measure. **Scaling** defines the unit of measure for a coordinate system. In this chapter, you will use a coordinate system expressed in inches because, most likely, you are accustomed to thinking of a piece of paper in inches. Later in this chapter, you will set the ScaleMode to inches using the constant vbInches.

The Print Method and Printer Buffer

One method supported by the Printer object is the Print method. When you call the Print method, the information is not immediately sent to the printer. Rather, the information is stored in the printer buffer. The **printer buffer** is an area of the computer's memory that holds printed output before it is sent to the printer. When the printer buffer becomes full, the information is sent to the printer.

Syntax	[*object.*]**Print** *outputlist*
Dissection	■ The **Print** method prints text to the object—a form, printer, or the Immediate window. If you call this method without an object, the text will print to the form from which it was called. The Print method accepts optional arguments that define the text to be printed and specify the format of the text. If an object is specified, you must separate the object and Print method with a period.
	■ The *outputlist* describes the text to be printed and defines its format.

Although the Print method sends information to the printer buffer, the information may not actually be printed until the printer buffer is full. As a result, you need a way to force the contents of the printer buffer to print after you have finished printing the report. This goal is accomplished with the EndDoc method pertaining to the Printer object. To cause the remaining contents of the printer buffer to be printed, you use the following statement:

```
Printer.EndDoc
```

As mentioned, each report should have a title. To see how to send data to the printer, you will first print a simple report title. This title will appear at the top of each page. Before printing any text, you need to specify the font desired and the size of that font. For example, you can print different fonts and font sizes on the same page:

```
Printer.FontSize = 12
Printer.FontName = "Arial"
Printer.Print "12 point Arial font."
Printer.FontSize = 10
Printer.FontName = "Times New Roman"
Printer.Print "10 point Times New Roman font."
```

The previous statements print two lines on the same page. Each line, however, appears in a different font size and font.

You will now set the scaling for this chapter's report and its font characteristics. Because this task needs to be done only once, you will perform it in the Form_Load event procedure for the main form. Then you will print the report title.

To set the report characteristics and print the report title:

1 Activate the Code window for the form named **frmMain,** then select the **Form_Load** event procedure. To set the printer properties for the report, enter the following statements in this procedure:

```
Printer.ScaleMode = vbInches
Printer.FontSize = 12
Printer.FontName = "Arial"
```

2 Create a general **Private Sub** procedure with no arguments named **PrintPageTitle** in the form named **frmMain,** then enter the following statements (shown in bold) to print the page title. Remember that to create a general procedure without using Add Procedure, you must move the cursor to the end of the Code window and type in the procedure name and components.

```
Private Sub PrintPageTitle ()
    Printer.Print "Pacific Bank — Loan Amortization"
End Sub
```

3 In the **cmdPrint_Click** event procedure, enter the following statements (shown in bold) at the end of the procedure to call the PrintPageTitle procedure. These statements cause the contents of the printer buffer to be flushed and print the report.

```
    . . .
        End If
        PrintPageTitle
        Printer.EndDoc
    End Sub
```

4   Test the program. Click the **Print** command button. When the Print Options dialog appears, click the **OK** button to accept the default options. A page should print with the text "Pacific Bank – Loan Amortization" appearing at the top of the page. End the program to return to design mode.

At this point, the page title prints in the upper-left corner of the page. To align this text, you need to perform several arithmetic computations to determine where the text should appear.

Formatting the Page and Column Titles

A well-designed report includes titles that are evenly spaced on the page. You need two pieces of information to center a page title. First, you need to know the width of the page. Second, you need to know the width of the title. You can determine the width of the page by using one of the input values from the Print Options dialog. By default, this value is 8.5 inches and is stored in the text box named txtWidth on the form named frmPrint. To determine the width of the text, you can use the TextWidth method supported by the Printer object, as shown in the following statements:

```
Dim psngWidth As Single
psngWidth = Printer.TextWidth( _
    "Pacific Bank — Loan Amortization")
```

To Center Titles

Earlier in this chapter, you set the ScaleMode property of the Printer object to inches. Thus all measurements concerning the printer will be expressed in inches. When the program calls the TextWidth method, it uses the current font, font size, and ScaleMode to determine the width of the text as it will be printed on the page. This value will be expressed in inches.

Once you know the width of the line and the width of the page, you can compute the proper x coordinate of the beginning of the line, as shown in the following statements:

```
psngWidth = Printer.TextWidth( _
    "Pacific Bank — Loan Amortization")
Printer.CurrentX = ( 8.5 — psngWidth) / 2
```

Figure 6-11 illustrates how these statements work. The first statement determines the number of inches required to print the message. The second statement sets the *x* coordinate so that the string will be centered horizontally on the page.

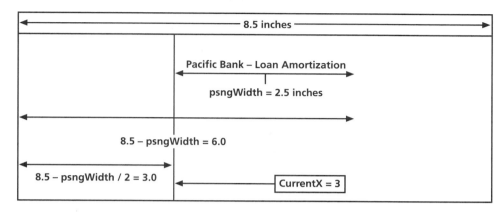

Figure 6-11: Centering data on the page

In the next step, you will print the page title so that it appears centered across the top of the page and ensure that the column titles are spaced evenly across the page. You print the report titles in the PrintTitles general procedure; the final titles will appear as shown in Figure 6-12.

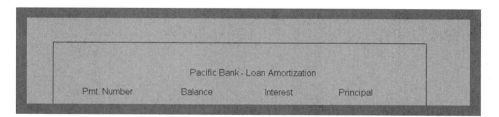

Figure 6-12: Column titles

Each time you call the Print method of the Printer object, it updates the current *x,y* position to reflect the current print position. If you print a line at a CurrentY property value of 1, the Printer object adjusts the CurrentY property value so that the next line prints just below that line. The Printer object also updates the CurrentX property value. Whenever a line is printed, the CurrentX property value is reset to 0. When you print the column titles, each title should appear on the same line, so the CurrentY property value must be reset each time a title is printed.

The report described here will contain four different columns. To simplify the process of aligning the columns, constants have already been declared in the main form to specify the right margin of each column. Each column title will be aligned to this margin, as shown in the following constant declarations:

```
Private Const csngCol1 As Single = 2#
Private Const csngCol2 As Single = 3.5
Private Const csngCol3 As Single = 5#
Private Const csngCol4 As Single = 6.5
```

These constants define the right margin for each column. The right margin of the first column is at 2 inches, and the second right margin is at 3.5 inches. The third right margin is at 5 inches, and the fourth is at 6.5 inches. To align each column title to the right margin, you will use a technique similar to the one used to center the report title on the page.

```
Printer.CurrentX = csngCol1 - _
     Printer.TextWidth("Pmt. Number")
```

In the preceding statement, csngCol1 contains the right margin of the first column. The last character of the column title should appear at the right margin. The width of the text is subtracted from this value and stored in the CurrentX property, which causes the column heading to be right-justified, as shown in Figure 6-13.

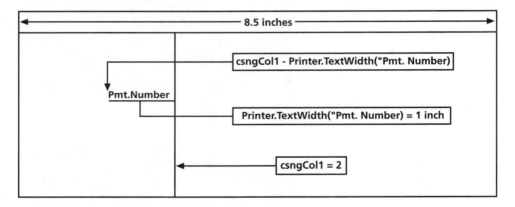

Figure 6-13: Right-justifying data on the page

You can now proceed to write the code to print the report and column titles.

To print the report and column titles on the amortization schedule:

1 Activate the Code window for the form named **frmMain,** then locate the **general** procedure named **PrintPageTitle.** Enter the following statements (shown in bold) in the procedure:

```
Dim psngWidth As Single
Dim psngLastY As Single
psngWidth = Printer.TextWidth( _
    "Pacific Bank - Loan Amortization")
Printer.CurrentX = _
    (Val(frmPrint.txtWidth) - psngWidth) / 2
Printer.CurrentY = frmPrint.txtTop
Printer.Print "Pacific Bank - Loan Amortization"
Printer.Print
psngLastY = Printer.CurrentY
Printer.CurrentX = csngCol1 - _
    Printer.TextWidth("Pmt. Number")
Printer.Print "Pmt. Number"
Printer.CurrentY = psngLastY
Printer.CurrentX = csngCol2 - _
    Printer.TextWidth("Balance")
Printer.Print "Balance"
Printer.CurrentX = csngCol3 - _
    Printer.TextWidth("Interest")
Printer.CurrentY = psngLastY
Printer.Print "Interest"
Printer.CurrentX = csngCol4 - _
    Printer.TextWidth("Principal")
Printer.CurrentY = psngLastY
Printer.Print "Principal"
Printer.Print
```

2 Test the program. Enter a loan amount of **1000.00,** an annual interest rate of **.10,** and a term of **1.** Click the **Print** command button to display the Print Options dialog. Accept the default options and click the **OK** button. The report and column titles should appear across the top of the report. End the program to return to design mode.

You have written several lines of code to center and print the report and column titles. Before proceeding, examine this code in more detail.

```
psngWidth = Printer.TextWidth( _
    "Pacific Bank - Loan Amortization")
Printer.CurrentX = _
    (Val(frmPrint.txtWidth) - psngWidth) / 2
Printer.CurrentY = frmPrint.txtTop
Printer.Print "Pacific Bank - Loan Amortization"
Printer.Print
```

These statements print the first line of the report title. The first statement determines the width of the text so that it can be centered on the page. The second statement determines the *x* coordinate where the text will be printed. To calculate this value, the width of the text is subtracted from the width of the page. The page width is stored in the text box named txtWidth on the form named frmPrint. This form then needs to be loaded. The intermediate result is divided by 2 to obtain the *x* coordinate. The *y* coordinate is determined using the top margin, also specified on the Print Options dialog. Next, the report title text is printed, followed by a blank line. The column titles are then printed.

```
psngLast Y = Printer.CurrentY
```
no space

This statement sets the variable psngLastY to the CurrentY property of the Printer object. Each time text is printed, the Printer object changes both the CurrentX and CurrentY properties. In this case, the CurrentY property is changed such that the next item printed will appear on the next line. This effect is not wanted, however, as each column title should appear on the same line (that is, at the same current *y* position). Thus the current *y* position of the line should be saved so that it can be reset for each subsequent column.

```
psngLastY = Printer.CurrentY
Printer.CurrentX = csngCol1 - _
    Printer.TextWidth("Pmt. Number")
Printer.Print "Pmt. Number"
Printer.CurrentY = psngLastY
Printer.CurrentX = csngCol2 - _
    Printer.TextWidth("Balance")
Printer.Print "Balance"
Printer.CurrentX = csngCol3 - _
    Printer.TextWidth("Interest")
Printer.CurrentY = psngLastY
Printer.Print "Interest"
Printer.CurrentX = csngCol4 - _
    Printer.TextWidth("Principal")
Printer.CurrentY = psngLastY
Printer.Print "Principal"
```

The first column is printed such that its right margin is two inches from the left side of the page. This value is stored in the constant csngCol1. The width of the text in the column is subtracted from that value to determine the current *x* position.

In these lines, the vertical position (CurrentY property) is reset so that the text will appear on the same line as the text printed in the first column. Then we calculate the *x* coordinate by subtracting the length of the text string from the constant csngCol2. This value is 3.5 inches. The process is repeated for the third and fourth columns.

You have now printed the column titles. The next step is to print the amortization schedule itself.

Printing the Amortization Schedule (Detail Lines)

The task of writing the code to print each detail line in the amortization schedule consists of three parts. First, you must compute the payment of a loan. You will use the PMT function, an intrinsic function similar to the FV function you used in Chapter 2, to perform this calculation. Second, using the loan payment, you will write a loop that will execute for each payment made. For each payment, you need to calculate the portion applied to the principal and the portion is applied to the interest. Once you compute the necessary information (payment, interest, and principal), you can perform the third part of the task—printing the detail line to the report.

Syntax	**Pmt**(*rate, nper, pv*[, *fv*[, *type*]])
Dissection	■ The **Pmt** function is an intrinsic function that computes the payment of a loan or annuity having a fixed interest rate and a fixed number of time periods.
	■ *rate* defines the interest rate.
	■ *nper* defines the number of periods.
	■ *pv* defines the present value of the loan or annuity.
	■ *fv* defines the future value of the loan or annuity.
	■ *type* indicates when the payments are due.
Code Example	`psngPmt = Pmt(.01,12,1000,0)`
Code Dissection	The preceding statement computes the payment of a $1000 loan for 12 months at 1 percent interest per month.

We can break the computation of the amortization schedule down into six steps:

1. Use the input values in the Pmt function to compute the payment on the loan. This task is done once. The remaining steps are part of a loop. This loop will execute for each payment. Thus, if the term of the loan is 24 months, the loop will execute 24 times.
2. Compute the portion of the current payment that is applicable to the monthly interest. To determine this value, you multiply the current balance of the loan by the monthly interest rate.
3. Compute the portion of the current payment that is applicable to the principal. To determine this value, you subtract the interest pertaining to the payment from the payment amount itself.

4. Recompute the loan balance. To accomplish this task, you subtract the principal from the current loan balance. Each time through the loop, the loan balance is reduced by the amount of the payment applied to principal.
5. Print the payment number, current loan balance, interest, and principal on the report each time through the loop.
6. When all of payments have been processed, the loop should exit.

Consider the following statements, which determine the monthly interest rate, loan term expressed in months, and the payment on the loan. These tasks occur only once, so they are outside of the loop.

```
psngInterestRate = Val(frmMain.txtInterestRate) / 12
psngLoanAmount = Val(frmMain.txtLoanAmount)
pintTermMonths = Val(frmMain.txtTermYears) * 12
psngPayment = Pmt(psngInterestRate, pintTermMonths, _
    -psngLoanAmount)
psngStartBalance = psngLoanAmount
```

The first three statements convert the input values into numeric data types. Because the payment is expressed in months and the input values are expressed in years, we divide the interest rate by 12 and multiply the term of the loan by 12. Again, the process is similar to the one you used with the investment calculator in Chapter 2. Next, we compute the payment by calling the Pmt function. Then, the starting balance (psngStartBalance) is set to the value of the loan amount. The For loop then begins.

```
For pintCurrentMonth = 1 To pintTermMonths
    psngInterest = psngStartBalance * psngInterestRate
    psngPrincipal = psngPayment — psngInterest
    ' Code to print the starting balance,
    ' interest, and principal will be inserted here.
    psngStartBalance = psngStartBalance — psngPrincipal
Next
```

The For loop executes for each payment (pintTermMonths). Thus, if the term of the loan was 5 years, pintTermMonths would contain the value 60, which is the number of payments. In this loop, the variable pintCurrentMonth indicates the payment number. This variable is considered the counter for the loop.

For each payment, the program computes the interest by multiplying the starting balance by the monthly interest rate. It calculates the principal by subtracting the interest from the payment. The code to print these values on the detail line will execute. Finally, the new starting balance is determined by subtracting the principal from the previous starting balance. The loop then executes again.

Printing the Detail Lines

Once the information for the detail lines has been computed, you need to write the code to print each detail line. This task requires careful analysis. Each field on the detail line should appear directly under its respective column title. Because the value in each field is a numeric value and because the report must be aesthetically pleasing, you need to format all values appropriately. The payment number should be formatted as Integer; the remaining values should be formatted as Currency. Remember that this printout does not use a monospace font. That is, different characters may take up a different amount of space on the page. Consequently, the starting x coordinate for each column may vary based upon the data stored in the field to be printed. You will adjust the x coordinate so that the columns will appear right-justified.

In this example, as noted, the columns will be formatted in one of two ways. The payment number column will be formatted as Integer. The remaining three columns will be formatted as Currency. Because the starting balance, interest, and principal columns all share exactly the same formatting characteristics, you can create a general procedure to print each column, as shown in the following statements:

```
Private Sub PrintSngField (psngData As Single, _
    psngXRight As Single, psngY As Single)
    Dim psngWidth As Single
    Dim pstrData As String
    pstrData = Format(psngData, "Currency")
    psngWidth = Printer.TextWidth(pstrData)
    Printer.CurrentX = psngXRight - psngWidth
    Printer.CurrentY = psngY
    Printer.Print pstrData
End Sub
```

This general procedure will be used to print each currency value. It accepts three arguments: the input value to print, the x coordinate describing the right-most position of the column, and the y coordinate. The code in the procedure first formats the single-precision number and stores the result in the string variable pstrData. The TextWidth method pertaining to the Printer object determines the width of this string. Next, the x,y coordinates are set. Finally, the data are printed.

You now have all of the tools necessary to print the page title, the column titles, and the detail lines on the report.

To print the detail lines on the report:

1 Activate the Code window for the form named **frmMain**.

2 Enter the following statements (shown in bold) in the **cmdPrint_Click** event procedure:

```
If frmPrint.Response = vbCancel Then
    Exit Sub
End If
psngInterestRate = Val(frmMain.txtInterestRate) / 12
psngLoanAmount = Val(frmMain.txtLoanAmount)
pintTermMonths = Val(frmMain.txtTermYears) * 12
psngPayment = Pmt(psngInterestRate, pintTermMonths, - _
    psngLoanAmount)
psngStartBalance = psngLoanAmount
PrintPageTitle
For pintCurrentMonth = 1 To pintTermMonths
    psngLastY = Printer.CurrentY
    Call PrintIntField(pintCurrentMonth, csngCol1, _
        psngLastY)
    Call PrintSngField(psngStartBalance, csngCol2, _
        psngLastY)
    psngInterest = psngStartBalance * psngInterestRate
    Call PrintSngField(psngInterest, csngCol3, _
        psngLastY)
    psngPrincipal = psngPayment - psngInterest
    Call PrintSngField(psngPrincipal, csngCol4, _
        psngLastY)
    psngStartBalance = psngStartBalance — psngPrincipal
    psngTotalInterest = psngTotalInterest + psngInterest
Next
Call PrintSngField(psngTotalInterest,_
    csngCol3,Printer.CurrentY + .2)
Printer.EndDoc
```

3   Create a **Private Sub** procedure in the form **frmMain** named **PrintSngField** and enter the following statements:

```
Private Sub PrintSngField (psngData As Single, _
    psngXRight As Single, psngY As Single)
    Dim psngWidth As Single
    Dim pstrData As String
    pstrData = Format(psngData, "Currency")
    psngWidth = Printer.TextWidth(pstrData)
    Printer.CurrentX = psngXRight - psngWidth
    Printer.CurrentY = psngY
    Printer.Print pstrData
End Sub
```

4   Create a **Private Sub** procedure in the form **frmMain** named **PrintIntField** and enter the following statements:

```
Private Sub PrintIntField(pintData As Integer, _
    psngXRight As Single, psngY As Single)
    Dim psngWidth As Single
    Dim pstrData As String
    pstrData = CStr(pintData)
    psngWidth = Printer.TextWidth(pstrData)
    Printer.CurrentX = psngXRight - psngWidth
    Printer.CurrentY = psngY
    Printer.Print pstrData
End Sub
```

5   Test the program. Enter a loan amount of 1000.00, an interest rate of .10, and a term of 5 years. The data should be printed on multiple pages. End the program to return to design mode.

This program, as it presently exists, has a flaw. In your printout, all of the detail lines will not fit on a single page. The report is cut short at the end of the first page. To resolve this problem, you must modify the program so that when a page becomes full, the printer advances to the next page, prints the page and column headers again, then prints the remaining detail lines.

Printing a New Page

To force the Printer object to advance to the next page, you must call the NewPage method. To call this method, you use the following statement:

```
Printer.NewPage
```

To determine when to call the NewPage method, you need to know when the current page is full—that is, when the last detail line has printed at the bottom margin of the current page. This task can be accomplished by adding a decision-making statement to the cmdPrint event procedure. Just before a detail line prints, the If statement should test the current y position. If it is greater than the bottom margin, then the printout should advance to the next page and print page headers at the top of the new page, as shown in the following If statement:

```
If Printer.CurrentY >= frmPrint.txtHeight - _
    frmPrint.txtBottom - frmPrint.txtTop Then
    Printer.NewPage
    PrintPageTitle
    psngLastY = Printer.CurrentY
End If
```

This If statement tests the CurrentY property to ensure that the next line printed will fit within the margins defined for the page. Again, these values are stored in the text boxes on the form named frmPrint. The top and bottom margins are therefore subtracted from the height of the page. If the current y position is greater than this value, then the statements within the If statement execute.

The statements found in the If statement perform three tasks. First, they call the NewPage method to advance the printer to the next page. Second, they print the report and column titles at the top of the new page. Third, they reset the variable psngLastY to correct the y coordinate for the new page.

You can now write the statements to generate a new page when necessary.

To print a new page:

1   Activate the Code window for the form named **frmMain**.

2 Enter the following statements (shown in bold) in the **cmdPrint_Click** event procedure:

```
For pintCurrentMonth = 1 To pintTermMonths
    psngLastY = Printer.CurrentY
    If Printer.CurrentY >= frmPrint.txtHeight - _
        frmPrint.txtBottom - frmPrint.txtTop Then
        Printer.NewPage
        PrintPageTitle
        psngLastY = Printer.CurrentY
    End If
    Call PrintIntField(pintCurrentMonth, csngCol1, _
        psngLastY)
```

3 Test the program by entering a loan with a term of 5 years or greater. The data should appear on multiple pages. End the program to return to design mode.

Printing Graphical Objects

In addition to printing textual data, the Printer object supports additional methods for printing graphical images and drawing lines. The process for drawing a line is very similar to printing text, for instance you simply specify the endpoints of the line.

Syntax	*object*.**Line** [**Step**] (x1, y1) [**Step**] (x2, y2), [*color*], [**B**][**F**]
Dissection	■ The **Line** method prints a box or line on a report.
	■ The *object* represents an instance of the predefined Printer object.
	■ The optional **Step** argument indicates the coordinates are relative to the CurrentX and CurrentY properties pertaining to the Printer object.
	■ The *x1* and *y1* arguments indicate the starting point of the line.
	■ The *x2* and *y2* arguments indicate the ending point of the line.
	■ The optional *color* argument specifies a color for the line. This option is useful only when you are using a color printer.
	■ If the optional **B** argument is used, then the pattern drawn is a box instead of a line.
	■ If the optional **F** argument is used, then the box fills with the color specified for the line. The **F** argument can be used only in conjunction with the **B** argument.

Code Example	`Printer. Line (0.5, 0.5) — (7.5, 10), , B`
Code Dissection	This statement draws a box around the page because the B argument is used. Had this argument been omitted, the statement would have drawn a diagonal line.

Closely related to the Line method are the DrawStyle and DrawWidth properties. The DrawStyle property determines how the line is drawn. By default, the Line method draws a solid line. You can change the DrawStyle property, however, to draw dotted and dashed lines. By default, the width of a line is 1 pixel, but you can modify the DrawWidth property to draw a wider line. Thus, to set the line width, you would use the following statement:

```
Printer.DrawWidth = 5
```

You can now modify the report to draw a box around each page.

To draw a box:

1   Activate the Code window for the form named **frmMain**. Locate the **Form_Load** event procedure and enter the following statement (shown in bold) at the end of the procedure:

```
Printer.FontName "Arial"
Printer.DrawWidth = 10
```

2   Locate the **PrintPageTitle** general procedure and enter the following statement (shown in bold) to draw a box around the page:

```
Dim psngLastY As Single
Printer.Line (0.5, 0.5)-(7.5, 10), , B
psngWidth = Printer.TextWidth( _
    "Pacific Bank - Loan Amortization")
```

3   Test the program. Enter a loan amount of **1000.00**, a term of **1** year, and an interest rate of **.10**. Print the amortization schedule. A border should be printed around the report. End the program to return to design mode.

You have now completed the programming for this chapter. You have printed both text and graphics to the Printer object. In addition, you can format and align that text.

S U M M A R Y

To add an existing form to a project:

■ Click **Project, Add Form**. Click the Existing tab on the dialog to display the Open dialog. From this dialog you can select the form to add.

To remove a form's borders and set the startup position:

■ Set the StartUpPosition property as necessary and set the BorderStyle property to 0 - None.

To change the startup object:

■ In the Project Properties dialog, select the General tab. Set the startup object to the desired form module.

To display a form using the Show method:

■ Call the Show method using the following syntax:
object.**Show** [*style*]

To create a timer:

■ Create an instance of the Timer control on the form. Set the Interval property to the number of milliseconds that should elapse between Timer events. The Timer control responds to the Timer event. Write code for the Timer event as necessary.

To display and hide a modal form:

■ Call the Unload method to unload a form. Call the Hide method to make a form invisible but keep the form in memory. To display the form as a modal form, call the Show method with the vbModal argument.

To create a Do statement:

■ **Do [While|Until]** *condition*
   statements
Loop

To create a For statement:

■ **For** *counter* = *start* **To** *end* [**Step** *increment*]
   [*statement-block*]
   [**Exit For**]
   [*statement-block*]
Next [*counter*]

To move a control instance or form, call the Move method with the following syntax:

■ *object*.**Move** *left*, [*top*], [*width*], [*height*]

To repaint an object on the screen, call the Refresh method:

■ *object*.**Refresh**

To print text to a report, call the Print method:

■   [*object.*]**Print** *outputlist*

To determine the width of text, use the TextWidth property:

■   Printer.TextWidth

To draw a box or line in a report, call the Line method:

■   *object.***Line** [**Step**] (*x1, y1*) [**Step**] (*x2, y2*), [*color*], [**B**][**F**]

Q U E S T I O N S

1. What is the name of the object used to send information to the default printer?
    a. Output
    b. Printer
    c. Print
    d. Device
    e. None of the above.

2. What are the property names used to specify the *x* and *y* positions on a printed page?
    a. X and Y
    b. Xaxis and Yaxis
    c. Xcoordinate and Ycoordinate
    d. CurrentX and CurrentY
    e. None of the above.

3. What is the name of the property used to set the scaling for the printer?
    a. Scale
    b. Measure
    c. Distance
    d. Mode
    e. ScaleMode

4. What is the name of the method used to advance the printer to the next page?
    a. Page
    b. NextPage
    c. NewPage
    d. EndDoc
    e. EndPage

5. What is the name of the method to send any remaining contents of the printer buffer to the printer?
    a. Page
    b. NextPage
    c. NewPage
    d. EndDoc
    e. EndPage

6. Write the statement(s) to determine the width of the text string "This is a string" and store the result in the variable psngLength.

7. Write the statement(s) to set the printer scaling to inches.

8. Write the statement(s) to set the *x,y* position of the printer to 1 inch and 2 inches, respectively.

9. Write the statement(s) to advance the printer to the next page.

10. Write the statement(s) to print the line of text "This is a line of text" to the printer.

E X E R C I S E S

 In this exercise, you will create a program that prints a depreciation schedule for an asset using the straight-line depreciation method. For this exercise, assume that the page size is 8½ by 11 inches. Three input values are required to compute the depreciation: the original cost of the asset, the life of the asset, and the value of the asset at the end of its useful life (known as the salvage value). To compute the depreciation schedule, you will subtract the salvage value from the cost of the asset, giving the amount to depreciate. The amount to depreciate is divided by the life of the asset to give the amount to depreciate each year. Figure 6-14 shows the completed input form for this program.

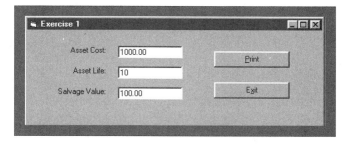

Figure 6-14: Exercise 1 – completed form

a. Run the executable file named **Chapter.06\Exercise\Sample\Ex1.exe**. Set the drive designator as necessary. Enter the values shown in Figure 6-14, and click the **Print** button on the form to print the depreciation schedule. The report contains a report title and column headers. Also, the columns are aligned and the data is centered on the page.

b. Start Visual Basic and create a new project, if necessary. Change the Caption property of the form to **Exercise 1**. Change the Name property to **frmEx1**. Save the form and project using the names **Chapter.06\Exercise\frmEx1.frm** and **Chapter.06\Exercise\Ex1.vbp**, respectively. Set the drive designator as necessary.

c. Create the input objects on the form, as shown in Figure 6-14.

d. In the **Form_Load** event procedure, write the necessary statements to set the characteristics of the printout. Set the ScaleMode to **inches**, the font size to a **12 point font**, and the font to **Arial**.

e. Create a general procedure to print the page title. The page title should contain a line with the text **Depreciation Schedule** centered on the page. A blank line should print after the page title.

f. Following the blank line, print the column titles. The column titles consist of two lines each. There are four columns. The first column should contain the text **Year**. The second column should contain the text **Start Value** on separate lines. The third column should contain the text **Depreciation Amount** on separate lines, and the last column should include the text **End Value** on separate lines. To simplify the programming for the remainder of the exercise, declare four constants to identify the right margin (*x* coordinate) of the four columns.

discovery ▶

g. In the **Click** event procedure for the Print command button, write the code to calculate and print the depreciation schedule. This event procedure should use a For statement that executes for each year of the asset's life. For each year, the beginning value of the asset needs to be printed, along with the depreciation amount and the ending value of the asset. Also, print the current year on the line. To print the output, consider implementing the procedures **PrintSngField** and **PrintIntField** mentioned in this chapter.

h. Test the program.

i. Correct any mistakes and save your work again, if necessary.

2. In this exercise, you will develop a program that creates a simple tax table in multiple columns. The form shown in Figure 6-15 indicates the input fields for the tax table, which include the minimum value, the maximum value, and the increment. These values will be used in a For statement. The program should print the tax amount from the minimum value to the maximum value. Each iteration of the loop should be incremented by the value of the increment. For each value, multiply the amount by the tax rate. Each printed page should have four columns: the first column is a value, the second column is the tax, the third and fourth columns are the same as the first and second columns. Thus, when the report prints, the first two columns should be printed until the page is full. The second two columns should then be printed. If all of the values will not fit on one page, then the program should print a second page. The report should be printed with 1-inch top and bottom margin. For this exercise, assume that the paper size is 8½ by 11 inches.

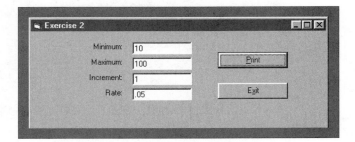

Figure 6-15: Exercise 2 – completed form

a. Run the executable file named **Chapter.06\Exercise\Sample\Ex2.exe**. Set the drive designator as necessary. Enter the values shown in Figure 6-15 and click the **Print** button on the form to print the depreciation schedule. The report contains a report title and column headers. The columns are aligned, and the data is centered on the page.

b. Start Visual Basic and create a new project, if necessary. Change the Caption property of the form to **Exercise 2**. Change the Name property to **frmEx2**. Save the form and project using the names **Chapter.06\Exercise\frmEx2.frm** and **Chapter.06\Exercise\Ex2.vbp**, respectively. Set the drive designator as necessary.

c. Create the input objects on the form, as shown in Figure 6-15.

d. In the **Form_Load** event procedure, write the necessary statements to set the characteristics of the printout. Set the ScaleMode to **inches**, the font size to a **12 point font**, and the font to **Arial**.

discovery ▶

e. The logic for the printing requires some careful thought. First, you must print the first two columns containing a value and taxable amount. When the columns reach the bottom margin, the program should print the next two columns until the bottom margin is reached. When this event occurs, you should advance to the next page and begin printing the first two columns on the next page. Thus, you must keep track of which column is being printed and test that current y position before printing to determine whether the printout should be advanced to the next column or to the next page.

f. Test the program.

g. Correct any mistakes and save your work again, if necessary.

3. ABC Company wants a program prototype with an animated splash screen. The splash screen should appear for three seconds, then display a main form. On the main form, you will display the current time, updating it each second.

   a. Run the executable file named **Chapter.06\Exercise\Sample\Ex3.exe**. Set the drive designator as necessary. The splash screen appears for three seconds, then the main form appears. The main form contains a label that displays the current time of day. The time is updated each second.

   b. Start Visual Basic and create a new project, if necessary. Change the Caption property of the form to **Exercise 3**. Change the Name property to **frmEx3**. Save the form and project using the names **Chapter.06\Exercise\ frmEx3.frm** and **Chapter.06\Exercise\Ex3.vbp**, respectively. Set the drive designator as necessary.

   c. Add a second form to the project. Set the name of this form to **frmSplash**. Set the properties so that no border appears on the form at run time. Also, make this form become the startup object.

   d. Create a label on this splash screen. Change the caption of the label to **Exercise 3**. Animate the label so that it moves from left to right across the top of the screen.

   e. Create a **Timer** control instance on the splash screen. Set the interval so that the **Timer** event occurs **every three seconds**. When the Timer event occurs, the program should display the form named **Chapter.06\Exercise\frmEx3.frm** and unload the splash screen.

   f. On the form named **frmEx3**, create an instance of the **Timer** control. Set the interval of the timer so that it occurs **every second**.

discovery▶   g. Create a **label** at the bottom of the form. Write code to display the time of day in this label. In this way, the time of day should be updated every second.

   h. Correct any mistakes and save your work again, if necessary.

Reading and Writing Text Files into List Boxes and Arrays

Creating a Quotation System for Star Plant Supply

case ▶ Star Plant Supply provides plants to landscaping firms. Its customers require a written price estimate or quote before placing an order. Star Plant Supply currently uses a printed price list and quote forms to record customer quotes. Because business is growing and workers must look up the price of each item manually, quotes are often tardy and erroneous. The company would like a computerized system that will help keep up with the volume of quotes and compute the pricing information automatically. A product price list already exists in an electronic text file in which each product and its corresponding price are listed on a single line. This file is updated when the prices change or when new items are added. Once complete, the new program will read this text file and use the information to produce price quotes for customers.

Previewing the Quotation System

To preview the completed quotation system:

1   Start Visual Basic, then load the project **Chapter.07\Complete\Star_C.vbp**. Set the drive designator as necessary. The completed program reads a text file assumed to be on the A: drive. If you are running the program from a different drive or directory, modify the following statement in the Form_Load event procedure:

```
Open "A:\Chapter.07\Complete\Product2.txt" For Input As #1
```

2   Run the program. The form will appear, as shown in Figure 7-1. Note that the form illustrates an order already in progress.

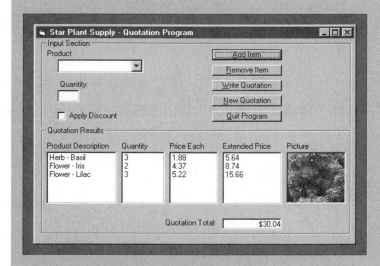

Figure 7-1: Completed quotation program

The quote system in this chapter reflects good user interface design principles. The screen is divided into two sections. The upper section handles input; the lower section is reserved for output. To visually identify these areas, a frame surrounds each section. In this case, the frames are not used to group together a control array of option buttons. Rather, they merely visually separate the input and output sections of the form. We could have used the Shape control for this purpose as well.

3   Click the **Product** combo box located in the upper-left corner of the form. The list will drop down and display the products.

4   Select the product named **Herb - Mint**.

5   Enter **1** in the **Quantity** text box.

6 Click the **Add Item** command button. The program will look up the price of the selected item and multiply it by the quantity requested so as to compute the extended price. Next, the output section of the form displays the item, the quantity ordered, the price, and the extended price. Finally, the quote total is computed and displayed in the output section of the form.

7 Select other products and add them to the quote. With each new product selection, the product, quantity ordered, price, and extended price are added to the output list boxes at the bottom of the form. Due to disk space limitations, some items will not have corresponding pictures; instead, the word "none" will display.

8 Select the product **Herb - Mint** in the output section of the form, then click the **Remove Item** command button. Upon the removal of the item, the quotation total is updated.

9 Click the **New Quotation** command button to clear the contents of the output list boxes.

10 End the program, then exit Visual Basic.

SECTION A
objectives

In this section you will:

- Create instances of the ComboBox and ListBox controls to work with lists

- Read information from a text file into a combo box at run time

- Create arrays to store a series of variables

- Add and remove items to and from a list box

Working with Lists of Data

The ComboBox Control

The Label and TextBox controls, which you used in previous chapters, stored a single item of data. Other controls, such as the ComboBox control, can work with lists of data or multiple data items.

The partially completed project file for this chapter contains objects that you have used in the past, such as frames, labels, text boxes, and command buttons.

To open the partially completed quote program:

1   Start Visual Basic, then open the project file named **Chapter.07\Startup\ Star_S.vbp**. Set the drive designator as necessary. Activate the form named **frmStar.frm**. It resembles Figure 7-2.

input Quantity text box

input section

Apply Discount check box

output section

output Quotation Total label

command buttons

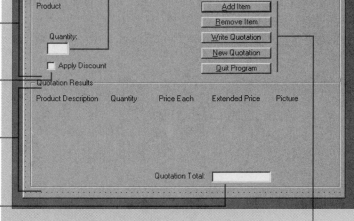

Figure 7-2: Initial quotation screen

As shown in Figure 7-2, the form contains an input and output section. The input section contains command buttons and a text box for the user to enter the quantity ordered for a particular item. In addition, it contains a check box with which the user can apply a discount. The output section contains descriptive labels for the objects you will create in this chapter. It also contains a label to display the quote total.

The end user of this program will select an item from a list of products in inventory, but will not need to type the name of each item every time a bid is prepared. To implement this type of interface, you will use a combo box.

Syntax	ComboBox
Definition	A **ComboBox** control displays a list of items from which the user selects one item. The standard prefix for a combo box is "cbo".
Properties	■ Combo boxes come in three styles. The style is set with the **Style** property. Setting the Style property to 0 - Dropdown Combo allows a user to select an item from a drop-down list of suggested choices or to type in a new item. No items will appear until the user clicks the list arrow at the right of the combo box. Setting the Style property to 1 - Simple Combo displays a text box and a list that does not drop down. Instead, the list shows all choices at all times. If the list will not fit inside the combo box, a scroll bar appears. The user can then specify a value for the combo box that does not appear in the list of suggested choices in the text box. Setting the Style property to 2 - Dropdown List allows a user to select an item only from a preset drop-down list of choices. As with the drop-down combo box, this list does not appear until the user clicks the list arrow at the right of the combo box.
	■ The **List** property specifies the items stored in the combo box. You can set the List property at design time using the Properties window. To add or remove items at run time, you can call the AddItem and RemoveItem methods. These methods update the List property.
	■ The **Sorted** property, when set to True, displays the items in alphabetical order even if they were not added in alphabetical order. If set to False, the items appear in the order in which they were added.
	■ The **ItemData** property is a list of Long Integer values containing the same number of items as the control's List property. You can use the numbers associated with each item to identify the list items. Thus the ItemData property can serve as an index into another array or list. When you insert an item with the AddItem method, an item is simultaneously inserted into the ItemData array.
	■ The **NewIndex** property works in conjunction with the ItemData property. If you are placing items in a sorted list, each new item is added to the list in alphabetical order. To determine where an item was inserted, you use the NewIndex property. It returns the index of the item most recently added to the combo box or list box.

- The **ListIndex** property is an Integer value that identifies the currently selected item in a combo box. The first item in the list has a ListIndex property value of zero (0), the second item has a value of one (1), and so on. If no item is selected, the ListIndex property has a value of negative one (-1).

- The **ListCount** property is an Integer value that returns the number of items in a list. If the list is empty, the value of the ListCount property is zero (0); otherwise, its value indicates the number of items in the list.

- The **Text** property contains the text of the currently selected item. If no item is selected, then the Text property remains blank.

Methods

- The **AddItem** method adds an item to the list at run time, which updates the List property.

- The **Clear** method removes all items from the list. Calling this method causes the ListCount property to be set to zero (0). At the same time, the ListIndex property is set to negative one (-1).

- The **RemoveItem** method removes one item from the list. This procedure causes the List property to be updated and the ListCount property to be decremented by 1.

The Style property determines the visual appearance of the combo box. Figure 7-3 shows the different styles of combo boxes that could appear on a form.

Dropdown Combo and Dropdown List ComboBox objects

Simple Combo ComboBox object

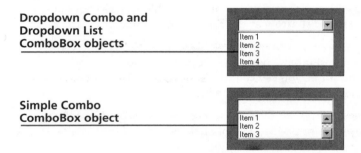

Figure 7-3: Types of ComboBox objects

In developing Star Plant Supply's program, you will add items to the combo box at run time, when the form loads, so you will not set the List property in the Properties window at design time. The items will appear in the list in the same order as they appear in the input file, so you will not set the Sorted property or use the ItemData property. Because the user will only select items from the list rather than adding new items, and because the form does not have enough room to display each item in the list, you will use a Dropdown List combo box.

To create a combo box:
1   Click the **ComboBox** control ▣ on the toolbox and draw an instance of it, as shown in Figure 7-4.

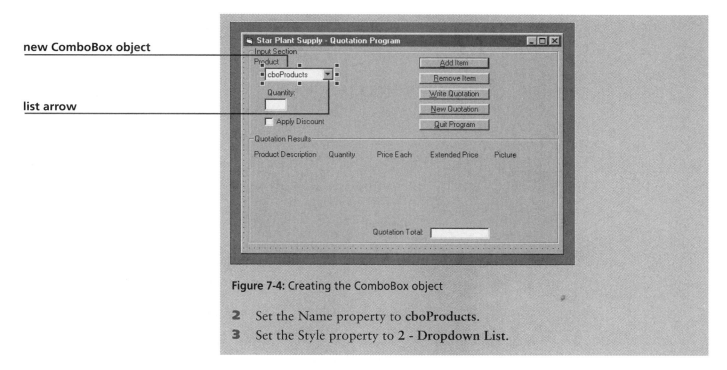

Figure 7-4: Creating the ComboBox object

2   Set the Name property to **cboProducts**.

3   Set the Style property to **2 - Dropdown List**.

Later, you will write the necessary code to add items to the combo box when the form loads. This information currently appears in the price list. Thus you will not set the List property at design time.

In addition to developing the combo box used for input, you must create the output objects. These output objects will also display information in the form of a list.

The ListBox Control

After the user selects a product from the combo box, specifies a quantity ordered, and clicks the Add Item command button, the item, quantity ordered, price, and extended price are displayed in the output section of the form. Because a given quote can contain several items, the program must be able to show information for several items at once. This goal can be accomplished with the **ListBox** control.

The ListBox and ComboBox controls share many of the same properties. The user cannot enter new items into a list box by typing in information, however. Rather, the programmer must add items at design time by setting the List property or at run time by calling the AddItem method of the list box. You now will create the list boxes that display the quote information.

The standard prefix for a list box is "lst". Because you are creating list boxes to store the quoted products, quantity selected, price, and extended price, you will name the objects lstQuotedProduct, lstQuotedQty, lstQuotedPrice, and lstQuotedExtPrice, respectively.

To create the ListBox objects:

1   Click the **ListBox** control 🔲 on the toolbox and draw an instance of a list box under the Product Description label, as shown in Figure 7-5. Set the Name property to **lstQuotedProduct**. Note that the first character of the object name is a lowercase "L", not the numeral "1."

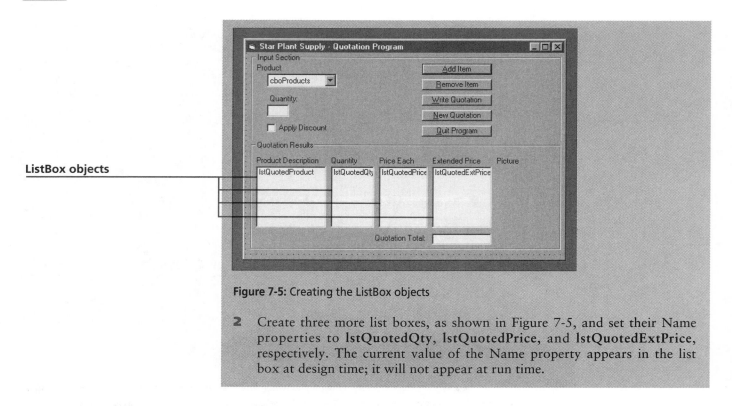

Figure 7-5: Creating the ListBox objects

2 Create three more list boxes, as shown in Figure 7-5, and set their Name properties to **lstQuotedQty**, **lstQuotedPrice**, and **lstQuotedExtPrice**, respectively. The current value of the Name property appears in the list box at design time; it will not appear at run time.

The price list includes one product and its corresponding price on each line. A change in a price or the addition of a new item to the inventory prompts an update of this list. Figure 7-6 shows a printout of the first nine items in the price list.

Flower - Iris	4.37
Flower - Lilac	5.22
Herb - Mint	1.88
Shrub - Juniper	4.18
Shrub - Boxwood	9.22
Tree - Ash	43.80
Tree - Pine	28.60
Tree - Oak	33.84
Tree - Olive	19.20

Figure 7-6: Price list for Star Plant Supply

Before your quote program can read the text file that contains the price list, it must be reformatted. To use the text file with Visual Basic, the tabs must be removed. Also, each field must be separated from the others by a comma, and the spaces between the fields must be removed. The product names must be enclosed in quotation marks because they contain text, rather than numbers. Note that numeric data—in this case, the prices—is not enclosed in quotation marks.

To complete Star Plant Supply's program, you will use a text file that has already been correctly formatted for the quote program.

Processing Text Files

When the quote program starts, it must initially load all of the products from the text file into the combo box that lists these products.

In Chapter 5, you accessed a table in a database by creating an instance of a Data control and using the methods of the Data control and the Recordset object to navigate through the records. Unlike a database, a text file is not manipulated using objects. Instead of calling the methods of an object like a recordset, you must use Visual Basic statements to open a text file and read its data. Once a text file is open, you can read it from beginning to end. This strategy for accessing a text file is called **sequential access**.

Note, however, that a program cannot explicitly locate a specific line in a text file without reading all of the lines preceding it. Also, it is not possible to move backward through a file when reading it sequentially.

Opening a Text File

When you open a text file, you must explicitly open the file and tell Visual Basic which operations to perform on it. You open a text file with the Open statement.

Syntax	**Open** *"pathname"* **For [Input	Output	Append] As** #*filenumber*
Dissection	■ The **Open** statement opens a file.
	■ The *pathname* contains a string describing the name and location of the file that you want to open. This string must be enclosed in quotation marks if you enter text, though you omit the quotation marks if you use a variable.
	■ You must include one of three options—For Input, For Output, or For Append—in the Open statement, or Visual Basic will generate a syntax error. If the file is opened **For Input**, the file must already exist. Your program can read text from the file, but cannot write to it. If the file opened **For Output**, your program can write to the file, but cannot read from it. If the file opened For Output does not exist, Visual Basic will create it; if the file does exist, its existing contents will be deleted when the file is opened. The end user will not be asked to confirm the deletion. As the programmer, you can opt to display a message box before opening the file For Output that asks for confirmation from the end user. The For Output option is useful if you want to rewrite an existing file entirely. If the file is opened **For Append**, information written to the file will be appended to the end of the file. If the file does not exist, Visual Basic will create it. Unlike a file opened For Output, the existing contents of a file opened For Append will not be deleted.
	■ To read from a file opened For Output or For Append or to write to a file opened For Input, you must close the file and open it again using the desired option.
	■ The required *filenumber* argument is an arbitrary Integer number you assign as a reference to the file while it is open. The filenumber must be preceded by the # (pound) character. If you do not specify a filenumber, Visual Basic will generate a syntax error. This argument must be preceded by the **As** keyword.

| **Code Example** | ```
Dim pstrFile As String
pstrFile = "A:\Chapter.07\Startup\Product.txt"
Open "A:\Chapter.07\Startup\Product.txt" For Input As #1
Open pstrFile For Input As #1
``` |
| **Code Dissection** | The preceding statements open the file named Product.txt For Input. The filenumber assigned to the open file is 1. Both Open statements have an equivalent effect, but the first uses a text string and the second uses a variable. |

Programming tip

Although you can use any Integer number for the filenumber, starting the filenumber at #1 for the first open file and #2 for the second open file will make your program more understandable. Although you can maintain several open files at once, you cannot open an infinite number of files. Windows determines how many total files can remain open simultaneously. Because this number varies from system to system, it is a good practice to close a file once you have finished reading from it or writing to it.

Because the information contained in the text file must be loaded before the user can prepare any quotes, the program should read the text file and store the list of products into the combo box when the program first begins. You will therefore open the file in the form's Load event procedure.

To open a text file for reading:

1   Open the Code window for the **Form_Load** event procedure, then enter the following code in the window. Replace the path name as necessary, depending on the location of the file Product.txt.

```
Open "A:\Chapter.07\Startup\Product.txt" For Input As #1
```

This statement opens the price list file, Chapter.07\Startup\Product.txt. Because you will be reading the file, you opened it For Input. As the first open file, its filenumber is #1.

Reading a Text File

After opening the file For Input, the program needs to read each product from the file into the Product combo box. You could enter all the items at design time by setting the combo box's List property, but then you would have to make any changes to the list of products by modifying the value of the List property via the Properties window. Because modifying the program is not a task generally performed by the end user, reading the products from a file at run time is the best solution. The salespeople at Star Plant Supply can then update the text file in WordPad when they must add or remove a product or when the prices change. As long as the price list is kept current, every time the user runs the program, it will read the current information from the text file.

Programming tip

If the contents of a combo or list box are likely to change, read the items at run time from a text file or database table. If the contents will not change, set the List property at design time.

Visual Basic can use an Input # statement to read text files when each field in a line is separated, or delimited, by a comma, and when string information is enclosed in quotation marks. This type of text file, known as an **ASCII-delimited file**, is supported by most word processing, spreadsheet, and database programs. Figure 7-7 shows part of the ASCII-delimited file for Star Plant Supply's quote program.
```

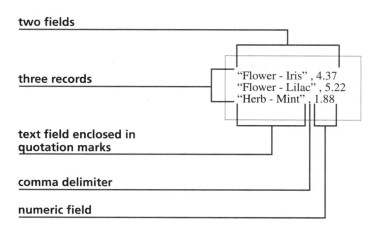

two fields

three records

"Flower - Iris" , 4.37
"Flower - Lilac" , 5.22
"Herb - Mint" , 1.88

text field enclosed in quotation marks

comma delimiter

numeric field

Figure 7-7: ASCII-delimited file with two fields

As shown in Figure 7-7, the input text file contains two items of information separated by a comma. Each item can be thought of as a field. The first field contains text; text fields should always be enclosed in quotation marks. The second field is numeric; it is not enclosed in quotation marks. Each line in the file represents a record. Figure 7-7 displays three records.

When you create an ASCII-delimited file, make sure that each record contains the correct number of fields. If a particular field in a record contains no information, create a blank entry by placing two commas next to one another. Also, each line in an ASCII-delimited file must end with a carriage return, including the last line. Typically, if the input file is not correct, the program will generate a run-time error indicating that you tried to read past the end of file.

Syntax	Input #*filenumber, varlist*
Dissection	■ The **Input #** statement reads a line of text from an open file. When information in the input file is separated by commas, each item is considered a field, just as in a database. Each field in the text file must be separated by a comma and any text strings in the file must be enclosed in quotation marks.
	■ The *filenumber* can be any valid filenumber assigned by the Open statement. It is preceded by the # character.
	■ The optional *varlist* comprises a list of variables, separated by commas, consisting of assigned values that are read from the file. The data type of each variable must correspond to the data type in the respective field.

Generally, you should read a text file just after opening it; therefore the program should read the file immediately after opening it in the Form_Load event procedure. To accomplish this task, you will create a variable to temporarily store the information read from the text file before adding it to the Product combo box.

To read a text file, you will create a Do loop that calls the Input # statement repeatedly until the program reaches the end of the file. To identify the end of file, you will use the EOF function.

Syntax	EOF(*filenumber*)
Dissection	■ The **EOF** function takes one argument—the *filenumber* assigned to a file when it was opened. The EOF function returns the Boolean value True if filenumber is at the end of the file; it returns False otherwise. ■ The *filenumber* contains the Integer number of the open file.
Code Example	``` Do Until EOF(1) = True ' Statements to read a record from the file. Loop ```
Code Dissection	The preceding Do loop tests whether *filenumber* 1 is not at the end of file. If the end of file has been reached, the loop exits. Otherwise the statements in the loop execute and test the condition again.

In this situation, we chose a Do loop rather than a For loop because the program does not know in advance how many records appear in the file. If you knew the number of lines in advance, you could write a For loop to iterate from the first line to the last line. Recall from Chapter 6 that a For loop can be used only when you know how many times the loop must execute. Otherwise, you must employ a Do loop.

To read a text file:
1 Make sure that the Code window for the **Form_Load** event procedure is active, then enter the following statements (shown in bold) in the event procedure:

```
Dim pstrProduct As String
Dim psngPrice As Single
Open "A:\Chapter.07\Startup\Product.txt" For Input As #1
Do Until EOF(1) = True
    Input #1, pstrProduct, psngPrice
Loop
```

These statements read each record from the text file and load each field into the variables named pstrProduct and psngPrice. At this point, the loop is incomplete. Although the information in the file is read into the variables, the program overwrites their values each time through the loop. Later in this section, you will see how to store the information pertaining to each record into the program.

```
Dim pstrProduct As String
Dim psngPrice As Single
```

The Dim statements declare two local variables. The variable pstrProduct will store the name of each product. The variable psngPrice will store the price of each product, which you will use later in this section.

```
Do Until EOF(1) = True
     Input #1, pstrProduct, psngPrice
Loop
```

The EOF function determines when the end of file is reached, allowing the program to exit the Do loop. The EOF function returns the value True if the end of file has been reached; otherwise it returns the value False. The argument 1 is the filenumber corresponding to the open file.

In the Input statement, the filenumber #1 is associated with the file opened upon execution of the Open statement. Each time the program reads a line from the file, the values read are stored in the variables pstrProduct and psngPrice. If the input file included more than two fields on a line, you would have stored the other fields in additional variables separated by commas. Because the number of variables in the Input statement must correspond to the number of fields in the file, we must include the variable psngPrice here, even though the program does not use this variable at this point.

The Loop statement sends the program back to the Do statement to determine whether it has reached the end of file.

The AddItem Method

To this point, the text file has been read into the computer's memory, but the description of each product needs to appear in the combo box. The AddItem method works with both the ComboBox and ListBox objects and is used to add an item to the list of choices at run time.

Syntax	*object.***AddItem** *text*
Dissection	■ The *object* represents an instance of the ComboBox or ListBox controls.
	■ The **AddItem** method adds an item to the list of items at run time.
	■ The *text* argument represents the individual item to be added to the list. Each item will appear in the combo box or list box when the program runs. To add five different items to a list, for example, you must call the AddItem method five times with different text strings. You can store numeric data in a list box or combo box. If you store numeric data, however, then the data is converted to a string before it is inserted into the list or combo box.
Code Example	`cboProducts.AddItem "Item 1"`
Code Dissection	The preceding statement adds an item to the combo box named cboProducts. The text of the item is "Item 1". After calling this method, the List property is updated to reflect the newly added item. The ListCount property is updated as well.

You now can write the statement to call the AddItem method that will store the contents of the variable pstrProduct into the combo box. This statement should execute each time a record is read from the input file, so the code that adds the item to the combo box should appear inside the Do loop.

To call the AddItem method:

1 Make sure that the Code window for the **Form_Load** event procedure is active, then enter the following statement (shown in bold) into the event procedure, just after the Input # statement and just before the Loop statement:

```
Do Until EOF(1) = True
    Input #1, pstrProduct, psngPrice
    cboProducts.AddItem pstrProduct
Loop
```

2 Enter the following statement in the **cmdExit_Click** event procedure to end the program:

```
Unload Me
```

Whenever a program finishes reading from or writing to a file, it should close the file. Because Windows limits the number of files that can remain open at one time, closing unused files will ensure that adequate file numbers remain. Also, each open file consumes some amount of memory. Depending on the amount of memory in your computer, too many open files can slow down your computer.

Closing a Text File

When the program finishes reading a file, it should explicitly close the file using the Close statement.

Syntax	**Close** *filenumberlist*
Dissection	■ The **Close** statement explicitly closes one or more files.
	■ If you do not specify a *filenumberlist*, any files opened with the Open statement will be closed. If you are working with several files, then including such a Close statement just before the program exits will guarantee that all files are closed.
	■ The arguments can consist of one or more filenumbers separated by commas.
Code Example	`Close #1, #2` `Close`
Code Dissection	The first statement closes file #1 and file #2. The second statement closes all open files.

Programming

tip

• • • • • • • • • • • • • • •

▶ Whenever you have finished processing a file, use the Close statement to explicitly close the file. This approach will prevent corruption of a file in the event of a power failure or an improperly terminated program.

You currently have one file—Product.txt—open, and it is associated with the filenumber #1. You now need to write the code to close this file.

To close an open text file:

1 Open the Code window for the **Form_Load** event procedure, then enter the following statement (shown in bold) just before the End Sub statement:

```
    Loop
    Close #1
End Sub
```

When the running program reaches this statement, it will close the Product.txt file. The filenumber #1 will no longer be associated with the file. If a program needs to read the file again, it must reopen the file with the Open statement.

You have now completed the programming to open the text file, read all of the records, and add the description of each product to the combo box named cboProducts. After reading in all of the records, the program closes the file. You now should test the Do loop to see whether the products in the text file are read into the Product combo box correctly.

To test the Do loop:

1 Save the project, then run it.

2 Click the list arrow on the rightmost side of the Product combo box. Your screen should match Figure 7-8.

products from text file stored in combo box

Figure 7-8: Combo box with products

help

• • • • • • • • • • • • • • •

▶ If the products are loaded in the combo box correctly, make sure that your code matches the code in the previous steps. If incorrect information appears, make sure that the Input # statement lists both variables. Make any necessary corrections, then repeat Steps 1 and 2.

The Product combo box now displays the products that Star Plant Supply sells. Because all of the products will not fit into the combo box simultaneously, a scroll bar appears so that the user can scroll through the list.

3 Test the **Quit Program** button to end the program.

Every time you run the program, the information in the first field of the Product.txt file will appear in the Product combo box. Now, you must write the code to store the prices corresponding to these products.

Creating an Array to Store Information

In programs you have written until this point, you declared variables that can store only a single item of information, such as an interest rate or the term of a loan. In the quote program, you must store the price for each product sold by Star Plant Supply; thus you will store multiple prices. When the user selects an item from the Product combo box, the program should look up the corresponding price for that product. The company sells many different products, so you would need many different variables to store the information. Although creating different variables does not present a problem in this case, consider a company that sells 500 or 5,000 products. The situation becomes further complicated when you add more products, because you would need to declare additional variables. The solution is to declare a variable that can store several items.

You have seen how you can group several objects of the same type together in a control array. Each object in a control array has the same name and is referenced with a unique Index property value. An array can also group variables. An **array** is a variable that contains a list of several items, each having the same data type. Each item in an array is called an **element**. Each individual element is referenced by a unique index number known as a **subscript**. Thus an array is simply a variable that contains many elements of the same data type. To access an individual element in an array, you use the array name and the subscript to reference the element.

You can create an array to store the prices of all of the items in one variable, just as you can store many items in one combo or list box. Figure 7-9 illustrates the relationship between the information stored in the array and the combo box. In Figure 7-9, the array is named msngPrices. This name uses the standard conventions for naming variables—the first character, "m", denotes that the array is a module-level variable and the prefix "sng" indicates that the array stores single precision numbers.

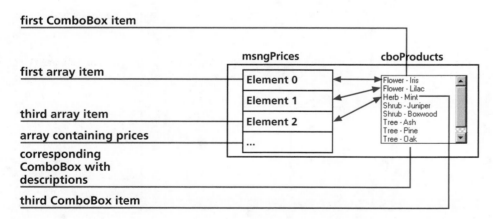

Figure 7-9: Relationship between an array and a combo box

In Figure 7-9, the array msngPrices contains three elements, with subscripts 0 through 2, that correspond to the product descriptions stored in the cboProducts combo box. Thus the price for the first product, Flower - Iris, is stored in the first element of msngPrices, which is element 0.

To create an array, you use a Dim, Private, or Public statement, just as you would to declare any variable. To declare an array for use in a single module, you include a Private statement in the general declarations section of the module.

Syntax	**Private** *array-name*([*lower-bound* **To**]*upper-bound*) **As** *datatype*
Dissection	■ The **Private** statement declares a module-level array. ■ The *array-name* can consist of any valid variable name. ■ The *lower-bound* defines the subscript of the first element of the array. If you do not specify a lower-bound, it will be set to 0 by default. The keyword **To** specifies the range of the array. ■ The *upper-bound* defines the subscript of the last element of the array. ■ The array can be declared as any valid *datatype* using the keyword **As**.
Code Example	`Private mintValues(0 To 3) As Integer` `Private msngValues(1 To 4) As Single`
Code Dissection	Both of the preceding statements declare an array with four elements. In the first statement, the subscripts range from 0 to 3. In the second statement, the subscripts range from 1 to 4. The first statement declares an array of integers, and the second declares an array of single precision numbers.

For Star Plant Supply's program, you need to create an array to store the price for each product corresponding to the description loaded into the Product combo box. Like any variable, an array declared in the general declarations section of a form module becomes available to all procedures in the module if you use the Private keyword. You cannot declare a Public array in a form module. If you declare an array inside a procedure by using the Dim statement, the array will be considered local to the procedure and can be referenced inside that procedure only. Because many procedures will access the array in the quote program, you must declare the array in the general declarations section.

Like variables, arrays consume memory. Too large an array will waste memory, because Visual Basic allocates memory for each element in the array regardless of whether the program stores a value in that element.

You should make an attempt to estimate accurately the number of elements in the array for your program. Star Plant Supply anticipates that it will sell at most 100 different products, so you should declare an array that holds 100 items. You do not need to store a value in each element of an array immediately, but rather can add values later. Running the program with some empty array elements will not cause an error. With the module-level array that holds the prices, you will use the Single data type and the name msngPrices.

To declare an array:

1 Activate the general declarations section of the Code window for the form module, then enter the following statement (shown in bold) in the Code window:

```
Option Explicit
Private msngPrices(0 To 99) As Single
```

The array msngPrices contains 100 elements. The first element (subscript) is 0, and the last element is 99. Each element in the array is defined as a Single data type, which is the appropriate data type because the prices will contain a decimal point.

Storing Information in an Array

After declaring an array, you need to store information—the price for each item—in it. Each price will correspond to an item in the Product combo box, as shown in Figure 7-9, but your array will include 100 elements (instead of 3).

In storing data in and retrieving data from an array, you are interested in a specific element rather than the contents of the entire array. In this case, the array stores the price for each product in the inventory. To look up a price in the array, you will search for the price of a particular item rather than all of the prices. The price of each product must be stored in the array such that the first item in the Product combo box corresponds to the price contained in the first element of the array.

The procedure for loading the prices into the array resembles the procedure for loading the products into the combo box. Because all of the products and corresponding prices must be placed into the computer's memory before the salesperson can write a quote, the array should be loaded at the same time that the products are loaded into the combo box. To accomplish this task, you will modify the existing Form_Load event procedure to add the necessary statements for loading prices into the array. To keep track of the current array element, you will create a variable that will serve as a subscript. Because a subscript always contains a whole number and the array includes only 100 elements, you will declare this variable as an Integer. If the array needed to store more than 32,767 elements, then you would declare this variable as a Long. Each time through the Do loop, the subscript must be incremented by 1. In the example that follows, the variable is used much like a counter.

To store data into an array:

1   Activate the Code window for the **Form_Load** event procedure, then add the following statements (shown in bold) to the event procedure:

```
Dim psngPrice As Single
Dim pintCurrentItem As Integer
pintCurrentItem = 0
Open "A:\Chapter.07\Startup\Product.txt" For Input As #1
Do Until EOF(1) = True
    Input #1, pstrProduct, psngPrice
    cboProducts.AddItem pstrProduct
    msngPrices(pintCurrentItem) = psngPrice
    pintCurrentItem = pintCurrentItem + 1
Loop
```

This code will load the prices from the text file into the array.

```
Dim pintCurrentItem As Integer
pintCurrentItem = 0
```

In this code, the variable pintCurrentItem is used as an array subscript, which is always a whole number. Because the program should load the first line of the text file into the first element of the array, you initialized the pintCurrentItem variable to zero.

```
msngPrices(pintCurrentItem) = psngPrice
pintCurrentItem = pintCurrentItem + 1
```

Each time the program reads a line from the input file, it assigns the variable used in the Input # statement, psngPrice, to an array element in msngPrices. This element corresponds to the product contained in the Product combo box. To reference a specific element in an array, you use the subscript to identify a specific element of the array. Because the variable pintCurrentItem was initialized to zero, the first value of psngPrice will be stored at element position 0—the lower bound of the array. Next, pintCurrentItem is incremented explicitly by 1. As a result, the next time through the loop, the value of psngPrice will be stored in the next element.

Now that you have written the necessary code to read the product descriptions into the list box and the corresponding prices into the array, you must write the statements to look up the appropriate price in the array when a salesperson clicks a product in the combo box. In addition, the program needs to copy the selected product description and price into the ListBox objects used for output when the user clicks the Add Item command button. To accomplish this task, you can take advantage of the ListIndex property of the ComboBox object.

The ListIndex property is an Integer value that identifies the currently selected item in a list or combo box. The expression List1.ListIndex returns the Integer index for the currently selected item in the ListBox object named List1. This approach resembles the way in which you reference an element in an array with a subscript; with an array, however, you do not use a property. You can assign a value to the ListIndex property for a list or combo box. In this way, you set the active item for the list. For example, if you wanted to make the currently selected item become the first item of a list box, you would set its ListIndex property to zero. To deselect all items in the list, you would set the ListIndex property to negative one (-1).

Adding an item to the quote is the most common event that a user will trigger in this program. To allow salespersons to press the Enter key and thereby add an item to the quotation, the Default property of the Add Item command button is set to True. Next, you need to program the Add Item command button to look up the price for the selected product and store the product and price information in the output list boxes. The description for the selected product resides in the Text property of the cboProducts combo box and must be added to the Product

Description output list box. In addition, you must add the item's price to the Price Each output list box. This information should be formatted with two decimal places, so you will use the Format statement with the Fixed argument. You will program the quantity list box later in this section.

To call the AddItem method pertaining to a list box:

1 Activate the Code window for the **cmdAdd_Click** event procedure, then enter the following statements in the event procedure:

```
If cboProducts.ListIndex > -1 Then
    lstQuotedProduct.AddItem cboProducts.Text
    lstQuotedPrice.AddItem _
        Format(msngPrices(cboProducts.ListIndex), _
        "Fixed")
    cboProducts.ListIndex = -1
End If
```

Each time the user clicks a product in the Product combo box and then clicks the Add Item command button, this code will place the new information into the Product Description and Price Each output list boxes.

The code to add an item is enclosed in an If statement. This If statement checks that the user has selected an item in the combo box. If no product is selected—that is, if ListIndex = -1—then no attempt is made to add an item to the quotation. If the If statement was omitted and no product was selected, a run-time error would occur.

```
lstQuotedProduct.AddItem cboProducts.Text
```

This statement adds the text of the currently selected item in the Product combo box to the output list box named lstQuotedProduct.

```
lstQuotedPrice.AddItem _
    Format(msngPrices(cboProducts.ListIndex), _
    "Fixed")
```

This statement uses the array you created to locate the price for the selected product. It references the value of the ListIndex property of the currently selected product in the Product combo box, and that value then becomes the subscript referenced in the msngPrices. Figure 7-10 shows how this process works. To display the prices with two decimal places, you used the Format function with the Fixed argument.

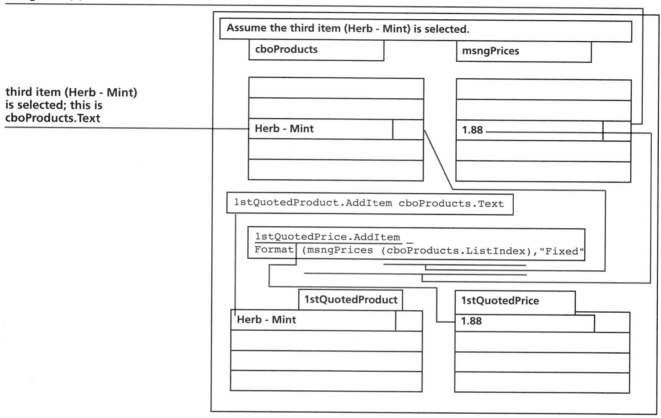

third element— msngPrices(2)

third item (Herb - Mint) is selected; this is cboProducts.Text

Figure 7-10: Adding the product and price to the output lists

```
cboProducts.ListIndex = -1
```

This statement sets the ListIndex property of the combo box to -1, which deselects the item in the Product combo box. The combo box is thereby cleared for the next product selection.

You now should test the program to determine whether the Add Item command button works properly. When clicked, this button should add the selected product and its corresponding price to the quotation and then deselect the active item in the Product combo box.

To test the Add Item command button:

1 Save the project, then run it.

2 Click the list arrow in the Product combo box, then click the product **Herb - Mint**.

3 Click the **Add Item** command button. Your screen should match Figure 7-11.

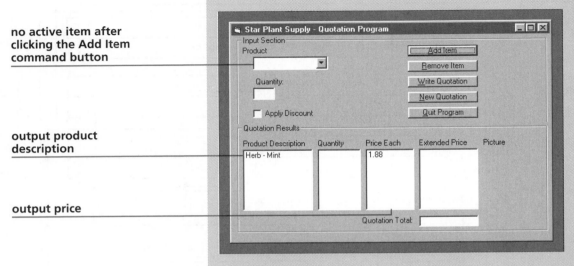

no active item after clicking the Add Item command button

output product description

output price

Figure 7-11: Testing the Add Item command button

4 Scroll through the Product list, then click the product **Tree - Oak**.

5 Press the **Enter** key to verify that the Add Item button acts as the default button. Tree - Oak is added to the Product Description output list, and 33.84 is added to the Price Each output list.

6 Click the **Add Item** button while no product is selected. Nothing should be added to the output list boxes.

7 End the program.

Now you are ready to place the quantity ordered and the extended price in the corresponding output list boxes as each item is added. This action should occur when the user clicks the Add Item command button. When the user selects an item in the combo box and enters the quantity ordered, the quantity ordered must be added to the Quantity list box and the extended price computed. The extended price is stored in a local variable, named psngExtPrice. Because this variable is used by this procedure only, you declare it to be local. Because it will store prices, you declare it as a Single data type. To compute the extended price, you look up the correct price in the msngPrices array and multiply that value by the quantity ordered. The output should be displayed with two decimal places, so you will use the Format statement with the Fixed argument. The result is then displayed in the Extended Price list box.

To write the code to display output in the list boxes:

1 Activate the Code window for the **cmdAdd_Click** event procedure, then add the following statements (shown in bold) to the event procedure:

```
Private Sub cmdAdd_Click()
    Dim psngExtPrice As Single
    If cboProducts.ListIndex > -1 Then
        If IsNumeric(txtQty.Text) Then
            lstQuotedProduct.AddItem cboProducts.Text
            psngExtPrice = (txtQty.Text) * _
                msngPrices(cboProducts.ListIndex))
            lstQuotedPrice.AddItem _
                Format(msngPrices(cboProducts.ListIndex), _
                "Fixed")
            lstQuotedQty.AddItem txtQty.Text
            lstQuotedExtPrice.AddItem Format(psngExtPrice, _
                "Fixed")
            cboProducts.ListIndex = -1
            txtQty.Text = vbNullString
        End If
    End If
End Sub
```
(handwritten: Val inserted before (txtQty.Text))

This code copies the quantity from the Quantity text box in the input section to the Quantity list box in the output section when the user clicks the Add Item command button. It also computes the extended price and places it in the Extended Price list box in the output section. The additional If statement checks that txtQty contains a number. If you omitted this statement, the user could enter an invalid character, which would cause a run-time error.

```
Dim psngExtPrice As Single
psngExtPrice = (txtQty.Text) * _
    msngPrices(cboProducts.ListIndex))
```
(handwritten: Val inserted before (txtQty.Text))

The first statement creates a local variable, psngExtPrice, to store the temporary extended price computed in this procedure. The local variable you declared stores the extended price of the product. To compute the extended price, the ListIndex property of the Product combo box acts as the subscript of the array. If the user selects the first item in the combo box, the ListIndex property will have the value zero. Thus zero would be the subscript for the array because it represents the first element of the array. The desired array element is multiplied by the quantity requested and stored in the variable psngExtPrice. After computing the extended price, the program can add the items to the output list boxes.

```
lstQuotedQty.AddItem txtQty.Text
lstQuotedExtPrice.AddItem Format(psngExtPrice, _
    "Fixed")
```

The first statement adds the quantity of the specific item (stored in the Text property of the Quantity text box) to the lstQuotedQty list box. The second statement adds the computed extended price to the lstQuotedExtPrice list box by calling the AddItem method. To display the extended price with two decimal places, you called the Format function with the Fixed argument.

```
txtQty.Text = vbNullString
```

This statement sets the Text property of the txtQty text box to a blank value, which clears the Quantity text box and readies the form for the next product and quantity to be added.

Next, you should test the program to verify that it adds the output to the correct ListBox objects, computes the extended prices properly, and resets the input combo and text boxes.

To test the extended price and quantity output:

1   Save the project, then run it.

2   Enter the products and quantities shown in Figure 7-12.

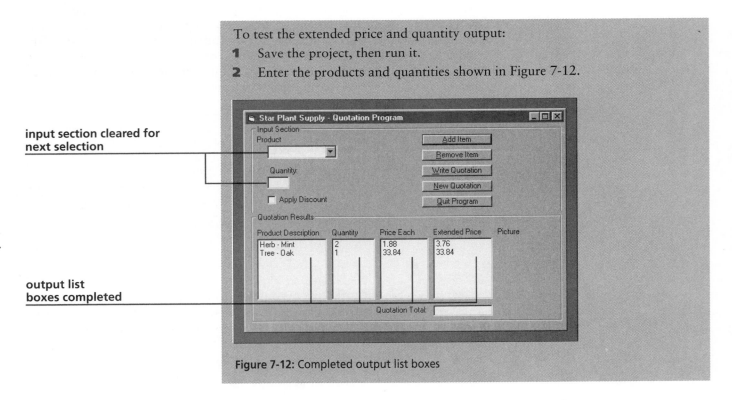

input section cleared for next selection

output list boxes completed

Figure 7-12: Completed output list boxes

The product description, quantity, price, and extended price should appear in the Quotation Results section on the form. The quotation total contains no information because you have not yet written the code to compute this value.

3 Try to add an item without specifying a quantity. The If statement should prevent the addition of an item without an accompanying quantity.

4 End the program.

You have now completed the statements to store each product's description, quantity, individual price, and extended price in the output list boxes. Your next task is to update the quotation total each time the user adds an item. To perform this task, you will create another Do loop.

Looping Through the Items in a List Box

In previous chapters, you used the Change or LostFocus event of an object to call a general procedure that calculated totals each time the value of the object changed or the focus moved to a different object. The ListBox object, however, does not support the Change event. Consequently, the program must update the total when the user clicks the Add Item command button. You will write a Do loop to examine each item in the extended price list box.

Earlier, you learned how to use a Do loop with the EOF function to examine each line of a text file repetitively until the end-of-file condition is reached. In that situation, the program did not know the number of lines in the text file. Rather, the loop terminated when the end-of-file condition was True. You could use a Do loop to step through each item in the Extended Price list box by creating a variable to be used as an index. Another ListBox property, the ListCount property, is an Integer that contains the number of items in a list box or combo box. If the list or combo box is empty, the ListCount is zero; otherwise, its value indicates the number of items in the list. Because you know in advance how many items appear in the list, you can employ a For loop. This For loop will examine each item in the list.

When used with an index, the List property of the ListBox and ComboBox acts like an array.

Syntax	*object*.**List**(*index*)
Dissection	■ The **List** property references the text in each item of a list box or combo box.
	■ You use the *index* of an item with the **List** property just as you would use the subscript for an array. The first list item has an index of zero.
Code Example	`pstrItem = lstMyList.List(0)` `lstMyList.List(0) = "New Text"`
Code Dissection	The first statement references the text stored in the first item of the list box named lstMyList; the text is stored in the variable named pstrItem. The second statement stores the string "New Text" in the first item of the list box named lstMyList.

For Star Plant Supply's quote program, you will create a loop that steps through all items in the Extended Price list box, allowing the program to compute the quotation total. The first item in the list box has an index of zero.

The ListCount property indicates how many items appear in the list. To compute the index value of the last item in the list, you simply subtract 1 from the ListCount property.

You now have the information needed to identify the start and end conditions of the For loop. You can use the List property with the index to reference the item that the program should examine. This index will serve as the counter for the For loop. The index of the first item in a list box is always zero, so the For loop should start at zero (0) and end when all of the items have been examined (ListCount - 1). The following generic code segment illustrates how to examine each item in a list box using a For loop:

```
For pintCurrent = 0 to lstDemo.ListCount —1
     ' Statements
Next
```

Using a For loop and the properties of the list box, you can compute the quotation total by adding together the extended prices in the Extended Price list box. You will declare a variable, named psngTotal, to serve as an accumulator that stores the quotation total. Because the variable will be used only by this procedure, you declare it as a local variable. Each time through the loop, the program must add the extended price to the accumulator. When the loop ends (each item has been examined), the result should be formatted with two decimal places and a leading dollar sign and displayed in the lblTotal label. Thus you will use the Format statement and store the result in the Caption property of lblTotal.

Because the program also must recompute the quotation total when the user removes a product, you can write the necessary code once in a general procedure and then call that procedure whenever the total needs to be recalculated. That is, the general procedure is called whenever an item is added to the quote or when an item is removed from the quote. You will name this procedure ComputeTotal to communicate its purpose. Because the program consists of a single form, and multiple procedures will use the general procedure, you will declare the procedure as Private.

To compute the quotation total using a For loop:

1 Make sure the Code window is active. Create a new **Private** general **Sub** procedure named **ComputeTotal**, then enter the following statements in the Code window:

```
Dim psngTotal As Single
Dim pintCurrentItem As Integer
psngTotal = 0
For pintCurrentItem = 0 To _
    lstQuotedExtPrice.ListCount - 1
    psngTotal = psngTotal + _
    CSng (lstQuotedExtPrice.List(pintCurrentItem)
Next
lblTotal.Caption = Format(psngTotal, "Currency")
```

With the For loop, these statements use a counter (pintCurrentItem) to examine each value in the Extended Price list box and add the value to an accumulator (psngTotal).

```
Dim psngTotal As Single
Dim pintCurrentItem As Integer
psngTotal = 0
```

These statements declare two local variables that exist only while the procedure is running. The variable psngTotal serves as an accumulator. Each time the program steps through an item in the Extended Price list box, it adds the extended price to psngTotal. The variable pintCurrentItem acts as the counter in the For loop. You initialize this variable by setting psngTotal to zero. The For loop then initializes the value of the counter pintCurrentItem automatically.

```
For pintCurrentItem = 0 To _
    lstQuotedExtPrice.ListCount - 1
    psngTotal = psngTotal + _
        lstQuotedExtPrice.List(pintCurrentItem)
Next
```

Programming

tip

It is a good practice to initialize variables explicitly before the program begins processing. This approach gives the reader of your program a clear indication of the desired value of the variable when the procedure starts.

The For loop steps through each item in the lstQuotedExtPrice list box by starting at item zero—that is, the start value of the For loop. You could use a similar For loop to review all elements in an array because you know the number of elements (indicated by the array subscript).

The List property of the list box retrieves the textual contents of the list box—in this case, the extended prices—and adds them to the total variable. Remember that the List property resembles an array in some ways; it requires an index of the element. In this case, the index is the loop's counter, pintCurrentItem.

When the program reaches the Next statement, it increments the value of pintCurrentItem by 1. If the new value of the counter is less than or equal to ListCount - 1, then the statements inside the For loop execute again. This process continues until no more items remain in the list box, which means that the counter has reached the end value, ListCount - 1, and the For loop exits. No Exit statements are needed to exit a For loop; it automatically exits when the end value of the counter is reached.

```
lblTotal.Caption = Format(psngTotal, "Currency")
```

This statement formats the quotation total with two decimal places and a leading dollar sign.

Now that you have written the ComputeTotal general procedure, you need to call it explicitly. The Add Item command button's Click event procedure controls the action that occurs when a product is added to the quotation. To update the quotation total whenever a new product is added to it, you call the general procedure from the Add Item command button's click event procedure.

To call the ComputeTotal general procedure:

1 Activate the Code window for the **cmdAdd_Click** event procedure, then add the following statement (shown in bold) to the procedure.

```
      End If
      ComputeTotal
End Sub
```

2 Test the program by entering the products and quantities shown in Figure 7-13.

enter these quantities

select these products

displays the total of the
extended prices

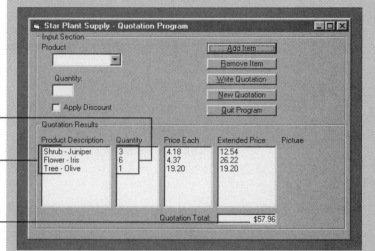

Figure 7-13: Testing the quotation total

3 Make sure that your extended prices and quotation total match those shown in Figure 7-13.

4 End the program.

5 Save the project and exit Visual Basic.

help

If the program fails to compute the quotation total, verify that you called the ComputeTotal procedure in the cmdAdd_Click event procedure. If the quotation total is not correct, check the code for the For loop in the ComputeTotal procedure. Make any necessary corrections, then repeat Steps 1 and 2.

You have now completed the first phase of the quote program. The salespeople can add products, quantities, and prices to a quote and see the new total of the quote with each addition. They also can create quotes electronically and with a minimal amount of typing. By preserving the contents of the text file containing the product and price information, they can print a copy of the file when one is needed.

Q U E S T I O N S

1. Which of the following is a valid style for a combo box?
   a. Dropdown combo
   b. Simple combo
   c. Dropdown list
   d. All of the above.
   e. None of the above.

2. Which of the following properties is supported by the combo box?
   a. List
   b. ListIndex
   c. Count
   d. Both a and b.
   e. All of the above.

3. Which of the following is a valid option for the Open statement?
   a. For Input
   b. For Output
   c. For Read
   d. Both a and b.
   e. All of the above.

4. What is the name of the method to add an entry to a list or combo box?
   a. AddList
   b. AddEntry
   c. AddItem
   d. Add
   e. None of the above.

5. Which of the following statements is true about arrays?
   a. They contain multiple elements of the same data type.
   b. An element is referenced using a subscript.
   c. A subscript must be of the String data type.
   d. Both a and b.
   e. All of the above.

6. Write the statement to open the file named C:\Text.txt for reading.

7. Create a Do loop to read file #1. Assume that the file has one field and that it is an Integer. Read the field into the array named pintFirst.

8. Create a For loop to add the integers 1 through 10 to the list box named lstInteger.

9. Write the statement(s) to deselect the current item in the list box named lstProducts.

10. Create a loop that will print to the Immediate window all of the items in the list box named lstCurrent.

In this section you will:

■ Clear the contents of a list box at run time

■ Remove specific items from a list box

■ Create arrays with rows and columns

■ Display pictures at run time

■ Write a text file

Doing More with List Boxes and Arrays

Modifying the Program

You have created a good program, but Star Plant Supply's salespeople still need additional features. First, they would like the ability to clear the contents of the output list boxes so that they can prepare new quotes. Second, they would need the capability to delete a particular item from a quote. Third, users need to specify discounted prices for customers having a large sales volume. Fourth, they would like the capability to display pictures corresponding to each item. Finally, the salespeople need a way to write the quote results to a file that can be formatted and then printed using a word processing program.

Star Plant Supply often gives its customers a discount depending on their annual purchasing volume, so the program must to be able to apply the discount. You will program an Apply Discount check box that will enable the user to apply a discount to the price charged, when appropriate. The company also would like to display pictures of the different products on the form for those occasions when the customer visits the office. This way, customers can see the products they are ordering. Next to the output list boxes, you will therefore include a picture box, which will display pictures of the various products. You need to complete the programming for the New Quotation, Remove Item, and Write Quotation buttons, as well as the Apply Discount check box and picture box.

Clearing the Contents of a List Box

After the salesperson completes a quote, the program needs to reset all of the output list boxes and the quotation total so as to begin a new quote for a new customer. The New Quotation command button will be used to ready the form for another quote. It should remove all of the items from the ListBox objects and set the quotation total to zero again. You can delete all of the items from the list boxes using the Clear method on each of the four ListBox objects.

Syntax	*object.***Clear**
Dissection	■ The *object* can be a ListBox or ComboBox object.
	■ The **Clear** method removes all of the items from the combo box or list box.
Code Example	`lstQuotedProduct.Clear`
Code Dissection	The preceding statement removes all of the items from the list box named lstQuotedProduct.

You now can write the code for the New Quotation command button. You will call the Clear method for each list box, clearing the contents of the quantity, the selected item in the combo box, and the quotation total.

To program the New Quotation command button:

1   Open the project file named **Chapter.07\Startup\Star_S.vbp** in the folder on your Student Disk, if necessary. Set the drive designator as necessary.

2   Open the Code window for the **cmdNewQuotation_Click** event procedure, then enter the following statements in the event procedure:

```
lstQuotedProduct.Clear
lstQuotedQty.Clear
lstQuotedPrice.Clear
lstQuotedExtPrice.Clear
lblTotal.Caption = vbNullString
txtQty.Text = vbNullString
cboProducts.ListIndex = -1
```

These statements clear the input and output objects in preparation for another quotation.

```
lstQuotedProduct.Clear
lstQuotedQty.Clear
lstQuotedPrice.Clear
lstQuotedExtPrice.Clear
```

These four statements call the Clear method to delete all of the items in the output list boxes.

```
lblTotal.Caption = vbNullString
txtQty.Text = vbNullString
cboProducts.ListIndex = -1
```

These statements erase the value of the Caption property of the Label object used for the quotation total, clear the contents of the Quantity text box, and deselect the active item in the Product combo box. It is essential to clear the Quantity text box and the Product combo box because, if the user selects a new product or enters a new quantity and does not click the Add Item button to add those selections to the output and to clear these objects, they would still be selected.

Now you should test the program to ensure that the code for the New Quotation command button works properly.

To test the New Quotation command button:

1 Test the program by entering the products and quantities shown in Figure 7-14.

objects will be blank
after clicking the New
Quotation button

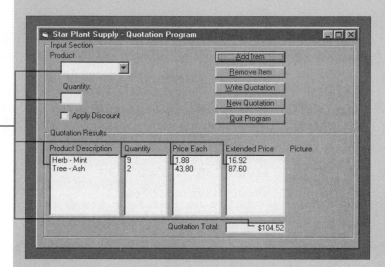

Figure 7-14: Testing the New Quotation command button

2 Click the **New Quotation** command button. Each line in the output list boxes should be erased. The Quotation Total label becomes blank, and no product appears selected in the Product combo box.

3 End the program.

If the output lists and quotation total do not clear, check the code for the New Quotation command button and make sure that you called the Clear method for each output ListBox object and set the text box's Text property to an empty string. Make any necessary corrections, then repeat Steps 1 and 2.

Now that you have used the Clear method to remove all items from a list box, you can write the statements that will allow the user to remove an individual item from the output list boxes.

Removing a Specific Item from a List Box

Just as you used the AddItem method to add an item to a list box, you can use the RemoveItem method to delete a specific item from a list box.

Syntax	*object*.**RemoveItem** *index*
Dissection	■ The *object* is any valid ListBox or ComboBox object.
	■ The **RemoveItem** method takes one argument—the *index* of the item you want to delete. If you want to remove the first item, the index is zero; if you want to remove the second item, the index is one; and so on.
	■ The *index* must be an existing item in the list box. If you attempt to remove a nonexistent item, a run-time error will occur.
Code Example	`lstQuotedProduct.RemoveItem 0`
Code Dissection	This statement removes the first item from the list box named lstQuotedProduct.

The program calls the RemoveItem method for each output list box when the user clicks the Remove Item command button. You will use a procedure-level Integer variable representing the ListIndex property as the index argument for each call to the RemoveItem method. After the deletion of an item from the quotation, you need to recompute the total; you will therefore call the ComputeTotal general procedure you wrote earlier.

To remove an item from a list box:
1 Activate the Code window for the **cmdRemove_Click** event procedure, then enter the following code:

```
Dim pintIndex As Integer
pintIndex = lstQuotedProduct.ListIndex
If pintIndex > -1 Then
    lstQuotedProduct.RemoveItem pintIndex
    lstQuotedQty.RemoveItem pintIndex
    lstQuotedPrice.RemoveItem pintIndex
    lstQuotedExtPrice.RemoveItem pintIndex
    ComputeTotal
End If
```

These statements remove the selected item from the output ListBox objects and recompute the quotation total.

```
Dim pintIndex As Integer
pintIndex = lstQuotedProduct.ListIndex
```

The preceding two statements declare the variable pintIndex and store the index of the currently selected item in that variable. When the program calls the RemoveItem method on the active item in the list, the ListIndex property is set to negative one (-1) because the active item no longer exists. If you try to use the ListIndex property, rather than the temporary variable, as the argument to the RemoveItem method when its value is -1, the program would generate a run-time error because the program attempts to remove a nonexistent item.

```
If pintIndex > -1 Then
    lstQuotedProduct.RemoveItem pintIndex
    lstQuotedQty.RemoveItem pintIndex
    lstQuotedPrice.RemoveItem pintIndex
    lstQuotedExtPrice.RemoveItem pintIndex
    ComputeTotal
End If
```

The preceding code uses an If statement to determine whether an item is selected in the lstQuotedProduct list box. If no item is selected, the value of the ListIndex property and of pintIndex is negative one (-1), so no attempt will be made to remove an item. Next, you call the RemoveItem method for each of the four output list boxes. Then, because an item was removed, the program recomputes the quotation total by calling the ComputeTotal general procedure.

You now should test the program to verify that the Remove Item command button's Click event works properly.

To test the Remove Item command button:

1 Test the program by entering the products and corresponding quantities into the quotation, as shown in Figure 7-15.

2 Click the product **Tree - Oak** in the output list box, as shown in Figure 7-15.

3 Click the **Remove Item** command button. The program should remove the item Tree - Oak from the output lists and recompute the quotation total.

4 Make sure no product is selected in the Product Description list box.

5 Click the **Remove Item** command button. No item should be removed from the lists and no error generated because the If statement tested whether nothing was selected.

enter these two products and quantities

select this item to be removed

total will update after clicking the Remove Item button

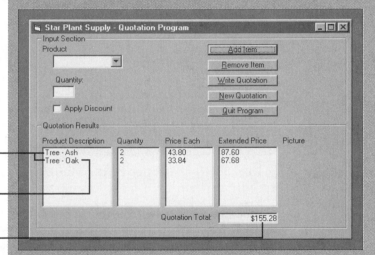

Figure 7-15: Testing the Remove Item command button

6 End the program.

help

• • • • • • • • • • • • • • • • • • •

▶ If a run-time error occurs or if the selected items were not deleted from the list and the quotation total was not recalculated, verify that the code for the Remove Item command button's Click event procedure matches the code shown in the previous steps. Make any necessary corrections, then repeat Steps 1 through 5.

Salespeople can now quickly search for each product and see a quote without worrying about looking up the wrong price or making a computational error. With the Remove Item command button, they can delete items from the quote without starting over from scratch.

The salespeople would also like the program to compute a discount for customers with a large annual sales volume. To accomplish this goal, you need to program the Apply Discount check box that indicates whether a discount should be applied and to create an array that can hold both the regular and discounted prices.

Creating a Two-Dimensional Array

One way to keep track of both regular prices and discounted prices is to declare a second price list array that contains the discounted prices. Another option is to create one array that provides two columns for each price field. One column will contain the regular price, and the other column will hold the discounted price. The resultant two-column array is called a **two-dimensional array**.

The "two-dimensional" in "two-dimensional array" refers to the rows and columns. The one-column array you created in Section A to hold the prices for the products was a one-dimensional array because it contained only rows. In the two-dimensional array for regular and discounted prices, one dimension—the rows—will hold the information for each element in the array and the other dimension—the columns—will hold the regular prices in one column and the discounted prices in a second column. Figure 7-16 shows part of the two-dimensional array for the regular and discounted prices.

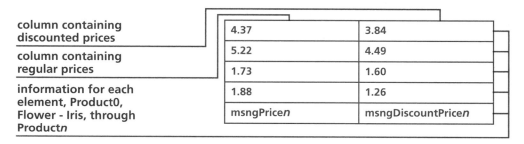

column containing discounted prices

column containing regular prices

information for each element, Product0, Flower - Iris, through Productn

4.37	3.84
5.22	4.49
1.73	1.60
1.88	1.26
msngPrice*n*	msngDiscountPrice*n*

Figure 7-16: Two-dimensional array

Like the one-dimensional array you created earlier, a two-dimensional array is not an object. Rather, it is a variable that contains elements. In a two-dimensional array, you make a reference to an individual element using a subscript, just as you do with a one-dimensional array. On the other hand, you must supply a subscript for each dimension of the array. A two-dimensional array therefore has two subscripts: one identifying the row number and the other identifying the column number. The syntax to create a two-dimensional array is similar to the syntax to create a one-dimensional array.

Syntax	**Private** *arrayname*([*lowerbound* **To**] *upperbound*, [*lowerbound* **To**] _ *upperbound*) **As** *datatype*
Dissection	■ This statement declares a form-level array with the name *arrayname*, which can be any valid variable name. ■ The first subscript is the range of rows; the second is the range of columns. The first *lowerbound* defines the element in the first row of the array. The second *lowerbound* defines the element in the first column of the array. If you do not specify a *lowerbound*, it will be set to zero by default. ■ The first *upperbound* defines the element in the last row of the array. The second *upperbound* defines the element in the last column of the array. ■ The *datatype* can be any valid Visual Basic data type.
Code Example	```Private msngPrices(0 To 99, 0 To 1) As Single```
Code Dissection	The preceding statement declares a two-dimensional array with 100 rows and 2 columns. Each element in the array is of the Single data type.

In addition to declaring a two-dimensional array, you must also reference elements in the array. The syntax to reference a two-dimensional array is similar to the syntax to reference a one-dimensional array, with the exception that two subscripts are used.

```
msngPrice = msngPrices(0,0)
msngPrice = msngPrices(99,1)
```

The first statement references the first row and column in the array msngPrices. The second statement references the last row and column.

For Star Plant Supply's program, you need to change the price array msngPrices so it has two columns. The first column will store the regular prices, and the second column will hold the discounted prices.

To declare a two-dimensional array:

1 Activate the **general declarations** section of the Code window for the form module, then change the declaration of the array **msngPrices**:

```
Private msngPrices(0 To 99,0 To 1) As Single
```

This statement declares a two-dimensional array consisting of 100 rows and two columns. It can store 100 products in its rows for each of the two different prices.

Next, you need to write the statements to load the array. The text file contains the discounted prices separated by commas. You will create a variable named psngDiscountPrice, which stores the discounted prices, and modify the Input # statement in the Form_Load event procedure so that it reads the entire contents of the new file. The first subscript refers to the rows, as in the original array. The second subscript refers to the columns. The first column can be referenced by using a subscript of zero. The second column has a subscript of one.

To reference a two-dimensional array:

1 Activate the Code window for the **Form_Load** event procedure, then change the Open statement so that it reads the file named **Product2.txt** rather than the file named Product.txt. This file contains an additional field that stores the discounted prices. It also contains a field holding the name of a bitmap file. You will use this field later in the chapter.

2 Enter the following variable declarations (shown in bold) into the **Form_Load** event procedure just after the other variable declarations:

```
Dim pintCurrentItem As Integer
Dim psngDiscountPrice As Single
Dim pstrPicture As String
```

Later in this section, you will use the variable pstrPicture to store the file names containing pictures of Star Plant Supply's products. Because the field appears in the text file, you have to read it now.

3   Modify the Input # statement as follows:

```
Input #1, pstrProduct, psngPrice, _
    psngDiscountPrice, pstrPicture
```

4   Change the existing msngPrices statement in the event procedure, and add the new msngPrices statement to match the following code:

```
msngPrices(pintCurrentItem, 0) = psngPrice
msngPrices(pintCurrentItem, 1) = psngDiscountPrice
```

These changes to the Form_Load event procedure will load the price information into a two-dimensional array.

```
msngPrices(pintCurrentItem, 0) = psngPrice
msngPrices(pintCurrentItem, 1) = psngDiscountPrice
```

These two statements place the values of the variables into each column of the array msngPrices. The first statement stores the regular prices in the first column (column 0), and the second statement stores the discounted prices in the second column (column 1). The row is defined by the variable pintCurrentItem and set by the For loop.

Now you can program the Apply Discount check box and modify the Add Item command button so that the program will use the correct price depending on whether the Apply Discount check box is checked. To do so, you need to write an If statement that determines the value of the check box. You will use this information to decide whether to use the regular or discounted price.

To program the discount:

1   Activate the Code window for the **cmdAdd_Click** event procedure, then modify the code to include an If statement to determine whether the program should use the discounted or regular price. The If statement sets the variable psngExtPrice and calls the AddItem method; make sure to add the column subscripts to the msngPrices array.

```
lstQuotedProduct.AddItem cboProducts.Text
If chkDiscount.Value = vbChecked Then
    psngExtPrice = (txtQty.Text) * _
        msngPrices(cboProducts.ListIndex, 1))
    lstQuotedPrice.AddItem _
        Format(msngPrices(cboProducts.ListIndex, 1),"Fixed")
Else
    psngExtPrice = (txtQty.Text) * _
        msngPrices(cboProducts.ListIndex, 0))
    lstQuotedPrice.AddItem _
        Format(msngPrices(cboProducts.ListIndex, 0),"Fixed")
End If
```
(handwritten annotations: "Val" above txtQty.Text in both occurrences)

This code uses an If statement to apply a discount if the user has checked the Apply Discount check box. If this object is not checked, then the regular prices are used. You now can test whether the program computes the regular and discounted prices correctly.

To test the discounted prices:

1 Test the program by clicking the **Apply Discount** check box to select it.

2 Enter the products and corresponding quantities into the quote, as shown in Figure 7-17.

enter these products

enter these quantities

verify the prices are the same

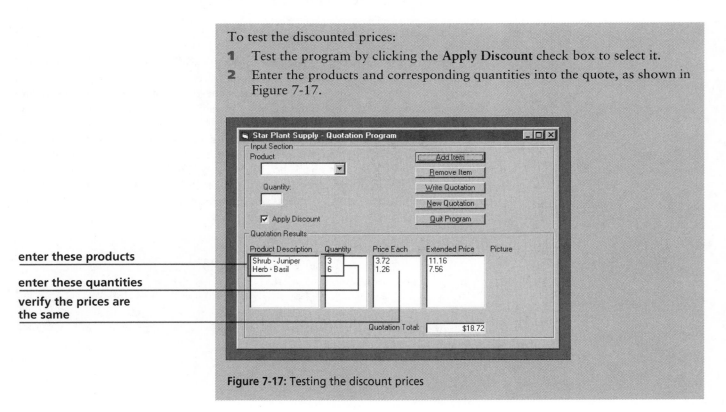

Figure 7-17: Testing the discount prices

The program should apply the discount and display the discounted price for each selected product.

3   Verify that the discounted prices match those shown in Figure 7-17.

4   End the program.

> **If a run-time error occurs, make sure that you changed the number of array dimensions in the general declarations section of the form module. Also, verify that you changed the array dimensions in the Form_Load event procedure and added the statement to load the discounted price. Finally, make sure that you modified the Open statement to read Product2.txt. Check that the If statement in the Add Item command button's Click procedure is correct. Make any necessary corrections, then repeat Steps 1 through 3.**

Now the program will calculate the quotations at the regular price or at the discounted price.

Star Plant Supply would also like to display product pictures for customers who visit the company's office. At some point, the company will have pictures of all of the products, but currently it has only a few images to display.

Adding Pictures to a Form

You can use either a PictureBox object or an Image object to display pictures on a form. The PictureBox object supports more events and properties than the Image object. For example, a picture box can respond to a Change event as well as a Click event. In contrast, the Image control cannot respond to a Change event. Unlike with the Image control, however, the Stretch property does not apply to the picture box. Fortunately, the pictures used in this program are all the same size, so you can create an instance of the PictureBox control that matches the size of the pictures.

As with the Image control, you could assign the pictures to the picture box by setting the Picture property in the Properties window at design time. With that approach, however, your program could display only one picture. Because you want the picture displayed to depend on the active product, you should therefore set the Picture property with code rather than with the Properties window.

Another price list file, Product2.txt, includes a field containing the file name of the picture. The program must be able to load the file containing the picture when the user selects an item in the Product combo box.

As noted earlier, all elements in an array must be of the same data type. Here, you need to store different types of information in the same array: In the first and second columns, you will store numbers representing the regular prices and discounted prices. In the third column, you will store strings (picture file names). On the surface, this setup seems to violate the Visual Basic "rule" of storing variables of the same data type in an array. Another option, however, will allow you to include prices and file names in the same array.

Arrays of Variant Data

Visual Basic supports the **Variant** data type, which can store all of the different data types, including Integer, Single, and String. The Variant data type cannot store Fixed length strings or user-defined types. If you declared a variable named var1 as a Variant data type, it could contain the values 1, 1.05, TRUE, "Hello", or "C:\Windows\waves.bmp". Visual Basic accomplishes this goal by storing the data type of the variable within the variable itself. If you place an Integer in a Variant array or variable, the variable is an Integer Variant data type. If you later store a String in the Variant array or variable, the variable becomes a String Variant data type. Variant variables, as well as members of Variant arrays, can change their data type while a program is running.

To store both the prices and the picture file names, you will create a two-dimensional Variant array having three columns. The first and second columns use Single Variant data types to store the regular prices and discounted prices, and the third column is treated as a String Variant data type that stores the picture file names.

To declare an array of the Variant data type, you use the Private, Public, or Dim statements, as you have done before.

To modify the code so that it will work with both pictures and prices, you need to transform the two-dimensional array msngPrices, which contains prices (Single data type), into a two-dimensional array of variants (Single and String data types). You also need to add a third column to hold the picture file names from the text file.

Programming

tip

. . . .

▶ Because Visual Basic stores the data type of a variable inside the variable and must determine the type of data stored in a Variant variable whenever it references the variable, operations on Variant variables are performed much more slowly than operations on Integer or Single variables. Consequently, you should use Variant variables only when necessary.

To declare a Variant array:

1 Open the **general declarations** section of the Code window for the form module, then change the declaration for **msngPrices** in the window:

```
Dim msngPrices( 0 To 99,0 To 2) As Variant
```

Now that you have declared the three-column array of a Variant data type, you can write the code to load the picture file names into its third column. The specific picture should appear when the user clicks a product so that a customer in the office can see the product being quoted. To load the picture, you will modify the Form_Load event procedure.

In the new three-column array, the first subscript still represents the rows, and the second subscript represents the columns. The regular prices are represented by the column subscript 0; the discounted prices are represented by the column subscript 1; and the picture file names are represented by the column subscript 2.

To load the file names into the Variant array:

1 Create a PictureBox object, as shown in Figure 7-18.

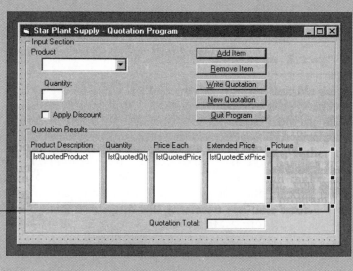

new PictureBox object

Figure 7-18: Creating the PictureBox object

2   Set the Name property to **picFlower**.

3   Activate the Code window for the **Form_Load** event procedure.

4   Add the following line of code (shown in bold) to the Do loop immediately after the **Input #** statement. The new statement stores the file name of the picture into msngPrices.

```
Input #1, pstrProduct, psngPrice, _
    psngDiscountPrice, pstrPicture
msngPrices(pintCurrentItem, 2) = pstrPicture
cboProducts.AddItem pstrProduct
```

This statement stores the picture file names into the third column of the array. Now you can write the code to display a picture in the picture box when the user clicks an item in the Product combo box. When the user clicks a product, the program loads the corresponding picture using its file name by calling the LoadPicture function at run time.

Syntax	*object*.**Picture** = **LoadPicture**(*filename*)
Dissection	■ The **Picture** property of any valid *object* can be set using the **LoadPicture** function. ■ The *filename* can be any file name containing a picture.
Code Example	picFlower.Picture = LoadPicture("A:\Chapter.07\Startup\Iris.bmp")
Code Dissection	The preceding statement loads the picture stored in the file "A:\Chapter.07\Startup\Iris.bmp" into the PictureBox named picFlower.

The third column of the array contains the file names of the pictures that will be displayed in the quotation program. You will use the ListIndex property of the Products combo box as a subscript of the array to look up the correct file name.

To load the pictures into the picture box:

1   Activate the Code window for the **cboProducts_Click** event procedure, then enter the following code in the window:

```
If cboProducts.ListIndex > -1 Then
    picFlower.Picture = _
        LoadPicture(msngPrices _
        (cboProducts.ListIndex, 2))
End If
```

When the user clicks an item in the Product combo box, this code will display the corresponding picture in the picture box. The If statement determines whether an item is selected in the Product combo box. The subsequent statements are called only if an item is selected (ListIndex > -1). The second statement calls the LoadPicture function with one argument—the file name of the picture to load. The file names are stored in the third column of the array msngPrices. To determine the current row, the program uses the current index (ListIndex property) of the Product combo box.

Now you should test the new picture box and the code you added to the Product combo box's Click event procedure.

To test the picture box:

1   Test the program by clicking **Flower - Iris** in the Product combo box. The picture of the selected product should appear in the PictureBox object, as shown in Figure 7-19.

selected product

picture appears in
PictureBox object

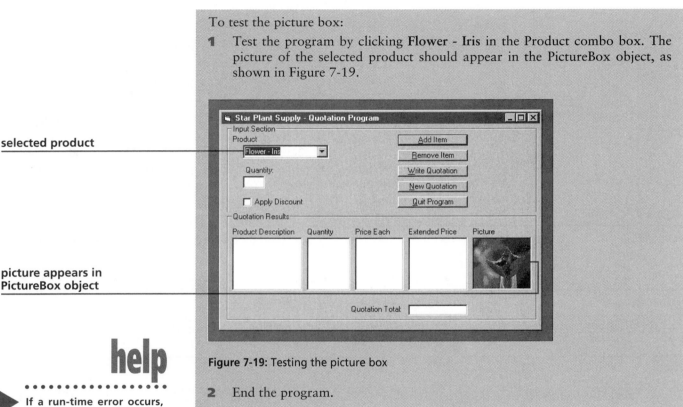

Figure 7-19: Testing the picture box

2   End the program.

help

• • • • • • • • • • • • • • •

▶ If a run-time error occurs, you probably failed to change the dimensions of the array or forgot to change the data type from Single to Variant. Check your code, verify that you added the LoadPicture function to the Click event, make any necessary corrections, then repeat Step 1.

Your program will now display pictures, when they are available. The program performs this task by setting the Picture property of the PictureBox object at run time.

Writing to a Text File

Sometimes customers may want a printed copy of a quote or they may want to use the information produced by this quote program in word processing documents.

Visual Basic supports a Write # statement that will write text to ASCII-delimited files, which can then be read by most word processing, spreadsheet, and database programs. You used the same type of file to read text into the quote program when you called the Input # statement.

When you write to a text file, just as when you read one, you must first open the file with the Open statement. In Section A, you used the Open statement For Input to read the text file containing the product and price information. This time you will combine the Open statement with the For Output option so that you can write to a file. Then, you can use the Write # statement to write information from the program to the text file. Remember—if the file already exists when you open it For Output, it will be overwritten. As with other files you open, you must close a text file when you have finished writing to it.

Syntax	**Write #**_filenumber_, [_outputlist_]
Dissection	■ The **Write #** statement writes to a file that already has been opened For Output or For Append. It also inserts commas between each item in the _outputlist_ and places quotation marks around strings as they are written to the file. It writes numeric data using the period (.) as the decimal separator. Files written with the Write # statement can easily be read with the Input # statement.
	■ The _filenumber_ is a valid filenumber created by an Open statement.
	■ Each item in the _outputlist_ usually comprises a variable or object property in your program that has been separated by a comma. The _outputlist_ is similar to the _inputlist_ of the Input # statement.
	■ In the file, Visual Basic will insert commas between the fields and surround String variables with quotation marks.
| **Code Example** | ```
Open "A:\Chapter.07\Startup\Text.txt" For Output As #1
Write #1, "Field1",123.45
``` |
| **Code Dissection** | The previous statements open the file "A:\Chapter.07\Startup\Text.txt" for output and write a record to the file. The first field is a text field, and the second is a number. |

You will add statements to the Write Quotation command button to ensure that clicking this button creates a text file of the quote output. That way, the user can read the file into a word processing program and format it. To perform this task, you need to open the file For Output and create a For loop to examine every item in the output list boxes, just as you did to include every item in the ComputeTotal general procedure. Inside the For loop, you will use the Write # statement to write the contents of each output list box—Product Description, Quantity, Price Each, and Extended Price—to the text file. Because you have no open files, you can reuse filenumber 1.
```

To write the code to create a text file of the current quotation output:

1   Open the Code window for the **cmdWriteQuotation_Click** event procedure, then enter the following statements:

```
Dim pintCurrentItem As Integer
Dim pstrFileName As String
pstrFileName = _
    InputBox("Enter the filename", "Write File")
If pstrFileName <> vbNullString Then
    Open pstrFileName For Output As #1
    For pintCurrentItem = 0 To _
        lstQuotedExtPrice.ListCount - 1
        Write #1, _
            lstQuotedProduct.List(pintCurrentItem), _
            Val(lstQuotedQty.List(pintCurrentItem)), _
            Val(lstQuotedPrice.List(pintCurrentItem)), _
            Val(lstQuotedExtPrice.List(pintCurrentItem))
    Next
    Close #1
End If
```

The code to write an ASCII-delimited file resembles the code to read the same type of file. You open the file, use a loop to write each line in the file, and close the file once all lines have been written. To allow the user to specify the folder and file name, you call the InputBox function to get a string that will be used as a file name:

```
pstrFileName = _
    InputBox("Enter the filename", "Write File")
If pstrFileName <> vbNullString Then
    Open pstrFileName For Output As #1
```
└ app.path &

This statement opens the file using the Open statement if a file name was specified and assigns the active filenumber. Instead of opening the file For Input (reading the file), you open the file For Output (writing the file). This option overwrites the contents of the file if the file already exists. To append information to a file, you use the For Append option.

```
For pintCurrentItem = 0 To _
    lstQuotedExtPrice.ListCount - 1
    Write #1, _
        lstQuotedProduct.List(pintCurrentItem), _
        Val(lstQuotedQty.List(pintCurrentItem)), _
        Val(lstQuotedPrice.List(pintCurrentItem)), _
        Val(lstQuotedExtPrice.List(pintCurrentItem))
Next
```

The For loop steps through each item in the output list box lstQuotedExtPrice, starting at zero and ending at the end of the list (ListCount - 1). It writes a line for each item quoted. Each line written contains the four items from the output list boxes, with Visual Basic inserting a comma between each item. Because the program treats the items in a list box as strings, these statements call the Val function on the quantity, price, and extended price fields; thus they are converted to numbers and written without quotation marks.

Next, you should test the program again to verify that the Write Quotation command button works correctly.

To test the Write Quotation command button:

1 Test the program by entering the products and corresponding quantities, as shown in Figure 7-20.

enter these products
and quantities

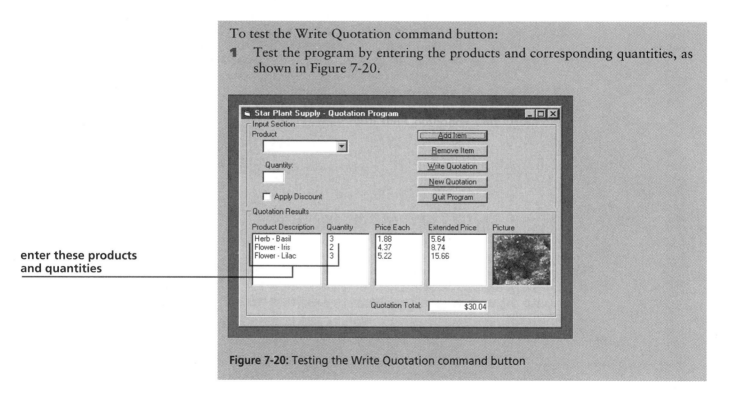

Figure 7-20: Testing the Write Quotation command button

2 Click the **Write Quotation** command button. An input box should appear, enabling you to enter the file name.

3 Enter the file name **A:\Chapter.07\Startup\Quote.txt**, then click the **OK** button.

The program output should be written to the file Quote.txt in the Chapter.07\Startup folder. This file should contain the information shown in Figure 7-21. You can open it in WordPad or any other word processing program.

"Herb - Basil" , 3,1.88,5.64
"Flower - Iris" , 2,4.37,8.74
"Flower - Lilac" , 3,5.22,15.66

Figure 7-21: Contents of text file

4 End the program, save it, then exit Visual Basic.

5 Open the file **Quote.txt** in your word-processing program and compare it to Figure 7-21. Exit your word-processing program.

Star Plant Supply's quote program is now complete. When the user starts the program, the text file containing the price list loads into the computer's memory. When the user selects a product in the Product combo box, a picture of the product (if one exists) appears in the picture box. The user can enter a quantity and click the Add Item command button to display the product description, the quantity, the price per product, and the extended price in the output section of the form. The price per product can either be the regular price or the discounted price, based on the customer's volume of sales. To have the program determine the discount, the user clicks the Apply Discount check box. The user can clear one or all of the products from the output section of the quotation program. The quotation total will be updated with every change to the output section of the form. Finally, the salesperson can write the quotation to a text file, which he or she can format and print in a word processing program.

SUMMARY

This chapter covered two significant topics. First, it described the use of the ListBox and Combo Box controls. These controls are very similar and are used to store lists of data. Second, it explained how to read and write text files.

To open a text file:

■ Open the file for input using the following statement.
  Open *"pathname"* **For [Input | Output | Append] As** #*filenumber*

To read a text file:

■ After a text file has been opened using the Open statement, use the Input # statement.
Input #*filenumber, varlist*

To close a file:

■ Use the Close statement.
Close *filenumberlist*

To write a text file:

■ Use the Write # statement on a file that has been opened For Output or For Append.
Write #*filenumber, varlist*

To load a picture at run time:

■ Load the picture into a picture box control using the following statement:
*Object.***Picture = LoadPicture** (*filename*)

To declare a one-dimensional array:

■ Use the Private statement to create a module-level array. Use the Dim statement inside a procedure to create an array that remains local to the procedure.
Private *array-name*([*lower-bound* **To**]*upper-bound*) **As** *datatype*

To declare a two-dimensional array:

■ **Private** *arrayname*([*lowerbound* **To**] *upperbound*, [*lowerbound* **To**] _
upperbound) **As** *datatype*

To loop through the items of a list box:

■ Create a For loop that iterates from 0 to the value of the list box's ListCount property – 1.
■ Inside the For loop, use the list property to examine each item.
*object.***List**(*index*)

To add an item to a list box at run time:

■ Call the AddItem method of the list box.
*object.***AddItem** *text*

To clear the contents of a list box:

■ Use the Clear method on the list box.
*object.***Clear**

To remove a specific item from a list box:

■ Call the RemoveItem with the *index* argument. The *index* identifies which item to remove.
*object.***RemoveItem** *index*

Q U E S T I O N S

1. Which method removes all of the entries from a list or combo box?
   a. RemoveItem
   b. Clear
   c. Delete
   d. Remove
   e. None of the above.

2. Which method removes a single item from a list or combo box?
   a. RemoveItem
   b. Clear
   c. Delete
   d. Remove
   e. None of the above.

3. Which of the following statements is true about two-dimensional arrays?
   a. They have one subscript.
   b. They have two subscripts.
   c. They consist of rows and columns.
   d. Both a and c.
   e. Both b and c.

4. What is the name of the statement used to write to a text file?
   a. Output
   b. Save
   c. Print
   d. Write
   e. None of the above.

5. Which of the following statements is true about Variant variables?
   a. They can store different kinds of data.
   b. The data type is stored inside the variable.
   c. Programs using them run more slowly than programs using Integer or Single variables.
   d. None of the above.
   e. All of the above.

6. Write the statement(s) to remove all items from the list box named lstDemo.

7. Write the statement(s) to remove the current item from the list box named lstDemo.

8. Write the statement(s) to declare a two-dimensional array with 10 rows and 2 columns having the Single data type.

9. Write the statement(s) to save the array named pstrMessages having subscripts ranging from 0 to 100 to the text file named C:\Messages.txt.

10. Write a loop to examine each element of the array named psngValues. Assume that the array has subscripts ranging from 0 to 49. For each element examined, print the value of the array element to the immediate window.

E X E R C I S E S

1. Valley Computer Supply carries a wide variety of computers and computer accessories. Its business manager keeps a list of these computers and accessories in a sequential file, with each computer appearing on a separate line. This file is used to produce a variety of reports and to answer customer questions about the vendors with which Valley Computer Supply does business. The company would like to use this file for a particular report, but the list is not sorted alphabetically by product name, as this report requires. You will write a program to sort the list using the Sort property of an invisible list box. Figure 7-22 shows the completed form.

Figure 7-22: Exercise 1 – completed form

   a. Run the executable file named **Chapter.07\Exercise\Sample\Ex1.exe**. Set the drive designator as necessary. Click the **Start Sort** command button. When the Input Box appears, enter the file name **Chapter.07\Exercise\Computer.txt**. Set the drive designator as necessary. When the second input box appears, enter the file name **Chapter.07\Exercise\Sorted.txt**.

   b. Start WordPad or any other word processing program, then examine the file named **Chapter.07\Exercise\Computer.txt**. Replace drive designator as necessary. This file contains the unsorted list of computer names. Exit WordPad or the word processing program without saving the file. Open the file named **Sorted.txt**. Note that its contents are sorted.

   c. Start Visual Basic and create a new project. Save the form using the name **Chapter07\Exercise\frmEx1.vbp** and the project with the name **Chapter07\ Exercise\Ex1.vbp**.

   d. Change the form's caption to **Valley Computer Supply – Sort**.

   e. Create a command button with the caption **Start Sort** and the name **cmdStartSort**. Make it become the default button for the form. Position and size all objects as shown in Figure 7-22.

   f. Create a working **Exit** command button for which **Alt+X** is the hot key.

discovery ▶

   g. Draw a list box on the form. Set its name to **lstSort**, and set its properties so that the list box will be sorted and invisible at run time.

   h. All of the processing will occur when the user clicks the cmdStartSort button, so you need to write your code and declare all of the variables in the button's Click event procedure.

   i. Open the Code window for the **cmdStartSort_Click** event and declare three local String variables: **pstrComputerName** will hold the computer name as it is placed into the list box, **pstrInputFileName** will hold the name of the input file, and **pstrOutputFileName** will hold the name of the output file. Declare a local Integer variable named **pintCount** to be used within a For loop that writes to the output file.

j. Using the InputBox function with the prompt **Enter Input Filename**, store the user's response in the variable called **pstrInputFileName**.

k. Using the InputBox function with the prompt **Enter Output Filename**, store the user's response in the variable called **pstrOutputFileName**.

l. Open the file referenced by **pstrInputFileName** for input using the results obtained with the InputBox function. Remember to assign a valid filenumber to the file.

m. Create a loop to read each computer name and add it to the previously created list box. Because only one computer name appears on each line, the Input # statement should store the field in the variable **pstrComputerName**. To store the computer names in the list box, you need another statement that will add an item to the **lstSort** list box. The text of this item resides in the variable **pstrComputerName**.

n. Open the file referenced by the variable **pstrOutputFileName** for output using the results obtained with the InputBox function.

o. Write a loop that will step through all items in the list box and write those items to the output file. Remember that the first item in a list box is designated as 0. To discover how many items are in the list box, you can use the ListCount property. Inside the For loop, create a Write # statement that will write the correct item to the output file. You can use the List property with the pintCount variable as its argument, which is set by the For loop, to indicate the correct item.

p. Close all files.

q. Change the caption of the **Start Sort** command button so that it indicates the number of records sorted, followed by a space and the string Records Sorted. You will need to concatenate the two strings to achieve this effect. Remember that the ListCount property of the lstSort object contains the number of items in the list box—that is, the number of items sorted.

r. Test the program. The program will request an input and output file name. The Start Sort button now should say 11 Records Sorted if you use the text file in the **Chapter.07\Exercises\Computer.txt** folder. Set the drive designator as necessary.

s. Open WordPad or any other word processing program and look at the sorted **Sorted.txt** file in the **Chapter.07\Exercise** folder on your Student Disk. The names of the computers should have been sorted by the invisible list box's Sorted property. After you have viewed the file, exit WordPad or the word processing program.

2. Sundown Hospital is a small regional hospital that serves as a primary care center. The hospital admits approximately 20 individuals per day and would like a method of storing and recalling information for inpatients. This program should display previous patient information and accept new patient information. It should also store the information in a sequential file for later use and be able to call up the information quickly by reading the sequential file into a two-dimensional array. Occasionally, the hospital loses power to the admitting station. In such an event, the staff would like to be able to start the program and recover all of the admitted patient data; therefore, after adding each new patient, the program will append that information to the sequential file and close the file so that it cannot be corrupted.

The admitting interface form has already been completed. You will now add the code that will perform the tasks. Figure 7-23 shows the completed form.

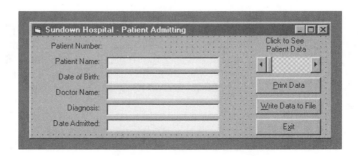

Figure 7-23: Exercise 2 – completed form

a. Run the executable file named **Chapter.07\Exercise\Sample\Ex2.exe**. Set the drive designator as necessary. When the form loads, the text file named **Patient.txt** is read into an array. Information on the first patient is then displayed in the text boxes on the form. Use the scroll bar to locate different patients.

b. Start Visual Basic and create a new project. Save the form with the name **frmEx2.vbp** and the project with the name **Ex2.vbp**.

c. Create the objects on the form, as shown in Figure 7-23. Open the general declarations section of the Code window for the form module. Declare a two-dimensional string array of 50 rows and 6 columns named **mstrPatients**. The first element of the array should be (1,1), not (0,0).

d. In the Form_Load event procedure, open the file named **Chapter.07\Exercise\ Patient.txt** for input. Set the drive designator as necessary. Write a loop that reads the information from the file into the newly created two-dimensional array **mstrPatients**. Use the variable **pintRow** as a counter that will be incremented by 1 each time through the loop. The loop should exit when it reaches the end of file.

e. Inside the loop, write an Input # statement that reads the file into the different rows and columns of the array **mstrPatients**. The file Patient.txt has six fields, so the Input # statement will accept six arguments. The first argument will be **mstrPatients(mpintRow,1)**. Remember that the lower bound of the array is (1,1), not (0,0). Increment the counter each time before executing the Loop statement.

f. Write the code to close the text file.

g. Create a general procedure that displays the current patient. Use the Value property of the scroll bar **hsbPNumber** as the array subscript to place the patient information into the corresponding text boxes and labels on the form. The names of the objects correspond to the columns, as follows:

lblPatientNumber	Column 1, value of the scroll bar hsbPNumber
txtPatientName	Column 2
txtDOB	Column 3
txtDoctorName	Column 4
txtDiagnosis	Column 5
txtDateAdmitted	Column 6, time when the patient was admitted

h. As the final part of the Form_Load event procedure, call the general procedure you just wrote to display the information for the first patient.

i. Write the code for the **Write Data to File** command button. When it is clicked, this command button should append the information for the patient shown on the screen to the file **Chapter.07\Exercise\Patient.txt**. Hint: Open the file For Append. Write the contents of the six objects to the fields in the file you just opened, making sure that you write them in the same order.

j. Write the code to close the file.

k. Write the code for the scroll bar so when the user changes its value, the current patient information (stored in the two-dimensional array) will appear in the text boxes and labels. To accomplish this task, you simply call the general procedure you already wrote.

l. Program the **Exit** button.

m. Set the initial focus to **txtPatientName**.

n. Run the program. The sequential file Patient.txt already includes some sample patient data. Click the scroll bar to advance through the existing patient data to a blank screen. Type in patient data of your choice for five patients. After you type in the information for each patient, click the **Write Data to File** command button. Review the patient data by clicking the scroll bar.

o. Exit the program.

p. Run the program again and observe that clicking the scroll bar causes the data you entered to be appended to the file and loaded into the data array in the program for use by Sundown Hospital's admitting staff.

q. Add a command button to the form with **&Print Data** as its caption. Name this button **cmdPrint**. In the **cmdPrint_Click** event, write a nested For loop using the Print method that will print the two-dimensional patient array to the printer. The external part of the nested For loop should include an If statement that tests for a null (empty) string in the first column of the next row of the array.

r. Write the external part of the nested For loop that will vary the row of the array from one (1) to the number of records you have in the file (use the scroll bar to check this number if you do not remember how many records exist).

s. Write the internal part of the For loop that will vary the column from one (1) to six (6) and call the Print method of the Printer object to print each element in the array's current row. The Print statement in the nested For Next statement will take the form of Printer.Print PatientTbl(Row, Column);. The ";" turns off the automatic line feeds.

t. Write a Printer.EndDoc statement after the last Next statement that will send the output to the printer.

u. Run the program. Click the **Print Data** command button and examine your output. No line feed should appear after each patient's six fields print. Add a line containing the Printer.Print statement between the two Next statements, click the command button again, and observe the results.

v. Save the project, then exit Visual Basic.

3. Super Office sells office supplies to the public. The customer service manager for Super Office would like a program that reads a sequential data file containing item names and prices. The item names should appear in a list box, and the prices should be placed in a one-dimensional array that can hold up to 10 Single data type items. The program will have buttons to select an item and to add it to the current purchase. It should also include a button to remove a purchased item. Another button should reset the form in preparation for another order, and a final button should end the program. Figure 7-24 shows the completed form for the program.

Figure 7-24: Exercise 3 – completed form

a. Run the executable file named **Chapter.07\Exercise\Sample\Ex3.exe**. Set the drive designator as necessary. When the form loads, the text file named **Office.txt** is read into a list box and the prices are loaded into an array. Select an item from the list box and enter a quantity ordered. Click the **Add Purchase** command button to add the selected item to the output list boxes. Add a second item. Select an item in the output section's Product list box and click the **Remove Item** command button. As items are added and removed, the program recomputes the order total. Click the **Reset** button to clear the form in preparation for another order.

    b. Start Visual Basic and create a new project. Save the form with the name **frmEx3.frm** and the project with the name **Ex3.vbp**.

    c. Create the objects on the form, as shown in Figure 7-24.

    d. In the Form_Load event procedure, write the necessary code to read the input file **Chapter.07\Exercise\Office.txt**. Set the drive designator as necessary. The input file contains two fields: a product name and the product price. Read the product names into the input list box and the corresponding prices into an array.

    e. Write the code for the **Add Purchase** command button. This button should verify that an item is selected and a quantity ordered is selected. If either of these conditions is not met, you should display a message box. Otherwise, you should add the information to the output list boxes. This information includes the item description, quantity ordered, price, extended price, and sales tax. Compute the sales tax at a rate of 5 percent.

    f. Create a procedure named **ComputeTotal** that computes the order total. The value is the sum of the extended price and sales tax for each of the selected items.

    g. Write the statement to compute the order total when an item is selected.

    h. Write the code for the **Remove Item** command button. It should verify that a product name in the output list box is selected. If it is, the program should remove the old order total and recompute the new order total.

    i. Write the code for the **Reset** command button. This button should clear all of the output list boxes, the order total, and the quantity ordered.

    j. Program the **Exit** command button.

    k. Create a **PictureBox** object to display a logo using a graphic file of your choice.

    l. Use WordPad or any other word processing program to create a sequential data file with at least five items and prices. Save the file as **Office.txt** in the **Chapter.07\Exercise** folder. Set the drive designator as necessary.

    m. Test the program. Verify that items can be added and removed and that the order total is recomputed each time. Also, test the Reset command button.

    n. Save the project, then exit Visual Basic.

4. Consumers Catalog Sales sells specialty items directly to its customers around the world. The company would like to have a program that displays customer address data (Customer Name, Address 1, Address 2, City, State or Province, Zip Code or Postal Code, and Country) and permits the addition of new customer data to the file. The data is stored in a sequential file and read into a two-dimensional array with 50 rows and 7 columns.

The program should load the existing customer names into a combo box so that they can be selected by the user. The ItemData property of the ComboBox object will store the row location of the customer information contained in the array. This arrangement is necessary because the combo box will sort the names in the box, and the sorted combo box list will not reflect the sequence of the array information.

Your program should have four command buttons. The first should clear the contents of the text boxes and deselect the current item from the combo box. The second should add new data to the ASCII-delimited file. Each time you add a new record, it should be written to both the array and the sequential file. (*Hint:* Use the ListIndex property of the ComboBox object with the ItemData property to directly reference information in the array.) A third command button should print a mailing label for the customer displayed on the screen. The fourth command button should end the program. Figure 7-25 shows the completed form.

Figure 7-25: Exercise 4 – completed form

a. Create the sequential data file with at least five records using addresses of your choice in WordPad or any other word processing program. Make sure that each record includes seven fields, separated by the comma delimiter, and that you press the Enter key after each line. Save the file as **Consumer.txt** in the **Chapter.07\Exercise** folder. Set the drive designator as necessary.

b. Run the executable file named **Chapter.07\Exercise\Sample\Ex4.exe**. Set the drive designator as necessary. When the form loads, the text file named **Consumer.txt** is read into a list box. Select a **Customer Name** from the combo box. The information for the customer appears.

c. Start Visual Basic and create a new project. Save the form with the name **frmEx4.frm** and the project with the name **Ex4.vbp**.

d. Create the objects on the form, as shown in Figure 7-25.

e. In the **Form_Load** event procedure, write the code to open the newly created file named **Consumer.txt**. This file contains seven fields. Read each of these fields into a two-dimensional array and then close the file.

discovery    f. In the **Form_Load** event procedure, add the first field (the name) to the combo box. Also, set the ItemData property so that it contains the index of the row of the array corresponding to the item in the combo box.

g. In the **Click** event procedure for the combo box, write the code to display the information pertaining to the selected customer name. You will need to use the ItemData property of the selected item. The value of this property contains the row index in the array holding the customer information. Using the current row and the corresponding column, display the information in the text boxes.

discovery    h. Write the code for the **Add New Data** command button. It should locate the first unused row in the array. To determine the first unused row, search through each row until you find a row where the first column contains an empty string. Store the current value of each text box in the current row.

discovery ▶   i. Write the code for the **Update** command button. When clicked, this button should save the current contents of the text boxes to the proper array row.

j. Write the code for the **Save** command button. This button should write the text file **Consumer.txt** from the contents of the array. Write only those array elements that are in use. You can determine their status by testing that the current row and first column contains a null string.

k. Program the **Exit** command button.

l. Test the program.

m. Save the project, then exit Visual Basic.

o b j e c t i v e s

In this case you will:

■ Create a comprehensive calculator
■ Program multiple control arrays

Utility Solutions

Creating a Calculator

case ▶ Utility Solutions is a computer software company that develops, manufactures, and distributes software packages for clients all over the world. The company is creating a set of utility programs, and would like you to create the calculator program for this set. Figure EC1-1 shows the completed form for the calculator.

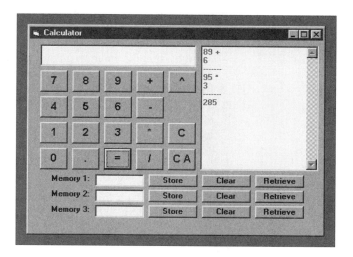

Figure EC1-1

As you can see in Figure EC1-1, the calculator consists of numeric buttons (0 through 9, and a decimal point) and operator buttons (+, -, *, /, ^). As the user clicks each numeric button, the digit corresponding to the button must be displayed in the text box at the top of the form. A text box at the right of the form must work like the paper tape on an adding machine. When the user clicks an operator button, the contents of the top text box must be copied to the tape (the right text box) and cleared from the top text box. Finally, three text boxes at the bottom of the form must work like the memory buttons on a calculator. The command buttons next to these memory text boxes are used to store, clear, and retrieve values to and from each memory location. The memory button should store the current value of the paper tape.

The following list describes some characteristics of the calculator:

- The user must be able to enter numbers using a numeric keypad (command buttons on the form). As each individual digit is entered, it must be concatenated to the current number displayed in the text box at the upper-left part of the form. Clicking the button 1, then the button 2 would cause the values of 1 and then 12 to appear in the text box. If a decimal point is entered, it must also be displayed in the text box. A number can contain only one decimal point; the button should be disabled once the user enters the decimal point. Once an operation is performed on the number, the decimal point button should be enabled again.

- The user should be able to use the keyboard to type numbers directly into the top text box, and switch back and forth between using the buttons and the keyboard.

- Once a number has been entered, the user should be able to perform an operation on it. Operations include addition, subtraction, multiplication, division, and exponentiation. Each time the user clicks an operator button, the current number stored in the top text box should be cleared.

- Whenever the user clicks an operator button, the information should also be displayed in another text box, as an adding machine would display the information on a paper tape. Each time an operation like addition or subtraction is performed, the result should appear on the tape as well. Refer to Figure EC1-1 for a sample of the tape.

- Just as calculators have a memory to store and retrieve values, Utility Solutions' calculator should support a memory function. Its calculator, however, should support three memory locations instead of just one.

- The user should be able to store a number into one of the three memory locations by clicking the corresponding command button to the right of the memory location. To retrieve a number from memory into the current number text box at the top of the form, the user should have access to a Retrieve command button. When the user clicks the Retrieve command button, the number should remain in memory. The Clear command button should clear the appropriate memory location. The Store command button should store the current value of the adding machine tape into the corresponding memory location.

- The calculator must include a Clear button and a Clear All button. The Clear button should clear the current number from the top text box as well as the contents of the tape, but should leave the contents of the values stored in memory. The Clear All button should clear the contents of the previous items as well as the memory locations.

Consider the following guidelines as you develop the calculator program:

- Test each function as it is developed. For additional help finding errors in your programs, refer to "Appendix A: Debugging."

- You can divide the command buttons into three groups. Organize each group as a separate control array. The first group consists of the buttons that the user will click to enter the numbers 0 through 9 and a decimal point. The second group includes the operators, such as + and –.

- Each time the user clicks a number on the keypad, the program can use the index of the control array to determine the value of the number. Pay attention to the value you assign to the Index property for each element in this control array. You can simplify the code considerably.
- By placing all of the operators into another control array, you can localize the functionality of the different mathematical operations. You can think of the task of adding the numbers 1 and 2 as one operator, addition, and two operands, the numbers 1 and 2. Your program must be able to deal with the case in which the user enters the first number in an expression. The addition operation should not be performed until the user has entered the second number. The two numbers should then be added together and the result displayed on the tape.
- Because the user must be able to both click buttons and type numbers on the keypad to store values in the current number text box, you need to validate that the user types in either a number or a decimal point at the keyboard. You can use the KeyPress event pertaining to the form to accomplish this validation.
- Be sure to validate user input. The user should not be able to enter characters into the text box. The only valid characters are the numbers 0 through 9 and a decimal point.

1. Run the executable file named **ExtraCases\Project1\CalcDemo.exe**. Set the drive designator as necessary. Enter numbers using both the command buttons and the keyboard. Click on the operators to add, subtract, multiply, and divide values. These operations can be performed only by clicking the corresponding command button. Also, store and retrieve values from the three different memory locations. Click the Close button to exit the program.
2. Start Visual Basic.
3. Save the form and the project using the names **ExtraCases\Project1\frmCalculator.frm** and **ExtraCases\Project1\Calculator.vbp**, respectively. Set the drive designator as necessary.
4. Create the objects shown on the form in Figure EC1-1. To simplify the programming process, create different control arrays as indicated earlier. The text stored in the top text box should be right-justified. The text boxes representing the memory locations should be configured such that the user cannot directly edit the textual contents.
5. Write the code to store digits into the current text box at the top of the form.
6. Write the statements to perform arithmetic operations on the current numbers. If the operation is the first operand in an expression, then display only the operand in the tape text box. Otherwise, perform the operation and display the result in the tape text box. Each time an operation is performed, your program should clear the contents of the current number text box.
7. Write the statements for the **Clear** and **Clear All** command buttons.
8. Write the statements for the command buttons to store, clear, and retrieve values from the three memory locations.
9. Test the program by using each number and each operator. Verify that each memory location works correctly.
10. Correct any mistakes and save the project again, if necessary.
11. Create an executable file named **ExtraCases\Project1\Calculator.exe**.
12. Exit Visual Basic.

o b j e c t i v e s

In this case you will:

- Create an inventory management system that interacts with a database
- Locate records using the Recordset object
- Add, change, and delete data using the Data control and recordset
- Create a menu system
- Validate input data

Industrial Paper

Creating an Inventory Management System

case ▶ Industrial Paper sells wholesale printing products on a national scale. The company is currently creating an inventory management system. One necessary component of this system is the ability to manage the list of parts, their cost, sales price, and other information. The user must be able to add, change, and delete items from the price list.

A splash screen should appear when the program first begins. Figure EC2-1 shows the splash screen at design time.

Figure EC2-1

The splash screen should contain two lines, as shown in Figure EC2-1. When the form loads, the logo should appear in the upper-left corner. The image used for this logo is **ExtraCases\Project2\IPLogo.wmf**. When the form becomes activated, the picture box should move from the upper-left corner of the screen to the right, then down until it appears above the text "Industrial Paper." Figure EC2-1 shows its final position. The splash screen should appear for three seconds. You should use a Timer control to accomplish this task.

After the splash screen appears, the main form should appear, as shown in Figure EC2-2. Note that the form is shown at design time.

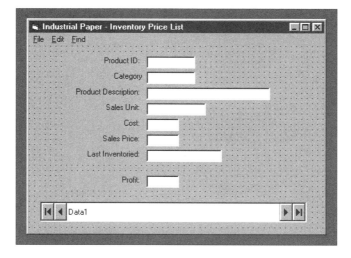

Figure EC2-2

The text boxes shown in Figure EC2-2 correspond to the fields in the database's Inventory table, named tblInventory. You will create and assign meaningful names for all text boxes on the form.

For each menu item you create, you must assign an access key and a shortcut key. The menu for the main form contains three menus:

- The **File** menu should include only one menu item: the **Exit** command, which displays a message box that requests confirmation from the user to exit the program.
- The **Edit** menu should contain the following commands: **Add**, **Edit Record**, **Update Record**, **Delete**, and **Cancel**. Assign hot keys and shortcut keys for each of these menu items.
- The **Find** menu should contain menus to locate the **First, Next, Previous,** and **Last** record in the database. To accomplish this task, you will call the methods of a Recordset object. Remember that a reference to the recordset is stored in the Recordset property pertaining to the Data control. You will assign shortcut keys and hot keys for each of these menu items.
- The menu commands and text boxes must be enabled and disabled as follows: When the program starts, only the Edit menu's Add, Edit Record, and Delete commands are enabled. When the user clicks the Add or Edit Record command, only the Update Record and Cancel commands are enabled. The user can modify the fields, then click Update Record to record the changes to the database or click Cancel to abandon the changes.
- The Find menu commands should not produce an error when BOF or EOF is reached. If the user tries to find a record that would cause BOF to be True, the program should locate the first record. If the user tries to find a record that would cause EOF to be True, the program should locate the last record.
- The text boxes are locked (the Locked property is set to True) unless the user is adding a new record or editing an existing record. Whenever the user changes the current record, the first text box (containing the Product ID) should receive focus.

The database is named **ExtraCases\Project2\IP.mdb**. In this exercise, you will use the table named **tblInventory**. Figure EC2-3 lists the field names and the data type of each field.

Field Name	Data type
fldID	Long
fldCategory	Text
fldDescription	Text
fldSalesUnit	Text
fldCost	Single
fldSalesPrice	Single
fldLastInventoried	Date

Figure EC2-3

The database does not include a field in which to store the profit. This value needs to be computed at run time each time a record is located.

A Data control should connect the program to the database. With the exception of the Profit text box, all of the text boxes correspond to the fields in the database. When the user attempts to edit a record or save any changes to the database, you should validate the user's input. If it is invalid, a message box should be displayed describing the error. The following fields should be validated as indicated:

- The Product ID should contain only numbers.
- The Product Description must be less than 50 characters.
- The Sales Unit must be a number.

- The Cost and Sales Price both must be numbers.
- The Last Inventoried field should be a date.

As you develop the program, consider the following suggestions to help you solve the problem. These ideas are only suggestions; you may find other ways to solve the problem.

- To enable and disable the menus items based on whether a record is being edited, consider creating a Function or Sub procedure that enables and disables all of the menus simultaneously based upon the edit state. Then, you can call this function when the user begins and ends editing the current record. Also, when a record is not being edited, you may want to lock the text boxes in this procedure.
- Consider validating the entire user input simultaneously through the Data control's Validate event. Remember to cancel the Update that caused the Validate event to occur. Otherwise, if you attempt to add or update invalid data, a database error might occur.
- You must compute the gross profit each time the current record changes. Consider using the Reposition event of the Data control for this purpose.

1. Run the executable file named **ExtraCases\Project2\IPDemo.exe**. Set the drive designator as necessary. Note that the splash screen is animated and appears for three seconds. Use the Find menu to locate different records. Use the Edit menu to add, change, and delete records. For the executable program to work correctly, the database file **IP.mdb** must reside in the same folder as the executable file.
2. Start Visual Basic.
3. Create a splash screen for the project. Make sure it is the startup object. Create the objects on the splash screen as shown in Figure EC2-1. Animate the picture box so it moves from left to right across the top of the form, then down until the bottom of the picture reaches the top of the company name. Save the form using the name **ExtraCases\Project2\frmSplash**. Write the code to display the main form after the splash screen has appeared on the screen for three seconds. Use a **Timer** control for this purpose.
4. Create the main form for the program. Create the text boxes, labels, and menu system on the form, as shown in Figure EC2-2. Save the form using the name **ExtraCases\Project2\frmIPMain**.
5. Create an instance of the **Data** control on the form. Set the properties so that the data control connects to the table named **tblInventory** in the database named **ExtraCases\Project2\IP.mdb**.
6. Set the properties to bind the text boxes to the **Data** control.
7. Create the code for the **Exit** menu. It should exit the program after displaying a message box requesting confirmation from the user.
8. Create the code for the **Find** menu commands to locate the first, next, previous, and last records. Remember to test for beginning and end of file (a current record should always exist). Disable and enable each menu item as described in the first bulleted list in this case.
9. Create the code for each command on the **Edit** menu. The program should have two edit states—a record is or is not being edited. Write the code to disable and enable the appropriate menu items based upon the current state as described in the first bulleted list in this case. Write the code to add change and delete records. Be sure to validate user input before updating the current record.
10. Calculate the gross profit each time a new record is located. Format the result with a leading dollar sign and two decimal places.
11. Test the program.
12. Correct any mistakes and save the project again, if necessary.
13. Create an executable file named **ExtraCases\Project2\IP.exe**.
14. Exit Visual Basic.

In this case you will:

- Create a customer service survey application
- Program arrays
- Read and write a text file
- Work with multiple forms

Computronics

Creating a Customer Service Survey

case▶ Computronics conducts customer satisfaction surveys every six months. Currently, telephone customer service representatives must write the responses to each survey question on a piece of paper. Computronics would like to automate this system so that the customer service representatives can enter the information directly into the computer as they ask each question.

The program you write will include four forms: two forms that make up the questionnaire, a splash screen that appears when the program first begins, and a main form. These four forms are shown in Figures EC3-1, EC3-2, EC3-3, and EC3-4, respectively.

Figure EC3-1

The splash screen contains the program name and a Timer control. Figure EC3-1 shows the splash screen at design time.

Figure EC3-2

As shown in Figure EC3-2, the main form for the program contains the buttons to create a new survey, open an existing survey, save a survey, and locate the different responses. Each survey will consist of 500 responses. Each respondent is asked a series of eight questions, and data accuracy is important. In most cases, you will use the most appropriate Visual Basic control so that the user cannot enter invalid data for a particular question. For example, you will use a check box for questions that have a Yes/No answer. In other situations, the user will enter dates and text into text boxes. The program must then validate this information.

A single form is not large enough to show all of the questions. Therefore, you will divide the questionnaire into two forms or pages. A command button on each form will allow the user to move between pages.

Figure EC3-3

As shown in Figure EC3-3, different types of control instances are used for different types of questions. This page, for example, uses option buttons.

Figure EC3-4

As shown in Figure EC3-4, the user can select items from several list boxes.

The main form should always remain visible. When the program first begins (after the splash screen has disappeared), the main form should be the only form visible. After the main form appears, you can open or create a survey, causing the first page used to store survey responses to appear. Each survey response has two pages. The first page contains a button to display the second page. The second page includes a button to display the first page. Only one of the two pages should be visible at any time.

The main form contains several command buttons that control the processing for the program. The program should process the data pertaining to each survey in the following manner. Each six-month survey should be stored as an ASCII-delimited file, and each survey should be stored in a separate file. When the user clicks the Open Survey command button, an input box should appear, allowing the user to select a file. The code in your program should open the text file, and its data should be read into a Variant array.

The Variant array that receives the data should be 500 elements in size (the maximum number of responses) and have nine columns (subscripts 0 through 8). The first column will indicate that an array element represents a valid survey response. The remaining columns will store the eight survey questions. Each question, as it appears on the page, is represented by different types of control instances. The array that stores the information pertaining to each response will store each question as an Integer number. Page 1 and Page 2 of the data entry form will display all questions pertaining to a single response.

The customer service representatives also need a way to move from response to response. If the user clicks the Previous Response button, then the program should look up the array element pertaining to that response. The contents of that array element should appear in the control instances created on the two forms corresponding to each question. The program must also save the current response into the array before locating the previous response.

If the customer service representative clicks the Next Response button, the program should determine whether the user wants to create a new response or view an existing response. The first column of the array should be treated as a Boolean value to indicate whether the response is in use. If the response is a new one, then the control instances on the pages of the data entry forms should be set to default values. Otherwise, the program should look up the values in the array and set the control instances so that they reflect the value of the current response.

If the customer service representative clicks the Save Survey button, the contents of the array should be saved to a text file. An input box will get the name of the file from the user.

The user should be able to open an existing survey file, edit it, and add responses to it. Certain data items contain text. Validate the data in the following manner:

- Question 3 must be a number within the range of 18–100.
- Question 4 must be a number.
- Question 5 must be a valid date.

1. Run the executable file named **ExtraCases\Project3\CompDemo.exe**. Set the drive designator as necessary. Note that the splash screen appears for three seconds. Click the **New Survey** button to create a new survey, then complete at least two questions. Click the **Save Survey** button and save the survey to a text file. Click the **Exit** command button on the main form to exit the program.
2. Start Visual Basic.
3. Create a new project. Add a splash screen to the project. On the form, create a timer and the objects shown in Figure EC3-1. Write the code to wait three seconds and then display the main form. Save the splash screen form using the name **ExtraCases\Project3\frmSplash.frm**. Set the drive designator as necessary.
4. Create the main form, as shown in Figure EC3-2. Create the command buttons on the form. Save the form using the name **ExtraCases\Project3\frmMain.frm**. Set the drive designator as necessary.

5. Add a form representing the first page of the survey and name it **frmPage1.** Save the form using the name **ExtraCases\Project3\frmPage1.frm**. Create the objects on the form, as shown in Figure EC3-3.

6. Add another form representing the second page of the survey and name it **frmPage2.** Save the form using the name **ExtraCases\Project3\frmPage2.frm**. Create the objects on the form, as shown in Figure EC3-4.

7. Save the project using the name **ExtraCases\Project3\Comp.vbp**.

8. On each of the two survey response pages, write the code to navigate between them. Only one of the two forms should be visible at any given time.

9. Write the code in the **LostFocus** event procedures for each text box to validate user input. If the input is not valid, display a message box and return the focus to the invalid text box.

10. Write the code for the **New Survey** command button. This code should initialize the Variant array.

11. Write the code for the **Open Survey** command button to open an existing survey. This code should get a file name from the user by means of an input box. The contents of this file should then be read into the Variant array.

12. Write the code to save an existing survey. This code should save the contents of each array element to a text file. It should get the name of the text file by means of an input box and execute when the user clicks the **Save Survey** command button.

13. Write the code to save the current response to the array. You may want to create a general procedure for this purpose. This code should execute whenever the user clicks the **Previous Response** or **Next Response** command button.

14. Write the code to read the current row in the array into the current response (the control instances on the two data entry pages). You may want to create a general procedure for this purpose. This code should also execute when the user clicks the **Previous Response** or **Next Response** command button.

15. Write the code to set default values for the control instances on the data entry form. For the list boxes and option buttons, the default value should consist of the first value in the list or the first value in the option group.

16. When the user selects the previous or next response, the current response should be saved to the array. If the selected response is a new one, then the program should set the control instances on the data entry forms to their default values. If it is an existing response, then the program should read the values from the current array element.

17. Program the **Exit** command button. In this command button, write the code to verify that the current survey was saved to disk and that no changes to the array remain unsaved. To implement this functionality, declare a Boolean variable. When changes are made, set this variable to indicate that unsaved changes exist. When the current survey is saved, reset this variable to indicate that no unsaved changes exist.

18. Test the program.

19. Correct any mistakes and save the project again, if necessary.

20. Create an executable file named **ExtraCases\Problem3\Survey.exe**.

21. Exit Visual Basic.

Examining Database Objects and the Structured Query Language (SQL)

Creating a Payroll Program for Paymaster

case ▶ Paymaster Payroll Services processes the payroll for more than 150 companies which find it more cost effective and efficient to outsource this task. You have been assigned the job of creating several components of a new Visual Basic payroll program to replace Paymaster's existing software.

In this chapter, you will complete the following tasks:

- ■ Create a user interface to add, change, and delete database records without the aid of the Data control.
- ■ Write code to read an ASCII file containing an employee ID and the number of hours worked into a database table. Using that data, the program will compute the gross pay, payroll taxes, and net pay for each employee having a record in the ASCII file. Instead of calculating that information one record at a time, the program will include statements that operate on an entire group of records at once.
- ■ Write code to select a group of records having specific characteristics from a database.

Previewing the Completed Payroll Application

In Chapter 5, you used a Data control and bound controls to interact with a database. In this chapter, you will learn how to add, change, and delete records programmatically without the aid of the Data control. Also in Chapter 5, you used the Recordset object to navigate through database records and edit those records. The Recordset object, however, is only one object supported by the Microsoft Jet database engine. In fact, every table, field, query, and recordset in a database is stored as an object in the database. You can use these objects, in addition to the Recordset object, to manipulate the data in a database.

To preview the completed payroll application:

1   Start Visual Basic and load the project file named **Chapter.08\Complete\ Pay_C.vbp**. Set the drive designator as necessary. For the program to locate the database correctly, you must store the program on the floppy drive and the database named **Paymast.mdb** must reside in the same folder as the project file.

2   Run the program. The main form for the program is shown in Figure 8-1. (Note that the figure appears at run time with records loaded from the database.)

text boxes display data from database

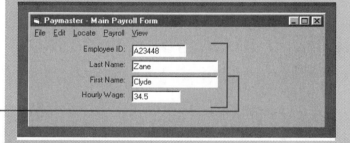

Figure 8-1: Completed main form

3   As shown in Figure 8-1, the main form contains text boxes to display the information pertaining to an employee. This information includes the employee ID, last and first name, and hourly wage. The Locate menu contains items to locate different records. Click these menu items to move to the first, next, previous, and last records in the table. Note that the records are not sorted—that is, they appear in the same order in which they were added to the table.

4   The Edit menu contains the options to add, edit, and delete records. It also contains menu items to update and cancel changes. Click **Edit**, then click **Add Record** to add a new record. Enter an employee ID of **A123**. Enter your last and first name into the appropriate text boxes. Enter **12.44** as the hourly wage.

5   Click **Edit**, then click **Update Record** to record your changes to the database table.

6   Click **Locate**, then click **First** to locate the first record in the table.

7   Click **Edit**, then click **Edit Record** to enable editing on the current record.

8 Change the contents of the current record.

9 Click **Edit**, then click **Cancel Edit** to cancel your most recent changes to the current record and to restore the original contents.

10 Click **Locate**, then click **Last** to locate the last record. This record contains your name.

11 Click **Edit**, then click **Delete** to delete the record you added to the database.

12 The Select Records form is used to select different records from the database. With this form, you can select specific fields from a table, sort the selected records, and select specific records based on the date that the employee was paid. Click **View**, then click **Select Records Form** on the main menu to activate the Select Records form, which is shown in Figure 8-2. The form contains check boxes to select specific database fields and an option group to define the method for sorting the data. The Date Paid text box is used to select records having a specific pay date. The text box at the bottom of the form displays the selected output.

check these boxes

sort by last name

click to select

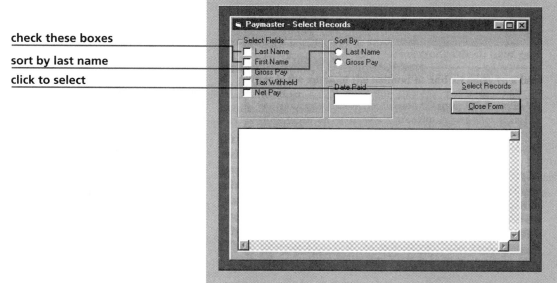

Figure 8-2: Completed Select Records form

As shown in Figure 8-2, the form contains three frames to group the input areas. You use the Select Fields frame to specify the fields to select from the database table. The Sort By frame contains two option buttons to indicate how the records will be sorted, and the Date Paid frame allows the user to select only those records having a particular date paid.

13 Click the **Last Name** and **First Name** check boxes in the **Select Fields** frame. Click the **Last Name** option button in the **Sort By** frame. Click the **Select Records** command button. The text box at the bottom of the form displays the selected fields of the selected records. Note that the records are now sorted by last name.

14 End the program and exit Visual Basic.

In addition to these two forms, the payroll program contains functions to modify and delete several records at a time. Because these functions do not have a visual component, you will not preview them at this time.

SECTION A
objectives

In this section you will:

- Understand the objects that make up a database
- Use default methods and properties
- Understand the Recordset object

Creating and Using Recordsets Programmatically

Preparing to Use Data Access Objects

In Chapter 5, you used the Data control and its DatabaseName and RecordSource properties to open a database and create an instance of the Recordset object. The recordset was created implicitly by the Data control at run time; you did not explicitly write code for it. In contrast, in this chapter you will open a database and manipulate its objects without the aid of the Data control. In other words, you will write code to operate with Data Access Objects.

The **Data Access Objects (DAO)** hierarchy consists of collections, which contain zero, one, or many objects of the same type. A **collection**, like an array, is a grouping of like objects. Some objects contain other collections, which in turn contain still other objects. DAO is considered a hierarchy because the collections and objects are related in such a way that they form a hierarchical inverted tree structure.

Before you can reference DAO objects with code, you must make the corresponding object library available to the project. An **object library** provides information to Visual Basic about a group of objects such as DAO. Object library files have the extension ".olb". When you used the Data control earlier, this control made the DAO object library available to you implicitly. Because you will not use the Data control in this chapter, you must explicitly establish a reference to the object library using the References dialog.

To make the DAO object library available to your program:

1 Start Visual Basic and open the project named **Chapter.08\Startup\Pay_S.vbp**. Set the drive designator as necessary.

2 Click **Project**, then click **References** to open the References dialog, as shown in Figure 8-3.

click OK to close the dialog

click Microsoft DAO 3.51 Object Library to make objects available to the project

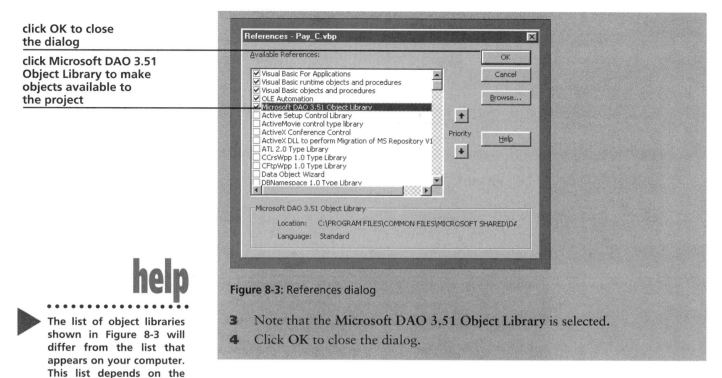

Figure 8-3: References dialog

3   Note that the **Microsoft DAO 3.51 Object Library** is selected.

4   Click **OK** to close the dialog.

help

• • • • • • • • • • • • • • • •

The list of object libraries shown in Figure 8-3 will differ from the list that appears on your computer. This list depends on the software installed on the computer.

Once you create a reference to the DAO object library, it will appear in the Object Browser and you can reference the DAO objects with code. That is, you can write code to open databases and recordsets using the methods contained in the DAO library.

The DAO Hierarchy

The **DBEngine** object appears at the top of the DAO hierarchy. It provides a reference to all other objects in the DAO hierarchy and acts as the interface to the Microsoft Jet database engine. You do not declare or create an instance of the DBEngine object; rather, it is predefined. This case is a rare situation where you do not declare an object variable before using it.

Accessing the Microsoft Jet database engine creates a session; this session is later destroyed when you close the Microsoft Jet database engine. A **session** contains all databases opened by a user. In the DAO hierarchy, a session is analogous to a Workspace object in the Workspaces collection.

When the predefined DBEngine object is created for you, the Workspaces collection and a single Workspace in that collection, known as the Default Workspace, are created as well. The **Default Workspace** is a Workspace object that is created automatically when you connect to the Microsoft Jet database engine. Usually, only one session is necessary for a user; hence the Workspaces collection includes only one Workspace object.

Figure 8-4 shows the relationship between the DBEngine object and the Workspaces collection.

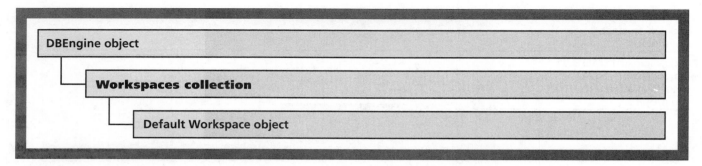

Figure 8-4: Relationship between DBEngine and Workspaces

To reference a collection that is contained by another object, you use the same syntax as you use to reference an object's properties or methods.

Syntax	*objectname.collectionname*
Dissection	■ The *objectname* can be any object, such as the DBEngine object, that contains a reference to a collection. An object may contain references to multiple collections. ■ The *collectionname* can be any collection contained by an object.
Code Example	`DBEngine.Workspaces`
Code Dissection	The previous statement fragment references the Workspaces collection pertaining to the DBEngine object.

Although you can reference a collection, you also need a way to reference an individual object stored in a collection. Most collections allow you to reference an individual object in a collection in two ways:

■ You can use a numeric index. This process is much like using a subscript to reference an element of an array. The numeric index is a numbering system starting at 0 or 1, and incremented by 1 for each object in the collection. That is, every collection is either a **zero-based** or **one-based** collection, depending on the collection and its time of creation. Whenever you use a collection, check its Help page to determine whether 0 or 1 is used to reference the first item in the collection. This inconsistency is historical. Older collections are numbered starting at 0; new collections follow the more intuitive numbering system that begins with 1.

■ You can use a **string key** that uniquely identifies an object in the collection. A string key provides a more intuitive way to reference each object in the collection. Instead of using a numeric index, which carries no inherent meaning, a string key describes the object in the collection.

To use a numeric index or a string key to reference an individual object contained in a collection, you use the Item method:

Syntax	*objectname* = [*parentobjectname*].*collectionname*.**Item**(*index*)
Dissection	■ The **Item** method takes one argument—a numeric *index* or a *string key*—and returns a reference to the specified object from the collection.

- The *objectname* is an object of the same type as the object stored in the collection.

- The *parentobjectname* is the name of an object that provides a reference to the collection.

- The *collectionname* can be any valid collection.

- The *index* can be a numeric index or string key. If it consists of a numeric index, it must be an Integer number. If the collection supports a string key, *index* can contain a text string enclosed in quotes or a String variable.

| **Code Example** | ```
Set mwsCurrent = DBEngine.Workspaces.Item(0)
Set mwsCurrent = DBEngine.Workspaces.Item _
    ("#Default Workspace#")
``` |
| **Code Dissection** | These two statements return a reference to the first Workspace object in the Workspaces collection, which is the Default Workspace. In this case, mwsCurrent references a Workspace object. The equivalent assignment statements assign mwsCurrent so that it references the Default Workspace. This workspace always has a numeric index of zero (0) and a string key of "#Default Workspace#". The choice of which statement to use is a matter of personal preference, although the second seems more intuitive because it uses the string key.

To assign an object reference, you use the Set statement. To assign an ordinary variable, you omit the Set statement. Note that the Set statement is used in the preceding assignment statements because you are not assigning ordinary variables. Rather, you are assigning object references. |

Because the Workspaces collection is zero-based, the Default Workspace (the first item in the collection) has a numeric index of 0. The string key for the Default Workspace is "#Default Workspace#". Now that you know how to reference a collection and a specific object in a collection, you can call the methods and reference the properties pertaining to that object.

Default Methods and Properties

Most objects support either a default method or a default property. **Default methods** and **default properties** allow you to call a method or reference a property pertaining to an object without explicitly specifying the name of the method or property. Using default methods and properties in a program offers two advantages:

- Default methods and properties can considerably reduce the amount of typing.
- The code that executes when you implicitly call a default method or property differs from the code that executes when you specify the default method or property explicitly. Statements that implicitly use default methods or properties execute approximately 25 percent faster than those that specify the default method or property explicitly.
```

The Item method is the default method of the Workspaces collection. Thus the following equivalent statements will produce the same results as the previous two statements that referenced the Default Workspace. The choice of using a numeric index or string key remains a matter of personal preference. Note that the Item method is the default method for most collections.

```
Set mwsCurrent = DBEngine.Workspaces(0)
Set mwsCurrent = DBEngine.Workspaces("#Default Workspace#")
```

In the previous two statements, the Item method was omitted because it is the default method. Notice that no period (.) separates the object name from the method name. Because you are still assigning an object reference, you include the Set statement. You have used other controls that supported default properties. For example, the default property of a text box is the Text property. Figure 8-5 lists selected controls and their default properties.

Control	Default Property
CheckBox	Value
ComboBox	Text
Image	Picture
Label	Caption
ListBox	Text
OptionButton	Value
PictureBox	Picture
ScrollBar	Value
TextBox	Text

Figure 8-5: Default properties

The following statements to reference the Text property of the text box named txtCurrent have the same effect, although the statement that uses the default property will execute more quickly:

```
txtCurrent = "This is a line of text."
txtCurrent.Text = "This is a line of text."
```

In the DAO hierarchy, collections contain object references. Those objects, in turn, contain references to other collections and objects. For example, each Workspace object contains a reference to the Databases collection.

Opening a Database Programmatically

When you open a database, a Database object is created and added to the Databases collection. You use this object to reference the data in a physical database file. If one database is open, the Databases collection contains a reference to one Database object. If two databases are open, the Databases collection contains a reference to two Database objects. Thus a program can open several databases concurrently. Figure 8-6 shows the relationship between the Workspaces and Databases collections and the objects that they contain.

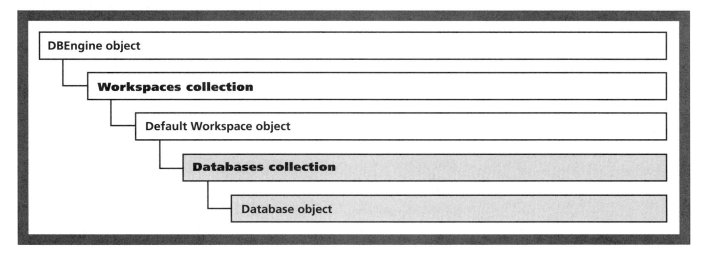

Figure 8-6: Databases collection and Database object

The database programs you wrote in Chapter 5 used the Data control to implicitly open a database and create a Recordset object. You now know how to reference the Default Workspace object. The Workspace object, like other objects, supports a fixed set of methods and properties. One such method is OpenDatabase, which can be used to open an existing database.

Syntax	**Set** *database* = *workspace*.**OpenDatabase** (*dbname* [, *options*] [, *read-only*] [, *connect*])
Dissection	■ When you call the **OpenDatabase** method, the Jet Database engine creates a new Database object. A reference to the new Database object is created in the Databases collection, and a reference to a Database object is stored in the variable *database*.
	■ The variable *database* must be declared as a Database or as a generic Object variable.
	■ The variable *workspace* contains the reference to the workspace, usually the default workspace, where the database will be opened.
	■ The variable *dbname* must contain either a text string or a variable that represents the folder and file name of the database to be opened.

- The *options* argument can be either True or False. If True, then the database is opened in exclusive mode, meaning that no other user can open the same database until the current session ends. If False, the database is opened in shared mode, meaning that multiple users can access it. If you do not specify *options*, multiple users can access the database.

- The optional *read-only* argument can be True or False. If True, then you can read data from the database but cannot change the data. If False (the default), data can be both read and written.

- The optional *connect* argument is used to specify information such as passwords.

| **Code Example** | ```
Public gdbCurrent As Database
Set gdbCurrent = DBEngine.Workspaces(0). _
        OpenDatabase("A:\Chapter.08\Startup\Paymast.mdb")
``` |
| **Code Dissection** | The preceding statements will open the database named Paymast.mdb in the Chapter.08\Startup folder. The Database data type is an object, so you use the Set statement in the assignment statement. |

Like other object variables, DAO objects such as Workspace and Database objects have standard prefixes indicating the object's type. The Database object uses the "db" prefix. In the previous statements, this object was assumed to be a global variable, so the prefix "g" was used to denote the variable's scope.

You previously saw that the Workspaces collection supported a default method—the Item method. In addition to supporting a default method or property, many objects and methods support a default collection or object. For example, the OpenDatabase method refers to the Default Workspace by default. Furthermore, the default object pertaining to the workspace is DBEngine. Consequently, we can shorten the previous Set statement to the following statement:

```
Set gdbCurrent = _
    OpenDatabase("A:\Chapter.08\Startup\Paymast.mdb")
```

The preceding syntax is valid because the OpenDatabase method by default applies to the Default Workspace object stored in the Workspaces collection. This statement adds the newly opened database object to the Databases collection and stores a reference to the Database object in the object variable gdbCurrent.

In the payroll program, multiple procedures in multiple forms will use the object variable representing the Database object, so it must be declared as a Public variable in the general declarations section of a Form module. Because the program will access the database every time it runs, the database should be opened when the startup form is loaded.

To open the database for Paymaster's program:

1 Enter the following statement in the general declarations section of the Form module named **frmPay**:

```
Public gdbCurrent As Database
```
```

2 Enter the following statement in the **Form_Load** event procedure for the form named **frmPay**. Remember to change the path name as necessary depending on where you have installed the database file. Also, if you have copied the database file from the CD-ROM, set the file properties as read-write; otherwise, an error will occur.

```
Set gdbCurrent = _
    OpenDatabase("A:\Chapter.08\Startup\Paymast.mdb")
```

The first statement declared the variable gdbCurrent as a Database type object variable. Because the variable is an object variable, the assignment statement shown in Step 2 must use the Set statement. The second statement opened the database and set the Database object variable to reference the open database; the OpenDatabase method consequently creates an instance of the Database object. A reference to this database instance is stored in the object variable gdbCurrent.

Once a Database object exists, you can call its methods to create recordsets and manipulate the data in the open database.

Programming the Recordset Object

The Database object contains a reference to several other collections and objects. For example, each Database object contains a reference to the Recordsets collection. This collection contains a reference to zero or more Recordset objects representing the open recordsets in a database. One Recordset object exists for each open recordset in a database. You can open several recordsets at the same time. Figure 8-7 shows the relationship between the Recordsets collection and Recordset object to the other objects in the DAO hierarchy.

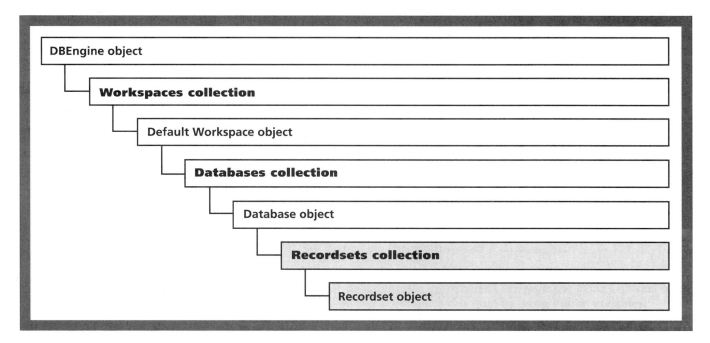

Figure 8-7: Recordsets collection and Recordset object

After opening a database, you can write code to explicitly open a recordset. In reality, when you write code to open a recordset, you are performing the same task carried out by the Data control when it opens a recordset. To explicitly create a recordset, you call the OpenRecordset method pertaining to the Database object. When the OpenRecordset method is called, a recordset is both created and opened.

Syntax	**Set** *recordset* = *object*.**OpenRecordset** (*source* [, *type*] [, *options*] [, *lockedits*])
Dissection	■ The **OpenRecordset** method creates a new recordset.
	■ A reference to the newly created recordset is stored in *recordset*.
	■ *object* represents a Database object variable.
	■ The *source* argument is either the name of a database table to be opened or an SQL SELECT statement. You will learn how to write SQL SELECT statements in Section C of this chapter.
	■ The optional *type* argument indicates the type of recordset to create.
	■ The *options* argument contains additional options that control the creation of the recordset.
	■ The optional *lockedits* argument is used in multiuser environments when multiple users must access the same database at the same time.
| **Code Example** | ```
Private mrstCurrent As Recordset
Set mrstCurrent = gdbCurrent.OpenRecordset("tblEmployees")
``` |
| **Code Dissection** | The preceding statement assumes that gdbCurrent is a Database object variable. The OpenRecordset method is called with a single argument: the name of a table in a database. In this statement, the name of the table is "tblEmployees". This value could also be stored in a string variable containing the table name. Finally, the left-hand side of the assignment statement contains a recordset object variable. Again, because an object reference is being assigned, the Set statement must be used. |

The OpenRecordset method, which is very similar to the OpenDatabase method, creates an instance of the Recordset object. A reference to this instance is then stored in the object variable. In this case, the object variable is named mrstCurrent.

As you move into the next step of your programming, consider the database tasks you performed in Chapter 5. You used the Recordset object in conjunction with the Data control to locate, add, change, and delete records. To accomplish these tasks, you created bound text boxes. That is, you set the DataField and DataSource properties of the text boxes so that they displayed information from the recordset created by the Data control. You can perform the same processing in Paymaster's program without the Data control; that is, your code can load data into the text boxes and save that data to the open recordset. In this situation, the text boxes are implemented as unbound controls.

When developing the code that will allow the user to locate, add, change, and delete records from a database table, you must prevent the user from attempting an impossible database operation. For example, the user should not be able to delete a record when no current record exists. The user must also be prohibited from updating a record that has not been enabled for editing. In addition, the user must be able to abandon editing and cancel any changes that were made to the current record. While these limitations may seem difficult to program, in reality their programming is quite straightforward.
```

To provide the user with this type of flexibility, all editing functions appear as menu items. The Edit menu contains menu items to add, change, and delete records. The Locate menu is used to find records. Your program will enable and disable these menu items as necessary so that the user cannot execute a command that will cause a run-time error.

Whether a menu item is enabled or disabled depends on the program being in one of two situations or states. In the first state, a record is being edited; the user should therefore be restricted to recording the edits or abandoning them. In the second state, a record is not being edited; the user should therefore be limited to locating records, adding new records, or changing and deleting existing records.

You can disable and enable menu items based upon the current edit state of the program by creating a Sub procedure. When the program starts, the edit state should reflect the fact that a record is not being edited.

To set the edit state:

1   Activate the Code window for the form named **frmPay**, if necessary.

2   Create a **Private** general procedure named **SetEditState** that accepts one argument, a Boolean value. Enter the following code in the procedure:

```
Private Sub SetEditState(pblnEditing As Boolean)
    If pblnEditing Then
        mnuLocate.Enabled = False
        txtEmployeeID.Locked = False
        txtLastName.Locked = False
        txtFirstName.Locked = False
        txtHourlyWage.Locked = False
        mnuEditAdd.Enabled = False
        mnuEditRecord.Enabled = False
        mnuEditUpdate.Enabled = True
        mnuEditCancel.Enabled = True
        mnuEditDelete.Enabled = False
    Else
        mnuLocate.Enabled = True
        txtEmployeeID.Locked = True
        txtLastName.Locked = True
        txtFirstName.Locked = True
        txtHourlyWage.Locked = True
        mnuEditAdd.Enabled = True
        mnuEditRecord.Enabled = True
        mnuEditUpdate.Enabled = False
        mnuEditCancel.Enabled = False
        mnuEditDelete.Enabled = True
    End If
```

3 When you start the program, the edit state should reflect the fact that a record is not being edited. Enter the following statements (shown in bold) to open the recordset and call the general procedure to set the edit state in the form's **Form_Load** event procedure:

```
Set gdbCurrent = _
    OpenDatabase("A:\Chapter.08\Startup\Paymast.mdb")
Set mrstCurrent = gdbCurrent.OpenRecordset("tblEmployees")
Call SetEditState(False)
```

4 Save and test the program. When the program starts, the File, Locate, Edit, Payroll, and View menus should be enabled. On the Edit menu, the Update Record and Cancel Edit menu items should be disabled. These options indicate that a record has not yet been enabled for editing.

5 End the program to return to design mode.

The statements in Step 2 enable or disable the appropriate menu items depending on whether the edit state is True or False. They also lock or unlock the text boxes accordingly. The statements in the Form_Load event procedure explicitly open the recordset and set the edit state, indicating that a record is not being edited.

Now that you have set the edit state for the program, you are ready to write the code for the menu items to locate, add, change, and delete records. You will accomplish this task without the aid of the Data control.

Referencing the Fields in the Recordset Object

The key to working with a recordset programmatically is to realize that the program code must explicitly copy data from the recordset to the unbound text boxes. The code must also save data contained in the text boxes back to the recordset. In this chapter, the text boxes are not bound to a Data control. Rather, they are used in an unbound mode. Reflecting this setup, you need to write code to move data between the text boxes and the recordset.

In Chapter 5, you used a bound text box to display a field from a recordset; because you are not using a Data control here, however, you need a mechanism to reference a specific field in a recordset directly and to store the field contents in an unbound text box. To reference a field in a recordset, you use the following syntax.

Syntax	*recordsetname*![*fieldname*]
Dissection	■ *recordsetname* must be an existing recordset.
	■ *fieldname* is a field in the recordset.

Earlier in this chapter, you wrote statements to open a database and a recordset, based upon a table in that database. A reference to this recordset is stored in the variable named mrstCurrent. The following statement reads the contents of a field in that recordset and stores the contents of that field in the corresponding text box:

```
txtEmployeeID = mrstCurrent![fldEmployeeID]
```

This statement reads the contents of the fldEmployeeID field from the mrstCurrent recordset and stores the value in the txtEmployeeID text box. Note that the variable referencing the recordset is followed by an exclamation point. The field name, enclosed in square brackets, follows the exclamation point. fldEmployeeID is a field in the table named tblEmployees—the table you used when you opened the recordset. The preceding statement reads the employee ID for the current record; recall from Chapter 5 that a recordset always maintains a current record and that the current record pointer identifies this record. Finally, notice that this assignment statement does not use the Set statement. You are copying actual data into the text box rather than assigning an object reference, so you omit the Set statement.

When the program starts, the current record pointer references the first record in the recordset, and that record should be loaded into the text boxes on the form. Because the text boxes are not bound to a Data control, you must explicitly write the code to communicate information between the recordset and the unbound text boxes. Also, whenever the current record changes for any reason, the current record needs to be loaded into the text boxes. Because this task must be performed in several circumstances, you can create a general procedure to load the current record into the text boxes on the form and then call that procedure as necessary whenever the current record changes.

To load a recordset's current record into an unbound text box:

1 Activate the Code window for the form named **frmPay**, if necessary.

2 Create a **Private** general procedure named **LoadCurrentRecord** that accepts no arguments. Enter the following code in the procedure:

```
Private Sub LoadCurrentRecord()
    txtEmployeeID = mrstCurrent![fldEmployeeID]
    txtLastName = mrstCurrent![fldLastName]
    txtFirstName = mrstCurrent![fldFirstName]
    txtHourlyWage = mrstCurrent![fldHourlyWage]
End Sub
```

3 After the form loads, the recordset will open because of the statements you already wrote. These statements cause the current record pointer to locate the first record automatically. You can copy the information from the current record into the text boxes by calling the general procedure you just wrote from the Form_Load event procedure. Enter the following statement (shown in bold) in the **Form_Load** event procedure just after the statement to open the recordset:

```
Set mrstcurrent = gdbCurrent.OpenRecordset("tblEmployees")
Call LoadCurrentRecord
```

4 Save and test the program. When the form loads, the recordset should open. The general procedure should then be called to display the current record in the text boxes. The contents of the current record should appear as shown in Figure 8-8.

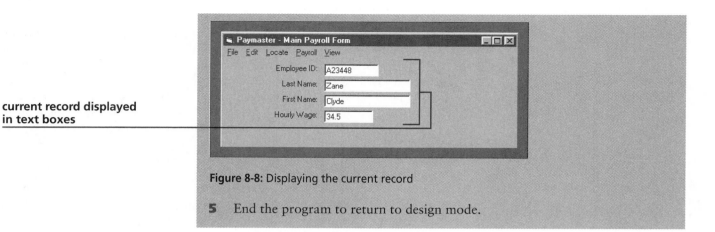

current record displayed in text boxes

Figure 8-8: Displaying the current record

5 End the program to return to design mode.

In addition to loading the current record into the text boxes, the user will change the contents of the text boxes and want to save those modifications. The syntax to write a field to a recordset is the same as the syntax to read a field. Consider the following statements:

```
mrstCurrent.Edit
mrstCurrent![fldEmployeeID] = txtEmployeeID
mrstCurrent.Update
```

Remember that you must enable editing on a record before changing its contents. Thus the first statement calls the recordset's Edit method to enable editing on the current record. The next statement reads the contents of the text box named txtEmployeeID and stores its contents in the corresponding recordset field. After saving the value, the program calls the Update method to write the changes back to the database. Remember that changes to a recordset do not become permanent until the Update method is called.

To save data to the recordset's current record:

1 Activate the Code window for the form named **frmPay**, if necessary.

2 Create a **Private** general procedure named **SaveCurrentRecord** that accepts no arguments. Enter the following code in the procedure:

```
Private Sub SaveCurrentRecord()
    mrstCurrent![fldEmployeeID] = txtEmployeeID
    mrstCurrent![fldLastName] = txtLastName
    mrstCurrent![fldFirstName] = txtFirstName
    mrstCurrent![fldHourlyWage] = txtHourlyWage
End Sub
```

These statements read the contents of each text box and store them in the appropriate fields of the recordset. Note that the code neither enables editing of the current record nor updates the change. This task will be left to other procedures, as you will see next.

Calling the Methods of the Recordset Object

Now that you have developed the general procedures to read and write recordset data, you can write the code to add, change, and delete records and to update the edit state as necessary. To accomplish this task, you can call the two general procedures you just created with the techniques you used in Chapter 5 to add, change, and delete records in a recordset.

To add, change, and delete records from a recordset:

1 Activate the Code window for the form named **frmPay**, if necessary.

2 Enter the following statements (shown in bold) in the **mnuEditAdd_Click** event procedure:

```
Private Sub mnuEditAdd_Click()
    mrstCurrent.AddNew
    Call ClearCurrentRecord
    Call SetEditState(True)
End Sub
```

3 Enter the following statements (shown in bold) in the **mnuEditCancel_Click** event procedure:

```
Private Sub mnuEditCancel_Click()
    mrstCurrent.CancelUpdate
    Call LoadCurrentRecord
    Call SetEditState(False)
End Sub
```

4 Enter the following statements (shown in bold) in the **mnuEditDelete_Click** event procedure:

```
Private Sub mnuEditDelete_Click()
    mrstCurrent.Delete
    mrstCurrent.MoveFirst
    Call LoadCurrentRecord
    Call SetEditState(False)
End Sub
```

5   Enter the following statements (shown in bold) in the **mnuEditRecord_Click** event procedure:

```
Private Sub mnuEditRecord_Click()
    mrstCurrent.Edit
    Call SetEditState(True)
End Sub
```

6   Enter the following statements (shown in bold) in the **mnuEditUpdate_Click** event procedure:

```
Private Sub mnuEditUpdate_Click()
    Call SaveCurrentRecord
    mrstCurrent.Update
    Call SetEditState(False)
End Sub
```

7   Save and test the program. Click **Edit**, then click **Add Record** to create a new record.

8   Enter an employee ID of **A9999**. Enter your last and first name in the name fields. Enter an hourly wage of **12.34**.

9   Click **Edit**, then click **Update Record** to record the changes.

10   Click **Locate**, then click **First** to locate the first record. Click **Locate**, then click **Last** to locate the last record—that is, the record you just added. The procedures to locate different records have already been created for you. If you are not familiar with these procedures, refer to Chapter 5.

11   Click **Edit**, then click **Edit Record** to enable editing on the current record. Make changes to the record, click **Edit**, then click **Cancel Edit** to abandon the changes. The record should be restored to its original contents.

12   Click **Edit**, then click **Delete** to remove the record you just added.

13   End the program to return to design mode.

You have now completed the programming for this section. Your newly written code allows the user to add, change, and delete records from the database without using the Data control. When to use the Data control and when not to use it is somewhat subjective and often a matter of programmer preference. In general, when you want to closely manage the processing of a recordset, you should not use the Data control; on the other hand, using the Data control generally requires that you write far less code.

Q U E S T I O N S

1. To use DAO objects in a program, you must _____.
   a. add the DAO control to the toolbox
   b. create a reference to the DAO object library using the Project References dialog
   c. create an instance of the Workspaces collection
   d. create an instance of the DBEngine object
   e. None of the above.

2. The _____ method opens a database, and the _____ method opens a recordset.
   a. NewDatabase, NewRecordset
   b. CreateDatabase, CreateRecordset
   c. OpenDatabase, OpenRecordset
   d. OpenDatabase, CreateRecordset
   e. None of the above.

3. The _____ property is the default property for a text box, and the _____ property is the default property for a label.
   a. Name, Name
   b. Caption, Text
   c. Change, Click
   d. Click, Change
   e. Text, Caption

4. Which of the following statements about default methods and properties is true?
   a. Using a default property or method causes the statement to execute about 25 percent faster.
   b. Using a default property or method saves typing.
   c. There is no performance difference with default methods and properties.
   d. Both a and b.
   e. Both b and c.

5. Which of the following statements about collections is true?
   a. They can be zero-based.
   b. They can be one-based.
   c. An item in a collection can be referenced with a string key.
   d. An item in a collection can be referenced with a numeric index.
   e. All of the above.

6. Which of the following is a DAO object?
   a. DBEngine
   b. Workspace
   c. Database
   d. Recordset
   e. All of the above.

7. Write the statement to declare a variable named mdbQuestion. Then write the statement to open the database named "C:\Question.mdb" and store a reference to it in the variable you just declared.

8. Assume that mdbQuestion is a database variable that contains a reference to an open database. Write the statement to declare a variable named mrstQuestion. Open the recordset using the table named "tblQuestion", and store a reference to the open recordset in the variable mrstQuestion.

9. Assume that mrstQuestion is a recordset and fldName is a field in that recordset. Write the statement to read the contents of the field and store its value in the text box named txtQuestion.

10. Assume that mrstQuestion is a recordset and fldName is a field in that recordset. Write the statement to read the contents of the text box named txtQuestion and store its value in the recordset field. Also, write the statements to enable the recordset for editing and save the changes to the recordset.

SECTION B
objectives

In this section you will:

- Use the SQL language to manipulate the records in a database table
- Use the INSERT statement to add records to a table
- Use the UPDATE statement to change the contents of existing records
- Use the WHERE clause to restrict the records that are selected with an SQL statement
- Use the DELETE statement to remove records from a table

Writing SQL Statements

Writing SQL Statements

Most database management systems provide two models to manipulate information in a database. In the **navigational model** (discussed in Chapter 5), you move forward and backward through records or locate records in a recordset using a method such as FindFirst or FindNext. The Microsoft Jet database engine also supports the **relational model**, which allows a single statement to perform an action on several records simultaneously and is implemented using the Structured Query Language (SQL).

The American National Standards Institute (ANSI) has defined a standard for the **Structured Query Language (SQL)**, which is widely used in database applications. This language supports a set of statements that allow you to add, change, and delete data in a database. When a program will execute an SQL statement, you do not need to write code to navigate through the records in a recordset individually. Rather, the program executes a statement that will operate on one or more rows of data at the same time.

Most implementations of SQL contain extensions. That is, each vendor supplying a version of SQL adds enhancements that it believes improve its product. Despite this proliferation of extensions, most parts of the language are consistent from one database vendor to another.

SQL consists of three Data Definition Language statements and four Data Manipulation Language statements. **Data Definition Language (DDL)** statements change the structure of a database. **Data Manipulation Language (DML)** statements add, change, and delete records in a database table or query. In this section, you will learn how to use the four DML statements. Figure 8-9 lists the DML statements and a brief description of their purposes.

SELECT	Retrieves one or more rows from a database table or query
INSERT	Inserts rows into a database table
UPDATE	Changes the contents of one or more existing columns
DELETE	Removes one or more rows from a database table

Figure 8-9: DML statements

Notice that the DML statements appear in uppercase letters. The standard naming convention for SQL statements calls for use of capital letters for all SQL keywords such as **INSERT** and **UPDATE**.

DML statements can be grouped into two types of queries:

- A select query returns records from a database and stores them in a Recordset object as a result of a SELECT statement.
- An action query performs an action on a database table or query but does not return any records. Possible actions include adding, updating, and removing records. Action queries do not return a recordset.

Paymaster Payroll Services receives payroll information from its customers in the form of ASCII-delimited files. The first step in computing the payroll, therefore, is to read the ASCII file into the database table that contains the time sheets. Figure 8-10 shows the format of this ASCII file.

Employee ID	Hours Worked
"A23448"	40
"A44228"	30
"A55433"	30.5

Figure 8-10: Fields in the ASCII File

As shown in Figure 8-10, the ASCII file contains two fields. The first field is a string containing the employee ID, and the second field is a numeric field containing the hours worked.

In Chapter 7, you learned how to write a Do loop to read records from a sequential file into list and combo boxes. In this chapter, you will read the sequential file into a database table so as to compute the payroll. Thus you need to write a Do loop to read each record from the sequential file, just as you did in Chapter 7. For each record read from the ASCII file, you need to insert a record in the database. Instead of calling the methods of a recordset, you will use the INSERT statement, which will be called for each record in the text file.

Inserting Database Records with the INSERT Statement

Two forms of the INSERT statement exist. The first appends a single record to a table, and the second appends multiple records. The syntax for the first form follows.

Syntax

INSERT INTO *target* [(*field1*[, *field2* [, ...]])]
VALUES (*value1*[, *value2*[, ...]])

Dissection

- The *target* is the name of the table or query where the records will be appended.
- For each *field* in the *target*, the **INSERT INTO** statement will store data in the *field*.

- The values stored in the fields are specified through the **VALUES** clause using *value1*, *value2*, and so on. Each value is inserted such that *value1* corresponds to *field1*, *value2* corresponds to *field2*, and so on. The number of fields and values must be the same. Commas separate each field and value. Text data are enclosed by quotation marks, unlike numeric data. Pound signs (#) surround the Date fields. If you need to embed a single quotation mark into a string, you can use "Chr(34)", which is the code for the single quotation mark character.

Code Example	```INSERT INTO tblPayroll```
	``` (fldEmployeeID,fldHoursWorked,fldDatePaid)```
	``` VALUES ('A32147',40,#2/23/99#)```

Code Dissection	This statement illustrates the use of the INSERT statement. Although the previous statement is formatted on multiple lines, it will be stored in a Visual Basic variable as a consecutive string of characters. A record is inserted into the table named tblPayroll. Three fields are inserted: fldEmployeeID, fldHoursWorked, and fldDatePaid. The value for the first field, A32147, is a string; the value for the second field, 40, is numeric; and the value for the third field, 2/23/99, is a date value. Note that this SQL statement is not a legal Visual Basic statement. In a moment, you will see how to adapt an SQL statement so that it can be written as a Visual Basic action query.

If you do not specify a field and a corresponding value for a field, a Null value is inserted for the missing columns. If the number of fields does not correspond to the number of values, a run-time error occurs.

To execute a statement that returns records (a select query), you use the OpenRecordset method. To execute an action query, you call the Execute method, which is also supported by the Database object. The **Execute** method executes an SQL statement that runs an action query.

Syntax	*object*.**Execute** *source* [, *options*]
Dissection	■ The **Execute** method performs an action query on an open database. ■ The *object* must be a Database object. The Database object is usually created using the OpenDatabase method. ■ The *source* is a string containing the SQL statement or the Name property value of a QueryDef object. ■ The optional *options* argument contains one or more constants to determine the characteristics of the statement. For more information about these constants, see the Help page for the Database object's Execute method.
Code Example	```gdbCurrent.Execute "INSERT INTO tblPayroll " & _``` ``` (fldEmployeeID) VALUES 'A1234' "```
Code Dissection	The preceding statement assumes that the database gdbCurrent is a Database object variable that references an open database. The first argument—the *source* argument—is a string containing the INSERT statement. This statement inserts a record into the table named tblPayroll with one field named fldEmployeeID. The fldEmployeeID field has a value of A1234. Because it is a text field, the data is enclosed in single quotation marks.

As part of the payroll program, you will write the structure of the Do loop to read the ASCII-delimited file, test the loop, and write the INSERT statement to insert each record into the appropriate database table. You must declare two local variables to hold the two fields from the ASCII file. The input file, Paymast.txt, is stored in the Chapter.08\Startup folder.

To write the structure of the Do loop to read the ASCII-delimited input file:

1   Activate the Code window to the **Click** event procedure for the menu item named **mnuPayrollReadASCIIFile** on the form named **frmPay.**

2   Enter the following statements (shown in bold) into the event procedure. Replace the drive designator as necessary, depending on where the database is installed.

```
Private Sub mnuPayrollReadASCIIFile_Click( )
    Dim pstrEmployeeID As String
    Dim psngHoursWorked As Single
    Open "A:\Chapter.08\Startup\Paymast.txt" For Input As #1
    Do Until EOF(1)
        Input #1, pstrEmployeeID, psngHoursWorked
    Loop
    Close #1
End Sub
```

Because the input file contains two fields (employee ID and hours worked), you declared two variables to store the information. employee ID is a string, and hours worked is a number that may contain a decimal point. The Do loop reads the input file into the two variables named pstrEmployeeID and psngHoursWorked until it reaches the end-of-file. At that point, nothing is done with the variables.

The next step in the programming process is to create the INSERT statement that will add a new record to the table using the contents of the variables. When you create an INSERT statement in Visual Basic, you first must store the INSERT statement in a String variable and then use that variable as an argument to the Execute method. Storing the INSERT statement in the String variable requires that you concatenate each part of the INSERT statement to build the string.

For this INSERT statement, you will insert three fields into the table named tblPayroll. The first field, fldEmployeeID, is a string. The second field, fldHoursWorked, is a Single data type. The third field, fldDatePaid, is a Date data type. Remember that when you use an INSERT statement to insert a string, you must enclose the string in single quotation marks. When you insert a date, you must enclose the date in pound signs. No characters surround numeric data. The following code segment shows how to create the string to insert a record into the table named tblPayroll:

```
pstrSQL = "INSERT INTO tblPayroll " & _
    "(fldEmployeeID,fldHoursWorked,fldDatePaid)" & _
    " VALUES ('" & pstrEmployeeID & "'" & "," & _
    psngHoursWorked & "," & "#" & pdatDatePaid & "#" & ")"
```

Notice that the local variable is named pstrSQL. The word SQL in all capital letters may seem to violate the standard naming conventions of capitalizing only the first character of each word. SQL keywords, however, always appear in capital letters—a convention also followed with variable names. Note also that spaces are embedded into the string. For example, a space follows the table named tblPayroll and a space precedes the VALUES clause. If you omit these embedded spaces, the Jet Engine cannot decode the INSERT statement and a run-time error will occur.

The most difficult part of executing an SQL statement from Visual Basic involves the creation of the String variable in which to store the SQL statement. Because the string can become quite lengthy, you must either use continuation lines so that each line will fit into the Code window or use several assignment statements to build the string. Which option to use is a matter of personal preference. When the number of continuation lines exceeds four or five, however, you should consider writing multiple assignment statements to improve readability.

The first line of the preceding code contains the INSERT statement followed by the required table name (tblPayroll). The next line contains the field names in the table. Note that these field names are enclosed in parentheses. The next three lines deserve careful examination. Because the field, pstrEmployeeID, is a text string, we must enclose this value in single quotation marks. These characters must be inserted manually into the string. For example, if the value of pstrEmployeeID contains the value A12345, the code segment

```
" VALUES ('" & pstrEmployeeID & "'"
```

will produce the following string:

```
VALUES ('A12345'
```

The next line concatenates the value of psngHoursWorked to the string. Because this value is a number, no quotation marks are used. This format applies to all types of numbers.

The final line builds the part of the text string in which to store the date paid. Because the data type of this field is a Date, pound signs must surround the value. For example, if the value of the variable pdatDatePaid is 2/23/99, then the code segment

```
"#" & pdatDatePaid & "#"
```

will produce the following string:

```
#2/23/99#
```

Thus, if the value of pstrEmployeeID is A12345, the value of psngHoursWorked is 30, and the value of pdatDatePaid is 2/23/99, the value of the String variable pstrSQL would be

```
INSERT INTO tblPayroll
    (fldEmployeeid,fldHoursWorked,fldDatePaid)
    VALUES ('A12345',30,#2/23/99#)
```

This string was formatted on multiple lines but is stored as a continuous string of characters in the String variable. You used continuation lines to create the string variable pstrSQL. You can also write multiple assignment statements to accomplish the same task:

```
pstrSQL = "INSERT INTO tblPayroll "
pstrSQL = pstrSQL & "(fldEmployeeID,fldHoursWorked,fldDatePaid)"
pstrSQL = pstrSQL & " VALUES ('" & pstrEmployeeID & "'" & ","
pstrSQL = pstrSQL & psngHoursWorked & ","
pstrSQL = pstrSQL & "#" & pdatDatePaid & "#" & ")"
```

Whether you use continuation lines or multiple assignment statements, the end result is the same—you create a string containing a valid SQL statement.

Several ways are available to write the string concatenation performed in the preceding statements. For example, consider the following equivalent statements:

```
pstrSQL = pstrSQL & "#" & pdatDatePaid & "#" & ")"
pstrSQL = pstrSQL & "#" & pdatDatePaid & "#)"
```

Both statements store the same string in the variable pstrSQL, but they concatenate the strings differently. Exactly how you concatenate the strings is a matter of personal choice. As you write more programs, you will eventually develop your own preference and style.

Now that you know how to build the String variable containing the INSERT statement, you can enter the code into the existing Do loop. After creating the String variable, you will call the Execute method of the Database object to execute the INSERT statement. This INSERT statement will create a new record with three fields: Employee ID, Hours Worked, and Date Paid. The Employee ID and Hours Worked fields are stored in the variables used in the Input # statement. The program specifications require that the user specify the value of the Date Paid field through an input box.

To write the statements to build the INSERT statement and to call the Execute method:

1   On the form named **frmPay**, activate the Code window to the **Click** event procedure for the menu item named **mnuPayrollReadASCIIFile**, if necessary.

2 Enter the following statements (shown in bold) in the event procedure:

```
Dim pstrEmployeeID As String
Dim psngHoursWorked As Single
Dim pdatDatePaid As String
Dim pstrSQL As String
pdatDatePaid = InputBox("Enter date paid", _
    "Paymaster", Date)
Open "A:\Chapter.08\Startup\Paymast.txt" For Input As #1
Do Until EOF(1)
    Input #1, pstrEmployeeID, psngHoursWorked
    pstrSQL = "INSERT INTO tblPayroll " & _
        "(fldEmployeeID,fldHoursWorked,fldDatePaid)" & _
        " VALUES ('" & pstrEmployeeID & "'" & "," & _
        psngHoursWorked & "," & _
        "#" & pdatDatePaid & "#" & ")"
    gdbCurrent.Execute pstrSQL
Loop
```

Each time a record is read from the text input file named Paymast.txt and stored in the two variables, the program builds the string pstrSQL containing the correct INSERT statement. Once the string is complete, it calls the Execute method on the open database. The Execute method requires one argument, a string containing the action query to be executed. In this case, the action query is an INSERT statement.

You should now verify that the records in the text file were read correctly. A form has already been created to view records in the table named tblPayroll. You will use that form to verify that each record was read correctly.

To verify that the file Payroll.txt was read correctly:

1 Save and run the project.

2 Click **Payroll**, then click **Read ASCII File** on the main form's menu bar.

3 When the input box appears, click **OK** to accept the current date supplied by your computer.

4 On the main form, click **View**, then click **Payroll Form** on the menu bar to open the payroll form. Scroll through the records to verify that three records with the current date exist. Note that the database also includes records having a date paid of 3/24/99 and 3/25/99. Ignore these records.

5 End the program to return to design mode.

Now that you have inserted the Employee ID, Hours Worked, and Date Paid fields into the Payroll table, you must compute the gross pay, payroll taxes, and net pay from the information just read by the program. You can accomplish this goal using the UPDATE statement.

Updating Database Records with the UPDATE Statement

The UPDATE statement is used to change the contents of one or more rows from one or more fields in a table or query. Consider a situation where you need to change the contents of several records in a table. To carry out this task, you could create a Recordset object and a corresponding Do loop to examine each record in the recordset. Each time you wanted to change the contents of a field, you would call the Edit method of a recordset, set the field contents, and call the Update method on the Recordset object.

This technique, which uses the navigational model, will work, but you could also use the relational model. That is, you can write an SQL UPDATE statement that will update many rows using the same statement. The UPDATE statement has the following syntax:

Syntax	**UPDATE** *tablename* **SET** *fieldname = newvalue*[, *fieldname = newvalue*] ...
Dissection	■ The *tablename* is the name of an existing table or query. ■ The *fieldname* is a field from the table or query specified by *tablename*. ■ The *newvalue* can be a literal value or expression.

Code Example	```
	pstrSQL = "UPDATE tblPayroll " & _
	    "SET fldLastName = 'Smith' " & _
	    " WHERE fldEmployeeID = 'A12345' "
	gdbCurrent.Execute pstrSQL
	``

Code Dissection	The preceding statements update the field named fldLastName in the table named tblPayroll. The value is set to Smith. The WHERE clause ensures that the program updates only the record having an Employee ID of A12345. You will learn about the WHERE clause next.

The expression in an UPDATE statement resembles an assignment statement. That is, it has a left-hand side and a right-hand side. The left-hand side contains the name of a field in the table or query to be updated. The right-hand side combines field names, properties, literal values, or variables that evaluate to a single value. Figure 8-11 shows examples of valid expressions given the fields fldGrossPay (a number), fldEmployeeID (a string), and fldDatePaid (a date).

Expression	Description
fldEmployeeID = 'A1234'	Sets the value of the field named fldEmployeeID to the string "A1234".
fldEmployeeID = 'A' & '1234'	Produces the same result as the previous expression using string concatenation.
fldTaxesWithheld = 24.23	Sets the value of the field fldTaxesWithheld to the value 24.23.
fldTaxesWithheld = fldGrossPay * .20	Sets the value of the field fldTaxesWithheld to the value of the field fldGrossPay * the constant value .20.
fldTaxesWithheld = fldGrossPay * fldTaxRate	Sets the value of the field fldTaxesWithheld to the value of the field fldGrossPay * the value stored in the field fldTaxRate.
fldDatePaid = #7/22/98#	Sets the value of the field fldDatePaid to the date value 7/22/98.

Figure 8-11: Expressions in an UPDATE statement

The first step in computing the payroll involved loading the information from the text file. Now you will use that information to compute the gross pay, taxes withheld, and net pay. To compute the gross pay, you multiply the hourly rate by the hours worked. To compute the taxes withheld, you multiply the gross pay by the tax rate. Finally, to compute the net pay, you subtract the taxes withheld from the gross pay. These fields do not appear in the same table, however, so a query has already been developed. Figure 8-12 shows the two tables used in the query.

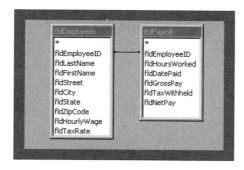

Figure 8-12: Paymaster query

For more information about queries, refer to Appendix C.

The UPDATE statement works much like the INSERT statement you wrote in the previous steps. First, the UPDATE statement performs an action query. That is, it updates fields in a table rather than selecting rows from a table and returning them as a Recordset object. Unlike the INSERT statement, however, the UPDATE statement operates on many rows rather than on a single row. When you used a recordset, you performed operations inside a Do loop once for each record in a recordset. When you use an UPDATE statement, it selects all rows to update and then performs the specified operation on each row selected. Figure 8-13 shows how the UPDATE statement works.

desired rows are
selected

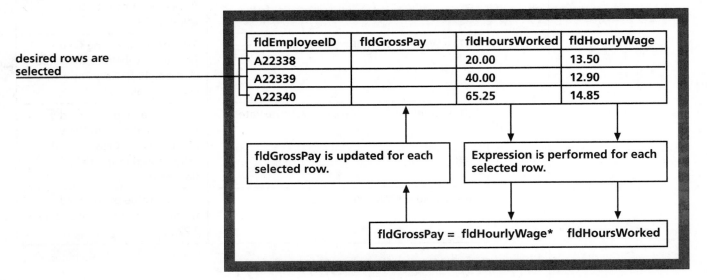

Figure 8-13: How the UPDATE statement works

To use the UPDATE statement, you first build a string and then submit that string as an argument to the Execute method. The following code segment shows the statement to build the string that will update the field named fldGrossPay by multiplying fldHourlyWage by fldHoursWorked for every record in the query named qryEmployeesPayroll:

```
Dim pstrSQL As String
pstrSQL = "UPDATE qryEmployeesPayroll " & _
    "SET fldGrossPay = fldHourlyWage * fldHoursWorked"
```

The first argument of the UPDATE statement indicates the table or query to be updated. The expression after the SET statement provides the value part of the UPDATE statement as an expression. It multiplies fldHourlyWage by fldHoursWorked and stores the result in fldGrossPay. The statement performs this action for every row in qryEmployeesPayroll rather than on a single row.

Because you want to compute the payroll only for the records you just added, you will use the Date Paid field to select specific records from tblPayroll in the

UPDATE statement. You can accomplish this goal with a WHERE clause. A **WHERE** clause contains an expression much like the expression in an If statement. That is, the expression evaluates to True or False. A WHERE clause has the following syntax:

Syntax

WHERE *conditionlist*
The *conditionlist* has the following syntax:
fieldname operator value

Dissection

- The *fieldname* indicates the field from the table or query used in the SELECT statement.

- The *operator* works like the operator in an If statement's condition.

- The *value* can be a variable, a property, or a literal value. If it is a date, then it must be enclosed in pound signs (#). If it is a string, then the value must be enclosed in single quotation marks (').

- Multiple conditions can be concatenated using the **And** and **Or** statements.

When used in an UPDATE statement, the expression in the WHERE clause is tested for every row in the table or query. If the expression is True, the program updates the record as described by the SET part of the UPDATE statement. If the expression is False, the program ignores the record. Figure 8-14 shows several examples of WHERE clauses.

Expression	Description
WHERE fldEmployeeID = 'A1234'	Returns the record(s) with an employee ID of A1234.
WHERE fldTaxesWithheld > 50.00	Returns the record(s) having a value in the Taxes Withheld field greater than $50.00.
WHERE fldTaxesWithheld >= 50.00 And fldTaxesWithheld <= 100.00	Returns the record(s) having a value in the Taxes Withheld field between $50.00 and $100.00.
WHERE fldTaxesWithheld > 50.00 Or fldGrossPay > 500.00	Returns the record(s) having a value in the Taxes Withheld field greater than $50.00 or having a value in the field fldGrossPay greater than $500.00.
WHERE fldDatePaid = #7/22/98#	Returns the record(s) having a value in the Date Paid field of 7/22/98.

Figure 8-14: Expressions in a WHERE clause

Next, you should create the UPDATE statement to update the gross pay for each payroll record just read when you executed the INSERT statement. To accomplish this goal, you must create a String variable containing the correct UPDATE statement with a WHERE clause to restrict the rows updated to those rows that were just loaded. Those rows have a specific date paid.

To write the UPDATE statement to compute the gross pay:

1   In the form named **frmPay**, activate the Code window to the **Click** event procedure for the menu item named **mnuPayrollComputePayroll**.

2   Enter the following statements (shown in bold) in the event procedure:

```
Dim pstrSQL As String
Dim pstrDatePaid As String
pstrDatePaid = InputBox("Enter date paid", _
    "Paymaster", Date)
pstrSQL = "UPDATE qryEmployeesPayroll " & _
    "SET fldGrossPay = " & _
    "fldHourlyWage * fldHoursWorked " & _
    " WHERE fldDatePaid = " & "#" & _
    pstrDatePaid & "#"
gdbCurrent.Execute pstrSQL
```

These statements declare the String variable used as the argument to the Execute method and the String variable to store the date paid. After the program builds the string representing the SQL statement, it calls the Execute method.

```
pstrSQL = "UPDATE qryEmployeesPayroll " & _
    "SET fldGrossPay = " & _
    "fldHourlyWage * fldHoursWorked" & _
    " WHERE fldDatePaid = " & "#" & _
    pstrDatePaid & "#"
```

This UPDATE statement updates the column fldGrossPay in the query qryEmployeesPayroll by multiplying the column fldHourlyWage by the column fldHoursWorked. It updates only those records having a date paid matching the value specified.

You will now verify that the UPDATE statement works correctly.

To verify that the UPDATE statement updates the proper records:

1   Save and test the program. Click **Payroll**, then click **Compute Payroll** on the main form's menu bar.

2   Click **OK** in the input box to use the current date.

3   Click **View**, then click **Payroll Form** on the menu bar. Scroll through the records on the form and verify that the gross pay was computed for each of the three employees. Ignore the records having a date paid of 3/24/99 and 3/25/99.

4   End the program to return to design mode.

Although the UPDATE statement you just wrote updates the Gross Pay field, you must also compute the Taxes Withheld and Net Pay fields. To accomplish this task, you need to write two more UPDATE statements in the same event procedure.

To compute the taxes withheld, you multiply the gross pay (computed in the last step) by the tax rate. To compute the net pay, you subtract the taxes withheld from the gross pay.

To write the UPDATE statement to compute the taxes withheld and the net pay:

1 In the form named **frmPay**, activate the Code window to the **Click** event procedure for the menu item named **mnuPayrollComputePayroll**.

2 Append the following statements (shown in bold) to the event procedure just before the End Sub statement:

```
pstrSQL = "UPDATE qryEmployeesPayroll " & _
    " SET fldTaxWithheld = " & _
    "fldGrossPay * fldTaxRate" & _
    " WHERE fldDatePaid = " & "#" & _
    pstrDatePaid & "#"
gdbCurrent.Execute pstrSQL

pstrSQL = "UPDATE qryEmployeesPayroll " & _
    " SET fldNetPay = fldGrossPay - fldTaxWithheld" & _
    " WHERE fldDatePaid = " & "#" & _
    pstrDatePaid & "#"
gdbCurrent.Execute pstrSQL
```

These UPDATE statements update the fields fldTaxWithheld and fldNetPay for those records having the same date paid, as specified by the user.

```
pstrSQL = "UPDATE qryEmployeesPayroll " & _
    " SET fldTaxWithheld = " & _
    "fldGrossPay * fldTaxRate" & _
    " WHERE fldDatePaid = " & "#" & _
    pstrDatePaid & "#"
gdbCurrent.Execute pstrSQL
```

This UPDATE statement multiplies fldGrossPay by fldTaxRate and stores the result in the field fldTaxWithheld. It updates only those records where the value of the field fldDatePaid matches the variable pstrDatePaid. Because fldDatePaid is a Date data type, pound signs (#) must enclose the value of the variable. Once the UPDATE statement is built and stored in the string pstrSQL, the program calls the

Execute method and updates the records in the database query.

The second UPDATE statement that you typed in Step 2 is identical to the first, but subtracts fldTaxWithheld from fldGrossPay to compute fldNetPay. You will now run the program again to test these two new UPDATE statements.

To verify that the UPDATE statement updated the fields properly:

1 Save and test the program. Click **Payroll**, then click **Compute Payroll** on the main form.

2 Click **OK** in the input box to use the current date.

3 Click **View**, then click **Payroll Form** on the menu bar to open the form and display the payroll records. Scroll through the records on the form to verify that the Tax Withheld and Net Pay fields were computed for each of the employees. Ignore the records having a date paid of 3/24/99 and 3/25/99.

4 End the program to return to design mode.

In addition to updating records in a table or query using an SQL statement, you can delete records.

Removing Database Records with the DELETE Statement

The DELETE statement allows you to remove one or more rows (records) from a table. Although you could create a recordset and call the Delete method for each record you want to delete, you can also call the DELETE statement once to remove several records—just as you called the UPDATE statement once to update several records. The syntax of the DELETE statement follows.

Syntax	**DELETE ***
	    FROM *tableexpression*
	    WHERE *criteria*

Dissection	■ The **DELETE** statement removes one or more records from a table or query.
	■ The *tableexpression* is the name of the table from which records are deleted. *Tableexpression* is preceded by the FROM keyword.
	■ The *criteria* is an expression that determines which records to delete and has the same format as the WHERE clause in the UPDATE statement. That is, the expression contained in *criteria* must evaluate to True or False. If True, the record is deleted. If False, the record is ignored.
Code Example	`DELETE * FROM tblPayroll WHERE fldDatePaid = #3/22/99#`
Code Dissection	The preceding statement deletes all records from the table named tblPayroll where the field named fldDatePaid has a value of 3/22/99. Note that the program assumes that the value is a date because it is enclosed in pound signs (#).

The length of time that Paymaster Payroll Services maintains payroll information in its database depends on the customer. Each month, the company backs up the database. Then, it deletes obsolete payroll records from the table named tblPayroll.

You will now write the DELETE statement to remove those payroll records that were entered on the same date specified by the user. To accomplish this task, you will build a DELETE statement in a String variable. Because the DELETE statement performs an action query rather than returning rows in a recordset, you call the Database object's Execute method just as you did for the UPDATE and INSERT statements.

To delete obsolete payroll records from the database:

1 On the form named **frmPay**, activate the Code window to the **Click** event procedure for the menu item named **mnuPayrollDeleteOldPayroll**.

2 Enter the following statements in the event procedure:

```
Dim pstrSQL As String
Dim pstrDatePaid As String

pstrDatePaid = InputBox("Enter date paid", _
    "Paymaster", Date)
pstrSQL = "DELETE * FROM tblPayroll " & _
    " WHERE fldDatePaid = " & _
    "#" & pstrDatePaid & "#"
gdbCurrent.Execute pstrSQL
```

After declaring local variables to hold the SQL string containing the DELETE statement and the date paid entered by the user, you called the InputBox function to get the correct date from the user. Then, you built the string containing the DELETE statement. This statement will delete all records from the table tblPayroll for which the value of the field named fldDatePaid is less than or equal to the date paid value entered by the user. You should now test these statements to ensure that the DELETE statement works correctly.

To test the DELETE statement:

1 Save and test the program. Click **Payroll**, then click **Delete Old Payroll** on the menu bar.

2 Click **OK** in the input box to select the current date.

3 All payroll records you created in the previous steps should have been deleted. Click **View**, then click **Payroll Form** to verify that no records appear with the same date paid as the current date.

4 End the program to return to design mode.

Your program now performs all tasks necessary to insert records into a table from an ASCII file. It uses an UPDATE statement to compute the gross pay, taxes withheld, and net pay. It also has a feature to delete old payroll records.

QUESTIONS

1. Which of the following statements about SQL is true?
   a. SQL statements use the navigational model.
   b. SQL statements use the relational model.
   c. SQL statements consist of Data Manipulation Language statements and Data Definition Language statements.
   d. Both a and c.
   e. Both b and c.

2. What is the name of the method that runs an SQL action query?
   a. SELECT
   b. OpenRecordset
   c. Run
   d. Execute
   e. Do

3. What is the name of the SQL statement that adds a new record to a database table?
   a. ADD
   b. INSERT
   c. NEW
   d. ADDITEM
   e. None of the above.

4. What is the name of the SQL statement that changes the contents of a record in a table or query?
   a. EDIT
   b. UPDATE
   c. CHANGE
   d. MODIFY
   e. WRITE

5. What is the name of the SQL statement that removes a record from a table or query?
   a. DELETE
   b. REMOVE
   c. KILL
   d. SELECT
   e. None of the above.

6. Which of the following statements about variables in SQL statements is true?
   a. Strings are enclosed in double quotation marks.
   b. Dates are enclosed by ampersand characters.
   c. Numeric data is enclosed by single quotation marks.
   d. All of the above.
   e. None of the above.

7. Assume that gdbCurrent is a database variable that references an open database. Write the code to insert a record into that database. Assume that the table is named tblCurrent and that the fields are named fldID, fldName, and fldDate. The first field is an Integer, the second is a String, and the third is a Date. Use the value "1234" for the first field, "John Smith" for the second field, and 12/1/2001 for the date.

8. Using the same information presented in Question 7, write the statements to update the name associated with the ID 1234 to "Jane Smith".

9. Using the same information presented in Question 7, write the code to update the date associated with the ID 1234 to 12/31/2001.

10. Using the information presented in Question 7, write the statements to delete ID 1234.

Selecting Data with the SELECT Statement

The SELECT Statement

The SELECT statement is used to retrieve a set of records from a database. It can also be used to retrieve records from multiple tables or queries. When you use a SELECT statement with a database like Microsoft Access, you can type the statement into one window and view the results of that statement into another window. When you use the SELECT statement with Visual Basic, however, the statement serves as an argument to the OpenRecordset method (the same method you used in Section A of this chapter). When the program calls the OpenRecordset method, the SELECT statement executes and the resultant rows are retrieved and stored in a Recordset object. You can then scroll through these records and change the contents of a recordset by calling the recordset's methods as you have done in the past.

The SELECT statement has several parts. Rather than examining the entire syntax of the statement, you will examine it in its simplest form, then write more complex SELECT statements using the various options. The basic syntax (which does not produce a valid Visual Basic statement) for the SELECT statement follows.

Syntax	**SELECT * FROM** *tableexpression*
Dissection	■ The * (asterisk) indicates that every field from the table should be selected.
	■ The *tableexpression* can be an existing table or query name preceded by the keyword FROM.
Code Example	`SELECT * FROM qryEmployeesPayroll`
Code Dissection	This statement selects all records from the query named qryEmployeesPayroll. It is not a valid Visual Basic statement, however. In a moment, you will see how to adapt a SELECT statement for use with Visual Basic.

This form of the SELECT statement will retrieve all records and fields from a table or query. To use this SELECT statement in Visual Basic, you enclose the statement in a String variable just as you did with the other SQL statements. This String variable, however, serves as an argument to the OpenRecordset method instead of the Execute method, because you are running a select query rather than an action query.

The first step in executing a SELECT statement is to create the actual SELECT statement and store it in a String variable. To select all rows from the query named qryEmployeesPayroll, you would write the SELECT statement and store it in a variable with the following syntax:

```
pstrSQL = "SELECT * FROM qryEmployeesPayroll"
```

Because the SELECT statement you will write in this section will include many different clauses, you will write the statement so that it stores each individual clause in a separate String variable. Once you have created all of the necessary clauses, you will concatenate them into a String variable containing the entire SELECT statement.

You will need a variable to store the entire SELECT statement, another to store the FROM clause, and another to hold the individual fields selected by the user. In addition, you will need a local object variable to store the recordset that will be opened when the program calls the OpenRecordset method. Instead of using an existing table or query name as an argument to the OpenRecordset method, however, you will use a String variable containing the SELECT statement. Each Recordset object has a place in the DAO hierarchy, and each Database object contains a Recordsets collection. For each open recordset, a reference exists to a Recordset object in the Recordsets collection. Thus you need to know an object's place in the DAO hierarchy so that you can reference it with code.

As your first step, you will develop a simple version of the SELECT statement to select all the fields from the query named qryEmployeesPayroll.

To create a Recordset object using an SQL statement:

1   Open the Code window to the **cmdSelect_Click** event procedure on the form named **frmSel**, then enter the following statements (shown in bold):

```
Private Sub cmdSelect_Click( )
    Dim pstrSQL As String
    Dim pstrFROM As String
    Dim pstrFields As String
    Dim prstCurrent As Recordset

    pstrFields = " *"
    pstrFROM = " FROM qryEmployeesPayroll"

    pstrSQL = "SELECT" & pstrFields & pstrFROM
    Set prstCurrent = _
        frmPaymasterPayroll.gdbCurrent.OpenRecordset(pstrSQL)
End Sub
```

These statements declare the String variables to store the SELECT statement and to store the clauses that constitute the SELECT statement. They also call the OpenRecordset method to open a recordset.

A closer examination of the code you just typed is in order.

```
Dim pstrSQL As String
Dim pstrFROM As String
Dim pstrFields As String
Dim prstCurrent As Recordset
```

The first statement declares the variable pstrSQL to store the entire string for the SELECT statement. The variable pstrFROM will store the FROM clause, and pstrFields will store the fields selected by the user. You will use the object variable prstCurrent to reference the open recordset.

Consider the following code:

```
pstrFields = " *"
pstrFROM = " FROM qryEmployeesPayroll"
pstrSQL = "SELECT" & pstrFields & pstrFROM
```

These three statements build the SELECT statement. Because you want to select all fields from the query, you used the asterisk (*) character instead of specifying individual fields. Notice that a space precedes this character. It is necessary to insert a space between the SELECT statement and the fields. The next statement builds the FROM clause. You are selecting records from the query named qryEmployeesPayroll. The next statement concatenates the SELECT statement to the fields and the FROM clause. After the string is concatenated, the variable pstrSQL contains the following string:

```
SELECT * FROM qryEmployeesPayroll
```

The final statement opens the recordset and stores a reference to it in the variable prstCurrent.

```
Set prstCurrent = _
    frmPaymasterPayroll.gdbCurrent.OpenRecordset(pstrSQL)
```

In this assignment statement, you are again assigning an object reference, so you use the Set statement. Note that the variable gdbCurrent is the Database object variable. This variable was declared on the form frmPaymasterPayroll. Thus, to reference this variable, you must also specify the form name.

Once you have opened the recordset, each record should be displayed in the multiline text box found at the bottom of the form. The information will be arranged in columns, making the data in each field easy to read. Because the user should have the option of selecting a different combination of fields to display, you need a way to determine both the number of fields and the name of each field in the recordset at run time. You will learn this next.

In Section A of this chapter, you saw how to reference a specific field in a recordset. The Recordset object also supports a Fields collection. That is, one Fields collection exists for each Recordset object. That Fields collection contains zero or more Field objects identifying the field name, its size, and its data type. Figure 8-15 shows the relationship between the Fields collection and the Field object, and the relationship of both to the DAO hierarchy.

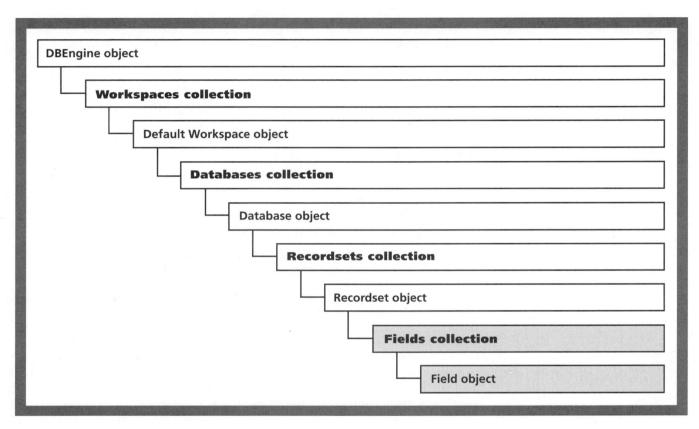

Figure 8-15: Fields collection and Field object

In the previous sections of this chapter, we described a few of the collections that make up the DAO hierarchy, though we said little about how to use those collections. In Section A, you saw how to reference a particular field in a record-set. In reality, a field is an object that is part of the Fields collection pertaining to the Recordset object. Assuming that a recordset named prstCurrent is open, you would use the following statement fragment to reference the Fields collection:

```
prstCurrent.Fields
```

In practice, you are not generally interested in the Fields collection itself. Rather, you wish to work with the individual Field objects stored in the Fields collection. From the program you wrote in Chapter 7, you know how to use a For loop to examine the individual elements in an array. To examine the individual objects in a collection, you use a variation of the For loop called a For Each loop.

Syntax	**For Each** *element* **In** *group*
	    [*statements*]
	    [**Exit For**]
	    [*statements*]
	Next [*element*]

Dissection	■ The **For Each** loop iterates through each object in a collection. ■ The required *element* is an object variable or Variant. Each time through the For Each loop, it contains a reference to an object in the collection. ■ The *group* contains the collection to examine. ■ The *statements* execute each time through the loop. ■ The optional **Exit For** statement is generally used inside an If statement and causes the loop to exit. ■ The **Next** statement marks the end of the For Each loop.
Code Example	``` Dim pfldCurrent As Field For Each pfldCurrent in prstCurrent.Fields Debug.Print pfldCurrent.Text Next ```
Code Dissection	This For Each loop references all of the fields in the recordset named prstCurrent. It works much like an ordinary For loop. Instead of using a counter, however, the For Each loop examines individual objects in a group of objects. In the preceding statements, the group of objects is the Fields collection supported by the Recordset object. Each time through the loop, the program examines a particular Field object in the collection. Thus, the first time through the loop, pfldCurrent references the first Field object in the collection. The next time through the loop, pfldCurrent references the second Field object. The process continues until all of the Field objects in the collection have been examined.

As you will see in the next set of steps, you can use the For Each loop to print each of the fields in a particular recordset. First, however, you will examine the properties pertaining to the Field object.

A Field object, like any object, supports a set of properties. The **Name** property contains the name of the field in the recordset, the **Size** property defines the number of bytes used to store the data in the field, the **Text** property contains the actual field data, and the **Type** property indicates the data type of the field.

For fields containing textual data, the width of a column should match the size of the field (stored in the Size property of the Field object). For numeric fields, the column width should be 15 spaces—adequate to display the field names and the data.

The first line of the text box will display the field names selected by the user. The corresponding field data for each record will appear under the field names. In the following steps, you will examine the Fields collection pertaining to the Recordset object. For each field, you must print the field name in a column. Because you are examining each item in a collection, you can write a For Each loop. To make the program as modular as possible and to minimize the size of the event procedure for the Select Records command button, you will create a general procedure to print the column titles. The general procedure will take one argument—the active recordset whose fields you want to print.

To print the column titles:

1 Be sure the Code window is active for the form named **frmSel**.

2 Create a **Private Sub** procedure named **PrintFields**.

3 Enter the following statements into the procedure:

```
Private Sub PrintFields(prstArg As Recordset)
    Dim pfldCurrent As Field
    Dim pstrLine As String
    Dim pintSpaces As Integer
    Dim pintCounter As Integer

    For Each pfldCurrent In prstArg.Fields
        pstrLine = pstrLine & pfldCurrent.Name

        If pfldCurrent.Type <> dbText Then
            pintSpaces = 15 - Len(pfldCurrent.Name)
        Else
            pintSpaces = pfldCurrent.Size - _
                Len(pfldCurrent.Name)
        End If

        For pintCounter = 0 To pintSpaces
            pstrLine = pstrLine & " "
        Next
    Next
    txtSQLOutput = pstrLine & vbCrLf
End Sub
```

These statements examine each field in the Fields collection pertaining to the Recordset object. A reference to this object is passed as an argument to the Sub procedure. The program determines the data type for each Field object in the collection. If the data type is Text, then it sets the width of the column to the number of characters in the string. Otherwise, the width is set to exactly 15 characters.

Examine the code you just typed more closely.

```
Dim pfldCurrent As Field
Dim pstrLine As String
Dim pintSpaces As Integer
Dim pintCounter As Integer
```

In these statements, you delcare the variable pfldCurrent as a Field object used to reference each field in the Fields collection. The variable pstrLine will contain the line for the column names displayed in the multiline text box. The variables pintSpaces and pintCounter will be used in a For loop to insert the correct number of spaces in the column.

```
For Each pfldCurrent In prstArg.Fields
```

The For Each loop steps through each Field object in the recordset's Fields collection. Each time through the loop, it sets the variable pfldCurrent to the current Field object. When no more fields in the Fields collection remain, the loop terminates.

```
pstrLine = pstrLine & pfldCurrent.Name
```

Inside the For Each loop, the name of the current field, which is stored in the Name property of the Field object named pfldCurrent, is appended to the string containing the line. The field name will therefore appear as a title for the column.

```
If pfldCurrent.Type <> dbText Then
    pintSpaces = 15 - Len(pfldCurrent.Name)
Else
    pintSpaces = pfldCurrent.Size - _
        Len(pfldCurrent.Name)
End If
```

The last part of the code determines the type of the field using an If statement. The field's type, which is stored in the Type property of the Field object, is compared with the intrinsic constant dbText. If the field's type is not Text, the program sets the variable pintSpaces to 15 minus the length of the column name. These spaces will be appended to the column name to ensure that the column uses exactly 15 characters. If the field contains text, the field's size is used as the column width. The length of the field is subtracted from the size of the field to determine the number of spaces to append to the column to make it the correct width.

```
    For pintCounter = 0 To pintSpaces
        pstrLine = pstrLine & " "
    Next
Next
```

Once the program has determined how many spaces to append to the column, the correct number of spaces must be added on to the line containing the column names. This task was accomplished using a For loop to count the number of spaces and append them to the line.

```
txtSQLOutput = pstrLine & vbCrLf
```

Performance
tip

• • • • • • • • • • • • • • • • •

▶ Instead of using the variable pstrLine to create the line, you could have stored each string in the text box individually; however, it is considerably faster to store values in variables than in properties. When you will use the value of a property frequently, you should create a variable of the proper type and read or write data to the property only when necessary to improve performance.

The final statement in the procedure stores the line containing the column names in the text box txtSQLOutput. The default property for a text box is Text, so you do not need to specify the property name.

Now that you have developed the Sub procedure to print the column headings, you must write the code to call the procedure when the user clicks the Select Records command button. Then, you should test the program.

To call the Sub procedure to print the column titles:

1   Open the Code window to the **cmdSelect_Click** event procedure for the form named **frmSel**, then enter the following statements (shown in bold) just before the End Sub statement:

```
Set prstCurrent = _
    frmPaymasterPayroll.gdbCurrent.OpenRecordset(pstrSQL)
Call PrintFields(prstCurrent)
```

2   Save and test the program. Click **View**, then click **Select Records Form** on the main form's menu bar.

3   Click the **Select Records** command button on the form to print the column titles, as shown in Figure 8-16.

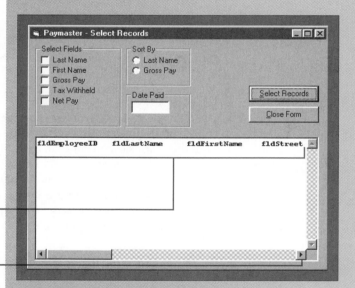

field titles

use scroll bars to see all the titles

help

• • • • • • • • • • • • • • • • •

▶ If the column titles do not appear, verify that you called the PrintFields function in the Click event procedure for the Select Records command button. If a run-time error occurs, verify that the code in the PrintFields general procedure matches that indicated in the preceding steps.

Figure 8-16: Printing the column titles

4   End the program to return to design mode.

Now that you have displayed the columns in the text box, you need to create another loop to print each record in the recordset. To accomplish this task, you will create a Do loop to examine each record. For each record, each field in the recordset's Fields collection must be printed. Thus you will create a For Each loop inside of the Do loop. To keep the Click event procedure for the Select Records command button small, you will create another general procedure to print the contents of each record.

To print the records in the recordset:

1 Be sure the Code window is active for the form named **frmSel**.

2 Create a **Private Sub** procedure named **PrintRecords**.

3 Enter the following statements into the procedure:

```
Private Sub PrintRecords(prstArg As Recordset)
    Dim pfldCurrent As Field
    Dim pstrLine As String
    Dim pintSpaces As Integer
    Dim pintCounter As Integer

    Do Until prstArg.EOF

        For Each pfldCurrent In prstArg.Fields
            pstrLine = pstrLine & pfldCurrent

            If pfldCurrent.Type <> dbText Then
                pintSpaces = 15 - Len(pfldCurrent)
            Else
                pintSpaces = pfldCurrent.Size - _
                    Len(pfldCurrent)
            End If

            For pintCounter = 0 To pintSpaces
                pstrLine = pstrLine & " "
            Next
        Next
        txtSQLOutput = txtSQLOutput & pstrLine & vbCrLf
        pstrLine = vbNullString

        prstArg.MoveNext
    Loop
End Sub
```

4 Enter the following statement (shown in bold) into the **cmdSelect_Click** event procedure just before the End Sub statement:

```
Call PrintFields(prstCurrent)
Call PrintRecords(prstCurrent)
```

Like the For Each loop you wrote for the PrintFields general procedure, this For Each loop steps through each field in the current recordset record and prints the contents of the field. This task is performed for each record in the recordset. This general procedure uses the same variables as those employed in the PrintFields general procedure.

Let's examine the code that you just typed.

```
Do Until prstArg.EOF
```

This Do loop serves as the main loop for the procedure. The variable prstArg represents the recordset created by the OpenRecordset method and the SELECT statement. This recordset is passed as an argument to the procedure. The For Each loop then examines each record in the recordset.

```
For Each pfldCurrent In prstArg.Fields
```

The Recordset object supports a Fields collection. This For Each loop examines each Field object in the Fields collection (stored as a collection in the Recordset object). A reference to the Field object is stored in the variable pfldCurrent.

```
pstrLine = pstrLine & pfldCurrent
```

The String variable pstrLine contains the line that will appear in the text box. This statement appends the contents of the current field to the string variable. The default property of the Field object is the Value property—that is, the contents of the field. You could use the syntax pfldCurrent.Value, but using the default property will make the program run faster and reduce typing.

```
If pfldCurrent.Type <> dbText Then
    pintSpaces = 15 - Len(pfldCurrent)
Else
    pintSpaces = pfldCurrent.Size - _
        Len(pfldCurrent)
End If
```

This If statement determines a column's width. If the data type of the column is Text, represented by the constant dbText, then the width of the column matches the width of the underlying data. If the data type is not Text, then the width of the column is 15. For each type of field, the variable pintSpaces contains the number of spaces that must be appended to make the column widths the same.

```
For pintCounter = 0 To pintSpaces
    pstrLine = pstrLine & " "
Next
```

This For loop, which uses the variable pintSpaces as the counter, appends to the output line the necessary number of spaces to align the next column.

```
txtSQLOutput = txtSQLOutput & pstrLine & vbCrLf
pstrLine = vbNullString
prstArg.MoveNext
```

The last three statements display the line stored in the variable pstrLine in the text box. Note that the line is appended to the existing text box contents and that the line ends with a carriage return. Next, the procedure reinitializes the current line (pstrLine). Finally, the last statement in the loop calls the MoveNext method to locate the next record in the recordset.

Now you will save your work and test whether the recordset correctly locates and prints each field.

help

If the field data do not appear under the column titles, verify that you called the PrintRecords function in the Click event procedure for the Select Records command button. If a run-time error occurs, verify that the code in the PrintRecords general procedure matches the code indicated in the preceding steps.

field titles

use scroll bars to see all the titles

To test that the fields are being displayed under the appropriate field titles:

1 Save and test the program. Click **View**, then click **Select Records Form** on the main form's menu bar. Click the **Select Records** command button on the form to print the column titles and the payroll records, as shown in Figure 8-17.

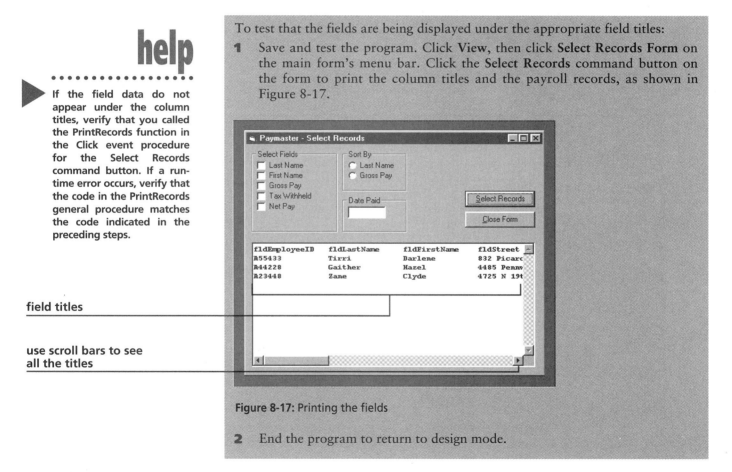

Figure 8-17: Printing the fields

2 End the program to return to design mode.

In addition to printing all rows, the program should have the ability to restrict the rows displayed to a specific date paid. To accomplish this task, you need to know how to create a WHERE clause with a SELECT statement.

Using the WHERE Clause with a SELECT Statement

Often, you will want to limit the number of records retrieved by a SELECT statement. In this payroll program, the user should have the ability to select records from a specific pay period. He or she should also be able to select all of the records depending on whether a value appears in the Date Paid text box. You can accomplish the former goal by selecting only those records with a specific date stored in the fldDatePaid. To write this form of a SELECT statement, you use the WHERE clause.

The WHERE clause employed here has the same syntax as it did in the UPDATE and DELETE statements. When combined with the SELECT statement, it produces the following syntax.

Syntax	**SELECT * FROM** *tableexpression* [**WHERE** *conditionlist*]
Dissection	■ This form of the SELECT statement is identical to the first form, but now contains the WHERE clause. The optional WHERE clause requires one argument—*conditionlist*. The *conditionlist* restricts the number of rows returned by the SELECT statement.
| **Code Example** | ```
SELECT * FROM qryEmployeesPayroll
WHERE fldDatePaid = #2/2/99#
``` |
| **Code Dissection** | This SELECT statement retrieves all records from the query named qryEmployeesPayroll having a date paid of 2/2/99. |

You now need to create a WHERE clause and append it to the SELECT statement so that the user can select records for a specific date paid. Because the information in the Date field is stored as a Date data type rather than as a string or number, you need to enclose the date inside the pound (#) characters. Instead of writing the code to step through each record to determine whether the date is correct, you can use the SELECT statement to examine each record and return only those records for which the condition in the WHERE clause is True.

As presently written, the SELECT statement has a limitation. Although it will retrieve the records having a date paid value of 2/2/99, the user cannot select another date. To avoid this problem, you can build the parts of the SELECT statement at run time and then create the recordset. Concatenating a string, as you have done in the past, will accomplish this task.

To create the WHERE clause to select a specific date paid:

1 Open the Code window to the **cmdSelect_Click** event procedure for the form named **frmSel**, then enter the following statement (shown in bold) just after the declaration for the variable pstrFROM:

```
Dim pstrFROM As String
Dim pstrWHERE As String
```
```

2 Enter the following statements (shown in bold) just after the line that builds the FROM clause:

```
pstrFROM = " FROM qryEmployeesPayroll"
If txtDatePaid = vbNullString Then
    pstrWHERE = " "
Else
    pstrWHERE = " WHERE fldDatePaid = " & "#" & _
        txtDatePaid & "#"
End If
pstrSQL = "SELECT" & pstrFields & pstrFROM & _
    pstrWHERE
```

3 Save and test the program. Click **View**, then click **Select Records Form** on the main form's menu bar.

4 Enter **3/24/99** as the date, then click **Select Records**. Your form should look like Figure 8-18. Note that the order of the records may differ from Figure 8-18.

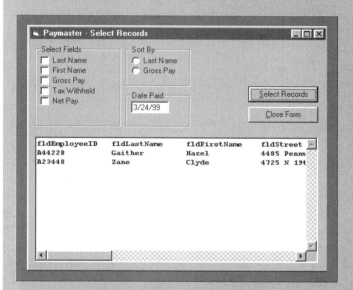

Figure 8-18: Printing the selected records

5 End the program to return to design mode.

The If statement determines whether a value appears in the text box named txtDatePaid. If one exists, the program creates a WHERE clause to select only records with a specific date paid. Otherwise, all records are selected. Note that the WHERE clause is stored in the string pstrWHERE and appended to the statement to create the pstrSQL variable.

Creating an ORDER BY Clause to Sort Records

In addition to determining which records are returned to the recordset, you can specify the order in which those records are returned. The ORDER BY clause is usually the last clause specified in the SELECT statement. This clause is followed by one or more field names and the optional keywords ASC or DESC. If you use ASC, the records are returned in ascending sequence. If you use DESC, they are returned in descending sequence. If you omit these keywords, ASC is assumed. If the clause includes multiple field names, commas must separate each field. This form of the SELECT statement has the following syntax.

Syntax	**SELECT * FROM** *tableexpression* [**WHERE** *conditionlist*] [**ORDER BY**] *field1* [**ASC** | **DESC**][, *field2* [**ASC** | **DESC**][, ...]]
Dissection	■ The **ORDER BY** clause accepts one or more fields separated by commas. Each *field* can be sorted in ascending or descending order depending on whether the optional **ASC** or **DESC** keyword is used. If the keywords are omitted, the **ASC** option is assumed. ■ If you specify multiple fields, the first field is sorted. If duplicate values appear, the values in the second field will be sorted.
Code Example	`SELECT * FROM qryEmployeesPayroll` `    ORDER BY fldLastName`
Code Dissection	This statement sorts, in ascending order, the records based upon the contents of the field named fldLastName.

The user should be able to sort the selected records by either the employees' last names or the amount of gross pay for the period. To accomplish this task, you must add an ORDER BY clause to the SELECT statement you have already created. Two option buttons have already been created on the form in the control array named optOrderBy. If the user selects the first option button, the program should sort the records by the Last Name field. If the user selects the second option button, it should sort the records by the Gross Pay field.

To sort the selected records:

1   Open the Code window to the **cmdSelect_Click** event procedure for the form named **frmSel**, then enter the following statement (shown in bold) just after the declaration for the variable pstrWHERE:

```
Dim pstrWHERE As String
Dim pstrORDERBY As String
```

2   Enter the following statement (shown in bold) just before the statement that assigns the string representing the SQL SELECT statement and modify the statement that stores the value in the variable pstrSQL as indicated:

```
If optOrderBy(0) = True Then
    pstrORDERBY = " ORDER BY fldLastName"
Else
    pstrORDERBY = " ORDER BY fldGrossPay"
End If
pstrSQL = "SELECT" & pstrFields & pstrFROM & _
    pstrWHERE & pstrORDERBY
```

3   Save and test the program. Click **View**, then click **Select Records Form** on the menu bar.

4   Click the **Last Name** option button, then click the **Select Records** command button. The records should be sorted in ascending order by last name.

5   Click the **Gross Pay** option button, then click the **Select Records** command button. The records should be sorted in ascending order by gross pay.

6   End the program to return to design mode.

These statements cause the records returned by the SELECT statement to be sorted, either by last name or by gross pay.

```
If optOrderBy(0) = True Then
    pstrORDERBY = " ORDER BY fldLastName"
Else
    pstrORDERBY = " ORDER BY fldGrossPay"
End If
```

The option group optOrderBy contains two option buttons. If the first option button is active, the program sorts the records by last name. Otherwise, it sorts them by gross pay. The ORDER BY clause is stored in the variable pstrORDERBY and will be used in the SELECT statement.

```
pstrSQL = "SELECT" & pstrFields & pstrFROM & _
    pstrWHERE & pstrORDERBY
```

You modified the SELECT statement to incorporate the ORDER BY clause before calling the OpenRecordset method.

Selecting Specific Fields from a Table or Query

The SELECT statements you have written so far have retrieved all of the fields from a single table or query. It is possible, however, to select individual fields from a table or query using a version of the SELECT statement.

Syntax	SELECT [*table.*]*field1* [**AS** *alias1*][, [*table.*]*field2* [**AS** *alias2*] [, ...]] **FROM** *tableexpression* [**WHERE**...]
Dissection	■ The names of the fields are specified using *field1*, *field2*, . . . Each field is separated from the others by a comma. If you include more than one field, the fields are retrieved in the order listed. ■ If the names of the column headers should differ from the original field names, specify the **AS** *alias* clause.

You will use the check boxes already created on the form to allow the user to select all or some of the fields from the underlying query. To accomplish this goal, you will write If statements to determine which check boxes are checked, then build a string containing a list of fields accordingly. You also will remove the line that stores the asterisk (*) character in the string strFields.

To write the statement to select specific fields from the query:

1   Open the Code window to the **cmdSelect_Click** event procedure for the form named **frmSel**.

2   Remove the following statement:

```
pstrFields = " *"
```

3   Enter the following statements (shown in bold) in place of the statement you just deleted:

```
pstrFields = " fldEmployeeID"
If chkLastName = vbChecked Then
    pstrFields = pstrFields & ",fldLastName"
End If
If chkFirstName = vbChecked Then
    pstrFields = pstrFields & ",fldFirstName"
End If
If chkGrossPay = vbChecked Then
    pstrFields = pstrFields & ",fldGrossPay"
End If
If chkTaxWithheld = vbChecked Then
    pstrFields = pstrFields & ",fldTaxWithheld"
End If
If chkNetPay = vbChecked Then
    pstrFields = pstrFields & ",fldNetPay"
End If
```

4 Save and test the program. Click **View**, then click **Select Records Form**.

5 Check the box shown in Figure 8-19, then enter the value **3/24/99** as the date. Click the **Select Records** button. Your output should look like Figure 8-19.

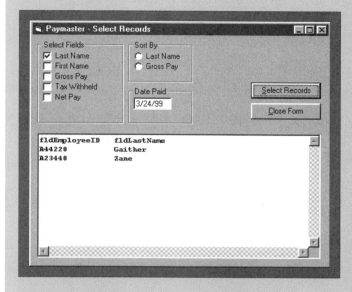

Figure 8-19: Printing the selected fields

6 End the program to return to design mode.

7 Exit Visual Basic.

You have now completed the payroll program. The user can read data from a text file and insert records into the database. He or she can also compute the payroll and delete obsolete records. Finally, the user has extensive flexibility in selecting records from the database.

S U M M A R Y

This chapter introduced two key concepts: the DAO hierarchy and how to use the SQL language with Visual Basic.

To make the DAO object library available to a program:

■ Click **Project**, then click **References** to open the References dialog.

■ Select **Microsoft DAO 3.51 Object Library** from the list of references.

■ Click **OK** to add the object library and to close the dialog.

To open a database programmatically:

■ Call the OpenDatabase method:
   Set *database* = *workspace*.**OpenDatabase** (*dbname, options, read-only, connect*)

To open a recordset programmatically:

■ Call the OpenRecordset method:
  Set *recordset* = *object*.**OpenRecordset** (*source, type, options, lockedits*)

To reference a field in a recordset:

■ Enter the recordset name, followed by an exclamation point (!), followed by the field name enclosed in square brackets:
  recordsetname![*fieldname*]

To insert a record into a database using the SQL insert statement:

■ Create a string representing the INSERT statement.
  INSERT INTO *target* [(*field1*[, *field2* [, ...]])]
       VALUES (*value1*[, *value2*[, ...]])
■ Call the Execute method using the string argument.

To execute an SQL action query:

■ Call the Execute method with a string argument containing the action query:
  object.**Execute** *source, options*

To update database records using the SQL UPDATE statement:

■ Create a string representing the UPDATE statement:
  UPDATE *tablename*
       SET *fieldname* = *newvalue*[, *fieldname* = *newvalue*] ...
■ Call the Execute method using the string argument.

To remove database records using the SQL DELETE statement:

■ Create a string representing the DELETE statement:
  DELETE *
       FROM *tableexpression*
       WHERE *criteria*
■ Call the Execute method using the string argument.

To select records from a database using the SQL SELECT statement:

■ Create a string representing the SELECT statement:
  SELECT [*table*.]*field1* [**AS** *alias1*][, [*table*.]*field2* [**AS** *alias2*] [, ...]]
       FROM *tableexpression*
       [**WHERE**...][**ORDER BY**] *field1* [**ASC** I **DESC**][, *field2* [**ASC** I **DESC**][, ...]]
■ Call the OpenRecordset method using the string argument.

 # Q U E S T I O N S

1. What is the name of the statement to execute a select query?
    a. RETRIEVE
    b. GET
    c. EXECUTE
    d. SELECT
    e. None of the above.

2. Which of the following is a valid clause in a SELECT statement?
   a. WHERE
   b. ORDER BY
   c. FROM
   d. ALL
   e. None of the above.

3. What is the name of the loop that examines the objects in a collection?
   a. For
   b. For Each
   c. For All
   d. For One
   e. Do Each

4. Which of the following statements about the ORDER BY clause is true?
   a. The ASC option will sort the records in ascending order.
   b. The DESC option will sort the records in descending order.
   c. The ASC and DESC options cannot be used in the same statement.
   d. The ASC and DESC options can be omitted.
   e. All of the above.

5. The FROM clause in a SELECT statement is used to _____.
   a. specify where the file is located on the disk
   b. specify the name of the database used
   c. specify the name of a table or query
   d. Both b and c.
   e. None of the above.

6. Assuming that mdbCurrent is an object variable that references an open database, write a SELECT statement and open a recordset named mrstCurrent to select all records from the table named tblMaster.

7. Assuming that mdbCurrent is an object variable that references an open database, write a SELECT statement and open a recordset named mrstCurrent to select only those records where the field named fldID is equal to 3. Assume that fldID is a number.

8. Assuming that mdbCurrent is an object variable that references an open database, write a SELECT statement and open a recordset named mrstCurrent to select all records from the table named tblMaster. Sort the records in descending order based upon the contents of the field named fldName.

9. Assuming that mdbCurrent is an object variable that references an open database, write a SELECT statement and open a recordset named mrstCurrent to select all records from the table named tblMaster. Select only the fields named fldID and fldLastName. Sort the records in ascending order based upon the contents of the field named fldName.

E X E R C I S E S

1. In addition to computing payroll information, Paymaster Payroll Services needs to be able to update information about each employee. Specifically, it needs a program with a menu. The commands on the menu should support functions to locate, add, change, and delete records. Unlike in the programs you created in Chapter 5 to accomplish this task, you will create Database and Recordset objects explicitly and use unbound text boxes to manipulate the data. Figure 8-20 shows the completed form for this project.

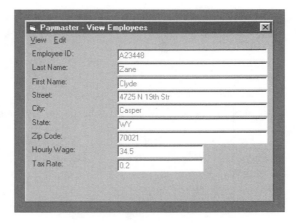

Figure 8-20

In this exercise, you will use the table named **tblEmployees**. This table contains the following fields: **fldEmployeeID, fldLastName, fldFirstName, fldStreet, fldCity, fldState, fldZipCode, fldHourlyWage,** and **fldTaxRate**.

a. Run the executable file **Chapter.08\Exercise\Ex1.exe**. Set the drive designator as necessary. For the completed application to work correctly, the database **Paymast.mdb** must reside in the same folder as the executable file. End the program.

b. Start Visual Basic and create a new project, if necessary.

c. Set the appropriate property so that the title bar of the form contains the text **Paymaster – View Employees**.

d. Set the Name property of the form to **frmEx1**.

e. Save the form as **frmEx1.frm** and the project as Paymaster **Ex1.vbp** in the **Chapter.08\Exercise** folder. Set the drive designator as necessary.

f. Create the labels and text boxes on the form, as shown in Figure 8-20.

g. Create the menu system for the program. The **View** menu should include the following menu items: **First, Next, Previous,** and **Last**. The **Edit** menu should include the following menu items: **Add, Edit, Update, Cancel,** and **Delete**.

h. In the general declarations section of the form module, create a variable named **mdbCurrent** that stores a reference to a Database object. Declare this variable as a Private variable. Declare a second variable named **mrstCurrent** to store a reference to a Recordset object.

i. Write the statement to open the database named **Chapter.08\Exercise\Paymast.mdb** when the form is loaded. Set the drive designator as necessary. In the same event procedure, open a recordset for the table named **tblEmployees**. Store a reference to the recordset in the object variable named **mrstCurrent**.

j. Because you are using unbound controls, you cannot rely on the Data control to store the current record in the text boxes, nor can you rely on the Data control to save the text box contents back into the recordset. Instead, you must write the code to provide this functionality. Create two general procedures named **LoadCurrentRecord** and **SaveCurrentRecord**. The first procedure should load the fields from the current record into the corresponding text boxes. The second procedure should perform the reverse task, saving the contents of the text boxes into the fields of the recordset.

k. Create the code for the menu items on the **View** menu. These menu items should locate the First, Next, Previous, and Last records. Each time you position the current record, call the **LoadCurrentRecord** procedure to display the current record in the text boxes. Ensure that your program accounts for BOF and EOF and that a current record always exists.

l. Create the code for the menu items on the Edit menu. When the user clicks the **Add** menu item, the program should create a new record in the recordset and clear the contents of the text boxes. When the the user clicks the **Edit** menu item, it should enable editing on the current record. When the user clicks the **Update** menu item, it should call the **SaveCurrentRecord** procedure to save the current text box contents to the recordset and save the recordset changes. When the user clicks the **Cancel** menu item, it should cancel any updates and restore the recordset's current record to the text boxes. When the user clicks the **Delete** menu item, it should delete the current record and locate the last record.

m. To prevent the user from attempting an impossible action, enable and disable the menu items as necessary. Lock the text boxes unless the user is currently editing a record.

n. Save and test the program. Exit Visual Basic.

2. Steel Fabricators purchases raw steel to fabricate beams and other parts used in large buildings. It purchases its steel from many overseas sources. Due to currency fluctuations in the countries in which the steel is purchased, the price must frequently be changed for each item from a particular country. Prices can be changed upward or downward depending on the country of origin. Steel Fabricators needs a program to update the prices and to view the price list. When complete, the main form for the program should look like Figure 8-21.

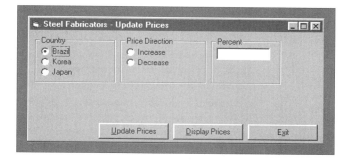

Figure 8-21

a. Run the executable file named **Chapter.08\Exercise\Ex2.exe**. The form contains option buttons to select a country as well as option buttons to change prices. In addition, a text box enables the user to indicate the percentage amount of the price change. When the user clicks the **Update Prices** command button, the prices for a particular country increase or decrease by the percentage amount specified. The **Display Prices** command button displays the current price list, and the **Exit** command button ends the program. Note that for this executable program to run, the database file **Steel.mdb** must reside in the same folder as the executable file. The price entered should be a decimal value between 0 and 1. For brevity, the percentage has not been checked for errors. End the program.

b. Start Visual Basic and create a new project, if necessary.

c. Set the form name to **frmEx2** and the caption to **Steel Fabricators - Update Prices**.

d. Save the form as **frmEx2.frm** and the project as **Ex2.vbp** in the **Chapter.08\Exercise** folder. Set the drive designator as necessary.

e. In the general declarations section of the form module, create a variable named **gdbCurrent** that can store a reference to a Database object.

f. Open the database named **Chapter.08\Exercise\Steel.mdb** when the form loads. Set the drive designator as necessary. Store a reference to the open database in the object variable named **gdbCurrent**.

g. Create a command button to exit the program.

h. Create a Frame object and set its caption to **Country**.

i. Create a control array of three option buttons named **optCountry**. Set the captions of these option buttons to **Brazil, Korea,** and **Japan**.

j. Create a second Frame object with the caption **Price Direction**.

k. Create a control array of two option buttons named **optDirection** in the frame. Set the captions of these option buttons to **Increase** and **Decrease**.

l. Create a Frame object with the caption **Percent** and a text box inside the frame named **txtPercent**.

m. Create two command buttons: one to update prices and another to display a form containing the price list. Set the names and captions as necessary.

n. In the command button to update prices, write the statements in the Click event procedure to determine which option button the user has selected and to store the selected country name in a String variable.

o. Write the statements to store the price change percentage in a variable having the Single data type. If the new price represents an increase, the number should be positive. If the new price represents a decrease, multiply the number by -1 to make it negative.

p. In a local String variable, store an UPDATE statement that will update the field named **fldItemPrice** in the table named **tblPriceList** where the field named **fldCountry** is the same as the selected country. The price stored in fldItemPrice should be increased or decreased by the percentage amount specified by the user.

q. Create a form that will display and locate the records from the table named tblPriceList. You can create this form manually or use the Data Form Wizard to accomplish this task. Save the form using the name **frmPrices.frm**. Use the fields named **fldItemNumber**, **fldCountry**, **fldItemDescription**, and **fldItemPrice**.

r. Program the second command button on the main form to display the newly created form as a modal form.

s. Test the program by displaying the original price list, then increasing and decreasing the prices by different percentages.

t. Save the forms and project again. Exit Visual Basic.

3. Kismet Real Estate Sales is a residential real estate brokerage firm. Each month, it receives the sales transactions in the area for the past year in an ASCII file. When the company receives this ASCII file, rather than replacing existing records in the database, it removes all of the records and then reads the ASCII file into a table. Sales agents then use the data to perform comparative price analyses. Figure 8-22 shows the completed main form.

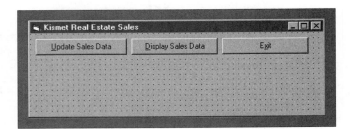

Figure 8-22

a. Run the executable file **Chapter.08\Exercise\Ex3.exe**. The main form contains three command buttons. The **Update Sales Data** button removes all the records from the table named **tblSales**, then reads the ASCII file named **Kismet.txt**. For each record in the ASCII file, a record is inserted into the database table. The **Display Sales Data** command button displays the records from the table named **tblSales**. Note that for the executable application to function correctly, the database file **Kismet.mdb** and the text file **Kismet.txt** must reside in the same folder as the executable file. End the program.

b. Start Visual Basic and create a new project, if necessary.

c. Set the name of the form to **frmEx3** and set the form's caption. Save the form as **frmEx3.frm** and the project as **Ex3.vbp**. Set the drive designator as necessary. Set the form's caption as shown in Figure 8-22.

d. In the general declarations section of the Form module, create a variable named **mdbCurrent** that can store a Database object. Then, using that variable, open the database named **Chapter.08\Exercise\Kismet.mdb** when the form loads. Set the drive designator as necessary.

e. Create two command buttons on the form. The first will delete the existing records from the sales table, then read the ASCII file containing the new data into the same table. The second will open another form to display the sales data.

f. Create a third command button to exit the program.

g. In the Click event procedure for the first command button, create the necessary variables and write the statements to delete all records from the database table named **tblSales**.

h. Inside the same event procedure, open the file **Kismet.txt** for input and create a Do loop to read each record in the file. Inside the Do loop, include a statement to read the fields in each record into a local variable. The input file contains five fields that correspond to the fields in the table tblSales: **fldArea, fldAddress, fldDateSold, fldSalesAmount,** and **fldSquareFeet**. The fields are stored in the input file in that order.

i. Create a local String variable to hold an SQL statement. In this variable, store an INSERT statement that will insert each of the five fields into the table named tblSales. Note that fldArea and fldAddress are String variables, fldDateSold is a Date data type, fldSalesAmount is a Single data type, and fldSquareFeet is an Integer data type. This task should be performed inside the Do loop.

j. Execute the INSERT statement.

k. Create a form based on the table named tblSales. Write the statements to locate and display the records in the table. You can create the form manually or use the Data Form Wizard. Save the form using the name **frmtblSales**. In the main form, write the code for the **Display Sales Data** command button, which displays this new form as a modal form.

l. Test the program. Run the program to verify that the INSERT and DELETE statements work correctly and that the second form displays the records from the underlying table. Save the project again, if necessary, and exit Visual Basic.

4. Lester International maintains several databases. It requires a program that will allow the company's programmers to open any database file and execute SQL SELECT statements. The developers should be able to execute SELECT statements in one window and display the results of the query in another window. Each of these windows will be implemented as a text box. Figure 8-23 shows the completed form for the program.

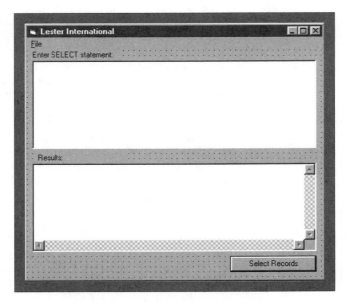

Figure 8-23

a. Run the executable file **Chapter.08\Exercise\Ex4.exe**. The form contains two text boxes. In the text box at the top of the form, you enter SQL SELECT statements. The results of a SELECT statement appear in the text box at the bottom of the form. Click **File**, then click **Open** on the menu bar to display an input box. Enter the database file named **Chapter.08\Exercise\Steel.mdb**, setting the drive designator as necessary. Enter the following SELECT statement in the text box at the top of the form: "SELECT * FROM tblPriceList". The results appear in the text box at the bottom of the form after you click the **Select Records** button. End the program.

b. Start Visual Basic and create a new project, if necessary.

c. Set the name of the form to **frmEx4** and set the form's caption. Save the form as **frmEx4.frm** and the project as **Ex4.vbp** as shown in Figure 8-23. Set the drive designator as necessary.

d. In the general declarations section of the form module, create a variable named **mdbCurrent** that stores a Database object.

e. Create the menu system for the program. The menu system consists of a **File** menu with two menu items: **Open** and **Exit**.

f. Create the objects on the form, as shown in Figure 8-23. These objects include two text boxes, labels to identify those text boxes, and a command button.

g. Write the code for the **Open** menu item. When clicked, this menu item should display an input box so that the user can enter the name of a database file to open. If the user enters a file, then execute the necessary code to open the database and store a reference to the database in the object variable mdbCurrent. Otherwise, exit the procedure. Also, create an error handler for the procedure so that if the user enters an invalid file name, the program will not crash.

h. Write the code for the **Exit** menu item.

discovery ▶

i. Write the code for the **Select Records** command button. This button, when clicked, should execute the SELECT statement entered in the text box at the top of the form. That is, it should open a recordset and display the records in the text box at the bottom of the form. Because the program cannot predict in advance which table or fields will be selected, you must use the Fields collection pertaining to the Recordset object to display the results of the SELECT statement. Also, write the code to format the results so that each field appears left-justified in a column.

j. Test the program using one of the databases from this chapter. Enter SELECT statements to ensure that the program works correctly.

k. Save your work. Exit Visual Basic.

Using Custom Controls to Open Files and to Interact with a Database

Creating an Event Registration System for Starlight Events

case ▶ Starlight Events provides event registration and meeting planning services for trade associations and other groups that hold conventions. The company manages both mail-in and telephone reservations for the meetings, banquets, and other functions occurring at these events.

Starlight Events wants to maintain a separate database for each client. When that client's event ends, Starlight Events will back up the database to tape. Because many clients use the company's services only once or on an infrequent basis, this method of backing up the client's data to tape will minimize the disk space consumed by the event registration system.

Previewing the Event Registration Program

The structure of Starlight Events' database and the layout of the tables for this program are defined and saved in the Chapter.09\Startup folder on the Student Disk. The database contains three tables: tblEvents, which contains a unique Event ID number, an event description, and the date of the event; tblPeople, which contains the names and addresses of each convention participant; and tblRegistration, which contains the event registrations. The tables are designed so that a person can register for multiple events. Each Event ID in the table tblEvents must be unique. Likewise, each Member ID in the table tblPeople must be unique. In the table tblRegistration, fldMemberID and fldEventID collectively specify a unique event registration record. Figure 9-1 shows the database tables and their relationships.

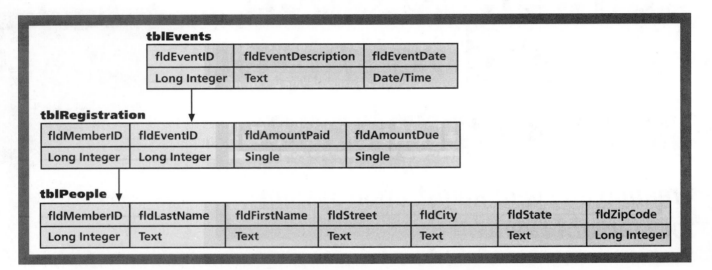

Figure 9-1: Tables and relationships in the Starlight Events database

The completed program allows the user to review the event descriptions in a combo box. When the user selects an event description, the program displays the event registrations applicable to the selected event. The user can then add, change, and delete the individual registrations.

Before previewing the application, you must verify that one of the controls used by the application is available to the program. If this control is unavailable, you will not be able to run the completed example, nor will you be able to complete the hands-on steps in the chapter. This project uses the DBGrid control, which is not installed automatically by Visual Basic. Thus you may need to install the DBGrid control on your system. If Visual Basic 5.0 was previously installed on your computer, the following steps may be unnecessary.

To make the DBGrid control available on your computer:

1 Insert the Visual Basic CD-ROM into your computer.

2 On the CD-ROM and using Windows Explorer, locate the folder named Common\Tools\Vb\Controls. Set the drive designator as necessary, depending on the drive assigned to your CD-ROM device.

3 If you are using Windows 95 or Windows 98, copy the files named **dbgrid.reg** and **DBGrid32.ocx** to the folder named **Windows\System**. If you are using Windows NT, copy the files to the folder named **Winnt\System**. Remember to set the drive designator as necessary.

4 Start an MS-DOS window and locate the folder named **Common\ Tools\Vb\Regutils** on the CD-ROM. To start an MS-DOS window, activate the Start menu, select **Programs**, then click **MS-DOS prompt**. To locate a specific folder, use the CD command. If the CD-ROM were in the E: drive, for example, the following statement would locate and change the directory to the correct folder:

```
CD E:Common\Tools\Vb\Regutils
```

5 Enter the following commands to register the DBGrid control on your computer:

```
Regsvr32.exe DBGrid32.ocx
RegEdit C:\Windows\System\DBGrid.reg
```

After entering the first command, a dialog will appear indicating that the command was successful. After entering the second command, a dialog will appear asking you to verify that you want to update the Registry. Click **Yes**.

6 Type **Exit** to close the MS-DOS window.

The preceding steps copy and register the DBGrid control on your system. If you are working in a lab, contact your system administrator to accomplish this task.

To preview the completed application:

1 Start **Visual Basic** and open the project **Chapter.09\Complete\Slight_C.vbp**. Set the drive designator as necessary.

2 Open **Project Explorer**, if necessary, to view the form named **frmStarlightEvents**. The completed form at design time looks like Figure 9-2.

combo box

grid

CommonDialog
control

Data controls

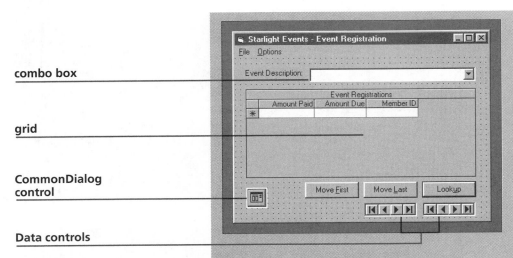

Figure 9-2: Completed form for Starlight Events

As shown in Figure 9-2, the user selects an event from a combo box. In addition, a grid displays the event registrations pertaining to the selected event. The form also includes two instances of the Data control, which are used to bind the combo box and grid to a database. Finally, a new control is presented: the CommonDialog control. Although invisible to the user at run time, this control displays dialogs to open and save files. In Starlight Events' program, the CommonDialog control will display dialogs allowing the user to open a particular database file and set fonts.

3 Run the program. On the menu bar, click **File**, then click **Open** to open a database file. The database is not opened when the program is run. In the Open dialog, select the folder named **Chapter.09\Complete**, then select the file named **Slight.mdb**. Again, set the drive designator as necessary. After the file is opened, the form's controls become visible.

4 Click on the combo box list arrow, select the event named **Visual Basic programming seminar – Beginning**, then click the **Lookup** command button. When the button is clicked, notice that only those event registrations pertaining to the selected event description appear on the screen.

5 Click the **Move Last** and **Move First** command buttons. Notice that the current record indicator in the grid is updated.

6 Click **Options**, then click **Fonts** on the menu. The Font dialog appears, allowing you to select different fonts and font attributes. Select a different font and click the **OK** button. The selected font in the combo box and grid is updated.

7 End the program and exit Visual Basic.

SECTION A
objectives

In this section you will:

- Learn the types of controls used by Visual Basic
- Add an ActiveX control into a project
- Display multiple records with the DBCombo control
- Display multiple rows and columns with the DBGrid control
- Locate records programmatically using the DBGrid control

An Introduction to ActiveX Controls

Types of Controls

Throughout this book, you have used intrinsic controls from the toolbox to create a user interface. Intrinsic controls, which are part of Visual Basic, are included in the executable files Visual Basic produces. Visual Basic supports two additional types of controls: ActiveX controls and insertable objects.

- You can use ActiveX controls as you develop more complex applications in Visual Basic. **ActiveX controls** work like the other controls you have used previously, but are not part of Visual Basic. Rather, they utilize a standard technology called component object modules. **Component object modules (COM)** allow the programmer to use a control or object with various programming languages, including Visual Basic. The code for these controls is contained in separate files with the extension .OCX, .DLL, or .EXE, rather than being stored in the executable file produced by Visual Basic.
- **Insertable objects** allow you to write programs to manipulate another application's objects from within Visual Basic. For example, both a Microsoft Excel Worksheet object and a Microsoft Word Document object can be inserted into a Visual Basic program. You can add these objects to the toolbox as controls or reference them programmatically as objects.

You can extend the functionality of Visual Basic by using and creating a variety of ActiveX controls. The Professional and Enterprise editions of Visual Basic supply several ActiveX controls. Additionally, software vendors sell different controls to perform specific tasks such as faxing or generating bar codes. ActiveX controls are frequently referred to as custom controls.

Making an ActiveX Control Available to a Project

When you start Visual Basic, it automatically adds intrinsic controls such as text boxes, scroll bars, and combo boxes to the toolbox. If you want to use an ActiveX control as well as the intrinsic controls, you must add the ActiveX control to the project by using the Components dialog. The new ActiveX control will then appear in the toolbox. When you add an ActiveX control to a project, a line is added to the project file, indicating that the control should be used; thus you need not add the ActiveX control to the toolbox each time you load the project.

In this chapter, you will use three ActiveX controls. The first control, **CommonDialog**, is used to open and save files. When you open and save files in different Windows applications, such as Microsoft Word or Visual Basic, you may have noticed that the dialogs look very similar. This similarity arises because they all rely on the same standard dialog to perform these tasks.

The second control, **DBGrid**, displays several rows of data (records) at the same time. That is, the control does not display a single record and field from a table or query, but displays multiple records and fields simultaneously. Like other bound controls you have used, the DBGrid control can be bound to an instance of the Data control in the same manner that a text box is bound.

The third control, **DBCombo**, works like the intrinsic ComboBox control, but can read and write data from a database table. Closely related to the DBCombo control is the **DBList** control. It extends the functionality of the ListBox control just as the DBCombo control extends the functionality of the ComboBox control.

For this project, you need to add the CommonDialog, DBList, DBCombo, and DBGrid controls to the toolbox and project file. In general, you can add ActiveX controls as you decide to use them or all at once.

To add ActiveX controls to a project:

1 Start Visual Basic and open the project **Chapter.09\Startup\Slight_S.vbp**. Set the drive designator as necessary.

2 Open the **Project Explorer**, if necessary, and view the form named **frmStarlightEvents**. The form should look like Figure 9-3.

existing menu

existing label

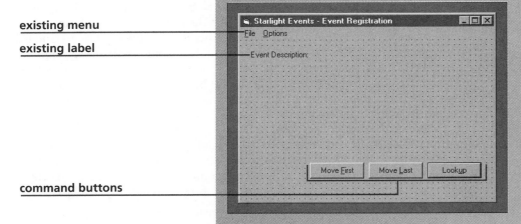

command buttons

Figure 9-3: Initial form for Starlight Events

As shown in Figure 9-3, the menu system and command buttons have already been created. You will create the other control instances during the hands-on steps in this chapter.

3 Click **Project** on the menu bar, then click **Components**. The Components dialog appears, as shown in Figure 9-4. Note that the Controls tab may contain different controls depending on the controls installed on your system.

Controls tab is active

click Browse to look
for other controls

click these three check boxes
to include the controls in
the project

controls on your system are
displayed on the controls
list box

the file name and path of the
highlighted control

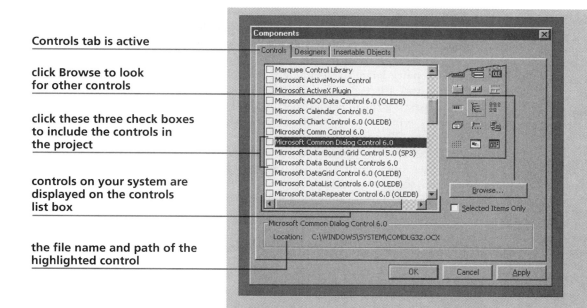

Figure 9-4: Components dialog

4 Click the box to the left of the **Microsoft Common Dialog Control 6.0**
   check box. Use the scroll bars to locate the control, if necessary.

5 Click the box to the left of the **Microsoft Data Bound Grid Control 5.0
   (SP3)** check box.

6 Click the box to the left of the **Microsoft Data Bound List Controls 6.0**
   check box.

7 Click **OK** to add the ActiveX controls to your project. Notice that four new
   controls appear in the toolbox. The DBList and DBGrid controls are both part
   of the Microsoft Data Bound List Controls and are added as a single unit.

Because the ActiveX controls have been permanently added to the project file,
you will not need to add them to the toolbox again for this project. When the
project loads again, the CommonDialog, DBList, DBCombo, and DBGrid controls will appear in the toolbox automatically.

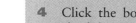

If the Microsoft Data
Bound Grid Control 5.0
(SP3) check box does not
appear in the Components
dialog, click the Browse
button to activate the Add
ActiveX control dialog. If
you are using Windows 95
or Windows 98, locate the
Windows\System folder. If
you are using Windows NT,
locate the Winnt\System
folder. Select the control
named Dbgrid32.ocx, then
click the Open button to add
the control to the project. If
the file Dbgrid32.ocx does
not appear in this folder,
you must copy the control
using the steps given previously in this chapter.

Once an ActiveX control appears in the toolbox, you can create an instance of
it by clicking the control in the toolbox and drawing that instance on the form,
just as you did with intrinsic controls. You can then set the ActiveX control's
properties at design time or at run time, depending on the needs of your program.

Performance
tip

• • • • • • • • • • • • • • • •

When creating programs with several control instances, you should consider limiting the number and quantity of ActiveX controls. For each type of ActiveX control you use, Visual Basic must load the ActiveX control when the form is loaded. This process causes your program to take longer to load. Also, it will consume more memory. If your system has inadequate memory or if the program is very large, your program may run more slowly.

Programming
tip

• • • • • • • • • • • • • • • •

Because the DBCombo and DBList controls are so similar, they are stored in a single OCX file and added on the toolbox as one unit. In fact, both controls share much of the same code.

Unlike the intrinsic controls you used in previous chapters, most ActiveX controls support an additional dialog called Property Pages. To set design-time properties that may not be available via the Properties window, you use **Property Pages**. The Property Pages for a control contain multiple tabs; each tab represents a separate **Property Page**. Each ActiveX control supports a unique set of Property Pages. To activate the Property Pages for an ActiveX control instance, right-click the control instance, then click Properties on the shortcut menu. You can also use the Properties window to activate the Property Pages pertaining to a specific ActiveX control. To accomplish this task, activate the Properties window for the desired ActiveX control. Locate the property named "(Custom)". In the Value column, click the properties button. The Property Pages will appear.

Note that some properties may be set only in the Properties window while other properties may be set only via the Property Pages.

Displaying Multiple Records with the DBCombo and DBList Controls

Starlight Events wants to be able to look at all registrations for a given event. Before viewing the registrations, however, the user must select a particular event from the list contained in the table tblEvents.

The DBList ActiveX control works like the intrinsic ListBox control in that it displays a list of items. The DBList control, however, can read and write data from a database. The DBCombo ActiveX control works like the intrinsic ComboBox control in that both can display a drop-down list of items. Like the DBList control, the DBCombo control can also read and write data from a database.

Both the DBCombo and DBList controls obtain their information from a Recordset object created by the Data control. Thus you must set the RowSource property of both controls to a valid instance of a Data control. The ListField property pertains to both the DBCombo and DBList controls and specifies which field in the recordset should appear in the control instance at run time. This property can be set only using the Properties window at design time. Like other controls, these ActiveX controls have standard prefixes: "dls" for the DBList control and "dbc" for the DBCombox box.

Syntax	DBList, DBCombo
Properties	■ The **BoundColumn** property specifies a column in the source Data control.
	■ The **BoundText** property contains the value identified by the bound column. When a record is selected, the value in its corresponding BoundColumn is stored in the BoundText property.
	■ The **RowSource** property contains the name of a Data control and identifies the source table or query.
	■ The **ListField** property is a field in the table or query identified by the Data control. The field specified in the ListField property will appear in the DBList or DBCombo control.
	■ The **Text** property is set to the value identified by the ListField property. When an item in the list is selected, it is stored in the Text property. The Text property is the default property for the DBCombo and DBList controls.

- The **MatchEntry** property controls how the DBCombo control or the DBList control searches through the list based on user input. You can set the MatchEntry property to one of two constants. If set to **dblBasicMatching**, the control searches for the next match containing the character entered by using the first letter of the entries in the list. Repeatedly typing the same letter cycles through all the entries in the list beginning with that letter. If set to **dblExtendedMatching**, the control searches for an entry that matches all entered characters. The search is performed each time the user types an additional character. When the MatchEntry property is set to dblExtendedMatching and the user enters a backspace or waits more than a few seconds, the matching string is reset.

- The **Style** property can be set to one of three values. If it is set to **0-dbcDropdownCombo** or **1-dbcSimpleCombo**, the user can select from the list of choices or enter a new item. The 0-dbcDropdownCombo setting saves space on the form because the list portion closes when the user selects an item. If the Style property is set to **2-dbcDropdownList**, the user must select a choice from the existing list of choices.

You will now create a DBCombo box that displays information from the table named tblEvents. You will first create a Data control instance, then set its properties to connect to the database. Next, you will create an instance of the DBCombo control and set its properties. Because users should be able to see the event descriptions for each event in the table, you will set the value of the ListField property to the field named fldDescription. Because the DBCombo box will not be used to add new events, you will set the Style property to 2-dbcDropdownList.

To display database data using the DBCombo control:

1 Create an instance of the Data control at the bottom of the form, as shown in Figure 9-5. Set the Name property to **datEvents** and the DatabaseName property to **Chapter.09\Startup\Slight.mdb**. Set the drive designator as necessary.

2 Set the RecordSource property to **tblEvents**. Because the user will not interact with the Data control at run time, change the Visible property to **False**.

3 Create an instance of the DBCombo control on the form, as shown in Figure 9-5.

new DBCombo instance

new Data control instance

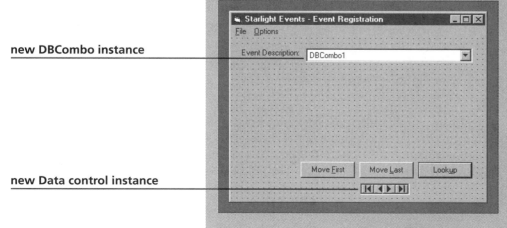

Figure 9-5: Creating an instance of the DBCombo control

4   Change the Name property to **dbcEvents**.

5   Set the RowSource property to **datEvents**, the ListField property to **fldEventDescription**, and the MatchEntry property to **1-dblExtendedMatching**.

6   Change the value of Style property to **2-dbcDropdownList** to prevent the user from trying to add a new event.

7   Set the TabIndex property to 0 so that DBCombo control instance will be the first object to receive focus when the program runs.

8   Remove the text from the **Text** property for the DBCombo control instance. The Text property will be set automatically at run time when the user selects an item from the list. The list will be populated automatically because you bound the DBCombo control instance to an instance of the Data control.

These steps will display the rows contained in the field fldEventDescription in the DBCombo object at run time. You now can test your program to verify that the records are loaded correctly.

To test the DBCombo control:

1   Save the project, then run it.

2   Click the **list arrow** in the combo box to display the records. Your form should look like Figure 9-6.

click the list arrow to display the records in the table

event descriptions are displayed

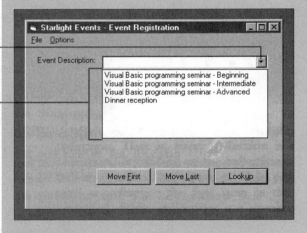

Figure 9-6: Testing the DBCombo object

3   End the program to return to design mode.

help

If no records appear in the DBCombo box, check the DatabaseName and RecordSource properties pertaining to the Data control. Also, verify that the RowSource property for the DBCombo box is set to datEvents and the ListField property is set to fldEventDescription. Repeat Steps 1 and 2.

The BoundColumn and BoundText properties enhance the usefulness of the DBCombo and DBList controls by allowing them to store the value of another field for the selected record in a property. For example, even though the DBCombo box displays the event description, you can store the value of the Event ID in another property of the control instance. The BoundColumn property specifies a column in the source Data control; the BoundText property contains the value identified by the bound column. When the user selects a record, the value stored in the corresponding BoundColumn is stored in the BoundText property; thus, when a user selects an item from the DBCombo list, the value of the BoundText property is set based on the BoundColumn.

Figure 9-7 illustrates the relationships among the ListField, Text, BoundColumn, and BoundText properties.

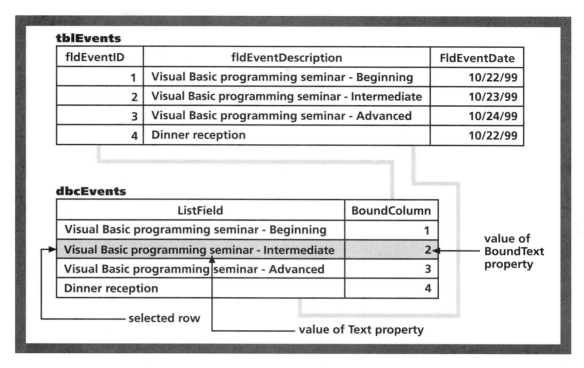

tblEvents

fldEventID	fldEventDescription	FldEventDate
1	Visual Basic programming seminar - Beginning	10/22/99
2	Visual Basic programming seminar - Intermediate	10/23/99
3	Visual Basic programming seminar - Advanced	10/24/99
4	Dinner reception	10/22/99

dbcEvents

ListField	BoundColumn
Visual Basic programming seminar - Beginning	1
Visual Basic programming seminar - Intermediate	2
Visual Basic programming seminar - Advanced	3
Dinner reception	4

value of BoundText property

selected row

value of Text property

Figure 9-7: The ListField, BoundColumn, Text, and BoundText properties

When a user selects an event description from the DBCombo box, the program should display all event registrations having the corresponding Event ID. The event registrations are stored in the table named tblRegistration. That table includes the Event ID for the registration, but not the event description. At run time, therefore, your program should allow the user to select an event description from the DBCombo control instance. You will need to write code to store the corresponding Event ID in the BoundText property of the DBCombo box. Later in the section, you will use this property to select all corresponding Event IDs from the registration table.

To store the Event ID when the user selects an event description:

1 Activate the **Properties window** for the DBCombo box named **dbcEvents**. Note that you must use the Properties window rather than the Property Pages because the BoundColumn property cannot be set via the Property Pages.

2 Set the BoundColumn property to **fldEventID**. Note that this property was set to fldEventDescription, the default value of the ListField property.

When an event description is selected at run time, the BoundText property will be set to the corresponding Event ID because of the BoundColumn property. The program should be able to display all event registrations corresponding to a specific Event ID.

Starlight Events would like to view several registrations on the screen at one time. You can use the DBGrid control to display information as it would appear in a spreadsheet—that is, with each field in a column and several records appearing at the same time. You will learn how to do this next.

Using the DBGrid Control to Display Multiple Rows and Columns

Like the other bound controls used to this point, the DBGrid control displays information from a database based on a Data control's Recordset object. The DBGrid control displays all of the rows and selected columns at the same time. It can display field names as column headers, or you can specify your own column headers.

The DBGrid control can store a fixed number of columns (1700) and any number of rows. The number of rows varies based on the configuration of your system. The intersection of a row and column in a DBGrid control is called a **cell**. Like other controls, the DBGrid control uses a standard prefix—"dbg". To load the rows and columns appearing in the DBGrid automatically at run time, you can connect the DBGrid to a Data control and set the DataSource property:

Syntax	DBGrid
Properties	■ The **AllowAddNew** property can be set to True or False. If set to True, the user can add new records to the recordset, and the last row displayed in the DBGrid control remains blank to permit the user to enter new records. If set to False, new records cannot be added, and no blank line appears in the last row. If the underlying recordset is not updatable, however, new records cannot be added even when the AllowAddNew property is True.
	■ The **AllowUpdate** property can be set to True or False. If set to True, the user can modify data in the DBGrid; otherwise, data cannot be modified. Note that the Recordset object may not permit updates even if the AllowUpdate property is True. In this case, a trappable error occurs when the user tries to change a record.
	■ The **AllowDelete** property can be set to True or False. If set to True, the user can delete records from the DBGrid; otherwise, records cannot be deleted. Again, if the underlying recordset is not updatable, then records cannot be deleted and a trappable error occurs if the user tries to delete one.
	■ The **DataSource** property is set to the name of an existing Data control. All rows and columns in the recordset created by the Data control will appear in the DBGrid control.
	■ The **Row** property identifies the active row. The first active row is zero (0), the second is one (1), and so on.
	■ The **Column** property identifies the active column. The first active column is zero (0), the second is one (1), and so on.
	■ The **Caption** property will cause a caption to appear in the DBGrid on its own line just above the column headers.
	■ The **HeadLines** property is a value between 0 and 10, and identifies the number of lines displayed in the column headers.
	■ The **BorderStyle** property, if set to **1 - Fixed Single**, draws a border around the region of the DBGrid control. If set to **0 - None**, no border is drawn.
	■ The **RowDividerStyle** describes the characteristics of the line separating each row and column. For a description of the valid settings, see the Help topic "RowDividerStyle property."
	■ The **TabAction** property controls the behavior of the Tab key while the DBGrid control has input focus.

Because Starlight Events wants to view all registrations pertaining to an event simultaneously, you will display the registrations in an instance of the DBGrid control. To do so, you need to create a second Data control and make it refer to the table tblRegistration instead of the table tblEvents. Once the second Data control exists, you can create the DBGrid control instance and set its DataSource property so that it can display the records in the recordset. Unlike the other bound controls used to this point, the DBGrid control displays information for multiple fields; therefore, no DataField property exists to specify a particular field.

Like other bound controls, the underlying Data control for a DBGrid control can be either visible or invisible at run time. When the Data control is visible, clicking the buttons on the Data control will update the current record pointer. When the current record pointer is updated, the current record indicator in the DBGrid control will be updated accordingly.

To create an instance of the DBGrid control:

1 Create an instance of the Data control at the bottom of the form, as shown in Figure 9-8. Set the Name property to **datRegistration** and the DatabaseName property to **Chapter.09\Startup\Slight.mdb**. Set the drive designator as necessary.

2 Set the RecordSource property to **tblRegistration**. Because the user will not interact with the Data control at run time, set the Visible property to **False**.

3 Click the **DBGrid** control ⊞ on the toolbox and draw an instance of the control on the form, as shown in Figure 9-8.

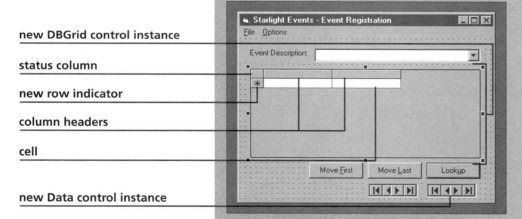

new DBGrid control instance

status column

new row indicator

column headers

cell

new Data control instance

Figure 9-8: DBGrid object

4 Activate the Properties window and set the Name property to **dbgRegistration**.

5 Set the DataSource property to **datRegistration**—the name of the Data control you just created.

When the DBGrid control is created, by default it displays two rows and three columns at design time. Each column has an empty column header. Inside the column header, you can display a prompt describing the column. When the program runs, the DBGrid control will connect to the recordset created by the Data control and display all the columns and rows. The title for each column will match the name of the field in the table. Status information appears to the left of the second column. At design time, an asterisk (*)—the symbol for a new row—appears in the status column.

Just as other controls can receive focus and become the active object, so, too, can each cell in the DBGrid control become the active cell. The active cell is identified by the Row and Col properties.

At run time, you can use a variety of techniques to navigate through the rows and columns displayed on the screen. You can click the mouse in a cell to activate it. You can change the active cell to the previous or next row using the Up and Down arrow keys. The Left and Right arrow keys allow you to change the active cell to that in the previous and next columns, respectively. The Home key will change the active cell to the first column in the current row. To view rows not displayed on the screen, you can use the scroll bars or press the Page Up or Page Down keys. By default, you cannot use the Tab key to move from cell to cell. Pressing the Tab key causes the DBGrid to lose focus and the next control instance to receive focus.

To test the DBGrid control:

1   Save the project, then run it. Your screen should resemble Figure 9-9.

column headers

current record indicator

scroll bars to locate records

cells

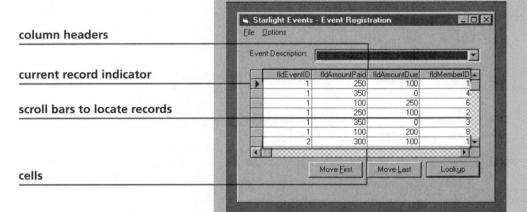

Figure 9-9: Testing the DBGrid object

Notice the columns and rows are displayed in the DBGrid object. By default, the DBGrid displays the field names in the column header and the current record indicator is positioned on the first row when the object is first activated.

2   Click the **DBGrid** control instance on the form to make it the active object.

3   Use the arrow keys to locate different cells. The Left and Right arrow keys activate the previous and next columns, respectively. The Up and Down arrow keys activate the previous and next rows, respectively. Note that pressing the Left arrow key in the first column or the Right arrow key in the last column has no effect. Also note that pressing the Up arrow key in the first row or the Down arrow key in the last row has no effect.

4   Use the scroll bar to locate rows not visible in the control instance.

5   Press the **Tab** key. Notice that the DBGrid control instance loses focus.

6   End the program to return to design mode.

help

• • • • • • • • • • • • • • • • • • •

If no information is displayed in the DBGrid control instance at run time, verify that the DatabaseName and RecordSource properties of the second Data control (datRegistration) are correct and that the DataSource property for the DBGrid control is set to the name of the correct Data control.

The DBGrid control now displays multiple records and multiple fields from the table. You can also use the scroll bars to locate records that are not initially visible on the screen.

Changing the Behavior of the Tab Key in the DBGrid Control

The DBGrid control can be configured such that the Tab key will behave differently when the control has focus. The TabAction property determines the behavior of the Tab key while the DBGrid control is the active object. By changing the value of the DBGrid's TabAction property, you can make the Tab key change the input focus from cell to cell, rather than cause the DBGrid to lose focus and another object to receive focus. The TabAction property has three possible settings. You can set these constants at run time or use the Property Pages to set them at design time:

- If the TabAction property is set to the constant **dbgControlNavigation** (the default), pressing the Tab key will cause the next control instance on the form to receive focus.
- If it is set to the constant **dbgColumnNavigation**, pressing the Tab key will move the focus to the cell in the next or previous column. If the last column in the DBGrid is active, then pressing the Tab key will cause focus to change to the next control instance on the form.
- If the TabAction property is set to the constant **dbgGridNavigation**, pressing the Tab key will cause the input focus to move from the current cell to the next or previous column. The WrapCellPointer property determines what happens when the Tab key is pressed when the last column is active. If the WrapCellPointer property is set to True, pressing the Tab key will change the focus from the active cell to the first column in the next row; if it is set to False, pressing the Tab key will have no effect.

Starlight Events has decided to let users change these properties at run time. To help you implement Starlight Events' decision, three menu items have already been created to change the behavior of the Tab key. These menu items will toggle the navigation methods between Control, Column, and Grid. When the user selects Grid navigation, the WrapCellPointer should be False to keep the user from accidentally adding new records to the database.

To change the behavior of the Tab key when the DBGrid control has focus:

1   Activate the Code window for the **mnuTabtoNewControl_Click** event procedure and enter the following statement:

```
dbgRegistration.TabAction = dbgControlNavigation
```

2   Enter the following statement into the **mnuTabtoNextCellinGrid_Click** event procedure:

```
dbgRegistration.TabAction = dbgGridNavigation
```

3   Enter the following statement into the **mnuTabtoNextColumn_Click** event procedure:

```
dbgRegistration.TabAction = dbgColumnNavigation
```

Programming

tip

• • • • • • • • • • • • • • •

▶ Note that the names of the menu items violate the naming conventions; if you adhered to the conventions, however, one of the names would be mnuOptionsTab BehaviorTabtoNewControl, causing an undue amount of typing to reference a menu name with code. When an object name is longer than 20 to 30 characters, consider using only the menu item name or abbreviating the name.

These statements set the TabAction property, as desired by the user, to one of the three possible values at run time.

You can now test the program to see the different results caused by pressing the Tab key.

To test the changes to the TabAction property:

1   Save the project, then run it.

2   Click **Options**, point to **Tab Behavior**, then click **Tab to Next Column**.

3   Click a cell in the first column, then press the **Tab** key repeatedly. The input focus should move forward from cell to cell until the active cell is a cell in the last column. When the active cell is a cell in the last column of the grid, the DBGrid control instance should lose focus.

4   Click **Options**, point to **Tab Behavior**, then click **Tab to Next Cell in Grid**.

5   Click a cell in the first column of the grid, then press the **Tab** key repeatedly. Note that when the active cell is a cell in the last column of the grid, nothing should happen.

6   Click **Options**, point to **Tab Behavior**, then click **Tab to New Control**.

7   Click a cell in the first column of the grid, then press the **Tab** key. The DBGrid control instance should lose focus.

8   End the program to return to design mode.

In addition to using the arrow keys to locate different records in the DBGrid, you can use the methods of the underlying Data control for this purpose, just as you did in previous chapters.

Locating Records Programmatically

When the DBGrid control is bound to a Data control, the DBGrid is linked to the recordset created by the Data control. As a result, you can call the methods of the underlying Data control and its recordset programmatically. For example, to program the command buttons on the form that locate the first and last records shown in the DBGrid control, you can call the MoveFirst and MoveLast methods of the Data control's Recordset property. When you call these methods, the contents of the DBGrid control are updated automatically along with the current record indicator in the DBGrid.

Starlight wants a user to be able to click a button that will locate the first or last record in the DBGrid. To accomplish this task, you will program the Move First and Move Last command buttons.

To locate the first and last records in the DBGrid:

1   Activate the Code window for the **cmdMoveFirst_Click** event procedure and enter the following statement:

```
datRegistration.Recordset.MoveFirst
```

2   Activate the Code window for the **cmdMoveLast_Click** event procedure and enter the following statement:

```
datRegistration.Recordset.MoveLast
```

These statements operate on the underlying Recordset object created by the Data control and will locate the first and last record in the recordset. You should now test the program to verify that the Move First and Move Last command buttons work correctly.

To test the command buttons:

1   Save and run the program. Test your work by clicking the **Move Last** and **Move First** command buttons to verify that the current record is repositioned correctly. The current record is identified by the arrow in the left margin of the DBGrid control instance.

2   End the program to return to design mode.

When you ran the program, you may have noticed that the information in the DBGrid control is poorly formatted. First, the numeric columns are not aligned properly. Second, the names of the columns are not descriptive names; they match the names of the underlying database fields. You can set additional properties pertaining to the DBGrid control to overcome these deficiencies.

Formatting Columns in the DBGrid Control

The DBGrid control gives you considerable flexibility in formatting the object's contents. To create the most intuitive user interface, you should change the names of the columns from the names of the database fields to names that hold more meaning for the user. Starlight Events also wants a caption to appear above the columns. To change this formatting, you must activate the Property Pages pertaining to the DBGrid control. By default, the DBGrid control does not display the different fields in the table in the column headers until the program runs. To modify the layout of each column, you must first explicitly retrieve the field names from the underlying table or query. Only then can you format the columns.

To select and format the columns in the DBGrid:

1   Activate the form named **frmStarlightEvents**, if necessary.

2   Right-click the DBGrid control instance, then click **Retrieve Fields** on the shortcut menu to load the field names into the control instance. The DBGrid control will look up the fields in the underlying database table. Notice that the field names are displayed in the column headers of the DBGrid control instance, as shown in Figure 9-10.

column names displayed in column headers after retrieving fields

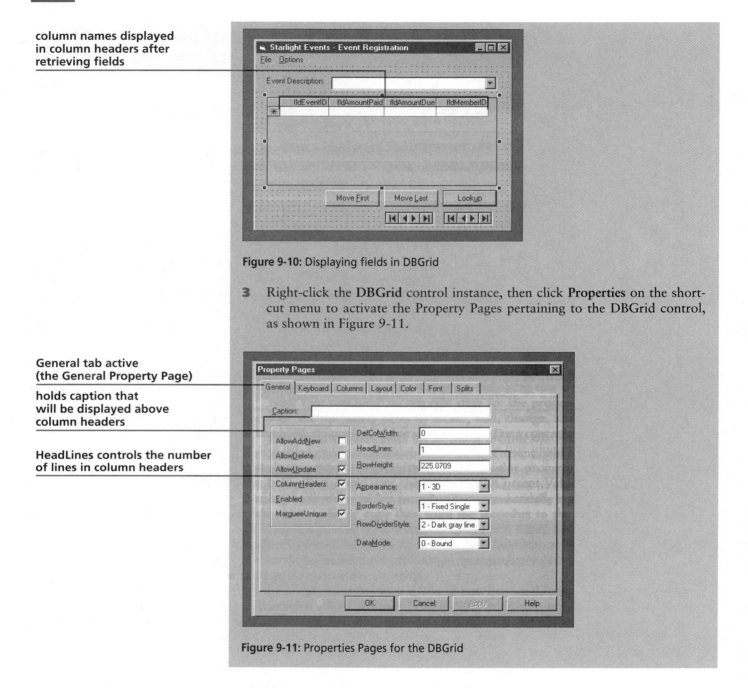

Figure 9-10: Displaying fields in DBGrid

3 Right-click the **DBGrid** control instance, then click **Properties** on the short-cut menu to activate the Property Pages pertaining to the DBGrid control, as shown in Figure 9-11.

General tab active (the General Property Page)

holds caption that will be displayed above column headers

HeadLines controls the number of lines in column headers

Figure 9-11: Properties Pages for the DBGrid

The Property Pages for the DBGrid control define both the general appearance of the object on the form and the appearance of each column. The General tab on the Property Pages defines properties, such as Caption, HeadLines, BorderStyle, and RowDividerStyle, that apply to all columns in the DBGrid. Starlight Events wants a caption to appear in the control instance and one line of text to appear in each of the column headers that identifies the data beneath the column.

To set the general properties for the DBGrid control:

1   Make sure that the **General** tab on the Property Pages is active.

2   Set the Caption property to **Event Registrations**.

Note that the HeadLines property is 1, which is the default.

3   Click the **Apply** button.

The caption should appear in the DBGrid control instance. If the Property Pages obscure the form, move the Property Pages so that you can see the changes in the DBGrid control instance.

Now that you have performed the general formatting of the DBGrid control, you need to format the individual columns. The Columns tab on the Property Pages defines the behavior of each column in the DBGrid. It defines the properties for the Column objects in the Columns collection pertaining to the DBGrid. The Columns collection is a zero-based collection, containing a reference to one Column object for each column in the DBGrid. The Column object supports properties pertaining to an individual column, including the column's caption, the field to be displayed, a default value (if any), and the format of the data displayed in the column. These properties pertain to the Column object belonging to the DBGrid control—*not to the DBGrid control itself.*

The Columns tab on the Property Pages is used to define the title, format, and field of each column displayed in the DBGrid. The Column list box is used to select a column.

The following properties can be set on the Columns tab:

■   The **Caption** property contains the text displayed at the top of the column (the column header).

■   The **DataField** property works like the DataField property of a text box. It identifies the field for a table or query. This property is set automatically when the fields are retrieved.

■   The **DefaultValue** property is a placeholder in which you can program an event that will set a default value of a column.

■   The **NumberFormat** property defines how numeric data in a column are displayed. The formats are the same as the named formats used in the Format statement.

To use the Columns tab on the Property Pages, you first select a column using the Column list box, then set the properties for the column. You can then format each of the columns in the DBGrid control. Note that you will not need to set the DataField property—when you loaded the fields in the previous steps, the DBGrid control automatically set this property for you. You should now set the caption for each column and specify a Currency format for the Amount Due and Amount Paid columns because they represent monetary values.

To format the columns in the DBGrid control:

1   Make sure the **Property Pages** for the DBGrid object are open. Click the **Columns** tab to activate it. By default, input focus is set to the Column list box and the first column "Column0 (fldEventID)" is active.

2   Set the Caption property for the column "Column0 (fldEventID)" to **Event ID**.

3   For the columns **Column1 (fldAmountPaid)** and **Column2 (fldAmountDue)**, set the NumberFormat property to **Currency**. Set their Caption properties to **Amount Paid** and **Amount Due**, respectively. To select a column, select the desired column in the Column list box.

4   For the column **fldMemberID**, set the Caption property to **Member ID**.

5   Click **OK** to close the Property Pages. Your form should look like Figure 9-12.

general caption

column captions

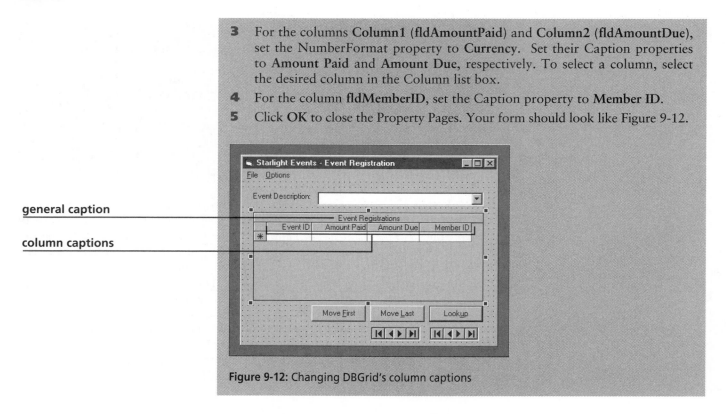

Figure 9-12: Changing DBGrid's column captions

The Layout tab on the Property Pages provides options that are similar to the options on the Columns tab. On the Layout tab, you use the Column list box to select a column, then set the properties that define the layout of the column. Again, these properties pertain to a column rather than to the DBGrid control itself.

- The **Split** property is an object used to split the region of the DBGrid into multiple panes, much as you would split a spreadsheet in Microsoft Excel.
- If the **AllowSizing** property is set to True, the mouse pointer changes to a double-headed arrow when positioned over the row divider. At run time, the user can resize the rows and columns by dragging the row and column separators.
- The **Alignment**, **Visible**, and **Width** properties work like the properties having the same names pertaining to the other controls you have used.

Starlight Events would like the numeric data to be right-justified so that the decimal points align. The columns can be aligned using the Alignment property on the Property Pages Layout tab. In addition, the DBGrid control currently displays the Event ID field in the registration table. Because the user will always enter registration information for the event selected in the DBCombo box, the value of this field will match that of the Event ID stored in the BoundText property of the currently selected item from the DBCombo box. To improve the user interface, it is suggested that you do not display this column. Even when a column is not visible in the DBGrid control, you can still reference it using Visual Basic code.

In addition to making the Event ID column invisible, Starlight Events wants the other numeric columns to be right-justified. The DBGrid control sets the alignment based on the data type of the field and the Numeric format selected on the Columns tab. You must verify that the correct alignment applies to each of the Numeric fields.

To align the numeric data and make the Event ID column invisible:

1   Open the **Property Pages** for the object named **dbgRegistration**.

2   Click the **Layout** tab, as shown in Figure 9-13. Depending upon the exact size of the DBGrid control instance you created on the form, the value of the Width property may vary slightly.

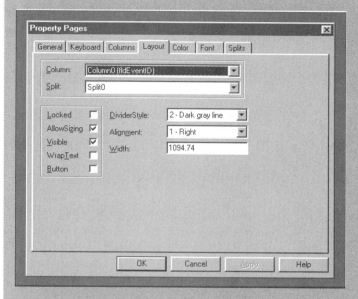

Figure 9-13: Changing DBGrid's column layout

3   Use the Column list box to select the column named **Column0 (fldEventID)**.

4   Click the **Visible** check box to remove the check and make the column invisible.

5   Click the **Apply** button.

6   Use the Column list box to select the column named **Column3 (fldMemberID)** and verify that the Alignment property is set to **1 - Right**.

7   For the fields **fldAmountPaid** and **fldAmountDue**, verify that the Alignment property is set to **1 - Right**.

8   Click **OK** to close the Property Pages.

Next, you should test the program to verify that the columns are formatted correctly. The Event ID column should not be visible, and the Amount Paid and Amount Due columns should be formatted with two decimal places and aligned at the decimal point.

To test the formatting of the DBGrid control:

1   Save the project, then run it.

The information in the DBGrid control should look like Figure 9-14.

numeric columns
right-justified

currency format

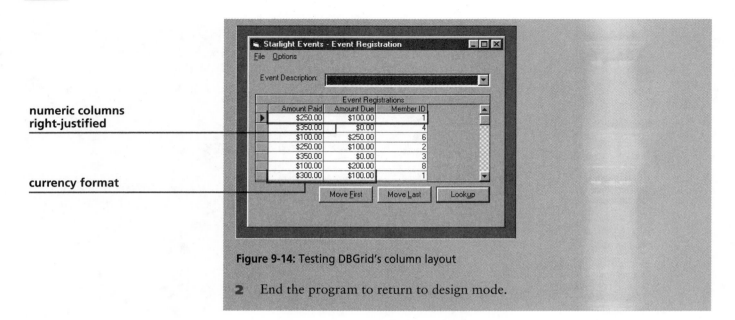

Figure 9-14: Testing DBGrid's column layout

2   End the program to return to design mode.

Your next step is to resize the columns. To accomplish this task, you could set the Width property by specifying a number for the Width on the Layout tab on the Property Pages. You could also resize the columns interactively by making the control User Interface active. **User Interface (UI) active** means that you can insert, move, delete, and resize the individual columns by dragging their borders instead of using the Property Pages to set the values.

To make the control instance UI active, right-click the mouse button over an instance of the DBGrid control to activate the shortcut menu, then click Edit. The control instance will remain UI active until it ceases to be the active object. Once the control instance is UI active, you can perform the following tasks:

- Remove columns by activating a column, right-clicking the mouse over an instance of the DBGrid control, then clicking Cut.
- Insert new columns by activating a column, right-clicking the mouse over an instance of the DBGrid control, then clicking Insert. The new column is inserted to the left of the active column.
- Add a column to the end of the list of columns by right-clicking the mouse over an instance of the DBGrid control, then clicking Append.
- Resize a column by positioning the cursor over the column dividers, holding down the left mouse button, then dragging the column to increase or decrease its width.
- Resize the height of a row by positioning the cursor over a row divider, then dragging the row up or down.

You will now practice changing the size of the rows and columns.

To modify row and column sizes:

1   Activate the instance of the **DBGrid** control, right-click the mouse on the control instance, then click **Edit** to make the control UI active.

2   Move the cursor to the first column separator, as shown in Figure 9-15. Notice that the cursor will appear as a ↔.

3   Hold down the left mouse button, then drag the column to the left to decrease its size.

4   Move the cursor to the column divider between each of the column separators. Increase and decrease the size of the columns to familiarize yourself with the process.

5   Resize the object until it is the size shown in Figure 9-15.

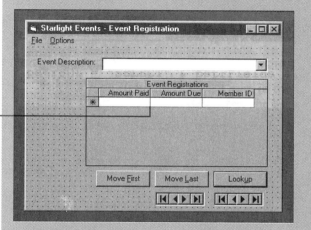

column separator

Figure 9-15: Resizing DBGrid's columns

Now that you have set the DBGrid's properties, you need to write the code that will synchronize the current selection in the DBCombo box with the records displayed in the DBGrid. Currently, the DBGrid displays all records in the recordset. Starlight Events wants to see only the registrations for the currently selected event.

Because the information displayed in the DBGrid is based on the Recordset object created by the datRegistration Data control, you must change the records in this recordset whenever the user selects a different event. In the past, you have set the RecordSource property of the Data control to a table or query at design time. You can also set the RecordSource property at run time, then call the Refresh method pertaining to the Data control. When you call the Refresh method, the Data control uses the value of the DatabaseName and RecordSource properties to create a new Recordset object and store a reference to the newly created recordset in the Data control's Recordset property. In addition to specifying a table or query name, you can create a SELECT statement of the same form that you used in Chapter 8, then set the RecordSource property to the SELECT statement. When the program calls the Refresh method, the SELECT statement executes and a new recordset is created.

The Lookup command button is defined as the default button so that users can select an event description from the DBCombo object and then press the Enter key. You therefore need to write the statement to refresh the recordset in the Click event procedure for this command button.

To select only event registrations for the current event:

1 Activate the Code window for the **cmdLookup_Click** event procedure.

2 Enter the following statements into the procedure:

```
Dim pstrSQL As String
If dbcEvents.Text <> vbNullString Then
    pstrSQL = "SELECT * FROM tblRegistration " & _
        " WHERE fldEventID = " & dbcEvents.BoundText & _
        " ORDER BY fldMemberID "
    datRegistration.RecordSource = pstrSQL
    datRegistration.Refresh
    dbgRegistration.Visible = True
End If
```

These statements create the necessary SQL statement and store it in the variable pstrSQL. Then, by setting the RecordSource property and calling the Data control's Refresh method, the Data control creates a new recordset. Notice that these statements are all enclosed in an If statement. The If statement verifies that an item is selected from the DBCombo object.

The code that you just typed requires careful examination:

```
If dbcEvents.Text <> vbNullString Then
    pstrSQL = "SELECT * FROM tblRegistration " & _
        " WHERE fldEventID = " & dbcEvents.BoundText & _
        " ORDER BY fldMemberID "
```

These statements create the SQL SELECT statement using the same technique employed in Chapter 8. The SELECT statement is built only if the user selects an item in the DBCombo box. Note that the Event ID corresponding to the selected event description is stored in the BoundText property of the DBCombo box. This value is used to create the WHERE clause for the SELECT statement. Because Starlight Events keeps its paper records sorted by Member ID, the records appear in the same order because of the ORDER BY clause.

```
datRegistration.RecordSource = pstrSQL
datRegistration.Refresh
dbgRegistration.Visible = True
```

The first statement assigns the SELECT statement, which is stored in the variable pstrSQL, to the RecordSource property of the Data control corresponding to the DBGrid control. The second statement causes the SELECT statement to execute. When the recordset is refreshed, the selected records will automatically appear in the DBGrid control instance. The final statement makes the DBGrid control instance visible. Later in the chapter, you will write the statements to make the DBGrid control instance invisible when the program first begins.

Whenever a user selects an event description in the DBCombo box object and clicks the Lookup command button, these statements will execute. Only the registrations for the Event ID corresponding to the event description will be selected and stored in the new recordset. Those records will then appear in the DBGrid control.

You can now test the program to verify that the code you just wrote works correctly.

To test the Lookup command button:

1 Save the project, then run it.

2 Click the **list arrow** in the Event Description combo box to display the event descriptions and select the description **Visual Basic programming seminar - Beginning**.

3 Press the **Enter** key to execute the code you just wrote in the Lookup button's Click event procedure. Because the Lookup command button is the default object, you can simply press Enter to execute the button's Click event procedure. Your form should look like Figure 9-16. Note that the DBGrid control contains six records.

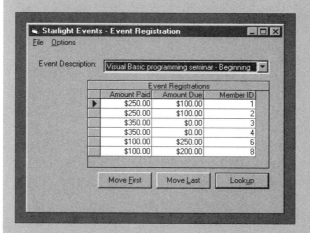

Figure 9-16: Modifying the Recordset object at run time

4 End the program to return to design mode.

help

If all records continue to be selected, check the code you just wrote and verify that it matches the code in the preceding steps. Then repeat Steps 1 through 3. If scroll bars appear, the height of the DBGrid control you created may be smaller than the one shown in Figure 9-16. In that case, use the scroll bars to display the remaining records.

After the user selects an event from the DBCombo object, the corresponding event registrations now appear in the DBGrid control instance. In addition, you have improved the user interface by formatting the numeric columns and modifying the captions. Because you programmed the menu items to change the behavior of the Tab key while the DBGrid control is active, the user can customize the behavior of the control according to his or her personal preference.

QUESTIONS

1. Which of the following is a valid control type?
   a. Intrinsic controls
   b. Standard controls
   c. ActiveX controls
   d. Both a and c.
   e. Both b and c.

2. Which of the following statements about ActiveX controls is true?
   a. They support Property Pages.
   b. They are added to a project using the Components dialog.
   c. The code for an ActiveX control is stored in an OCX file.
   d. All of the above.
   e. None of the above.

3. Which of the following is a valid ActiveX control supported by Visual Basic?
   a. DBList
   b. DBCombo
   c. DBGrid
   d. Common Dialog
   e. All of the above.

4. The field specified in the _____ property will be displayed in the DBList or DBCombo control.
   a. RecordSource
   b. ListField
   c. List
   d. FieldName
   e. Text

5. The intersection of a row and a column in the DBGrid control is called a(n) _____.
   a. rectangle
   b. cell
   c. point
   d. intersection
   e. None of the above.

6. Which of the following properties determines whether a user can add, change, or delete records in the DBGrid control?
   a. AllowAdd, AllowChange, AllowRemove
   b. AllowAddNew, AllowUpdate, AllowDelete
   c. AddNew, Update, Delete
   d. Add, Change, Delete
   e. None of the above.

7. Which of the following statements about the DBGrid control is true?
   a. Columns can be resized.
   b. You cannot change the contents of a column header.
   c. You cannot change the alignment of a column.
   d. All of the above.
   e. None of the above.

8.   Which of the following events does the DBGrid control support?
    a. BeforeInsert, BeforeUpdate, AfterInsert
    b. BeforeAdd, AfterAdd, BeforeChange, AfterChange
    c. Add, Change, Delete
    d. All of the above.
    e. None of the above.

9.   Which of the following can be used to set the properties of an ActiveX control?
    a. Properties window
    b. Property Pages
    c. Code window
    d. Both a and b.
    e. All of the above.

10. How do you make the DBGrid control become UI active?
    a. Click Edit from the control's shortcut menu.
    b. Set the UIActive property using the Properties window.
    c. Set the UIActive property using the Property Pages.
    d. All of the above.
    e. None of the above.

SECTION B
objectives

In this section you will:

- Modify data with the DBGrid control
- Add records with the DBGrid control
- Validate data with the DBGrid control
- Delete records with the DBGrid control
- Use the CommonDialog control to open files and set fonts
- Use the Controls collection

Programming the DBGrid and CommonDialog Controls

Modifying Data with the DBGrid Control

The DBGrid control allows the user to add, change, and delete records. As the user moves from cell to cell or from row to row, events pertaining to the DBGrid control occur, allowing your program to validate user input. Additionally, other events occur as the user adds, changes, and deletes records. Some of these events pertain to actions involving the current row (record) in the DBGrid. Other events relate to actions involving a specific column. In response to these events, the code in your program can then execute validation code, such as code that requests user confirmation before record deletion. As events are generated for the DBGrid control, corresponding events may be generated for the underlying Data control. As you develop your program, you may write validation code in the events pertaining to the DBGrid control or to the underlying Data control.

The DBGrid control supports a copy buffer much like the Data control's copy buffer. Changes made to the current record are stored in the DBGrid control's copy buffer. When the user changes the current cell from one row to another, the fields in this copy buffer are written to the Data control's copy buffer.

Three properties determine whether a user can add, change, and delete records—AllowAddNew, AllowUpdate, and AllowDelete, respectively. For the user to add a new record to the DBGrid control and the underlying recordset, the AllowAddNew property must be set to True either at run time or at design time using the General tab on the Property Pages. The AllowUpdate property must be set to True for the user to update a record, and the AllowDelete property must be set to True for the user to delete a record.

Because Starlight Events wants users to be able to add, change, and delete records directly from the DBGrid control, you must set the AllowAddNew, AllowUpdate, and AllowDelete properties to True.

To set the properties to add, change, and delete records:

1 Make sure that the DBGrid control instance is the active object.

2 Right-click the mouse button, then click **Properties** to activate the Property Pages for the object.

3 Make sure that the General tab on the Property Pages is active.

4 Make sure that the **AllowAddNew, AllowUpdate**, and **AllowDelete** check boxes are checked. The Enabled check box, which is checked by default, sets the Enabled property for the control instance. When enabled, the control instance can receive focus and respond to events. When disabled, the control instance cannot receive focus or respond to events.

5 Click the **OK** button to apply the changes and close the Property Pages.

When these check boxes are checked, the user can add, change, and delete records. Before modifying the data in the DBGrid control instance, you need to better understand the events and other objects supported by this control.

DBGrid Events and Objects

To add a new record to the DBGrid control, the user clicks a column in the last row of the DBGrid. This row, which is marked with an asterisk (*), is displayed only if the AllowAddNew property is set to True. As the user enters information into each of the columns, several events occur. Some of these events pertain to the entire row; others pertain to individual cells. Your program can respond to these events and validate user input. The following list describes the events pertaining to an entire row (record) and the order in which they occur when the user adds a record:

1. The **BeforeInsert** event occurs when the user enters the first character in a new row in the DBGrid.

2. The **BeforeUpdate** event occurs after the user enters data in each field but before he or she moves to a different row or different object on the form. You can write code in this event procedure to validate input. If a field contains invalid data, your program code can set the Cancel argument in the event procedure to True to cancel the update. Setting the Cancel argument to True in the BeforeUpdate event has the same effect as setting it to True in the Validate event for the Data control.

3. The **AfterUpdate** event occurs after the record is written to the underlying database table. If the BeforeInsert or BeforeUpdate events were canceled (that is, if the Cancel argument was set to True in the event procedure), this event will not occur.

4. Finally, the **AfterInsert** event occurs. If the BeforeInsert or BeforeUpdate events were canceled (that is, if the Cancel argument was set to True in the event procedure), this event will not occur.

The DBGrid control supports a Columns collection, which in turn contains a reference to Column objects. Each column object is used to reference a particular column in the DBGrid control instance. At run time, you can write code to reference the cells in the current row using the Column object. You can reference the zero-based Columns collection by numeric index or with a string key. The string key has the same value as the field name. One Column object exists for each column in the DBGrid control, regardless of whether the column is visible. The Column object supports a Value property, which contains the value displayed in the column for the currently selected row. The Value property is the default property.

When the user attempts to add a new record, the Amount Due and Amount Paid fields must be validated to ensure that they contain numeric data. Also, the Member ID field must be validated to ensure that the Member ID exists in the table named tblPeople. Finally, the Event ID must be stored in the Event ID column even though the column does not appear on the screen. Remember that the value for the current Event ID is stored in the BoundText property of the DBCombo box.

To illustrate the syntax for referencing a column in the Columns collection, assume that fldEventID is the first column in the Columns collection. For this case, the following four statements would be equivalent:

```
dbgRegistration.Columns(0).Value = 100
dbgRegistration.Columns(0) = 100
dbgRegistration.Columns("fldEventID").Value = 100
dbgRegistration.Columns("fldEventID") = 100
```

Programming

tip

The Value property of the Column object is the default property. Using the default property will save typing and improve the program's performance. Using the string key will improve the program's readability.

When a user tries to add a record, the Event ID from the DBCombo box must be stored in the first column of the active row in the DBGrid control. You must write code to perform this task, because this column is invisible to the user. Your code can use the Columns collection with an index of zero (0) or the string key "fldEventID" to specify the column.

To store the current Event ID into the current column:

1   Activate the Code window to the **dbgRegistration_BeforeUpdate** event procedure.

2   Enter the following statement into the Code window:

```
dbgRegistration.Columns("fldEventID") = _
    dbcEvents.BoundText
```

This statement assigns the current Event ID, which is stored in the BoundText property of the DBCombo box, to the Event ID column in the DBGrid. You used the Columns collection with the string key fldEventID to specify the column. Alternatively, you could have used the index zero (0).

Validating Data with the DBGrid Control

Starlight Events wants its program to validate that the data entered or changed in the Amount Paid or Amount Due fields is a positive number. Also, when the user deletes a record, a message box should appear requesting confirmation from the user before the record actually is removed.

The DBGrid control supports events to validate the information stored in a specific cell. When you wrote code for the Data control's Validate event, you included statements to validate all of the necessary fields in the recordset in a single event procedure. The process of validating data with the DBGrid control is similar to the process you used when you programmed the Data control's Validate event. One significant difference exists, however. With the DBGrid control, certain events occur on a cell-by-cell basis. As a result, you can write code to validate user input for a particular cell (field), rather than writing code to validate an entire row (record).

The following list summarizes some events supported by the DBGrid control when validating the contents of a cell:

- The **BeforeColUpdate** event occurs when a cell loses focus and before the changed data is copied to the DBGrid's copy buffer. Your program therefore has an opportunity to validate changes made to the column and to advise the user if any errors occur. If an error arises, you can display a message box and set the Cancel property to True to prevent the update.
- The **BeforeColInsert** and **AfterColInsert** events work like the BeforeUpdate and AfterUpdate events. These events can be canceled by setting the Cancel argument to True.

When a user changes the contents of the Amount Paid or Amount Due fields, the input should be validated to ensure that each field contains a positive numeric value. To accomplish this task, you can write code to respond to the BeforeColUpdate event. The BeforeColUpdate event supports three arguments:

- The **ColIndex** argument is an Integer value identifying the column. The ColIndex of the first column is zero (0), the second is one (1), and so on. You use the ColIndex argument to find the currently selected column. The ColIndex has the same value as the corresponding index in the Columns collection.
- The **OldValue** argument contains the value of the cell before it was changed.
- The **Cancel** argument, when set to True, cancels the event. The contents of the cell are automatically restored to the old value and focus returns to the cell in the control.

The BeforeColUpdate event occurs after changes are made to a cell and before another cell becomes active. Meanwhile, the ColIndex argument contains the index of the column that is ready to become inactive. In the BeforeColUpdate event procedure, you can write a Select Case statement to determine the current column and validate the fields as necessary. You now are ready to develop the statements to validate any changes made to the Amount Paid and Amount Due fields.

To write the code to validate changes before updating a column:

1 Activate the Code window for the **dbgRegistration_BeforeColUpdate** event procedure.

2 Enter the following statements in the Code window:

```
Select Case ColIndex
    Case 1
        If Not (IsNumeric _
            (dbgRegistration.Columns(ColIndex).Value)) Then
            Call MsgBox ("Cannot Update Amount Paid.")
            Cancel = True
        End If
    Case 2
        If Not (IsNumeric _
            (dbgRegistration.Columns(ColIndex).Value)) Then
            Call MsgBox ("Cannot Update Amount Due.")
            Cancel = True
        End If
End Select
```

These statements verify that the Amount Paid and Amount Due columns contain valid numbers. The program calls the BeforeColUpdate event procedure whenever the user changes the contents of a cell and moves to another cell. To determine the current column, the ColIndex is passed as an argument to the event procedure. The first column has a ColIndex value of zero (0), the second has a value of one (1), and so on.

Consider part of the code that you just typed:

```
Select Case ColIndex
    Case 1
        If Not (IsNumeric _
            (dbgRegistration.Columns(ColIndex).Value)) Then
            Call MsgBox ("Cannot Update Amount Paid.")
            Cancel = True
        End If
```

These statements execute when the argument ColIndex has a value of one (1), which represents the Amount Paid column. To obtain the current value of this column, your program selects the current column from the Columns collection of the DBGrid object. By specifying the Value property, it obtains the value stored in the current column. If the Value property did not contain a valid number, then the code you wrote would display a message box and set the value of Cancel to True.

This action effectively cancels the update operation. The old value is restored in the contents of the cell and focus returns to the column.

Consider the following code to validate the Amount Due column:

```
Case 2
    If Not (IsNumeric _
        (dbgRegistration.Columns(ColIndex).Value)) Then
        Call MsgBox ("Cannot Update Amount Due.")
        Cancel = True
    End If
```

These statements have the same effect as the preceding statements but use the third column rather than the second one. Thus the message was changed appropriately. You now are ready to test the code you just wrote to verify that the Amount Due and Amount Paid fields are properly validated.

To verify the code for the BeforeColUpdate event:

1 Save and run the program. Select the event named **Visual Basic programming seminar – Intermediate** in the DBCombo box.

2 Click the **Lookup** button to locate the corresponding event registrations.

3 Change the Amount Paid field in one of the rows to **32.33.3** and try to move the cursor to another cell. A message box should appear with the note "Cannot Update Amount Paid".

4 Click **OK** in the message box. The previous value in the Amount Paid field is restored and focus returns to the Amount Paid cell.

5 Change the Amount Due field in one of the rows to **32JK** and try to move the cursor to another cell. The message box appears with the note "Cannot Update Amount Due".

6 Click **OK** in the message box. The previous value in the Amount Due field is restored and focus returns to the Amount Due cell.

7 End the program to return to design mode.

Now that you can validate changes for the Amount Due and Amount Paid fields, you need to write the code to validate the Member ID field to ensure that it contains a member ID found in the table named tblPeople. To accomplish this task, you can add statements to the Select Case statement you just wrote to look up, in the table tblPeople, the Member ID typed by the user. These statements will create a SELECT statement, then open a recordset. If the recordset contains a record, then the member is on file, and the record can be added or updated. If the recordset is empty, then no corresponding member exists in the table tblPeople, and the update should be canceled.

You now can proceed to write the statements to validate the Member ID field.

To verify that a member exists in the table tblPeople:

1 Activate the Code window for the **dbgRegistration_BeforeColUpdate** event procedure.

2 Enter the following statement to declare a String and Recordset variable as the first and second statements in the event procedure:

```
Dim pstrSQL As String
Dim prstCurrent As Recordset
```

3 Append the following statements in the Code window just before the End Select statement:

```
Case 3
    pstrSQL = "SELECT * FROM tblPeople " & _
        " WHERE fldMemberID = " & _
        dbgRegistration.Columns(ColIndex).Value
    Set prstCurrent = _
        DBEngine.Workspaces(0).Databases(0). _
        OpenRecordset(pstrSQL)
    If prstCurrent.RecordCount = 0 Then
        Call MsgBox ("Member ID Not Found.")
        Cancel = True
    End If
    Set prstCurrent = Nothing
```

These statements execute when the user changes the value of the Member ID field. First, they create a SELECT statement to try to find a matching Member ID in the table named tblPeople. If a record is found, the update continues. Otherwise, the program displays a message box and cancels the update.

Consider one part of the code you just wrote:

```
pstrSQL = "SELECT * FROM tblPeople " & _
    " WHERE fldMemberID = " & _
    dbgRegistration.Columns(ColIndex).Value
```

This statement creates the SELECT statement to select any records from the table tblPeople, where the Member ID is the same as the Member ID in the current cell. This value appears in the third column of the DBGrid.

Consider the following code to create an instance of a Recordset object:

```
Set prstCurrent = _
   DBEngine.Workspaces(0).Databases(0). _
   OpenRecordset(pstrSQL)
```

This statement creates the recordset. In Chapter 8, you called the OpenDatabase method to explicitly open a database. You then called the OpenRecordset method pertaining to the Database object to explicitly create an instance of the Recordset object. Here, the statement does not open a database or create a Database object variable. Because you have not explicitly created a Database object variable, you have no object with which to call the OpenDatabase method. A reference to an open database created by the Data control does exist, however; you can use the first database in the Databases collection. The first Database object is stored in the Default Workspace, which is the first Workspace object in the Workspaces collection. The Workspaces collection is a member of the DBEngine object.

Consider the following code, which displays a message if the user enters an invalid Member ID:

```
If prstCurrent.RecordCount = 0 Then
   Call MsgBox ("Member ID Not Found.")
   Cancel = True
End If
```

When the recordset is created, the RecordCount property contains the number of records in the recordset. If it is zero (0), there are no records, the message box is displayed, and the update is canceled.

Consider the following code to destroy the recordset object:

```
Set prstCurrent = Nothing
```

Because the recordset will not be reused, the program explicitly destroys it by setting the value of the object to Nothing. You can now test the code you have written by attempting to add a new record.

To add a new event registration and test the Member ID validation statements:

1 Save and run the program. Using the combo box, select the event named **Visual Basic programming seminar - Beginning**, then click **Lookup**.

2 Create a new record by clicking the first column in the last row with the asterisk (*) in the column indicator. Enter **100.00** for the amount paid. Enter **200.00** for the amount due. Enter the value **10222** for the Member ID. The form should look like Figure 9-17.

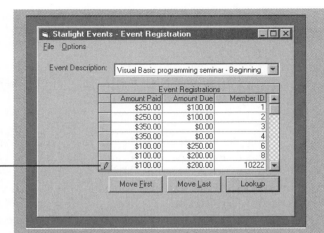

current record indicator indicates the record is being edited

Figure 9-17: Adding a new record to the DBGrid

3 Press the **Up arrow** key to move the current record indicator to the previous record, causing the BeforeUpdate event to occur.

4 Because this member is not on file, the message box should appear explaining the cause of the error. The text in the message box contains the string "Member ID Not Found." Click **OK** in the message box. Note that the value 10222 disappears from the Member ID field and focus returns to that cell.

5 Enter the value **9** for the Member ID and press the **Up Arrow** key to locate the previous record. The record you just entered will be added because that member is on file.

6 End the program to return to design mode.

The program now adds and updates registration information. If the user enters invalid data in a cell, then an appropriate message box appears on screen. You now need to write the code to display a message box that will confirm record deletion before proceeding.

Deleting Records with the DBGrid Control

By setting the AllowDelete property to True on the Property Pages General tab, the DBGrid control will allow the user to delete records by clicking a record in the record indicator column and then pressing the Delete key. To prevent the user from accidentally deleting a record, a message box should be displayed immediately before the record is actually removed from the underlying recordset.

The DBGrid control supports two events pertaining to record deletion:

■ The **BeforeDelete** event occurs just before the removal of a selected record from the database. If the Cancel argument is set to True, it will cancel the deletion and the AfterDelete event will not occur.

■ The **AfterDelete** event occurs immediately after the record is deleted.

To write the statements to confirm deletion:

1   Activate the Code window for the **dbgRegistration_BeforeDelete** event procedure.

2   Enter the following statements into the Code window:

```
Dim pintAnswer As Integer
pintAnswer = MsgBox _
    ("Are you sure you want to delete this record?", _
    vbYesNo)
If pintAnswer <> vbYes Then
    Cancel = True
End If
```

These statements display a message box asking the user to confirm the deletion of the currently selected record. If the user clicks the Yes button, the current record will be deleted; otherwise, the Cancel argument is set to True and the record will not be deleted.

You can now test the code you just wrote.

To test the statement to confirm deletion:

1   Save and run the program.

2   Locate the row containing Member ID 9 and click one of the cells corresponding to that record.

3   Click the record selector column, as shown in Figure 9-18, to select the Member ID 9 row. You added this record in the preceding steps. The entire record should appear highlighted.

click here to select the record

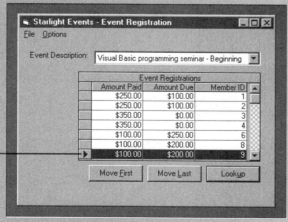

Figure 9-18: Deleting a record from the DBGrid

4 Press the **Delete** key. The message box should appear, requesting that you confirm the deletion.

5 Click **Yes**. The message box closes and the record is removed from the DBGrid control and the underlying recordset.

6 End the program to return to design mode.

Although the program you have written for Starlight Events works well for a single client, the user cannot select a specific database so as to choose a different client. Because one database exists for every client, the program should allow the user to select a specific database in any folder on any drive. The user should be able to modify that database's event registrations. To accomplish this task, you can create an instance of the CommonDialog control allowing the user to select a particular database for use.

Creating an Open Dialog Using the CommonDialog Control

The CommonDialog control is an ActiveX control used to display six standard dialogs. Each of these dialogs performs a specific function, as shown in Figure 9-19.

Dialog	Description
File Open	Allows you to select a file to be opened by specifying the drive, directory, and file
File SaveAs	Allows you to select a file to be saved by specifying the drive, directory, and file
Change Colors	Allows the user to select a color for a color palette or create a custom color
Change Fonts	Allows the user to select a font, and its size, color and style
Print	Allows the user to specify that output should be printed
Access Help	Starts the Windows Help program WINHLP32.EXE and displays a help file

Figure 9-19: Standard dialogs

As with the other controls you have used, you must create an instance of the CommonDialog control on a form before you can use it in your program. Once an instance exists, you can call the object's methods using Visual Basic code. You can also set properties at design time using the Properties window and Property Pages, or at run time by writing Visual Basic code.

Programming
tip

● ● ● ● ● ● ● ● ● ● ● ● ● ● ● ●

▶ Generally, a program needs
only one instance of the
CommonDialog control. You
can set its properties such
that at run time, it will
perform different tasks like
opening or saving files,
sending data to the printer,
or setting fonts and colors.
Using only one instance of
the CommonDialog control
will cause your program
to consume less memory,
thereby improving its
performance.

Unlike other controls you have used, the CommonDialog control does not appear on the form at run time; hence, its position on the form is unimportant. This control appears only at design time to remind the programmer that a valid instance of the control exists. At that time, you can click it to activate the Properties window and Properties Pages.

Starlight Events does not want a specific database to be opened or displayed on the form when the event registration system first starts. Rather, it wants the user to select a menu item so as to choose a database in a dialog. The CommonDialog control allows you to use standard dialogs to open, save, and print files and to set colors and fonts. Because the CommonDialog control is an ActiveX control, it must be added to the toolbox. You performed this operation at the beginning of the chapter. The CommonDialog control uses the standard prefix "cdl".

To create an instance of the CommonDialog control:

1 Click the **CommonDialog** control 🔲 on the toolbox, and draw an instance of the control on the form.

Because the control instance does not appear at run time, its exact position is unimportant. You should place it, however, so it does not obscure another control instance on the screen. Also, the size of the control is irrelevant. No matter what size you specify for the instance of the CommonDialog control, it will appear as a small square about the same size as the control on the toolbox.

2 Activate the Properties window and set the Name property to **cdlOne**.

3 Click the **Value** column of the Custom property, then click the **Properties** button [...] to open the Property Pages pertaining to the CommonDialog control, as shown in Figure 9-20.

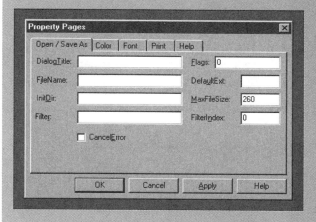

Figure 9-20: CommonDialog control Property Pages

The CommonDialog control supports six different dialogs to perform six different common tasks. Its Property Pages support different tabs to organize the properties that apply to each of the different dialogs. At this time, you need to set the properties that will describe the characteristics of the Open dialog that users will see when they select a specific file to open. The following list describes the effect of setting each of the different properties for the Open (or Save As) dialog:

- The **DialogTitle** text box specifies the title that appears on the Open (or Save As) dialog.
- If you want a default file name to appear in the **Filename** text box when the Open (or Save As) dialog appears at run time, set the **Filename** property to the name of the file.
- The **InitDir** text box defines the initial directory that will be scanned for files.
- To select only files with a specific file name extension, you can use the **Filter** property. The Filter property provides a list of options in the Files of type list box. The user can click one of these options to display files of a particular type. The syntax of the Filter property is described below.

Syntax	*object*.**Filter** [= *description1|filter1|description2|filter2...*]
Dissection	<ul><li>The *object* must be a valid instance of a CommonDialog object.</li><li>The **Filter** property is used to restrict the file suffixes that appear in the Open (or Save As) dialog.</li><li>Each filter consists of a description and a corresponding filter. The *description* appears in the list box on the Open (or Save As) dialog. The *filter* should be a three-character file extension. Files having that extension will be displayed in the Look in list box. A vertical bar separates each filter and description. Do not put spaces between the vertical bars, as they will appear in the description or be used in the filter. The description should briefly indicate the file type followed by the name of the file extension enclosed in parentheses.</li></ul>
Code Example	`cdlOne.Filter = "Access Database (*.mdb)|*.mdb|All Files|*.*"`
Code Dissection	The preceding statement will set the Filter property of an object named cdlOne to look for Microsoft Access databases or all files.

The following properties are supported by the CommonDialog control:

- The **FilterIndex** property works with the Filter property. It is useful for specifying a default filter when multiple filters exist. Each filter has a unique index beginning with zero (0); thus, to set the second filter to the default filter, you should set the FilterIndex property to zero (0).
- The **CancelError** property is used to determine whether the user clicked the OK button or the Cancel button. If set to True, a run-time error will be generated when the user clicks the Cancel button. You then can write an error handler to perform the appropriate processing.
- The **Flags** property further controls the behavior of the different dialogs.

Depending on the application, you may want the user to be able to select multiple files or create a new file. For more information on the Flags property, see the CommonDialog Control Constants Help topic.

The following list describes some of the valid flags pertaining to the Open dialog:

- The flag **cdlOFNCreatePrompt** specifies that the dialog will prompt the user to create a new file.
- The flag **cdlOFNFileMustExist** indicates that the user can select only existing files. If the user specifies a nonexistent file, a warning message appears.

Programming

tip

● ● ● ● ● ● ● ● ● ● ● ● ● ● ● ● ●

▶ Generally your program will open files of a specific type. In this section, you are opening files that have the extension ".mdb" (Microsoft Access database); thus you want only files that have the extension ".mdb" to appear in the list box by default. A user may have changed a file's extension, however, so you must also give the user the opportunity to look at all files.

■ The flag **cdlOFNoChangeDir** indicates that the user cannot change directories.
■ The flag **cdlOFNPathMustExist** indicates that the path must already exist.

Now you are ready to set the properties of the CommonDialog control so that it will open files with the ".mdb" extension and look in Chapter.09\Startup folder by default. It is suggested that you set the caption of the dialog to Open Database. If the user clicks the Cancel button, no database should be opened.

To set the design-time properties of the CommonDialog control:

1 Make sure the Property Pages for the CommonDialog control is still open and that the **Open / Save As** tab is active.

2 Type **Open Database** in the DialogTitle text box.

3 Type **A:\Chapter.09\Startup** in the InitDir text box. Change the drive designator as necessary.

4 Type **Microsoft Access database (*.mdb)|*.mdb|All Files|*.*** in the Filter text box.

5 Make sure the value for the FilterIndex property is **0**, its default setting.

6 Click the **CancelError** check box to select it.

7 Click **OK** to close the Property Pages and apply the properties to the CommonDialog control instance.

Now that you have set the properties for the CommonDialog control, you need to call a method to display the appropriate dialog. The user will not interact with the CommonDialog control.

Displaying the Open Dialog on the Screen

Next, you must write the code that will display the Open dialog when the user makes a File | Open menu selection. One of six standard dialogs is displayed, depending upon which of several methods is called.

When the CommonDialog's ShowOpen method is called, a dialog similar to the one shown in Figure 9-21 will appear on the screen.

DialogTitle property value displayed in title bar

InitDir property displayed in Look in list box

no default file name selected

Filter property determines Files of type

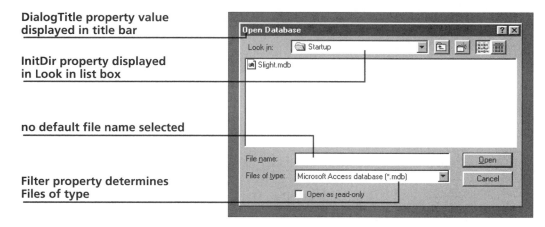

Figure 9-21: File Open dialog

Unlike with other controls you have used, the user does not interact with the instance of the CommonDialog control you created on the form. Instead, the dialog opens when your program calls one of the methods applicable to the control. The CommonDialog control supports six methods, each of which displays a different dialog when it is called. Figure 9-22 describes these different methods.

Method	Description
ShowColor	Specifies different colors for objects
ShowFont	Specifies different fonts for text
ShowHelp	Displays help information
ShowOpen	Opens files
ShowPrinter	Prints files
ShowSave	Saves files

Figure 9-22: Methods of the CommonDialog control

In this section, you are using the CommonDialog control to open an existing database, so you need to call the ShowOpen method. When this method is called, the Open dialog will appear on the screen. The CommonDialog control's windows are modal, just like a message box or input box. That is, the user must either select a file to open or click the Cancel button before interacting with the other forms in the program. Because you set the CancelError property to True, a run-time error will occur if the user clicks the Cancel button in the CommonDialog control. You therefore need to write an error handler. If the user specifies a file name, the database should open; otherwise, the code to open the database should not execute.

To call the ShowOpen method:

1 Activate the Code window for the **mnuFileOpen_Click** event procedure. (Remember that you can click Open on the File menu while in design mode to activate the Code window for this event procedure.)

2 Enter the following statements in the Code window:

```
On Error GoTo ErrorHandler
    cdlOne.ShowOpen
    Exit Sub
ErrorHandler:
```

When the program calls the ShowOpen method, Visual Basic will display the Open dialog created by the CommonDialog control so that the user can select the desired file name. The Open dialog closes when the user clicks the OK or Cancel button.

The CommonDialog control does not actually open a file for you. Rather, it provides a way for the user to specify a file name to be opened. You still must write the code that will connect the program to the user-specified database file. To accomplish this task, you set the DatabaseName and RecordSource properties of each Data control at run time and then call the Refresh method to create the recordset.

When the user selects a file name using the Open dialog, which appears when the CommonDialog control's ShowOpen method is called, that file name is stored in the FileName property of the CommonDialog control. You can use this value to set the DatabaseName property of each Data control. You then need to call the Refresh method to load the information correctly into the recordset.

To open a database at run time:

1 Make sure the Code window for the **mnuFileOpen_Click** event procedure still is active.

2 Enter the following statements (shown in bold) in the event procedure:

```
On Error GoTo ErrorHandler
    cdlOne.ShowOpen
    datEvents.DatabaseName = cdlOne.FileName
    datEvents.Refresh
    datRegistration.DatabaseName = cdlOne.FileName
    Exit Sub
ErrorHandler:
End Sub
```

These statements set the current database to the file name indicated by the user. If no file name is selected (that is, the user clicked the Cancel button), a run-time error will occur and no file will open.

Consider the code you just typed to explicitly open a database selected by the user:

```
datEvents.DatabaseName = cdlOne.FileName
datEvents.Refresh
```

The first statement takes the file name stored in the FileName property of the CommonDialog control and stores it in the DatabaseName property of the first Data control. The second statement calls the Refresh method of the Data control. It refreshes the recordset, so that the records in the database table are loaded into the recordset.

Consider the following line of code:

```
datRegistration.DatabaseName = cdlOne.FileName
```

This statement selects the database for the data control bound to the DBGrid control. The recordset for this control will be refreshed when the user selects an event description from the DBList control.

Using the Controls Collection

In the current version of your program, all the control instances are visible even though the user has not selected a database to open. Starlight Events wants the visible controls to remain hidden until the user successfully opens a database. Only then should the control instances become visible. One way to accomplish this task is to set the Visible property to True for each control individually after the database loads. A collection called the Controls collection contains a reference to one Control object for each control instance created on a form. Even though Starlight Events' form has only a few visible objects, the following discussion in this section will serve to illustrate the use of the Controls collection.

The Controls collection works like other collections you have encountered in earlier chapters. This zero-based collection contains a reference to Control objects. For each control instance created on a form, there exists one Control object in the Controls collection. The Controls collection has one property, Count, which specifies the number of Control objects in the collection.

Syntax	*object*.**Controls**(*index*)
Dissection	■ The *object* can be any form in your program.
	■ One **Controls** collection exists for each form. If you omit the object, the current form is assumed.
	■ The *index* can be a numeric index, starting at zero (0), or a string key. The string key for a control instance is the same as the Name property of the control instance.

Instead of writing several statements to make each control instance on a form visible or invisible, you can write a For Each loop to examine each control in the Controls collection. Inside this loop, you will determine the type of control and set the Visible property as necessary.

Before writing this loop, your program must determine the type of control involved. Each menu item is a Control object in the Controls collection. If you set the Visible property to False for all controls, then the menus would also become invisible. A Visual Basic keyword, called TypeOf, allows you to determine the type of any object. This keyword is used in an If statement and has the following syntax:

Syntax	**If TypeOf** *objectname* **Is** *objecttype* **Then**
	    [*statements*]
	End If

Dissection	■ The *objectname* can be any object reference. For example, the *objectname* could be an instance of a control drawn on the form or an object variable.
	■ The *objecttype* is any valid type of object, including objects you draw on a form, DAO objects, or any other type of object. The type of a menu title or menu item is "menu", and the type of a command button is "CommandButton".
Code Example	```If TypeOf control Is Menu Then` ` ' statements to execute if the control is a menu.` `End If```
Code Dissection	The preceding If statement uses a placeholder, *control*, to determine whether the current control type is a menu. If it is, then the statements inside the If statement execute. Otherwise, they do not execute.

For Starlight Events' project, you will make all objects (except for the menu items) invisible when the program starts. When a database opens, the DBCombo and DBGrid controls should become visible. This strategy will improve the user interface because the user will not be able to select an event or work with event registrations until he or she has opened the database.

You could write one For Each loop in the Form_Load event procedure to make the control instances invisible and another For Each loop in the mnuFileOpen event procedure to make the control instances visible when the database opens. Because these loops are identical, however, it will take less code overall to create a general procedure that accepts one argument: a Boolean value to determine whether the controls should become visible or invisible.

To write the general procedure to make the controls visible or invisible:

1 Make sure that the Code window is active.

2 Create a general procedure having the name **SetVisible**, the scope **Private**, and the type **Sub**.

3 Enter the following statements into the general procedure:

```
Private Sub SetVisible(pblnArg As Boolean)
Dim pctlCurrent As Control
    For Each pctlCurrent In Controls
        If Not (TypeOf pctlCurrent Is Data _
            Or TypeOf pctlCurrent Is CommonDialog _
            Or TypeOf pctlCurrent Is Menu) Then
            pctlCurrent.Visible = pblnArg
        End If
    Next
End Sub
```

This Sub procedure sets the Visible property of each control in the Controls collection to True or False depending on the value of the argument pblnArg.

Consider the following lines of code to examine the control instances on the form:

```
Dim pctlCurrent As Control
For Each pctlCurrent In Controls
```

The first statement creates a local variable of type Control for use as the member in the For Each loop. The For Each loop examines each control in the Controls collection. Each time through the loop, a reference to the current Control object is stored in the variable pctlCurrent. You can reference pctlCurrent just like any other control instance drawn on the form. That is, you can set or read its properties and call its methods.

Consider the following code to determine the type of control:

```
If Not (TypeOf pctlCurrent Is Data _
    Or TypeOf pctlCurrent Is CommonDialog _
    Or TypeOf pctlCurrent Is Menu) Then
        pctlCurrent.Visible = pblnArg
End If
```

This If statement uses the TypeOf keyword to determine the type of control stored in the variable pctlCurrent. Three types of controls should not have their Visible property changed at run time: the Menu objects, the Data controls, and the CommonDialog control. Consequently, your If statement tested whether the control type matches one of these three types. The Not keyword causes the Visible property to be set if it finds a match. Note that the CommonDialog control does not support the Visible property. If you try to set the Visible property for the CommonDialog control, a run-time error will occur.

You now need to write the statements to call this general procedure when the form loads so that the objects will be invisible. To accomplish this task, you will call the general procedure you just wrote with the argument False when the form loads. You will also call the procedure with the argument True when a database opens successfully, allowing the control instances to become visible.

To make the objects invisible when the form loads and visible when a database opens:

1 Activate the Code window for the **Form_Load** event procedure and enter the following statement:

```
Call SetVisible(False)
```

2 Activate the Code window for the **mnuFileOpen_Click** event procedure and enter the following statement (shown in bold) just after the ShowOpen method is called:

```
cdlOne.ShowOpen
Call SetVisible(True)
```

These statements make the controls invisible when the form first loads and visible after a database opens. You can now test the program again to verify that it works properly.

To verify that the controls are visible and invisible at the proper times:

1 Save and run the program. Note that the menus are the only objects visible on the form when the program first starts.

2 Click **File**, then click **Open** on the form's menu bar.

3 Select the file name **Slight.mdb** in the **Chapter.09\Startup** folder. Set the drive designator as necessary. The bound DBCombo and DBGrid control instances, command buttons, and labels should become visible.

4 End the program to return to design mode.

In a further improvement of the user interface, Starlight Events would like the user to be able to customize the font and font size for the text appearing in the DBCombo and DBGrid objects.

Understanding Screen and Printer Fonts

Fonts are classified as either screen or printer fonts. While some common fonts are installed on nearly all computers, some computers have unique fonts that may not always be available on other machines. The printer fonts available to a system depend on the type of printer and the fonts installed on the printer. Be aware that the screen and printer fonts supported may differ from system to system.

You can determine the fonts available on your system by looking at the following two objects:

- The **Screen** object allows you to manipulate the form and control instances on the screen.
- The **Printer** object represents the default printer on the system.

Each object supports two properties that allow you to determine the fonts applicable to each object:

- The **FontCount** property returns the number of fonts available for the screen or active printer.
- The **Fonts** property returns a list that works much like a zero-based collection. You reference a specific font name by supplying a numeric index from 0 to FontCount - 1.

Thus, if you want to print all the screen fonts on the system to the Immediate window, you could use the following For loop:

```
Dim pintCount As Integer
For pintCount = 0 To Screen.FontCount - 1
    Debug.Print Screen.Fonts(pintCount)
Next
```

This For loop steps through each of the screen fonts and prints the name of the font to the Immediate window.

Starlight Events wants each user to have the opportunity to change the font used in the DBCombo and DBGrid controls. Both controls support the Font object, which in turn supports the following properties:

- The **Bold** property can be True or False. If set to True, the font is boldface. Otherwise, it is not.
- The **Italic** property can be True or False. If set to True, the font is italic. Otherwise, it is not.

Programming tip

The Fonts property is not a collection of Font objects. It merely returns a list of the fonts installed; therefore, you cannot use a For Each loop to iterate through the list.

- The **Name** property identifies the name of the font. The list of available fonts may vary from computer to computer.
- The **Size** property identifies the size of the font in points.
- The **StrikeThrough** property can be True or False. If True, a line is drawn through the font. If False, no line is drawn.
- The **Underline** property can be True or False. If True, the font is underlined. If False, the font is not underlined.

Using the Font object and these properties, you can change the current font and attributes of the DBCombo box. The following statement sets the size of the font in the DBCombo box named dbcEvents to 10 points:

```
dbcEvents.Font.Size = 10
```

Note the syntax of this statement. You are referencing the Font object pertaining to the object named dbcEvents. The Font object, in turn, supports the Size property.

At run time, users should be able to select a menu item to display the common dialog applicable to fonts. When the user selects a font or its attributes, the font appears in both the DBGrid and DBList control instances. You can write code to display the Font dialog for the user by calling the ShowFont method pertaining to the CommonDialog control. You can then use the following properties to set the font for other visible objects on the form:

- The **FontBold** property can be True or False, indicating that the font should appear in a boldface or standard typeface.
- The **FontItalic** property can be True or False, indicating that the font should appear italicized or normal.
- The **FontStrikethru** property can be True or False, indicating whether the font should appear with a line through each character.
- The **FontUnderline** property can be True or False, indicating whether the font should be underlined.
- The **FontName** property identifies the name of the font.
- The **FontSize** property identifies the size of the font in points.

When you use the CommonDialog control with the ShowFont method, you must first set the Flags property to tell the CommonDialog control whether you want to display screen fonts, printer fonts, or both. The Flags properties can have the following values:

- If set to **cdlCFScreenFonts**, only the screen fonts will appear in the Font dialog.
- If set to **cdlCFPrinterFonts**, only the printer fonts will appear in the Font dialog.
- If set to **cdlCFBoth**, then both the printer and screen fonts will appear in the Font dialog.

Before calling the ShowFont method, you must set the Flags property to one of these values; otherwise, a run-time error will occur. In addition to these values, several other flags can be set to control the font's appearance in the CommonDialog control. For more information, see the Help information on the Flags property for the Font dialog.

After you set the Flags property for the CommonDialog control and call the ShowOpen method, you need to use the relevant properties of the CommonDialog control to set the font characteristics of both the DBCombo and DBGrid controls. Because you are working with several properties, you must write an assignment statement for each one. That is, you will need to write the following statements to set the properties for the DBCombo box:

```
dbcEvents.Font.Bold = cdlOne.FontBold
dbcEvents.Font.Italic = cdlOne.FontItalic
dbcEvents.Font.Name = cdlOne.FontName
dbcEvents.Font.Size = cdlOne.FontSize
```

The With statement provides a way to select an object and apply it to many statements.

Using the With Statement

The With statement allows you to specify a series of statements to act on a specific object without specifying the name of the object. The With statement has the following syntax:

Syntax	**With** *object* 　　　　[*statements*] **End With**
Dissection	■ The *object* can be the name of any object. ■ One or more *statements* can be executed on the object. ■ Between the With and End With statements, you can nest additional With statements.

Code Example	```With dbcEvents```
	``` .Font.Bold = cdlOne.FontBold```
	``` .Font.Italic = cdlOne.FontItalic```
	``` . . .```
	```End With```

Code Dissection	Using a With statement, the preceding statements reference the various Font properties of the DBCombo box named dbcEvents.

Because each statement uses the Font object, you can modify the preceding With statement as follows to reduce typing:

```
With dbcEvents.Font
    .Bold = cdlOne.FontBold
    .Italic = cdlOne.FontItalic
    . . .
End With
```

You should now write the statements to change the font for both the DBCombo and DBGrid controls using the ShowFont method for the CommonDialog control and a With statement.

To change the font of the visible objects:

1 Activate the Code window for the **mnuOptionsFonts_Click** event procedure.

2 Enter the following statements into the event procedure:

```
cdlOne.Flags = cdlCFScreenFonts
cdlOne.ShowFont
With dbcEvents.Font
    .Bold = cdlOne.FontBold
    .Italic = cdlOne.FontItalic
    .Name = cdlOne.FontName
    .Size = cdlOne.FontSize
End With
With dbgRegistration.Font
    .Bold = cdlOne.FontBold
    .Italic = cdlOne.FontItalic
    .Name = cdlOne.FontName
    .Size = cdlOne.FontSize
End With
```

Now that you have written the statements to change the font and font characteristics of the two visible objects, you can test the program to verify that the font works properly.

To verify that the user can change the font of the visible objects:

1 Save and run the program. Click **File**, click **Open**, then select the database named **Slight.mdb** in the Open dialog. Click **Open** to open this database.

2 Click **Options**, then click **Fonts** on the form's menu bar to open the Font dialog.

3 Select a font, style, and size. Click **OK**. The font should appear in both the DBCombo and DBGrid controls.

4 End the program and exit Visual Basic.

You now have completed the program for Starlight Events. The user can add, change, and delete records in the DBGrid control. In addition, he or she can open any database by using the CommonDialog control's Open dialog. Finally, the user can customize the interface by changing the fonts.

S U M M A R Y

To make an ActiveX control available to a project:

■ Click Project, then click Components to activate the dialog. Check the ActiveX controls you want to add to the project.

To display multiple records with the DBCombo or DBList controls:

■ Create an instance of the Data control and set the DatabaseName and RecordSource properties.
■ Create an instance of the DBCombo or DBList control.
■ Set the RowSource property to the name of the Data control.
■ Set the ListField to the field you want displayed in the DBCombo or DBList box.
■ Set the BoundColumn property, if desired, so that the BoundText property will be loaded at run time.

To display multiple rows and columns with the DBGrid control:

■ Create an instance of the Data control and set the DatabaseName and RecordSource properties.
■ Create an instance of the DBGrid control.
■ Set the DataSource property to the name of the Data control.

To locate records programmatically using the DBGrid control:

■ Assuming that the DBGrid control is bound to an instance of a Data control, call the recordset's navigational methods, such as MoveFirst or MoveLast.

To add, change, or delete records using the DBGrid control:

■ Using the Property Pages, set the AllowAddNew, AllowUpdate, and AllowDelete properties.

To validate data with the DBGrid control:

■ Write code for the BeforeColUpdate and/or BeforeColInsert events. If the data is not valid, set the Cancel argument to True.

To create an Open dialog:

■ Create an instance of the Common Dialog control.
■ Set DialogTitle property to the caption that should appear in the title bar of the dialog.
■ Set the InitDir property to the directory that will be initially scanned for files.
■ Set the Filter property so as to restrict the files that are displayed.
■ Call the ShowOpen method pertaining to the Common Dialog control.

To use the Controls collection:

■ Create an object variable of type Control.
■ Create a For Each loop to examine each control in the Controls collection.
■ To restrict which controls are used, create an If statement using the TypeOf keyword.

To create a With statement, use the following syntax:

With *object*
    [*statements*]
End With

To examine screen and printer fonts:

- Create a For loop that begins at zero and continues to FontCount − 1.
- Use the value as an index to the Fonts list.

Q U E S T I O N S

1. Which of the following is a valid flag for the Open dialog?
   a. cdlOFNCreatePrompt
   b. cdlFileExists
   c. cdlChangeDir
   d. cdlPathExists
   e. All of the above.

2. Which of the following is a valid method of the Common Dialog?
   a. Open
   b. Save
   c. Print
   d. All of the above.
   e. None of the above.

3. Write the necessary statement to store the value "ABC" in the first column of the DBGrid control named dbgDemo.

4. Write the statement to set the filter for the CommonDialog control instance named cdlDemo to display text files with the suffix .txt.

5. Write the statement to display the Open dialog for the CommonDialog control instance named cdlDemo.

6. Write a loop to print the contents of the Name property for all control instances on a form.

7. Write the statement(s) to determine if the control named ctlCurrent is a text box. If it is, print the Text property to the Immediate window.

8. Write a loop to print all of the Printer fonts to the Immediate window.

9. Assuming that lblCurrent is an instance of the Label object, create a With statement to set the Top and Left properties to 100, and set the Caption property to "Demo".

10. Create an event procedure to confirm that the user wants to delete a record from the DBGrid control by using a message box.

E X E R C I S E S

1. Color Graphics, a graphic arts company, has several different computers and printers in its office. Each of these computers has different screen and printer fonts available. The company would like you to write a program to display in list boxes each of the available screen and printer fonts on a specific computer. When complete, your form should look like Figure 9-23.

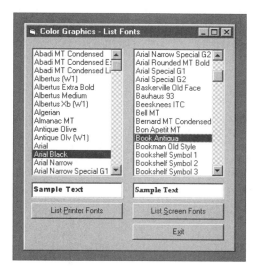

Figure 9-23: Exercise 1 – completed form

   a. Run the executable file named **Chapter.09\Exercise\Ex1.exe**. Set the drive designator as necessary. Click the **List Printer Fonts** command button. The fonts supported by the default printer appear in the list box. Click the **List Screen Fonts** list box. The screen fonts appear in the list box. In each list box, click on different fonts. As you click on each font, the font appears in the text box below the list box. End the program.
   b. Start Visual Basic and create a new project, if necessary.
   c. Set the caption of the form to **Color Graphics - List Fonts**, and set the name of the form to **frmColorGraphicsListFonts**.
   d. Save the form using the name **Chapter.09\Exercise\frmEx1.frm** and the project using the name **Chapter.09\Exercise\Ex1.vbp**. Set the drive designator as necessary.
   e. Create two command buttons on the form, as shown in Figure 9-23. Set the caption of the first command button to **List Printer Fonts** and the caption of the second command button to **List Screen Fonts**. Set the name of each command button as appropriate.
   f. Create a third command button to exit the program, and write the necessary code to exit the program when the user clicks this button.
   g. Create two list boxes named **lstPrinterFonts** and **lstScreenFonts**. The contents of each list box should appear in sorted order.

h. Create two text boxes below the list boxes, as shown in Figure 9-23.

i. In the **Click** event procedure for the **List Printer Fonts** command button, write a For loop to display each printer font in the List Printer Fonts list box. (Remember that you use the AddItem method to add an item to a list box at run time.) The printer fonts are stored in the Fonts property of the Printer object. The Fonts property is used with an index ranging from 0 to FontCount - 1.

j. In the **Click** event procedure for the **List Screen Fonts** command button, write a For loop to display each screen font in the corresponding list box. The fonts appear in the Fonts property of the Screen object.

k. Write the necessary code for each list box's **Click** event procedure so that when the user selects a font, the string Sample text appears in the corresponding text box in the selected font.

l. Test the program to verify that the appropriate fonts are loaded into the list boxes when the user clicks the corresponding command button. Also verify that when the user selects a font in one of the list boxes, the font name appears in that font in the text box below the list box.

m. Save the project, then exit Visual Basic.

2. Data Helpers is a consulting company that helps different businesses manage their data. One of the first tasks it performs is to examine the tables in an existing database, then the contents of those tables. The firm wants you to write a program that will allow the user to select a database to open. When a database is selected, the program should display each of the tables in that database. When a table is selected, each of the rows and columns should be displayed in a DBGrid. When complete, the form should resemble Figure 9-24.

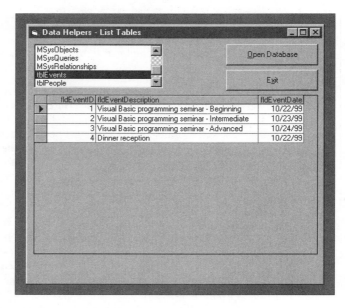

Figure 9-24: Exercise 2 – completed form

a. Run the executable file named **Chapter.09\Exercise\Ex2.exe**. Set the drive designator as necessary. Click the **Open Database** command button. Select the database named **Env.mdb** in the **Chapter.09\Exercise** folder. The tables in the database appear in the list box at the upper-left corner of the form. Click on the table named **tblCities** in the list box. The fields in the table appear in the DBGrid control instance. Do not select the tables with the prefix MSys. These are system tables and cannot be edited. End the program.

b. Start Visual Basic and create a new project, if necessary.

c. Set the form name to **frmDataHelpers**, and change the form's caption as shown in Figure 9-24.

d. Save the form using the name **Chapter.09\Exercise\frmEx2.frm** and the project using the name **Chapter.09\Exercise\Ex2.vbp**. Set the drive designator as necessary.

e. Add the **CommonDialog** and **DBGrid** controls to the project.

f. Create an instance of the CommonDialog control on the form and set the name of the object to **cdlOne**.

g. Using the correct Property Pages for the Open dialog, set the caption to **Open Database** and the initial directory to **Chapter.09\Exercise**. Set the drive designator as necessary. Set the Filter such that it locates only files with the extension ".mdb". If the user clicks the Cancel button, the CommonDialog control should generate a run-time error.

h. Create an instance of the Data control on the form and set the Name to **datAny**. Make the Data control invisible at run time.

i. Create a DBGrid control on the form and set the name to **dbgAny**. Connect this DBGrid control to the Data control you just created.

j. Create a list box on the form named **lstTables**.

k. Create two command buttons: one to open the database, and one to exit the program. Set the captions as shown in Figure 9-24.

l. Create two form-level variables: **mdbCurrent** with type Database, and **mdbTableDef** with type TableDef.

m. Write the necessary code to call the ShowOpen method pertaining to the CommonDialog control when the user clicks the Open command button. Because you set the properties such that clicking the Cancel button will generate a run-time error, you need to write an error handler for this procedure. If the user did not select a file, your code should exit the procedure. Write the necessary statement to open the database specified by the user if a run-time error does not occur. You need to call the OpenDatabase method on the file name returned by the CommonDialog control. Next, write a For Each loop to examine each table in the TableDefs collection of the database. For each table, add the name of the table to the list box. To accomplish this task, you can use the Name property of the current TableDef object.

n. When the user clicks a table in the list box, the contents of the table should be displayed in the DBGrid control. Set the necessary properties of the Data control to connect to the selected database and to a table in the database, then refresh the recordset. Because the DBGrid control is set up to connect to the Data control, all records in the selected table should be displayed.

o. Test the program by opening the database named **Env.mdb** in the **Chapter.09\Exercise** folder. Set the drive designator as necessary. The tables should appear in the list box. Click a table in the list box. The contents of the table should be displayed in the DBGrid control.

p. Save the program, then exit Visual Basic.

3. Intex Electronics is an electronics manufacturer. It makes memory and other chips for use in personal and other computers. The firm wants you to create a prototype form to examine pending orders and enter new orders. The final form will eventually interact with the company's database; this prototype form, however, will not. Figure 9-25 shows the completed form.

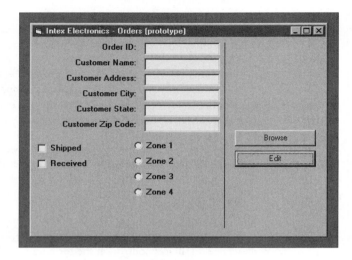

Figure 9-25: Exercise 3 – completed form

The form will operate in two modes as follows:
- In browse mode, all option buttons, text boxes, and check boxes should be disabled because they are used to add, change, and delete records only.
- In edit mode, the buttons and boxes should be enabled.

a. Run the executable file named **Chapter.09\Exercise\Ex3.exe**. Set the drive designator as necessary. Click the **Browse** button. The controls on the form are disabled. Click the **Edit** button. The controls on the form are enabled. End the program.

b. Start Visual Basic and create a new project, if necessary.

c. Set the form name to **frmIntexElectronics** and change the form's caption as shown in Figure 9-25.

d. Save the form using the name **Chapter.09\Exercise\frmEx3.frm** and the project using the name **Chapter.09\Exercise\Ex3.vbp.** Set the drive designator as necessary.

e. Create the labels, text boxes, command buttons, and option buttons shown in Figure 9-25. The option buttons should be members of a control array.

f. Create the necessary procedures and call them so that when the user clicks the Browse command button, the following will occur: If the type of the control is an option button, check box, or text box, the program should disable the button; if the control type is a label, it should change the font from bold to normal. When the user clicks the Edit button, the program should enable each option button, check box, and text box. It should also change the font of the label from normal to bold.

g. Save and test the project to verify that the control instances are enabled and disabled properly.

h. Exit Visual Basic.

4. Leopard Foods is a wholesale food distributor. The company would like you to create a form to help manage its inventory. Leopard Foods buys products directly from the manufacturers. The company therefore has the table tblManufacturer in the database called Leopard.mdb in the Chapter.09\Exercise folder. Each manufacturer has several products stored in the table tblProducts. These two tables are linked with the common field fldManufacturerID. Leopard Foods wants you to create a new form with two parts. The first part of the form should contain several bound text boxes to display information pertinent to the manufacturer. You need to use the Data control to navigate through the data for each manufacturer. Because this information will change, the program should disable the text boxes during this browse operation. Whenever a manufacturer is selected via a button on the Data control, the corresponding products should appear in the DBGrid control instance on the form. The user should be able to add, change, and delete records in the DBGrid control. When records are added or changed, the program should validate each input field. When records are deleted, it should display a message box to confirm the deletion. Figure 9-26 shows the completed form.

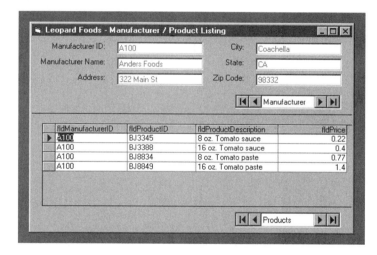

Figure 9-26: Exercise 4 – completed form

a. Run the executable file named **Chapter.09\Exercise\Ex4.exe.** Set the drive designator as necessary. Using the buttons on the Data control at the top of the form, move forward and backward to navigate through the recordset. As you locate different records, the corresponding records will appear in the DBGrid control at the bottom of the form. End the program.

b. Start Visual Basic and create a new project, if necessary.

c. Set the form name to **frmLeopard** and change the form's caption as shown in Figure 9-26.

d. Save the form using the name **Chapter.09\Exercise\frmEx4.frm** and the project using the name **Chapter.09\Exercise\Ex4.vbp.** Set the drive designator as necessary.

e. Make the DBGrid control available to the project.

f. Create the labels, text boxes, Data controls, and DBGrid control instance as shown in Figure 9-26.

g. For the Data control in the top section of the form, set the necessary properties to connect to the table named **tblManufacturer** in the database named **Leopard.mdb**.

h. Bind the text boxes at the top of the form so that they display the fields in the table named **tblManufacturer.**

i. For the Data control in the bottom section of the form, set the necessary properties to connect to the table named **tblProducts** in the database named **Leopard.mdb.**

j. Write the necessary code so that when the Data control representing the manufacturer is repositioned, the corresponding products will appear in the DBGrid. To accomplish this task, create a SQL SELECT statement that will select all of the products from the table named **tblProducts** when the field **fldManufacturerID** is the same as the manufacturer ID stored in the text box at the top of the form.

k. Create the necessary event procedures and set the necessary properties for the DBGrid control to allow deletion and to obtain confirmation from the user that a record should actually be deleted via a message box.

l. Create the necessary event procedure and set the properties so that if the user attempts to update the Price column in the DBGrid control, the program will validate the value to ensure that it contains a number.

m Test the project.

n. Save the project again, then exit Visual Basic.

Windows Common Controls

Creating a Part-Management System for Power Parts

case ▶ Power Programming Systems develops and sells computer software. The company is creating a comprehensive software package consisting of several utility programs. One utility program required comprises a text editor with the ability to create, open, and save files, as well as to apply formatting to the text. The formatting characteristics include setting the font and the font size; they also include font attributes such as setting the text to bold, italic, or underline. In addition, the user must be able to justify text. The program design requirements include the utilization of common programming elements such as a menu system, toolbars, and status bars.

Previewing the Completed Application

The completed application uses several new controls. A toolbar allows the user to execute many of the same commands found on the menu bar. A status bar indicates the state of specific keyboard keys. A rich text box displays formatted text. Figure 10-1 shows the control instances on the completed form.

justification buttons

toolbar with buttons

rich text box

status bar

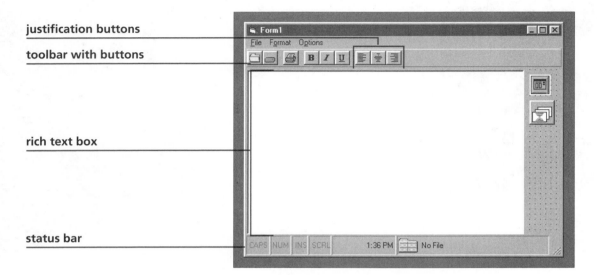

Figure 10-1: Completed form

To preview the completed application:

1 Start Visual Basic and open the project file named **Chapter.10\Complete\PPS_C.vbp**. Set the drive designator as necessary.

2 Run the program. Click **File**, then click **Open** on the menu bar. This menu item uses the CommonDialog control to open a file. Open the file named **Chapter.10\Complete\Demo.rtf**, again setting the drive designator as necessary.

3 Select the first line of text. Use the Bold, Italic, and Underline buttons on the toolbar to format this text.

4 Click the justification buttons to justify the text. As you click each button, the selected text becomes left-justified, centered, or right-justified.

5 Click **Format** on the menu bar, then click **Fonts**. The Font dialog should appear. Select a font and size, then click the **OK** button. The font attributes are applied to the selected text.

6 Resize the form. When the form is resized, the size of the rich text box changes to fill the region of the form.

7 Press the **Caps Lock, Num Lock, Insert,** and **Scroll Lock** keys on your keyboard. Note that the actual labels on these keys will vary depending on your keyboard. As each key is enabled or disabled, the status bar changes to show the updated state of each key. When a key is disabled, the status bar entry for that key appears shaded. When a key is enabled, the status bar entry for that key appears in a normal font.

8 Click **File**, then click **Exit** to end the program.

9 Exit Visual Basic.

In this section you will:

- Learn about the Windows Common Controls
- Create a status bar on a form
- Create a toolbar on a form using two new controls, the ImageList and Toolbar
- Apply formatting to text with the RichTextBox control

Using the Windows Common Controls

Introduction to the Windows Common Controls

Visual Basic supports a group of ActiveX controls called Microsoft Windows Common Controls. These controls, which are tightly coupled with the Windows interface, allow you to create, for example, toolbars and status bars that function much like the toolbars and status bars in other programs. The Microsoft Windows Common Controls include the TabStrip, Toolbar, StatusBar, ProgressBar, TreeView, ListView, ImageList, Slider, and ImageCombo controls.

With every ActiveX control, you must add the respective control reference to the project file before the control will appear in the toolbox and be available for use. In this section, you will use several ActiveX controls. You will add them to the project file all at once to save time. If necessary, however, you could add them individually.

To add the ActiveX controls to the project:

1 Start Visual Basic and open the project **Chapter.10\Startup\PPS_S.vbp**. Set the drive designator as necessary. Open the form window. Figure 10-2 shows the partially completed form. The menu system and common dialog have already been added to the form.

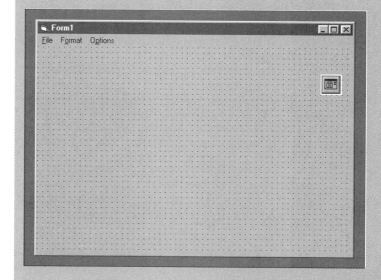

Figure 10-2: Partially completed form

Programming

tip

• • • • • • • • • • • • • •

The Microsoft Windows Common Controls are available only with the Professional and Enterprise editions of Visual Basic. The file MSComctl.ocx must exist on the computer to develop or run programs using the Microsoft Windows Common Controls 6.0. The file Richtx32.ocx must be present to use the RichTextBox control.

2 Click **Project**, then click **Components** on the menu bar to open the Components dialog. Verify that the Controls tab is selected.

3 Use the scroll bars to locate the **Microsoft Windows Common Controls 6.0** in the list box, then click the check box. Depending upon the configuration of your computer, another version of these controls may be present. Be sure not to select Microsoft Windows Common Controls 5.0. These controls were designed to operate with Visual Basic 5.0 and may not support all the properties and methods used in this chapter.

4 Click the check box for the **Microsoft Rich Textbox Control 6.0**.

5 Click **OK** to add the controls to the toolbox and close the Components dialog. This project also uses the CommonDialog control introduced in Chapter 9. This control has already been added to the project.

Now that you have added the necessary ActiveX controls to the project, you will continue the program's development by adding a status bar to the form.

Using the Status Bar Control

Many programs, such as Microsoft Word and Excel, support a status bar as a user interface element. A status bar typically appears at the bottom of a form and is commonly used to display information pertaining to the state of the program or of specific keys on the keyboard. For example, you can create a status bar that indicates the status of keys like Caps Lock, Insert, and others. You can also display information such as the time of day. To create a status bar, you use the StatusBar control, which is one of the Microsoft Windows Common Controls.

A status bar is divided into regions called **panels**. Each panel can contain text and/or a picture. A panel is implemented as a Panel object in the Panels collection (a one-based collection). As with most collections, you employ either a numeric index or a string key to reference a Panel object in the Panels collection. At design time, you add and remove individual panels through the control's Property Pages. The tabs on the Property Pages define the general characteristics of the status bar and the characteristics of each panel on the status bar. Like the objects in any other collection, Panel objects can be added and removed at run time using the Add and Remove methods pertaining to the collection. The standard prefix for the StatusBar is "sbr".

Syntax	**StatusBar**
Properties	■ The **Panels** property contains a reference to the Panels collection. The Panels collection, in turn, stores a reference to each Panel object used in the status bar.
	■ The **Style** property can be set to one of two constant values. If set to the constant value sbrSimple, the status bar appears as one large panel encompassing the entire region of the status bar. If set to sbrNormal (the default), the status bar displays all the Panel objects.
	■ The **SimpleText** property contains a text string that appears in the status bar only when the Style property is set to sbrSimple. Setting the Style property to sbrNormal causes this property to be ignored.

Events	■ The **PanelClick** event occurs when the user clicks any panel on the status bar. A reference to that panel is passed as an argument to the event procedure, allowing your program to respond accordingly. If a panel indicates the status of something, like a field being edited, responding to this event allows your program to change the status. In this situation, the panel works much like a command button.

After creating the status bar and setting the general properties, you create the individual panels and set the properties for each panel.

Syntax	**Panel**
Properties	■ The **AutoSize** property pertains to the Panel object and can have one of three constant values. If set to sbrNoAutosize, the panel has a fixed size. If set to sbrSpring, the sizes of all panels having an AutoSize property of sbrSpring are adjusted so that their widths are equal. If set to sbrContents, the size of the panel is adjusted so that the textual contents fit inside the panel. When the AutoSize property is set to sbrContents, the size will not decrease below the MinWidth property.
	■ The **Alignment** property determines the alignment of the text inside a specific panel. Text can be left-justified, centered, or right-justified.
	■ The **Bevel** property determines the appearance of the panel on the status bar. If set to sbrNoBevel, the panel appears flat on the status bar. If set to sbrInset or sbrRaised, the panel appears recessed or raised off the status bar, respectively.
	■ The **Index** and **Key** properties define the numeric index and string key used to identify a specific Panel object in the Panels collection.
	■ The **MinWidth** property is used only when the AutoSize property for the panel is set to sbrSpring or sbrContents. Its value specifies the minimum width of a particular panel.
	■ The **Style** property defines the behavior of an individual panel. This property differs from the property of the same name pertaining to the status bar itself. This Style property pertains to a Panel object, defining whether that object contains text and/or an icon. It is also used to display the status of keyboard keys like the Num Lock key, the Ins key, and the Shift key. Alternatively, the Style property can be set to display the date or time in a panel.
	■ The **Text** property contains the text displayed inside the panel.
	■ The **Width** property identifies the size of a panel.

One potential purpose of a panel on a status bar is to indicate the current state of specific keyboard keys. These indicators include whether the Caps Lock or Num Lock keys are pressed and whether the document is in Insert or Overwrite mode. By setting the Style property for a panel, you can display automatically the status of individual keyboard keys without writing any code. Figure 10-3 describes the different settings for the Style property.

sbrText	0	(Default). Text and/or a bitmap. Set text with the Text property.
sbrCaps	1	Caps Lock key. Displays the letters CAPS in bold when Caps Lock is enabled, and dimmed when disabled.
sbrNum	2	Number Lock. Displays the letters NUM in bold when the number lock key is enabled, and dimmed when disabled.
sbrIns	3	Insert key. Displays the letters INS in bold when the insert key is enabled, and dimmed when disabled.
sbrScrl	4	Scroll Lock key. Displays the letters SCRL in bold when scroll lock in enabled, and dimmed when disabled.
sbrTime	5	Time. Displays the current time in the system format.
sbrDate	6	Date. Displays the current date in the system format.
sbrKana	7	Kana. Displays the letters KANA in bold when scroll lock is enabled, and dimmed when disabled.

Figure 10-3: Panel constants pertaining to a Panel object

To create each of the Panel objects that will appear on the status bar, you will use the Panels tab on the control's Property Pages. Figure 10-4 shows the Panels tab on the Property Pages.

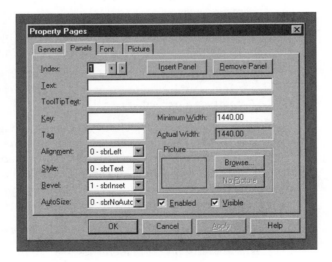

Figure 10-4: Panels Property Pages

To create a new panel, you click the Insert Panel command button. To remove a panel, you select the desired panel using the scroll bars and then click the Remove Panel command button. You can also select a specific panel by using the scroll bars and setting the individual properties as desired. To change the font of the text in the panels, you use the Fonts tab on the Property Pages. The Panels tab is also used to define any text that appears in a panel and associates a ToolTip with the panel.

To create a status bar:

1 Click the **StatusBar** control 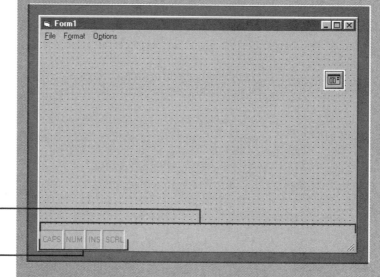 on the toolbox and create an instance of it on the form. By default, the status bar will appear across the bottom of the form.

2 Activate the Properties window for the status bar, then set the Name property to **sbrText**.

3 Set the Height property to **480**, then close the Properties window.

4 Right-click the status bar and select **Properties** from the shortcut menu to activate the Property Pages. Click the **Panels** tab. When the Panels tab first becomes activated, the Index is set to one (1) by default. This value designates the first Panel object in the Panels collection. Note that the Panels collection is a one-based collection because the first numeric index value is 1.

5 Set the Style property to **1 - sbrCaps**, the Minimum Width to **1**, and the AutoSize property to **2 - sbrContents**. When you set the minimum width of the panel, the panel's actual width may vary slightly from the width you specified.

6 Click the **Insert Panel** command button to insert a second panel. Use the scroll bars to the right of the Index text box to select Index number 2. Set the Style property to **2 - sbrNum**, the Minimum Width to **1**, and the AutoSize property to **2 - sbrContents**.

7 Click the **Insert Panel** command button again. Use the scroll bars to the right of the Index text box to select Index number 3. Set the Style property to **3 - sbrIns**, the Minimum Width to **1**, and the AutoSize property to **2 - sbrContents**.

8 Click the **Insert Panel** command button again and select Index number **4**. Set the Style property to **4 - sbrScrl**, the Minimum Width to **1**, and the AutoSize property to **2 - sbrContents**.

9 Click **OK** to apply the changes and close the Property Pages. The status bar should resemble the one shown in Figure 10-5.

status bar

4 panels

Figure 10-5: New status bar

10 Save and test the program. Press the **Caps Lock, Num Lock, Insert,** and **Scroll Lock** keys on the keyboard. As you press each key, the relevant panel on the status bar should be updated. When a key is enabled, the caption in the panel appears in a normal font. When a key is disabled, it appears shaded. End the program to return to design mode.

In addition to displaying the status of specific keyboard keys, you can display the date and time in a panel by setting the Style property to sbrDate or sbrTime. The system will automatically update the date and time; thus you do not need to write code to manually update these values.

To display the current time in the status bar:

1 Right-click the status bar and select **Properties** from the shortcut menu to activate the Property Pages. Click the **Panels** tab.

2 A new panel is inserted after the index of the currently selected panel. Use the scroll bars to select Index number **4**. Click the **Insert Panel** button to insert a new panel. Use the scroll bars to select panel number **5**.

3 Set the Alignment to **1 - sbrCenter**, the Style to **5 - sbrTime**, and the AutoSize property to **2 - sbrContents**.

4 Click **OK** to save your changes and close the Property Pages.

The StatusBar control itself will automatically update the panels you created in the status bar. You can also store text and images in the status bar. This text can be set at design time or at run time. For example, Microsoft Word places text in the status to indicate the current position within a document, while Microsoft Excel uses the status bar to inform the user when it is recalculating the spreadsheet and to provide instructional tips about what to do next. Both Word and Excel must update these values at run time as the status changes. In this chapter, you will use a text panel to indicate whether a text file is open and to list the name of the file being edited.

To create a text panel:

1 Right-click the status bar and select **Properties** from the shortcut menu to activate the Property Pages. Click the **Panels** tab.

2 Select Index number **5**, then click the **Insert Panel** button to create the new panel. Select Index number **6**.

3 Enter the character string **No File** into the Text property. Set the Style property to **0 - sbrText** and the AutoSize property to **1 - sbrSpring**.

4 Enter the character string **pnlText** into the Key property. You will later write code to use this string key to reference the panel at run time.

5 Click the **Browse** button in the Picture frame. In the Select picture dialog, select the picture named **Chapter.10\Startup\Cldsfold.ico**. Set the drive designator as necessary. Click **Open** to add the picture to the status bar.

6 Click **OK** to close the Property Pages and to update the status bar.

In addition to setting the properties pertaining to a Panel object at design time, you can write code to manipulate the contents of the status bar at run time. One common task is to update the contents of a textual panel as the program's status changes. In this chapter, you will write code to update the contents of the panel you just created using the Property Pages. This code will display the currently open file. In addition, you will write code to display a different picture to indicate that a file is indeed open. To accomplish this task, you need the ability to reference a particular Panel object in the Panels collection. The syntax involved is identical to the syntax you have used to reference other objects in other collections. Consider the following statements:

```
sbrText.Panels("pnlText").Text = "A:\Chapter.10\Startup\File.txt"
sbrText.Panels("pnlText").Picture = _
    LoadPicture "A:\Chapter.10\Startup\Openfold.ico"
```

These two statements set the text and picture of a panel in the status bar named sbrText. A panel is referenced via the Panels collection (sbrText.Panels). To reference a particular panel, you use the string key you defined when you initially created the panel. You could have also used the numeric index pertaining to the panel; thus the following statement fragment provides a reference to a Panel object in the Panels collection:

```
sbrText.Panels("pnlText")
```

Once this reference exists, you can set the properties for the particular panel. In these statements, you are resetting the Text and Picture properties, thereby altering the textual contents and the image displayed in the status bar. You will write this code later in the chapter when you open and close files. Now that you have created the status bar for the program, you will move on to another of the Windows Common Controls—the Toolbar control.

GUI

tip

Generally, each button on a toolbar should correspond to a menu item, although this one-to-one relationship is not a requirement. When a menu item is used frequently, creating a corresponding toolbar button will improve the user interface by allowing the user to gain quick access to a commonly used function.

Creating a Toolbar with the ImageList and Toolbar Controls

In earlier chapters of this book, you have used command buttons and menu items to execute Click event procedures. Command buttons are useful when a form contains only a few buttons. When the number of command buttons becomes excessive, however, menu items provide a better way to reduce form clutter. In addition to allowing the user to click command buttons and menu items to perform tasks, you can enhance a program's user interface by adding a **toolbar** to a form. Toolbars that you create in Visual Basic work like toolbars in other Windows programs. Clicking a button on the toolbar causes an event procedure to execute.

A toolbar button works much like a command button. When the user clicks the toolbar button, an event occurs; however, instead of generating a different Click event for each button, a ButtonClick event is generated for the toolbar. The code you write for the ButtonClick event procedure must first determine which button was clicked. It must then carry out the corresponding action depending on the button clicked. The buttons on a toolbar operate in one of four ways:

- A button's default behavior is to appear unpressed or raised off the surface of the toolbar and, when clicked, to appear pressed while the ButtonClick event procedure is running. When the event procedure ends, the button appears unpressed again. This type of button is well suited to tasks such as opening and saving files.
- A button can work like a toggle switch. That is, a button can appear unpressed or pressed, depending on its status. "Pressed" generally indicates on; "unpressed" generally indicates off. A toggle button is suitable for describing the status of an object, such as a font being bold or normal.
- A button can be part of a group of buttons, with only one button from the group appearing pressed at any time. Conceptually, the effect resembles the use of option buttons in an option group. This type of button is useful for describing a mutually exclusive list. For example, when aligning the text in a paragraph, the paragraph can be left-justified, right-justified, or centered, but only one option is valid at any time.
- A button can be configured to display a submenu. In this case, the button works much like a menu title on the menu bar.

It is also possible to display other control instances, such as text and combo boxes, on a toolbar. For example, you can place a list of fonts or a list of font sizes in a combo box.

When you create a toolbar in Visual Basic, you use two complementary controls:

- The **ImageList** control stores a collection of bitmap or icon images that appear on Toolbar control. The ImageList control has the standard prefix of "ils". Like the CommonDialog control, the ImageList control is not visible at run time.
- The **Toolbar** control contains a Buttons collection that stores a reference to Button objects. Each button on the toolbar represents a Button object. The icon displayed on a button corresponds to an image stored in an ImageList control. The Toolbar control has the standard prefix of "tbr".

Using the ImageList Control

The ImageList control supports the ListImages property, which stores a collection of bitmap or icon images in the ListImages collection. The ListImages collection is a one-based collection that works like other collections you have used; it stores a reference to zero or more ListImage objects. You can reference each individual ListImage object in the ListImages collection by using a numeric index or a string key. Each ListImage object usually contains a bitmap or icon. As with other ActiveX controls, you set the properties for the ImageList control by using either the Properties window or the control's Property Pages. Figure 10-6 illustrates the relationships among the ImageList control, the ListImages property, and the ListImage objects in the ListImages collection.

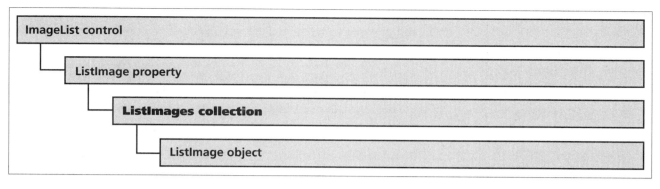

Figure 10-6: Relationship between ListImages collection and ListImage object

As Figure 10-6 demonstrates, the ImageList control supports a ListImage property, which stores a reference to the ListImages collection. This collection, in turn, stores a reference to ListImage objects. You can now create the ImageList control, set its name, and display the Property Pages.

To create an ImageList control instance:

1   Click the **ImageList** control ⬚, and draw an instance of the control on the form. Note that the ImageList control is not visible at run time, so it does not matter where you place the control instance. As with the CommonDialog control, the size of the ImageList is fixed at design time.

2   Using the Properties window, set the Name property to **ilsText.**

3   Right-click the control instance, then select **Properties** on the shortcut menu. The Property Pages appear, as shown in Figure 10-7.

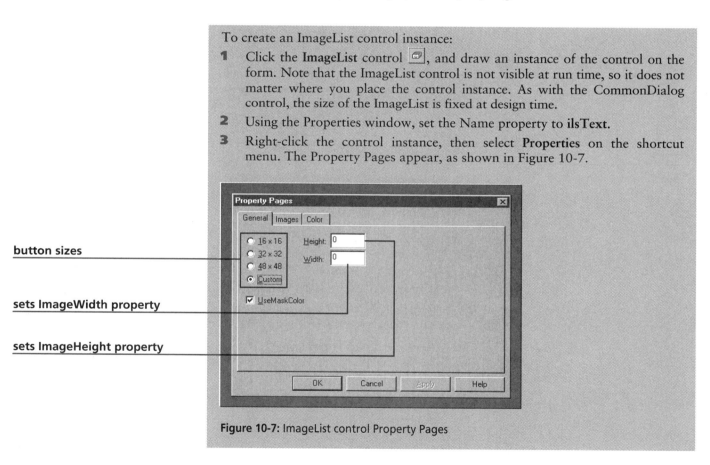

Figure 10-7: ImageList control Property Pages

As the first step in using the ImageList control, you define the height and width of each image you will ultimately store in the control instance. The General tab on the Property Pages contains the properties that apply to all images stored in the control instance. Each image must be the same size. The ImageHeight and ImageWidth properties define the height and width of each image. The values of these properties are defined in terms of pixels. You must set these properties before you add any images to the ImageList control. If you try to set either of these properties after adding an image, a dialog will appear indicating that the property is read-only—that is, indicating that you cannot change the property once images have been added to the image list. Typically, most icons are either 16 * 16 pixels or 32 * 32 pixels. The General tab on the Property Pages will allow you to select one of these default sizes or to customize the size of the icons.

In this chapter, you will use the standard 16 * 16 pixel button size. The resulting button will be the same size as the buttons found in Microsoft Word and Excel (and in many other programs).

> To set the general properties for the ImageList:
> **1** Click the **16 * 16** button on the General tab in the Property Pages.
> **2** Click the **Apply** command button in the Property Pages to apply the changes.

Once you have set the general properties, you can add each image to the ImageList control and specify the properties pertaining to each individual image. You can add the images and set their properties either at design time by using the Property Pages or at run time by writing code. When you use the Property Pages, each ListImage object is added automatically to the ListImages collection. If you perform this task at run time, you must call the Add method pertaining to the ListImages collection, then set the properties of each individual ListImage object. This method, which works much like the Add method pertaining to other collections, has the following syntax:

Syntax

object.**Add**([*index*,] [*key*,] *picture*)

Dissection

- The required *object* is the name of a ListImages collection.

- You call the **Add** method pertaining to the ListImages collection for each image you want to add.

- The optional *index* argument is an integer specifying the numeric position of the image in the collection. If this argument is omitted, the image is appended to the end of the collection.

- The optional *key* argument is a unique string that identifies each ListImage object. If you try to specify a duplicate key, an error will occur. The key argument works just like a string key for other collections.

- The required *picture* argument is the name of the picture to add to the collection. You typically load a picture with the LoadPicture function, which is the same function you used with the PictureBox control.

Code Example

```
ilsText.ListImages.Add _
    LoadPicture(1,"Print","A:\Chapter.10\Print.bmp")
ilsText.ListImages.Add _
    LoadPicture(,"Bold","A:\Chapter.10\Bold.bmp")
```

Code Dissection

Both of the preceding statements add an image to the ImageList control named ilsText. The first statement adds the image such that the numeric index is one (1) and the string key is "Print". The second statement adds the image such that the string key is "Bold". Because the code does not specify the numeric index, the image is added to the end of the ListImages collection.

Using the Property Pages, you can insert images to and remove images from the underlying ListImages collection. As shown in Figure 10-8, the Images tab in the Property Pages contains two command buttons to accomplish this task.

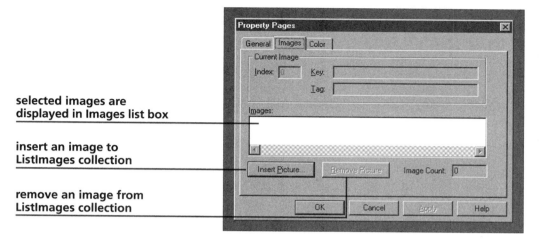

selected images are displayed in Images list box

insert an image to ListImages collection

remove an image from ListImages collection

Figure 10-8: Images Property Pages

Programming

tip

• • • • • • • • • • • • • • • •

▶ Use a string key to describe the purpose of each image. This approach will improve the program's readability.

To add an image, you click the Insert Picture command button. This button activates a common dialog, allowing you to select a bitmap or icon file. Each image added to the collection appears in the Images list box. When adding images to the Images list, you can set the Key property to the string key that you will use to reference the individual ListImage objects in the ListImages collection. As in any collection, each string key in the collection must be unique. Furthermore, string keys are case-sensitive. Thus the string key "Print" differs from the string key "print". The system automatically sets the numeric index when you add an image. Even though you can type a value into the Index text box, any changes you make will not be recorded. Rather, the Property Pages set the index value for you.

To remove ListImage objects from the collection, you use the Remove Picture command button.

You now need to add each image to the ImageList control instance. The design specification for Power Programming Systems' program requires that the user be able to execute common tasks from the toolbar. These tasks include opening, saving, and printing files. Other tasks involve describing the font and the font attributes (bold, italic, and underline). The final three tasks will left-justify, center, and right-justify text. You need to add images for each of these tasks first to the ImageList control and then to the toolbar.

To add the ListImage objects to the ImageList:

1   Activate the Property Pages for the ImageList control, if necessary. Click the **Images** tab on the Property Pages to activate it.

2   Click the **Insert Picture** command button to open the Select picture dialog.

3   Select the image named **Openfold.ico** in the **Chapter.10\Startup** folder. Set the drive designator as necessary.

4   Click the **Open** button to display the image. The dialog closes and the image appears on the Images list on the Property Pages.

5 Set the Key property to **Openfold**. Be careful to set the case of the string key properly. You will use the string key later in the chapter when you associate this image with a toolbar button.

6 Repeat Steps 2 through 5 to insert the images named **Print.bmp**, **Drive.ico**, **Bold.bmp**, **Italic.bmp**, and **Underln.bmp** with their Key properties set to **Print**, **Drive**, **Bold**, **Italic**, and **Underline**, respectively. Again, note that the Key property is case-sensitive.

7 Repeat Steps 2 through 5 to insert the images named **Left.bmp**, **Center.bmp**, and **Right.bmp**. Set their Key properties to **Left**, **Center**, and **Right**, respectively. The Images Property Page should now look like Figure 10-9.

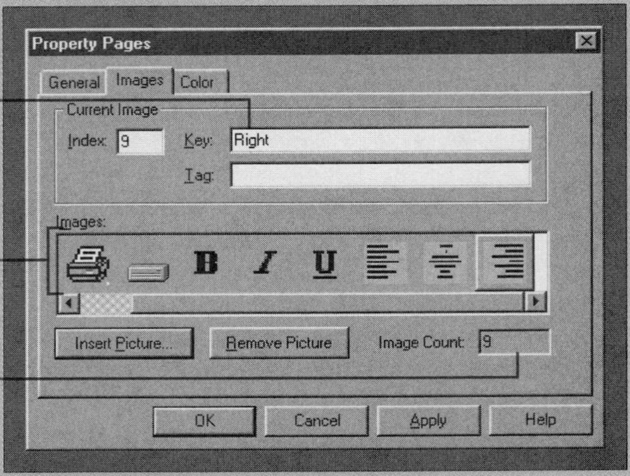

string key is set

images displayed

number of images

Figure 10-9: Adding images to the ImageList control

8 Click the **OK** command button to close the Property Pages.

After adding the images to the ImageList control, you can create the toolbar and add buttons to it. For each button, you can store a reference to an image stored in the ImageList control.

Using the Toolbar Control

When you create a toolbar on a form, it usually occupies the entire width of the form and appears underneath any existing menu. Like the ImageList control, the Toolbar control supports Property Pages with which you set design-time properties. The General tab on the Property Pages contains the properties applicable to the entire toolbar, and the Buttons tab contains the properties that pertain to each individual button.

Syntax	Toolbar

| Properties | ■ The **Align** property defines the toolbar's position on the form. Its settings work differently depending upon whether the toolbar is created on an MDI form or a non-MDI form. You will learn about MDI forms in Chapter 11. If this property is set to the constant vbAlignTop (the default value in an MDI form), the toolbar appears at the top of the form, just beneath the menu, if |

one exists. If it is set to vbAlignBottom, the toolbar appears at the bottom of the form. The width of the toolbar will match the width of the form. If the Align property is set to vbAlignLeft or vbAlignRight, the toolbar appears vertically along the left or right side of the form. If it is set to vbAlignNone, the toolbar's size and position depend on values indicated in the Properties window.

- The **Appearance** property can be set to 0 - ccFlat or 1 - cc3D. By default, it is 1- cc3D, which causes the toolbar to appear raised off the surface of the form. Otherwise, it is not raised off the form's surface. Note the BorderStyle property must be set to 1 - ccFixedSingle for the toolbar to appear raised.

- The **BorderStyle** property can be set to 0 - ccNone or 1 - ccFixedSingle. If it is set to None (the default), no border appears surrounding the toolbar. If it is set to Fixed Single, a border appears.

- The **ButtonHeight** and **ButtonWidth** properties define the height and width, respectively, of each button on the toolbar. Each button must be the same height and width.

- The **Height** and **Width** properties define the height and width, respectively, of the Toolbar object.

- The **ImageList** property is set to the name of an ImageList control instance already created on the form. Once you have bound a toolbar to an ImageList by setting the toolbar's ImageList property, you cannot delete the images in the relevant ImageList control.

- In addition to the ImageList property, you can associate the toolbar with two other ImageList control instances. The DisabledImageList property defines the images that appear when a toolbar button is disabled. The HotImageList property defines the images that appear when the user moves the mouse pointer over a particular button. When you use these properties, each ImageList must contain the same number of images with the same string keys.

- The **ShowTips** property determines whether a ToolTip is displayed for each toolbar button.

You can now create the toolbar and set its general properties. Your toolbar will appear across the top of the form. Its height should match the size of the buttons you just stored in the ImageList control. Also, the toolbar should appear raised off the form.

To set the general properties for the toolbar:
1   Click the **Toolbar** button 🔲 in the toolbox and create an instance of the toolbar on the form. The toolbar will appear across the top of the form automatically. You cannot move this object unless you change the value of the Alignment property.
2   Set the Name property to **tbrText** using the Properties window.
3   For the new Toolbar instance, activate the **General** tab on the Property Pages.
4   Set the ImageList property to **ilsText**.
5   Set the BorderStyle property to **1 - ccFixedSingle**.
6   Verify that the Appearance property is set to **1 - cc3D**.

7 Click **Apply** to record the changes. The toolbar should match that shown in Figure 10-10. Note that the Property Pages may obscure the form. Move the Property Pages window so that you can see the entire toolbar.

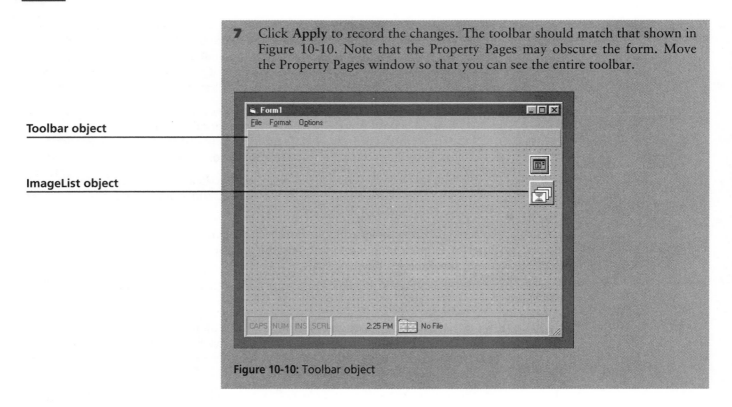

Toolbar object

ImageList object

Figure 10-10: Toolbar object

A toolbar can have zero or more buttons. The Buttons property of the Toolbar object references a Buttons collection. The Buttons collection, in turn, contains a reference to zero or more Button objects, each representing a button on the toolbar. The Buttons collection is a one-based collection that can be referenced by an integer or a string key, like other collections.

Syntax	Button
Properties	■ If the button should contain text, you must set the **Caption** property. Buttons usually do not have a caption, but rather store icons or bitmap images.
	■ The **Key** property defines the string key for the button. You use the string key when writing code to identify which button was clicked by the user.
	■ The **Image** property stores either the numeric index or the string key of the corresponding image found in the ListImages property of the ImageList control. A toolbar must be associated with an ImageList control instance before the Image property can be set.
	■ The read-write **ToolTipText** property contains a string and defines the ToolTip for a particular button.
	■ The **Value** property has two possible values. If set to 0 - tbrUnpressed, the button is not pressed; if set to 1 - tbrPressed, the button is pressed. You can read and write this property at run time to determine or change the status for a particular button.
	■ The **Visible** and **Enabled** properties make the button visible/invisible and enable/disable the button, respectively.
	■ The **Style** property controls the appearance of a button and how a button interacts with other buttons on the toolbar.

The behavior of an individual button is controlled by the Style property. This property can be set to one of six constants:

- If the Style property is set to **tbrDefault**, the button is not dependent on any other buttons. That is, it does not belong to a group. When the ButtonClick event procedure corresponding to the button is running, the button appears recessed. When the event procedure ends, the button returns to its normal appearance.

- If the Style property is set to **tbrCheck**, the button works like a toggle switch. When clicked, it appears recessed. When clicked again, the button returns to its normal appearance. When it has a pressed appearance, the button has a constant value of tbrPressed. When it does not appear pressed, the button has the constant value of tbrUnpressed.

- If the Style property is set to **tbrButtonGroup**, the user can select only one button from among a group of buttons. When a button in a group is clicked, the button appears recessed and all other buttons in the group are no longer recessed. It is possible for no button in a group to appear recessed. When you create a button group, you should surround the buttons that constitute the group on each side by a separator button (that is, the Style property is set to tbrSeparator).

- If the Style property is set to **tbrSeparator**, a button is created eight pixels wide. This button visually separates the buttons in a group and serves the same purpose as a separator bar between two menu items. It is also used to identify the buttons in a button group.

- If the Style property is set to **tbrPlaceholder**, the toolbar includes a blank space in which you can display other control instances. You can set the Width property to define the exact width of the placeholder button.

- If the Style property is set to **tbrDropdown**, the button will cause a drop-down menu to be displayed in the same way that a menu title displays a drop-down menu.

After setting the general properties for the toolbar, you need to create the individual buttons on it and then individually specify the properties for those buttons. For Power Programming Systems' program, you need to create nine buttons corresponding to the nine pictures in the ImageList control instance already created on the form. You will also create separator buttons to visually group buttons. To add the buttons on the toolbar, you use the Buttons tab in the Property Pages, as shown in Figure 10-11.

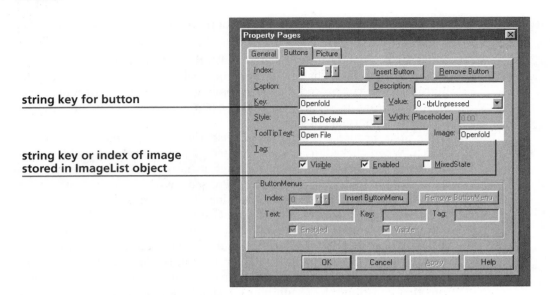

string key for button

string key or index of image stored in ImageList object

Figure 10-11: Buttons Property Pages

To add a button on the toolbar, you click the Insert Button command button on the Buttons tab of the Property Pages. To delete a button from the toolbar, you select the index of the desired button, then click the Remove Button command button. Each button on a toolbar is associated with a particular numeric index and string key. The combination of these values uniquely identifies a Button object in the Buttons collection. Note that the Buttons collection is separate from the ListImages collection. The Buttons collection contains information about a particular button and the string key or numeric index of the buttons' images stored in the ListImages collection. Figure 10-12 depicts this relationship.

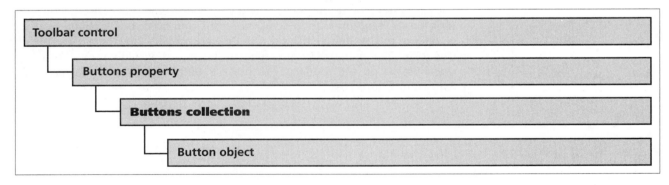

Toolbar control

Buttons property

Buttons collection

Button object

Figure 10-12: Relationship between the Buttons collection and Button object

As shown in Figure 10-12, the Toolbar control supports a Buttons property, which contains a reference to the Buttons collection. This collection, in turn, contains references to the Button objects in the collection. You can now add the buttons on the toolbar to open, save, and print files, as well as the buttons to format and justify text.

To add the buttons to the toolbar:

1   Make sure that the Buttons tab of the toolbar's Property Pages is active.

2   Click the **Insert Button** command button.

3   Make sure that the Index is set to **1**.

4   Set the Key to **Openfold** and the ToolTipText to **Open File.**

5   Set the Image to **Openfold.** Again, remember that the Image and Key properties are case-sensitive.

Note that the Key and Image properties are set to the same value; these values could differ, however. The Key property refers to the string key you will use to reference the particular toolbar button. The Image property refers to the string key of the image in the ImageList control instance.

6   Click the **Apply** button to save your changes to the toolbar.

7   Click the **Insert Button** command button and make sure that the Index is set to **2**. Set the Key to **Drive**, the ToolTipText to **Save File**, and the Image to **Drive**.

8   Click **Apply** to save your changes to the toolbar. As you add each button, it will appear on the toolbar. Note that you may need to move the Property Pages to see the effect on the toolbar.

9   Click the **Insert Button** command button to insert a button with an Index set to **3**.

10 Set the Style to **3 - tbrSeparator.** Because you will not reference this button with code or attach an image to the button, you do not need to set any other properties for it.

11 Click **Apply.**

12 Click the **Insert Button** command button. Make sure that the Index value is set to **4**. Set the Key to **Print**, the ToolTipText to **Print File**, and the Image to **Print**.

If a message box appears with the message "Element not found," verify that the Image property has been set correctly. If it has, open the Property Pages for the ImageList control instance, and verify that you set the Key property correctly for the image.

The Key values for these collections are case-sensitive. If you get an error message while trying to set the Image property, make sure that the case matches that of the key you specified when you created the ImageList control.

The buttons to change the formatting (bold, italic, underline) of text will work like toggle switches. When clicked, the text should be formatted appropriately. That is, when the user clicks the Bold button, text should be formatted in a bold typeface and the button should appear recessed, indicating that the bold typeface is applied. When the user clicks this button again, the bold formatting should be removed, and the button should no longer appear recessed. To accomplish this task (and similar ones for italic and underline formatting), you need to set the Style properties of these buttons to tbrCheck.

To create the bold, italic, and underline formatting buttons:

1   Make sure the **Buttons** tab on the Toolbar's Property Pages is active and Index 4 (the last button) is selected.

2   Click the **Insert Button** command button to insert a button with an Index of 5.

3   Set the Style to **3 - tbrSeparator.**

4   Click the **Insert Button** command button. The Index of the new button should be 6.

5   Set the Key to **Bold**, the Style to **1 - tbrCheck**, the ToolTipText to **Bold**, and the Image to **Bold**.

6   Click **Apply.**

7 Click the **Insert Button** command button again. The Index of the new button should be **7**.

8 Set the Key to **Italic**, the Style to **1 - tbrCheck**, the ToolTipText to **Italic**, and the Image to **Italic**.

9 Click **Apply**.

10 Click the **Insert Button** command button. The Index of the new button should be **8**.

11 Set the Key to **Underline**, the Style to **1 - tbrCheck**, the ToolTipText to **Underline**, and the Image to **Underline**.

12 Click **OK** to apply the changes and close the Property Pages.

Finally, you need to create the buttons to justify text. Text can be left-justified, centered, or right-justified. Because only one setting is valid at any time, the buttons should operate as a group. Thus a separator button must appear between these text-justification buttons and the formatting buttons.

To create the buttons to justify text:

1 Open the Toolbar's Property Pages to the **Buttons** tab. Make sure that the index of the currently selected button is **8**. Click the **Insert Button** command button to insert a button with an Index of **9**.

2 Set the Style to **3 - tbrSeparator**.

3 Click the **Insert Button** command button. The Index of the new button should be **10**.

4 Set the Key to **Left**, the Style to **2 - tbrButtonGroup**, the ToolTipText to **Left**, and the Image to **Left**.

5 Click **Apply**.

6 Click the **Insert Button** command button again. The Index of the new button should be **11**.

7 Set the Key to **Center**, the Style to **2 - tbrButtonGroup**, the ToolTipText to **Center**, and the Image to **Center**.

8 Click **Apply**.

9 Click the **Insert Button** command button. The Index of the new button should be **12**.

10 Set the Key to **Right**, the Style to **2 - tbrButtonGroup**, the ToolTipText to **Right**, and the Image to **Right**.

11 Click **OK** to apply the changes and close the Property Pages. The toolbar should now resemble Figure 10-13.

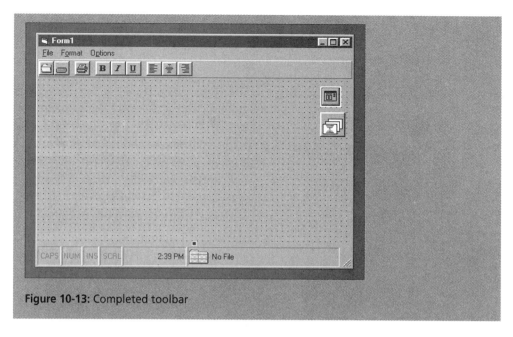

Figure 10-13: Completed toolbar

Now that the toolbar exists, you need to create the other objects on the form to display the files that the user will edit. To accomplish this task, you will use a control that works much like the TextBox control you have used in earlier chapters.

Using the RichTextBox Control

The RichTextBox control works much like the intrinsic TextBox control you have employed in previous chapters, except that it can display data in Rich Text Format. (The RichTextBox control can also read and write ASCII files.) Rich Text Format (RTF) is a standardized file format that is compatible with many word-processing programs. Rich Text Format files support different fonts and character formatting. The standard prefix for a RichTextBox control is "rtf".

Figure 10-14 shows a segment of a Rich Text Format file. As you can see from Figure 10-14, formatting directives for the text are embedded into the file. The RichTextBox control will interpret these formatting directives and display the formatted text inside the region of the rich text box. Like a text box, the RichTextBox control can be used as a bound control. That is, by setting the DataSource and DataField properties, you can instruct the RichTextBox control to interact with a field in a database. The rich text box can operate in an unbound mode as well.

```
{\rtf1\ansi\deff0\deftab720{\fonttbl{\f0\fswiss MS Sans Serif;} {\f1\froman\fcharset2
Symbol;} {\f2\fswiss;} {\f3\fswiss Arial;} }
{\colortbl\red0\green0\blue0;}
\deflang 1033\pard\plain\f2\fs24 This text appears in the Rich Text Box control.
\par Text can be\plain\f2\fs24\b Bold, \plain\f2\fs24\b\i Italic\plain\f2\fs24\b , \plain\f2\fs24
or\plain\f2\fs24\b \plain\f2\fs24\b\ul underline. \plain\f2\fs24\ul
\par
\par \pard\qc\plain\f2\fs24\ul Text can be centered
\par
\par \plain\f3\fs20\b Text can appear in different Fonts\plain\f0\fs17
\par }
```

Figure 10-14: Rich Text Format file

The RichTextBox control also supports methods to read and write plain text and RTF files without the aid of a database. In addition, it supports methods to explicitly open and read a file.

Syntax	**RichTextBox**
Properties	■ The **DataSource** property is used to create a bound control. It should be set to a Data control instance created on the form.
	■ The **DataField** property is used in conjunction with the DataSource property to create a bound control. It is set to a field in the recordset specified by the Data control.
	■ The **MultiLine** and **ScrollBars** properties have the same purposes as the properties of the same name pertaining to a text box.
	■ The **RightMargin** property sets the rightmost limit for the text that appears on a line. It is measured in twips.
	■ The **SelAlignment** property determines the alignment of the selected text between the left and right margins. If set to rtfLeft (the default), the text is left-justified. If set to rtfCenter, the text is centered between the left and right margins. If set to rtfRight, the text is aligned along the right margin.
	■ The **SelBold**, **SelItalic**, and **SelUnderline** properties set or return the font attributes of the currently selected text. If its value is True, the selected attribute is applied. If the value is False, the selected attribute is not applied. If the value is Null, the selected text contains a mixture of the font attributes.
	■ The **SelFontName** and **SelFontSize** properties set or return the font name and font size of the selected text or insertion point.
Methods	■ The **LoadFile** method reads a text or RTF file from the disk into a rich text box.
	■ The **SaveFile** method writes the contents of a rich text box to a file on the disk.
	■ The **SelPrint** method sends the contents of the rich text box to a printer. If text is selected, then only the selected text is sent to the printer. If no text is selected, the entire contents of the rich text box are printed.
Events	■ The **Change** event occurs when the user modifies the contents of the rich text box.
	■ The **SelChange** event occurs when the user selects different text or the insertion point changes.

You are now ready to create the rich text box, setting the general properties so that scroll bars will appear if the entire contents of a text file cannot fit in the region of the rich text box.

To create an instance of the RichTextBox control:

1 Click the **RichTextBox** control button 🔲 on the toolbar. Create an instance of the RichTextBox control using Figure 10-15 as a reference.

2 Using the Properties window, set the Name property to **rtfText**.

3　Remove the text from the Text property.

4　Verify that the MultiLine property is set to **True** and set the ScrollBars property to **3 - rtfBoth**.

RichTextBox control instance

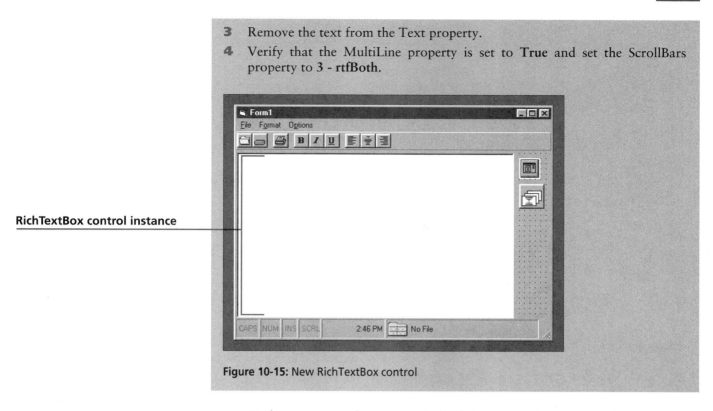

Figure 10-15: New RichTextBox control

At this point, you have created all of the control instances on the form. Your next step is to write the code necessary to open, close, and print files. You will also write the code to change the formatting of the text by clicking buttons on the toolbar or selecting an item on the menu.

QUESTIONS

1. Which of the following statements pertaining to a status bar is true?
   a. It is divided into regions called panels.
   b. Only one panel can be visible at a time.
   c. All panels must be exactly the same size.
   d. Both a and c.
   e. All of the above.

2. What is the name of the event that occurs when the user clicks a panel on the status bar?
   a. Click
   b. PanelClick
   c. Change
   d. Panel
   e. None of the above.

3. Which of the following formatting attributes does the status bar support?
   a. Raised panels
   b. Different fonts for individual panels
   c. Different colors for individual panels
   d. All of the above.
   e. None of the above.

4. Which of the following statements about a toolbar is true?
   a. It contains zero or more buttons that are stored as Button objects in the Buttons collection.
   b. A toolbar button can be configured to work like a toggle switch.
   c. A toolbar button can be configured as a group such that only one button in the group appears pressed at a time.
   d. None of the above.
   e. All of the above.

5. Which of the following statements about the ImageList control is true?
   a. The control is visible at run time.
   b. All images must be bitmaps.
   c. Images can be different sizes.
   d. None of the above.
   e. All of the above.

6. What is the name of the toolbar button constant that makes a button work like a toggle switch?
   a. tbrCheck
   b. tbrBoolean
   c. tbrToggle
   d. tbrOnOff
   e. None of the above.

7. Which of the following statements about the relationship between the ImageList control and the Toolbar control is true?
   a. There is no relationship between the two controls.
   b. The ImageList control contains the images displayed in the Toolbar control.
   c. The toolbar should be created before the ImageList control.
   d. The order in which the Toolbar and ImageList controls are created is not important.
   e. None of the above.

8. Which of the following statements about the RichTextBox control is true?
   a. The control can be used in either a bound or unbound mode.
   b. The control cannot read plain text files and supports only Rich Text Format files.
   c. All text must have the same font.
   d. All of the above.
   e. None of the above.

9. Which of the following is a characteristic of a Rich Text Format file?
   a. Color is supported.
   b. Font attributes like bold, italics, and underline are supported.
   c. There is no difference between a Rich Text Format file and a plain text file.
   d. Both a and b.
   e. All of the above.

10. Which methods are used to read and write files using the RichTextBox control?
    a. ReadFile, WriteFile
    b. Read, Write
    c. LoadFile, SaveFile
    d. Load, Save
    e. None of the above.

SECTION B
objectives

In this section you will:

- Write code to print the contents of the RichTextBox control
- Read and write rich text files
- Apply formatting to rich text files
- Program a toolbar

Programming the Windows Common Controls

Printing an RTF File

You can print the contents of a rich text box by calling the SelPrint method supported by the RichTextBox control. The SelPrint method has the following syntax:

Syntax	*object*.**SelPrint**(*hDC*)
Dissection	■ The *object* must be the name of a RichTextBox control instance.
	■ The **SelPrint** method prints the selected contents of the rich text box. If no text is selected, the method prints the entire contents of the rich text box. If text is selected, only the selected text prints. If you use the Printer object as the destination for the text from the RichTextBox control instance, you must first initialize the device context of the Printer object by printing a zero-length string.
	■ The required *hDC* argument is the device context of the desired printing device. This value is stored in the hDC property of the Printer object. A device context is a link connecting a Windows application, a device driver, and a device such as a printer.
Code Example	``` Printer.Print "" rtfText.SelPrint(Printer.hDC) ```
Code Dissection	When you call the SelPrint method, the contents of the rich text box are sent to the default printer.

Because you must print the contents of a rich text box in two ways—from either a menu item or a toolbar button—you need to create a general procedure to perform the task, then call the general procedure when the user clicks either the menu item or the button.

You can now create the general procedure, then call it from the proper menu item. You will program the toolbar later in the chapter. An instance of the CommonDialog control already exists on the form. The CommonDialog control was discussed in Chapter 9. In this example, one instance of the CommonDialog control will be used to open, save, and print files.

To print an RTF file using the RichTextBox control:

1 Open the Code window and create a Private general procedure named **PrintFile** that accepts no arguments. Set the Type to **Sub** and the Scope to **Private**.

2 Insert the following statements in the procedure:

```
On Error GoTo Cancel_Error
    cdlText.Flags = cdlPDReturnDC + cdlPDNoPageNums
    cdlText.ShowPrinter
    rtfText.SelPrint cdlText.hDC
    Exit Sub
Cancel_Error:
```

3 Locate the **mnuFilePrint_Click** event procedure, then enter the following statement:

```
Call PrintFile
```

These statements cause the entire contents or the selected text in the rich text box to be sent to the printer.

The code that you just typed requires careful analysis.

```
On Error GoTo Cancel_Error
```

This statement establishes the error handler for the procedure. If the user clicks the Cancel button on the Print dialog, the CommonDialog control instance will generate a run-time error. The code in the procedure will cause it to exit without printing the file.

Consider the following code to set the Flags property:

```
cdlText.Flags = cdlPDReturnDC + cdlPDNoPageNums
```

This statement sets the flags needed for printing. The flag cdlPDReturnDC returns the device context of the printer in the hDC property pertaining to the common dialog. The flag cdlPDNoPageNums disables the Pages option button in the Print dialog.

Finally, consider the following code:

```
cdlText.ShowPrinter
rtfText.SelPrint cdlText.hDC
```

The first statement displays the Print dialog. The second statement sends the contents of the RichTextBox control instance to the printer. The device context is determined using the hDC property of the common dialog.

You now should test the code that you just wrote to verify that the information prints correctly.

To print the contents of the rich text box:

1 Save and test the program. Enter a line of text in the RichTextBox control instance.

2 Click **File**, then click **Print**. Click **OK** in the Print dialog. The text should be sent to the printer.

3 End the program to return to design mode.

In addition to printing and saving files, Power Programming Systems' program must be able to open existing files and save files to the disk.

Opening and Saving Rich Text Files

Your next step is to write the code to open and save files. As with the printing operation, the user should be able to execute these functions by clicking either a menu item or a button on the toolbar. Thus you will create two general procedures that will be called when the user clicks the menu item or the toolbar button. Each procedure will use the CommonDialog control instance.

Although you could use the Open statement to open a text or rich text file and to read the contents of that file into the rich text box with a Do loop, it is much easier to call the SaveFile and LoadFile methods. These methods have the same syntax.

Syntax	*object*.**LoadFile** | **SaveFile** *pathname* [, *filetype*]
Dissection	■ The *object* must be any valid instance of a RichTextBox control.
	■ The **LoadFile** or **SaveFile** methods are called on the RichTextBox control and will read and write a text file or a rich text file, respectively.
	■ The required *pathname* argument must contain the folder and file name of the file to load in the control instance.
	■ The optional *filetype* argument must be an Integer constant specifying the type of file to be loaded. If set to 0 - rtfRTF (the default), the file is assumed to be a valid RTF file. If set to 1 - rtfText, a text file is loaded.
Code Example	``` rtfText.LoadFile "A:\Chapter.10\Startup\Demo.txt" rtfText.SaveFile "A:\Chapter.10\Startup\Demo.txt" ```
Code Dissection	The preceding statements read and write the text file named Demo.txt.

To improve the program's user interface, you will also write code to detect unsaved changes in the rich text box. You can accomplish this task by creating a module-level Boolean variable. When the file is saved, this variable should be set to False. When the Change event pertaining to the RichTextBox control occurs, the variable should be set to True.

To open and save Rich Text Format files:

1 Enter the following variable declaration statement in the **general declarations** section of the form module:

```
Private mblnDirty As Boolean
```

2 Create a **Private Sub** procedure named **OpenFile**. This procedure should accept no arguments. Enter the following statements. Note that in the following steps, the InitDir property is set to reference the A: drive. Change the drive designator as necessary depending on the location of your files.

```
On Error GoTo Cancel_Error
    Dim pintReturn As Integer
    If mblnDirty Then
        pintReturn = MsgBox("Abandon Changes", vbYesNo + vbQuestion)
        If pintReturn = vbNo Then
            Exit Sub
        End If
    End If
    With cdlText
        .Flags = cdlOFNExplorer + cdlOFNPathMustExist + _
            cdlOFNFileMustExist
        .Filter = "Text Files (*.txt)|*.txt|RTF Files (*.rtf)|*.rtf"
        .FilterIndex = 2
        .CancelError = True
        .InitDir = "A:\Chapter.10\Startup"
        .ShowOpen
    End With
    Me.Caption = cdlText.FileTitle
    rtfText.LoadFile cdlText.FileName
    sbrText.Panels("pnlText").Text = cdlText.FileName
    sbrText.Panels("pnlText").Picture = _
        LoadPicture("A:\Chapter.10\Startup\Openfold.ico")
    Exit Sub
Cancel_Error:
```

3 Create a **Private Sub** procedure that accepts no arguments named **SaveFile,** then enter the following statements:

```
On Error GoTo Cancel_Error
    With cdlText
        .Filter = "Text Files (*.txt)|*.txt|RTF Files (*.rtf)|*.rtf"
        .FilterIndex = 2
        .InitDir = "A:\Chapter.10\Startup"
        .ShowSave
        rtfText.SaveFile .FileName
        Me.Caption = .FileName
    End With
    sbrText.Panels("pnlText").Text = cdlText.FileName
    sbrText.Panels("pnlText").Picture = _
        LoadPicture("A:\Chapter.10\Startup\Openfold.ico")
    mblnDirty = False
    Exit Sub
Cancel_Error:
```

4 Enter the following statement in the **mnuFileOpen_Click** event procedure:

```
Call OpenFile
```

5 Enter the following statement in the **mnuFileSave_Click** event procedure:

```
Call SaveFile
```

6 Enter the following statement in the **rtfText_Change** event procedure:

```
mblnDirty = True
```

The OpenFile general procedure you just wrote displays the Open dialog using the CommonDialog control. Consider the following code in the OpenFile procedure:

```
If mblnDirty Then
    pintReturn = MsgBox("Abandon Changes", vbYesNo + vbQuestion)
    If pintReturn = vbNo Then
        Exit Sub
    End If
End If
```

Before attempting to open a file, the program tests the variable mblnDirty to determine whether any changes to the existing contents of the RichTextBox control instance are unsaved. If any exist, the program displays a message box requesting confirmation from the user that the unsaved changes should be abandoned. If the user wants to abandon the changes, the procedure continues; otherwise, it exits.

Carefully evaluate the following code:

```
Me.Caption = cdlText.FileTitle
rtfText.LoadFile cdlText.FileName
```

If the user does not press the Cancel button, the form's caption is set to the file name of the selected file, and the LoadFile method is called with one argument—the full path name for the file to be opened.

Consider another section of the code:

```
With cdlText
    .Flags = cdlOFNExplorer + cdlOFNPathMustExist + _
        cdlOFNFileMustExist
    .Filter = "Text Files (*.txt)|*.txt|RTF Files (*.rtf)|*.rtf"
    .FilterIndex = 2
    .CancelError = True
    .InitDir = "A:\Chapter.10\Startup"
    .ShowOpen
End With
    Me.Caption = cdlText.FileTitle
    rtfText.LoadFile cdlText.FileName
    sbrText.Panels("pnlText").Text = cdlText.FileName
    sbrText.Panels("pnlText").Picture = _
        LoadPicture("A:\Chapter.10\Startup\Openfold.ico")
```

These statements use the same techniques introduced in Chapter 9 to display the Open dialog. First, they set the flags pertaining to the CommonDialog control. The filter is set such that both plain text and RTF files will appear in the Open dialog. The FilterIndex property allows RTF files to become the default. The initial directory that will be scanned for files is set as well. Finally, the program calls the ShowOpen method to display the Open dialog. The status bar is updated so that the file name appears in the panel named pnlText, and the picture is changed to an open folder to indicate that the file is open.

The SaveFile procedure works much like the LoadFile procedure. The Filter, FilterIndex, and InitDir properties are set prior to calling the ShowSave method pertaining to the CommonDialog control. If the user did not click the Cancel button, then the program calls the SaveFile method.

```
rtfText.SaveFile .FileName
```

Finally, because no unsaved changes exist, the variable mblnDirty is set to False. This variable will be set to True in the Change event procedure for the RichTextBox control.

You can now test this code to verify that the files can be opened and saved.

To test the open file and save file commands:

1 Save and test the program. Click **File**, then click **Open** on the menu bar to display the Open dialog. Select the file **Chapter.10\Startup\Demo.rtf** and click the **Open** button. Remember to set the drive designator appropriately. The contents of the file should appear as shown in Figure 10-16.

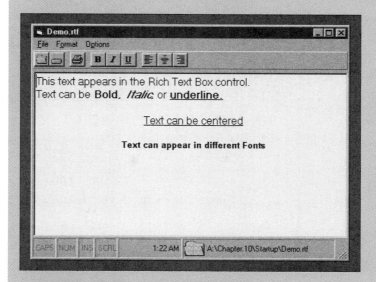

Figure 10-16: Formatted text in rich text box

2 Change the contents of the file. Click **File**, then click **Save** to save the file with the name **Chapter.10\Startup\Demo1.rtf**. Again, set the drive designator as necessary. The form's caption changes to reflect the new file name.

3 End the program to return to design mode.

In addition to opening and saving files, the user must be able to create a new file. This process is very simple. You can create an If statement just as you did in the OpenFile procedure to determine whether any changes are unsaved, and then obtain confirmation from the user about abandoning them. If the user wants to create a new file, you can clear the contents of the rich text box by setting the Text property to a null string. The statement to carry out this task is the same as the one you used with an intrinsic text box. Finally, you set the caption of the form to indicate that a new document is being edited.

You must also consider the state of the editor when the form first loads. One option would be to hide the rich text box to indicate that no file is being edited. The other option would be to set the caption of the form to New Document, thereby giving the user the impression that a new document had been automatically created. In this chapter, you will use this second technique (although the decision is somewhat arbitrary). Another task to perform when the form loads is to set the right margin to the width of the rich text box.

To initialize the editor and create new files:

1 Activate the Code window for the **Form_Load** event procedure and enter the following statements:

```
rtfText.RightMargin = rtfText.Width
mblnDirty = False
Me.Caption = "New Document"
sbrText.Panels("pnlText").Text = "New Document"
sbrText.Panels("pnlText").Picture = _
    LoadPicture("A:\Chapter.10\Startup\Clsdfold.ico")
```

2 Activate the Code window for the **mnuFileNew_Click** event procedure and enter the following statements:

```
Dim pintReturn As Integer
If mblnDirty Then
    pintReturn = MsgBox("Abandon Changes?", _
        vbYesNo + vbQuestion)
    If pintReturn = vbNo Then
        Exit Sub
    End If
End If
Me.Caption = "New Document"
rtfText.Text = vbNullString
mblnDirty = False
```

3 Save and test the program. Click **File,** click **Open,** then open the file named **Chapter.10\Startup\Demo.rtf.** Set the drive designator as necessary. Make changes to the file but do not save it. Click **File,** then click **New** to create a new file. A message box should appear, asking if you want to abandon the changes. Click **Yes.** The contents of the rich text box should be cleared and the caption of the form reset. End the program to return to design mode.

Consider the code you just wrote to create a new file:

```
rtfText.RightMargin = rtfText.Width
mblnDirty = False
Me.Caption = "New Document"
```

These statements set the right margin of the rich text box to the width of the rich text box. The variable mblnDirty is set to False indicating that no unsaved changes exist. Finally, the caption of the form is set.

```
sbrText.Panels("pnlText").Text = "New Document"
sbrText.Panels("pnlText").Picture = _
    LoadPicture("A:\Chapter.10\Startup\Clsdfold.ico")
```

These statements set the text in the status bar's pnlText panel to "New Document" and load the picture named "Clsdfold.ico" into the same panel.

```
Dim pintReturn As Integer
If mblnDirty Then
    pintReturn = MsgBox("Abandon Changes?", _
        vbYesNo + vbQuestion)
    If pintReturn = vbNo Then
        Exit Sub
    End If
End If
Me.Caption = "New Document"
rtfText.Text = vbNullString
mblnDirty = False
```

These statements test the value of the Boolean variable mblnDirty to determine whether unsaved changes exist. If any remain, a message box appears requesting confirmation from the user. If the user elects to abandon unsaved changes or if no unsaved changes exist, then the caption of the form is set, the contents of the rich text box are cleared, and the variable mblnDirty is reset to indicate that no changes remain unsaved.

A flaw currently exists with your program: If the user resizes the form, then the size of the rich text box will not be resized accordingly.

Resizing a Form

In previous chapters, you did not deal with the problem of resizing a form. In this program, if the user resizes the height or width of the form, the size of the rich text box should change in tandem so that the width of the rich text box matches the width of the form. If the user resizes the height of the form, the height of the rich text box should be adjusted accordingly so that the bottom of the rich text box appears just above the status bar. To solve this problem, you can write code that will respond to the form's Resize event. Consider the following statements:

```
rtfText.Height = Me.Height - 1650
rtfText.Width = Me.Width - 100
rtfText.RightMargin = rtfText.Width
```

Whenever the user resizes the form, the height and width of the rich text box change. The height of the status bar, toolbar, and menu bar combined is 1650 twips. This value is subtracted from the height of the form. The bottom of the rich text box therefore appears just above the top of the status bar. The width of the rich text box is set so that it is 100 twips less than the width of the form. The form's border is approximately 100 twips wide. If you do not subtract this value, the scroll bars for the rich text box, when they appear, will be cropped along the right side of the screen. The final statement of the preceding code sets the right margin of the rich text box. This consideration will become important when you write the code to right-justify and center text. In this example, the right margin of the text is the same as the rich text box.

To resize a control at run time:

1   Enter the following statements in the **Form_Resize** event procedure:

```
rtfText.Height = Me.Height - 1650
rtfText.Width = Me.Width - 100
rtfText.RightMargin = rtfText.Width
```

2   Save and test the program. Resize the form both vertically and horizontally. The size of the rich text box should be adjusted to fill the region of the form. End the program to return to design mode.

The next step in the program's development is to format the contents of the rich text box.

Formatting a Rich Text Box

The user will format text in the RichTextBox control by selecting the desired text, then applying the desired formatting attribute such as bold, italic, or underline. As the programmer, you will write code to apply the formatting attribute by setting a property pertaining to the rich text box. The RichTextBox control supports several properties to change the formatting of selected text. Your code can set the SelBold,

SelItalic, SelStrikethru, or SelUnderline properties to change the font style. These properties can have one of three values:

- If set to **Null**, the selected text contains characters having a mix of the selected font style. To determine whether the value is Null, you can use the IsNull classification function.
- If set to **True**, all characters in the selection or the character following the insertion point have the selected font style applied.
- If set to **False** (the default), neither the characters in the selection nor the character following the insertion point have the selected font style applied.

Power Programming Systems' program will allow the user to apply different formats in two ways: (1) by selecting text in the rich text box, then clicking the Bold, Italic, or Underline buttons on the toolbar, or (2) by using the equivalent menu commands. Also, when the user moves the insertion point in the rich text box or selects different text, the buttons on the toolbar and corresponding menu items must be updated to reflect the formatting attributes of the currently selected text.

You need a way to determine when the user selects different text or changes the insertion point so that your program can update the buttons on the toolbar and the items on the menu bar appropriately. For example, if the selected text is bold, the Bold button on the toolbar should appear recessed. If the selected text is not bold, this button should appear raised. The corresponding menu item should become checked or unchecked accordingly.

The RichTextBox control supports the SelChange event to accomplish this task. This event occurs whenever the selected text changes or the insertion point moves. As with a toolbar button, you need a way to represent a menu item so that it can indicate one of two states at any time. That is, the Bold menu item should be either checked or unchecked and should be synchronized with the corresponding toolbar button. To create a menu item that can be checked or unchecked, you set the Checked property to True in the Menu Editor at design time. You can then read and write the property as needed, just as you can set the state of a button on the toolbar as needed.

To set the value of the Checked property for the menu item named mnuFormatBold to True or False at run time, you can use the following two statements:

```
mnuFormatBold.Checked = True
mnuFormatBold.Checked = False
```

The first statement checks a menu item, and the second statement unchecks it.

In addition to applying formatting characteristics with menus and toolbar buttons, the user should have a third option—using the common dialog. You can write the code to accomplish this task in many different ways. Consider the task as consisting of two parts. In the first part, you apply particular formatting attributes to selected text. In the second part, you update the state of the toolbar buttons and menu items. In this chapter, you will create general procedures to update the menu item and toolbar button pertaining to a specific formatting attribute. The first general procedure will update the bold attribute, the second the italic attribute, and the third the underline attribute. When the user selects text in the rich text box or changes the insertion point, your program must call these three procedures to update the status of the menu items and toolbar buttons. When the user clicks a menu item or toolbar button, you will also call another set of general procedures to apply the formatting attribute. Finally, you need to write the code to display the Font dialog, update the formatting of the selected text, and update the toolbar buttons and menu items.

To update the menu items and toolbar buttons used for formatting:

1 Create a general **Private Sub** procedure named **BoldStatus** that accepts one argument: a Boolean variable named **pbln**. Enter the following statements into the procedure:

```
Private Sub BoldStatus(pbln As Boolean)
    If pbln Then
        mnuFormatBold.Checked = True
        rtfText.SelBold = True
        tbrText.Buttons("Bold").Value = tbrPressed
    Else
        mnuFormatBold.Checked = False
        rtfText.SelBold = False
        tbrText.Buttons("Bold").Value = tbrUnpressed
    End If
End Sub
```

2 Create a general **Private Sub** procedure named **ItalicStatus** that accepts one argument: a Boolean variable named **pbln**. Enter the following statements into the procedure:

```
Private Sub ItalicStatus(pbln As Boolean)
    If pbln Then
        mnuFormatItalic.Checked = True
        rtfText.SelItalic = True
        tbrText.Buttons("Italic").Value = tbrPressed
    Else
        mnuFormatItalic.Checked = False
        rtfText.SelItalic = False
        tbrText.Buttons("Italic").Value = tbrUnpressed
    End If
End Sub
```

3 Create a general **Private Sub** procedure named **UnderlineStatus** that accepts one argument: a Boolean variable named **pbln**. Enter the following statements into the procedure:

```
Private Sub UnderlineStatus(pbln As Boolean)
    If pbln Then
        mnuFormatUnderline.Checked = True
        rtfText.SelUnderline = True
        tbrText.Buttons("Underline").Value = tbrPressed
    Else
        mnuFormatUnderline.Checked = False
        rtfText.SelUnderline = False
        tbrText.Buttons("Underline").Value = tbrUnpressed
    End If
End Sub
```

4 Enter the following statements in the **SelChange** event procedure for the RichTextBox object named **rtfText**:

```
If rtfText.SelBold = True Then
    Call BoldStatus(True)
Else
    Call BoldStatus(False)
End If


If rtfText.SelItalic = True Then
    Call ItalicStatus(True)
Else
    Call ItalicStatus(False)
End If


If rtfText.SelUnderline = True Then
    Call UnderlineStatus(True)
Else
    Call UnderlineStatus(False)
End If
```

5 Save and test the program. Open the file named **Chapter.10\Startup\Demo.rtf**, setting the drive designator as necessary. Select text with each of the three different formatting attributes (bold, italic, and underline). As you select text having these attributes, check whether the corresponding toolbar button appears pressed or unpressed. Also, verify that the corresponding menu item on the format menu appears checked or unchecked.

6 End the program to return to design mode.

Consider carefully the code you just wrote. Each of the general procedures works the same way.

```
Private Sub BoldStatus(pbln As Boolean)
    If pbln Then
        mnuFormatBold.Checked = True
        rtfText.SelBold = True
        tbrText.Buttons("Bold").Value = tbrPressed
    Else
        mnuFormatBold.Checked = False
        rtfText.SelBold = False
        tbrText.Buttons("Bold").Value = tbrUnpressed
    End If
End Sub
```

The BoldStatus procedure accepts a Boolean argument indicating that the formatting attribute should be applied or not applied. If the formatting attribute should be applied, then the corresponding menu item is checked and the corresponding toolbar button is set so that the button appears recessed. Otherwise, the menu item appears unchecked and the toolbar button appears unpressed.

```
tbrText.Buttons("Bold").Value = tbrPressed
```

This statement requires careful analysis. At design time, you set the string key for each button using the Property Pages. The string key for the Bold button, for example, was set to "Bold". Thus this statement sets the value of the Bold button so that it appears pressed.

The program will call the SelChange event procedure whenever the user changes the insertion point in the rich text box or selects different text:

```
If rtfText.SelBold = True Then
    Call BoldStatus(True)
Else
    Call BoldStatus(False)
End If


If rtfText.SelItalic = True Then
    Call ItalicStatus(True)
Else
    Call ItalicStatus(False)
End If


If rtfText.SelUnderline = True Then
    Call UnderlineStatus(True)
Else
    Call UnderlineStatus(False)
End If
```

This procedure checks the three formatting attributes of the selected text. If the attribute is applied, then the program calls the corresponding general procedure with the necessary argument to update the menu item and toolbar buttons.

Next, you need to write the code that will execute when the user wants to apply a particular format to selected text. Again, selecting a menu item or clicking a toolbar button will accomplish this task. You need to create three general procedures, one for each formatting attribute. Consider the following general procedure to deal with the bold formatting attribute:

```
Private Sub FormatBold()
    If rtfText.SelBold = True Then
        rtfText.SelBold = False
        Call BoldStatus(False)
    Else
        rtfText.SelBold = True
        Call BoldStatus(True)
    End If
End Sub
```

If the currently selected text is already bold, then this code removes the formatting. Otherwise, this attribute is applied. The program calls this general procedure when the user clicks the corresponding menu item or toolbar button. You can now create the three general procedures to apply or remove each of the three formatting attributes and call those procedures when the user clicks the relevant formatting menu items. Again, you will program the toolbar later in the chapter.

To apply formatting to the rich text box:

1 Create a general **Private Sub** procedure named **FormatBold** that accepts no arguments and enter the following statements:

```
If rtfText.SelBold = True Then
    rtfText.SelBold = False
    Call BoldStatus(False)
Else
    rtfText.SelBold = True
    Call BoldStatus(True)
End If
```

2 Create a general **Private Sub** procedure named **FormatItalic** that accepts no arguments and enter the following statements:

```
If rtfText.SelItalic = True Then
    rtfText.SelItalic = False
    Call ItalicStatus(False)
Else
    rtfText.SelItalic = True
    Call ItalicStatus(True)
End If
```

3 Create a general **Private Sub** procedure named **FormatUnderline** that accepts no arguments and enter the following statements:

```
If rtfText.SelUnderline = True Then
    rtfText.SelUnderline = False
    Call UnderlineStatus(False)
Else
    rtfText.SelUnderline = True
    Call UnderlineStatus(True)
End If
```

4   Enter the following statement in the **mnuFormatBold_Click** event procedure:

```
Call FormatBold
```

5   Enter the following statement in the **mnuFormatItalic_Click** event procedure:

```
Call FormatItalic
```

6   Enter the following statement in the **mnuFormatUnderline_Click** event procedure:

```
Call FormatUnderline
```

This code sets the bold, italic, or underline formatting attributes. Each procedure works in the same way. If the formatting attribute is already applied, the procedure removes it. If the formatting attribute is not applied, the procedure applies it. This code also calls each of the three general procedures from the corresponding menu items.

Another way in which the user can apply formatting is to use the common dialog. The Font dialog should appear when the user clicks Format, Fonts on the menu bar. After the user selects the desired font characteristics, you need to apply the formatting and update the status of the corresponding menu items and toolbar buttons.

To apply formatting using the CommonDialog control:

1   Enter the following statements in the **mnuFormatFonts_Click** event procedure:

```
On Error GoTo Cancel_Error
    cdlText.Flags = cdlCFScreenFonts + cdlCFEffects
    cdlText.CancelError = True
    cdlText.ShowFont
    rtfText.SelFontName = cdlText.FontName
    rtfText.SelFontSize = cdlText.FontSize

    rtfText.SelBold = cdlText.FontBold
    If cdlText.FontBold = True Then
        Call BoldStatus(True)
    Else
        Call BoldStatus(False)
    End If

    rtfText.SelItalic = cdlText.FontItalic
    If cdlText.FontItalic = True Then
        Call ItalicStatus(True)
    Else
        Call ItalicStatus(False)
    End If

    rtfText.SelUnderline = cdlText.FontUnderline
    If cdlText.FontUnderline = True Then
        Call UnderlineStatus(True)
    Else
        Call UnderlineStatus(False)
    End If

    Exit Sub

Cancel_Error:
```

2   Save and test the program. Enter text in the rich text box and select it. Click **Format, Fonts** to display the Font dialog. Select a different font name, font size, and formatting attributes, then click the **OK** button to apply the formatting.

3   End the program to return to design mode.

The following statements display the Font dialog. If the user clicks the OK button, the formatting attributes are applied. Otherwise, the event procedure exits.

```
cdlText.Flags = cdlCFScreenFonts + cdlCFEffects
cdlText.CancelError = True
cdlText.ShowFont
```

These three statements set the necessary properties for the common dialog. The first sets the flags to use the screen fonts. The second generates a run-time error if the user clicks the Cancel button on the dialog, and the third displays the Font dialog.

Consider the following two lines of code:

```
rtfText.SelFontName = cdlText.FontName
rtfText.SelFontSize = cdlText.FontSize
```

These statements set the font name and font size for the currently selected text. Evaluate these statements:

```
rtfText.SelBold = cdlText.FontBold
If cdlText.FontBold = True Then
    Call BoldStatus(True)
Else
    Call BoldStatus(False)
End If
```

These statements apply the bold formatting attribute to the selected text or at the insertion point. Once the formatting attribute is applied, the code updates the corresponding menu item and toolbar button.

Now that you have written the code to apply bold, italic, and underline formatting to text, you need to write the code to justify the selected text in the rich text box. Three justification schemes are possible: left-justified, right-justified, or centered. This task is accomplished by setting the SelAlignment property to one of three constants: rtfLeft, rtfRight, or rtfCenter.

```
rtfText.SelAlignment = rtfLeft
rtfText.SelAlignment = rtfRight
rtfText.SelAlignment = rtfCenter
```

In this example, you will create a general procedure to justify the text. The procedure will accept one argument: a text string to indicate how the text should be justified. The program will call this general procedure when the user clicks a toolbar button. You will program the toolbar buttons in a moment.

To justify text in the rich text box:

1   Create a general **Private Sub** procedure named **Justify** that accepts one argument, a string named **pstr**, and enter the following statements in the procedure:

```
Private Sub Justify(pstr As String)
    Select Case pstr
    Case "Left"
        rtfText.SelAlignment = rtfLeft
    Case "Right"
        rtfText.SelAlignment = rtfRight
    Case "Center"
        rtfText.SelAlignment = rtfCenter
    End Select
End Sub
```

This procedure accepts one argument, a string. This string is expected to contain one of the three following values: Left, Right, or Center. Depending on the string value, the SelAlignment method is called with the appropriate constant to align the text. Remember, for centered or right-justified text, the RightMargin property is used to determine how the text will be positioned.

Programming a Toolbar

When you added the buttons to the toolbar using the Property Pages, the Button objects were added to the Buttons collection automatically. Of course, you can create them with code by creating instances of Button objects, setting the properties, and then adding each object to the collection. You then can write code to determine which button was clicked or to change the state of the button as necessary.

In Power Programming Systems' program, when the user clicks a button, the code should first determine which button was clicked. Each Button object supports a Key property—that is, the value of the button's string key you set using the Property Pages. To this point, you have written general procedures to open, save, and print files. You have also written the general procedures to format text. Your program must now call these procedures when the user clicks a particular toolbar button.

Unlike a command button, neither the toolbar nor an individual button responds to a Click event. Rather, when the user clicks a button on the toolbar, a ButtonClick event occurs for the entire toolbar. One argument is passed to the ButtonClick event procedure—a reference to a Button object indicating which button was clicked. This Button object comes from the toolbar's Buttons collection. To program the toolbar, you need to write the code for its ButtonClick event procedure. The Key property of the Button object contains the unique string key for the button. You can use this string key in a Select Case statement to call the appropriate general procedure when the user clicks a button. Consider the following statements for the ButtonClick event procedure:

```
Private Sub tbrText_ButtonClick(ByVal Button _
    As MSComctlLib.Button)


    Select Case Button.Key
        Case "Openfold"
            Call OpenFile
        Case "Print"
            Call PrintFile
        . . .
    End Select
```

In this code, a reference to the clicked toolbar button is passed to the ButtonClick event procedure. The Key property is used as the condition in the Select Case statement; it contains the string key corresponding to the button. Thus a case would exist for each button on the toolbar. The code for each case calls the same general procedure as the corresponding menu item.

To program the toolbar:

1   Activate the Code window for the **ButtonClick** event procedure for the toolbar named **tbrText** and enter the following statements into the event procedure:

```
Select Case Button.Key
    Case "Openfold"
        Call OpenFile
    Case "Print"
        Call PrintFile
    Case "Drive"
        Call SaveFile
    Case "Bold"
        Call FormatBold
    Case "Italic"
        Call FormatItalic
    Case "Underline"
        Call FormatUnderline
    Case "Left"
        Call Justify("Left")
    Case "Center"
        Call Justify("Center")
    Case "Right"
        Call Justify("Right")
End Select
```

These statements determine which button is clicked. Depending on the button, the appropriate general procedure is called to open files or format text. You can now test the program to verify the text is being formatted and the buttons updated correctly.

To test the toolbar:

1 Save and test the program. Open the file named **Chapter.10\Startup\Demo.rtf**, setting the drive designator as necessary.

2 Select some text from the rich text box, then apply and remove formatting to the text. Repeat this step for each of the three formatting buttons.

3 Click the **Print** button to verify that the procedure prints correctly.

4 End the program to return to design mode.

Another formatting attribute supported by the RichTextBox control is color. To set the color for text, you use the SelColor property. Again, you can use the Color dialog pertaining to the CommonDialog control to obtain color instructions from the user.

To set the color of selected text:

1 Enter the following statements in the **mnuOptionsColor_Click** event procedure:

```
On Error GoTo Cancel_Error
    cdlText.ShowColor
    rtfText.SelColor = cdlText.Color
Cancel_Error:
```

2 Save and test the program. Enter and select text. Click **Options**, then click **Color** to activate the Color dialog. Select a color. Click **OK**. This color should be applied to the selected text.

3 End the program to return to design mode.

4 Exit Visual Basic.

The code you just wrote displays the Color dialog. If the user presses the Cancel button, the error handler will execute and the color will not be set. Otherwise, the color of the selected text will be changed based upon the setting in the common dialog.

You have now completed the programming for this chapter. You have learned how to use the StatusBar, ImageList, and ToolBar controls. You have also learned how to load and save files to the rich text box and format the contents of the rich text box.

S U M M A R Y

This chapter introduced several new controls, including the StatusBar, ImageList, Toolbar, and RichTextBox controls. The StatusBar control displays an informative status bar, usually spanning the bottom of the form. The ImageList control stores graphical images for use by other controls, including the Toolbar control. The Toolbar control displays a toolbar, usually across the top of the form and beneath the menu bar, if one exists.

To add the Microsoft Windows Common Controls to a project:

- Click Project, then Components to activate the Components dialog.
- Select Microsoft Windows Common Controls 6.0 and close the dialog.

To implement a status bar on a form:

- Create an instance of the StatusBar control on a form.
- Activate the Property Pages for the status bar.
- Set the general properties pertaining to the status bar.
- Activate the Panels tab. To insert a panel, click the Insert Panel command button, then set the Style and Minimum Width as necessary.

To implement the ImageList control:

- Create an instance of the ImageList control on the form. Note that this control instance is not visible at run time.
- Activate the Property Pages for the control instance.
- On the General tab, set the size of the images to be stored in the control instance.
- On the Images tab, click the Insert Picture command button to add an image. Set the Key property as necessary to define a string key for the image. This string key is case-sensitive.
- Continue to add images as necessary.

To implement the Toolbar control:

- Create an instance of the Toolbar control on the form.
- Activate the General tab on the Property Pages.
- Set the Align property to define where the toolbar appears on the form.
- Set the BorderStyle property to define the border surrounding the toolbar.
- Set the ImageList property to the name of the ImageList control instance created on the same form.
- Set the Appearance property to make the toolbar appear flat or raised on the form.
- Activate the Buttons tab on the Property Pages.
- To add a button, click the Insert Button command button.
- For each button you create, set the Image property to the string key or numeric index of the button in the ImageList control instance.
- Set the Style property to define the button's behavior.
- Set the Key property to the string key you will use to reference the button with code.
- Set the ToolTipText property to add a ToolTip for the button.

To print a rich text file from the RichTextBox control, use the following syntax:

object.**SelPrint**(*hDC*)

To open or save a file from the RichTextBox control, call the LoadFile or SaveFile method with the following syntax:

object.**LoadFile** | **SaveFile** *pathname, filetype*

To set the formatting attributes pertaining to the rich text box:

■   Set the SelBold property to apply or remove the bold formatting attribute.
■   Set the SelItalic property to apply or remove the italic formatting attribute.
■   Set the SelUnderline property to apply or remove the underline formatting attribute.

To set justified text in a rich text box:

■   Set the SelAlignment property to one of the following constants: rtfLeft, rtfRight, or rtfCenter.

To program a toolbar:

■   Create code for the toolbar's ButtonClick event procedure. This code typically consists of a Select Case statement, with one case existing for each button. Each case should rely on either the numeric index or string key of the button.

Q U E S T I O N S

1. What are the possible values for the SelBold, SelItalic, and SelUnderline properties pertaining to the RichTextBox control?
    a. SelectBold, SelectItalic, SelectUnderline
    b. Bold, Italic, Underline
    c. Selected, UnSelected
    d. Null, True, False
    e. None of the above.

2. What is the name of the event procedure that occurs when the user clicks a toolbar button?
    a. Click
    b. Button
    c. ButtonClick
    d. Icon
    e. None of the above.

3. Assume that rtfDemo is an instance of a rich text box. Write the statements to read and save the file named C:\Demo.rtf.

4. Create a Resize event procedure that will make a rich text box named rtfDemo the same size as the form.

5. Write the necessary statements to remove the bold, italic, and underline formatting attributes from the rich text box named rtfDemo.

6. Assume that tbrDemo is a toolbar and "Check" is the string key for a button on the toolbar. Write the statements to make the button appear pressed and unpressed.

7. Assume that rtfDemo is a rich text box. Write the statements to left-justify, right-justify, and center selected text in this rich text box.

8. Write the statement to set the right margin of the rich text box named rtfDemo to the width of the rich text box.

9. Assume that tbrDemo is a toolbar with four buttons having string keys of "Top", "Bottom", "Left", and "Right". Create an event procedure to determine which button was pressed and call the general procedures "SetTop", "SetBottom", "SetLeft", and "SetRight" as appropriate.

E X E R C I S E S

1. Currency Conversion Systems operates currency exchange centers at airports around the world. It needs a program to convert the currency of one country to the currency of another. The program will have two forms. On the main form, the user can select two different currencies using a toolbar. After selecting two currencies, the user can enter the amount of the source currency, then click a command button to convert the dollar amount from the source currency to the destination currency. The main form for the program appears in Figure 10-17.

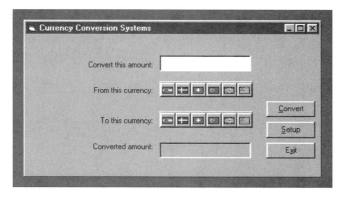

Figure 10-17: Exercise 1 – completed main form

     a. Run the executable file named **Chapter.10\Exercise\Ex1.exe**. Set the drive designator as necessary.

     b. Click the **Setup** command button on the main form to activate the dialog shown in Figure 10-18. Note that Figure 10-18 is shown at design time, so one additional text box appears at the bottom of the form to store the conversion factor of U.S. dollars. This value is always 1 and is hidden from the user at run time.

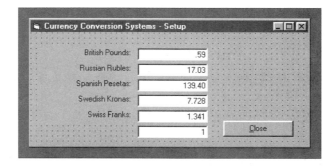

Figure 10-18: Exercise 1 – completed setup form

c. Default values have already been entered in the form, as shown in Figure 10-18. These values represent the currency exchange rates from a foreign currency to U.S. dollars. Close the dialog. On the **From this currency** toolbar, click a flag to select a country. On the **To this currency** toolbar, click a flag to select a country. Enter a numeric amount in the **Convert this amount** text box, and click the **Convert** button to perform the currency conversion calculation. Exit the program.

d. Start Visual Basic and create a new project named **Ex1.vbp**. Create two forms named **frmEx1.frm** and **frmSetup.frm**, respectively. Save these files to the folder **Chapter.10\Exercise**. Set the drive designator as necessary.

e. On the form named **frmSetup**, create the objects shown in Figure 10-18. Write the code for the **Close** command button to hide the form. Do not unload it, as you will need the values in the text boxes to perform the currency conversion calculations.

f. Add the ImageList and Toolbar controls to the toolbox.

g. On the main form, create an instance of the ImageList control and load the following images from the **Chapter.10\Exercise** folder: **Flgspain.ico, Flgswed.ico, Flgswitz.ico, Flgturk.ico, Flguk.ico,** and **Flgusa02.ico**. Set the Key and other properties as necessary. Set the Name property of the ImageList control to **ilsFlags**. The images should be 16*16 pixels in size.

h. Create a toolbar named **tbrSource**. Load the images you created in Step g into the control instance. Set the Key properties of these images to **Flgspain, Flgswed, Flgswitz, Flgturk, Flguk,** and **Flgusa02**. Set the properties so that the toolbar is not aligned and has the same size as the toolbar shown in Figure 10-17. Make sure that all the buttons belong to the same button group.

i. Create a second toolbar named **tbrDestination**. Set the properties to the same values as those used for the first toolbar.

j. Create the text boxes, labels, and command buttons on the main form.

k. Write the code for the **Setup** command button to display the setup form as a modal dialog.

l. Write the code for the **Exit** command button to exit the program.

m. Declare two module-level variables named **mintSource** and **mintDestination**. Both variables should be of type Integer.

n. In the ButtonClick event procedure for the first toolbar (**tbrSource**), write a Select Case statement to set the value of the module-level variable mintSource to a value between 1 and 6, depending upon which flag is clicked. Repeat this process for the toolbar named **tbrDestination**, setting the value of the variable **mintDestination**.

discovery ▶

o. Write the code for the Convert command button to convert the currency value in the text box based upon the source and destination flags that are clicked. Use the variables **mintSource** and **mintDestination** to accomplish this task. The procedure should validate that the text box contains a number and that a flag is clicked in both toolbars. Display a message box if the input is invalid.

p. Conversion of the currency values requires two steps. The first step should convert the source currency into U.S. dollars; the second should convert that value into the destination currency. To convert the source currency to U.S. dollars, you can divide the user-entered value by the conversion value for the corresponding currency stored on the setup form. To determine the source currency, use the variable **mintSource** in a Select Case statement. After converting the source currency to U.S. dollars, convert the value to the destination currency by multiplying the dollar-converted value by the conversion rate for the destination currency.

q. Save and test the program to verify that it properly converts the currency values.

r. Exit Visual Basic.

2. Mathematical Engineers needs a program to determine whether a number is a prime number. A prime number is evenly divisible only by 1 and itself. Thus the number 7 is a prime number because it is evenly divisible by only 1 and 7.

a. Run the executable file named **Chapter.10\Exercise\Ex2.exe**. Set the drive designator as necessary. Figure 10-19 shows the main form for this program after a prime number has been entered.

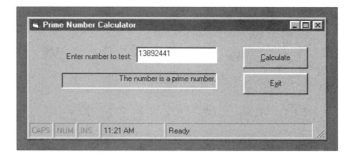

Figure 10-19: Exercise 2 – completed form

As shown in Figure 10-19, the program contains a status bar indicating the state of various keyboard keys. It also displays the time of day. If the user tries to determine whether a large number is a prime number, the calculation will take more than a few seconds. Therefore, the rightmost panel in the status bar displays the message **Ready** or **Working**. Enter the number **13892441,** as shown in Figure 10-19. Click the **Calculate** button. The status bar displays the message "Working" while the computation takes place. The number is a prime number, so the message "The number is a prime number." eventually appears in the label below the text box and the message "Ready" appears in the status bar when the calculations end. Exit the program.

    b. Start Visual Basic and create a new project named **Ex2.vbp.** Set the form name to **frmEx2.** Save these files to the folder **Chapter.10\Exercise.** Set the drive designator as necessary.

    c. Create the labels, text boxes, and command buttons on the form as shown in Figure 10-19.

    d. Create a status bar as shown in Figure 10-19. The first three panels should display the status of the Caps Lock, Num Lock, and Ins keys. The fourth panel should display the time of day.

    e. Create the fifth panel for the status bar. Set a string key for the panel so that you can reference the panel with code. Also, set the initial text to **Ready.** Change the necessary property so that the panel spans the width of the form.

    f. Write the code for the Exit command button to exit the program.

    g. The bulk of the processing occurs in the Calculate command button. This code will determine whether a number entered by the user is a prime number. You can use the following logic to perform this calculation. First, determine whether the number is a Long Integer by calling the CLng function. If the number is not valid, use an error handler to display an appropriate message to the user. To determine whether the number is prime, create a For loop that iterates from 2 to the number entered by the user minus 1. Thus, if the user entered the number 125, the loop should iterate from 2 to 124. Inside the For loop, use the Mod operator to determine whether a number entered by the user is evenly divisible by the current number in the loop. Assuming that plngPrime contains the prime number, the following code illustrates the general structure of the loop:

```
For plngTemp = 2 to plngPrime - 1 then
    If (plngPrime Mod (plngTemp)) = 0 then
        ' Not a prime number / Exit the For loop
    Else
        ' Number may be prime; continue to evaluate.
    End If
Next
```

    h. In the same event procedure, write the code to display the message **Working** in the status bar while the event procedure is executing. When the event procedure is complete, display the message **Ready** in the status bar.

   i.   Save and test the program. Use the same prime number you used when you ran the completed program to verify that the calculation works correctly and the status bar is updated.

   j.   Exit Visual Basic.

3.   Data Techniques requires a database program that allows the user to add, change, and delete database records. To accomplish this task, you can use the same techniques you have used in previous chapters; the company, however, requires this program to display information in a status bar and to utilize a toolbar to execute common functions such as locating different records. The main form for the program is shown in Figure 10-20.

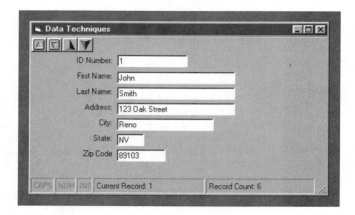

Figure 10-20: Exercise 3 – completed form

   a.   Run the executable file named **Chapter.10\Exercise\Ex3.exe**. Set the drive designator as necessary. For the program to run correctly, the database file named DT.mdb must reside in the same folder as the executable program.

   b.   As shown in Figure 10-20, the form contains toolbar buttons to locate different records. It also contains a status bar to indicate the current record. End the program.

   c.   Start Visual Basic and create a new project named **Ex3.vbp**. Set the form name to **frmEx3**. Save these files to the folder **Chapter.10\Exercise**. Set the drive designator as necessary.

   d.   Create an instance of the Data control on the form. Set the necessary properties to connect to the table named **Chapter.10\Exercise\DT.mdb**. Connect to the table named **Mailing List** in the database.

   e.   Create the bound text boxes shown in Figure 10-20. Set the necessary properties to display the following table fields: **fldMailingListID**, **fldFirstName**, **fldLastName**, **fldAddress**, **fldCity**, **fldState**, and **fldPostalCode**.

   f.   Create a status bar on the form, as shown in Figure 10-20. The first three panels should display the status of the Caps Lock, Num Lock, and Ins keys. The final two panels should indicate the current record and the number of records in the table, respectively. Set the string keys for these panels to **pnlCurrent** and **pnlCount**, respectively, so that you can reference the panels in your code.

   g.   In the **Reposition** event procedure pertaining to the Data control, write the necessary statements to display the current record and record count as shown in Figure 10-20. To determine the current record, you can use the AbsolutePosition property pertaining to the Data control's Recordset object.

   h.   Create an instance of the ImageList control on the form to store icon files for the toolbar. Use 16*16 icons. Add the following icons to the image list from the **Chapter.10\Exercise** folder: **Arw01dn.ico**, **Arw01up.ico**, **Arw03dn.ico**, and **Arw03up.ico**. Set the string key for each button so that you can easily associate each button with the Toolbar control instance you will create in a moment.

i. Create an instance of the toolbar on the form with four buttons. Each of these buttons should operate as a normal button. They will be used to locate the records in the Data control's recordset. Associate the four buttons with the buttons in the ImageList control.

j. Write the code in the appropriate toolbar event procedure to locate records when the user clicks a button. The first two up/down arrows should locate the previous and next records. The other two arrows should locate the first and last records. Create a ToolTip for each button. Write the code in this procedure to check for BOF and EOF conditions.

k. Save and test the program. Verify that each button works correctly and that the status bar is updated properly.

l. Exit Visual Basic.

4. Manta Seafood needs a program to create, edit, and print memos stored in RTF format. The program should open, save, and edit memos. In addition, it should print a memo. Figure 10-21 shows the completed form for this program.

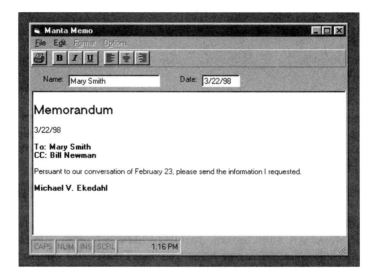

Figure 10-21: Exercise 4 – completed form

a. Run the executable file named **Chapter.10\Exercise\Ex4.exe**. Set the drive designator as necessary. For the program to run correctly, the database file named Manta.mdb must reside in the same folder as the executable program. Click **Edit**, then click **Add** to add a new record. Enter a name, the date, and some memo text. Click **Edit**, then click **Update** to update the record. Click **Edit**, then click **Locate Next** to locate the next record. Click **Edit**, then click **Locate Previous** to locate the previous record. The database initially contains only two records. Exit the program.

b. Start Visual Basic and create a new project named **Ex4.vbp**. Set the form name to **frmEx4**. Save these files to the folder **Chapter.10\Exercise**. Set the drive designator as necessary.

c. Add the Windows Common Controls and the RichTextBox control to the project.

d. Create an instance of the ImageList control. The folder **Chapter.10\Exercise** contains the following buttons: **Print.bmp, Bold.bmp, Italic.bmp, Undrln.bmp, Left.bmp, Right.bmp**, and **Center.bmp**. Add the images to the control instance, and assign a string key to each button.

e. Create a toolbar to display the buttons. The Print button should be of a normal style. The Bold, Italic, and Underline buttons should appear pressed when clicked and unpressed when clicked again. The Left, Right, and Center buttons should belong to the same button group. Create the necessary separator buttons as shown in Figure 10-21.

f. Create an instance of the Data control on the form. Bind this control to the database named **Manta.mdb** in the **Chapter.10\Exercise** folder.

g. Create two text box instances on the form. Bind them to the fields **fldName** and **fldDate**.

h. Create an instance of the RichTextBox control on the form. Bind this text box to the field named **fldMemo**.

i. Create the menu system for the program. The **File** menu should have two menu items named **Print** and **Exit**.

j. The **Edit** menu should have seven menu items with the captions **Add, Edit, Update, Cancel, Delete, Locate Next,** and **Locate Previous.**

k. The **Format** menu should have four menu items with the captions **Bold, Italic, Underline,** and **Fonts.**

l. The Options menu should have one item: **Color.**

m. Create an instance of the StatusBar control to display the state of the keyboard keys and the date, as shown in Figure 10-21.

discovery ▶

n. Using the techniques presented in the chapter, program the Format menu items so that they call general procedures to apply or remove the necessary formatting. Synchronize the menu items with the toolbar buttons.

discovery ▶

o. Program the **Edit** menu items. These items should call the necessary recordset methods to add, update, delete, enable editing, and cancel editing of the current record. Use the techniques presented in Chapters 5 and 8 to accomplish this task. Write the code to prevent a run-time error from occurring if the user tries to select a record that would cause BOF or EOF to be True. Also, create a general procedure to lock the text boxes and enable or disable the appropriate menu items depending upon whether a record is being edited.

p. Save and test the program.

q. Exit Visual Basic.

Creating a Multiple-Document Application

Creating the User Interface for ABC Concrete

case ▶ ABC Concrete owns cement trucks that supply concrete to construction sites. The company is in the process of automating the plant where it loads its trucks. The batch plant, as it is called, consists of 10 batch machines. Each batch machine contains large hoppers filled with cement, three types of sand, three types of gravel, and water.

When the plant receives an order, the batch machine's operator should be able to fill out a form to specify the type and quantity of the sand, gravel, cement, and water needed in the mix. After the operator records an order, it is sent to the batch machine for mixing. Management wants a program to record the volume (in cubic yards) of sand, gravel, and other materials that are used by each batch machine during the day. In addition, management wants to know the amount used by all the batch machines in a given day. Because some days are busier than others, only some of the batch machines may be operational at any given time. The program should allow the operator of an idle batch machine to remove the ordering form from the screen.

Previewing the Completed Application

The completed application in this chapter introduces two significant new concepts. First, the application is a multiple-document interface (MDI) application. That is, the windows that constitute the program are enclosed in another window. Second, in earlier programs you created only a single instance or copy of a form. In this program, however, you will create multiple instances of the same form at run time.

To preview the completed application:

1 Start Visual Basic and open the project file named **Chapter.11\ Complete\ABC_C.vbp**. Set the drive designator as necessary. Run the program. When you run the program, a new type of form, known as an MDI parent form, appears. Inside the MDI parent form, another form—the MDI child form—also appears. An MDI child form has distinctive characteristics—for example, it will always appear inside the region of the MDI parent form.

2 Move the MDI child form inside the region of the parent form. Note that you cannot move the visible region of the MDI child form beyond the region of the MDI parent form.

3 On the form's menu bar, click **Batch Machine Control**, then click **Start Batch Machine**. A second instance of the MDI child form appears inside the region of the outer form, as shown in Figure 11-1.

customized icons

MDI parent form

MDI child form
with focus

MDI child form
without focus

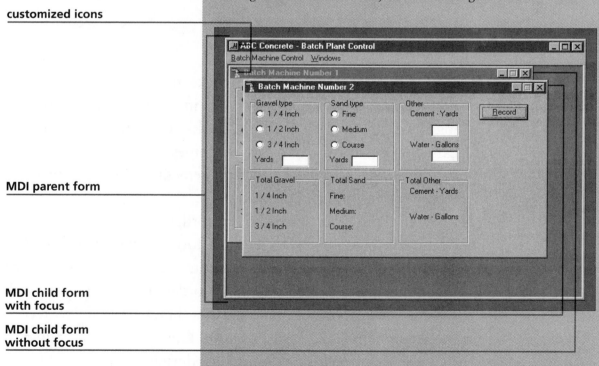

Figure 11-1: Completed MDI program

Figure 11-1 contains one MDI parent form. Inside the region of the MDI parent form, two instances of the MDI child form represent two active batch machines. Each form has a title bar with a caption. Only one MDI child form in a program can have input focus at a time. In Figure 11-1, Batch Machine Number 2 has input focus.

4 Click the **Minimize** button ⊟ on one of the MDI child forms. The form becomes iconified and appears at the bottom of the MDI parent form (rather than on the desktop).

5 Click the **Close** button ⊠ on the MDI parent form. Another form appears to display the material totals used for all machines. Close this window to end the program. Exit Visual Basic.

SECTION A
objectives

In this section you will:

- Create a user interface that operates with several instances of the same form, called a multiple-document application
- Create objects and object references
- Explicitly create objects
- Change the bounds of an array
- Create properties for a form
- Create an enumerated type with the Enum statement

Multiple-Document Interface Programming

Creating a Multiple-Document Application (MDI)

So far in this book, you have created single instances of standard forms. A standard form can appear anywhere on the visible screen and can be minimized independently of any other form. In this chapter, you will create multiple instances of the same form. These multiple form instances are related to one another in that they will all appear inside the region of another form. Programs like Microsoft Word and Microsoft Excel are MDI programs. In Microsoft Word, for example, you can open several documents at once. Each open document represents an instance of a form. The region of each document (form) appears inside another window. When you create an MDI program, you can use three different types of forms:

- An **MDI parent form** acts as a container for the program's MDI child forms. That is, the MDI child forms appear inside the region of the MDI parent form. An MDI parent form cannot be displayed as a modal form. One—and only one—MDI parent form can exist per project.
- An **MDI child form** always appears inside the region of the MDI parent form. An MDI child form cannot be displayed as a modal form.
- You can continue to use standard forms in an MDI program. **Standard forms** can appear anywhere on the screen and are not contained in the MDI parent window. They can be displayed as modal forms.

The Project Explorer displays a different icon for each type of form. Figure 11-2 shows the Project Explorer for the completed program with the three different form icons.

MDI child form

standard form

MDI parent form

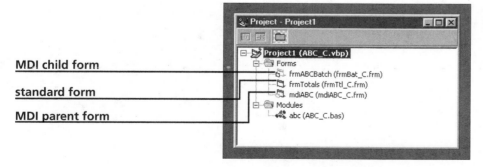

Figure 11-2: Form icons shown in Project Explorer

Like other forms, an MDI parent form supports properties and methods and can respond to events. In previous chapters, you have used the Initialize, Load, Activate, and GotFocus events with a standard form. In MDI programs (that is, programs with an MDI parent form), these events occur as follows:

- The **Initialize** event occurs first for the MDI parent form. You can place any startup code in this event.
- After the Initialize event, the **Load** event pertaining to the MDI parent form occurs. The Load event has the same effect for this form as it does for a standard form.
- After the Load event, the **Activate** event pertaining to the MDI parent form may occur depending on the status of the MDI child forms and standard forms. When the focus switches between two MDI child forms in a program, the Activate event occurs for the MDI child forms rather than for the MDI parent form. When the focus switches between an MDI child form and a standard form, the Activate event is generated in the MDI parent form.
- After the Activate event takes place, the **GotFocus** event occurs. Again, when the focus switches between two MDI child forms in a program, the GotFocus event occurs for the MDI child forms rather than for the MDI parent form.

An MDI child form is similar to the standard forms you have used in the past. A few exceptions exist, however:

- MDI child forms always appear inside the region of the MDI parent form.
- When you minimize an MDI child form at run time, the child form's icon will appear at the bottom of the MDI parent form rather than on the desktop.
- Menus for MDI child forms do not appear on the menu bar of the MDI child form. Rather, they appear on the menu bar of the MDI parent form.
- When you maximize an MDI child form, its title (stored in the caption property of the MDI child form) appears in brackets on the MDI parent form.

Because an MDI parent form acts as a container for MDI child forms, you do not create control instances like text boxes and command buttons on the MDI parent form. In fact, MDI parent forms can contain only certain types of control instances, such as menus, picture boxes, toolbars, and status bars. Although you can create control instances inside the region of a picture box, this practice is uncommon.

Characteristics of MDI Parent Forms

To create an MDI program, you add an MDI parent form to the project by using the Project menu's Add MDI Form menu item. Because a project can include only one MDI parent form, this menu item becomes disabled after you add the MDI parent form. After adding this form, you typically set its properties. The standard prefix for an MDI parent form is "mdi". The following list describes some of the properties supported by an MDI parent form:

- The **AutoShowChildren** property can be set to True or False. If set to True, an instance of the project's MDI child forms will appear when the program starts. If set to False, MDI child forms will remain hidden until explicitly displayed with the Show method.
- The **BackColor** property defines the background color of the MDI parent form. The default background color for an MDI parent form is dark gray.
- The **Caption** property defines the text displayed in the title bar of the MDI parent form.
- As in other forms, the **StartUpPosition** property controls where the form initially appears on the screen.

For ABC Concrete's program, the form to control a batch machine has already been created but the MDI parent form has not. The first step in developing the user interface is to add the MDI parent form and set its properties. You will set the form's caption and change its startup position so that it will appear in the center of the screen at run time. In addition, you will change the icon displayed in the upper-left corner of the form. When creating an MDI program, you generally want the MDI parent form to serve as the startup object, so you need to change the startup object with the Project Properties dialog.

All form types support the **Icon** property. By default, Visual Basic determines the icon displayed on a form, which is dependent upon the form type. You can change this icon by setting the Icon property to use a particular icon file. Icon files typically have the extension ".ico".

To create an MDI parent form:

1 Start Visual Basic and open the project named **Chapter.11\Startup\ABC_S.vbp**. Set the drive designator as necessary.

2 Click **Project**, then click **Add MDI Form**. The Add MDI Form dialog may appear, depending on the configuration of your system. If it does, click the **New** tab, then select **MDI Form**. Click **Open**. The New MDI parent form will appear.

Because a project can include only one MDI parent form, this option on the menu bar becomes disabled after you add the MDI parent form.

3 If necessary, open the **Properties** window for the MDI parent form you just created.

4 Set the Caption property to **ABC Concrete - Batch Plant Control**.

5 Set the Height property to **6945** and the Width property to **9600**, so the MDI child forms will fit in the region of the MDI parent form.

6 Set the Name property to **mdiABC**.

7 Click the Value column of the **Icon** property. Click the **Properties** button ⊡ to open the Load Icon dialog.

8 Click the **Look in** list box and locate the **Chapter.11\Startup** folder. Set the drive designator as necessary.

9 Click the file named **ABC.ico**, then click **Open**. The icon should appear in the upper-left corner of the MDI parent form's title bar.

10 Click **Project**, then click **Project1 Properties** to open the Project Properties dialog.

11 Make sure that the **General** tab is active.

12 Select **mdiABC** in the Startup Object list box, then click **OK** to close the dialog.

13 Save the form as **mdiABC_S.frm** in the folder **Chapter.11\Startup**. Set the drive designator as necessary.

Now that you have added the MDI parent form, you can create the menu system for it. Each standard form in a program can have its own menu system, and MDI programs are no exception. The menu system in an MDI program works in the following manner:

■ Only one menu bar appears at a time for both MDI parent and child forms. The menu bar always appears just under the title bar of the MDI parent form.

■ When no MDI child forms are open, the menu bar displays the menu pertaining to the MDI parent form.

■ When an MDI child form is open, the menu bar displays the menu pertaining to the MDI child form. If multiple MDI child forms are open simultaneously, the menu bar displays the menu pertaining to the active MDI child form.

To develop the menu system for the MDI parent form, you must create a menu item to create a new form instance when a batch machine starts up and another menu item to exit the program. The MDI parent form and MDI child forms will have separate menus. The menu for the MDI parent form will appear only when no batch machines are active.

To create the menu system for the MDI parent form:

1 Make sure that the MDI parent form is active. Use the **Tools** menu to activate the **Menu Editor** for the MDI parent form named **mdiABC**.

2 Create a menu title with a caption of **&Batch Machine Control** and a name of **mnuBatch**.

3 Create a menu item with a caption of **&Start Batch Machine** and a name of **mnuBatchStart**. Indent this menu item so that it will appear as a menu item for the menu title you just created.

4 Create another menu item with a caption of **E&xit** and a name of **mnuBatchExit**. Indent this menu item so that it will appear under the menu title. The Menu Editor should now look like Figure 11-3.

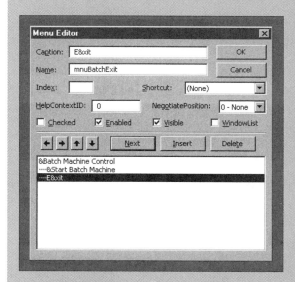

Figure 11-3: Menu system for MDI parent form

5 Click **OK** to close the Menu Editor.

The first menu item will start an instance of a batch machine when no batch machine is running. The second menu item will exit the program. Note that the names for each menu have been abbreviated to the first word of the menu item because using the full caption for the name would result in unreasonably long menu names.

The MDI parent form will display multiple MDI child forms. Each MDI child form, in turn, will control one of the active batch machines. The form representing a batch machine has not yet been set to operate as an MDI child form. To turn a form into an MDI child form, you set the MDIChild property of the desired form to True after adding the relevant MDI parent form to the project.

Characteristics of MDI Child Forms

The batch machine form should be the child form and appear inside the region of the MDI parent form. The MDIChild property for the MDI child form must therefore be set to True. In addition, because the child form should not be resized or maximized by the end user, you need to modify the buttons in the control box. The **control box** contains the Maximize, Minimize, Restore, and Close buttons that appear in the upper-right corner of the form's title bar. Several properties define whether a control box appears on a form and whether it contains buttons. These properties, which are discussed below, pertain to all forms:

- The **ControlBox** property can be True or False. If set to True, a control box appears on the form's title bar. If set to False, the control box will not appear.
- Whether the control box appears in the title bar depends upon the value of the form's **BorderStyle** property. If set to None, no buttons appear on the title bar because the title bar itself does not appear and the ControlBox, MinButton, and MaxButton properties are therefore ignored. If set to Fixed Dialog, then the control box cannot include a Maximize or Minimize button.
- The **MinButton** and **MaxButton** properties can be True or False. If the MinButton property is True, the Minimize button and Restore button will be displayed and active when the form is displayed and minimized. If the MaxButton property is True, the Maximize and Restore buttons will be displayed and active depending on the state of the form. Note that the appropriate buttons appear shaded when these properties are set to False.

In Visual Basic, all of these properties can be set only at design time. Trying to change them at run time will generate a run-time error. When the user clicks a button in the control box, the state of the window changes. That is, the window becomes maximized, minimized, or normal. When minimized, the form appears as an icon. When maximized, the form occupies the entire region of the MDI parent form. When normal, the form occupies some part of the MDI parent form. The **WindowState** property stores the current state of a form. The Intrinsic constants vbMaximized, vbMinimized, and vbNormal represent the three possible values for the WindowState property.

You will now modify the properties for the batch machine form so that it operates as an MDI child form. In addition, you will set the necessary properties to prohibit the form from being maximized or resized and to change the icon displayed in the form's title bar.

To create an MDI child form:

1   Open the form named **frmABCBatch** and activate the Properties window.

2   Set the MDIChild property to **True**. Note that the icon in the Project Explorer changes, indicating the form is an MDI child form. Set the MaxButton property to **False** to prevent the form from being maximized. Make sure the MinButton property is set to **True**.

3   Set the BorderStyle to **1 - Fixed Single** to prevent the form from being resized.

4   Set the Icon property to **Chapter.11\Startup\Faucet.ico**. Set the drive designator as necessary.

Now that you have set the design-time properties for both the MDI parent and MDI child forms, you need to show the MDI child form on the screen. To accomplish this task, you can call the Show method for the form named frmABCBatch inside the MDI parent form's Load event procedure. Because multiple MDI child forms may be open simultaneously, you need to write the code to set the caption of each child form at run time. You will use the caption "Batch Machine Number", followed by the number of the batch machine. In this case, the first batch machine started should contain a value of one (1).

To display an MDI child form:

1   Activate the Code window for the form named **mdiABC**, if necessary. Locate the **MDIForm_Load** event procedure. Because the program supports multiple forms, make sure that you activate the Code window for the correct form.

2   Enter the following statements into the event procedure:

```
frmABCBatch.Caption = "Batch Machine Number 1"
frmABCBatch.Show
```

Your program will now display an instance of the MDI child form inside the region of the MDI parent form and the user cannot resize the MDI child form. You will now test the program to verify that the forms are displayed correctly.

To test the MDI child form:

1   Save the project, then run it. An instance of the MDI child form should appear inside the region of the MDI parent form, as shown in Figure 11-4.

**Minimize
button enabled**

**Maximize
button disabled**

MDI child form

MDI parent form

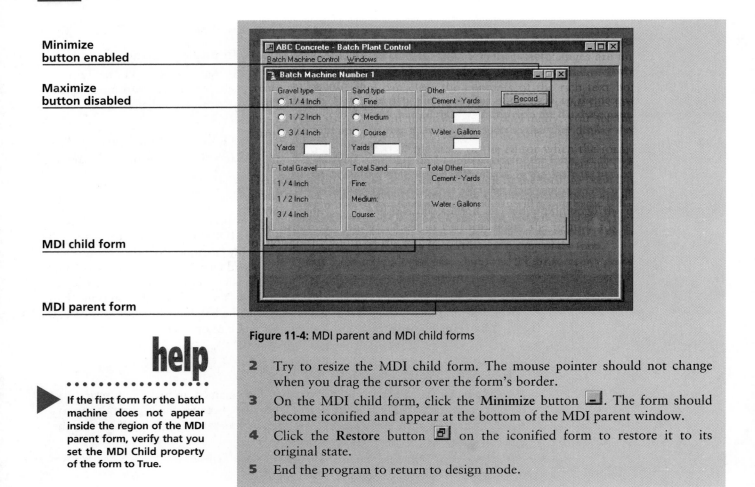

Figure 11-4: MDI parent and MDI child forms

help
• • • • • • • • • • • • • • • • •

▶ If the first form for the batch
machine does not appear
inside the region of the MDI
parent form, verify that you
set the MDI Child property
of the form to True.

2   Try to resize the MDI child form. The mouse pointer should not change
when you drag the cursor over the form's border.

3   On the MDI child form, click the **Minimize** button 🔲. The form should
become iconified and appear at the bottom of the MDI parent window.

4   Click the **Restore** button 🔲 on the iconified form to restore it to its
original state.

5   End the program to return to design mode.

Although the code you just wrote will display an instance of an MDI child
form inside the region of the MDI parent form, you still need a way to display
multiple instances of the same MDI child form simultaneously.

Understanding Object References

The term "class" has appeared throughout this book. A **class** is a template or
blueprint for an object. When you create an instance of a class, you create an
object from the class. For example, when you draw a command button or text
box on a form, you create an instance of the command button or text box from
the respective class. Like controls such as command buttons and text boxes, each
form in a project is also considered a class. The name of the class is the same as
the value stored in the form's Name property. ABC Concrete's program uses three
form classes: mdiABC, frmABCBatch, and frmTotals.

When a form loads or the program calls the Show method, an instance of the
class is created. In the programs you have created so far, you have created only
one instance of a particular form at a time. That is, only one copy of the form
displayed or hidden existed. Remember that a hidden form is active and that you

can access its objects programmatically, even though the form does not appear on the screen. Sometimes, however, it may be desirable to create multiple instances or copies of the same form and to display them on the screen at the same time.

Consider the program you are writing for ABC Concrete. The company's management wants a program to send orders to several batch machines, some of which may not be operating. Each batch machine accepts the same type of information. That is, each machine uses three types of gravel, three types of sand, cement, and water. One way to implement this user interface is to create one form class, then create an instance of the same form for each currently operating batch machine. Thus, if three batch machines were running, you would need three instances of the same form. At run time, the program will include one instance of the MDI parent form (mdiABC) and zero or more instances of the MDI child form (frmABCBatch).

When a form serves as the startup form or when you call the Show method on a form in a procedure like Sub Main, Visual Basic automatically creates an instance of the form from the corresponding class, thereby creating a form object. As part of this creation process, Visual Basic creates an object variable so that you can reference the form in code. For example, if you have a form named frmABCBatch, an instance of this form is created at run time along with an object variable of the same name. You then can set or retrieve properties and call the methods of the form object using statements such as the following:

```
frmABCBatch.Visible = True
frmABCBatch.SetFocus
```

You do not have to explicitly create an object variable to reference a form. Rather, for each form in a project, Visual Basic automatically creates an object variable with the same name as the form's class. When you reference the object variable for the first time, Visual Basic creates an instance of the form class so that you can reference the variable.

In earlier chapters, when you created object variables to store a reference to Database objects, you set them to reference an existing object; you did not create an object explicitly. Consider the following statement:

```
Dim dbCurrent As Database
```

When you declare an object variable using such a statement, an object (instance) is not created. Instead, an object variable is created that can reference an object of the specified type. Thus you cannot reference any properties or call methods using this object variable until it references an active Database object. In the past, before using the variable, you called the OpenDatabase method. The code in the OpenDatabase method created the object and stored a reference to that object in the object variable dbCurrent, as shown in the following statement:

```
Set dbCurrent = OpenDatabase("A:\MyDatabase.mdb")
```

You can also create multiple references to an object. That is, you can declare and assign multiple object variables so that they all reference the same object. Consider the following statements:

```
Dim db1 As Database
Dim db2 As Database
Dim db3 As Database
Set db1 = OpenDatabase("A:\MyDatabase.mdb")
Set db2 = db1
Set db3 = db1
```

In the preceding statements, the OpenDatabase method creates a Database object and stores a reference to the object in the variable db1. The second and third Set statements create two more references to the same Database object. A new object is *not* created. Figure 11-5 illustrates this process.

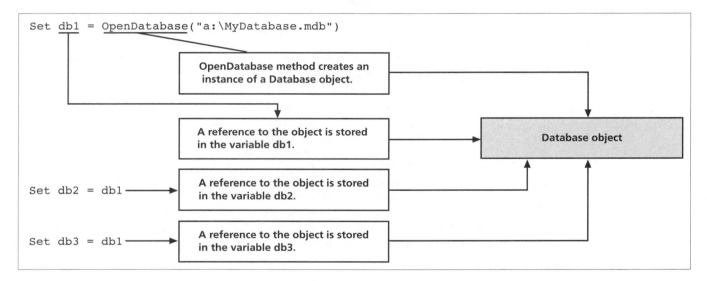

Figure 11-5: Creating multiple references to an object

In addition to declaring object variables of a specific type, you can declare generic object variables capable of storing references to different types of objects. You can use two different data types to store multiple types of objects as follows:

- The **Object** data type is a generic object data type and can store a reference to any type of object.
- The **Variant** data type can store a reference to any type of object or standard variable.

For example, if the object cmdRecord is a valid instance of a command button and lblPrompt is a valid instance of a Label object, then the following statements would be legal:

```
Dim objGeneric As Object
Set objGeneric = lblPrompt
Set objGeneric = cmdRecord
```

The first statement declares a generic object variable named objGeneric. The second statement causes the object variable to reference the label. The third statement causes the object variable to reference the command button. These statements do not create a new object, but rather create an additional reference to an existing object. You then can use the object variable to call the methods and set the properties of the underlying object using the object variable named objGeneric.

Using generic object variables can significantly degrade the performance of a program because of the process known as binding. **Binding** is the process of preparing to call a method or to set or read a property. The amount of time it takes to prepare to call the method or property is considered overhead and depends on the type of binding. Two types of binding exist:

- When you use a generic object variable of type Variant or Object, Visual Basic cannot determine the actual data type until run time. Thus, when you use a generic object variable to call a method or reference a property, Visual Basic must determine the actual object type at run time before calling a method or referencing a property. This process is called **late binding**.
- When you declare an object variable of a specific class, such as a command button or frmABCBatch, Visual Basic can determine the type of object before run time. Thus, at run time, the overhead to determine an object's type is eliminated. This process is called **early binding**.

Explicitly Creating Objects

To create a new object variable from a form's class, you do not use a method like Show as you have done previously to implicitly create the object. Rather, you must explicitly create the object. You can declare a new object variable and a corresponding object with the Dim, Public, Private, or Static statement and use of the New keyword. The syntax is identical to the syntax for the Dim, Public, Private, and Static statements you already have used, except that the New keyword is added to the declaration.

Syntax	{**Dim** | **Public** | **Private** | **Static**} *varname* [([*subscripts*])] [**As** [**New**] *type*]
Dissection	■ The optional **New** keyword, when used with the Public, Private, Dim, or Static statement, causes a new object variable of *type* to be created. The object does not actually exist until you reference it in code for the first time. You cannot use the New keyword to declare variables of any intrinsic data type, such as Integer or Single. It is used only to create objects.
Code Example	`Public frmInstance1 As New frmABCBatch`
Code Dissection	The preceding statement declares a Public variable that references a new instance (object) of the form class frmABCBatch; this variable is named frmInstance1.

The first time you reference the object named frmInstance1, either by setting a property or by calling a method, the instance is created automatically. In addition to using the Public, Dim, and Private statements to create an instance of an object and to store a reference to that instance in an object variable, you can use a variation of the Set statement. In the past, you have used the Set statement to assign an object reference to an object variable. You can also use the Set statement to create a new instance of an object from its class by using the New keyword.

Performance

tip

• • • • • • • • • • • • • • •

▶ Use object variables of a specific class whenever possible so that Visual Basic can use early binding. Early binding of object variables will significantly improve a program's performance. In addition to variables of type Object and Variant, objects of type Form and Control are late bound.

Syntax	**Set** *objectvar* = [**New**] *objectexpression* I **Nothing**
Dissection	■ The required *objectvar* argument contains the name of the object variable or property to be created.
	■ Using the optional **New** keyword will create a new instance of the object from the class name stored in *objectexpression*. If the variable *objectvar* already references an existing object, then that reference will no longer exist, and the new object and reference will be created. Just as you cannot use the New keyword in a Dim, Public, or Private statement to create objects of intrinsic data types such as Integer or Single, so you cannot use the New keyword with the Set statement to create an object having an intrinsic data type.
	■ The required *objectexpression* can contain an object variable or object type.
	■ Use of the optional **Nothing** keyword removes the association of *objectvar* from an object. By assigning Nothing to an object variable, you release all system and memory resources associated with the previously referenced object.
| **Code Example** | ```
Public frmInstance1 As frmABCBatch
Set frmInstance1 = New frmABCBatch
``` |
| **Code Dissection** | These two statements have the same effect as the Public statement with the As New keyword shown in the previous syntax. The first statement creates a variable of type frmABCBatch; the second statement actually creates an instance of the form class. |

Hidden Variables

Remember that for every form in a program, Visual Basic creates a variable with the same name as the form's class. This process is roughly equivalent to Visual Basic adding the following declaration to a form module in a project having a Name property of frmABCBatch:

```
Public frmABCBatch As New frmABCBatch
```

Visual Basic declares a **hidden variable** for you automatically, even though the declaration of the variable does not appear in the project. This declaration remains hidden because it changes each time you modify the Name property of the form. That is, if you changed the name of a form, the declaration discussed above would also change to the new form name.

The preceding statement declares an object variable named frmABCBatch from the class named frmABCBatch. To create two instances of the form named frmABCBatch, you could create two object variables. The following statements declare two object variables named frmABCBatch1 and frmABCBatch2 and create two objects of type frmABCBatch:

```
Public frmABCBatch1 As New frmABCBatch
Public frmABCBatch2 As New frmABCBatch
```

These statements create two separate instances of a form from the class named frmABCBatch. The first instance is named frmABCBatch1 and the second instance
```

is named frmABCBatch2. These are separate objects rather than multiple references to the same object. Consider the following statements:

```
Public frmABCBatch1 As New frmABCBatch
Public frmABCBatch2 As New frmABCBatch
Public frmABCBatchRef1 As frmABCBatch
Public frmABCBatchRef2 As frmABCBatch
```

The first pair of statements creates two form instances named frmABCBatch1 and frmABCBatch2 from the form class frmABCBatch. The second pair of statements declares two more object variables. No objects are created because you omitted the New keyword. Rather, the variables reference Nothing until a Set statement is used to cause them to reference an existing object.

```
Set frmABCBatchRef1 = frmABCBatch1
Set frmABCBatchRef2 = frmABCBatch2
```

The preceding statements create an additional reference to the objects frmABCBatch1 and frmABCBatch2. In other words, you can now use the object variables frmABCBatchRef1 and frmABCBatch1 to reference the first form object. The object variables frmABCBatchRef2 and frmABCBatch2 reference the second form object. Figure 11-6 illustrates this process.

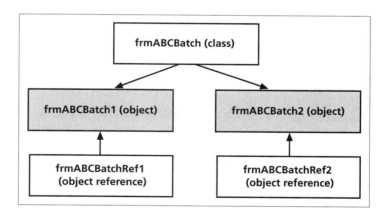

Figure 11-6: Creating multiple instances of a form and multiple references

Although a form is considered a class, a standard module is not. That is, you cannot create an instance of a standard module so as to use its variables and procedures.

Standard modules and class modules store their data differently. Each instance of a form has its own copy of the data stored in its properties. If you extend this concept to the control instances on a form, each such control instance (an instance of the control's class) has its own copy of its data stored in its properties. For example, the following statements would change the caption of each form:

```
frmABCBatch1.Caption = "First form instance"
frmABCBatch2.Caption = "Second form instance"
```

Each form object has its own copy of the Caption property. Setting the value of one form's caption, therefore, will not affect the caption of the other form. Only one copy of the variables in a standard module exists, however. When you destroy a form instance, its data are destroyed as well. Public and Private variables declared in the general declarations section of a standard module exist for the life of the program.

Changing the Lower Bound of an Array

Because the program in this chapter requires multiple instances of the form named frmABCBatch, you need an object variable to hold each individual form instance. To accomplish this task, you can create an object variable of type frmABCBatch for each form representing a batch machine. Each object variable then would store a reference to a form instance. Because you do not know how many batch machines will be active at any given time and because one program requirement is to be able to activate any number of batch machines, using multiple object variables will not allow the program to dynamically create an infinite number of batch machines (that is, form instances).

You have created arrays to store data types such as Integers and Variants. Visual Basic also allows you to create arrays to reference object variables. You can declare an array, then store a reference to each form instance into the array. In ABC Concrete's program, the title bar for each batch machine (MDI child form) should display the machine number. Because the batch machines are numbered starting from one, the programming task will become easier if the elements of each array corresponding to a form have the same number (subscript). That is, the first batch machine (machine number 1) should have an index of 1 in the array. To dimension an array with a lower bound of one, you could write the following statement:

```
Public gfrmABCBatchArray(1 to 10) As frmABCBatch
```

When it is more intuitive for all or most arrays in a program to have a lower bound of one, you can use the **Option Base** statement, which has the following syntax:

Syntax	**Option Base (0|1)**
Dissection	■ The **Option Base** statement must be used at the module level to declare the default lower bound for arrays declared in the module. This statement must appear before any procedure declarations in the module.
	■ If the default Option Base 0 is used, then the default lower bound for all arrays declared in that module is 0. If you do not declare an Option Base, or if you use the Option Base statement without an argument, then 0 is the lower bound for all arrays declared in that module.
	■ If you specify Option Base 1, then the default lower bound for all arrays declared in that module is 1.
	■ When necessary, you can explicitly declare the lower bound of an array to override the value of the Option Base. Consider the following: `Public gfrmABCBatchArray(2 To 11) As frmABCBatch`

Setting the Option Base in one module, however, does not change the Option Base in another module. Because each batch machine is numbered from one, you will change the default lower bound for the arrays in ABC Concrete's program to one (1) in each form and standard module.

> To change the default lower bound for all arrays in a module:
> **1** Activate the Code window to the general declarations section for the standard module named **ABC_S.bas**.
> **2** Enter the following statement as the first statement in the module after Option Explicit:
>
> ```
> Option Base 1
> ```
>
> **3** Enter the Option Base statement from Step 2 into the general declarations section of the forms named **mdiABC** and **frmABCBatch**.
> **4** Repeat the process for the form named **frmTotals**.

Because the array needs to be accessible from each instance of the batch machine form as well as from the MDI parent form, you need to declare the array as a Public variable in the standard module ABC_S.bas. To ensure that an instance of the form class will be created when the program references the object, you need to use the New keyword when you declare the array. One approach to creating the array involves creating an object variable for each of the 10 batch machines. Thus you could use the following statement:

```
Dim gfrmABCBatchArray(10) As New frmABCBatch
```

To save memory, however, you can create an array with no elements, then change the size of the array at run time as necessary. This process is called redimensioning an array. Visual Basic allows you to change the size of an array at run time using the ReDim statement.

Syntax

ReDim [**Preserve**] *varname*(*subscripts*) [**As** *type*]

Dissection

- You can use the **ReDim** statement to size or resize a dynamic array previously declared using a Private, Public, or Dim statement with empty parentheses (without dimension subscripts). You can call the ReDim statement repeatedly to change the number of elements and dimensions in an array. You cannot declare an array of one data type and later use ReDim to change the array to another data type unless the array is a Variant.

- If you use the optional **Preserve** keyword, any data stored in the array will be saved when the size of the last dimension changes. If you omit this keyword, the contents of each element will be destroyed.

- The required *varname* argument must contain the name of the variable. This variable should have been declared using the Dim, Private, Public, or Static statement. The required *subscripts* argument contains the new dimensions of the array and has the same syntax with which you are already familiar.

- The optional *type* may be any of the following data types: Byte, Boolean, Integer, Long, Currency, Single, Double, Date, String, Object, Variant, a user-defined type, or an object type.

In ABC Concrete's program, you will declare an array with no elements, then increase the size of the array and store a reference to the frmABCBatch object into the array each time a batch machine starts up (when an instance of the form is created). The array will contain objects of the form class named frmABCBatch.

To declare the array to store the form objects:

1 Open the Code window for the standard module named **ABC_S.bas**.

2 Enter the following statement into the general declarations section of the standard module just after the Option Base statement:

```
Public gfrmABCBatchArray( ) As New frmABCBatch
```

Programming

tip

• • • • • • • • • • • • • • •

▶ Visual Basic places some restrictions on the valid data types for Public variables declared in a form module. In particular, constants, fixed-length strings, and arrays cannot be declared as Public variables in a form module.

This statement declares an array named gfrmABCBatchArray to store object references based upon the class frmABCBatch. Note the components of the name. Because the variable is global, you used the "g" prefix, followed by the object's type frmABCBatch, followed by the suffix "Array". Each element in the array will store an instance of the form. Initially the array contains no elements. You will redimension the array later in this chapter when you create the form instances.

You can write code to change the size of the array when the MDI parent form loads, then create and display the first instance of the form representing the first batch machine started. In addition, you need to know which batch machine the form represents. To accomplish this task, you can use the Tag property, which has the following syntax:

Syntax	*object*.**Tag** = [*expression*]
Dissection	■ The **Tag** property stores an identification string in a form or control instance. This string is not used in any way by Visual Basic. Rather, it is used by a program to store information about an object that cannot be stored in an existing property.
	■ The *object* can be any control or form instance.
	■ The *expression* can be any string.
Code Example	gfrmABCBatchArray(1).Tag = 1
Code Dissection	The preceding statement assumes that element 1 of the array named gfrmABCBatchArray exists. It stores the value 1 in the Tag property.

Because the array is currently empty, it has a size of zero (0). To create the first object, you need to change the size of the array to 1 using the ReDim statement. You also will store the numerical value of the current batch machine in the Tag property. Later in this chapter, you will use this value to identify the current batch machine.

To create the first instance of the form for the batch machine:

1 Open the Code window for the **MDI** parent form, then activate the **MDIForm_Load** event procedure.

2 Remove the existing statements from the event procedure and replace them with the following statements:

```
ReDim gfrmABCBatchArray(1)
gfrmABCBatchArray(1).Tag = 1
gfrmABCBatchArray(1).Caption = _
    "Batch Machine Number 1"
gfrmABCBatchArray(1).Show
```

The first statement changes the number of elements in the array from zero to one. Because you declared the array with the New keyword, a new object is created automatically when the array is redimensioned. The second statement stores the value 1 in the Tag property. (You will use this value later in this chapter.) The Tag property is merely a string of characters; it is not used by Visual Basic. Rather, it gives your program a way to store information about a particular object. The third statement sets the caption for the new form instance. The final statement displays the MDI child form inside the region of the MDI parent form.

Now that you have written the statements to display the first instance of the MDI child form, you should test the program to ensure that it works correctly.

To test that the first instance of the batch machine is displayed correctly:

1 Save the project, then run it. Your form should resemble Figure 11-7.

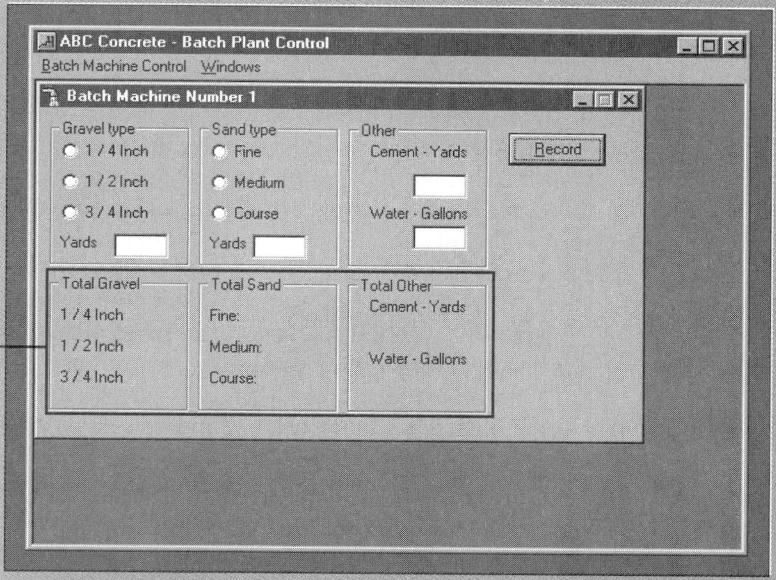

output section

Figure 11-7: MDI parent and child forms

2 End the program to return to design mode.

help

If the MDI child form does not appear, check the code you wrote for the MDI parent form's MDIForm_Load event.

Notice that the form in Figure 11-7 includes an output section containing three frames. The first frame contains objects to display the amount of the three different types of gravel used. The second frame contains objects to display the amount of the three different types of sand used. The third frame indicates the amount of cement and water used.

Each time the operator clicks the Record command button, the program should add the amount of each material used to an accumulator; it should then display the current value of each accumulator in the output section of the form. You need to declare the accumulators to store this information. Additionally, you need a set of the same accumulators for each form because you must keep track of the materials used for each batch machine. Although you could declare arrays in the standard module to hold this information, you can also store the information inside the form and reference it from other forms and modules.

Creating Form Properties

Remember that a form is a class and that, when a form is displayed, an instance of the form is created from the class. By adding a control instance to a form, you actually add a property to the form class. This property, which has the same name as the Name property of the new control instance, is a read-only property that you use to reference the object. As well as adding properties to a form with existing controls, you can create your own properties.

For example, you can store the data inside of the form and reference it from other modules by declaring Public variables in a form module. When you declare a Public variable in a form module, the variable behaves much differently than it does in a standard module. Public variables declared in a form module do not exist for the life of the program. Instead, they exist only while the specific instance of the form exists. Once the instance of the form is unloaded, the variables and their values are destroyed. Furthermore, each instance of a form has its own copy of the Public variable. In fact, Public variables declared in a form module are treated as properties of the form itself.

One important concept in object-oriented programming is encapsulation. **Encapsulation**, simply put, means placing an object's code and data in the same module. In ABC Concrete's program, you will encapsulate the form's data (the accumulators to determine the total amount of each type of sand, gravel, water, and concrete used) inside the form itself. You have dealt with encapsulation before by using controls such as a text box.

With a text box, for instance, the TextBox control is a class. When you draw multiple text boxes on a form, you create multiple instances of the TextBox class. Each instance of the text box maintains its own copy of the object's properties. Thus each text box has a Text property, but the Text property of each text box remains a separate value. All data related to a specific instance of a text box, and the procedures that act on that data, are encapsulated in the text box.

Public variables in form modules work in exactly the same way. When you declare a Public variable in a form module, it is considered a property of the form. You reference the property by using the variable's name. For example, assume you declared the following variable in the general declarations section for a form module:

```
Public YardsSandFine As Single
```

This variable name may seem to violate the naming conventions for a variable. The variable, however, is a property because it is declared as Public inside of a form module. Property names should consist of words, with the first letter of each word being capitalized. Abbreviate words only when the name of the property exceeds 20 to 30 characters.

For a valid instance of the form module named frmABCBatch1, for example, you would write the following statement fragment to reference the property:

```
frmABCBatch1.YardsSandFine
```

The program you are writing for ABC Concrete requires that you maintain an accumulator for each of the three types of sand and gravel. Two more accumulators are necessary to store the yards of cement and the gallons of water used. A simple way to accomplish this task is to declare Public variables in the form module. With this approach, you do not need to declare an array in the standard module and redimension the array each time a new batch machine starts up. This technique encapsulates the data in the form.

To create the accumulators for a batch machine:

1 Activate the Code window for the form named **frmABCBatch**, then enter the following statements in the general declarations section after the Option Base statement:

```
Public YardsSandFine As Single
Public YardsSandMedium As Single
Public YardsSandCoarse As Single
Public YardsGravelQuarter As Single
Public YardsGravelHalf As Single
Public YardsGravelThreeQuarter As Single
Public YardsCement As Single
Public GallonsWater As Single
```

These statements declare eight Public variables that are treated as form properties. The first three variables will accumulate the cubic yards of each type of sand used. The second three variables will accumulate each type of gravel used. The final two variables will accumulate the yards of cement and gallons of water used.

A unique copy of each variable will exist for each instance of the form. Also, when the form unloads, the instance of the form will be destroyed, so the variables will be destroyed as well.

Now that you have declared the accumulator variables, you need to write the statements to update their values when the plant receives an order. The first step in this process is to determine which option buttons representing the sand type and the gravel type are selected. To make your program more readable, you can create an enumeration. An **enumeration** allows you to create a set of constants and associate the constant values with names.

The Enum Statement

In the past, you have used intrinsic and user-defined constants in your programs to improve readability. Frequently, you have used an intrinsic constant and assigned the constant value to a property. In these cases, a fixed number of values can be assigned to the property. For example, you can represent the value of a check box by using any of three constants: vbChecked, vbGrayed, or vbUnchecked. Each of these constants can be represented as an Integer value: vbChecked = 1, vbGrayed = 2, and vbUnchecked = 0. When you use the Object Browser to view these different constants, you can see that the constants are actually an enumerated type named CheckBoxConstants. You can look at the Object Browser to verify the type name for the check box constants and the valid values for the type.

To look at the enumerated type for the check box constants and their possible values:

1   Click **View**, then click **Object Browser** on the menu bar to open the Object Browser.

2   Click **CheckBoxConstants** in the Classes section in the Object Browser. Your form should resemble Figure 11-8. Note that the Search Results section in the Object Browser may not appear, depending on your Visual Basic configuration.

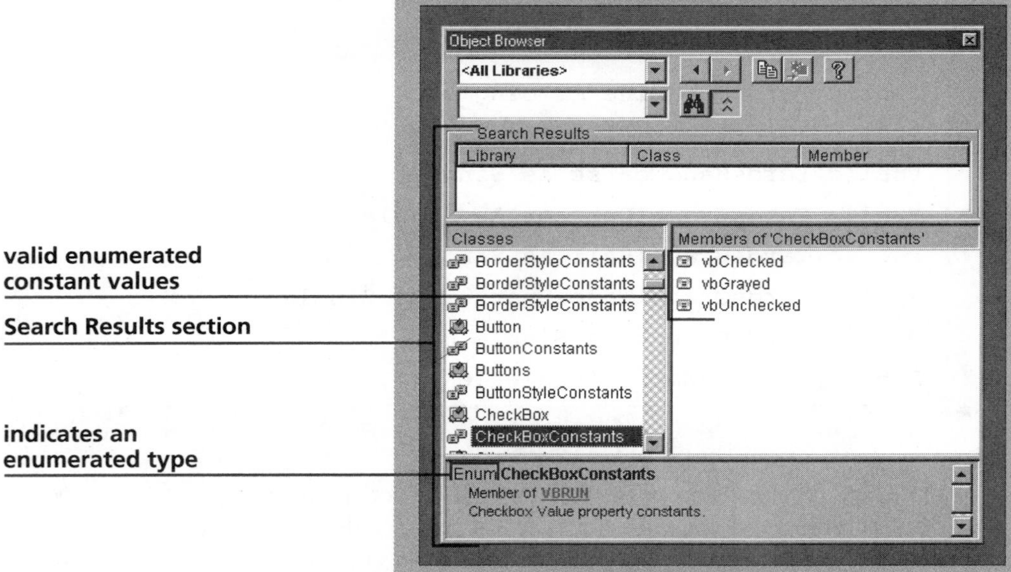

valid enumerated constant values

Search Results section

indicates an enumerated type

Figure 11-8: Enumerated type in Object Browser

CheckBoxConstants is an enumerated type, as indicated by the word Enum. This type has three valid values, which are listed in the Members section in the dialog.

3   Close the Object Browser.

In Visual Basic, you can create your own variables whose value should be one of a defined set of constants. This process is called an enumeration. For example, if you wanted to create a variable to represent the days of the week, you could declare an enumeration with the Enum statement.

Syntax	**[Public|Private] Enum** *name*
	membername [= *constantexpression*]
	membername [= *constantexpression*]
	…
	End Enum

Dissection	■ The optional **Public** keyword specifies that the enumerated type be visible throughout the project. The optional **Private** keyword specifies that the enumerated type be visible only within the module in which it is declared. The Public and Private keywords have the same effect when declaring enumerated types as they do when declaring variables with an intrinsic type such as Integer or Single.
	■ The **Enum** statement declares the type for an enumeration. It can appear only at the module level. Once you have declared the enumerated type, the type can be used to declare variables.
	■ The *name* represents the name of the enumerated type. It must adhere to the same rules as variable names.
	■ The *membername* is an element of an enumerated type. Visual Basic treats the member of an enumerated type much like a constant. When you declare variables of an enumerated type, they should assume only member values.
	■ The *constantexpression* contains the value of the member and is treated as a Long Integer. This value can be a number or another enumerated type. If you do not specify a *constantexpression*, the first member is assigned the value of 0, the second a value of 1, and so on.
	■ The **End Enum** statement exits the declaration block.

When you declare variables of a user-enumerated type, you should use the prefix "e" to denote an enumerated type. After declaring an enumerated type, you can then declare variables of that type or procedures that return the enumerated type. For example, if you wanted a variable to represent the days of the week, you could create seven constants, representing Sunday through Saturday. You can then declare a variable to store one of the seven constants, but nothing prohibits a programmer from assigning a value to the variable outside the defined range. To declare an enumerated type named eDaysOfTheWeek to store one of the seven constant values representing the days of the week, you would write the following statements:

```
Public Enum eDaysOfTheWeek
      Sunday
      Monday
      Tuesday
      Wednesday
      Thursday
      Friday
      Saturday
End Enum
```

These statements declare the enumerated type eDaysOfTheWeek. This enumerated type can store seven different values, represented by the numbers 0 through 6. Your code, however, can reference the type using the mnemonic constants Sunday through Saturday. Using enumerated types can significantly improve the readability of a program.

In the previous enumeration, the name Sunday has a value of 0, Monday a value of 1, and so on, because the constant expression was omitted. The following set of statements produce an equivalent result:

```
Public Enum eDaysOfTheWeek
        Sunday = 0
        Monday = 1
        Tuesday = 2
        Wednesday = 3
        Thursday = 4
        Friday = 5
        Saturday = 6
End Enum
```

The preceding statements actually do not create a variable. Rather, they define an enumerated type. You must declare a variable of the enumerated type before using the enumerated type. Thus, to declare a variable to store the values of an enumerated type, you use a Dim, Public, or Private statement.

```
Public eToday As eDaysOfTheWeek
```

Programming

. . . .

▶ **If you try to store a value other than the enumerated constants into the variable eToday, no run-time error will occur. Create enumerated types in your program whenever the value of a variable should assume only a finite set of values, such as days of the week or months of the year. This strategy will improve the readability of your program. Use caution when storing the intended constants in the enumeration, however.**

The preceding statement declares a Public variable that can be used by all modules in a program. The variable has the enumerated data type of eDaysOfTheWeek. It is intended to store the values 0 through 6, represented by the constant names Sunday through Saturday. After declaring this variable, you can use it in an assignment statement. For example, to set the variable eToday to Monday, you can use the following statement:

```
eToday = Monday
```

For your program, you can use enumerated types to represent the types of sand and gravel used by the batch machines. For example, ABC Concrete uses three sizes of gravel (quarter-inch, half-inch, and three-quarter-inch) and three types of sand (fine, medium, and coarse). Thus you can create one enumerated type for the types of gravel and another for the types of sand. Because all the different modules in your program will use these types, you should declare them in the standard module ABC_S.bas.

To declare enumerated types:

1 Open the Code window to the general declarations section of the standard module named **ABC_S.bas**.

2 Enter the following statements (shown in bold) into the Code window just after the Option Base statement:

```
Option Base 1
Public Enum eGravelType
    GravelQuarter
    GravelHalf
    GravelThreeQuarter
End Enum
Public Enum eSandType
    SandFine
    SandMedium
    SandCoarse
End Enum
```

These statements declare two enumerated types, named eGravelType and eSandType. The enumerated type eGravelType is represented by three constant values: GravelQuarter, GravelHalf, and GravelThreeQuarter. The enumerated type eSandType is also represented by three constant values. Each enumerated type begins with an Enum keyword and ends with the End Enum keyword. Collectively, this group of statements is referred to as an enumeration block.

Using enumerated types offers an advantage to the programmer, in that they appear in the Object Browser, and the Code window's IntelliSense technology will list the valid enumerated constants. You should now look at the Object Browser to review the enumerated type and the valid constant values.

To view an enumerated type in the Object Browser:

1 Click the **Object Browser** button 🔡 on the menu bar to open the Object Browser.

2 Select **Project1** in the Project/Library list box.

3 In the Classes section, click the type **eGravelType** you just created.

4 Click each constant in the Members of 'eGravelType' section to review the value of each constant. Your screen should look like Figure 11-9. Note that the Search Results section in the Object Browser may not appear, depending on your Visual Basic configuration.

Project1 selected

valid values for the type eGravelType

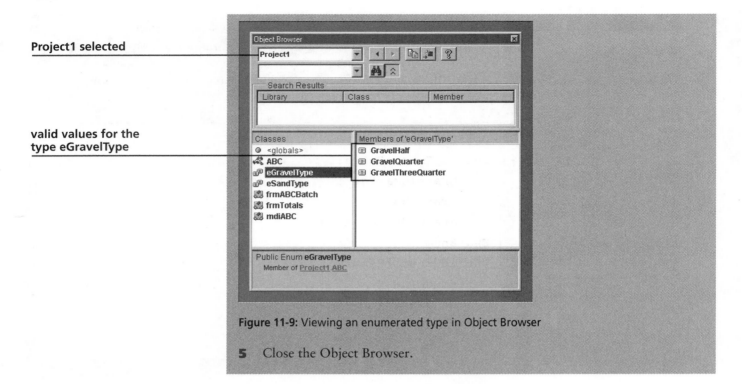

Figure 11-9: Viewing an enumerated type in Object Browser

5   Close the Object Browser.

Two groups of option buttons, named optGravelType and optSandType, have already been created for you. Each is a member of a control array. When the user clicks the Record command button, your program needs to determine which option button in each option group is active, then update the corresponding accumulator. Instead of using the numeric value representing the index in the control array, you can use the enumerated types you just declared. To declare a variable of an enumerated type, you can use the Public, Private, or Dim statement, just as you did with intrinsic data types.

You now need to declare two variables for the two enumerated types you just created. These variables will store the currently selected type of sand or gravel. Because the type of sand and gravel selected pertains to a specific batch machine, the variables should be declared in the form named frmABCBatch. These variables, however, will be used only by a specific form instance but by multiple procedures in the form; thus they should be declared as Private variables in the general declarations section of the form module.

To create enumerated variables:

1   Activate the Code window to the general declarations section of the form named **frmABCBatch**.

2   Enter the following statements in the Code window just after the Option
Base statement:

```
Private eSandSelected As eSandType
Private eGravelSelected As eGravelType
```

These statements declare two variables, each of which can store a constant of
the enumerated type. The variable eSandSelected can store the three valid values
for the types of sand, and the variable eGravelSelected can store the three valid
values for the types of gravel.

Now that you have declared the variables, you can write the code to set the
values of these variables depending on which option button is clicked. You can
either write an If statement in the cmdRecord_Click event procedure or write code
in the Click event procedure for each option button. In this chapter, you will set
the value inside the option button, although the choice is arbitrary.

To determine which type of sand currently is selected:

1   Make sure that the Code window is still active for the form module named
frmABCBatch.

2   Activate the Code window for the **optSandType_Click** event procedure,
then enter the following statements:

```
Select Case Index
    Case SandFine
        eSandSelected = SandFine
    Case SandMedium
        eSandSelected = SandMedium
    Case SandCoarse
        eSandSelected = SandCoarse
End Select
```

This Select Case statement uses the same structure as the Select Case statements you wrote in Chapter 4 to determine which option button in an option
group is selected. Instead of using the values 0, 1, and 2 for the Case statement,
however, you used the new enumerated constants. These constants make the
program more readable because they rely on a named value rather than a number.

You now can write the nearly identical statement for the option group containing the types of gravel.

To determine which type of gravel currently is selected:

1 Make sure the Code window is still active for the form module named **frmABCBatch.**

2 Activate the Code window for the **optGravelType_Click** event procedure, then enter the following statements:

```
Select Case Index
    Case GravelQuarter
        eGravelSelected = GravelQuarter
    Case GravelHalf
        eGravelSelected = GravelHalf
    Case GravelThreeQuarter
        eGravelSelected = GravelThreeQuarter
End Select
```

These statements work in the same way as the statements you just wrote. This block, however, uses the eGravelSelected enumerated type instead of the eSandSelected enumerated type.

Now that the values of the currently selected option buttons are stored in the variables eSandSelected and eGravelSelected, you can write the statements in the cmdRecord command button to update the accumulators. When the user clicks the command button, the program should update the totals for each type of gravel and sand used. In addition, it should update the amount of cement and water used. The type of sand selected is stored in the variable eSandSelected, and the type of gravel is stored in the variable eGravelSelected. These variables can hold the values of the corresponding enumerated type. An error will occur if you try to store a different value in one of these variables. When the accumulators are updated, the new value should be stored in the output section of the form. The output section contains several labels in which to store the information.

To update the accumulators for the types of sand and gravel and then display the results in the corresponding labels:

1 Make sure that the Code window for the form module named **frmABCBatch** is still active.

2 Select the **cmdRecord_Click** event procedure, then enter the following statements in the Code window:

```
Select Case eSandSelected
    Case SandFine
        YardsSandFine = YardsSandFine + _
            Val(txtSandYards)
        lblSandFine = YardsSandFine
    Case SandMedium
        YardsSandMedium = YardsSandMedium + _
            Val(txtSandYards)
        lblSandMedium = YardsSandMedium
    Case SandCoarse
        YardsSandCoarse = YardsSandCoarse + _
            Val(txtSandYards)
        lblSandCoarse = YardsSandCoarse
End Select

Select Case eGravelSelected
    Case GravelQuarter
        YardsGravelQuarter = YardsGravelQuarter + _
            Val(txtGravelYards)
        lblGravelQuarter = YardsGravelQuarter
    Case GravelHalf
        YardsGravelHalf = YardsGravelHalf + _
            Val(txtGravelYards)
        lblGravelHalf = YardsGravelHalf
    Case GravelThreeQuarter
        YardsGravelThreeQuarter = _
            YardsGravelThreeQuarter + _
            Val(txtGravelYards)
        lblGravelThreeQuarter = _
            YardsGravelThreeQuarter
End Select
YardsCement = YardsCement + Val(txtCementYards)
lblCement = YardsCement
GallonsWater = GallonsWater + Val(txtWaterGallons)
lblWater = GallonsWater
```

These statements update the values of the accumulators and store the current result in the corresponding output label objects. Once the program performs its basic functions, future enhancements to the application will validate the input in the text boxes; for this chapter, however, you may assume that the user enters valid input.

The first Select Case statement, which is reproduced below, uses the value of the enumerated variable eSandSelected as the test expression.

```
Select Case eSandSelected
    Case SandFine
        YardsSandFine = YardsSandFine + _
            Val(txtSandYards)
        lblSandFine = YardsSandFine
    . . .
```

Remember that the variable's value must be one of the valid constant values for the enumerated type. These constant values are used in each individual Case statement. This statement is more readable than one using Integer numbers, because it describes the purpose of the Case statement rather than providing a number without any inherent meaning. The statements for each case are very similar. The current number of yards of a specific type of sand is added to the corresponding accumulator. One case is used for each type of sand. For each case, the program updates the corresponding accumulator and stores the updated value in the corresponding output label. Note that the Caption property is the default property for a label; to improve performance, the word "Caption" is therefore omitted.

Consider the following code:

```
Select Case eGravelSelected
    Case GravelQuarter
        YardsGravelQuarter = YardsGravelQuarter + _
            Val(txtGravelYards)
        lblGravelQuarter = YardsGravelQuarter
    . . .
```

This second Select Case statement uses the variable named eGravelSelected for the test expression and updates the appropriate gravel accumulators.

Finally, consider this code:

```
YardsCement = YardsCement + Val(txtCementYards)
lblCement = YardsCement
GallonsWater = GallonsWater + Val(txtWaterGallons)
lblWater = GallonsWater
```

These statements update the accumulators representing the amount of cement and water used, then display the result in the corresponding labels.

Now that you have written the statements to update the accumulators, you need to test whether they are updated properly.

To verify that the accumulators are updated correctly:

1   Save and test the program. Click the **1 / 4 Inch** Gravel type option button, then click the **Fine** Sand type option button.

2   Enter 3 in the Yards text box in the Gravel type section, 2 in the Yards text box in the Sand type section, .5 in the Cement - Yards text box, and 35 in the Water - Gallons text box.

3   Click the **Record** command button. The values in the labels should be updated, as shown in Figure 11-10.

enter these values in the input section

update values shown in output labels

click Record to update accumulators

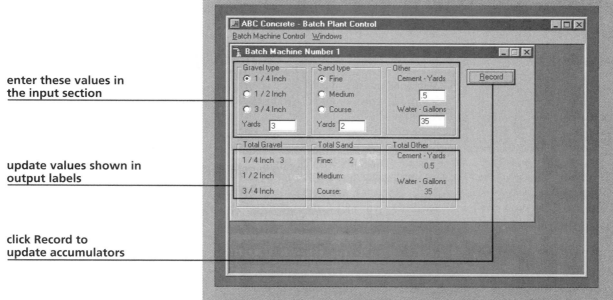

Figure 11-10: Testing the accumulators (1)

4   Repeat Steps 1, 2, and 3, selecting a **1 / 2 Inch** Gravel type and **Medium** sand. Repeat Steps 1, 2, and 3 again, selecting **3 / 4 Inch** Gravel type, and **Coarse** sand. Your form should look like Figure 11-11.

updated values shown in output labels

help

● ● ● ● ● ● ● ● ● ● ● ● ● ● ● ● ● ●

► If the accumulators are not updated properly, verify that the code you wrote for each option button and the code for the Record command button are correct. Repeat Steps 1 through 4.

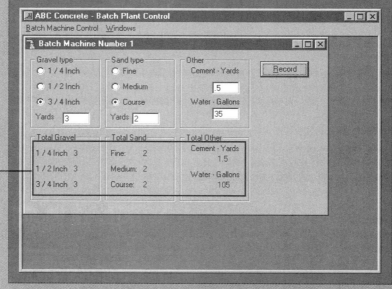

Figure 11-11: Testing the accumulators (2)

5 End the program to return to design mode.

The code you have written so far allows you to start the first batch machine by creating the first instance of the form class frmABCBatch. It also allows you to update the accumulators for each component by updating the Public variables in the form.

Q U E S T I O N S

1. Which of the following statements about MDI programs is true?
   a. They can have multiple MDI parent forms.
   b. They can have multiple MDI child forms.
   c. Standard forms cannot be used in MDI programs.
   d. All of the above.
   e. None of the above.

2. Which of the following statements about menus used with MDI forms is true?
   a. Only one menu bar is displayed for both the MDI parent and child form.
   b. When no MDI child forms are open, the menu bar displays the menu for the MDI parent form.
   c. When an MDI child form is open, the menu for the child form is displayed.
   d. All of the above.
   e. None of the above.

3. What is the name of the property used to turn a form into an MDI child form?
   a. Child
   b. MDI
   c. MDIChild
   d. SetChild
   e. None of the above.

4. Which of the following properties are used to determine the appearance of a control box and the appearance of any respective buttons?
   a. ControlBox, Max, Min, Resize
   b. ControlBox, Maximize, Minimize, Resize
   c. ControlBox, MinButton, MaxButton
   d. TitleBar, MinButton, MaxButton
   e. None of the above.

5. The _____ property stores the current state of a form.
   a. FormState
   b. FormStatus
   c. WindowStatus
   d. WindowState
   e. None of the above.

6. The process of preparing to call a method is called _____.
   a. Binding
   b. Setup
   c. Encapsulation
   d. Calling
   e. Preparation

7. Write a statement to create an instance of the form class named Form1, then store a reference to that instance in the object variable called frmInstance.

8. Write the statement to change the size of the array named ArrayDemo so that it has seven elements.

9. Create an enumerated type named eMonths having enumeration names of January, February, March, and so on. Create the enumeration such that January has a value of one (1), February (2), and so on.

10. Write the statement to declare a variable named Months having the enumerated type of eMonths.

In this section you will:

- Create multiple instances of a form
- Arrange MDI child forms
- Create a user-defined type
- Close an MDI program

Programming Multiple Form Instances

Creating Multiple Instances of a Form

Although the statements you just wrote are useful for starting the first batch machine, your program still needs the ability to operate multiple batch machines concurrently (that is, multiple instances of the same form). Each form instance should represent one of the active batch machines. A menu item on the batch machine form that starts a new batch machine has already been constructed for this purpose. You created a menu item on the MDI parent form to accomplish the same task. Now you will write a general procedure that is visible to both the MDI parent and child forms to start additional batch machines. This procedure should be declared as a Public procedure in the standard module so that it will be visible from both the MDI parent and child forms. It needs to increase the size of the array containing a reference to the batch machine form object by one. Then, it must create a new instance of the MDI child form and display it on the screen.

You have already learned how to use the ReDim statement to change the number of elements in an array from zero (0) to one (1) at run time. Now, however, you need a way to find out the number of elements in the array so that you will know the desired size of the array. One way to accomplish this task would be to declare a variable, then increment the variable each time a batch machine starts up. Visual Basic supports two intrinsic functions to obtain the current dimensions of an array without taking the additional steps of declaring and incrementing variables. Using these functions, you can compute the number of elements in a dimension of an array, then use the ReDim statement to change its size.

Syntax	**UBound**(*arrayname*[, *dimension*])
Dissection	■ The **UBound** function returns a Long Integer containing the largest available subscript for the indicated dimension of an array.
	■ The required *arrayname* argument is the name of an array that already has been declared.
	■ The optional *dimension* argument is a Long Integer indicating which dimension will be returned. This argument is one-based. That is, the first dimension is one (1), the second is two (2), and so on. If you do not specify a dimension, the value one (1) is assumed.

The LBound function works in the same way as the UBound function and returns a Long Integer containing the smallest subscript in a dimension in an array. It has the following syntax:

Syntax   **LBound**(*arrayname*[, *dimension*])

Before calling the UBound or LBound functions, a dimension must have been defined for the array; otherwise, a run-time error will occur. Thus you cannot call UBound or LBound on an array that has not been dimensioned. Given the following array declaration, the UBound function will return the values 50, 3, and 4, respectively. The LBound function will return 1, 0, and -3, respectively.

```
Dim ArrayOne(1 To 50, 0 To 3, -3 To 4)
UBound(ArrayOne, 1)
UBound(ArrayOne, 2)
UBound(ArrayOne, 3)
LBound(ArrayOne, 1)
LBound(ArrayOne, 2)
LBound(ArrayOne, 3)
```

By default, your array has a lower bound of one because you used the Option Base 1 statement, so the UBound function returns the number of elements in the array. To start an additional batch machine, you can call the UBound function, add one to the value returned by UBound, then use the result as the argument to the ReDim statement to increase the size of the array referencing each form object. In this situation, you need to increase the size of the array by one element. Because you do not want to destroy the existing objects in the array, you must use the Preserve keyword with the ReDim statement. As each additional batch machine starts up, the caption should contain descriptive text followed by the machine number.

To create additional form instances:

1   Activate the Code window for the standard module named **ABC_S.bas**.

2   Create a **Public Sub** procedure named **StartBatchMachine** that accepts no arguments, then enter the following statements into the general procedure:

```
Dim pintMachineCount As Integer
pintMachineCount = UBound(gfrmABCBatchArray)
pintMachineCount = pintMachineCount + 1
ReDim Preserve gfrmABCBatchArray(pintMachineCount)
gfrmABCBatchArray(pintMachineCount).Caption = _
    "Batch Machine Number " & pintMachineCount
gfrmABCBatchArray(pintMachineCount).Show
```

This code creates new form instances representing an active batch machine. The first statement declares a variable pintMachineCount to determine the number of active batch machines.

```
pintMachineCount = UBound(gfrmABCBatchArray)
pintMachineCount = pintMachineCount + 1
```

These two statements determine the current size of the gfrmABCBatchArray array by calling the UBound function. Because the array has a single dimension, the dimension argument pertaining to the UBound function is unnecessary. Remember that the first batch machine became activated when the MDI form loaded, so at least one batch machine is active when the program calls this procedure. Because the lower bound of the array is one, the UBound function returns the current number of active batch machines. The next statement increments the local variable by one. This new value will be used to change the size of the array.

```
ReDim Preserve gfrmABCBatchArray(pintMachineCount)
```

The ReDim statement increases the number of elements in the array gfrmABCBatchArray—that is, the value in pintMachineCount—by one. The use of the optional Preserve argument ensured that the existing object references would not be destroyed.

Consider the following:

```
gfrmABCBatchArray(pintMachineCount).Caption = _
    "Batch Machine Number " & pintMachineCount
gfrmABCBatchArray(pintMachineCount).Show
```

The first statement sets the caption of the form to the constant text "Batch Machine Number", followed by the batch machine number. Finally, the new form instance is displayed by calling the Show method. Note that the object does not actually exist until you set the Caption property.

You must call the general procedure you just wrote before the code will execute. The procedure must be called when the user wants to start a batch machine. Thus you will write the code for the Start Batch Machine menu item on the form named frmABCBatch. You also need to call this procedure from the MDI parent form menu.

To write the statements to start the batch machine from the forms mdiABC and frmABCBatch:

1 Activate the Code window for **frmABCBatch**, then locate the **mnuBatchStart_Click** event procedure. Enter the following statement into the event procedure:

```
Call StartBatchMachine
```

2 Activate the Code window for **mdiABC**, then locate the **mnuBatchStart_Click** event procedure. Enter the same statement into the event procedure.

The program can now start multiple batch machines. Each time the user clicks the Start Batch Machine menu item, the number of elements in the array containing each batch machine form instance is increased by one. Then, the new form instance is displayed inside the MDI parent form with an appropriate caption. That is, multiple instances of the same form derived from the form class named frmABCBatch will appear in the MDI parent form.

You should now test your code to verify that the program works correctly.

To verify that the program is creating multiple instances of the batch machine form:

1 Save the project, then run it. The first batch machine (MDI child form) should appear when the program starts.

2 Click **Batch Machine Control** on the form's menu bar, then click **Start Batch Machine** to start the second instance of the form.

3 Click **Batch Machine Control**, then click **Start Batch Machine** on the form's menu bar to start the third instance of the form. Your screen should resemble Figure 11-12.

first form instance
second form instance

third form instance

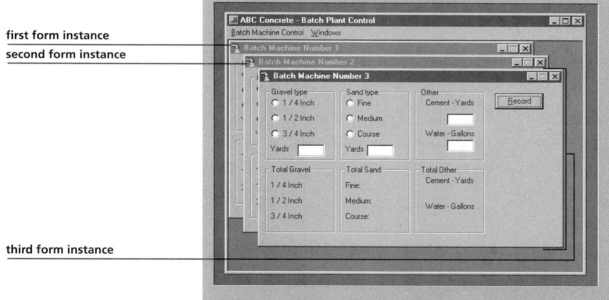

Figure 11-12: Creating multiple form instances

4 End the program to return to design mode.

Now that the user can start multiple batch machines, you must enhance the program to enable the user to manipulate the different form instances.

Arranging MDI Child Forms

Generally, the users of a program will open multiple instances of the same MDI child form, much as you might have multiple Microsoft Word documents open simultaneously. The MDI parent form supports a method that will resize and modify the position of all open MDI child windows.

Well-written MDI programs should allow the user to rearrange MDI child forms. MDI parent forms support the Arrange method, allowing you to cascade, tile, or arrange the icons of MDI child windows. The Arrange method accepts one argument—a constant describing how the windows should be arranged. These constants can be one of four values, as shown in Figure 11-13.

Constant name	Description
vbCascade	Cascades all nonminimized MDI child forms
vbTileHorizontal	Tiles all nonminimized MDI child forms horizontally
vbTileVertical	Tiles all nonminimized MDI child forms vertically
vbArrangeIcons	Arranges icons for minimized MDI child forms

Figure 11-13: Constants supported by the Arrange method

ABC Concrete's users have requested that they be able to cascade the forms and arrange the icons.

To write the code for the menu options to arrange the MDI child forms:
1 Activate the Code window for the Form module **frmABCBatch**.
2 Select the **mnuWindowsCascade_Click** event and enter the following statement:

```
mdiABC.Arrange vbCascade
```

3 Select the **mnuWindowsArrangeIcons_Click** event and enter the following statement:

```
mdiABC.Arrange vbArrangeIcons
```

In addition to these menu items, another menu item has the caption Show Window List. For this menu item, the WindowList property is set to True. When you set the WindowList property to True, the menu item will automatically list the different windows that are open.

When the user selects these menu items, the MDI child windows will be arranged accordingly. You should now test the program to verify that the menu items work correctly.

To test the menu items to arrange the MDI child windows:

1 Save and test the program. Start two additional batch machines by clicking **Start Batch Machine** twice on the **Batch Machine Control** menu.

2 Click the **Minimize** button ▭ in the control box of Batch Machine Number 2.

3 Click the **Cascade** menu item on the form's Windows menu. The forms should appear as shown in Figure 11-14.

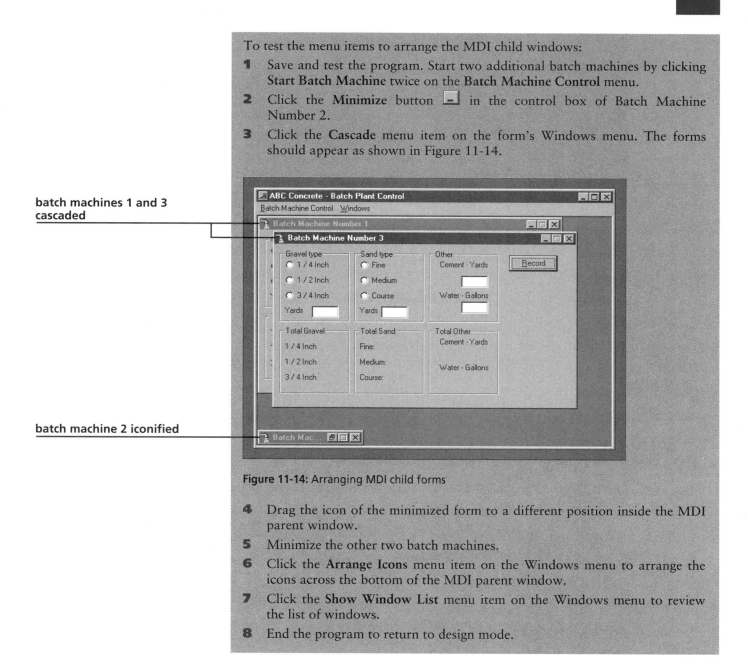

batch machines 1 and 3 cascaded

batch machine 2 iconified

Figure 11-14: Arranging MDI child forms

4 Drag the icon of the minimized form to a different position inside the MDI parent window.

5 Minimize the other two batch machines.

6 Click the **Arrange Icons** menu item on the Windows menu to arrange the icons across the bottom of the MDI parent window.

7 Click the **Show Window List** menu item on the Windows menu to review the list of windows.

8 End the program to return to design mode.

In addition to starting batch machines, your program must be able to shut them down. This task can be accomplished by unloading the form instance when the user clicks the Stop Batch Machine menu item pertaining to the MDI child form. Note that no such menu item appears on the MDI parent form. Because the menu for the MDI parent form will appear only when no batch machine is active, no machine will exist to shut down in this case.

Closing MDI Child Forms

Every time you create an object or object variable, memory and system resources are consumed. Thus, when you are finished with an object, you should release it to free up system memory. This recommendation applies to both the forms and the other object variables you create.

When a form instance is no longer needed, you use the Unload statement to remove the form from memory and to free up its associated system resources. Calling the Unload statement does not release all of the resources used by the form, however. To reclaim all the memory used by any type of object variable, you must set the variable to the keyword Nothing. When multiple references to an object variable exist, the memory for the object is not released until all the references are set to Nothing. For example, consider the following statements:

```
Private frmABCBatch1 As New frmABCBatch
Private frmABCBatch2 As frmABCBatch
Set frmABCBatch2 = frmABCBatch2
Set frmABCBatch2 = Nothing
Set frmABCBatch1 = Nothing
```

These statements create a single object with two references. That is, the variables frmABCBatch1 and frmABCBatch2 both reference the same object variable. When frmABCBatch2 is set to Nothing, the object continues to exist and can be referenced using the variable frmABCBatch1. Only when both object variables are set to Nothing is the memory for the object released. Figure 11-15 illustrates this process.

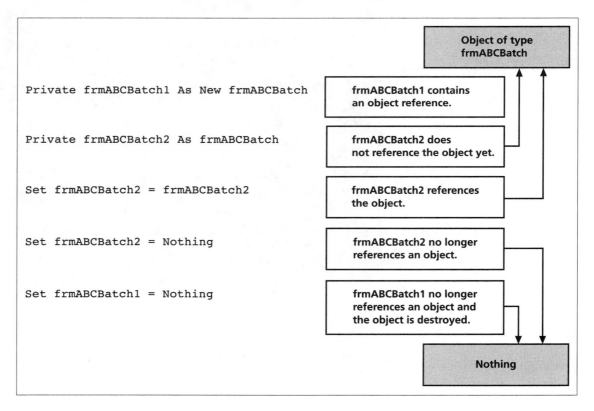

Figure 11-15: Releasing an object

You need a way to unload the active MDI child form when the user clicks the corresponding menu item or command button. One reference to the form object is stored in the global array. No information in the array indicates the active form, however. The Me keyword, on the other hand, can be used to refer to the active form, which is the form being unloaded. You now can write the statement to unload the active instance of the batch machine form, then test it.

To unload the active MDI child form:

1 Make sure the Code window is active for the Form module named **frmABCBatch**.

2 Enter the following statement into the **mnuBatchStop_Click** event procedure:

```
Unload Me
```

3 Save the project, then run it.

4 Start a second batch machine.

5 Click **Batch Machine Control** on the menu bar, then click **Stop Batch Machine**. The second form should close.

6 End the program to return to design mode.

While the procedures you just wrote create new instances of the form and destroy the existing instances, the program has several deficiencies. First, it makes no provision to shut down, then restart an existing batch machine. Instead, the StartBatchMachine general procedure just starts a new machine each time it is called. The program needs a way to shut down, then restart a batch machine. Additionally, you need a way to keep track of which machines are active and which machines are shut down and ready for restarting. ABC Concrete always starts the batch machines in numeric order. That is, Batch Machine Number 1 is started first and Batch Machine Number 2 is started second. If Batch Machine Number 1 were shut down, it would be restarted before Batch Machine Number 3 becomes active.

You could create multiple arrays to keep track of each item of information pertaining to a form, then redimension the array each time a new form instance is created. Alternatively, you could create a two-dimensional array such that each column would contain one item of information. Visual Basic, however, allows you to create your own data type. That data type can contain different items to keep track of information about the status of each batch machine. For ABC Concrete's program, this information includes the following items:

- A variable to determine whether a batch machine is active. That is, if a batch machine has been shut down, it is not active; if the batch machine is not shut down, it is active.
- A variable to determine whether an order has been recorded since the batch machine became active.

To accomplish this task, you can create a data type to hold this information, then create an array to store this newly defined data type such that the array includes one element for each batch machine.

Creating a User-Defined Type

In working with different database tables, you have operated on the different fields in a record as a group. It is possible to group variables together and then pass them to a function or procedure as a single argument, thereby making your program more readable. Variables can also be grouped to help you think of several variables as a collection of related items. To accomplish this task, you can declare your own data type, called a user-defined type, which is made up of different elements. The Type statement has the following syntax:

Syntax

[**Public** | **Private**] **Type** varname
   elementname [([*subscripts*])] **As** *type*
   [*elementname* [([*subscripts*])] **As** *type*]...
End Type

Dissection

■ The **Type** and **End Type** keywords identify a block containing statements to define each element that makes up a user-defined type.

■ A user-defined type can be Public or Private. If the type is **Public**, it is visible from all modules in a program. If it is **Private**, the type is visible only from the module in which it is declared. User-defined types declared in a standard module are considered Public if you omit the Public or Private keyword.

■ The *varname* is the name of the new user-defined type. It must conform to the standard naming conventions for variables.

■ The user-defined type can contain one or more elements identified by *elementname*. These elements can be any of the standard Visual Basic data types or another user-defined type.

■ You can create array elements by assigning a *subscript* to the *elementname*.

■ The **As** *type* clause specifies the data type of the element. *Type* can be any of the standard Visual Basic data types, an object type, or another user-defined type.

Programming tip

Visual Basic places a restriction on user-defined types. If you declare a user-defined type in a standard module, it can be Public or Private. If you declare a user-defined type inside a form module, the type must be Private. If you try to declare a Public user-defined type in a form module, you will receive a syntax error. Furthermore, the Type statement can be used only in the general declarations section of a form, class, or standard module. You cannot declare a user-defined type inside a procedure.

A user-defined type contains one or more members. Each member can be a specific type, object, or other user-defined type. The naming convention for user-defined types varies according to the size of the project. For small projects, you might give variables of a user-defined type the prefix "t". For large programs, consider a three-character prefix to identify a specific type; this prefix may resemble a three-character object prefix.

In ABC Concrete's program, you need to keep track of pertinent information about each MDI child form. This information includes whether a batch machine is active and whether an order has been recorded. Because this status information can be True or False, the variables can be Boolean values, as follows:

```
Type tMachineState
    Active As Boolean
    Dirty As Boolean
End Type
```

This user-defined type contains two elements. The first indicates whether a form (batch machine) is active. The second indicates whether an order has been recorded. If so, the totals in the accumulators need to be added to accumulators keeping track of the total of each product used for all the batch machines combined. You will create these accumulators in a moment. If no order has been recorded, you need not update the accumulators. Once the user-defined type is created, you can declare an array of this type.

To declare the user-defined type representing the machine state:

1 Open the Code window to the general declarations section of the module named **ABC_S.bas**.

2 Enter the following statements in the Code window just after the enumerated types:

```
Public Type tMachineState
    Active As Boolean
    Dirty As Boolean
End Type
```

Programming tip

"Dirty" is a common variable name for a Boolean value indicating that data have changed and some activity needs to occur.

The Type statement merely declares the new data type; it does not declare a variable of that type. This statement works much like the Enum statement, which creates an enumerated type rather than a variable. To declare a variable of a user-defined type, you can use the Dim, Public, or Private statement just as you did to declare other variables. Instead of declaring a variable As Integer or As Single, however, it is declared As *type*, where *type* is the new user-defined type.

To create a Public variable named MachineState as a tMachineState type, you can use the following statement:

```
Public MachineState As tMachineState
```

Programming tip

Note that the variable name is MachineState. This name is similar to a property. That is, no prefix indicates the data type. This naming convention was chosen because the syntax to store and retrieve values from a user-defined type is similar to the syntax to reference objects and properties. Adding a prefix to a user-defined variable is another common approach. As you write other programs, choose one standard and be consistent in your naming technique.

This syntax is identical to the syntax used to create object variables or variables having an intrinsic data type. Note that you can create Public variables of a user-defined type only in a standard module. If you try to declare a Public variable of a user-defined type inside a form module, a syntax error will occur.

Once you have declared a variable of a user-defined type, you need to know how to store and retrieve information from the individual elements in the type. To reference an element in a variable of a user-defined type, you specify the variable name followed by the member name, separated by a period (.). Thus, to set the value of the member named Active to True in the variable MachineState, you would use the following syntax:

```
MachineState.Active = True
```

You now need to declare a variable to store the state of each batch machine. Because you need a variable to store the information for each batch machine that has been started, you need to declare an array. Just as you can create an array of standard data types or objects, so too can you declare an array of user-defined types. This array will operate in conjunction with the array of form objects you have already created. When a batch machine is started and the array containing the form objects is redimensioned, the array containing the MachineState information will need to be redimensioned as well. You will therefore create the array such that it has zero elements when the program first starts—the same number of elements as the array containing the form objects.

To declare a variable of the user-defined type:

1 Activate the Code window for the standard module named **ABC_S.bas**, if necessary.

2 Add the following statement (shown in bold) to the general declarations section just after the statements declaring the user-defined type:

```
End Type
Public MachineState( ) As tMachineState
```

This statement declares an array named MachineState. Each member of the array is of the user-defined type tMachineState. Because you did not specify any dimensions for the array, it is initially empty. You can redimension this array, just as you redimensioned the array that stores a reference to each batch machine instance. Note that the MachineState array is declared as a Public variable in the standard module. As noted earlier, you cannot declare Public variables of a user-defined type inside a form module.

When a batch machine starts up, a new instance of the form is created and the array containing a reference to each form object is redimensioned. In addition to creating this new form instance, you need to redimension the array for the MachineState and set the Active state to True. You also need to set the Dirty state to False because no information has been yet recorded. This task should be performed when the first batch machine starts up, so you must add code to the MDIForm_Load event procedure for the MDI parent form.

In addition, the Dirty state should be set to True each time the program records a new order. You will use this information when the batch machine is shut down. When an order is recorded, the program should find the correct element in the array named MachineState, then set the Dirty flag to True. To accomplish this task, you will use the Tag property. This property should have the same value as the number of the batch machine. It also is the same value as the index for the corresponding element in the MachineState array. You can use this property with the Me object as an index to the array, as shown in the following statement:

```
MachineState(Me.Tag).Dirty = True
```

This statement uses the Tag property of the current form as an index to the MachineState array. The Dirty element of the user-defined type is set to True. You now can set the Dirty flag when the first machine starts up and the program records an order.

To set the Active and Dirty state when the first MDI child form starts:

1 Activate the Code window for the **MDIForm_Load** event procedure for the MDI parent form.

2 Enter the following statements (shown in bold) into the event procedure:

```
ReDim gfrmABCBatchArray(1)
ReDim MachineState(1)
MachineState(1).Active = True
MachineState(1).Dirty = False
```

3 Activate the Code window for **frmABCBatch**.

4 Enter the following statement into the **cmdRecord_Click** event procedure just after the Private statement (the beginning of the event procedure):

```
MachineState(Me.Tag).Dirty = True
```

When a batch machine starts up, the size of the MachineState array increases by one. For the first element, you set the Active flag to True indicating that the machine is active and the Dirty flag to False because no orders have been recorded. Upon receipt of an order, the Dirty flag is set to True.

Just as you have created arrays of Integer, Variant, and Object type, so too can you declare arrays of user-defined types and enumerated types.

Nesting User-Defined Types

User-defined types can be nested—that is, a user-defined type can contain a member that is itself a user-defined type. ABC Concrete's program should keep track of the total amount of the different types of sand and gravel used by the entire group of batch machines operating during the day. You can store most of this information in two user-defined types. One user-defined type will contain the types of sand and a second will hold the types of gravel. You can then create a third user-defined type containing two elements: one for the sand type and another for the gravel type.

To declare the user-defined types for the sand and gravel grand totals:

1 Activate the Code window to the general declarations section of the standard module named **ABC_S.bas**.

2   Enter the following statements (shown in bold) into the Code window just after the other existing Type declaration:

```
End Type
Public Type tGravel
     Quarter As Single
     Half As Single
     ThreeQuarter As Single
End Type
Public Type tSand
     Fine As Single
     Medium As Single
     Coarse As Single
End Type
Public Type tComponent
     Gravel As tGravel
     Sand As tSand
     Cement As Single
     Water As Single
End Type
```

3   Enter the following statement just after the final End Type statement to declare a variable of type tComponent:

```
Public Component As tComponent
```

These statements declare three user-defined types. The first describes the three types of sand, and the second indicates the three types of gravel. The final statement declares a third user-defined type made up of the other two user-defined types as well as variables representing the amount of cement and water used. In this example, the user-defined type is nested two levels. You can nest user-defined types, however, in as many levels as the program requires.

Now that you can declare an array of user-defined types, you need to know how to reference this array and its elements. When you reference a member of a user-defined type, the syntax looks identical to the syntax used to set and read properties. For example, to reference the Active and Dirty members of the first element in the MachineState array, you use the following syntax:

```
MachineState(1).Active
MachineState(1).Dirty
```

Because you used the Option Base 1 statement, the first element of the array has a subscript of 1. When using nested types, you add another period (.), followed by the subtype. For example, consider the following statements.

```
Component.Sand.Fine = 1.5
Component.Gravel.Quarter = 1.5
Component.Cement = 1.5
```

Because this variable is not an array, you do not use a subscript. The first statement references the component Sand, which is a user-defined type. Thus the program must select the appropriate member from the type of Sand. Another period is therefore added, followed by the Fine member of the Sand type. The second statement performs the same task on the Quarter member of the Gravel type. Because Cement is an intrinsic type (Single) rather than a user-defined type, no second period is required.

In addition to assigning values to the members of user-defined types, you can perform operations on all the elements of a user-defined type at once. For example, consider the following statements:

```
Dim Component1 As tComponent
Dim Component2 As tComponent
Dim ComponentSand As tSand
Dim ComponentGravel As tGravel
```

These statements declare the variables Component1 and Component2 of the type tComponent. The variable ComponentSand is of the type tSand, and the variable ComponentGravel is of the type tGravel. Remember that tSand and tGravel types are both members of tComponent. You can perform assignment statements on variables of a user-defined type, as long as the left-hand side of the expression is of the same type as the right-hand side of the expression. For example, all of the following statements are legal:

```
Component1 = Component2
Component1.Sand = ComponentSand
Component2.Gravel = ComponentGravel
```

In contrast, the following statements will cause a syntax error (a type mismatch error) because the left-hand side and right-hand sides of the expression do not have the same underlying data type:

```
Component1 = Component2.Sand
Component1.Gravel = Component2.Sand
ComponentSand = ComponentGravel
```

For ABC Concrete's program, you must tally all the materials used by each batch machine. That information is stored in the properties you defined for the form named frmABCBatch. Because this information will no longer exist after a form is unloaded, you must add the quantity used for each component to another set of accumulators that will continue to exist even after the instance of the batch form has been unloaded.

Now that you have declared the variable to store the grand totals for each material used during the day, you need to write the statements to update those totals. The only time it is necessary to update the grand totals for a batch machine is when the machine shuts down. Every form supports a **QueryUnload** event that allows to you update totals or perform other activities before the form unloads.

- The **QueryUnload** event occurs before a form unloads. Setting the Cancel argument to True cancels the event that triggered the Unload event. The UnloadMode argument contains a constant indicating why the QueryUnload event took place. Refer to the QueryUnload event Help topic for more information about these constants.
- If you do not cancel the QueryUnload event, then the **Unload** event will occur. You can, however, cancel this event as well by setting the Cancel argument to True.

Just as you have used a With block to write several statements that refer to the same object, so too can you use a With statement to refer to the members of a user-defined type. When you use a With statement to refer to a variable of a user-defined type, you specify the variable name, followed by the member name. If a member is itself a user-defined type, you follow the member name with a period (.), followed by its member name.

For ABC Concrete's program, the grand total of each component is stored in the variable Component, which is of type tComponent. You can use several variations of a With block to store the values in the Public variables into the members of this variable.

```
With Component
    .Sand.Fine = .Sand.Fine + YardsSandFine
    . . .
    .Gravel.Quarter = .Gravel.Quarter + YardsGravelQuarter
    . . .
    .Water = .Water + YardsWater
End With
```

Remember that the Sand and Gravel types are members of the tComponent type. These types, in turn, have their own members. Thus the With block has two levels. Because the Water type has no members, no period or member name follows the member water.

You can decompose the With block even further so as to reduce typing and make the program clearer, as shown in the following statements:

```
With Component
    With .Sand
        .Fine = .Fine + YardsSandFine
        . . .
    End With
    With .Gravel
        .Quarter = .Quarter + YardsGravelQuarter
        . . .
    End With
    .Water = .Water + YardsWater
End With
```

These statements have the same effect as the previous statements. Two With blocks, however, have been nested inside the main With block. Writing the code in this way provides a clearer indication of each subtype. It also improves the performance of the code slightly.

You now can write the necessary assignment statements inside a With block to update the value of the variable Component, which serves as the grand total accumulator. You will update this variable by using the Public variables in the current batch machine form. These Public variables accumulate the total amount used of each component each time the program records an order. This task should be performed just before the form unloads only if an order has been recorded; that is, it should be carried out if the Dirty flag is True. If the flag is False, then the form should be closed. If it is True, you should display a message box prompting the user for confirmation prior to updating the accumulators and closing the form.

To add the accumulators for a specific batch machine to the grand total accumulators:

1 Activate the Code window for the **Form_QueryUnload** event procedure for the form named **frmABCBatch**, then enter the following statements into the event procedure:

```
Dim pintReturn As Integer
If MachineState(Me.Tag).Dirty = False Then
    MachineState(Me.Tag).Active = False
    Exit Sub
End If
pintReturn = MsgBox("Do you want to shut down the machine" & _
    vbCrLf & "and record the material usage?", vbYesNo)
If pintReturn = vbYes Then
    With Component
        With .Sand
            .Fine = .Fine + YardsSandFine
            .Medium = .Medium + YardsSandMedium
            .Coarse = .Coarse + YardsSandCoarse
        End With
        With .Gravel
            .Quarter = .Quarter + YardsGravelQuarter
            .Half = .Half + YardsGravelHalf
            .ThreeQuarter = .ThreeQuarter + _
                YardsGravelThreeQuarter
        End With
        .Cement = .Cement + YardsCement
        .Water = .Water + GallonsWater
    End With
    MachineState(Me.Tag).Active = False
    MachineState(Me.Tag).Dirty = False
Else
    Cancel = True
End If
```

These statements first determine whether the program has recorded an order. If no order has been recorded, the form is unloaded automatically and the Active flag for the form is set to False. If an order has been recorded, the next statements ask the user to confirm that the machine should be shut down. If the user does not want to shut down the machine, the QueryUnload event is cancelled. Otherwise, the accumulators for the specific batch machine are added to the grand total accumulators. When the machine becomes inactive, both the Active and the Dirty flags are set to False.

The code you have written to create new form objects has a deficiency. The current version of the StartBatchMachine general procedure will not restart a batch machine that has been shut down previously. To correct this problem, you must modify the general procedure to determine if any inactive machines exist before redimensioning the array. To accomplish this task, you will replace the existing statements in the StartBatchMachine general procedure with statements to recycle elements in the batch machine array.

To locate the element in the array in which to place the new form instance:

1   Activate the Code window for the standard module named **ABC_S.bas**.
2   Locate the general procedure named **StartBatchMachine**.
3   Replace the existing statements so that the procedure contains the following statements:

```
Public Sub StartBatchMachine( )
    Dim pblnFoundInactive As Boolean
    Dim pintMachineCount As Integer
    Dim pintElement As Integer
    Dim pintMachine As Integer

    pintMachineCount = UBound(gfrmABCBatchArray)
    For pintMachine = 1 To pintMachineCount
        If MachineState(pintMachine).Active = False Then
            pintElement = pintMachine
            pblnFoundInactive = True
            Exit For
        End If
    Next
    If pblnFoundInactive = False Then
        ReDim Preserve MachineState(pintMachineCount + 1)
        ReDim Preserve _
            gfrmABCBatchArray(pintMachineCount + 1)
        pintElement = pintMachineCount + 1
    End If

    MachineState(pintElement).Active = True
    MachineState(pintElement).Dirty = False
    gfrmABCBatchArray(pintElement).Caption = _
        "Batch Machine Number " & pintElement
    gfrmABCBatchArray(pintElement).Show
    gfrmABCBatchArray(pintElement).Tag = pintElement
End Sub
```

These statements create a new instance of the MDI child form named frmABCBatch. If a batch machine has been shut down and the form closed, an empty element will appear in the array of forms. In this situation, the Sub procedure will reallocate the unused array element.

```
Dim pblnFoundInactive As Boolean
Dim pintMachineCount As Integer
Dim pintElement As Integer
Dim pintMachine As Integer
```

The preceding statements declare the local variables used by the Sub procedure. The first variable, pblnFoundInactive, is a Boolean variable that determines whether any machine was shut down previously. The variable pintMachine is used in a For loop, and pintElement contains the index of the machine being allocated.

```
pintMachineCount = UBound(gfrmABCBatchArray)
For pintMachine = 1 To pintMachineCount
    If MachineState(pintMachine).Active = False Then
        pintElement = pintMachine
        pblnFoundInactive = True
        Exit For
    End If
Next
```

These statements determine whether a machine was shut down by testing the Active flag for each batch machine. If an element in the array is inactive, then that batch machine can be restarted. Thus the batch machine to be used is stored in the variable pintElement, and the flag pblnFoundInactive is set to True indicating that the program should not allocate a new array element.

```
If pblnFoundInactive = False Then
    ReDim Preserve MachineState(pintMachineCount + 1)
    ReDim Preserve gfrmABCBatchArray(pintMachineCount + 1)
    pintElement = pintMachineCount + 1
End If
```

The preceding statements inside the If block execute only if the program failed to locate an inactive batch machine. In this situation, the size of both the MachineState and gfrmABCBatchArray arrays is increased by one. The new element in the array then becomes the active element.

```
MachineState(pintElement).Active = True
MachineState(pintElement).Dirty = False
gfrmABCBatchArray(pintElement).Caption = _
    "Batch Machine Number " & pintElement
gfrmABCBatchArray(pintElement).Show
gfrmABCBatchArray(pintElement).Tag = pintElement
```

These statements, which use the new array element or the recycled array element, set the value of the necessary flags and the form's caption. Once these properties have been set, they display the form. This function will be called when the user clicks the Start Batch Machine menu item from the batch machine control menu.

Remember that additional events occur when an MDI form and its MDI child forms are loaded. Still other events occur when an MDI form or its children are unloaded.

If an MDI child form is unloaded because of an Unload statement, or if the user closes the form by clicking the Close button in the form's control box, the following events will occur:

- The QueryUnload event occurs for the MDI child form.
- If the Cancel argument is not set to True in the QueryUnload event, the Unload event occurs in the MDI child form.

If an MDI parent form is unloaded, the following events will occur:

- The QueryUnload event occurs first for the MDI parent form. To cancel this event, the Cancel argument can be set to True.
- A QueryUnload event occurs for each MDI child form that is loaded. If that event is not cancelled, then an Unload event occurs for the MDI child form; this event can also be cancelled.
- If none of the MDI child forms cancels the QueryUnload or Unload event, then the Unload event occurs in the MDI parent form. This event also can be cancelled.

Figure 11-16 illustrates this process.

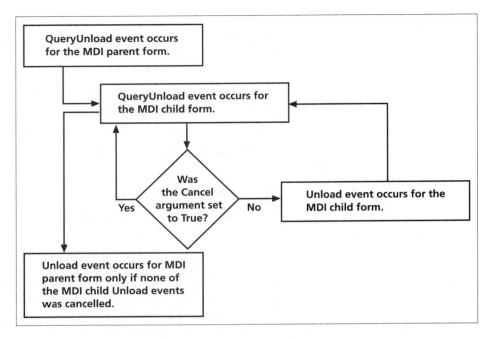

Figure 11-16: Unloading an MDI parent form and MDI child forms

You now should test the program to verify that each form is loaded and unloaded properly.

To test that the batch machines are loaded and unloaded correctly:
1 Save and test the program. Start two additional batch machines.
2 Close Batch Machine Number 1.
3 Start a batch machine. Batch Machine Number 1 should be restarted.
4 End the program to return to design mode.

Remember, when a form is unloaded, the Unload event occurs for a form. When the user wants to shut down a batch machine, the MDI child form representing the batch machine will be unloaded. Because the form instance will no longer exist, you must add the totals stored in the form's Public variable to the accumulators representing the grand totals for all the batch machines.

Closing an MDI Program

In addition to closing an individual MDI child form, the user may click the Close button on the MDI parent form to exit the program. If batch machines are active, a QueryUnload event will occur for each batch machine before the MDI parent form unloads. Prior to unloading the MDI parent form, management wants ABC Concrete's program to display another message box requesting confirmation from the user, then display a modal form containing the total quantity used of each component. This form has already been written. You need to display it on the screen before unloading the MDI parent form, however, and then copy the values of the grand total accumulators into the objects on the form. Figure 11-17 shows the Totals form.

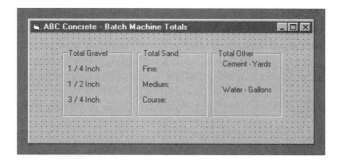

Figure 11-17: Totals form

Because you need to store the members of the Components variable, you can again use a With statement.

To store the values of the grand total accumulators in the labels on the form named frmTotals:

1   Activate the Code window for the form module named **frmTotals**. Select the **Form_Load** event, then enter the following statements into the event procedure:

```
Private Sub Form_Load( )
    With Component
        With .Sand
            lblSandFine = .Fine
            lblSandMedium = .Medium
            lblSandCoarse = .Coarse
        End With
        With .Gravel
            lblGravelQuarter = .Quarter
            lblGravelHalf = .Half
            lblGravelThreeQuarter = .ThreeQuarter
        End With
        lblCement = .Cement
        lblWater = .Water
    End With
End Sub
```

When the user exits the program either by clicking the Close button or by using the appropriate menu item, you often need to make sure that the MDI form and each of its children have had an opportunity to close any open files and perform any necessary processing before the program exits.

When an MDI form is unloaded (generally because you called the Unload statement on the MDI form), a QueryUnload event is generated first for the MDI forms. Then an Unload event occurs for each MDI child form. If any of these unload events is cancelled, then the Unload event for the MDI parent form will be cancelled as well and the MDI parent form will not be unloaded.

You now can write the code for the MDI form's QueryUnload event. This code, when executed, should display a modal form containing the grand totals. When this modal form is closed, you can exit the program. If any of the MDI child forms were not closed, then the program must cancel the QueryUnload event.

To display the grand totals when the MDI parent form is closed:

1   Activate the Code window for the MDI parent form named **mdiABC**, then enter the following statements into the **MDIForm_Unload** event procedure:

```
frmTotals.Show vbModal
```

2   Enter the following statements into the **mnuBatchExit_Click** event procedure for the MDI parent form:

```
Unload Me
```

You have now completed the program for ABC Concrete and should test it to verify that the accumulators are updated properly.

To test the grand total accumulators:

1   Save the project, then run it.

2   Start an additional batch machine.

3   Enter an order, then click **Record** for each batch machine.

4   Stop each batch machine. Answer **Yes** when the message box appears.

5   Click **Batch Machine Control**, then click **Exit** on the MDI parent form to exit the program.

The accumulators should be displayed in the Totals form.

6   Click the **Close** button on the Totals form. Exit Visual Basic.

ABC Concrete's program can now start and shut down each batch machine and operate with any number of batch machines. Each batch machine supports accumulators to tally the amount of each material used by that machine. When a machine is shut down, its totals are added to the totals for all the machines combined. Just before the program ends, it prints these totals.

S U M M A R Y

To create a multiple-document interface program:

■ Click Project, then click Add MDI Form to add an MDI parent form to the project. Set this form as the project's startup form.

■ Set the MDIChild property to True for the other forms in the project, so that they will operate as MDI child forms and appear inside the region of the MDI parent form.

■ Note that an MDI program can still support standard forms.

To modify the behavior of a form's control box:

■ To enable a form's control box, set the ControlBox property to True; otherwise, set it to False.

■ To enable the Minimize and Restore buttons, set the MinButton property to True.

■ To enable the Maximize and Restore buttons, set the MaxButton property to True.

■ Note that if a form's BorderStyle property is set to None, the control box will not appear.

To declare a generic object variable:

■ Using the Dim, Private, Public or Static statement, declare a variable of type Object or Variant.

To explicitly create an object, use one of the following declaration statements with the New keyword:

■ {**Dim** | **Public** | **Private** | **Static**} *varname* [([*subscripts*])] [**As** [**New**] *type*]

To change the default lower bound of the arrays in a module, add the Option Base statement to the beginning of the module:

Option Base (0|1)

To change the size of an array (redimension) at run time, call the ReDim statement:

■ **ReDim** [**Preserve**] *varname*(*subscripts*) [**As** *type*]

To determine the largest and smallest subscript for an array, call the UBound and Lbound functions, respectively:

■ **UBound**(*arrayname*[, *dimension*])

■ **LBound**(*arrayname*[, *dimension*])

To store additional information about a control or form instance, use the Tag property:

■ *object*.**Tag** = [*expression*]

To arrange the MDI child forms in a project:

■ Call the Arrange method with one of the following constants: vbCascade, vbTileHorizontal, vbTileVertical, vbArrangeIcons.

To close an MDI child form:

■ Call the Unload statement on the form. Respond to the QueryUnload and Unload events as necessary.

To create a user-defined type, declare the type with the Type statement:

[**Public | Private**] **Type** *varname*
   elementname [([*subscripts*])] **As** *Type*
    [*elementname* [([*subscripts*])] **As** *Type*]...
End Type

Q U E S T I O N S

1. What are the functions used to determine the largest and smallest subscript for an array?
    a. Max, Min
    b. Upper, Lower
    c. Maximum, Minimum
    d. UBound, LBound
    e. None of the above.

2. What is the name of the method used to organize the MDI child forms within the MDI parent window?
    a. Arrange
    b. Cascade
    c. Organize
    d. Tile
    e. List

3. What is the name of the event that occurs just before a form is unloaded?
    a. Unload
    b. BeforeUnload
    c. QueryUnload
    d. Unloading
    e. None of the above.

4. Public variables declared in a form module are considered _____.
    a. Methods
    b. Properties
    c. Events
    d. None of the above.
    e. All of the above.

5. The _____ statement is commonly used with user defined types.
    a. When
    b. Using
    c. With
    d. Group
    e. None of the above.

6. Write the statements to declare a user-defined type named tComponent having members named Part1, Part2, and Part3. Each member should have a data type of Integer.

7. Write the statement to declare a variable named Component having a type of tComponent.

8. Write the statements to store the members of the Component type in the Text properties of the text boxes named Text1, Text2, and Text3. Assume the same type you declared in Question 6.

9. Write the event procedure and statements to display a message box before the form named frmQuestion is unloaded. Depending on the user's response to the message box, either continue to unload the form or cancel the event.

10. Write the statements to determine the lower and upper bound of a one-dimensional array named pintQuestion. Store the lower bound in a variable named plngLower and the upper bound in a variable named plngUpper.

E X E R C I S E S

1. Communications, Inc., audits telephone charges for two major long-distance providers. The information manager has asked you to write a program to display the telephone charges. Each day the company receives an ASCII-delimited file from a long-distance company that must be analyzed. It wants to read the file into an array, then create a form to display each record in the array. The ASCII-delimited file has the following fields and data types:

Day of the week (Integer)
Year the call was started (Integer)
Month the call was started (Integer)
Day the call was started (Integer)
Year the call ended (Integer)
Month the call ended (Integer)
Day the call ended (Integer)
Hour the call was started (Integer)
Minute the call was started (Integer)
Second the call was started (Integer)
Hour the call ended (Integer)
Minute the call ended (Integer)
Second the call ended (Integer)
Originating area code (String)
Originating phone number (String)
Destination area code (String)
Destination phone number (String)

You will organize the information from the ASCII-delimited file with user-defined types. Figure 11-18 shows the completed form.

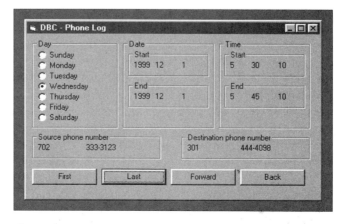

Figure 11-18: Exercise 1 – completed form

a. Run the executable file named **Chapter.11\Exercise\Ex1.exe**, setting the drive designator as necessary. For the program to run properly, the file dbc.txt must reside in the same folder as the executable file. Click the **First, Last, Forward,** and **Back** buttons to locate different records. As you click these buttons, the corresponding record appears in the form objects. Exit the program.

b. Start Visual Basic, then create a new project. Set the name of the form to **frmExt.frm** and the project name to **Ex1.vbp**. Set the form's caption as shown in Figure 11-18. Save the form in the **Chapter.11\Exercise** folder, setting the drive designator as necessary.

c. The first step in developing this program is to create the user-defined types representing the information stored in the ASCII file. Create an enumerated type representing the days of the week such that Sunday is zero (0), Monday is one (1), and so on.

d. Create a form-level user-defined type for the data consisting of the year, month, and day.

e. Create a form-level user-defined type for the time consisting of the hour, minute, and second.

f. Create a form-level user-defined type for the phone number consisting of the area code and phone number.

discovery ▶

g. Create a user-defined type representing the phone record. This record must contain the day of the week, call start date, call end date, call start time, call end time, source phone number, and destination phone number. Each of these members should be a user-defined type.

h. Declare an empty module-level array to hold the phone records. This array should be of the same type you declared in Step g.

i. When the form is loaded, the records in the ASCII-delimited file named **Chapter.11\Exercise\DBC.txt** must be read into the array. In the Form_Load event procedure, create a Do loop to redimension the array, read the information into the array, then increment the counter to read the new record into the next element of the array.

j. Create the frames as shown in Figure 11-18. Note that the frame containing the option buttons will be used as a container for those buttons.

k. Create labels inside each frame to hold the corresponding information.

l. Create the option buttons as shown in Figure 11-18. These option buttons should be part of a control array.

m. Create the four command buttons as shown in Figure 11-18.

n. Create a general procedure to locate different records in the array. This procedure should accept one argument, indicating which record to locate. Four valid values exist for this argument to locate the first, last, next, and previous records, respectively. You may want to create an enumerated type to accomplish this task.

discovery ▶

o. For each command button, write the necessary statements to call the general procedure such that the **First** command button will display the first record in the array, the **Last** command button will display the last record in the array, the **Forward** command button will display the next record in the array, and the **Back** command button will display the previous record in the array. *Hint*: You may want to create a second general procedure to actually display the current record. This general procedure would accept one argument—the record to display.

p. Write the necessary error-handling code to prevent the user from displaying a record that does not exist. This error-handling code should be placed in the **Forward** and **Back** buttons and should verify that the current record is not the first or last record.

q. Save the program, then test it to verify that the records are displayed correctly. Exit Visual Basic.

2. Atlantic Gaming owns several casinos across the United States. Each day coins from the slot machines must be rolled. Each casino has one or more machines to perform this task. The company would like you to write a program to keep track of the dollar amount of the coins rolled by each machine during each shift. In addition, the company would like to know the total amount of coins rolled by all machines. Figure 11-19 shows the MDI parent and child forms representing the coin machine.

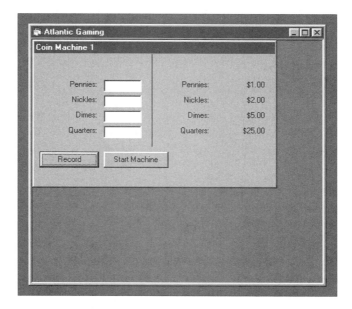

Figure 11-19: Exercise 2 – completed MDI parent and child forms

a. Run the executable file named **Chapter.11\Exercise\Ex2.exe**, setting the drive designator as necessary. When the program first begins, the first coin machine (MDI child form) appears. Enter Integer values in the text boxes for Pennies, Nickels, Dimes, and Quarters. Click the **Record** command button. The values are recorded in the output section on the right side of the form. Repeat the process. The new values you entered are added to the values in the output section on the right side of the form. Click the **Start Machine** command button to start a second instance of the coin machine form. Enter and record values for this machine. Click the **Close** button on the MDI parent form. The totals for each machine are added together and then displayed in the Totals form as shown in Figure 11-20. End the program.

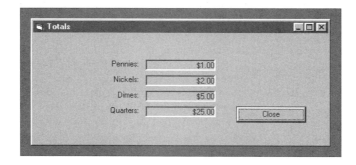

Figure 11-20: Exercise 2 – completed Totals form

b. Start Visual Basic and create a new project named **Ex2.vbp**. Create an MDI parent form and save this file using the name **MDIEx2.frm**. Create an MDI child form and save this file using the name **ChildEx2.frm**. Create a final standard form to display the totals and save it using the name **TTLEx2.frm**. Finally, create a standard module named **Ex2.bas**. Create the visible objects on the forms, as shown in Figures 11-19 and 11-20. Save the project using the name **Ex2.vbp**, setting the drive designator as necessary for all files. Save all the files in the **Chapter.11\Exercise** folder.

c. In the standard module, declare an array named **gfrmCoinMachineArray**. This array should have no elements initially and should store **frmChild** objects. Use the New keyword so that objects will be created upon redimensioning of the array. This array will store references to all of the open MDI child forms.

d. Set the Option Base in all forms and modules so that the initial array element is 1.

e. When the program first begins, the MDIForm_Load procedure should redimension the array you just created so that its size is 1. Remember, this array stores references to the MDI child form in the project. Write the necessary code to redimension the array, set the caption of the new MDI child form to "Coin Machine 1", and display the newly created form instance.

f. The design of this program takes advantage of the QueryUnload and Unload events pertaining to both the MDI parent and child forms. The program must keep track of the amount of coins for all of the coin machines. Thus these accumulators must be available to all active child forms. Declare four Public variables in the MDI parent form to store the four types of coins. Name these variables **TotalPennies**, **TotalNickels**, **TotalDimes**, and **TotalQuarters**.

g. Create four Private variables named **msngPennies**, **msngNickels**, **msngDimes**, and **msngQuarters** to serve as accumulators in the MDI child form. These variables will store the coin totals for the particular machine.

h. In the MDI child form, write the code for the **Record** command button to validate the input of the text boxes, update the value of the accumulators you created in Step g, and display the current value of these accumulators in the output labels when the user clicks this button.

discovery ▶

i. In the MDI child form, create the code **Start Machine** command button to open additional copies of the coin machine form. The procedure must determine how many coin machines are active, then create an additional instance of a coin machine. Thus you will need to redimension the global array created in Step c. Be sure that redimensioning the array preserves its existing contents. You may want to put this code in a general procedure.

j. Set the necessary properties for the MDIChild form so that the form cannot be resized. Also set the properties so that the control box is not visible.

discovery ▶

k. In the QueryUnload event procedure for the MDI child form, write the code to accumulate the total coin amounts on the current form in the grand total accumulators on the MDI parent form. Just before an instance of the MDI child form is unloaded, the form's current accumulator values should be added to the accumulators on the MDI parent form.

l. When the MDI parent form is unloaded, you need to display the grand total accumulators on the Totals form. The user will close the program by clicking the Close button on the MDI parent form's title bar. This action will cause the QueryUnload event to occur for each MDI child form. After all MDI child forms have been unloaded, the Unload event will occur for the MDI parent form. In this event procedure, write the code to display the grand total accumulators on the Totals form, then display the Totals form as a modal dialog.

m. On the Totals form, program the **Close** button so that the form will unload.

    n. Test the program by starting several machines, entering values, and recording them. Shut down the program by clicking the Close button on the MDI parent form. The value of the accumulators should be printed on the Totals form. Save your work, then exit Visual Basic.

3. Mentor Customer Tracking maintains address information for several companies. This address information is stored in the database named **Chapter.11\Exercise\Mentor.mdb**. A table named **tblCustomer** contains the following fields: **fldCustomerID, fldPersonName, fldAddress, fldCity, fldState,** and **fldZipCode.** Each Customer ID number has several names associated with it. Currently there are three different customers and, therefore, three Customer IDs. These customers have ID numbers of 1, 2, and 3.

    a. Run the executable file named **Chapter.11\Exercise\Ex3.exe**, setting the drive designator as necessary. When the program first begins, the MDI parent form appears. Click **File,** then click **Open** on the menu bar to display an input box. Enter the customer number "1" in the input box. An instance of the MDI child form appears inside of the MDI parent form, as shown in Figure 11-21. Click **File,** then click **Open** again to display an input box. This time, enter a Customer ID of "2". Click **OK** to close the dialog. A second instance of the MDI child form appears. Only those records pertaining to that customer appear, however. End the program.

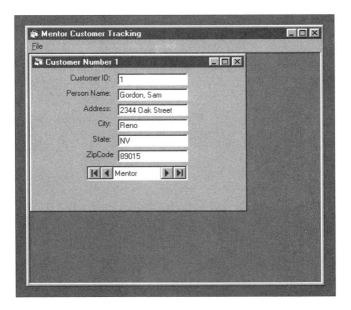

Figure 11-21: Exercise 3 – Completed form

    b. Start Visual Basic and create a new project named **Ex3.vbp**. Create an MDI parent form and save this file using the name **MDIEx3.frm**. Create an MDI child form and save this file using the name **ChildEx3.vbp**. Finally, create a standard module named **Ex3.bas**. Save the project and its files in the **Chapter.11\Exercise** folder, setting the drive designator as necessary.

    c. Create the visible objects on the MDI child form as shown in Figure 11-21. Set the Data control to connect to the table named **tblCustomer** and bind the text boxes to the fields in the table.

d. In the standard module named **Ex3.bas**, declare a Public array variable to store instances of the MDI child form.

discovery ▶

e. In the standard module, create a general procedure named **OpenCustomer**. This general procedure should redimension the array created in Step c. It should then display an input box to obtain the desired Customer ID from the user. Write an SQL SELECT statement to select the records for the desired customer once the Customer ID has been determined. Refresh the recordset pertaining to the Data control on the new form by setting the RecordSource property to the SQL SELECT statement you just wrote. Set the caption of the new form to the string "Customer Number", followed by the ID number of the selected customer.

f. On the MDI parent form, create a menu system having a **File** menu with two options, **Open** and **Exit**. The Open menu item should call the procedure you wrote in Step e. The Exit menu item should cause the program to exit.

g. Save and test the program. Open three MDI child windows for Customer ID numbers 1, 2, and 3. Use the buttons on the Data control to locate different records. Verify that only the records for the selected customer appear in the MDI child form.

h. Exit Visual Basic.

Programming with Class

Creating an Airport Management System for Airsoft

case ▶ Airsoft develops software for airports. One of its software programs under development will allow an airport to charge an airline two fees. The first, a landing fee, is charged when an airplane lands at an airport. This fee varies based on the size of the airplane and the time that it remains on the ground. The second fee is for any fuel purchased.

The airport fee program must keep track of the charges pertaining to an airplane from the time of its arrival through its departure. After an airplane leaves the airport, the charges incurred will be appended to a text file. This information will be used later by the airport's billing system to generate individual airline invoices.

Previewing the Completed Application

Like other applications you have created in this book, this application contains multiple form modules. It also contains a new type of module, called a class module. Although its role is not apparent from the user interface, this class module performs most of the processing in the program.

The form frmMain serves as the main form for the project. It contains buttons to record the arrival of an airplane at the airport and its subsequent departure. The code for these buttons calls methods in the class module to add and to remove the airplanes. Figure 12-1 shows the main form for the program when three airplanes are at the airport.

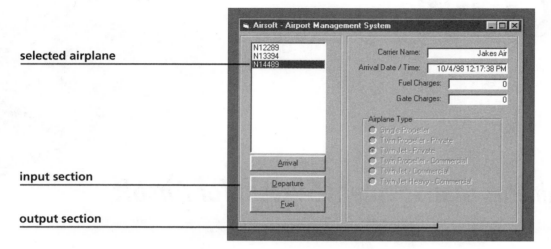

Figure 12-1: Completed main form

As shown in Figure 12-1, the main form contains two frames separating the form's input and output sections. The input section contains a list box displaying all of the airplanes currently at the airport. Clicking on an airplane in this list box updates the labels and option buttons in the output section of the form such that the information pertaining to the currently selected airplane appears. The input section also contains three command buttons to record the arrival of an airplane, its departure, and any fuel charges. The Arrival button activates the dialog shown in Figure 12-2.

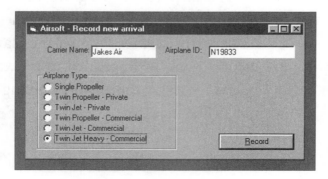

Figure 12-2: Completed Arrival dialog

This modal dialog records the arrival of an airplane at the airport. The user specifies the name of the airline (carrier) and a unique identification number for each airplane. The type of airplane is also recorded. When the user clicks the Record button, the airplane is added to this list box on the main form and the dialog closes.

When the user clicks the Departure button on the main form, the currently selected airplane is removed from the list box, and the charges pertaining to that airplane are appended to a text file.

The Fuel command button displays another dialog, shown in Figure 12-3, that records fuel charges pertaining to the currently selected airplane.

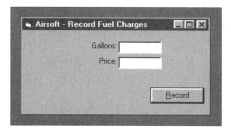

Figure 12-3: Completed fuel charges form

To preview the completed application:

1   Start Visual Basic and open the project named **Chapter.12\Complete\Air_C.vbp.** Set the drive designator as necessary.

2   Run the program.

3   Click the **Arrival** command button on the main form to activate the Record new arrival dialog. Enter the carrier name **Jakes Air** and an Airplane ID of **N23345**. Select an Airplane Type of **Single Propeller**. Click the **Record** button to close the dialog and record the arrival of the airplane at the airport. The Airplane ID appears in the list box on the main form.

4   In the list box, click the airplane you just added, then click the **Fuel** command button to activate the Record Fuel Charges dialog. Enter **150** gallons of fuel at a price of **1.45**. Click the **Record** command button to record the fuel charges for the current airplane and close the dialog. The fuel charges appear on the main form.

5   Click the Airplane ID again in the list box, if necessary, to select it, then click the **Departure** command button. The selected airplane is removed from the list box and the labels on the right side of the form are cleared.

6   End the program and exit Visual Basic.

SECTION A
objectives

In this section you will:

- Learn how to create a new type of module called a class module
- Create a collection using the Collection object
- Add and remove objects from a collection
- Create properties for a class module

Collections and Classes

Introduction to Class Modules

In Visual Basic, all objects are created from classes. You can create your own classes using a class module. A **class module** is a template for objects that you create, as opposed to predefined classes that have already been created for you. A class module has no visual interface; it contains only code. The code in a class module includes variables, Function procedures, and Sub procedures. These variables and procedures act as the properties and methods of the class. The description of the class is stored in a type library. A **type library** contains standard descriptions of objects, properties, methods, and collections.

Conceptually, a class module resembles a form module. Just as you create a form instance from a form class, so too can you create an instance of an object from a class module. The primary difference between a form and class module is that the class module has no visual interface.

An instance of a class module works much like a Recordset object. Once you create an instance of the class, you can read and write its properties and call its methods by writing code. The objects you create from the class support properties and methods that define the **interface** for the class, through which the programmer interacts with the class.

A class module differs from a standard module in some ways. For instance, the Public variables (data) declared in a standard module exist for the life of the running program and are available to all the modules in the program. With a class module, however, the data do not exist until an instance of the class is created. The same data are destroyed when the class instance is destroyed.

Visual Basic is an object-oriented programming language, and an object attempts to model the real-world behavior of some item. For example, you can envision a television's remote control or a telephone as an object. The data and the processes acting on those data are combined together or encapsulated. **Encapsulation** means that an object supports a fixed set of data items (properties) and processes act on those data items (methods).

For instance, a television's remote control supports data items, like the current channel and volume, and processes to act on these data items, like adjusting the volume or changing the channel. The capabilities of the remote control are therefore part of the remote control class. The interface for a remote control consists of the buttons on the remote control. You cannot perform any actions on a remote control without using this interface.

In addition to an object supporting properties, actions can be performed on an object by calling its methods. When you call a method, the code in that method may in turn set properties. For example, if you call a method to change the volume on a television, that method would change the value of the Volume property.

To create a new type of object, you first need to create a class module. To create a new class module, you add the module to the project by clicking Project on the menu bar, then clicking Add Class Module. This creation process is the same as the one you used to add form and standard modules. The newly created class module appears in the Project Explorer in the Class Modules folder. A project can include any number of class modules.

Like a form module, a class module supports a Name property that you should set to a value that will be meaningful to other programmers using the class. Because the class you will develop in this chapter represents an airplane at the airport, you will name it Airplane. You will now create this class module, set its Name property, and save it to the disk.

Programming tip

When you implement a task that may be performed by several programs, consider implementing it as a class. Each programmer using the class can then access it by using a well-defined interface.

help

If the Add Class Module dialog appears on the screen, select the **Class Module** icon, then click the **Open** button. To prevent the dialog from appearing in the future, check the Don't show this dialog in the future check box.

To create a class module:

1 Start Visual Basic, then open the project named **Chapter.12\Startup\Air_S.vbp**. Set the drive designator as necessary.

2 Click **Project**, then click **Add Class Module**.

The Code window for the class module should appear. The title bar of the Code window displays the name of the project and class. Note that the Code window for the class module has the same characteristics as the Code window for any other type of module. For example, you declare module-level variables in the general declarations section. You use the Object and Procedure list boxes to select event and general procedures.

3 Open the Project Explorer, if necessary. Note: A new folder should appear showing the class modules that are part of the project. This folder contains one module, Class1, because the project has one class module.

4 Open the Properties window for the new class module, if necessary by activating the Code window for the class module, then pressing F4.

5 Set the Name property to **Airplane**, then close the Properties window. The Code window should resemble Figure 12-4.

class name listed
in title bar

object list box

procedure list box

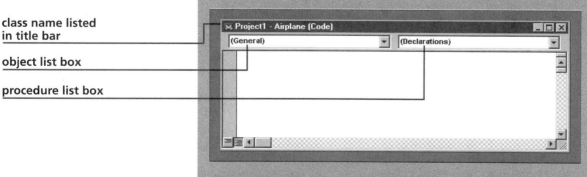

Figure 12-4: Code window for class module

6   Click **File**, then click **Save Airplane As** to open the Save File As dialog. Note the default suffix for a class module is ".cls". Accept the default file name, **Airplane.cls**, and save it in the **Chapter.12\Startup** folder. Set the drive designator as necessary. The Airplane class module appears in the Project Explorer as shown in Figure 12-5. Note that the Project Explorer may show some folders as being closed. Click on the folders to open them, if necessary.

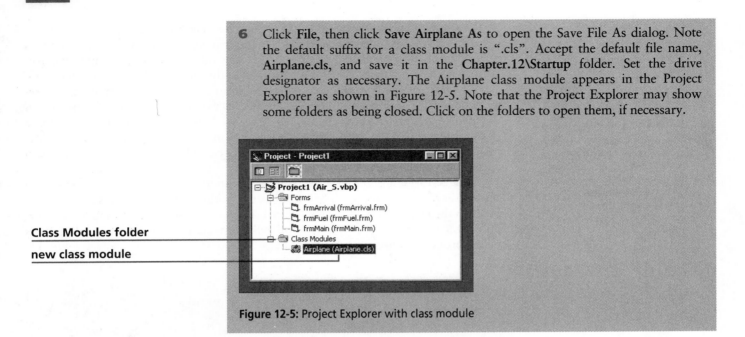

Figure 12-5: Project Explorer with class module

Although this project contains only one class module, more than one class module can be included in a project. The Name property of a class module defines the name of the class. For example, if you created a class module with a Name property of Airplane, you could create an instance of the class with the following statement:

```
Dim CurrentAirplane As New Airplane
```

This process is similar to the one you used with form modules. With form modules, you used the Name property of the form as the class name to create a new form instance. Just as with a form or standard module, a class module's Name property may differ from the file name stored on the disk. In the previous statement, you used the New keyword to create an instance of the class. If you omitted the New keyword, the newly created object variable would reference Nothing—that is, the object would not exist and the variable could not be used to set properties or call the object's methods.

Creating the Properties of a Class

Once you have created a class module, you can begin to develop its properties and methods. By declaring a Public variable in a form module, you create a property of the form. Similarly, by declaring a Public variable in a class module, you create a property of the class. This variable (property) is considered **exposed data**, meaning that the variable is visible to the programmer using the class. That is, exposed data are part of the class's interface. For example, consider again a television's remote control. It has a current channel property that is exposed to the user of the remote control.

Sometimes you may want only to use a variable inside a class module, but not to expose the variable to the programmer using the class. This strategy is called **data hiding**. When you declare a variable in a class module as Private, the variable can be used only by the code inside the class module. Thus the variable remains hidden inside the class module. You cannot reference it from other standard or form modules. Private variables (hidden data) in class modules work the same way as Private variables declared in form modules. A Private variable is not considered a property, nor does it form part of the class's interface.

The first step in programming a class module is to create its properties. The properties in a class module work just like the properties for other objects you have created. Once you create an instance of a class, you can read and write its properties and call its methods from other modules. For example, after creating an instance of a Recordset object, you can read properties like BOF and EOF and call methods like MoveFirst and MoveLast.

Just as choosing meaningful variable names will make your program more readable, so too will choosing meaningful names for properties and methods make it easier for other programmers using your class. Variable names in class modules must meet the same requirements as variable names in other modules. That is, they cannot contain spaces or special characters and must begin with a letter. The naming conventions for properties and methods differ from those applied to variables declared in standard modules, however. The following list describes the naming conventions for the properties and methods of class modules:

- Use whole words, with the first letter of each word being capitalized.
- If the name of a property or method seems too long (a subjective decision), use the first syllable of a word rather than other abbreviations.
- Use plural names for collections.
- When creating properties, use nouns such as AirplaneType.
- When creating methods, create the method's name using a verb for the first word, followed by a noun, such as AddAirplane.
- You cannot use the following names as property or method names: QueryInterface, AddRef, Release, GetTypeInfoCount, GetTypeInfo, GetIDsOfNames, or Invoke. Attempting to assign these names will generate a compilation error.

You do not use a unique Visual Basic statement to create properties for a class. Rather, you declare a Public variable of a specific data type as you have done in the past. For example, to create a property named AirplaneID to hold string values, you would write the following statement in the general declarations section of the class module:

```
Public AirplaneID As String
```

Once a property has been created, you can read and write that property by using code in a form or standard module. For example, to create an instance of the Airplane class and then set the property AirplaneID, you can use the following statements in a standard or form module:

```
Dim CurrentAirplane As New Airplane
CurrentAirplane.AirplaneID = "N23448"
```

These statements create a new instance of the Airplane class named CurrentAirplane, then set the AirplaneID property to the string literal "N23448". Note that you used the *object.property* syntax as you have done previously when referencing the properties of an object.

Programming tip

You cannot create properties declared as arrays or fixed-length strings. If you do, you will receive a syntax error. Trying to store a value of an incorrect data type into a property will generate a run-time error.

You are now ready to create the properties as Public variables in the class. The first property is the name of the airplane's carrier (airline), so you will use the name CarrierName. Each airplane has a unique identification number, known as the Airplane ID. In addition, the program needs to keep track of each airplane's departure date and time, both of which should be stored together in one property.

To create properties for a class module:

1 Make sure that the Code window for the class module named **Airplane.cls** is active.

2 Enter the following statements into the general declarations section of the Code window just after the Option Explicit statement. Note that the Option Explicit statement will not appear unless you have turned on the Require Variable Declaration option. To set this option, you click Tools, click Options, then select Require Variable Declaration on the Editor tab. The Option Explicit statement will only appear when new modules are subsequently created.

```
Public CarrierName As String
Public AirplaneID As String
Public DepartureDateTime As Date
```

The preceding Public variables are properties of the class you just created and thus are part of the class's interface. "CarrierName" will store the name of the airplane's carrier. "AirplaneID" will store the identification number. "DepartureDateTime" will store the airplane's departure date and time. These variables conform to the suggested naming conventions for properties—they are all nouns with the first letter of each word capitalized. The string "ID" was used as an acronym for Identification Number because the property name AirplaneIdentificationNumber is too long.

Using the Object Browser to Look at the Class

Throughout this book, you have used the Object Browser to examine the values of intrinsic constants supported by a class, such as when you looked at the acceptable values of a check box. You also have examined the enumerated and user-defined types in a project via the Object Browser. Now, however, you will use the Object Browser to view all the properties and methods of a class module. At this time, your class contains three properties. You can use the Object Browser to view these different properties just as you have in earlier chapters.

To view the properties of the class you just created:

1 Click the **Object Browser** button 🖾 on the toolbar.

2 Click the **Project/Library** list button, then select the project named **Project1** to view the classes applicable to the project.

3 Click the class named **Airplane** to view the members of the class, as shown in Figure 12-6.

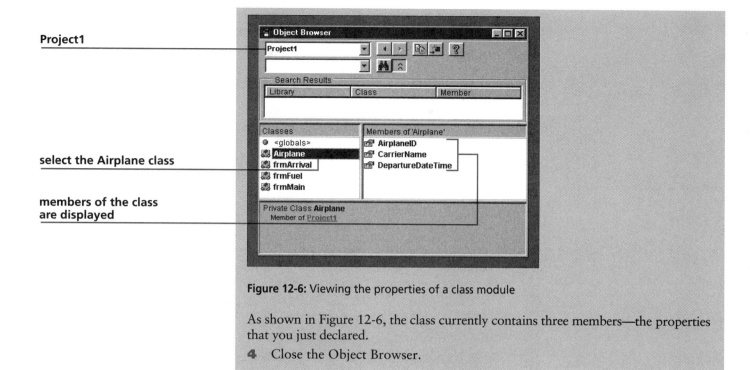

Project1

select the Airplane class

members of the class
are displayed

Figure 12-6: Viewing the properties of a class module

As shown in Figure 12-6, the class currently contains three members—the properties that you just declared.

4   Close the Object Browser.

Programming

tip

• • • • • • • • • • • • • • •

As you create additional properties and methods for a class, you can use the Object Browser to view them. Also, Visual Basic's IntelliSense technology will display suggestions as ToolTips in the Code window as you read and write properties and call methods.

Now that you have created the class module and its properties, you can begin to write code for the form that will create an instance of the class, then set the value of the class's properties. Just as a control or form is a class, and an object does not exist until you create an instance of the control or form, so too does an object not exist until you create an instance of the class.

Airsoft's program will create an instance of the Airplane class each time an airplane arrives at the airport. When the airplane departs, the information relating to the charges incurred will be saved to a text file. The instance of the class will then be destroyed.

In Chapter 11, you created an array to store a reference to multiple instances of a form class, then wrote code to add and remove objects from the array. Similarly, you could manage the Airplane class by including the following statement in the general declarations section of the form module to create an empty array to store Airplane objects:

```
Private mAirplaneArray( ) As New Airplane
```

Using this technique, you would need to redimension the array each time an airplane arrived, as well as keep track of which element in the array represents which airplane. Furthermore, when an airplane departs the airport, you would need to destroy the class instance representing that airplane and remove its reference from the array. While this technique would work, another technique allows you to store multiple instances of like objects. Just as you used predefined collections to obtain a reference to multiple object variables, so too can you create your own collection and then store object references in it.

Creating a Collection

Instead of using an array to store object references, you can create your own collections using the Visual Basic Collection object. The Collection object works much like the collections you have used in previous chapters. In those chapters, the individual object references contained in a collection were created for you, either automatically or by calling a method. For example, Visual Basic automatically stored a reference to each control instance created on a form in the Controls collection. By calling the OpenDatabase method pertaining to the Workspace object, you created a new instance of the Database object and stored a reference in the Databases collection. In this chapter, however, you must manage the members of the collection yourself. The Visual Basic Collection object stores references to objects. You can create collections to manage control instances or other like objects. In fact, a collection can store a reference to a different type of object in each member. In this case however, the programmer must keep track of what type of object is contained in each collection member.

Collection names should always be plural and usually match the name of the objects they reference. Thus a collection used to store references to Airplane objects should be called Airplanes. To create a collection to store the different airplanes at the airport, you could use the following statement:

```
Public Airplanes As New Collection
```

Programming

tip

. . . .

▶ Use collections instead of arrays to store references to like objects. Using a collection makes the program easier to write and easier to read.

This statement declares a collection named Airplanes that will store zero or more instances of the Airplane class. Because you used the New keyword, a new Collection object is created. If you omitted the New keyword, the object variable would exist but would reference Nothing. At this point, the collection is empty; that is, it does not yet contain a reference to any Airplane objects.

Although you could store CommandButton or Recordset object references in the Airplanes collection, that strategy would not make sense to another programmer using the class or collection. By convention, the Airplanes collection is used to store Airplane objects. That is, the collection name is plural and the name of the objects stored in the collection is singular.

To create a new collection:

1 Activate the Code window for the form named **frmMain.**

2 Enter the following statement in the general declarations section of the form module just after the Option Explicit statement:

```
Public Airplanes As New Collection
```

Because you used the New keyword, this statement creates a new Collection object named Airplanes. Had you omitted the New keyword, you would have to explicitly create a Collection object with a Set statement and the New keyword.

Remember that some collections are zero-based and others are one-based. All collections you create with the Collection object are one-based. The Collection object supports several properties and methods that allow you to add, remove, and locate objects.

Syntax	Collection
Properties	■ The read-only **Count** property returns a Long Integer containing the number of objects referenced in the collection. You cannot update this value directly. Rather, it is updated automatically when you add and remove items from the collection.
Methods	■ The **Add** method adds an item (object reference) to a Collection object.
	■ The **Item** method returns a specific item (object reference) from a Collection object through either a string key or a numeric index.
	■ The **Remove** method removes an item (object reference) from a Collection object.

Now that you know how to create a collection, you must learn how to add object references to the collection, locate those object references, and delete an object reference. The process of adding and deleting object references from a collection is very similar to adding and removing items from a list box at run time.

Adding Items to a Collection

To add an object reference to a collection, you explicitly call the Add method, which will add an item (object reference) to the specified collection.

Syntax	*object*.**Add** *item*[, *key*][, *before*	*after*]
Dissection	■ The **Add** method adds an item (object reference) to a collection.
	■ The required *object* is the name of a Collection object.
	■ The required *item* argument is the name of the object reference to be added to the collection.
	■ The optional *key* argument must be a unique string key that can be used instead of a positional numeric index to references an item in the collection.
	■ The optional *before* or *after* argument is an Integer or String specifying the relative position of the new item in the collection. You can specify a *before* position or an *after* position, but not both. The item to be added is placed in the collection before or after the item identified by the *before* or *after* argument, respectively. If an Integer, the *before* or *after* argument must be a number from one (1) to the value of the collection's Count property. If a String, the *before* or *after* argument must correspond to the string key specified when the relevant item was added to the collection. To specify which argument you are using, use the following syntax:
	before: = *value* or **after:** = *value*

Code Example	<pre>Dim CurrentAirplane As New Airplane
	Airplanes.Add CurrentAirplane "N12289"</pre>

Code Dissection	The previous statement assumes that CurrentAirplane is a valid instance of an Airplane object. A reference to this object is added to the Airplanes collection having a string key of "N12289".

Before you can add an Airplane object to the collection, you must create an instance of the object and store a reference to the object inside an object variable. Once the object and a reference to it exist, you must set the CarrierName and AirplaneID properties. Only then can you add the object to the collection.

The string key for each object in a collection must be unique. That is, two airplanes cannot have the same Airplane ID number. Therefore, you must ensure that the user does not add the same Airplane ID to the collection twice. Two techniques are available to ensure a unique Airplane ID number. With the first technique, you could try to find a match in the collection before adding an airplane to the collection. In the second technique, you can try to add the airplane to the collection. If you write code that attempts to add an object with a duplicate string key to a collection, a run-time error will occur. You could then write an error handler to trap this error. Operating under the assumption that the user will rarely attempt to add an existing airplane, you will create an error handler for Airsoft's program, because searching the collection each time an airplane is added will require more code and degrade the performance of your program.

You can now write the necessary statements to create a new Airplane object, set its properties, and then add the Airplane object to the Airplanes collection. To make the collection as easy to use as possible, the object references stored in the collection should be accessible using a string key. Because the Airplane ID is always unique, the string key should consist of the Airplane ID. This string key will be used later to reference individual items in the collection. Furthermore, because the string key will reference the objects referenced in the collection, you do not need to use the before or after arguments to specify the actual position of an object in the collection.

To add an Airplane object to the collection:

1 Activate the Code window for the form module named **frmMain**, if necessary.

2 Enter the following statements in the **cmdArrival_Click** event procedure:

```
On Error GoTo DuplicateAirplane
    Dim AirplaneNew As New Airplane
    frmArrival.Show vbModal
    AirplaneNew.CarrierName = frmArrival.txtName
    AirplaneNew.AirplaneID = frmArrival.txtID
    Airplanes.Add AirplaneNew, frmArrival.txtID
    lstAirplanes.AddItem frmArrival.txtID
    Exit Sub
DuplicateAirplane:
    MsgBox "Cannot add. Airplane ID already exists.", _
        vbOKOnly, "Error"
```

These statements create a new instance of the Airplane class to store the arriving airplane. Next, they display a modal form to get the information pertaining to the arriving airplane. This form, which has already been created for you, contains two text boxes named txtName and txtID, representing the name of the carrier and the Airplane ID number. Once the instance of the class has been created, the code stores the carrier in the CarrierName property and the Airplane ID number in the AirplaneID property. If the collection already contains that Airplane ID, the error handler executes and a message box is displayed.

```
On Error GoTo DuplicateAirplane
```

This statement creates the error handler for the procedure. Attempting to add an Airplane object to the Airplanes collection with a duplicate string key will invoke the error handler, and the object will not be added. Rather, a message box will appear advising the user of the error condition.

```
Dim AirplaneNew As New Airplane
frmArrival.Show vbModal
AirplaneNew.CarrierName = frmArrival.txtName
AirplaneNew.AirplaneID = frmArrival.txtID
```

These statements set the CarrierName and AirplaneID properties based on the information contained in the corresponding control instances on the form frmArrival. The object variable was created in the previous Dim statement.

```
Airplanes.Add AirplaneNew, frmArrival.txtID
lstAirplanes.AddItem frmArrival.txtID
Exit Sub
```

The first of these statements adds the object reference to the collection by calling the Add method. Notice that you used two arguments: the name of the object you want to add and the string key you will use to reference the object in the collection. The second statement adds the new Airplane ID to the list box. Later in the chapter, you will use this list box to allow the user to select an individual airplane and update its properties. After these statements execute, the Exit Sub statement causes the procedure to exit, thereby preventing execution of the error handler.

```
DuplicateAirplane:
    MsgBox "Cannot add. Airplane ID already exists.", _
        vbOKOnly, "Error"
```

In the preceding code, if a duplicate string key is detected, the error handler executes. It displays a message box advising the user that the airplane cannot be added because it already exists.

Using a collection to manage several objects is much easier than using an array because you do not need to explicitly change the size of the collection or determine exactly where to insert an item. The Collection object keeps track of this information automatically.

Note that the variable AirplaneNew is a local variable. When the cmdArrival_Click event procedure ends, this variable is destroyed. Another reference to the object was created when you added the object to the collection, however. Even though the variable AirplaneNew no longer exists when the procedure exits, the object continues to exist because the collection continues to maintain a reference to it. Figure 12-7 illustrates this process.

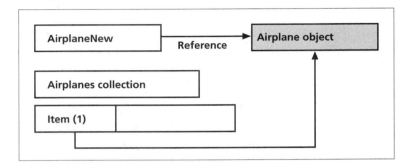

Figure 12-7: Storing an object reference in a collection

In its current form, your program will create a new instance of the Airplane class when the user clicks the Arrival command button. It also will display the Airplane ID number in the list box. You can now run the program to test that the instance of the class is created and that the list box is updated properly.

To test the program:

1   Save the project, then run it. Click the **Arrival** button to display the arrival form.

2   Enter the information as shown in Figure 12-8.

enter this carrier

enter this Airplane ID

click Record

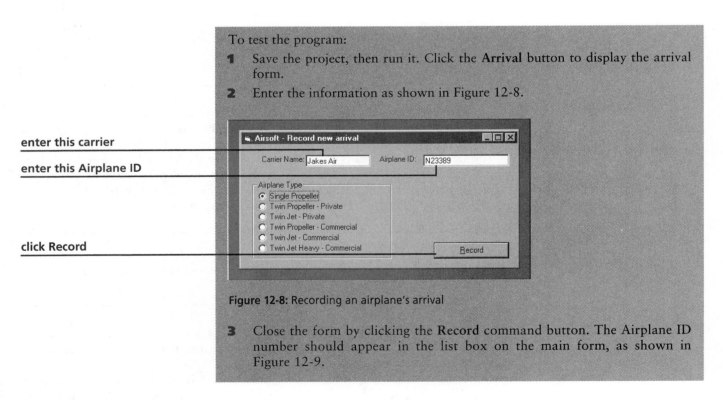

Figure 12-8: Recording an airplane's arrival

3   Close the form by clicking the **Record** command button. The Airplane ID number should appear in the list box on the main form, as shown in Figure 12-9.

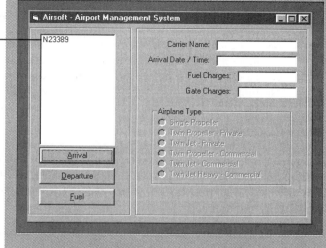

Airplane ID shown
in list box

Figure 12-9: New airplane shown in main form

4 Click the **Arrival** button again to display the arrival form. Enter the Airplane ID from Figure 12-9. The message box should appear indicating the airplane cannot be added. Click **OK**.

5 End the program to return to design mode.

help

● ● ● ● ● ● ● ● ● ● ● ● ● ●

▶ If the information does not appear in the list box, verify that the code for the Arrival command button's Click event matches the code shown in the previous steps.

Removing Items from a Collection

In addition to adding items to the Airplanes collection when an airplane arrives, you must write the code to remove an item from the collection when an airplane departs from the airport. To remove an item from a collection, you call the Remove method, which has the following syntax:

Syntax	*object*.**Remove** *index*
Dissection	■ The **Remove** method removes an object from the specified collection.
	■ The required *object* is a Collection object.
	■ The required *index* argument is an expression that specifies the position of an item in the collection. This index can consist of a number from one to the value of the collection's Count property (numeric index) or a string expression (string key). If the value provided for the index does not match an existing member of the collection, a run-time error will occur.
| **Code Example** | ```
Airplanes.Remove "N23389"
``` |
| **Code Dissection** | The preceding statement removes the Airplane object having a string key of "N23389" from the Airplanes collection. |
```

When the user clicks the Departure command button, the instance of the Airplane class should be terminated, the item removed from the collection, and the corresponding item deleted from the list box on the main form. To accomplish this task, you call the Remove method pertaining to the Airplanes collection with one argument: the Airplane ID used as the string key when the object was added to the collection. You do not need to explicitly destroy the Airplane object by setting it to Nothing. Because only one reference to the object appears in the Airplanes collection, calling the Remove method eliminates the only object reference.

To remove an Airplane instance from the Airplanes collection:
1   Activate the Code window for the form module named **frmMain**.
2   Select the **cmdDeparture_Click** event procedure, then enter the following statements:

```
Dim pstrIndex As String
If lstAirplanes = vbNullString Then
    MsgBox "No airplane selected.", vbOKOnly, "Error"
    Exit Sub
End If
pstrIndex = lstAirplanes
Airplanes.Remove (pstrIndex)
lstAirplanes.RemoveItem lstAirplanes.ListIndex
lblName = vbNullString
lblArrivalDateTime = vbNullString
lblFuel = vbNullString
lblCharges = vbNullString
```

These statements remove an Airplane object from the Airplanes collection. After the object is removed, the item is also deleted from the list box. If the user has not selected an item in the list box, then the procedure displays a message box and the procedure exits.

```
Dim pstrIndex As String
```

The above statement declares the variable pstrIndex to store the string key used to reference the individual object in the collection.

```
If lstAirplanes = vbNullString Then
    MsgBox "No airplane selected.", vbOKOnly, "Error"
    Exit Sub
End If
```

This If statement verifies that an item is selected in the list box. If not, it displays a message box so that the user cannot attempt to remove an airplane when none is selected. This approach prevents a run-time error generated by trying to remove a nonexistent item.

```
pstrIndex = lstAirplanes
Airplanes.Remove (pstrIndex)
lstAirplanes.RemoveItem lstAirplanes.ListIndex
```

If an item in the list box is selected, then the preceding statements execute. The first statement sets the variable pstrIndex to the text in the currently selected item in the list box. The next statement uses this variable to remove an Airplane object from the Airplanes collection. The final statement calls the RemoveItem method to remove the corresponding item from the list box.

Just before the procedure ends, it clears the contents of the output labels, indicating that no airplane is selected.

You can now test the program to verify that airplanes are removed from both the list box and the collection when the user clicks the Departure command button.

To test the Departure command button:

1　Save the project, then run it.

2　Click **Arrival** to activate the Record new arrival dialog. Type **Jakes Air** for the Carrier Name and **N23389** for the Airplane ID number.

3　Click **Record**.

4　Click **Arrival**, then type **International** for the Carrier Name and **N18566** for the Airplane ID number.

5　Click **Record**.

6　Click **N23389** in the list box, then click the **Departure** command button. The airplane should be removed from the collection and the list box.

7　Click **N18566** in the list box, then click the **Departure** command button.

8　Click the **Departure** command button again to verify that you cannot remove a nonexistent airplane.

9　Click **OK** to close the message box.

10　End the program to return to design mode.

Removing an item from a collection is considerably easier than performing the same operation on an array. You need not write code to locate the element in an array by examining each element individually. Instead, you can locate an item in the collection simply by using a string key.

In addition to adding and removing items from the Airplanes collection, the user must be able to click an Airplane ID in the list box so as to display information pertaining to the selected airplane in the output section of the form. Thus you need a way to reference a specific Airplane object in the Airplanes collection. You can accomplish this task by using either a numeric index or the string key with the Item method.

Finding an Item in a Collection

To locate an item in a collection, you can use a numeric index or a string key as you have done previously with other collections. Locating a particular object reference in a Collection is accomplished with the Item method.

Syntax	*object*.**Item**(*index*)
Dissection	■ The **Item** method returns a reference to a specific member in the collection.
	■ The *object* must be a valid instance of a Collection object.
	■ The *index* can be a numeric index or a string key.
| **Code Example** | ```
Dim CurrentAirplane As Airplane
Set CurrentAirplane = Airplanes.Item(1)
Set CurrentAirplane = Airplanes.Item("N23389")
``` |
| **Code Dissection** | The above statements assume that Airplanes is a collection containing references to Airplane objects. The first statement declares the object variable CurrentAirplane so that it can reference an Airplane object. The first Set statement returns a reference to the first Airplane object in the collection; the second Set statement returns a reference to the Airplane object having a string key of "N23389". |

When searching for an item in a collection, you must use a valid numeric index or string key. That is, if the collection contains two objects, the valid numeric index values are one (1) and two (2). If the user specifies an invalid index or string key, a run-time error will occur.

Like many other objects, the Collection object supports a default method—the Item method. Thus the following two statement fragments are equivalent:

```
Airplanes.Item(1)
Airplanes(1)
```

This default method also applies to referencing an item using the string key. Thus the following statements are equivalent:

```
Set CurrentAirplane = Airplanes.Item("N23389")
Set CurrentAirplane = Airplanes("N23389")
```

You can now write the statements to locate a specific airplane in the Airplanes collection, then display the information pertaining to that airplane. The only information you have recorded so far is the carrier name. Because the value in the list box was recorded at the same time that the Airplane object was added to the collection, you need not verify that the string key is valid. You will write the code for the list box's Click event procedure to locate the Airplane ID, then display the carrier name corresponding to that airplane.
```

To display the current airplane information when an airplane is selected:

1 Activate the Code window for the form module named **frmMain**.

2 Enter the following statements in the **lstAirplanes_Click** event procedure:

```
Dim AirplaneCurrent As Airplane
Set AirplaneCurrent = Airplanes(lstAirplanes)
lblName = AirplaneCurrent.CarrierName
```

The variable AirplaneCurrent references an Airplane object in the Airplanes collection. The first statement does not create an Airplane object because the New keyword was omitted. Rather, the object variable references an existing object (stored in the Airplanes collection). The second statement locates the desired object in the collection by using the currently selected item in the list box as the string key. Finally, the caption of the label lblName is set to the CarrierName property of the selected Airplane object.

You should now test the program to verify that you can select different Airplane IDs in the list box and display the corresponding carrier.

To test the Click event procedure for the lstAirplanes list box:

1 Save the project, then run it.

2 Click **Arrival** to activate the Record new arrival dialog, then type **Jakes Air** for the Carrier Name and **N23389** for the Airplane ID number.

3 Click **Record**.

4 Click **Arrival**, then type **International** for the Carrier Name and **N18566** for the Airplane ID number.

5 Click **Record**.

6 Click **N23389** in the list box. Jakes Air should appear in the Carrier Name text box.

7 Click **N18566** in the list box. International should appear in the Carrier Name text box.

8 End the program to return to design mode.

Your program can now add airplanes to the collection, delete airplanes, and locate airplanes. Next, you will compute the charges incurred by an airplane while it remains at an airport.

Hiding Data in a Class Module

Sometimes you may not want certain data in a class to be accessible to other modules. That is, you do not want the data to become part of the object's interface. In object-oriented terminology, this approach is called **data hiding**. By exposing only certain data as properties, you can change the inner workings of a class module without affecting the programs that use the class.

To hide data in a class module, you create Private variables. Private variables declared in a class module behave in the same way as Private variables declared in a form module. To declare a hidden variable, you use the Private statement. A variable that is declared in the general declarations section of the class module can be used by all procedures in the class module. Alternatively, you can use the Dim statement inside a procedure to declare a local variable. Local variables can be used only in the procedure where they are declared.

For Airsoft's program, you need several Private variables to store the data hidden in the class module. These data include the charges for fuel, other charges, and the total charges. You also need to store the departure date and time.

To declare the hidden variables in a class module:

1   Activate the Code window for the class module named **Airplane.cls**.

2   Enter the following statements into the general declarations section of the class module just after the Public variables:

```
Private msngCharges As Single
Private msngFuelCharge As Single
Private mdtmArrivalDateTime As Date
```

Each of these hidden variables uses the naming convention for variables, rather than the naming convention for properties. Because you declared these variables with the Private statement, they are neither properties nor part of the class's interface.

The variable msngCharges will store the accumulated charges accrued for each airplane from the time it arrives until the time it departs. The variable msngFuelCharge will store the charges for fuel. The variable mdtmArrivalDateTime will store the airplane's arrival date and time.

Class Initialization

Just as a form supports an Initialize event that occurs when an instance of the form is first created, so too can a class module respond to an Initialize event. Upon the creation of a new class instance, the Initialize event occurs. The arrival of a new airplane at the airport prompts the creation of a new instance of the Airplane class representing the airplane and the addition of the object reference to the Airplanes collection. You have not yet recorded the arrival time of the airplane in the class instance, however. Although you could create the instance of the class, then explicitly set a property as you did with the CarrierName and AirplaneID properties, you will instead program the Initialize event to record the arrival date and time in the variable you just created.

To record an airplane's arrival time when the class is initialized:

1   Activate the Code window for the class module named **Airplane.cls**, if necessary.

2   Choose **Class** in the Object list box. Enter the following statement in the **Initialize** event procedure:

```
mdtmArrivalDateTime = Now
```

> **Programming tip**
>
> • • • • • • • • • • • • • • • •
>
> ▶ Declare all properties together and all Private variables together so as to improve the readability of your programs.

This statement sets the hidden variable mdtmArrivalDateTime to the current date and time by calling the Now function. Once recorded, this information should never be changed. Part of the interface for the class requires that you be able to retrieve the arrival date and time. Because this information is currently hidden, you need a way for the form module to retrieve and display this information.

Creating Property Procedures

The form using the class module needs to read a property containing the arrival date and time. To satisfy this requirement, you will create the property that the code in other modules can read. Its value should never be set explicitly by a programmer using the class module, however. If you use a Public variable, nothing would prevent a programmer from manipulating the class so as to overwrite the value of the property. Furthermore, if you create a Public variable, the programmer using the class would have to explicitly set the arrival date and time each time an instance of the class was created.

To create a property that can be read but not written, you must create a Property procedure. **Property procedures** resemble Sub or Function procedures declared in a standard module. You do not explicitly call Property procedures as you do Sub or Function procedures, however. Rather, a Property procedure executes when you set or read the property. The name of the Property procedure is identical to the name of the property.

When you create a Property procedure by using the Add Procedure dialog, Visual Basic automatically declares two procedures—a Property Get procedure and a corresponding Property Let procedure. Property procedures usually work in pairs. That is, when you set the value of a property, the Property Let procedure executes; when you read the value of a property, the matching Property Get procedure executes. When the relevant property is an Intrinsic data type, the Property Get and Property Let statements will allow you to execute code when the property is read or written, respectively. If the property will set a reference to an object variable, the Property Set procedure is used instead of the Property Let procedure. Notice that the syntax for a Property procedure is very similar to the syntax for a Sub or Function procedure, except that it contains slightly different keywords. The Property Get statement has the following syntax:

Syntax	[**Public** | **Private**] [**Static**] **Property Get** *name* [(*argumentlist*)] [**As** *type*]
	     [*statements*]
	     [*name = expression*]
	     [Exit Property]
	     [*statements*]
	     [*name = expression*]
	 End Property

Dissection	■ If you include the **Public** keyword, the Property procedure is visible to all other procedures in all other modules. If you include the **Private** keyword, the Property procedure is visible only to the procedures in the module where it was declared. If you use the **Static** keyword, the value of the local variables declared in the Property procedure will be preserved between calls to the procedure. ■ The *name* argument defines the name of the property and follows the standard naming conventions for property names.

- When setting a property requires arguments, the *argumentlist* allows you to pass one or more arguments used to set the property.

- Inside the Property procedure, any number of *statements* may be executed when the property is set.

- The *type* argument identifies the data type returned by the Property procedure.

- The **Exit Property** statement works much like the Exit Sub statement, causing the Property procedure to exit before the last statement in the procedure executes.

- The **End Property** statement identifies the end of the Property procedure, just as the End Sub statement identifies the end of a Sub procedure.

To create a Property procedure, you can use the Add Procedure dialog as you have done previously. The Add Procedure dialog will create both the Property Let and Property Get procedures. Alternatively, you could manually enter the Property procedure(s) into the Code window. You now need to create the Property procedures to read the values of the ArrivalDateTime property.

To create the ArrivalDateTime Property procedures:

1 Activate the Code window for the class module named **Airplane.cls**, if necessary.

2 Click **Tools**, then click **Add Procedure** to open the Add Procedure dialog.

3 Set the Name to **ArrivalDateTime**, as shown in Figure 12-10. Click the **Property** option button in the Type section of the dialog. Because the procedure should be visible to other modules, click the **Public** option button in the Scope section of the dialog. The Property Get and Property Let procedures of this name will be added to the project.

procedure type is Property

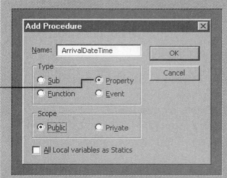

Figure 12-10: Adding a Property procedure

4 Click the **OK** button to close the Add Procedure dialog.

These steps created the ArrivalDateTime Property procedures, as shown in the following statements:

```
Public Property Get ArrivalDateTime() As Variant


End Property


Public Property Let ArrivalDateTime(ByVal vNewValue As Variant)


End Property
```

Note that the Add procedure dialog created both the Property Get and Property Let procedures. Because the Property procedures do not contain any code, however, nothing will happen if you write statements to set or read the properties. You now need to write the code to read the property.

Creating a Read-Only Property

Although the Add Procedure dialog created the Property Let and Property Get procedures, the programmer should not be able to set the property. A property that can be read but not written is known as a **read-only property**. To make a Property read-only, you can omit any code for the Property Let procedure. If the programmer tried to set the property, however, nothing would happen. A better technique employs an error message to notify the programmer that the read-only property cannot be written. To generate an error if the programmer attempts to set the read-only property, you remove the Property Let procedure.

To write the code for the read-only property ArrivalDateTime:

1 Activate the Code window for the class module named **Airplane.cls**, if necessary.

2 Locate the Property Let **ArrivalDateTime** procedure and remove the entire procedure.

3 Locate the Property Get **ArrivalDateTime** procedure and enter the following code, shown in bold. Note that the Property Get procedure returns a Variant by default. Make sure to change the return type to a Date instead of a Variant. Although a Variant will work, the resulting procedure will run more slowly.

```
Public Property Get ArrivalDateTime( ) As Date
    ArrivalDateTime = mdtmArrivalDateTime
End Property
```

The Property Get procedure stores the hidden variable mdtmArrivalDateTime in the property named ArrivalDateTime. Remember that the hidden variable was initialized in the Class_Initialize event procedure. This statement will execute when the property is read. The new Property procedure illustrates the use of hidden variables within a class module. When the programmer tries to read the ArrivalDateTime property, the corresponding Property Get procedure will execute and retrieve the value from the hidden variable. Because no corresponding Property Let procedure exists, the property is read-only. If the programmer tries to write a value to the property, an error will occur because the procedure does not exist.

Now that you have created the Property procedure, you can write the necessary statements to display the arrival date and time on the form by reading the property and storing the value in the corresponding label. Because this operation should occur whenever the user selects an airplane from the list box, you must add statements to the Click event procedure for the list box.

To display the arrival date and time on the form:

1   Activate the Code window for the form named **frmMain**, then locate the **Click** event procedure for the list box named **lstAirplanes**. Enter the following statement (shown in bold) into the event procedure just before the End Sub statement:

```
lblName = AirplaneCurrent.CarrierName
lblArrivalDateTime = AirplaneCurrent.ArrivalDateTime
```

2   Save the project, then run it.
3   Click the **Arrival** command button.
4   Enter **Jakes Air** as the Carrier Name and **N1288** as the Airplane ID number, then click the **Record** command button.
5   Click the **N1288** item in the list box. The carrier name and arrival date and time should appear as depicted in Figure 12-11.

carrier name displayed
selected airplane
arrival date and
time displayed

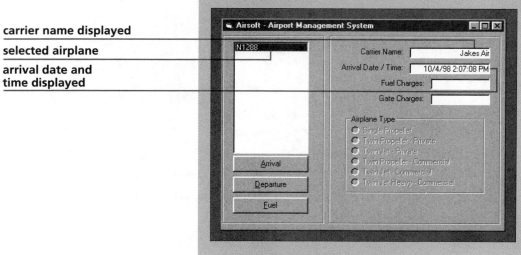

Figure 12-11: Displaying the arrival time

6   End the program to return to design mode.

Airsoft's program now supports an Airplane class. This class supports properties to identify the Carrier Name and the Airplane ID. Another read-only property describes the arrival date and time. You can create instances of the class each time an airplane arrives and terminate those instances when an airplane departs. Also, your program can keep track of each object reference using a collection instead of an array.

Q U E S T I O N S

1. Which of the following statements regarding property names is true?
   a. They can contain spaces.
   b. They cannot contain spaces.
   c. Whole words should be used.
   d. Both a and c.
   e. Both b and c.

2. Which of the following techniques to implement a property for a class is valid?
   a. Create a Public variable in a class module
   b. Create a Private variable in a class module
   c. Create Property procedures
   d. Both a and c.
   e. Both b and c.

3. Which of the following statements regarding the Collection object is true?
   a. Objects must be of the same type.
   b. Objects can be referenced only using a numeric index.
   c. The lower bound of a collection is zero (0).
   d. All of the above.
   e. None of the above.

4. Which of the following methods are supported by the Collection object?
   a. Add
   b. Item
   c. Count
   d. Remove
   e. All of the above.

5. Which keyword is used to declare a hidden variable in a class module?
   a. Public
   b. Private
   c. Dim
   d. Both a and c.
   e. Both b and c.

6. What is the name of the event that occurs when an instance of a class is created?
   a. Load
   b. Activate
   c. Paint
   d. Initialize
   e. None of the above.

7. What are the names of the statements used to declare Property procedures?
   a. Property Let
   b. Public Function
   c. Property Get
   d. Both a and c.
   e. All of the above.

8. Assume that the object variable NewAirplane represents a valid instance of the Airplane class. Write the necessary statement(s) to add an object reference to the Airplanes collection having a string key of "N9999".

9. Write the necessary statement(s) to remove an item from the Airplanes collection having a string key of "N9999".

10. Create a read-only property named ID that reads the contents of the hidden variable named mstrID.

In this section you will:

- Create read-write properties using Property procedures
- Generate a run-time error in a class module
- Set the default property for a class
- Create a write-once property
- Create a method
- Terminate a class instance

Property Procedures and Methods

Creating Read-Write Properties

Sometimes a property should both be read and written. Properties that allow you to store a value in the property and then read that value from the same property are called read-write properties. Although a Public variable can serve this purpose, it has limitations. For example, you cannot execute code in response to reading or writing a property when using a Public variable. Such a task may be necessary to ensure that the programmer attempted to set the property to a valid value. In those cases, Property procedures should execute when the property is read or written. To accomplish this task, you can create a Property procedure as you did in Section A, but you must write code for both the Property Let and Property Get procedures instead of just the Property Get procedure. In this section, you will develop a property to represent the airplane type. Each airplane is classified as one of six different types. You will then use the type of airplane to compute the charges.

You could create an Integer property and store the values one through six to represent each type, or you could use a description stored in a String property. To make the class module as robust as possible and to validate the input most easily when the programmer sets the property, you can create an enumerated type as you did in Chapter 11. This enumerated type will describe each type of aircraft. The six different types of aircraft are based on the plane's size, number of engines, and ownership (commercial or private). Because these data pertain to the class, you should declare the enumerated type in the class module itself. To ensure that other modules can use the enumerated type, the type should be declared as a Public enumeration, which helps encapsulate the data within the class.

To declare the enumerated type describing the type of aircraft:

1 Activate the Code window for the class module named **Airplane.cls**, then enter the following statements in the general declarations section of the class module just after the Option Explicit statement:

```
Public Enum AirplaneType
    atSinglePropeller
    atTwinPropellerPrivate
    atTwinJetPrivate
    atTwinPropellerCommercial
    atTwinJetCommercial
    atTwinJetHeavyCommercial
End Enum
Private atAirplaneType As AirplaneType
```

These statements declare an enumerated type named AirplaneType. Six valid values exist for this enumeration. Because the enumerated type is declared as Public, it can be used not only by the class, but also by any other modules that use the class. The final statement declares a hidden variable named atAirplaneType. You will create Property procedures to set and retrieve the values of this type so as to validate any input from the user. These read-write properties will allow you to store a value in the property and read the value from the same property. You can implement read-write properties using Public variables or a Property Get and corresponding Property Let procedure.

It is important to know when to create a Public variable to represent a property and when to create a Property procedure. You should create a Public variable when:

- The property is a read-write property.
- The property does not need to be validated when set. For example, if a property has a data type like Boolean, the property is self-validating. That is, an error will occur if you try to assign a value to the property other than True or False.

You should create a Property procedure when:

- The property is read-only or should not be changed once it has been set initially.
- The property has a set of values that can be validated.
- Some action needs to occur when a property is read or written.

In Airsoft's program, Property procedures offer a better option than creating a Public variable. With Property procedures, you can validate the value set by the user. You now need to create the Property Let and Property Get procedures for the AirplaneType property. The Property Let statement has a syntax almost identical to the Property Get syntax.

Syntax	[**Public** | **Private**][**Static**] **Property Let** *name* [(*arglist*)]
	    [*statements*]
	    [**Exit Property**]
	    [*statements*]
	End Property

Dissection	■ The **Property Let** procedure may be Public, Private, or Static. If you include the Public keyword, then the Property procedure is visible to all other procedures in all other modules. If you include the Private keyword, the Property procedure is visible only to the procedures in the module where it was declared. If you include the Static keyword, then the value of the local variables declared in the Property procedure will be preserved between calls to the procedure. ■ The *name* argument identifies the name of the Property procedure and thus the name of the property. In situations when you want to execute one procedure when a property is set and another procedure when a property is read, you declare both a Property Get and Property Let procedure with the same name. ■ The *arglist* contains the arguments passed to the Property procedure. It has the same syntax as the *arglist* employed with ordinary Function and Sub procedures. ■ The **Exit Property** and **End Property** statements exit the procedure without completing it and signify that you have reached the last statement in the procedure, respectively.

The AirplaneType Property Let procedure must verify that the input value is a valid airplane type. If it is, the value of the hidden variable corresponding to the property should be set. If it is invalid, the Property procedure should generate a run-time error. The programmer using the class module can then write an error handler to trap this error and produce an error message, if necessary.

When you use Property Let and Property Get procedures to create a read-write property, the arguments of the paired properties must match. Consider the Property procedure necessary to read and write the airplane type. When setting the property, the Property Let procedure must accept one argument—the type of airplane. When reading a property, the corresponding Property Get procedure must return an argument, which also is the airplane type. Thus you would use the following declarations for the two Property procedures:

```
Public Property Let AirplaneType(ByVal atType As AirplaneType)
Public Property Get AirplaneType( ) As AirplaneType
```

In all cases, the Property Let procedure takes one more argument than the corresponding Property Get procedure. The Property Get procedure also returns a value. The final argument in the Property Let procedure must be of the same data type as the return value of the Property Get procedure. Both procedures are of the same type. Figure 12-12 illustrates this process.

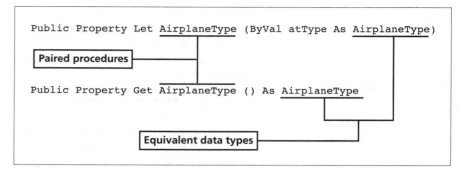

Figure 12-12: Property Let and Property Get arguments

Generating a Run-Time Error

The programs you have written so far have responded to run-time errors caused by conditions such as type mismatches or numeric overflows. In Airsoft's Airport Management System, the Property procedure must be able to communicate an error condition to another procedure if it receives invalid data. One way to accomplish this goal is for the Property procedure to generate a run-time error if the program receives invalid input. To carry out this task, you can generate a run-time error that the module using the class can then trap. To generate a run-time error, you use the Err object with the Raise method.

Syntax	**Err.Raise** *number* [, *source*] [, *description*] [, *helpfile*] [, *helpcontext*]
Dissection	■ The **Raise** method always is called on the required **Err** object.
	■ The required *number* argument contains a Long Integer that identifies the error. Visual Basic errors (both Visual-Basic-defined and user-defined errors) are in the range of 0 to 65,535. When setting the Number property to your own error code in a class module, you add your error code number to the vbObjectError constant.
	■ The optional *source* argument contains a string expression naming the object or application that generated the error. When setting this property for an object, you use the form *project.class*. If you do not specify the *source*, the programmatic ID of the current Visual Basic project is used.
	■ The optional *description* argument is a string describing the error. If unspecified, the program examines the value in *number*. If it can be mapped to a Visual Basic run-time error code, the string that would be returned by the Err object is used as the *description*. If no Visual Basic error corresponds to *number*, the "Application-defined or object-defined error" message is generated.
	■ The optional *helpfile* and *helpcontext* arguments define the file containing help information.

Often you will call a function or method without using all of the arguments. In this situation, you can specify each argument by name by giving the argument name, followed by the characters := followed by the value. For example, to use only the Number argument and the Description argument pertaining to the Err.Raise method, you would use the following statement:

```
Err.Raise Number:=3, Description:="Invalid airplane type"
```

The Property Let procedure to set the AirplaneType property must validate the value of the argument that receives it. If it is a valid AirplaneType, the hidden variable named atAirplaneType should be set; otherwise, the Property procedure should generate a run-time error. The corresponding Property Get procedure sets the property to the value of the hidden variable. You can now write the Property Get and Property Let procedures for the AirplaneType property.

To write the code for the Property Let and Property Get Procedures:

1 Activate the Code window for the class module named **Airplane.cls,** if necessary.
2 Move the cursor to the end of the module.
3 Enter the following statements to create the Property Let procedure. Note that you can enter the procedure manually instead of using the Add procedure dialog.

```
Public Property Let AirplaneType(ByVal atType As AirplaneType)
    Select Case atType
        Case atSinglePropeller, atTwinPropellerPrivate, _
            atTwinJetPrivate, atTwinPropellerCommercial, _
            atTwinJetCommercial, atTwinJetHeavyCommercial
        Case Else
            Err.Raise Number:=3, _
                Description:="Invalid airplane type"
    End Select
    atAirplaneType = atType
End Property
```

4 Enter the following statements to create the Property Get procedure:

```
Public Property Get AirplaneType( ) As AirplaneType
    AirplaneType = atAirplaneType
End Property
```

5 In the general declarations section of the form module named **frmArrival,** enter the following statement:

```
Public SelectAirplaneType As AirplaneType
```

These statements create the Property procedures to read and write the AirplaneType property and to validate the argument when the user writes a value to the property.

```
Public Property Let AirplaneType(ByVal atType As AirplaneType)
```

This statement creates the Property Let procedure named AirplaneType. The procedure accepts one argument—the enumerated type AirplaneType.

```
Select Case atType
    Case atSinglePropeller, atTwinPropellerPrivate, _
        atTwinJetPrivate, atTwinPropellerCommercial, _
        atTwinJetCommercial, atTwinJetHeavyCommercial
    Case Else
        Err.Raise Number:=3, _
            Description:="Invalid airplane type"
End Select
```

The Select Case statement validates the argument atType. If it has a valid value, then the variable atAirplaneType is set to the type specified by the user. This hidden variable will be used when the corresponding Property Get procedure reads the property. If an invalid argument is passed to the Property procedure, the Case Else statement executes and an error is raised. This error will cause a message to be displayed with the description "Invalid airplane type". In a moment, you will write the code to process the error.

```
atAirplaneType = atType
```

The preceding statement sets the value of the hidden variable atAirplaneType to the value of the argument specified by the user only if an error is not raised.

```
Public Property Get AirplaneType( ) As AirplaneType
    AirplaneType = atAirplaneType
End Property
```

The preceding procedure executes when the AirplaneType property is read. It stores the hidden variable atAirplaneType in the AirplaneType property.

You now need to write the statements to set the airplane type when an airplane arrives and to display the current airplane type when the user selects an airplane in the list box.

To write the code to read and write the AirplaneType properties:

1   Open the Code window for the form named **frmMain**.

2 Enter the following statement (shown in bold) in the **cmdArrival_Click** event procedure:

```
. . .
AirplaneNew.CarrierName = frmArrival.txtName
AirplaneNew.AirplaneID = frmArrival.txtID
AirplaneNew.AirplaneType = _
     frmArrival.SelectAirplaneType
```

This statement sets the AirplaneType property for the current airplane to the currently selected option button in the form named frmArrival. When this property is set, the AirplaneType Property Let procedure executes. If you try to store an invalid airplane type into the AirplaneType property, however, a run-time error will be generated.

You must still create the event procedure in the frmArrival form to set the Public variable SelectAirplaneType to one of the valid airplane types whenever the user clicks an option button on the form.

To set the airplane type:
1 Activate the Code window for the form named **frmArrival**.
2 Enter the following statements in the **optAirplaneType_Click** event procedure:

```
Select Case Index
    Case atSinglePropeller
        SelectAirplaneType = atSinglePropeller
    Case atTwinPropellerPrivate
        SelectAirplaneType = atTwinPropellerPrivate
    Case atTwinJetPrivate
        SelectAirplaneType = atTwinJetPrivate
    Case atTwinPropellerCommercial
        SelectAirplaneType = atTwinPropellerCommercial
    Case atTwinJetCommercial
        SelectAirplaneType = atTwinJetCommercial
    Case atTwinJetHeavyCommercial
        SelectAirplaneType = atTwinJetHeavyCommercial
End Select
```

3 Activate the code window for the form named frmMain, then select the **lstAirplanes_Click** event procedure. Then, enter the following statement (shown in bold) just before the End Sub statement:

```
lblArrivalDateTime = AirplaneCurrent.ArrivalDateTime
optAirplaneType(AirplaneCurrent.AirplaneType) = _
    True
```

This statement reads the AirplaneType property for the currently selected airplane. Remember that this value must be one of the valid values for the enumerated type AirplaneType. It serves as an argument to set the corresponding option button.

4 Save the project, then run it.

5 Record two airplane arrivals with the following information: Carrier Name of **Jakes Air**, Airplane ID number of **N23389**, and Airplane Type of **Twin Propeller - Commercial**; Carrier Name of **International**, Airplane ID number of **N23904**, and Airplane Type of **Twin Jet Heavy - Commercial**.

6 Select the second airplane, as shown in Figure 12-13. The date and time on your form will differ from those in Figure 12-13.

airplane type

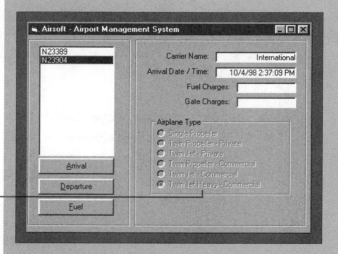

Figure 12-13: Testing the airplane type

7 End the program to return to design mode.

help
· · · · · · · · · · · · · ·
▶ If the airplane type is not displayed as shown in Figure 12-13, verify that the code you wrote in the previous steps is correct.

Setting the Default Property

Just as objects like text boxes and command buttons can have a default property or method, so too can a class have a default property or method. This property or method will execute whenever you reference the object without explicitly specifying the object or property name. Selecting the Procedure Attributes menu item on the Tools menu or using the Object Browser sets the default property.

Because the AirplaneID property will be used more than any other property, you will set it to be the default property of the class.

To set the default property to Airplane ID:

1　Open the Object Browser.

2　In the **Project/Library** list box, select the project named **Project1**.

3　In the **Classes** list box, select the class named **Airplane**.

4　In the **Members of 'Airplane'** list box, click the member named **AirplaneID**, as shown in Figure 12-14.

Project1 selected

Airplane class selected

AirplaneID
member selected

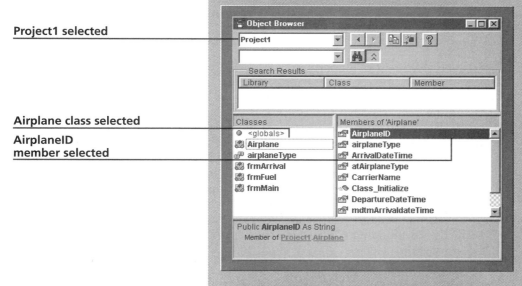

Figure 12-14: Setting a default property

5　Right-click **AirplaneID**, then select the item named **Properties** to activate the Procedure Attributes dialog.

6　Click the **Advanced** command button to expand the Procedure Attributes dialog.

7　Click the **User Interface Default** check box, as shown in Figure 12-15.

click this check box

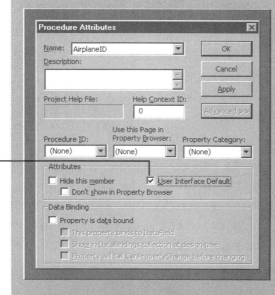

Figure 12-15: Setting the default property

8 Click **Apply**, then click **OK** to close the dialog.

9 Close the Object Browser.

The AirplaneID property is now the default property.

In the current version of the program, the AirplaneID property is a read-write property implemented using a Public variable. Once set, however, the property should not be changed. If the programmer accidentally changes the value of this property, the value would correspond to neither the string key in the collection nor the value in the list box.

Creating a Write-Once Property

When creating a property that will be used as a key, it is often desirable to create the property such that, once it is written, it cannot be written again. The result is a **write-once property**. Although Visual Basic does not explicitly support write-once properties, you can write code to implement a property as a write-once property.

For Airsoft's program, you will implement the AirplaneID property as a write-once property to ensure that any programmer using the class does not accidentally set the property to a different value at a later date. To accomplish this goal, you need to remove the Public variable named Airplane ID, replace it with a corresponding hidden variable, and create Property Let and Property Get procedures.

To implement a write-once property:

1 Activate the Code window for the class named **Airplane.cls**.

2 Remove the following line from the general declarations section:

```
Public AirplaneID As String
```

3 Replace the line with the following declaration statement:

```
Private mstrAirplaneID As String
```

4 Create a **Public** Property procedure named **AirplaneID**. Note that you can use the Add Procedure dialog or create the procedure by hand. If you use the Add Procedure dialog, be sure to change the argument and return values as necessary.

5 Enter the following statements into the **Property Get** procedure:

```
Public Property Get AirplaneID( ) As String
    AirplaneID = mstrAirplaneID
End Property
```

6 Create and enter the following statements into the **AirplaneID Property Let** procedure:

```
Public Property Let AirplaneID(ByVal pstrArg As String)
    If mstrAirplaneID = vbNullString Then
        mstrAirplaneID = pstrArg
    Else
        Err.Raise 1, , _
            "Cannot reset the write-once property AirplaneID."
    End If
End Property
```

These statements implement the AirplaneID property as a write-once property instead of a read-write property using a Public variable. This change strengthens the class (that is, makes it more robust). The code is very similar to the code used to create an ordinary read-write property in that it uses both Property Get and Property Let procedures. The Property Get procedure reads the value of the hidden variable named mstrAirplaneID. The Property Let procedure is more complicated. If the value of the hidden variable has not been set, its value will be an empty string. The If statement therefore tests whether the hidden variable is empty. If it is, then the property is set; otherwise, an error is raised.

Creating a Method

In addition to setting and retrieving properties and/or executing code when those properties are read and written, you can create methods for a class. You can create two types of methods in Visual Basic:

- Function methods that return a value
- Sub methods that do not return a value

Creating a Public Function or Sub procedure within a class module creates a Function or Sub method, respectively. The syntax is the same as the syntax to create Public Function and Sub procedures in other modules. To call a method, you use method syntax rather than the syntax to call a Function or Sub procedure. Consider the following procedure declaration in a class module:

```
Public Sub AddFuel(ByVal Gallons As Single, _
    ByVal Price As Single)
End Sub
```

This statement declares a method named AddFuel. The AddFuel method takes two arguments, both having a data type of Single: the number of gallons of fuel and the price of the fuel. To call the method, you would use the following statements:

```
Dim AirplaneCurrent As New Airplane
AirplaneCurrent.AddFuel 100, 1.34
```

These statements declare a new object named AirplaneCurrent, then call the AddFuel method with two arguments. The first represents 100 gallons of fuel, and the second represents a price of $1.34 per gallon.

Just as it is important to determine whether to use a Public variable or Property procedure to create a property, so too is it important to determine whether to create a property or a method. Use the following guidelines when deciding which is appropriate:

- Create a property when referring to data about an object.
- Create a method when referring to an action that the object should perform.
- When it is not clear whether you are referring to data or an action, use your best judgment.

Sub Methods

Sub methods, like Sub procedures, do not return a value. They can accept zero or more arguments of different types, however. To declare a Sub method, you create a Public Sub procedure in a class module. The name of the Sub procedure should match the method name. Note that you cannot assign the same name to both a method and a property. If you do, a syntax error will occur.

One method for the Airport Management System will compute the charges for fueling the plane. This method will accept two arguments—the number of gallons of fuel added and the price per gallon. It will compute the dollar amount of fuel used, then set the value of a Private variable. Next, this variable will be read by a read-only property. Remember that to create a read-only property, you must create a Property Get procedure and omit the corresponding Property Let procedure.

To create the AddFuel method:

1 Activate the Code window for the class module **Airplane.cls**, then insert a Sub procedure named **AddFuel**. Set the Scope to **Public**. Again, you can use the Add Procedure dialog or create the procedure manually.

2 Enter the following statement into the Sub procedure:

```
Public Sub AddFuel(ByVal Gallons As Single, _
    ByVal Price As Single)
    msngFuelCharge = Gallons * Price
End Sub
```

3 Insert a **Public Property Get** procedure named **FuelCharge**, then enter the following statement into the procedure:

```
Public Property Get FuelCharge( ) As Single
    FuelCharge = msngFuelCharge
End Property
```

The first statements create a method named AddFuel that accepts two arguments: the number of gallons of fuel and the cost per gallon. The gallons of fuel used are multiplied by the cost per gallon, and the result is stored in the hidden variable named msngFuelCharge. The Property procedure will retrieve the value of this hidden variable and store the result in the FuelCharge property.

Although the Sub procedure resembles a general procedure, it is considered a method because it was declared as Public in a class module. Thus, if you wanted to call the method, you must supply a valid Airplane object. If the variable CurrentAirplane was a valid instance of an Airplane object, you could call the method with the following statement:

```
AirplaneCurrent.AddFuel 2040, 1.44
```

You now need to write the statements to call this method and read the newly created property. When the user clicks the Fuel command button, the program should get the number of gallons of fuel used and the price, then call the AddFuel method. This information then should be displayed on the form along with the other charges.

A form named frmFuel was created to record the fuel charges; this form works much like the one that records the arrival of an airplane. It retrieves the gallons of fuel and the price from the user, then stores the information into text boxes named txtGallons and txtFuel, respectively. You now need to display this form as a modal form when the user clicks the Fuel command button, then call the AddFuel method. After calling the method, you can display the fuel charges.

To record and display the fuel charges:

1 Open the Code window for the form named **frmMain**, activate the **Click** event procedure for the **cmdFuel** command button, then enter the following statements (shown in bold) in the event procedure:

```
Private Sub cmdFuel_Click( )
    Dim AirplaneCurrent As Airplane
    If lstAirplanes = "" Then
        MsgBox "Please select airplane", vbOKOnly
    Else
        frmFuel.Show vbModal
        Set AirplaneCurrent = Airplanes(lstAirplanes)
        AirplaneCurrent.AddFuel frmFuel.txtGallons, _
            frmFuel.txtPrice
        lblFuel = AirplaneCurrent.FuelCharge
    End If
End Sub
```

2 Enter the following statement at the end of the **lstAirplanes_Click** event procedure:

```
lblFuel = AirplaneCurrent.FuelCharge
```

3 Save the project, then run it.

4 Record an airplane arrival using the carrier name **Jakes Air** and the airplane ID **N23389.**

5 Select the airplane ID in the list box, then click the **Fuel** command button.

6 Enter **1000** gallons and a price of **1.43** per gallon, then click **Record** to close the form. The fuel charges should be displayed in the main form. For brevity, this value has not been formatted.

7 End the program to return to design mode.

The statements added in the previous steps display the form to get the fuel information from the user only if an airplane currently is selected. The AddFuel method is then called, and the FuelCharge property is displayed in the corresponding label on the main form.

In addition to computing the fuel charge, Airsoft's program must calculate the landing charges. The landing charges are based on the airplane type and the length of time that the airplane remains on the ground. Each time the user selects an airplane, the program should display the current landing charges.

Function Methods

Function methods work just like Sub methods, except that Function methods return a value. This operation is identical to that of a function in a standard module. For Airsoft's program, you need a Function method to compute the total charges incurred by an airplane. Figure 12-16 illustrates the schedule for the airplane charges.

Airplane type	Charge per minute
Single Propeller	.25
Twin Propeller Private	.44
Twin Jet Private	.92
Twin Propeller Commercial	1.21
Twin Jet Commercial	1.84
Twin Jet Heavy Commercial	2.42

Figure 12-16: Airplane charges

To compute the total charges:

1 Make sure the Code window is active for **Airplane.cls**.

2 Insert a **Public Function** procedure named **ComputeCharges**, then enter the
following statements in the procedure:

```
Public Function ComputeCharges( ) As Single
    Dim psngCharges As Single
    Dim plngElapsedMinutes As Long
    plngElapsedMinutes = DateDiff("n", _
        mdtmArrivalDateTime, Now)
    Select Case atAirplaneType
        Case atSinglePropeller
            psngCharges = plngElapsedMinutes * 0.25
        Case atTwinPropellerPrivate
            psngCharges = plngElapsedMinutes * 0.44
        Case atTwinJetPrivate
            psngCharges = plngElapsedMinutes * 0.92
        Case atTwinPropellerCommercial
            psngCharges = plngElapsedMinutes * 1.21
        Case atTwinJetCommercial
            psngCharges = plngElapsedMinutes * 1.84
        Case atTwinJetHeavyCommercial
            psngCharges = plngElapsedMinutes * 2.42
    End Select
    ComputeCharges = psngCharges
End Function
```

These statements declare a method named ComputeCharges. This method
takes no arguments and returns a value of the Single data type.

```
Dim psngCharges As Single
Dim plngElapsedMinutes As Long
```

The above statements declare two variables. The first stores the dollar amount
of the charges, and the second stores the number of minutes that the airplane has
been at the airport.

```
plngElapsedMinutes = DateDiff("n", _
    mdtmArrivalDateTime, Now)
```

This statement calls the DateDiff function to determine the number of minutes that the airplane has been at the airport. The first argument "n" tells the DateDiff function that you want to determine the number of minutes elapsed. The second argument consists of the hidden variable mdtmArrivalDateTime, which contains the arrival date and time of the airplane and was set in the Class_Initialize event procedure. The final argument is the current date and time. Using these arguments, the DateDiff function computes the number of elapsed minutes from the time an airplane arrived to the current time.

```
Select Case atAirplaneType
    Case atSinglePropeller
        psngCharges = plngElapsedMinutes * 0.25
    Case atTwinPropellerPrivate
        psngCharges = plngElapsedMinutes * 0.44
    Case atTwinJetPrivate
        psngCharges = plngElapsedMinutes * 0.92
    Case atTwinPropellerCommercial
        psngCharges = plngElapsedMinutes * 1.21
    Case atTwinJetCommercial
        psngCharges = plngElapsedMinutes * 1.84
    Case atTwinJetHeavyCommercial
        psngCharges = plngElapsedMinutes * 2.42
End Select
```

The preceding statements determine the charges by multiplying the number of minutes that the airplane remained at the airport by the charge per minute.

```
ComputeCharges = psngCharges
```

The final statement sets the return value for the method. Its syntax is identical to the syntax you have used with other Function procedures.

Now that you have created the method, you need to call it whenever the user selects an airplane. The method should display the value in the corresponding lblCharges label on the form.

To call and test the ComputeCharges method:

1 Activate the Code window for the form named **frmMain**.
2 Locate the **lstAirplanes_Click** event procedure, then enter the following statement just before the End Sub statement:

```
lblCharges = AirplaneCurrent.ComputeCharges
```

3 Save the project, then run it.

4 Click the **Arrival** command button, then enter the **Jakes Air** as the carrier name and **N23389** as the Airplane ID.

5 Click the **Record** button.

6 Wait at least one minute, then click the **Airplane ID** in the list box. The charges should be displayed in the Gate Charges on the main form.

7 End the program to return to design mode.

Terminating a Class Instance

As presently written, the program terminates the instance of the Airplane class when the user clicks the Departure command button. Just before the instance of the class is terminated, the information about the current airplane charges must be recorded so that it can be used by another program. In the same way that the Initialize event occurs before the instance of the class is created, the Terminate event occurs just before the instance is destroyed. You will append the charges pertaining to an airplane to a text file when an airplane leaves the airport. The airport's billing system will later use this file to produce monthly invoices.

One way to implement this functionality is to create a property containing the file name to be written and to write the file in the Terminate event. This option would require that the Terminate event validate the file before opening it. If the file name is invalid, the event needs to raise an error. Alternatively, you could call a method with the file name as an argument and write the file in that method. This implementation would require that you check that the information had been written. If it was not, an error again would need to be raised. Otherwise, the information would be lost.

In this situation, your decision of which implementation to use is a subjective one. In the Airport Management System, you will use the latter approach because it gives the user slightly more control over when the information is written to the disk.

To write the information pertaining to an airplane when the instance is terminated:

1 Activate the Code window for the class module **Airplane.cls**.

2 Enter the following statement into the general declarations section of the class module after the Option Explicit statement:

```
Private mblnRecordWritten As Boolean
```

3 Enter the following statements (shown in bold) into the **Class_Terminate** event procedure:

```
Private Sub Class_Terminate( )
    If mblnRecordWritten = False Then
        Err.Raise 3, "Airsoft.Airplane", _
            "Data not written to disk."
    End If
End Sub
```

These statements declare a hidden variable named mblnRecordWritten. Because this variable must be available to the Class_Terminate event and the method you will write in a moment, you declared it in the general declarations section of the class module. Because the variable is Private, it is not part of the class's interface.

The If statement determines whether the record has been written. If it has, the program terminates the instance; otherwise, it raises an error. Because you have not yet created a method to write the record and set the variable mblnRecordWritten to True, the Terminate event will always generate an error. You should test your program to verify that the Terminate event tests the variable mblnRecordWritten correctly.

To test the program and the Terminate event:

1 Save the project, then run it.

2 Enter an Airplane arrival.

3 Click the **Airplane ID** in the list box.

4 Click the **Departure** command button. The Class_Terminate event should generate an error, as shown in Figure 12-17.

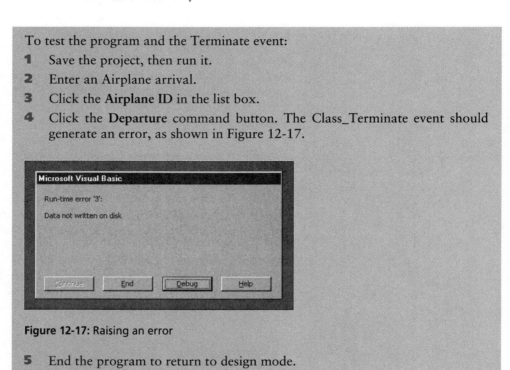

Figure 12-17: Raising an error

5 End the program to return to design mode.

You now need to create the method that will write the text file and write statements to call the method when the user clicks the Departure command button.

To write the airplane record to a file:

1 Activate the Code window for the **Airplane** class module, if necessary.

2   Create a **Public Sub** procedure named **WriteAirplane**. Enter the following statements into the Sub procedure:

```
Public Sub WriteAirplane(ByVal pargOutputFile As String)
    Open pargOutputFile For Append As #1
    Write #1, mstrAirplaneID, CarrierName, msngCharges, _
        msngFuelCharge, mdtmArrivalDateTime, _
        DepartureDateTime, atAirplaneType
    Close #1
    mblnRecordWritten = True
End Sub
```

3   Activate the Code window for the form named **frmMain**.

4   Enter the following statement (shown in bold) in the **cmdDeparture_Click** event procedure just before the statement that removes the current airplane from the collection. Change the drive designator as necessary.

```
Airplanes(lstAirplanes).WriteAirplane _
    "A:\Chapter.12\Startup\Airplane.txt"
Airplanes.Remove (pstrIndex)
```

5   Save the project, then run it.

6   Record two airplane arrivals and departures.

7   End the program to return to design mode.

8   Start NotePad and verify the contents of the text file.

9   Exit NotePad.

10   Exit Visual Basic.

These statements declare the method to write the information to the text file as specified by the String argument to the WriteRecord method. The last statement calls the method to append the record to the file named Airplane.txt.

S U M M A R Y

To create a class module:

■   Click Project, then click Add Class Module.

■   Set the Name property to the name that the programmer will use to reference the class.

To create a property in a class:

■ Declare a Public variable in a class module with the following syntax:
Public *variablename* **As** *type*

To create and use a collection:

■ Declare a variable of type Collection.
■ Call the Add method to add an item to the collection with the following syntax:
object.**Add** *item*[, *key*][, *before* | *after*]

■ Call the Item method to reference a specific element in a collection:
object.**Item**(*index*)

■ Call the Remove method to delete an item from the collection:
object.**Remove** *index*

To hide data in a class module:

■ Declare a Private variable in a class module.

To create a read-only property:

■ Create a Property Get procedure using the following syntax. Omit the corresponding Property Let procedure.
[**Public** | **Private**] [**Static**] **Property Get** *name* [(*argumentlist*)] [**As** *type*]
  [*statements*]
  [*name = expression*]
  [**Exit Property**]
  [*statements*]
  [*name = expression*]
End Property

To create a read-write property:

■ Create both a Property Let and Property Get procedure. Use the following syntax for the Property Let procedure:
[**Public** | **Private**][**Static**] **Property Let** *name* [(*arglist*)]
  [*statements*]
  [**Exit Property**]
  [*statements*]
End Property

To create a write-once property:

■ Generate a run-time error if the property has already been written. Use a Static Boolean variable or test for an initial condition to determine whether the property has been previously written.

To generate a run-time error, call the Raise method on the Err object:

Err.Raise *number*[, *source*][, *description*][, *helpfile*][, *helpcontext*]

To set a default property or method for a class module:

- Open the Object Browser.
- In the Project/Library list box, select the project.
- In the Classes list box, select the desired class name.
- In the Members list box, select the desired property or method.
- Activate the Procedure Attributes dialog, then click the Advanced command button.
- Click the User Interface Default check box.

To create a method:

- Write a Public Sub procedure to create a method that does not return a value.
- Write a Public Function procedure to create a method that returns a value.

QUESTIONS

1. Under what circumstances should you create Property procedures?
   a. The values of a property can be validated.
   b. An action needs to occur when the property is read or written.
   c. The property is a read-only or write-once property.
   d. All of the above.
   e. None of the above.

2. Which statements are used to create Property procedures?
   a. Property Sub, Property Function
   b. Property Read, Property Write
   c. Property Let, Property Get
   d. Property Input, Property Output
   e. None of the above.

3. What is the name of the method used to purposely generate a run-time error?
   a. Error
   b. Raise
   c. Trap
   d. ErrorHandler
   e. None of the above.

4. To set the Default property for a class, you _____.
   a. Create a Property procedure with the keyword Default
   b. Use the Default statement
   c. Use the Procedure Attributes dialog
   d. All of the above.
   e. None of the above.

5. How do you create a method?
   a. Create a Public Sub or Public Function procedure in a class module.
   b. Create a Private Sub or Private Function procedure in a class module.
   c. Declare a Method procedure.
   d. Create a Function Set procedure.
   e. None of the above.

6. What is the name of the event that occurs when a class instance is destroyed?

a. End

b. Unload

c. Hide

d. Terminate

e. Destroy

7. What are the guidelines to help you decide when to create a property or method?

a. When referring to data about an object, create a property.

b. When referring to an action, create a method.

c. There is no difference between properties and methods.

d. Both a and b.

e. None of the above.

8. Create a read-write Boolean property named Valid. Implement the property using Property procedures and store the value in the hidden variable named mblnValid.

9. Create a write-once property named ID. Raise an error if a programmer attempts to write the property more than once.

10. Create a method named Volume to compute the volume of a cube. This method should accept three arguments: length, width, and height. The code in the method should multiply the values of these arguments together and return the volume.

E X E R C I S E S

1. Text Processors performs word-processing and data entry tasks for a number of clients. The company wants a program that will count the number of characters, words, and lines in a text file. Because several other programs will use this utility program, the company would like these functions implemented as a class module. The class module should have one method that will open a text file for input. The same method should also count the number of characters, words, and lines. The programmer should be able to read these values using read-only properties. After creating the class module, you will need to develop a form to test the program. This form should include a CommonDialog control instance to open a file as specified by the user. Then, it should call the method in the class module to open the file. Finally, the information in the read-only properties of the class should appear in the labels on the form. Figure 12-18 shows the completed form.

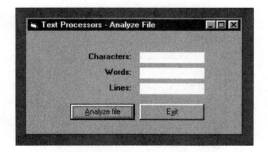

Figure 12-18: Exercise 1 – completed form

a. Run the executable file named **Chapter.12\Exercise\Ex1.exe**, setting the drive designator as necessary. Click the **Analyze file** command button. When the Open dialog appears, select the name of a text file residing on your computer. Click **Open**. The number of lines, words, and characters in the text file will appear on the form. Exit the program.

b. Start Visual Basic, then create a new project.

c. Create a class module named **Ex1.cls**, making sure to include the **Option Explicit** statement. Set the Name property for the class to **StringProcessor**.

d. Set the form to **frmEx1.frm**. Save the form, class module, and project in the **Chapter.12\Exercise** folder. Use a project name of **Ex1.vbp**. Set the drive designator as necessary.

e. Create a method named **OpenFile**. This method should accept one argument—the full path name of the file to be opened.

f. In the **OpenFile** method, write the necessary statements to open the file, then count the number of characters, words, and lines. *Note*: A word is a sequence of characters separated by a space. A line is terminated with a newline character. This information needs to be stored in hidden variables.

g. Create three read-only properties named **Characters, Words**, and **Lines**. These properties should return the number of characters, words, and lines, respectively, stored in the corresponding hidden variables. *Note*: You should create Property procedures rather than Public variables.

h. Create the form objects as shown in Figure 12-18. You can use the CommonDialog control to get a file name from the user and then pass the name to the class module. The first command button should create an instance of the class, then call the method to open and read the file. Finally, it should read the properties and store the information in the corresponding labels.

i. Test the program by creating a small text file in NotePad. Run the program using the text file.

j. Exit Visual Basic.

2. Forte Systems performs statistical analysis and marketing surveys. The company wants a class module that stores a list of numbers. Once the list of numbers is created, the company wants to be able to determine the maximum number in the list, the minimum number in the list, and the sum of all numbers in the list. The class should contain a Private array to store the list of numbers. When the class is initialized, the number of elements in the array should be set to zero. The class will support a method, named AddItem, that will accept one argument—a numeric value to add to the list. Three other methods named Max, Min, and Sum will return the maximum, minimum, and sum of the list, respectively. Figure 12-19 shows the completed form.

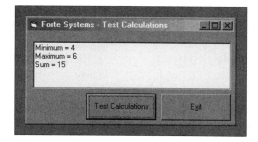

Figure 12-19: Exercise 2 – completed form

a. Run the executable file name **Chapter.12\Exercise\Ex2.exe**, setting the drive designator as necessary. Click the **Test Calculations** command button. The numbers 4, 5, and 6 are added to the collection, and the maximum number, minimum number, and sum printed. Exit the program.

b. Start Visual Basic, then create a new project.

c. Insert a class module in the project. Set the name of the class to **Statistical**. Save the class using the file name **Ex2.cls**.

d. Set the form name to **frmEx2.frm**. Save the form, class module, and project to the **Chapter.12\Exercise** folder. Use a project name of **Ex2.vbp**. Set the drive designator as necessary.

e. Declare a hidden array named **msngList** to hold the Single data type. Initially, the array should have no elements. You will need to redimension the array each time an element is added.

f. Write a statement to set the number of elements in the array to zero when the class is initialized.

g. Create a method named **AddItem** that accepts one argument, a Single data type to be added to the list. Write a statement to increase the size of the array by one, making sure that you preserve the existing array contents. Store the argument passed to the method in the new array element.

h. Create a method named **Maximum** that returns the largest number stored in the array. You will need to create a For loop to look at each element in the array. Inside the For loop, an If statement should determine whether the current item in the array is greater than the largest number.

i. Create another method named **Minimum**. This method will work just like the one you created in the previous step, but will return the smallest number in the list.

j. Create the final method named **Sum**. This method also needs to contain a For loop to look at each item in the list. You will need an accumulator to store the total value of all elements in the array. After all elements in the array have been examined, the method should return the total.

k. Write the code to test the methods created in the class module. Create a command button on the main form. The code in the command button should call the AddItem method several times with different numbers. After calling the AddItem method, you must call the Maximum, Minimum, and Sum methods and display the results in a multiline text box. Verify that the calculations are correct. Create a second button to exit the program.

3. MidTex International distributes automobile parts across the United States from its central Texas distribution facility. The company has a database containing inventory information. The company wants a program to update prices and delete old parts from a database. Company programmers should be able to call methods and read and write properties to work with this database, rather than having to learn how to use the SQL programming language. The inventory table (**tblInventory**) has the following fields:

fldPartNumber	String
fldQuantityInStock	Integer
fldCost	Single
fldSalesPrice	Single

You will need to create the following methods:

- The **Open** method should open a database.
- The **Insert** method should accept four arguments, which are the fields in the table, and insert a part number into the table.
- The **Delete** method should accept one argument, the part number, and remove the part number from the table.
- The **Update** method should accept four arguments, which are the fields in the table. Using the part number, the method should update the other three fields.

Figure 12-20 shows the completed form.

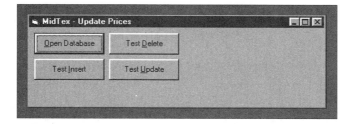

Figure 12-20: Exercise 3 – completed form

a. This program does not produce any visible output. Run the executable file named **Chapter.12\Exercise\Ex3.exe**, setting the drive designator as necessary. Click the Open Database command button. When the Open dialog appears, select the database named **Chapter.12\Exercise\MidTex.mdb**. Click **Open**. Click the **Test Insert** command button, then click the **Test Update** command button, then test the **Test Delete** command button. These command buttons call the methods in the class module to add, change, and delete a record, respectively. Exit the program.

b. Start Visual Basic, then create a new project.

c. Create a class module named **Ex3.cls**. Set the Name property to **Data**. Set the name of the test form to **frmEx3.frm**. Save the class and form. Save the project using the name **Ex3.vbp** in the **Chapter.12\Exercise** folder, setting the drive designator as necessary.

d. In the class module, create the code for the **OpenDB** method. This method should accept one argument, the file name of the database to open.

e. Create the code for the **Insert** method. This method should accept four arguments: part number, quantity in stock, cost, and sales price.

f. Create the code for the **Update** method. This method should accept the same arguments as the Insert method and update all fields.

g. Create the code for the **Delete** method. This method should accept one argument, the part number to delete.

h. Create the objects on the form as shown in Figure 12-20. Write the necessary code to test the method you created in the class module.

i. Save and test the program to verify that each method works correctly.

discovery ▶ 4. Shuffle Meister creates various computer card games. The company wants you to create a class module that will simulate shuffling of a deck of cards. The class module, when initialized, should create an array to store a deck of 52 playing cards. You should create a method named **Shuffle** to shuffle the deck of cards, as well as another method to deal the deck of cards. The latter method, named **DealCard**, should deal the next card off the deck. After creating the class module, you will develop a form to test the program. This form should contain a list box that displays the cards after they have been shuffled. You also will need a command button that, when clicked, will shuffle the deck of cards. Consider the following approaches to implement this program:

■ In the class module, declare an array of user-defined types. This array should contain 52 elements, each representing a card in the deck. The user-defined type should have two members: one representing the card (Ace, 2, 3, 4,...), and a second representing the suit of the card. In the Class_Initialize event procedure, store the cards in the array.

■ To shuffle the cards, call the Randomize function to seed the Visual Basic random number generator. In random order, copy the contents of the first array to a second array.

■ The deal card method should deal the cards from the second array.

a. Run the Executable file named **Chapter.12\Exercise\Ex4.exe,** setting the drive designator as necessary. Click the **Shuffle** command button. The cards are shuffled and appear in the left box at the left of the form as shown in Figure 12-21. Exit the program. Because the cards are shuffled randomly, the order of the cards in Figure 12-21 will differ from the order of the cards you see when you run the program.

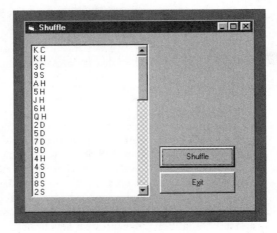

Figure 12-21: Exercise 4 – completed form

b. Create a new project and develop the application as described previously.
c. Save the form using the name **frmEx4.frm** and the project using the name **Ex4.vbp** in the **Chapter.12\Exercise** folder. Save the class module using the name **Ex4.cls.**

Compiling and Distributing Programs

Creating a Distributable Program for MathTek

case ▶ MathTek develops and distributes statistical software throughout the United States. Its software performs complex statistical and mathematical analysis. It also produces a list of random numbers. Many industries, including the gaming business, use random numbers. In this chapter, you will develop the entire software package in Visual Basic. The program's end users, however, will not necessarily have Visual Basic installed on their systems. Thus you must build an executable file and bundle the necessary support files such that the program can be distributed to and easily installed by the end users.

Previewing the Completed Application

The completed program in this chapter introduces four new concepts. First, it uses the **App** object to manage general program information. Second, the program uses the **Shell** function to execute other programs on the computer. Third, it illustrates how to compile a program and introduces the different compiler options that are available to you, the programmer. The compiler options can have a significant impact on the performance of your program. To enable you to more easily see the effect of compiler options, the program has been designed such that it performs an operation (producing a list of random numbers) that takes more than a few seconds. Fourth, the program illustrates how you can distribute a program to other computers.

Most programming languages support a random number generator. A **random number generator** is a function or group of functions that generates random numbers. Visual Basic's random number generator consists of two parts. First, a function initializes the random number generator. The **Randomize** function takes a numeric argument called a **seed**. The seed is used to generate a unique sequence of random numbers. A common value for the seed is the time of day or some other value that changes regularly. After initializing the random number generator, you call the **Rnd** function repeatedly to obtain a sequence of random numbers. The Rnd function generates random numbers between zero (0) and one (1). Consider the following code to generate a list of random numbers. In this procedure, the size of the random number list varies based upon user input stored in the text box named txtCount.

```
Private Sub cmdRandomize_Click()
    Dim plngCount As Long
    Dim datStart As Date
    Dim datEnd As Date
    Me.MousePointer = vbHourglass
    datStart = Now
    If IsNumeric(txtCount) Then
        Randomize (Time)
        ReDim msngNumbers(txtCount)
        For plngCount = 1 To CLng(txtCount)
            msngNumbers(plngCount) = Rnd
        Next
        datEnd = Now
    Else
        Exit Sub
        Me.MousePointer = vbNormal
    End If
    txtSeconds = DateDiff("s", datStart, datEnd)
    Me.MousePointer = vbNormal
End Sub
```

The code in this procedure uses a module-level dynamic array of Single precision numbers named msngNumbers. The event procedure named cmdRandomize_Click redimensions the array to the number of elements specified by the user. This value is read from the text box named txtCount. After the array is redimensioned, the procedure calls the Randomize function to seed the random number generator. To ensure that the seed will differ each time the Randomize function is called, the function's argument is set to the current time of day. The For loop then populates the array with random numbers by repeatedly calling the Rnd function. Although this procedure illustrates how to generate a list of random numbers, its primary purpose is to create a function that requires more than a few seconds to execute. Just before random number generation begins and just after the list is generated, the current time is stored in local variables. These variables are used to compute the elapsed time to generate the random number list.

To preview the completed application:

1   Start Visual Basic and open the project file named **Chapter.13\Complete\MT_C.vbp**. Remember to set the drive designator as necessary. The completed project contains three forms: a splash screen, a main form, and a dialog to indicate the program settings.

2   Start the program. The splash screen appears for three seconds, then the main form appears. Figure 13-1 depicts the splash screen at run time. Although this splash screen resembles the one you created in Chapter 6, the text displayed in each of the labels is read from a Visual Basic object called the App object.

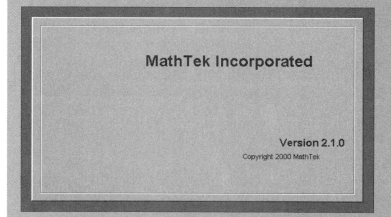

Figure 13-1: Splash screen at run time

3   After the splash screen closes, the main form appears. The main form is not intended to present any new programming topics, but rather to illustrate functions that execute for more than a few seconds. Such functions help you see the effect of compiling a program using different options and the effect of these different options on program performance. Figure 13-2 shows the completed main form.

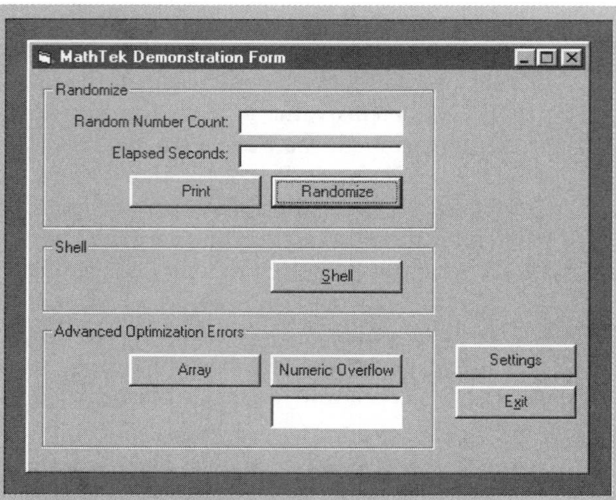

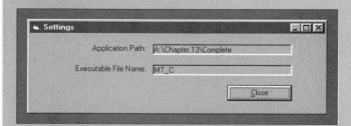

Figure 13-2: Main form

4   Enter a value of **10000000** in the Random Number Count text box, then click the **Randomize** button. Depending on the speed of your computer, this procedure will take about one to two minutes to execute. Note that while the procedure executes, the mouse pointer changes to an hourglass. This icon is a common user interface element indicating that the program is busy.

5   Click the **Settings** button. This button displays the Settings dialog, as shown in Figure 13-3. This dialog displays the path name of the application and the executable file name. This information is retrieved from the Visual Basic App object. Depending upon the drive and folder you are using, the path name of the executable file name may differ for your computer.

Figure 13-3: Settings dialog

6   Click the **Close** button on the Settings form.

7   End the program and exit Visual Basic.

The completed program also contains command buttons named Shell, Array, Numeric Overflow, and Print. You will use these command buttons later in the chapter.

In this section you will:

- Use the App object to read and write general program settings
- Use the Shell function to execute other programs from a Visual Basic program
- Create an executable program
- Optimize programs

Program Settings and Interprogram Communication

Using the App Object

Visual Basic supports the App object, which takes advantage of several properties that define information global to an application. This information includes the name of the application, legal copyright information, revision information, and much more. It can also be used to determine the path name of an executable file and the status of the application (that is, whether an instance of the application is already running). The properties pertaining to the App object are set at design time using the Project Properties dialog and cannot be set using code at run time. At run time, however, you write code to read these properties and display the information in your application.

Syntax	App
Properties	■ The **Comments** property returns a string containing comments about the program.
	■ The **CompanyName** property returns a string containing the name of the company or the creator of the program.
	■ The **EXEName** property contains the name of the executable file without the file extension or the path name.
	■ The **LegalCopyright** property returns a string containing copyright information about the application.
	■ The **LegalTrademark** property returns a string containing trademark information about the application.
	■ The **Major, Minor,** and **Revision** properties are read only at run time. They return the major release number, minor release number, and revision version number of the application. Each of these properties can assume a value between 0 and 9999.
	■ The **ProductName** property contains the product name of the running application.
	■ The **PrevInstance** property returns a Boolean value indicating whether an instance of the application is already running. If an application instance is running, then the value of this property is True; otherwise, it is False.

■ The **Path** property returns the path name of the application. This property is not available at design time.

■ The **Title** property returns the title of the application.

You set each of these properties at design time using the Make tab on the Project Properties dialog, as shown in Figure 13-4.

Application frame

Version Number frame

Version
Information frame

Type list box

Value text box

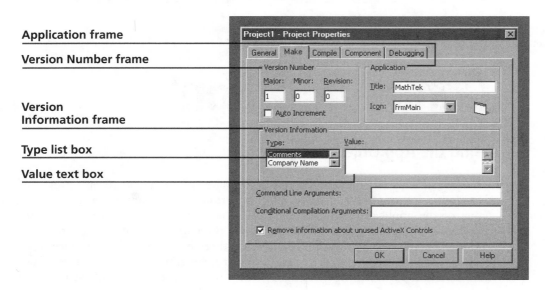

Figure 13-4: Make tab – Project Properties dialog

As shown in Figure 13-4, the Make tab contains three frames. The Version Number frame sets the Major, Minor, and Revision properties. The Application frame sets the Title property and the icon used for the application. The remaining properties are set via the Version Information frame. To set these properties, you select a property in the Type list box and enter the desired string in the Value text box. As indicated, these properties can be written only at design time and are read-only at run time. You will now set the properties pertaining to MathTek's application so as to display information on the program's splash screen and the Settings dialog.

To set the properties pertaining to the App object:

1 Start Visual Basic and open the project named **Chapter.13\Startup\MT_S.vbp**. Set the drive designator as necessary.

2 Click **Project**, then click **Project1 Properties** to activate the Project Properties dialog.

3 Click the **Make** tab on the Project Properties dialog.

4 In the Version Number frame, set the Major property to **2**, the Minor property to **1**, and the Revision property to **0**.

5 In the Application frame, set the Title to **MathTek**, if necessary.

6 In the Version Information frame, select **Company Name** in the Type list box, then enter the string **MathTek Incorporated** in the Value text box. Depending upon the settings for your computer, a default value may appear for the value of this property. This default value is derived from the system settings on your computer.

7 Select **Legal Copyright** in the Type list box, then enter the value **Copyright 2000 MathTek**

8 Click **OK** to save the property settings and close the dialog.

The properties pertaining to the App object serve several purposes. For instance, your application may read configuration files that are stored in the same directory as the application itself. The user, however, may have installed your application in a folder different from the one you intended. In this situation, you can use the App object's Path property to locate the path name of the running application. You could also use the various version-related properties to display information on the program's splash screen.

To read the properties pertaining to the App object:

1 Activate the code window for the form named **frmSplash**.

2 Enter the following statements in the **Form_Load** event procedure:

```
lblVersion = "Version " & App.Major & _
    "." & App.Minor & "." & App.Revision
lblCompany = App.CompanyName
lblCopyright = App.LegalCopyright
```

3 Activate the Code window for the form named **frmSettings**, then enter the following statements in the **Form_Activate** event procedure:

```
lblPath = App.Path
lblExeName = App.EXEName
```

4 Save and test the program. The startup object has been set to the splash screen. Additionally, an instance of the Timer control has been created to display the main form after the splash screen appears for three seconds. When the splash screen appears, the application settings should be displayed on it. These settings include the company name, legal copyright notice, and revision information including the major, minor, and revision numbers. After three seconds, the main form should appear.

5 Click the **Settings** button on the main form. The code has already been written to display the Settings form. Through this code, the path name and executable file name are retrieved from the App object and displayed on the modal Settings form.

6 Click the **Close** button on the Settings form to close the dialog.

7 End the program to return to design mode.

The statements in the Form_Load event procedure for the splash screen read the properties of the App object and display the relevant information in the labels. The statements in the Form_Activate event procedure for the Settings form display the application path and executable file name in the form's corresponding labels.

Executing Other Programs from Visual Basic

The programs you have created so far in this book have not interacted with other programs on the computer. That is, your Visual Basic programs have executed, but have not been able to execute any other programs. In fact, a Visual Basic program can execute any other program on the system by using the intrinsic Shell function.

Syntax	**Shell**(*pathname*[,*windowstyle*])
Dissection	■ The **Shell** function executes a program on the system.
	■ The required *pathname* argument must contain the full path name, including the drive designator, of the executable file.
	■ The optional *windowstyle* argument can contain a constant value indicating how the new window will appear to the user when it is opened. If this argument is set to the constant vbHide, the window remains hidden. If it is set to vbNormalFocus, the new window receives focus and is displayed at its original size and position. The constants vbMinimizedFocus and vbMaximizedFocus cause the window to appear as an icon or to be maximized, respectively. The constants vbNormalNoFocus and vbMinimizedNoFocus cause the active window to remain active and the new window not to receive focus, respectively.
| **Code Example** | ```
Dim pdblID As Double
pdblID = Shell("C:\demo.exe", vbNormalFocus)
``` |
| **Code Dissection** | The preceding code attempts to run the executable file named Demo.exe located in the root directory of drive C. If this file does not exist, the value zero (0) will be returned in the variable pdblID. Otherwise, the procedure returns the task ID of the new process. The window displayed by the executable program will appear with normal focus. Note that the Shell function returns a Variant Double value. |

The Shell function has many uses. In this chapter, you will create a general-purpose application of the Shell function where the user can select an .exe file using the CommonDialog control. The selected file then executes.

To execute a program with the Shell function:
1 Activate the Code window for the form named **frmMain**.
2 Click **Project**, then click **Components** to activate the Components dialog.
3 Use the scroll bars to locate the **Microsoft Common Dialog Control 6.0**, then click the check box to select it.
4 Click **OK** to close the Components dialog.
```

5 Create an instance of the CommonDialog control on the form named **frmMain** and set its Name property to **cdl1**. Set the CancelError property to **True**. Enter the following statements into the **cmdShell_Click** event procedure:

```
On Error GoTo ShellCancel:
    Dim pdblID As Double
    cdl1.CancelError = True
    cdl1.Filter = "Executable files (*.exe)|*.exe"
    cdl1.ShowOpen
    pdblID = Shell(cdl1.FileName, vbNormalFocus)
ShellCancel:
```

6 Save and test the program. Click the **Shell** command button, select an executable file, then open the file. The Shell function should execute the selected file.

7 End the program to return to design mode. Exit the executable program you ran as well.

The statements in the preceding steps are very simple. The user selects a file name using the CommonDialog control. The FileName argument is passed to the Shell function for execution. Using the constant vbNormalFocus ensures that the new window receives focus and is restored to its normal size and position. Because the code sets the CancelError property pertaining to the CommonDialog control to True, a run-time error will occur and be trapped if the user clicks the Cancel button.

Creating an Executable Program

As you created earlier programs in this book, you wrote and tested them inside the Visual Basic integrated development environment (IDE). This approach does not match how a user generally runs a program, however. In fact, the end user can run executable programs created with Visual Basic on computers that do not have Visual Basic installed. To create an executable program, you must compile it. **Compilation** is the process by which the Visual Basic statements you have written become converted into an executable file. This executable file can then be run directly, without the Visual Basic IDE.

The Compile tab in the Project Properties dialog allows you to specify how a program is compiled, as shown in Figure 13-5.

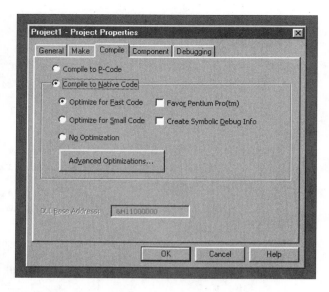

Figure 13-5: Compile tab – Project Properties dialog

Visual Basic will allow you to create two types of executable files: P-Code or native code executable files.

- **Native code** is executable code that corresponds to the instructions understood by the underlying processor. When your program is compiled into native code, it will run significantly faster than when it is run in the Visual Basic IDE.
- **P-Code** represents an intermediate step between the Visual Basic statements you write and native code. The letter "P" actually stands for "pseudo," although the terms "P-Code" and "pseudocode" are not synonymous. Visual Basic converts the P-Code representing a statement into native code before actually executing the P-Code statement.

Regardless of whether a program is compiled into P-Code or native code, the program requires the assistance of the Visual Basic run-time library named MSVBVM50.DLL.

Depending upon the characteristics of your program, the performance impact of using the two different options may or may not be significant. The following list describes the performance impact of native code and P-Code for various types of programs.

- If most of your program's execution time is spent referencing control instances and other objects, little performance difference exists between P-Code and native code.
- If most of your program's execution time is spent performing mathematical calculations, executing loops, and executing statements that do not reference objects or call object libraries, native code will run significantly faster than P-Code.

When you compile your program into native code, you have several options regarding the compilation process. These options can significantly impact both the speed of your program and the size of the executable file produced. These options include the following:

- If you select the **Optimize for Fast Code** option button, the compiler will create an executable file that will run faster but be larger. Use this option when disk space is plentiful. Usually, the increase in performance is worth the increased size of the executable file.

- If you select the **Optimize for Small Code** option button, the size of any executable file produced will be reduced at the expense of program performance. Use this option when disk space is very limited.
- If you select the **No Optimization** option button, no optimization will be performed.
- If you check the **Favor Pentium Pro(™)** check box, the executable file will contain instructions that will improve the program's performance when it runs on Pentium Pro CPUs. The code will still run on other CPUs, albeit much more slowly.
- If you check the **Create Symbolic Debug Info** check box, debugging information will be created so that the program can be debugged using Visual C++.
- The **Advanced Optimizations** command button opens the Advanced Optimizations dialog and provides additional flexibility in defining how the program is compiled. We will address these optimizations later in the chapter.

Once you set all the information pertinent to program compilation, you can build the executable file. This task is accomplished by clicking File, then clicking Make MT_S.exe on the menu bar. Once the executable file exists, you can run it by adding the program to the Start menu, using the Run command on the Start menu, or double-clicking the executable file using Windows Explorer. To compare the performance of P-Code, native code, and execution of a program inside of the Visual Basic IDE, you will compile the project into both native code and P-Code and then assess the resulting performance.

To set the compile information and create the executable file:

1 Click **Project**, then click **Project1 Properties**. Click the **Compile** tab.
2 Make sure that the **Compile to Native Code** option button is selected.
3 Click the **Optimize for Fast Code** option button, if necessary.
4 Click **OK** to apply the settings and close the Project Properties dialog.
5 Save the project.
6 Click **File**, then click **Make MT_S.exe**. Note that the executable file name is stored in the Project file. If you have changed this name, the file name on this menu item will differ.
7 The **Make Project** dialog appears as shown in Figure 13-6.

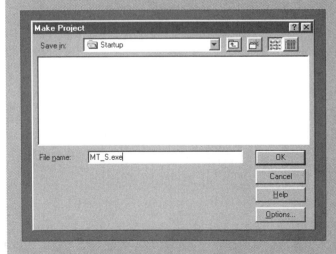

Figure 13-6: Make Project dialog

8 Select the **Chapter.13\Startup** folder on your Student Disk and set the name to **MTNative.exe**. Remember to set the drive designator as necessary.

9 Click **OK** to compile the project.

10 If a dialog appears indicating that the file already exists, click **Yes** to replace the existing file.

11 Click **Project**, then click **Project1 Properties**.

12 Click the **Compile** tab.

13 Make sure that the **Compile to P-Code** option button is selected.

14 Click **OK** to close the dialog. Save the project.

15 Click **File**, then click **Make MTNative.exe**. Select the **Chapter.13\Startup** folder on your Student Disk and set the name to **MTPCode.exe**. Again, set the drive designator as necessary. Note that Visual Basic remembers the name of the executable file you built in the previous steps, so you must change the executable file name from MTNative.exe to MTPCode.exe.

16 Click **OK** to close the Make Project dialog.

To visualize the performance impact of running the program in the Visual Basic IDE, running P-Code, and running native code, you should run each version with the same options. Because MathTek's program is mathematically intensive, you should expect that native code would run the fastest, followed by P-Code, then execution of the program in the IDE. Figure 13-7 shows the elapsed time to run this program on a Pentium P166 with 48 megabytes of memory.

Compiler Option	Execution Time
Visual Basic IDE	84.8 seconds
P-Code	72.6 seconds
Native code	68.2 seconds

Figure 13-7: Execution times

To execute the compiled program:

1 Test the program inside the Visual Basic IDE. When the main form appears, enter a random number count of **10000000**, then click the **Randomize** button. Note the elapsed time in the elapsed time output label.

2 End the program to return to design mode.

3 To run the program outside the IDE, click the **Start** button on the taskbar, then click **Run**. Enter the executable file named **MTPCode.exe**, setting the path name as necessary. Enter the same random number count you used in Step 1. Note the elapsed time in the output label. End the program by clicking the Exit button on the main form.

4 Repeat Step 3 using the file named **MTNative.exe**.

Depending upon the amount of memory in your computer and the speed of the processor, the native code executable file should run faster than the P-Code executable file. Both options should run significantly faster than the program running inside the Visual Basic IDE. Note, however, that your results may differ.

In addition to compiling a program into native code or P-Code, you can use the Advanced Optimizations dialog to further control compilation of a program.

Advanced Optimizations

The Advanced Optimizations dialog, shown in Figure 13-8, contains other options that can improve the performance of your program.

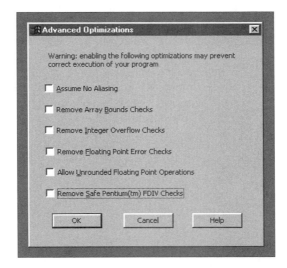

Figure 13-8: Advanced Optimizations dialog

By default, when you run a program, Visual Basic performs several validation checks as your program carries out arithmetic and array operations. For example, if your program tries to reference an invalid array element, or if you write code that performs an arithmetic operation that causes numeric overflow, a run-time error will occur; your program can then trap this error with an error handler. The run-time error occurs because Visual Basic checks the results of these operations. You can use the Advanced Optimizations dialog to eliminate these validation checks.

If you use the dialog to remove the validation checks, your program will run faster, but no run-time error will occur in the event of an overflow or array reference error. Rather, in the case of conditions like numeric overflow, the program will produce an incorrect result. Storing a value into an invalid array element will write the data to an area of the computer's memory that may be used by another variable. The program may therefore produce incorrect results or crash unexpectedly.

The following list describes the advanced optimizations pertaining to a program. Note that these optimizations affect only the compiled program—they do not affect the program while it is running inside the Visual Basic IDE.

- The **Assume No Aliasing** check box tells the compiler that the program does not use aliasing. Aliasing occurs when two variable names reference the same memory location. If you check this check box and aliases exist, your program may produce incorrect results.
- The **Remove Array Bounds Checks** check box causes the bounds of an array not to be validated when referenced. By default, whenever you reference an array, Visual Basic validates the value of the subscript to verify that it is within the array bounds. If it is not, a run-time error will occur that you can then trap with an error handler. If no validation of the bounds of an array

takes place, and your code sets an index to a value outside the array bounds, your code will write information to a memory address that may be used by other data. This problem can lead to incorrect results or cause the program to crash.

- The **Remove Integer Overflow Checks** check box causes the result of Integer arithmetic not to be validated to ensure that the value lies within a valid range. By default, if you store too large a number in an Integer variable, a run-time error will occur. If you check this box, however, no run-time error will occur and an invalid result will be produced.
- The **Remove Floating Point Error Checks** check box causes the results of floating-point (Single and Double data types) arithmetic not to be validated to ensure that they lie within a valid range. By default, if you store too large a number in a floating-point variable, a run-time error will occur. If you check this box, however, no run-time error will occur and an invalid value will be stored in the resultant variable.
- The **Allow Unrounded Floating Point Operations** check box causes floating-point operations to be performed more quickly. Significant rounding errors can occur, however.
- The **Remove Safe Pentium(™) FDIV Checks** check box deals with those Pentium processors with the FDIV bug. Some early Pentium processors contained a bug that, on very rare occasions, would cause floating-point division to produce incorrect results. By default, code is checked so as to generate only correct results.

To illustrate the effect of the advanced optimizations, you will create code that generates overflow and underflow errors.

To see the effect of advanced optimizations:

1 Enter the following statements in the **cmdOverflow_Click** event procedure on the main form:

```
Dim pintCurrent As Integer
pintCurrent = 99999
txtOverflow.Text = pintCurrent
```

2 Enter the following statements in the **cmdArray_Click** event procedure on the main form:

```
Dim pintCurrent(5) As Integer
pintCurrent(6) = 72
```

3 Click **Project**, then click **Project1** properties. Activate the **Compile** tab. Make sure that the **Compile to Native Code** button is clicked.
4 Click the **Advanced Optimizations** button.
5 In the Advanced Optimizations dialog, check the **Remove Integer Overflow Checks** and **Remove Array Bounds Checks** boxes. Click **OK** to close the Advanced Optimizations dialog. Click **OK** again to close the Project Properties dialog.
6 Click **File**, then click **Make MTPCode.exe**. Save the executable file using the name **MathError.exe** in the **Chapter.13/Startup** folder.

Consider carefully the statements you just wrote.

```
Dim pintCurrent As Integer
pintCurrent = 99999
txtOverflow.Text = pintCurrent
```

When inside the Visual Basic IDE, the second statement will cause a numeric overflow error because the largest value that can be stored in an Integer is 32,767. When the executable file is run, however, a run-time error will not occur because the executable file no longer checks for Integer overflow errors.

```
Dim pintCurrent(5) As Integer
pintCurrent(6) = 72
```

These statements will also cause a run-time error to occur when they are run inside the Visual Basic IDE. Because you have removed the array bounds checks, however, no run-time error will be produced when the executable file is run. To see the effect of these advanced optimizations, you will run the program both inside the Visual Basic IDE and an executable file.

To visualize the effects of the advanced optimizations:

1. Run the program inside the Visual Basic IDE.
2. Click the **Numeric Overflow** command button. An overflow run-time error occurs. Click the **Debug** button on the dialog to see the assignment statement that caused the error.
3. End the program, then run it again.
4. Click the **Array** command button. Again, an error message appears, indicating that an invalid subscript was referenced.
5. End the program.
6. Run the executable file you created in the previous steps (**MathError.exe**). Click the **Numeric Overflow** command button. Instead of generating a run-time error, an incorrect result (the value -31073) is stored in the text box.
7. Click the **Array** command button. Note that no run-time error occurs when the program references the invalid array element. Because the event procedure produces no visible output, you will see nothing on the screen.
8. Exit the program.
9. To prepare the program for deployment, compile the program again using the name **MT_S.exe**.
10. Because the file already exists, a dialog appears asking you to replace the file. Respond **Yes**.
11. Exit Visual Basic.

As you can see, you should use the advanced optimizations options only with great caution as your program may produce erroneous results.

Optimizing Programs

As you begin to create larger programs, you need to consider carefully performance issues. Although a program's performance is not exactly part of the user interface, a program that runs slowly will create negative user perceptions. For example, if it takes a long time to move from one form to another, the user may grow dissatisfied. Similarly, the user may become impatient if it takes several minutes to locate a database record. As you create programs, consider carefully the following performance issues:

- Minimize the time it takes to move from one control instance on a form to another. The user should be able to enter data into one control instance, tab to another control instance, and begin entering data immediately. Thus, if the user will enter several fields of data, you should validate the fields all at once, just before a record is recorded to a database, to minimize the time it takes to move from field to field.
- Be careful when accessing records in a database. In large database tables, make sure that you have created indexes on the appropriate fields. Without an index, searching for a record in a table containing many records can take several seconds to several minutes. In such a case, the user may not just be dissatisfied, but may think the program or computer has become frozen.
- When you cannot prevent an operation from taking more than a few seconds, consider displaying a status message on a form or object on the form to advise the user about the operation's progress and the estimated time of completion.

As a Visual Basic programmer, you can follow several guidelines to improve the overall performance of your program. These guidelines will be discussed next.

Control Selection and Use

Some controls consume more resources than others. For example, labels use far less Windows resources than text boxes. Thus, you should use text boxes only when the user must input information. Furthermore, use default properties when possible. If you do not explicitly specify the default property pertaining to a control, the affected statement will execute approximately 25% faster.

Use ActiveX controls only when you need their functionality. When a program uses an ActiveX control, the corresponding ".ocx" file must be loaded into memory along with the corresponding form. While this operation usually does not pose a problem, using several ActiveX different controls on a form can have a negative impact on performance as a form loads. In these cases, you can improve the perceived performance of the program by loading necessary forms all at once while a splash screen appears.

When using controls such as the CommonDialog control, create only one instance of the control and set its properties at run time to activate the different dialogs, rather than creating several instances of the control and setting the same properties at design time. Each control instance consumes memory and can diminish the overall performance of your program.

Data Type Selection

Using the proper data type for different variables can both improve the performance of the program and reduce the amount of memory required for it to run.

- Use Integer data types for counters when the value will not exceed 32,767.
- Use Integer arithmetic rather than floating-point arithmetic where possible. Arithmetic on integers is significantly faster than arithmetic on floating-point numbers.
- Avoid double-precision arithmetic when possible. Arithmetic on double-precision numbers is significantly slower than arithmetic on single-precision numbers. Double-precision numbers are needed only when you must store very small or very large numbers.
- Avoid the use of Variant data types. Each Variant variable consumes 16 bytes of memory, so excessive use of Variants can increase program size dramatically. Also, because Visual Basic must determine the current data type of a Variant variable when it is used, operations on Variant data are significantly slower.
- Do not use generic object variable types like Object, Form, or Control. These data types are late-bound, which increases overhead.

Array Management

In this book, you have created both fixed-size arrays and dynamic arrays with the ReDim statement. Each element in an array consumes memory. Therefore, if the size of the array will grow and shrink at run time, use dynamic arrays and reduce the size of the array as elements no longer become necessary. Again, choose the correct data type for an array.

Module Organization

When you produce an executable file containing several modules, including form modules, class modules, and standard modules, the module organization is preserved in the executable file. When you run a program consisting of several modules, all of the modules are not loaded into the computer's memory when the program starts. Rather, modules are loaded "on demand"—that is, a module loads only when your code calls a procedure in that module. In large programs containing several modules, you can organize your procedures so as to improve overall performance. For example, one set of procedures may be used frequently in a program. You can store all of these procedures in a single module so that they are loaded initially when the program is started. If no procedures in a specific module are ever called, however, then that module will not be loaded into the computer's memory.

In general, you should organize modules such that their procedures perform a set of related tasks. This will improve the performance of the program and tend to improve program readability.

Storing Data in Programs

Many programs store large amounts of constant data, such as tax tables, or constant strings. Storing these data in your application at design time will increase the amount of memory consumed by the program. If the information is used frequently, it may be wise to store the data directly into the program. If the information is used infrequently, you should consider reading it from a text or database file only when needed. This strategy will reduce the total memory required by the program.

Avoiding Dead Code

As you develop and modify programs over a period of time, you may replace general procedures with other procedures. Eventually, you may find that the program never uses certain general procedures and variables. Even though a variable or general procedure is never used, it will continue to consume memory in a program.

Note that unused constants do not appear in an executable file. Thus, no performance improvement results from removing unused constants. Comments are also removed from the program when you produce an executable file. Thus they have no impact on performance.

Q U E S T I O N S

1. Which of the following statements pertaining to the App object is true?
    a. The properties are read-only at run time.
    b. The properties are set by writing code.
    c. The properties contain general information about the program.
    d. Both a and c.
    e. All of the above.

2. How do you set the properties pertaining to the App object?
    a. Write code.
    b. Use the Make tab on the Project Properties dialog.
    c. Click Project, then click App Properties.
    d. Any of the above.
    e. None of the above.

3. How do you execute another program from your Visual Basic program?
    a. Call the Run function.
    b. Call the Execute function.
    c. Call the Program method.
    d. Call the Shell function.
    e. None of the above.

4. What type of executable file is produced by Visual Basic?
    a. Run-time code
    b. Native code
    c. P-Code
    d. Both a and b.
    e. Both b and c.

5. Which of the following is a valid type of optimization?
    a. Optimize for fast code.
    b. Optimize for small code.
    c. No optimization.
    d. All of the above.
    e. None of the above.

6. What happens if you check the Remove Integer Overflow Checks in the Advanced Optimizations dialog?
    a. A run-time error will arise if numeric overflow occurs.
    b. The program will crash.
    c. An incorrect result will be produced.
    d. Any of the above can occur.
    e. None of the above can occur.

7. Which of the following is a valid option on the Advanced Optimizations dialog?
    a. Remove Numeric OverFlow Checks
    b. Don't Check Text
    c. Allow Errors
    d. All of the above.
    e. None of the above.

8. Which of the following statements about program performance is true?
    a. Program performance has no impact upon user perception.
    b. Your program should minimize the time it takes to move from one control instance to another control instance.
    c. You should display a message when a long-running operation takes place.
    d. Both b and c.
    e. All of the above.

9. Which of the following statements related to control performance is true?
    a. Text boxes consume fewer resources than labels.
    b. ActiveX controls have no performance impact.
    c. The number of controls you use in a program has no impact on performance.
    d. All of the above.
    e. None of the above.

10. Which of the following statement(s) is (are) true about data type selection?
    a. Integer arithmetic consumes fewer resources than single precision arithmetic.
    b. Single precision arithmetic consumes fewer resources than double precision arithmetic.
    c. Operations on Variant data are very slow compared with operations on Integers.
    d. All of the above.
    e. None of the above.

In this section you will:

■ Build a package in preparation to deploy a program

■ Deploy a package

Creating Programs for Distribution

Deploying Applications

After you have compiled an application, you must prepare it for distribution. Most applications are executed on a computer other than the one where the application was developed. The process of distributing an application is referred to as **deployment**. Three types of media are commonly used to deploy an application:

■ Floppy disks
■ CD-ROM
■ World Wide Web (Internet distribution)

When you deploy your application, you must distribute not only the executable file you compiled, but also any support files required for the application to run correctly. Several types of support files exist:

■ If your program uses any ActiveX controls, the code for those controls is stored in a file with the extension .ocx. These files must be deployed with the application for it to run correctly.

■ If your program uses any dynamic link libraries (DLLs), these files must be deployed in conjunction with the application.

■ Programs you create may also use configuration files that must be deployed. For example, your program may require a database file or other configuration files.

The collection of files you deploy is referred to as a **package**. A package contains all files necessary to deploy a program to the end user. The **Package and Deployment Wizard** provides all the options needed to create a package representing a distributable program. The Package Deployment Wizard is not part of the Visual Basic IDE, but rather a stand-alone program that you run independently of Visual Basic. Like any other wizard, you interact with the Package and Deployment Wizard by completing a series of dialogs.

To start the Package and Deployment Wizard:

1 Make sure that Visual Basic is not running.

2 Click **Start**, highlight **Programs**, then **Microsoft Visual Basic 6.0**, then **Microsoft Visual Basic 6.0 Tools**, then click the **Package & Deployment Wizard**. The Package and Deployment Wizard dialog appears as shown in Figure 13-9.

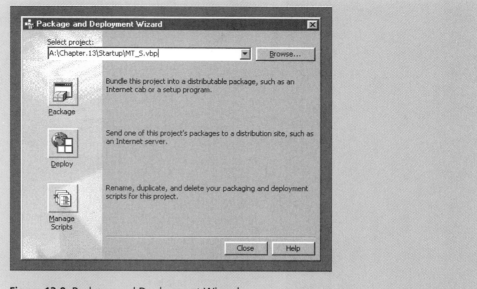

Figure 13-9: Package and Deployment Wizard

As shown in Figure 13-9, the Package and Deployment Wizard contains a list box allowing you to select the project you want to deploy. The projects shown in this list box will vary depending upon whether you have previously deployed packages. This list box may be blank. You can select the project to deploy with the Browse button. The dialog also contains three other buttons:

- The **Package** button is the first step in building a deployment package. This option collects all of the files necessary for the project to run on a different computer.
- After building the package, you use the **Deploy** button to actually deploy the project. The project can be deployed to floppy disks, a CD-ROM, a local folder, a network folder, or the Internet. The deployment options vary based upon the type of project involved.
- The **Manage Scripts** option allows you to modify the scripts used to build and deploy the package.

The first step in deploying a package is to build the package itself. You accomplish this task by clicking the Package button and completing several dialogs. The following list briefly describes each of the dialogs.

- When you build a package, the Package and Deployment Wizard creates a script containing the configuration settings for the package. You can select a packaging script from the **Packaging Script** dialog so as to take advantage of the previously saved settings pertaining to a particular package. If you have not previously built a package, no scripts will exist on the system and this dialog will not appear.
- You use the **Package Type** dialog to define the kind of package you want to create. For instance, you can create a Standard Setup Package—this type of package is later installed by the user when he or she runs the Setup.exe program. You can also create a dependency file—it lists information required by the run-time components in your application.
- You use the **Package Folder** dialog to specify where the package will be built. The folder can reside on a local drive or can consist of a folder on the network.

- The **Included Files** dialog allows you to list the files that will be included in the package. The Package and Deployment Wizard will automatically select the necessary run-time files. You can use the Add button on this dialog to add other files to the package. Such files might include configuration files or other support files like database and text files.
- The **Cab Options** dialog determines how the cabinet files are built. The files that make up the package are compressed and joined together into **cabinet files**, also known as **Cab files**. If you intend to distribute an application on floppy disks, you must use multiple Cab files, and the size of an individual Cab file must not exceed the size of the distribution medium (floppy disk).
- On the **Installation Title** dialog, you specify the title displayed when the end user runs the Setup program.
- When the end user runs the Setup program, that program will copy the necessary files to the user's hard disk. It will also add program items to the Start menu on the target machine. The **Start Menu Items** dialog contains options that enable you to specify where the application will appear on the Start menu. Note that the end user can change this destination.
- The **Install Locations** dialog allows you to change the default folder (location) where your application will be installed on the end user's computer.
- Some files you install with your application may be shared by other applications. In this situation, those files should be removed only when all applications using those files are deleted. The **Shared Files** dialog allows you to mark a file as "shared." If the user uninstalls an application, the shared file(s) will not be removed until all programs using the shared file are gone.
- The **Finished** dialog completes the process. Using this dialog, you can specify a script name. This script can be used again if you later create a package for the same application. All settings for the current package are saved, so you do not need to complete each of the dialogs the next time you create the package.

After you complete the necessary dialogs, the Package and Deployment Wizard will create the Cab files required to deploy the application. These Cab files contain your application and any dependent files needed for your application to run. After their creation, a final dialog appears indicating whether the package creation was successful.

The first step in building the package is to select the desired project. That project cannot be open in Visual Basic.

help

Note that this project must not be open in Visual Basic. If it is, an error dialog will appear. To fix the problem, activate Visual Basic and close the project.

To select a package to build:

1 Click the **Browse** button to open the **Open Project** dialog. Select the project file named **Chapter.13\Startup\MT_S.vbp**. Click the **Open** button to select the project. Set the drive designator as necessary. The selected project will appear in the Select project list box, which contains a list of packages you have built recently. Depending on whether the Package and Deployment Wizard has been used on your computer, this list may be empty initially.

Once you have selected the project to build, you must create the package file. If you have not previously compiled the project, the Package and Deployment Wizard will compile it for you. If you have already compiled the project, recompilation may not be necessary. If the project file is more recent than the corresponding executable file, the Package and Deployment Wizard will display a message asking if you want to recompile the project.

The information used to build a package is stored in a **script file**, which contains the configuration information related to the package. As you repeatedly build packages, you can use the script file rather than specify the package configuration repeatedly.

To build a package:

1 Click the **Package** button on the Package and Deployment Wizard dialog. If the project file is newer than the executable file, the wizard will display the dialog shown in Figure 13-10. Click **Yes** to recompile the project. Note that the file names in Figure 13-10 may vary depending upon the last executable file name you used in the previous section.

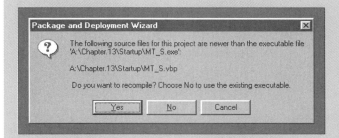

Figure 13-10: Package and Deployment Wizard dialog

2 After the project is recompiled, the Packaging Script dialog will appear, as shown in Figure 13-11. Again, the items in the Packaging Script list box will vary depending on whether the wizard has been used on your computer. If no scripts exist on your computer, the dialog shown in Figure 13-11 will not appear.

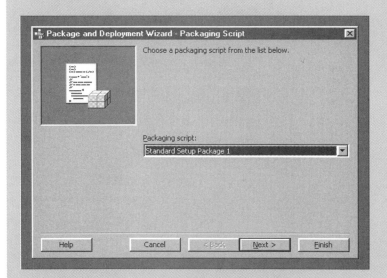

Figure 13-11: Packaging Script dialog

3 If the dialog shown in Figure 13-11 appears, select the (**None**), then click the **Next** button to activate the Package Type dialog shown in Figure 13-12.

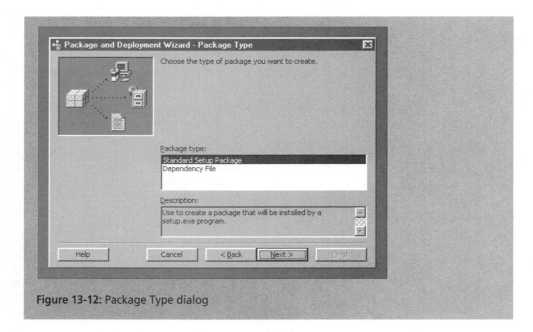

Figure 13-12: Package Type dialog

The wizard creates packages based upon the type of project. MathTek's project is a standard EXE project, which supports two package types. The **Standard Setup Package** type creates a package intended for installation by the Setup.exe project. The **Dependency File** type creates a file containing the components required for your program to run. In this chapter, you will create a Standard Setup Package.

To select the package type:

1   Select the **Standard Setup Package** in the Package type list box, then click the **Next** button to activate the Package Folder dialog shown in Figure 13-13. Note that the default drive is the same as the drive where the executable file resides.

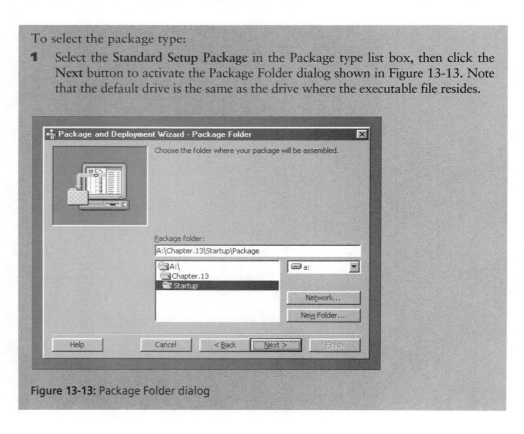

Figure 13-13: Package Folder dialog

The Package Folder dialog allows you to select the folder in which the package will be built. Because several files are used to build the package, and these files can be quite large, in most cases you cannot select a floppy disk directory to build the package. The wizard will allow you to change folders, create new folders if necessary, and select folders on the network.

To select the package folder:

1 Select the hard drive on your computer (typically C:). Note that you cannot use the floppy drive A: because the destination files will not fit on the floppy disk.

2 Click the **New Folder** button. When the New Folder dialog appears, enter the name **Package** in the text box and click **OK** to close the dialog. If you select an existing folder, a dialog will appear indicating that the existing contents will be destroyed. When this dialog closes, make sure that the package folder is selected and open.

3 Click the **Next** button to activate the Included Files dialog shown in Figure 13-14.

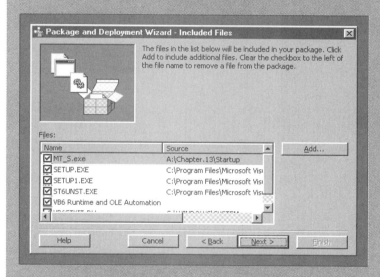

Figure 13-14: Included Files dialog

When you deploy your program, several files are required to make it run besides the program's executable file itself. The wizard examines the project to detect these files and lists them in the Files list box. Consider the dependent files for your current program:

- The file **COMDLG32.OCX** contains the code for the ActiveX CommonDialog control.
- The files **SETUP.EXE** and **SETUP1.EXE** contain the setup program.
- **MT_S** is your executable file.
- **ST6UNST.EXE** is used on the target computer to uninstall the software if necessary.
- The remaining files contain the necessary run-time files needed for Visual Basic programs to execute.

In addition to these files, you may want to deploy other files with your application. For example, if your program requires a database file, you can add it with this dialog. To deploy additional files, you click the Add button and select the desired file.

To select the included files:

1   The wizard has detected all files necessary for deployment of MathTek's program. Click the **Next** button to activate the Cab Options dialog shown in Figure 13-15.

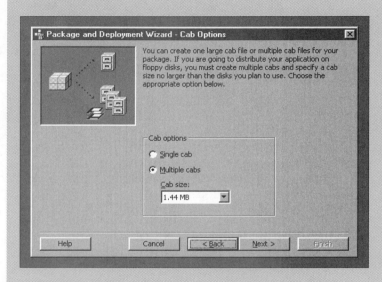

Figure 13-15: Cab Options dialog

The wizard stores the program's executable file and the dependent files using a standard file format called a cabinet (Cab) file. If you are distributing your program on a CD-ROM or the Internet, you can store all dependent files in the same Cab file. If you are distributing the program on floppy disks, each Cab file must fit on a single floppy disk so you must create multiple Cab files. Furthermore, the Cab file must be the same size or smaller than the capacity of the floppy disks you are using. For MathTek's program, you will use floppy disk distribution so you will create multiple Cab files.

To select the Cab options:

1   Click the **Multiple cabs** option button, if necessary.

2   Set the Cab size to **1.44 MB**, the default. If you are using low-density floppies, you would set the Cab size to **720 KB**.

3   Click the **Next** button to display the Installation Title dialog shown in Figure 13-16.

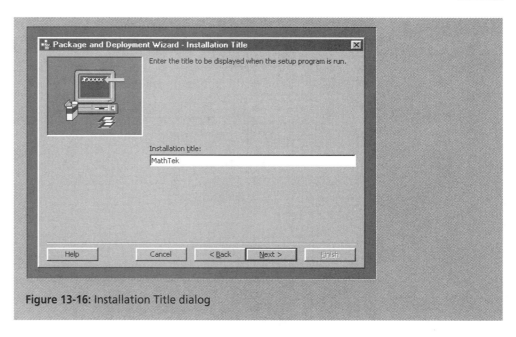

Figure 13-16: Installation Title dialog

When the user installs your deployed package on his or her computer, he or she will run a Setup program. This process is the same as the process you have likely used when you installed software on your own computer. When the Setup program is run, the Setup program automatically displays a program title. This title is set via the Installation Title dialog.

To set the installation title:

1 Enter the name **MathTek Statistical Demo** in the Installation Title dialog.

2 Click the **Next** button to activate the Start Menu Items dialog shown in Figure 13-17.

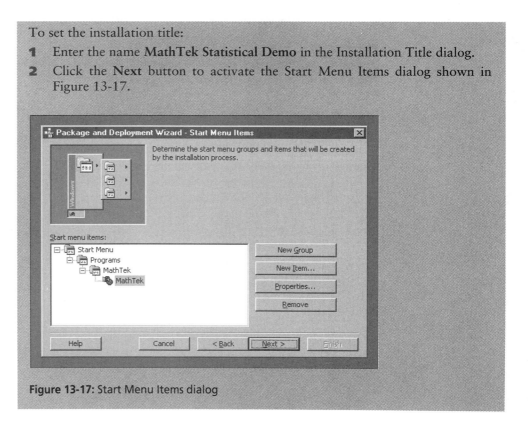

Figure 13-17: Start Menu Items dialog

The end users of your program are likely accustomed to running a program by selecting an entry from the Start menu. Your deployment must therefore add the necessary items to the Start menu. The wizard will set default Start menu items for you. You can modify these menu items as necessary depending on the needs of your program. You modify the Start menu items using the four command buttons on the dialog:

- The New Group button will create a new program group item.
- The New Item button will create a new program item in the currently selected program group.
- The Properties button will set the properties pertaining to the currently selected program group or program item.
- The Remove button will remove the currently selected program group or program item.

To set the program group and program item:

1 Select the default program group named **MathTek.** This is the second item from the bottom of the list. Click the **Properties** command button. The Start Menu Group Properties dialog appears as shown in Figure 13-18. Figure 13-18 shows the dialog after setting the name.

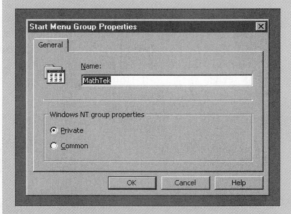

Figure 13-18: Start Menu Group Properties dialog

2 Note that the name is set to **MathTek.** Set the name to **MathTek Statistical Software.** Click the **OK** button to close the dialog.

3 Click the **MathTek** program item. This is the last item on the list. Click the **Properties** command button.

4 Set the name to **Random Number Demo.** Click **OK** to close the dialog.

5 Click the **Next** button to activate the Install Locations dialog shown in Figure 13-19.

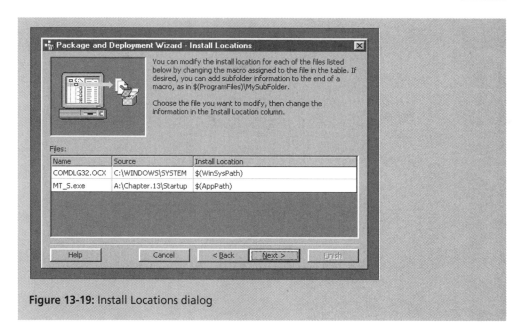

Figure 13-19: Install Locations dialog

The wizard uses macros to indicate where a package should be installed. Figure 13-19 lists two macros named $(WinSysPath) and $(AppPath). The following list describes the macros supported by the Package and Deployment Wizard:

- **$(WinSysPath)** installs the file in the folder \Windows\System when the end user's computer supports Windows 95 or Windows 98. When it uses Windows NT, the file is installed in the folder \Winnt\System32.
- **$(WinSysPathSysFile)** uses the same folder names as those used for the macro $(WinSysPath). The files are marked as system files, however, and are not deleted when the application is removed.
- **$(WinPath)** installs the file in the folder \Windows when the end user's computer supports Windows 95 or Windows 98. When it uses Windows NT, the file is installed in the folder \Winnt.
- **$(AppPath)** installs the file in the application path specified by the user. The default value for this macro is obtained using the Setup.lst file.
- **$(ProgramFiles)** installs the file in the application directory. This directory is typically \Program Files.
- **$(CommonFiles)** installs the file in the folder where shared files are stored most often. This directory is typically C:\Program Files\Common Files.

You do not need to change the default destinations for MathTek's program.

To select the install locations:

1 Click the **Next** button to select the default install locations and activate the Shared Files dialog shown in Figure 13-20.

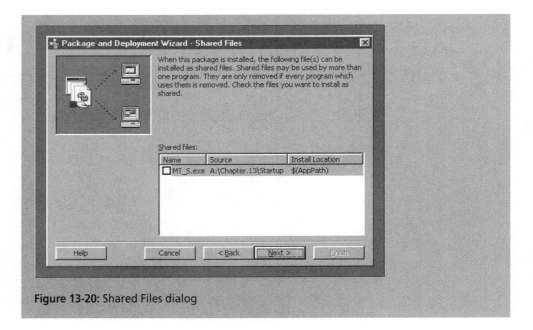

Figure 13-20: Shared Files dialog

In some situations, you may install files that are shared by multiple applications. If one such application is removed, the shared file must not be deleted because another application may require its use. To indicate that a file is a shared file, click the check box in the Shared files list. The file will be removed only when all programs using the file are deleted.

To mark a file as a shared file:

1 The application in this chapter has no shared files. Click the **Next** button to activate the Finished dialog shown in Figure 13-21. Figure 13-21 shows the script name after it has been set.

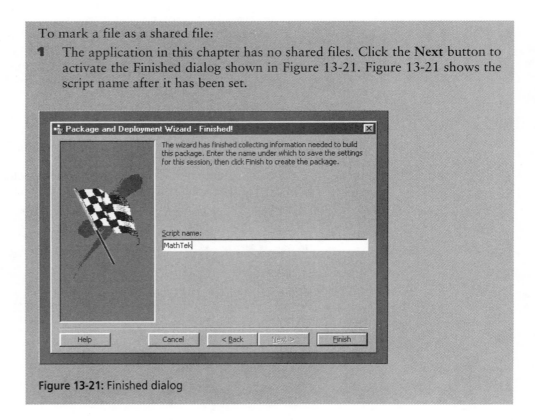

Figure 13-21: Finished dialog

The final step in building the package is to assign a name to the script created by the wizard. You can reuse this script when and if you need to rebuild the package.

To save the script:

1 Set the Script name to **MathTek** and click the **Finish** button to build the package.

2 This process takes a few minutes. As the wizard generates the Cab files, a dialog appears to indicate its progress. The Packaging/Report dialog then appears.

3 Click **Close** to close the dialog.

Deploying a Package

After you create a package, you must deploy it. Depending on how the package was created, you have several deployment options:

- You can deploy a package to floppy disks.
- You can deploy a package to a CD-ROM.
- You can deploy a package for distribution over the Internet.

To deploy a package, you complete a series of dialogs.

- The **Deployment Method** dialog allows you to specify the method for deploying the package. If you created multiple Cab files, you can distribute the package on floppy disks. If you selected a single Cab file, you can either deploy the package to a folder or publish it to a Web server.
- Different dialogs will appear depending on your deployment choice. If you deploy a package via floppy disks, the **Floppy Drive** dialog appears, allowing you to select the desired floppy drive. If you deploy a package to a folder, the **Folder** dialog appears, allowing you to select the drive and folder where the package will appear. Finally, if you select the **Web Publishing** option, you must choose which files to deploy as well as specify the destination URL where the package will appear.
- After you select the desired options, the **Finished** dialog appears. Again, you can save the deployment options to a script, which can be reused later when the package is deployed again.

MathTek's package is intended for floppy disk distribution. In the deployment phase, you will copy the necessary package (Cab) files to floppy disks. To complete the steps in the remainder of this section, you will need two blank floppy disks.

The dialogs in the deployment phase work much like the dialogs in the package phase. You specify the deployment information and then save it into a deployment script, which you can reuse later.

To begin deployment of the package you created:

1   Click the **Deploy** button on the Package and Deployment Wizard dialog to activate the Deployment Script dialog shown in Figure 13-22. If you have not previously deployed a package, this dialog will not appear because no deployment scripts pertaining to the application exist.

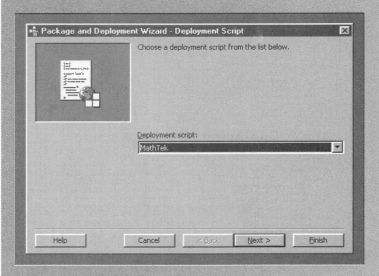

Figure 13-22: Deployment Script dialog

2   If the Deployment Script dialog appears, select (**None**) because you will be creating a new script.

3   Click the **Next** button to activate the Package to Deploy dialog shown in Figure 13-23.

Figure 13-23: Package to Deploy dialog

4 You have created a package named MathTek that you want to deploy. Select **MathTek** in the Package to deploy list box, if necessary, then click the **Next** button to select the Deployment Method dialog shown in Figure 13-24.

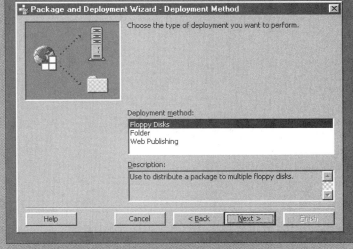

Figure 13-24: Deployment Method dialog

For MathTek's program, you will be deploying the application to floppy disks. Alternatively, you could deploy your package to a folder or the Internet.

To select the deployment method:

1 Verify that the **Floppy Disks** option is selected as the deployment method.

2 Click the **Next** button to display the Floppy Drive dialog shown in Figure 13-25.

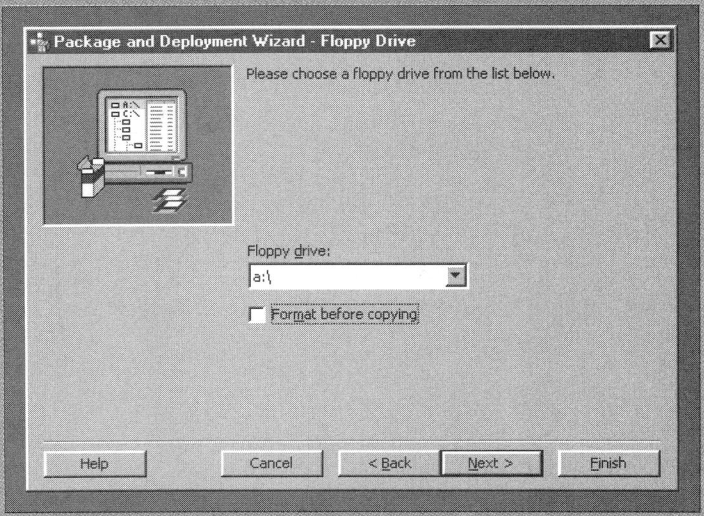

Figure 13-25: Floppy Drive dialog

3   Make sure that the **A:** drive is selected. If your floppies require formatting, check the **Format before copying** check box.

4   Click the **Next** button to display the Finished dialog shown in Figure 13-26.

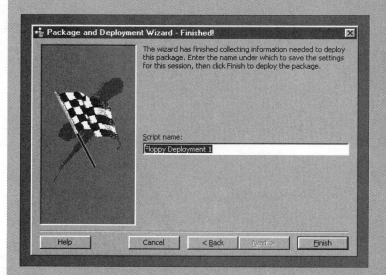

Figure 13-26: Finished dialog

5   Set the script name to **MathTek**.

6   Click the **Finish** button to begin copying the package to floppy disks. Dialogs will appear indicating when to insert and change floppies.

7   The Deployment Report dialog appears describing the copied files. Click **Close** to close the report. On the Package and Deployment Wizard dialog, click **Close** to end the program.

You have now completed the process of building and deploying the package for your application. Next, you will see how the end user will see your deployment.

To install the package:

1   Insert the first disk created by the Package and Deployment Wizard.

2   Click the **Start** button on the taskbar, then click **Run.**

3   Enter the file name **A:\Setup.exe** in the dialog, then click **OK.**

4   The Setup program will begin to copy the files to the hard disk in preparation for installation. Change disks when requested by the Setup program.

5   After the files have been copied, the Setup screen will appear, as shown in Figure 13-27. Click **OK.** The Setup program begins installing the files. Complete the remaining dialogs to install the program.

6   Click **Start**, highlight **Programs**, highlight **MathTek Statistical Software,** and select **Random Number Demo** to execute the program you just installed.

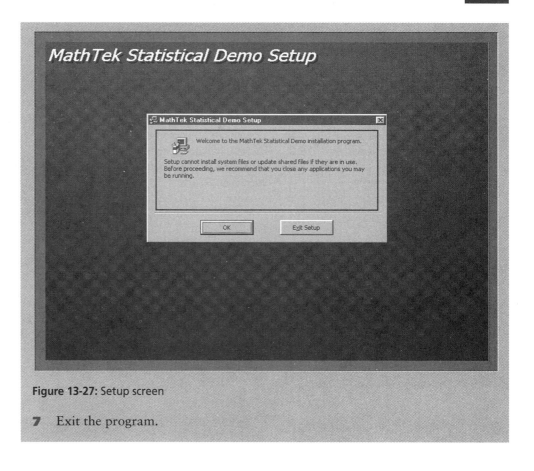

Figure 13-27: Setup screen

7 Exit the program.

S U M M A R Y

This chapter has presented several important topics. You learned how to set general application properties using the App object. You also saw how to execute other programs from Visual Basic using the Shell function. In addition, you learned how to compile programs and assess the effect of compilation options on program performance. Finally, you learned how to package and deploy applications.

To set the properties pertaining to the App object:

■ Click **Project,** then click **Project Properties**. Select the **Make** tab. Enter the version and application information.

To execute another program from a Visual Basic program, call the Shell function with the following syntax:

Shell(*pathname*[,*windowstyle*])

To create an executable program:

■ Click **Project,** then click **Properties**. Activate the **Compile** tab.
■ Set the compiler optimizations as necessary.
■ Click **File,** then click **Make** *projectname* on the menu bar to build the executable file.

To build a package:

- Make sure that the program for which you want to build a package is not open.
- Start the Package and Deployment Wizard.
- Click the Package button to begin building the package.
- Set the Package Type to define the type of package you want to create.
- Set the Package Folder to specify where the package should be built.
- Set the Cab options to indicate how the cabinet files should be created.
- Set the Installation Title.
- Set the Install Locations to specify where the application should be installed on the target computer.
- Specify any shared files used by multiple applications.

To deploy a package:

- Click the Deployment button on the Package and Deployment Wizard.
- Select the Deployment method.
- If deploying to floppy disks, specify the name of the disk drive and indicate whether to format the disks.
- Click the Finish button to make the floppy disks.

QUESTIONS

1. What is the term used to describe the distribution of a program?
   a. Distribution
   b. Release
   c. Target
   d. Deployment
   e. None of the above.

2. What is the tool used to deploy software?
   a. Setup Wizard
   b. Package and Deployment Wizard
   c. Install Wizard
   d. All of the above.
   e. None of the above.

3. Which of the following is contained in a package?
   a. The executable program
   b. Dependent files including .ocx files
   c. Other required files
   d. All of the above.
   e. None of the above.

4. Which of the following is a valid type of package?
   a. Standard Setup Package
   b. Dependency file
   c. Install package
   d. Both a and b.
   e. Both a and c.

5. If you are building a package to be distributed to floppy disks, you must
_____

    a. Create multiple Cab files.

    b. Create a single Cab file.

    c. Cab files are not used in floppy disk distributions.

    d. Create a link file.

    e. None of the above.

6. What is the purpose of the Install Locations dialog pertaining to the Package and Deployment Wizard?

    a. To define where the Cab files will be located

    b. To define which files will be included in the Cab files

    c. To define the default location where the application will be installed on the target computer

    d. All of the above.

    e. None of the above.

7. The information used to build a package is stored in a _____ file.

    a. Temporary file

    b. Form file

    c. Project file

    d. Script file

    e. None of the above.

8. Which of the following statements is true?

    a. A package must be built before it is deployed.

    b. Building a package and deploying it take place concurrently.

    c. You can specify package deployment options before building the package.

    d. Package deployment is accomplished inside the Visual Basic IDE.

    e. None of the above.

9. Which of the following is a valid package deployment destination?

    a. Floppy disks

    b. Folders

    c. The Web

    d. All of the above.

    e. None of the above.

10. When a package is deployed to floppy disks, which files are copied to the floppy disks?

    a. Setup.exe

    b. Cab files

    c. Build files

    d. Both a and b.

    e. Both a and c.

E X E R C I S E S

1. Magtronics sells industrial motors. The company maintains its price list in a database file. It would like a program to display this price list to its customers. This program will ultimately be distributed on floppy disks.

    a. Run the executable file named **Chapter.13\Exercise\Ex1demo.exe**, setting the drive designator as necessary. When the program first starts, a splash screen appears, as shown in Figure 13-28.

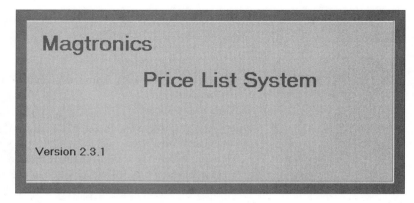

Figure 13-28: Exercise 1 – splash screen

After the splash screen appears for three seconds, the main form appears as shown in Figure 13-29.

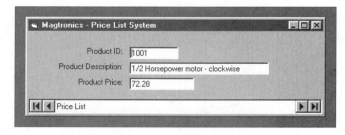

Figure 13-29: Exercise 1 – main form

b. Use the buttons on the Data control to locate different records. Exit the program.

c. Start Visual Basic and create a new project named **Ex1.vbp**. Add a splash screen to the project with a file name of **frmEx1sp.frm**. Save the main form with the name **frmEx1.frm**. Save both the form and project files.

d. Add the objects to the splash screen as shown in Figure 13-28. Set the necessary App object properties so that the major version of the software is **2**, the minor version is **3**, and the revision is **1**. Set the company name to **Magtronics** and the product name to **Price List System**. Write the code required to display the version, company name, and product name on the form.

e. Create a timer on the splash screen so that it appears for three seconds, then displays the main form.

f. Add the objects to the main form. The program should connect to the database named **Mag.mdb**.

The table used in the database is named **tblPriceList** and has fields named **fldID**, **fldDescription**, and **fldPrice**. Set the necessary properties to display this information on the form.

discovery ▶

g. In the Form_Load event procedure, write statements to set the Data control's Database name property such that the database file Mag.mdb is appended to the current path of the application. That is, the database opened should reside in the same folder as the application itself.

h. Compile the program into a native code executable file named **Ex1.exe**.

i. Exit Visual Basic.

j. Using the Package and Deployment Wizard, deploy the program and the necessary support files to floppy disks. Make sure that you also deploy the database file named **Mag.mdb**. This file should be distributed and saved on the target machine in the same folder as the application itself.

k. After you have built the distribution, test it by installing the program using the deployment floppy disks.

2. Tax Master sells property tax information. The company wants to distribute a program along with a text file containing the most up-to-date tax information for a given area.

a. Run the executable file named **Chapter.13\Exercise\Ex2demo.exe**, setting the drive designator as necessary. When the program first starts, a splash screen appears, as shown in Figure 13-30.

Figure 13-30: Exercise 2 – splash screen

After the splash screen appears for three seconds, the main form appears, as shown in Figure 13-31.

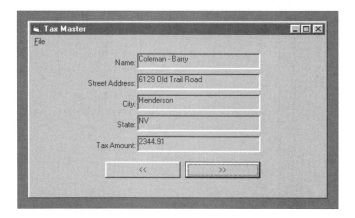

Figure 13-31: Exercise 2 – main form

b. Click **File**, then click **Open** on the main form's menu bar. Open the file named **Tax.txt**. Click the buttons on the form to locate different records. Click **File**, then click **Notepad**. Notepad should start and the text file should load. (Notepad must appear on your computer and be installed in the default location for this feature to work properly.) Exit the program.

c. Start Visual Basic and create a new project named **Ex2.vbp**. Add a splash screen to the project with a file name of **frmEx2sp.frm**. Save the main form with the name **frmEx2.frm**. Save both the form and project files.

d. Add the objects to the splash screen, as shown in Figure 13-30. Set the necessary App object properties so that the major and minor version numbers and the revision level are the same as those shown in Figure 13-30. Set the company name to **Tax Master** and the product name to **Tax Listing**. Write the code required to display the version, company name, and product name on the form.

e. Add the objects to the main form, as shown in Figure 13-31. Create a **File** menu with the following menu items: **Open, Notepad,** and **Exit**. Add an instance of the common dialog to the form.

f. In the main form, declare a user-defined type with the following members: **Name, Address, City, State,** and **Amount**. Declare an empty module-level array to store these user-defined types.

g. Write the code necessary to set the array dimension to zero when the form loads.

h. In the Open procedure, use the common dialog to open a file. Set its properties so that the program searches for a file in the same folder as the application's path. In the same procedure, create a Do loop to read the file entered by the user. As part of the Do loop, redimension the array and read the current record.

i. Create a general procedure to display the current array record into the form objects. This procedure should take one argument—the record to display.

j. Program the command buttons on the form. The button with the caption "<<" should display the previous record, and the button with the caption ">>" should display the next record. Write error-checking code so that if the user attempts to display the next record when the last record is the current record, a message box will appear. In addition, write the code to display a message box if the user attempts to display the previous record when the first record is the current record.

k. Program the Exit menu item.

l. Program the Notepad menu item. When the user clicks this item, the program should start Notepad with the current file name as an argument and load the file. Make sure that when the user clicks this menu item, Notepad receives input focus.

m. Compile the program into a native code executable file. Set the necessary options so that the program is optimized for speed and Integer overflow checks and array bounds checks are turned off.

n. Exit Visual Basic.

o. Using the Package and Deployment Wizard, deploy the program and the necessary support files to floppy disks. Make sure that you also deploy the text file named **Tax.txt**. This file should be distributed and saved on the target machine in the same folder as the application itself.

p. After you have built the distribution, test it by installing the program using the deployment floppy disks.

o b j e c t i v e s

In this case you will:

- Use several ActiveX controls
- Interact with a database using Data control instances
- Interact with a database programmatically using SQL statements
- Create multiple form and standard modules including MDI parent, MDI child, and standard forms

Monarch Roofing

Creating an Order Entry System

case ▶ Monarch Roofing manufactures roofing tiles that are sold to construction companies throughout the southwestern United States. In this case, you will create an order entry system for the company. This order entry system must allow the user to create a new order by specifying an existing customer, then specifying an order date and a requested shipping date. Once the order has been created, the user should be able to select items from inventory and add them to the order. In addition to entering new orders, the company wants users to be able to edit existing orders.

The information for the order entry system is stored in a Microsoft Access database that consists of four tables:

- The table tblCustomers contains the customer information, as shown in Figure EC4-1.
- The table tblInventory contains the inventory information, as shown in Figure EC4-2.
- The table tblOrderMaster contains general information about an order, as shown in Figure EC4-3.
- The table tblOrderDetail contains the different inventory items and quantities pertaining to the order, as shown in Figure EC4-4.

Name	Data Type
fldCustomerID	Long
fldCompanyName	Text
fldLastName	Text
fldFirstName	Text
fldAddress	Text
fldCity	Text
fldState	Text
fldZipCode	Text
fldPhone	Text
fldFax	Text
fldOrderLimit	Currency

Figure EC4-1: Structure of table tblCustomers

Name	Data Type
fldPartID	Long
fldDescription	Text
fldCost	Currency
fldSalesPrice	Currency
fldQtyInStock	Long

Figure EC4-2: Structure of table tblInventory

Column Name	Data Type
fldOrderID	Long
fldCustomerID	Long
fldOrderDate	Date/Time
fldShipDate	Date/Time

Figure EC4-3: Structure of table tblOrderMaster

Column Name	Data Type
fldOrderID	Long
fldPartID	Long
fldQtyOrdered	Long

Figure EC4-4: Structure of table tblOrderDetail

The relationships for the database also have been defined, as shown in Figure EC4-5.

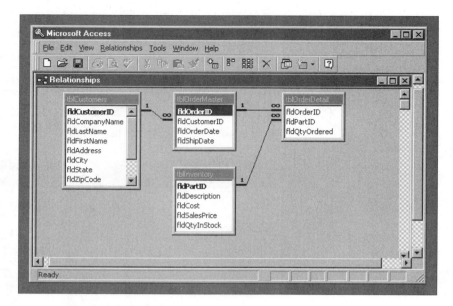

Figure EC4-5: Database relationships

Monarch Roofing's program should be an MDI program consisting of several forms. The following list describes the general purpose of each form:

■ A splash screen should display the company name and pertinent information about the program. Use the App object to display the revision information and product name on the splash screen.

■ The MDI parent form should display each of the different MDI child forms.

■ The Find form will be used to locate a customer by selecting a company. This form should be displayed as a modal form; thus it will not be an MDI child form.

■ The New Order form will be used to enter a new order into the system. It should be an MDI child form.

■ The Edit Order form will be used to view, and possibly change, the contents of an existing order.

When the program first starts, the Sub Main procedure should execute. The Sub Main procedure must be written in a standard module with the suffix ".bas". This procedure, which should be the startup object for the project, should perform the following tasks:

1. Display the splash screen.
2. Load all forms in the project.
3. Using an instance of the CommonDialog control, open the database as specified by the user. The common dialog should be configured such that it looks for the default file name Monarch.mdb in the folder containing the application. Use the App object to determine the application's path. Consider creating a Function procedure to open the database.
4. If a database was opened successfully, then continue to display the MDI parent form. If a database was not opened, then display a message box asking the user if he or she wants to try again. Depending on the user input, the code that you write should either exit the program or make another attempt to open a database.

The MDI parent form should include two menu titles. The first, **File**, contains one menu item—to exit the program. The second, **Orders**, contains two menu items—one to add a new order, and another to edit an existing order.

Before adding or editing an order, the user must locate an existing customer by using the Find form. The Find form is shown in Figure EC4-6.

Figure EC4-6: Find form

This Find form should provide considerable flexibility in searching for a company. As shown in Figure EC4-6, the company name is specified as an asterisk (*), which means to search for all companies. If the user specified "B*" as the search criteria, then all the company names starting with the letter "B" should be selected. When the user selects a company and clicks the LookUp command button, the program should generate a corresponding SELECT statement to create a Recordset object containing all companies that match the search criteria. You can use the LIKE clause of the SELECT statement to accomplish this task. Next, each record in the recordset should be displayed in the list box, as shown in Figure EC4-6. The user will then select a company by clicking the company name in the list box, then clicking the OK button. If the user clicks the Cancel button, the form should be hidden.

The form needs to communicate three items of information to other forms. First, a flag needs to be set indicating whether a company was found. A second flag should indicate the current customer ID, and the third flag should describe the company name. To improve the user interface for this form, consider resetting the default command button and focus as the user selects a company.

When adding an order, the New Order form should be displayed. This form is shown in Figure EC4-7.

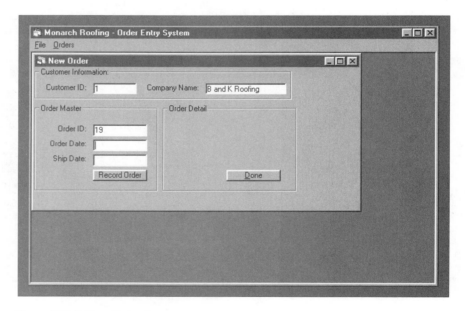

Figure EC4-7: New Order form

The New Order form consists of three sections. The first section displays the Customer ID and Company Name. The Customer ID and Company Name should not be edited from this form, as this information should have been determined by the Find form.

The second section contains the information pertaining to the table named tblOrderMaster and indicates the Order ID, Order Date, and Ship Date. In Figure EC4-7, the Order ID text box is already filled in. This field should always be filled in automatically by the program. That is, when the New Order form is displayed, a new Order ID should be generated. You can accomplish this task by determining the maximum Order ID value in the table named tblOrderMaster and then adding one to that value; you can use a SELECT statement for this purpose. The user should not be able to change the Order ID value. The default value for the Order Date should be the current date, as shown in Figure EC4-8.

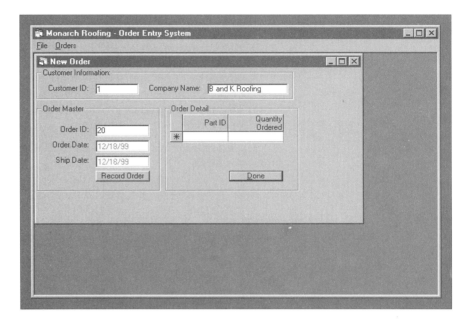

Figure EC4-8: Default value for order date

Once the user has entered the Order Date and Ship Date, the program should validate this information to ensure that both dates are valid. When the user clicks the Record Order command button, the new order should be added to the table named tblOrderMaster. Again, you can accomplish this task by writing an SQL INSERT statement. Do not use bound controls. After inserting the Order Master table information, the third section, which is order detail, should display an instance of the DBGrid control so that the user can proceed to specify the different inventory items and quantities desired for each item. The user then can specify the Part ID and Quantity Ordered for each item.

When the order is complete, the Done command button—found in the Order Detail section of the New Order form—should hide the form.

You can think of entering a new order as a series of steps:

1. Locate an existing Customer ID and a Company Name by displaying the Find form.
2. If a customer is found, then display the New Order form. Otherwise, do not.
3. Assign a new Order ID by finding the maximum Order ID in the table tblOrderDetail and adding one to that number.
4. After the order and ship date are entered, and the Record Order button is clicked, add the order to the current table.
5. Display an instance of the DBGrid control so that the user can specify order items and order quantities.

The Edit Order form will be used to view and edit an existing order. Figure EC4-9 shows this form.

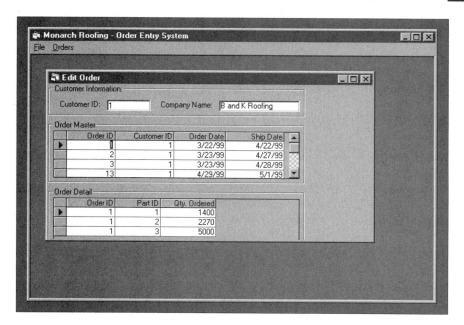

Figure EC4-9: Edit Order form

The Edit Order form displays the current customer and company just as the New Order form does. It also contains two DBGrid controls. The first should display the information from the Order Master table. Note that the program should display the records corresponding to the current Customer ID. When the user selects an Order ID, the detail information should appear in the other DBGrid control instance. If the user selects a different Order ID, then the records displayed in the second DBGrid should be updated accordingly.

You can think of editing an existing order as a series of steps:

1. Locate an existing Customer ID and a Company Name by displaying the Find form.
2. If a customer is found, then display the Edit Order form. Otherwise, do not display the current Customer ID and Company Name on the form.
3. When an Order ID is selected, display the pertinent information in the detail section.

As you develop this program, you may want to consider creating general functions in a standard module to build and execute the various SQL statements required by the program. Putting careful thought into the program's design will make the programming process easier. Complete the following general steps to develop the application:

1. To view the completed application, run the file **Monarch.exe** in the **ExtraCases\Project4** folder. Set the drive designator as necessary. For the completed application to run correctly, the database file Monarch.mdb must reside in the same folder as the executable file. Locate a company and prepare an order. Exit the program.

2. Start Visual Basic and create a new project.

3. Create a splash screen for the project. Use the App object to display the pertinent information on the splash screen.

4. Create the MDI parent form for the program and its menu items.

5. Create the Find form and its objects. Write code so that when the user clicks the Lookup command button, the companies matching the selected criteria will appear in the list box. When the user selects a company in the list box and clicks the OK button, the form should be hidden. You should also create a flag to indicate whether the user selected a company. You can implement this flag as a property in the form module or as a global variable in a standard module.

6. Create the New Order form and its objects. When this form appears initially, the Customer ID and Company Name should be filled in automatically. Also, the Order ID should be filled in automatically. Note that the Customer ID and Company Name are derived from the information specified in the Find form.

7. Create the Edit Order form and its objects. When this form appears, the Customer ID and Company Name should be filled in automatically. Again, this information should be derived from the Find form. Display the master and detail order information for the customer in two synchronized DBGrid control instances.

In this case you will:

- Create MDI parent, MDI child, and standard forms
- Create and use a Class module
- Create a toolbar
- Use arrays and collections
- Create enumerated and user-defined types
- Create multiple instances of a form

Lyons Bank

Creating a Customer Service Program

case ▶ Lyons Bank is an issuer of credit cards. Its customer service center employs 100 people to answer telephone calls from customers. Customers call the customer service center to check on their balances, available credit, and other account information.

Each time the center receives a call, certain information about the call is recorded in a text file. Each employee produces one text file during his or her shift. The company wants a program that will allow supervisors to view and summarize this information so as to better assess employee performance and the types of calls that are being received. Lyons Bank wants to find out the average duration of each type of call for each employee. Also, they want to be able to compute additional statistics for all employees.

Because the company has determined that many of the tasks related to processing the log files can be used by other programs, you should encapsulate the processing of the text file into a Class module.

The input data for the program are well defined. Each record in the text file has the format shown in Figure EC5-1

Field Description	Data Type
Call Type	Integer
Resolution Code	Integer
Start Time	Date
End Time	Date
Account Number	String

Figure EC5-1: Input text file format

The first two fields can have one of eight discrete values. The type of call can be a number between zero (0) and seven (7). The meaning of each value is shown in Figure EC5-2.

Call Type	Value
Lost Card	0
Check Balance	1
Limit Increase	2
Address Change	3
Payment Information	4
Additional Card	5
Cancel Card	6
Stolen Card	7

Figure EC5-2: Call types

The resolution of the call is represented by one of three Integer values. The meaning of each value is shown in Figure EC5-3.

Resolution Description	Resolution Code
Refer to Supervisor	1
Problem Solved	2
Call Back	3

Figure EC5-3: Resolution codes

The properties and methods of the class module have also been defined. When an instance of the class is created, a method should load an input file into the class. Each record should be stored in a private array of user-defined types, with the type corresponding to the format of the input file.

You also need to create an array to hold the summary information. After the log file is read, you need to store summary information in another private array according to the following guidelines:

- The summary array should have eight elements corresponding to each call type.
- You should create another user-defined type with six members for the elements: The first member of the user-defined type should identify the call type. The second member should contain the number of calls having that specified call type. The third member should contain the average duration of the calls of that type. The fourth, fifth, and sixth members should contain the count of calls referred to a supervisor, problems solved, and the calls to be returned, respectively.

You will create methods to locate different elements in the arrays and to summarize the information. In addition, you will create several properties so that the information can be displayed on the form.

Lyons Bank's program should operate as an MDI program with one type of MDI child form. Each MDI child form instance should display the information corresponding to a single text file stored in an instance of the class. That is, the information should represent the call activity for the work shift of a single employee. A supervisor should be able to open any number of MDI child forms. Each MDI child form should call the methods of a class. These methods should open files, load the information into memory, and locate different records.

The class should work much like a recordset. Each line read from the text file can be considered a record. You should store each record into an array, and then call methods like FindFirst, FindNext, FindPrevious, and FindLast to navigate through the array. When you read the properties representing an individual field, the value should be retrieved from the current record. Thus your class will implement the concept of a current record pointer.

The following list describes the properties of the class and their behavior:

- The **AccountNumber** property should be a read-only property that returns a string.
- The **StartTime** and **EndTime** properties should be read-only properties of the Date data type corresponding to the call's starting and ending times.
- The **CallType** property should be a read-only property. Valid values are the integers zero (0) through seven (7). You can use an enumerated type to represent these values.
- The **Count** property should be a read-only property containing the number of records in the class instance.
- The **Current** property should be a read-write property identifying the current record. When setting the Current property, the Property procedure should verify that the value lies within the acceptable range. That is, it should be between one (1) and the number of records in the array.
- The **CurrentSummary** property should be a read-write property identifying the current summary record. When setting the CurrentSummary property, the Property procedure should verify that the value lies within the acceptable range.

■ The **Duration** property should be a read-only property that computes the duration of the call by subtracting the end time of the call from its start time. This property should return a string. The format of the string should be the elapsed minutes and seconds of the call in the form mm:ss.

■ The **LogBOF** property should be a read-only property indicating that the beginning of file has been reached. It should be True when the first record is the current record.

■ The **LogEOF** property should be a read-only property indicating that the end of file has been reached. It should be True when the last record is the current record.

■ The **ResolutionCode** property should be a read-only property. Its valid values are the integers zero (0) through two (2). You can use an enumerated type to represent these values.

■ The **SummaryCallType** property should be a read-only property that returns the call type of the currently selected summary record.

■ The **SummaryCallCount** property should be a read-only property that returns the count of the calls corresponding to the SummaryCallType.

■ The **SummaryAverageDuration** property should be a read-only property that returns the average time of the call of the currently selected SummaryCallType.

■ The **SummaryReferToSupervisor**, **SummaryProblemSolved**, and **SummaryCallBack** properties should return the count of the resolutions for the selected SummaryCallType. All these properties should be read-only.

In addition to these properties, the class should support several methods to read the information from a file and to locate different records. The following list describes the methods of the class:

■ The **FindFirst**, **FindNext**, **FindPrevious**, and **FindLast** methods should locate the first, next, previous, and last detail records, respectively.

■ The **FindFirstSummary**, **FindNextSummary**, **FindPreviousSummary**, and **FindLastSummary** methods should locate the first, next, previous, and last summary records, respectively.

■ The **Load** method should accept one argument—the disk file to load into the class instance. This method should return True if the file was loaded successfully and False otherwise. This information should be stored in a private array. Each time the program loads a record, it should redimension the array. After the array is loaded, the information should be summarized and recorded in a second array.

The MDI parent form should have one menu title with the caption **File** and two menu items, **Open** and **Exit**. The Open menu item should generate several actions. First, an instance of the class and an instance of the MDI child form should be created. You can keep track of each form and class instance with collections. Once the instance of the class is created, the user should be able to specify a file name to be loaded. The name of the file should match the Employee ID number. Two sample data files with Employee ID numbers of 3248.txt and 3249.txt have been provided.

The MDI child form also should have a menu system. Its **File** menu should match that of the MDI parent form, with the addition of a **Close** menu item. The Close menu item should unload the instance of the form and destroy the corresponding instance of the class. Figure EC5-4 shows the MDI child form at run time inside the MDI parent form.

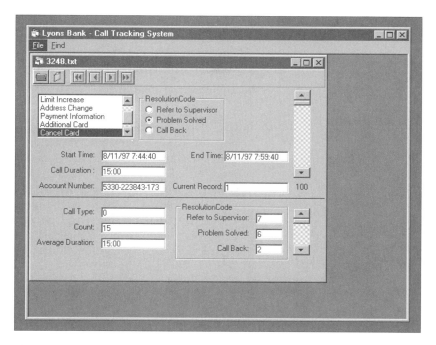

Figure EC5-4: MDI parent and child form at run time

As you can see from Figure EC5-4, the form is divided into two sections separated by a line. The first section displays detail information. The current call type appears in a list box, the current resolution code is displayed in an option group, and the start time, end time, and call duration are found in labels. In addition, the current record and account number are displayed. Note the vertical scroll bar shown on the right side of the form. This scroll bar should display the relative position of the current record pointer in the list of records. If the user moves the scroll bar, the current record should be updated accordingly, and the correct information should appear in the form. In addition, the user should be able to locate different records using the items on the Find menu and the buttons on the toolbar. The icons and bitmaps for the toolbar are stored in the **ExtraCases\Project5** folder on your Student Disk. They have the following file names: **First.bmp, Next.bmp, Last.bmp, Previous.bmp, Open.ico,** and **Close.ico**.

The second section of the form provides summary information. The scroll bar in this section should change the current call type and display the appropriate information, just as the scroll bar in the first section does.

In addition to including scroll bars to help the user locate information, the Find menu should contain menu items to locate the first, next, previous, and last summary and detail records.

Here are some hints to solving this problem:

■ Use an enumerated type for both the CallType and the ResolutionCode. This approach will make the program more readable and less error prone. Also, create a user-defined type to store the input records.

■ Create one collection to store each form instance and a second collection to store the class instance corresponding to the form. Use the Tag property of the form to keep track of the current form.

■ Make sure that you properly deal with the first and last summary and detail records. A common problem is to miss these records.

■ When an input file is read, load the detail array. Then, using that array as input, derive the information in the summary array. Note that these arrays should remain private to the Class module. The form accessing the Class module will retrieve elements using properties and methods.

Complete the following general steps to develop the application:

1. To view the completed application, run the file **ExtraCases\Project5\Credit.exe**. Click **File**, then click **Open**. Open the file named **3248.txt**. Note that you can also use the file named **3249.txt** for testing. Use the scroll bars to locate different summary and detail records. Exit the program.
2. Start Visual Basic.
3. Create a new project with an MDI parent form, an MDI child form, a Class module, and a standard module.
4. Create the menu systems and necessary objects for the MDI parent and child forms as described in the case and shown in Figure EC5-4.
5. Create the properties and methods of the Class module.
6. Save the forms and project.
7. Create an executable file for the project named **Lyons.exe**.
8. Test the program by using the input files.
9. Exit Visual Basic.

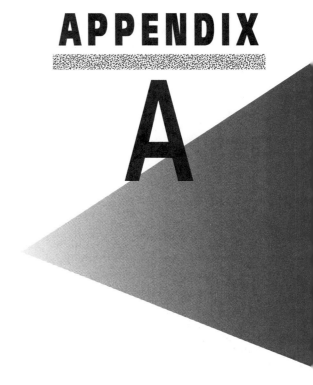
objectives

In this appendix you will:

- Locate and fix run-time errors
- Trace program execution
- Set breakpoints in code
- Use the Immediate window
- Add watch expressions
- Trace cascading events

Debugging

Techniques for Resolving Errors in a Visual Basic Program

Programming errors can occur when you are writing code or when you are running the program. A **programming error** (or **bug**) is any error that causes a program to end abnormally or to produce unexpected results.

Programming errors can be categorized into three different types: syntax errors, run-time errors, and logic errors. A **syntax error** occurs when you write a statement that Visual Basic cannot understand. For example, if you misspell a word such as "Private" when declaring a variable, Visual Basic will detect a syntax error. Syntax errors are generally detected when you enter statements in the Code window, when you run a program, or when you compile it. When you encounter a syntax error, look closely at the Visual Basic Help page that describes the statement or expression that caused the error, and make sure you have typed the statement correctly.

A **run-time error** arises from many sources. It can be caused when you use function arguments that have an incorrect data type. Trying to store data of the wrong data type into a property or variable can also generate a run-time error.

Run-time errors occur when your program is running and usually results from one of the following:

- A statement may attempt an invalid operation caused by an unexpected user action. For example, a user may have entered a letter into a text box when the program expected a number, and the program subsequently tried to use this value in an arithmetic expression without verifying the validity of the input first. These errors can be fixed by writing code to validate data, by creating error handlers for procedures, or both.

- Errors resulting from statements that attempt to store a value that is too large or too small into a variable cause numeric overflow or underflow. **Numeric overflow** conditions arise when an attempt is made to store a number that is too large in a variable of a particular data type; **numeric underflow** conditions arise when the number is too small. For example, the largest number that can be stored in an Integer is 32,767. Trying to store a number larger than this value will generate a run-time error. You resolve these types of errors by creating an error handler. An **error handler** or **error-handling routine** in your code determines whether it is reasonable for the program to continue processing.

A **logic error** occurs when the program does not perform as intended, but instead produces incorrect results. You generally notice logic errors at run time. For example, if you intended to compute the area of a rectangle, you would multiply the length of the rectangle by its width. If your program added the numbers rather than multiplying them, then the program would not generate the correct answer and you would have created a logic error.

The distinction between logic and run-time errors is sometimes unclear, because you might have coded an expression incorrectly. For example, a logic error would occur if you intended to add two numbers together but wrote statements to multiply them instead. When the program is run, the multiplication could generate a result that causes a numeric overflow error. In this situation, a logic error causes a run-time error.

To find and fix run-time and logic errors in program code, you must use a process called **debugging**. Visual Basic provides built-in tools that help you debug programs. The debugging tools described in this appendix will help you fix run-time and logic errors.

The Visual Basic Debugging Environment

Visual Basic checks for syntax errors when a program compiles and as it executes in the IDE. How a program is compiled and how errors are handled depend on settings in the Options dialog. These settings, which are saved to the Visual Basic environment, persist from one session of Visual Basic to the next. You should verify that they are correct before you begin to debug a program.

The Compile section of the General tab in the Options dialog contains two check boxes:

- If you check the **Compile On Demand** check box, Visual Basic will compile the current procedure and analyze it for syntax errors as it is run. A procedure will be compiled only when it is called for the first time. When the Compile On Demand option is selected, Visual Basic will not find all syntax errors until you execute all procedures in the program. While you

You may find it useful to display the Debug toolbar, which contains the more frequently used debugging commands. To display this toolbar, click View, then Toolbars, then Debug.

are writing and testing programs, checking this box will cause a program to start much faster. If you do not check the Compile On Demand check box, the syntax of the entire program is examined before any procedure begins executing.

■ If you check the **Background Compile** check box, the program will be compiled while the computer sits idle during run time. Background Compile can improve run-time execution speed the first time procedures are executed. This option is available only when Compile On Demand is checked.

Leaving the Background Compile option off will ensure that you realize the same results described in this appendix.

As with syntax errors, Visual Basic's handling of run-time errors depends on settings in the Options dialog. The Error Trapping section of the General tab contains three options to control the behavior of Visual Basic when a run-time error occurs:

■ When the **Break on All Errors** option button is selected, any run-time error will cause Visual Basic to enter break mode, open a dialog allowing you to activate the Code window, and display the line that caused the error in the Code window.

■ When the **Break in Class Module** option button is selected, errors in class modules will cause Visual Basic to enter break mode, allowing you to fix the error.

■ When the **Break on Unhandled Errors** option button is selected, Visual Basic will enter break mode when a run-time error that is not handled by an On Error statement occurs.

In this appendix, you will use the Break on Unhandled Errors setting so that any error handlers will execute without generating a run-time error.

To set the Compile and Error Trapping settings:

1 Start Visual Basic and open the project named **Appendix.A\RunTime.vbp**. Set the drive designator as necessary.

2 Click **Tools** on the menu bar, then click **Options** to open the Options dialog.

3 Click the **General** tab, as shown in Figure A-1.

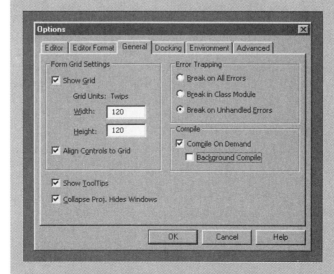

Figure A-1: Options dialog (General Tab)

4 If necessary, change the settings so that they match those shown in Figure A-1. The **Break on Unhandled Errors** and **Compile On Demand** options should be selected, and the **Background Compile** check box should not be checked.

Ignore the Form Grid Settings, Show ToolTips, and Collapse Proj. Hides Windows options.

5 Click the **OK** button to close the Options dialog and save the settings.

When you debug a program, you will likely have several windows open simultaneously, which might cause windows to obscure one another. Consider making the Immediate window and the Code window as small as possible so that you can see each on the screen. Also, try to keep windows from obscuring the toolbar. You will use the toolbar buttons often, and they might be hard to find if they are covered by another window.

Visual Basic's debugging tools consist of commands that allow you to suspend temporarily the execution of a program by entering break mode and to trace the execution of statements and procedures as they are called. You can execute each statement in the program line by line, with execution of the program halting when it reaches a specific statement or when the value of a variable or object changes.

When you suspend the execution of a program, your goal is to identify a particular problem. This process involves looking at the values of the variables and object properties in your program to see if they contain correct data. You can examine the contents of variables and objects using the Immediate, Watch, and Locals windows. You also use the Code window to examine the values of variables and to see which statement is currently executing. Using the debugging commands in conjunction with these windows as tools will help you locate and fix run-time and logic errors in your program.

Locating and Fixing Run-time Errors

Run-time errors can occur for many reasons. Unlike syntax errors, however, they do not occur during compilation of a program. Rather, these errors occur while a program is running and are caused by attempts to perform an operation such as storing data of the incorrect type into a variable or object property. Run-time errors also will arise if you perform invalid run-time operations on a database object like a Recordset. Because the problems with such operations are unknown until the program runs, the statements will not actually cause an error until they are executed.

When you write programs, you frequently can prevent run-time errors by writing code that carefully validates the correctness of user input before using that input in other parts of the program. Consider the following guidelines when writing code that processes input from the user:

- Validate numeric data entered into objects like text boxes before using it in computations. Use the IsNumeric and IsDate functions to check for valid numbers and dates, respectively.
- Required input, such as a first or last name, often must exist before certain other statements can execute. Compare the variable or object properties with the null string (vbNullString) to verify that the variable stores a valid value.
- Perform range checking to prevent overflow and other errors.

When a run-time error cannot be prevented, you should create an error handler in the procedure that will execute when the error occurs. Refer to the Help page for the OnError statement if you are unfamiliar with the process of creating an error handler. Inside the error handler, your code should determine the cause and severity of the error. Based on this information, it must decide which action to take. For example, a calculator program may receive user input that would cause a number to be divided by zero. In this case, the error handler should advise the user what happened, indicate the possible causes, and continue to let the user correct the problem.

When a run-time error occurs, one of two dialogs can open. One contains an OK button that, when clicked, activates the Code window and highlights the statement that caused the error. You can then edit the code to fix the error. The other dialog contains two items of information—an error number and a description. Error numbers are typically used by an error handler in your code. A well-designed program should alert the user to the problem and continue to run, even when the program encounters an error or the user gives the program invalid input.

To help identify the cause of a run-time error and how to fix it, always read the description of the error carefully to determine its nature. As a programmer, you can choose any of four actions in the second dialog:

- Click the **Continue** button to try to run the program from the point where the error occurred. Depending on the nature of the error, this option may be disabled, indicating that you cannot continue execution until you have fixed the problem.
- Click the **End** button to end the program. Visual Basic will then return to design mode.
- Click the **Debug** button to enter break mode and attempt to fix the program. The Code window will open and the statement causing the error will appear highlighted. After fixing any problematic statements, click the Start button on the toolbar to continue execution with the statement that caused the error. If the corrections require that you change variable declarations or add new variables or procedures, however, you must end the program and then restart it from the beginning.
- Click the **Help** button to get more information about the nature of the problem if you do not understand the meaning of the run-time error.

The underlying cause of a run-time error might stem from other statements in your program. As you analyze the error, you should therefore look at the statements preceding the run-time error to help identify the problem. When you write statements to perform arithmetic operations, for example, be careful to use the correct data type. If you use an Integer data type, the variable cannot store a number larger than 32,767. Attempting to store a number larger than that value in an Integer will generate a numeric overflow error. Generally, the solution to a numeric overflow error is to use a data type that can store a larger number or to check the user input to verify that it lies within a valid range. You also can write an error handler that will advise users of the problem so they can try to correct their input values.

Another kind of error, known as a **type mismatch error**, occurs when you try to store a character string in a numeric data type like Integer or Single. A type mismatch error can occur when a user enters invalid data into a text box that you intend to use as a number in other statements. To prevent a type mismatch error, call the IsNumeric or IsDate function on the user input. If the input is valid, then perform the desired processing; otherwise, display a message box advising the user to correct the input.

To find and fix overflow and type mismatch errors:

1 Run the program. Enter **.25** for the Interest Rate, **15000** for the Periods, and **1000000** for the Amount, then click the **Numeric Overflow** button. The Microsoft Visual Basic dialog opens with a run-time error message, as shown in Figure A-2.

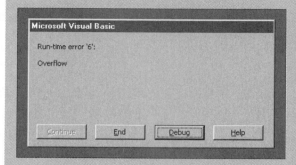

Figure A-2: Overflow error message

2 Click the **Debug** button to look at the statement that caused the error.

The line containing the error calls the PMT function. To allow the program to continue after it encounters this error, you can write an error handler that displays a message box describing the problem to the user. Although the program can continue to run, the PMT function will not produce accurate results.

3 Read the comments in the event procedure to create an error handler and to call the MsgBox function to fix the program.

4 Click the **End** button on the toolbar to end the program, then repeat Step 1.

The message box appears and the program handles the run-time error rather than terminating its execution.

5 Click the **OK** button to resume running the program.

6 Enter the text **abc** in the Interest Rate text box, then click the **Type Mismatch** button. When the run-time error occurs, click the **Debug** button.

This error is caused by an attempt to store text into an argument of the PMT function that can contain only numbers.

7 Read the comments in the command button's Click event procedure, then fix the program.

8 End the program and run it again. Repeat Step 6 to verify that the If statement validates the user input before calling the PMT function. If the input is not valid, then the program will not call the PMT function.

9 End the program.

In some cases, the statement that caused a run-time error may be only a symptom of the underlying problem. You found the cause of the previous errors by debugging the statement that generated the run-time error. A program will sometimes produce incorrect results but not generate a run-time error, however, or you may want to examine the statements that led to the run-time error. For example, if you called the PMT function with incorrect argument values, then the function call would generate a run-time error. You would need to first determine which argument was incorrect, then locate the statement that set the value of each of the various arguments.

Tracing Program Execution

Often, a program contains logic errors—that is, it produces incorrect results—but does not necessarily generate a run-time error. In addition, the actual cause of a run-time error is not always apparent. Debugging tools are most useful in these types of situations. When a program produces incorrect results, but you are not sure why, it may prove helpful to step through the statements in a program. Several commands allow you to follow the execution of a program line-by-line:

Programming tip

Function keys can be used instead of these toolbar buttons. You may find that you prefer using shortcut keys rather than the mouse. The F8 key is the shortcut for the Step Into button, Shift-F8 can be used instead of the Step Over button, and Ctrl-Shift-F8 can replace the Step Out button.

- The **Step Into** button allows you to execute one statement at a time. When you use this button, a single statement executes, then Visual Basic enters break mode. If the statement is a procedure call, the procedure declaration for the procedure that will be executed next appears highlighted in the Code window.
- The **Step Over** button works like the Step Into button. If the statement is a procedure call, however, then all statements in the procedure are executed, and Visual Basic enters break mode just before executing the statement following the procedure call.
- The **Step Out** button is similar to the Step Over button. When clicked, it executes all of the remaining statements in the current procedure.
- You also can alter the flow of execution during break mode by clicking a statement in the Code window, clicking Debug on the menu bar, then clicking Set Next Statement on the menu bar.

To use the Step Into button to examine statements and procedures:

1 Run the program. Click the **Exit** command button on the form. The word "program" in the message box is misspelled and the question lacks a question mark.

2 Click **Yes** in the message box to stop program execution and return to design mode.

3 Click **View, Toolbars, Debug** to display the Debug toolbar, if necessary.

Because you are not sure where the MsgBox function is called or where the prompt is set, you will step into the procedures in the program.

4 Click the **Step Into** button on the Debug toolbar to begin execution of the program. The Form_Load event procedure executes first, so the Code window becomes the active window and this procedure becomes highlighted, indicating that it will execute next. The next time you click the Step Into button, the first statement in the procedure will be highlighted.

5 Before executing the procedure, change the following statement from

```
mstrPrompt = "Do you really want to exit the porgram"
```

to

```
mstrPrompt = "Do you really want to exit the program?"
```

6 Click the **Step Into** button twice to execute the first statement in the procedure.

7   Continue clicking the **Step Into** button until the form appears. At this point, no procedure is executing. Rather, the program is waiting for the user to generate an event.

8   Click the **Exit** command button to generate the cmdExit_Click event. The Code window will become activated.

9   Continue to click the **Step Into** button until the message box appears. As you click the Step Into button, the statements become highlighted as they execute.

10   Click the **Yes** button in the message box.

11   Continue to click the **Step Into** button to execute the remaining statements in the ExitProgram procedure until the program ends and Visual Basic returns to design mode.

In addition to stepping through every statement in every procedure in a program, you can step through parts of a program or pause the program (enter break mode) and then continue executing statements one at a time. When debugging a procedure that calls other procedures, for instance, you do not have to trace through the statements in a procedure when you know it works correctly. Instead, you can use the Step Over button to execute all statements in a procedure and then suspend execution at the statement following the one that called the procedure. Furthermore, you can suspend execution at any time by clicking the Break button at run time.

To step into and step over a procedure:

1   Run the program. In run mode, the program will execute the statements without displaying them in the Code window.

2   Click the **Break** button on the toolbar. The toolbar disables the Break button, indicating that Visual Basic is in break mode. If you clicked one of the program's command buttons, Visual Basic would beep, indicating that the code for the button is not being executed.

3   Click the **Step Into** button to begin stepping through each statement in the program. Visual Basic will enter run mode.

At this point, no statement is executing. The form has been loaded and Visual Basic is waiting for an event to occur. When you generate an event, the Code window will become active again and you can continue to click the Step Into button to trace the program's execution.

4   Activate the form and click the **Exit** command button. The cmdExit_Click event procedure becomes highlighted in the Code window.

5   Click the **Step Into** button again. The ExitProgram general procedure becomes highlighted.

6   Click the **Step Over** button on the Debug toolbar. You already have verified that the ExitProgram general procedure works correctly. The procedure will execute and the message box will appear.

7   Click the **No** button to continue running the program.

When the ExitProgram general procedure finishes, Visual Basic will suspend execution and enter break mode at the statement following the call to the ExitProgram procedure. You can then continue to examine the code statement by statement.

8   Click the **End** button on the toolbar.

As you debug a program, you may find it useful to enter break mode and then step through each statement that you suspect is in error. When a general procedure appears to work correctly, you should step over it.

Setting Breakpoints

When you suspect that a problem is occurring in a particular procedure or that a particular statement is incorrect, you can suspend execution of the program at any executable statement by setting a breakpoint. A **breakpoint** is a program line at which you specify that the program stop execution and enter break mode. To set a breakpoint, you can locate the targeted statement in the Code window and then click the Toggle Breakpoint button or press the F9 key. The Toggle Breakpoint button is available only when the Code window is active.

When a breakpoint is set on a line, the line will appear in a highlighted color. To clear a breakpoint, click the line in question and click the Toggle Breakpoint button. When you run the program and it reaches a statement containing a breakpoint, Visual Basic will suspend execution of the program and enter break mode just before executing that statement. The line with the breakpoint will appear highlighted.

Once in break mode, you can use the Immediate window and the Step Into or Step Over buttons to identify problems in your code. You also can examine the values of variables and objects in the Immediate window. For example, if you determine that a function, such as PMT, is producing incorrect results, you might want to set a breakpoint just before the function is called and then look at the values of the arguments to determine the incorrect one.

To set a breakpoint:

1   Make sure that the program is in design mode. Activate the Code window for the **ExitProgram** general procedure, then move the cursor to the beginning of the following line:

```
pintReturnValue = MsgBox(mstrPrompt, mintButtons, mstrTitle)
```

2   Click the **Toggle Breakpoint** button 🖐 on the Debug toolbar.

The line appears highlighted in a different color.

3   Run the program. Click the **Exit** command button. The program will enter break mode just before executing the statement that calls the MsgBox function at which you set the breakpoint. You can now examine the statement.

Another IntelliSense feature is Visual Basic's ability to display, as a ToolTip, the current arguments to a function or the value of a variable. While the line containing the MsgBox function remains highlighted, move the mouse over the three function arguments named mstrPrompt, mintButtons, and mstrTitle. The values of these variables will appear in a ToolTip.

4   On the menu bar, click **Debug**, then click **Clear All Breakpoints** to clear the breakpoint you set in Step 2.

After setting a breakpoint, you will often want to examine the values of variables or the properties of objects. In addition to using the IntelliSense technology, you can use the Immediate window for this purpose.

Using the Immediate Window

You use the Immediate window to examine the values of variables and object properties and to change those values.

- You can call the Print method of the Debug object in a procedure. Calling this method causes the values of the arguments to be printed in the Immediate window.
- You can type Print statements directly in the Immediate window so as to examine the values of variables or object properties in the program. You can type statements in the Immediate window only while a program is in break or design mode. Most statements are valid only in break mode.
- You can execute a procedure by typing its name and arguments into the Immediate window.

Programming tip

. . . .

▶ **You can use a question mark (?) in place of the Print statement to save typing. In the Immediate window, the "?" has the same meaning as Print.**

To examine a program's values using the Immediate window:

1 Make sure that the Immediate window is active and that the program is in break mode. You may want to resize or move the Immediate and Form windows so that they do not obscure one another.

2 Type the statements into the Immediate window, as shown in Figure A-3. The value of the variable and the label's properties will print to the Immediate window. When you type in the ExitProgram statement, the ExitProgram procedure is called.

3 A message box appears. Click **No** to continue running the program.

enter these statements to display values

enter this statement to call the sub Procedure ExitProgram

```
Immediate
print mstrPrompt
Do you really want to exit the program?
print Label1.Visible
True
?Label1.Caption
Infinite Events
ExitProgram
```

Figure A-3: Immediate window

In addition to examining the values of properties and variables, you can use the Immediate window to set the values of properties and variables. When you change the values of variables in the Immediate window, the changes remain in effect only while the program is running. Once the program ends and Visual Basic enters design mode, those changes are lost.

To set properties and values from the Immediate window:

1 Make sure that Visual Basic is still in break mode.

2   Enter the following statements in the Immediate window, pressing the **Enter** key after each statement:

```
Label1.Caption = "New Caption"
mstrPrompt = "New prompt for the message box."
```

3   Run the program. The Infinite Events label at the bottom of the form now contains the text "New Caption."

4   Click the **Exit** command button. The message box displays the new prompt.

5   Click the **Yes** button to exit the program.

6   Run the program again. The change to the label's caption will be lost. Exit the program. The change to the message box prompt will also be lost.

Now you can set breakpoints explicitly at specific statements in a program—as many as you want. Furthermore, as you debug the program, you can add and delete breakpoints as necessary. For instance, if you remember that the Toggle Breakpoint button works like a switch, you can remove an existing breakpoint by clicking the line containing the breakpoint, then clicking the Toggle Breakpoint button. When you close the project or exit Visual Basic, all breakpoints disappear.

In addition to setting breakpoints, Visual Basic allows you to suspend the execution of a program by watching an expression.

Adding Watch Expressions

Watch expressions are similar to breakpoints, but allow you to suspend execution when a condition is True or when the value of an object or variable changes. Like breakpoints, watch expressions can be created, changed, or deleted while a program remains in design or break mode. Also like breakpoints, they are lost after you close a project or exit Visual Basic. The more watch expressions you define, the longer it will take the program to execute, because Visual Basic must check each watch expression for every statement that executes. Thus, when you debug a program, use watch expressions sparingly.

To add a watch expression to a project, you use the Add Watch dialog. Figure A-4 shows the Add Watch dialog.

enter expression to watch

define where to
watch expression

define what to do when
something happens to
the expression

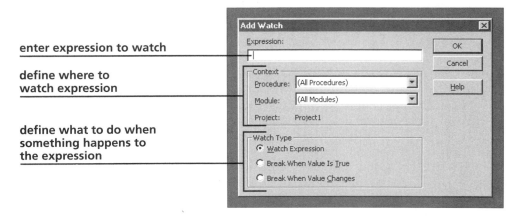

Figure A-4: Add Watch dialog

The Add Watch dialog contains three sections:

- The **Expression** text box is where you enter the expression you want Visual Basic to watch. If you want to watch the value of a variable, enter the variable name. To avoid typographical errors, you can copy the expression or variable from the Code window to the Add Watch dialog by means of the Windows Clipboard. The watch expression can consist of a variable, a property, or a procedure call.
- The **Context** section sets the scope of the expression to watch. It is especially useful if variables of the same name appear in different procedures. **Module** refers to the form module, standard module, or class module in a project that should be watched.
- The **Watch Type** section tells Visual Basic how to respond to the watch expression. If you select the **Watch Expression** option button, Visual Basic will display the value of the expression in the Watch window, but the program will not enter break mode when the expression becomes True or when it changes. Consider selecting the Watch Expression option button if you must print the value of a variable frequently when you reach a breakpoint. This option also helps trace the value of a variable when you use the Step Into button to watch the contents of a variable in detail. If you select the **Break When Value Is True** option button, Visual Basic will enter break mode whenever the expression is True. If you select the **Break When Value Changes** option button, Visual Basic will enter break mode whenever a statement changes the value of the watch expression.

The watch expressions you create appear in the Watches window. As their values change, the contents of the corresponding variables or expressions will appear as well. Figure A-5 shows the Watches window with the three watch expressions that you will create in this appendix.

watch expression but do not suspend execution

break when expression is true

break when expression has changed

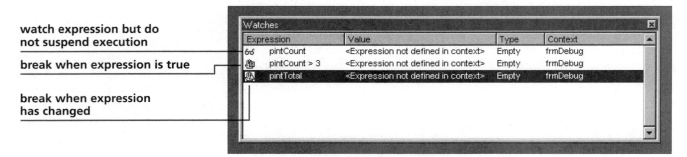

Figure A-5: Watches window

The Watches window contains four columns. The **Expression** column describes the watch expression and its type. The **Value** column displays the current value of the watch expression. Figure A-5 shows the Watches window while Visual Basic is in design mode; thus, the Value column contains the message "<Expression not defined in context>". Remember that local variables exist only while an event or local procedure remains active. When a procedure is not active, the value "Expression not defined in context" appears instead. The same message is displayed at design time. The **Type** column identifies the data type of the expression. The **Context** column defines the context of the watch expression—usually, the module name followed by the procedure.

When you create a watch expression, the Add Watch dialog tries to anticipate the context based on the active procedure in the Code window. If you want to watch a variable that is local to a specific procedure on a specific form, activate that procedure before setting the watch expression and Visual Basic will set the context for you.

To set a watch expression:

1   Activate the Code window for the **cmdAddList_Click** event procedure.
2   Click **Debug** on the menu bar, then click **Add Watch**.
3   Type **pintCount** in the Expression box.
4   In the Context section, make sure **frmDebug** is the module and **cmdAddList_Click** is the procedure.
5   In the Watch Type section, make sure that the **Watch Expression** option button is selected.
6   Click the **OK** button to add the watch expression.

A more complex expression that causes the program to enter break mode when an expression is True will help you discover why a For statement does not work correctly or why an array exceeds its bounds.

To set a watch expression that will enter break mode when the expression is True:

1   Click **Debug** on the menu bar, then click **Add Watch**.
2   Type **pintCount > 3** in the Expression text box. This expression will cause Visual Basic to enter break mode whenever pintCount is set to a value that is greater than three (3).
3   In the Context section, make sure **frmDebug** is the module and **cmdAddList_Click** is the procedure.
4   In the Watch Type section, click the **Break When Value Is True** option button to select it.
5   Click the **OK** button to add the watch expression.

In some circumstances, you might want to suspend the execution of a program when the value of a variable or expression changes. For example, if you are working with a payroll program that does not compute the gross wages correctly, you could write a watch expression to suspend execution whenever the value of the variable msngGrossWages (the variable assumed to store the gross wages) changes. This strategy would save time in locating the erroneous statement.

To set a watch expression that will enter break mode when an expression changes:

1   Click **Debug** on the menu bar, then click **Add Watch**.
2   Type **pintTotal** in the Expression text box.
3   Make sure **frmDebug** is the module and **cmdAddList_Click** is the procedure.
4   In the Watch Type section, click the **Break When Value Changes** option button to select it.
5   Click the **OK** button to add the expression.

Now that you have set the watch expressions, you can examine the values of these expressions as your program runs.

> **To test the watch expressions:**
>
> **1** Run the program. Click the **Add List** command button. The event procedure begins to execute. When one of the watch conditions becomes True, Visual Basic enters break mode. Then, the Watches window becomes active and the active watch expression is highlighted. The values of the watch expressions you created appear in the Watches window.
>
> **2** Continue to click the **Start** button ▶ until a run-time error occurs. Because Visual Basic is in break mode, the ToolTip displays the text "Continue." This error arose because one of the list items contains invalid data. Type the Print statements you used in previous steps in the Immediate window to find the item containing this invalid data. To correct the error, you could add the necessary statements to verify that the data consists of a valid number—perhaps by using a function such as IsNumeric.
>
> **3** End the program.

You can edit a watch expression when a program is in design or break mode. To edit a watch expression, click an expression in the Watches window, click Debug, then click Edit watch on the menu bar. Activating the Edit Watch dialog in this way allows you to change any of the settings in the watch expression.

You can delete a watch expression when a program is in design or break mode. To delete a watch expression, click the watch expression in the Watches window, then press the Delete key.

Tracing Cascading Events in a Program

In event-driven programs, improper logic can sometimes cause events to trigger one another indefinitely. Such a problem can arise when a statement causes a Change event in one object. That object, in turn, causes a Change event in a second object, and so on. If an object down the line causes a Change event in the first object, this program becomes circular—that is, the events will continue calling themselves indefinitely.

Consider this problem in a simple example involving two text boxes. After each text box receives input focus, it sets the focus to the other text box, and focus shifts back and forth between the two text boxes indefinitely. The program seems to lock up, and you cannot click any other object on the form while the text boxes continue updating one another. This phenomenon is called a **cascading event**. Whenever a program seems to lock up, you should press the Ctrl+Break keys, then check the relationship between the events in your program. Setting breakpoints and watch expressions might be the only way to determine the sequence of events.

> **To identify cascading events:**
>
> **1** Run the program. Click the text box containing the text **Text2**. The contents of the text boxes are updated each time a text box receives input focus. You cannot click the End button or the Exit command button to end the program.

2 Press the **Ctrl+Break** keys to stop the program and enter break mode.

3 In the **Text1_GotFocus** and **Text2_GotFocus** events, set a breakpoint in the line that reads **pintTimes = pintTimes + 1.**

4 Click the **Start** button ▶ to continue running the program. Again, the ToolTip is labeled "Continue."

5 Click the **Text2** text box. Visual Basic enters break mode and displays the Code window each time the variable pintTimes is updated in the GotFocus events of the text boxes.

6 Click the **Start** button ▶ several times to see the event procedures being called indefinitely.

7 Click the **End** button ■.

Identifying the exact cause of such a problem can prove difficult. You might need to set breakpoints or use the Step Into button in each suspect event procedure to see which events are called. The best solution to a cascading event problem, however, is prevention. You should use Visual Basic's debugging tools to diagnose errors interactively in your program. As the size of your programs grows, be sure to write and thoroughly test small pieces of code to fix any problems. As you continue developing the program, you can step over those smaller procedures that work properly.

When a variable has an expected value, try setting a watch expression that causes the program to enter break mode whenever the value of the variable changes. If a procedure seems to work incorrectly, set a breakpoint just before the first statement of the procedure, then trace each statement in the procedure, if necessary.

The Locals Window

The Locals window displays the local variables pertaining to the currently executing procedure. As the current procedure calls another procedure, the Locals window is updated to display the local variables pertaining to the new current procedure. Figure A-6 shows the Locals window.

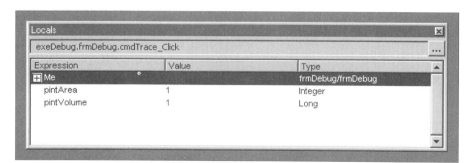

Figure A-6: Locals window

As shown in Figure A-6, the currently executing procedure is named cmdTrace_Click. It contains two local variables named pintArea and pintVolume. You can change the values of these variables by clicking the Locals window's Value column and changing the contents of the desired variable. To open the Locals window, you click View, then Locals Window on the menu bar.

S U M M A R Y

This appendix presented an overview of the tools that can be used to debug programs. These tools include tracing the execution of a program, setting breakpoints and watch expressions, and using the Immediate window. These tools are rarely used in isolation, but rather are most often used in conjunction with one another. As you become more familiar with these tools, you will likely develop your own techniques to debug programs.

To prepare a program for debugging:

■ Check the Compile On Demand check box. If you want to debug the code in an error handler, check the Break on Unhandled Errors option button. If you want to see all run-time errors, check the Break on All Errors option button. These options are located on the General tab of the Options dialog.

To trace the execution of a program:

■ To execute one statement at a time, click the **Step Into** button. To execute an entire procedure, click the **Step Over** button. To complete the execution of the current procedure, click the **Step Out** button.

To set or clear a breakpoint:

■ Activate the Code window and click the line where you want to set a breakpoint. Click the **Toggle Breakpoint** button. This action adds a breakpoint and highlights the line. To clear the breakpoint, repeat the process. All breakpoints will disappear when you exit Visual Basic.
■ Clicking Debug on the menu bar, then clicking Clear All Breakpoints will remove all breakpoints from the program.

To use the Immediate window:

■ While in break mode, enter print statements followed by an expression. The result of the expression prints.

To add watch expressions:

■ Click **Debug**, then click **Add Watch** to activate the Add Watch dialog. Enter the expression you want to watch. Enter the procedure to define the context. Set the watch type as desired. Depending on the watch type, Visual Basic will enter break mode when the value of an expression changes or when it becomes True.

objectives

In this appendix you will:

■ Create a program using the Application Wizard

■ Create a form using the Data Form Wizard

■ Add forms to a project using a template

Visual Basic Wizards

As part of the learning process, you have created programs by hand. In the process, you created one or more forms, added control instances and menus to those forms, and wrote code to accomplish specific tasks. You also created forms and control instances that interact with a database. You can automate the process of creating these common programming elements to some extent by using a wizard. A **wizard** is a series of dialogs that you complete to accomplish a complex task. Such dialogs allow you to create forms, add control instances and menus to those forms, and bind control instances to a database. When using a wizard, however, you neither create objects manually nor write code to determine the tasks performed by those objects. The wizard performs these steps for you. If you have used Microsoft Excel, you have likely taken advantage of a wizard to create graphs and perform other complex tasks. In this appendix, you will learn how to use Visual Basic's wizards.

In addition to wizards, Visual Basic supports **templates**. A template is a predefined form that performs a common task. For example, the template for a splash screen contains all of the control instances commonly associated with a splash screen. Instead of creating the splash screen from scratch, you can add the template to your project and modify it to suit your particular needs.

The Application Wizard

When you create a Visual Basic program, you begin by creating an empty project file with no visible objects or statements. You then create the necessary objects one at a time and write the code for those objects. A wizard can automate these tasks for you by helping to create a template for the different forms that make up a project. You can then expand on that template to make the program perform the specific tasks you desire.

The **Application Wizard** creates a functional project that you can execute. That is, it will generate the forms, menus, toolbars, and other program elements for you. After the Application Wizard creates the project, you can then modify the project's code and add additional control instances to perform any additional tasks you like. The Application Wizard can only create new programs, however. Although you can modify by hand programs created with the Application Wizard, you cannot use this wizard to modify programs.

Creating a project in Visual Basic with the Application Wizard is much like creating a document in Microsoft Word with a template. You select an item from the New Project menu to create the new project, then specify the characteristics of the project. In this appendix, you will create a program with the Application Wizard; you will not write any code.

To start the Application Wizard:

1   Click **File**, then click **New Project** on the menu bar. The New Project window appears, as shown in Figure B-1.

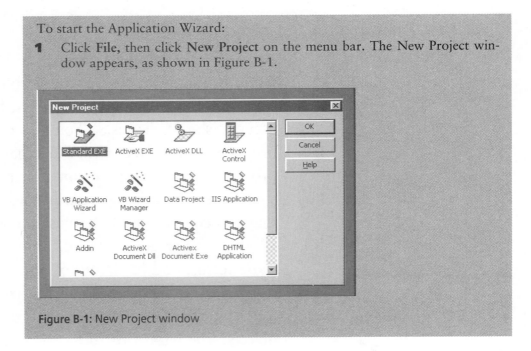

Figure B-1: New Project window

2 Click the **VB Application Wizard** icon, then click **OK**. The Introduction dialog opens, as shown in Figure B-2.

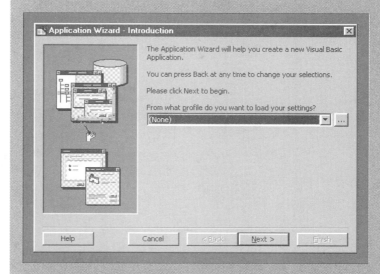

Figure B-2: Application Wizard—Introduction dialog

3 The Introduction dialog allows you to select a profile. A profile is generated when you save the options used to create a particular application. Because you have not used the Application Wizard before, you likely have no profiles on your computer. In this appendix, you will not create or use a profile. Click the **Next** button to create a new application without a profile. The Interface Type dialog appears, as shown in Figure B-3.

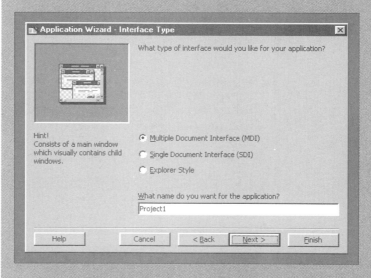

Figure B-3: Application Wizard—Interface Type dialog

4 In this dialog, you specify the name of your project and its type of interface. As shown in Figure B-3, you can create three different types of interfaces. In an application with an MDI interface, the windows that constitute the application appear inside of another window called a parent window. Both Microsoft Word and Excel use MDI interfaces. In an application with an SDI interface, the forms that make up the application can appear anywhere on the screen. In an Explorer Style interface, the user interface closely resembles the one used by the Windows Explorer program. In this appendix, you will use the Application Wizard to create a simple word processor with an MDI interface. Click **Multiple Document Interface (MDI)**, then click the **Next** button to activate the Menus dialog, as shown in Figure B-4.

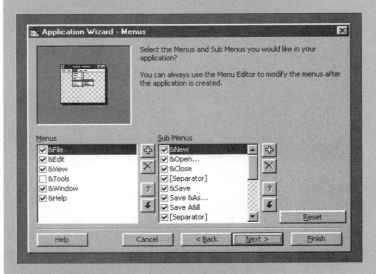

Figure B-4: Application Wizard—Menus dialog

5 As shown in Figure B-4, the Menus dialog contains options to define the menus used in the program. If you select the check box next to a menu, then that menu will be added to the project. If you do not check it, the menu will be omitted. To select or deselect a particular submenu, click the desired menu. The submenu pertaining to that menu will become activated. You can then check or uncheck the desired submenu check boxes. In this example, you will accept the default menus suggested by the Application Wizard. Click the **Next** button to activate the Customize Toolbar dialog, as shown in Figure B-5.

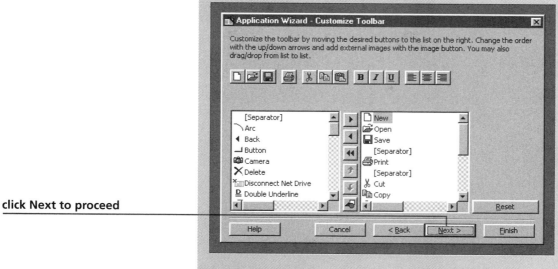

Figure B-5: Application Wizard—Customize Toolbar dialog

click Next to proceed

6 As shown in Figure B-5, the Application Wizard allows you to create a toolbar that will appear just below the menu created on the form. Again, you
will accept the default options. Click the **Next** button to activate the
Resources dialog, as shown in Figure B-6.

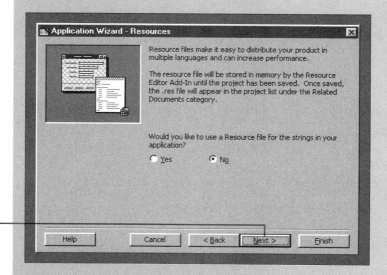

click Next to proceed

Figure B-6: Application Wizard—Resources dialog

7 A resource file allows you to save information with your program. The
Application Wizard has a default option, which does not include a resource
file for your program. Click the **Next** button to activate the Internet
Connectivity dialog, as shown in Figure B-7.

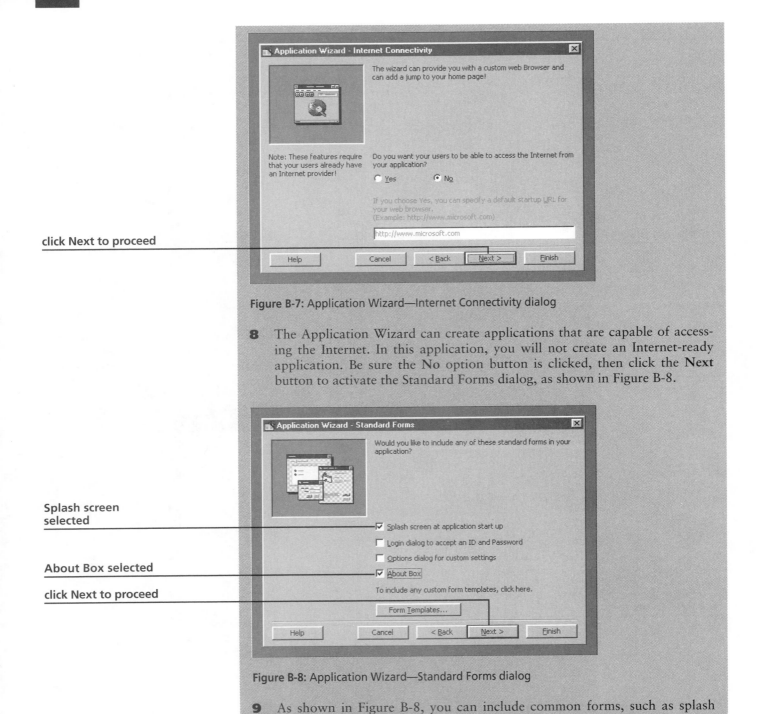

click Next to proceed

Figure B-7: Application Wizard—Internet Connectivity dialog

8 The Application Wizard can create applications that are capable of accessing the Internet. In this application, you will not create an Internet-ready application. Be sure the No option button is clicked, then click the **Next** button to activate the Standard Forms dialog, as shown in Figure B-8.

Splash screen selected

About Box selected

click Next to proceed

Figure B-8: Application Wizard—Standard Forms dialog

9 As shown in Figure B-8, you can include common forms, such as splash screens, in the application. Check the boxes shown in Figure B-8 to add a splash screen and an About Box to your project. Click the **Next** button to activate the Data Access Forms dialog, as shown in Figure B-9.

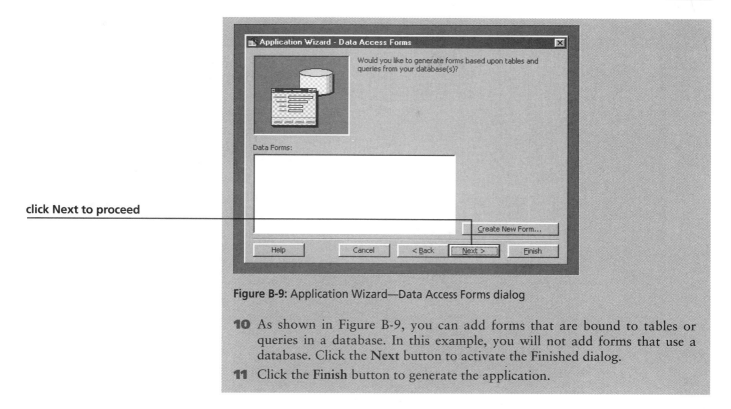

click Next to proceed

Figure B-9: Application Wizard—Data Access Forms dialog

10 As shown in Figure B-9, you can add forms that are bound to tables or queries in a database. In this example, you will not add forms that use a database. Click the **Next** button to activate the Finished dialog.

11 Click the **Finish** button to generate the application.

When you click the Finish button, the Application Wizard creates the forms that constitute the project. It also creates the specified objects on those forms and writes several lines of code. Upon its completion, the dialog shown in Figure B-10 will appear, indicating that the application has been created.

Figure B-10: Application Wizard—Application Created dialog

The Application Wizard has now created a functional program. It contains a menu, a toolbar, a splash screen, and several other program elements. You can now run the program to see what it does.

To execute the program created by the Application Wizard:

1 Run the program. The main form will appear, as shown in Figure B-11.

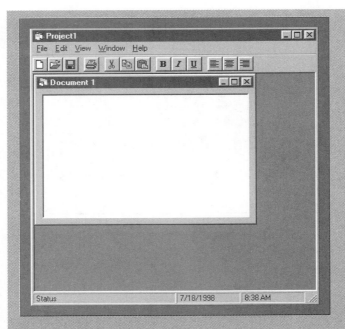

Figure B-11: Completed program

2 As shown in Figure B-11, the form contains a menu bar, a toolbar, a status bar, and a document window. This window is a simple word processor. One window contains the caption **Document1**. Enter your name in this window.

3 Buttons on the toolbar can apply formatting to your text. Select the text you entered and click the Bold, Italic, and Underline buttons to format the text.

4 The Application Wizard also created the code to open and save files. On the menu bar, click **File**, then click **Save**. The Save dialog appears, allowing you to specify the folder and file name.

5 End the program.

Although the Application Wizard wrote much of the code for your program, the code for some event procedures is incomplete. For example, if you try to execute certain menu commands, a message box will appear indicating that you need to write the code for that particular menu item. Also, you may want to change the code that executes when the user clicks certain menu items. In these cases, you can open the Code window for a particular form and write or modify code as necessary.

The Data Form Wizard

In addition to the Application Wizard, Visual Basic supports the Data Form Wizard. Unlike the Application Wizard, the Data Form Wizard is used to add a new form to an existing project rather than to create a new project. Like the Application Wizard, the Data Form Wizard can create new forms but it cannot modify existing ones. It creates forms based upon profile settings. These forms contain controls that are bound to a database table or query. The Data Form Wizard creates forms based upon Access or other types of databases.

The process of creating a form with the Data Form Wizard resembles the process of creating a new project with the Application Wizard. You simply complete a series of dialogs.

The **Database Type** dialog allows you to select an Access or a remote database. The **Database** dialog allows you to select the specific database to which the form will be bound. A form can be bound to only one database. After you select the database, the **Form** dialog appears, as shown in Figure B-12. This dialog allows you to specify the form name and its appearance.

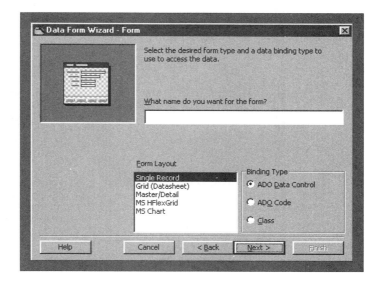

Figure B-12: Data Form Wizard—Form dialog

After you complete the Form dialog, the **Record Source** dialog appears. This dialog allows you to select the database table and the fields in that table that should appear on the form. Figure B-13 shows the Record Source dialog.

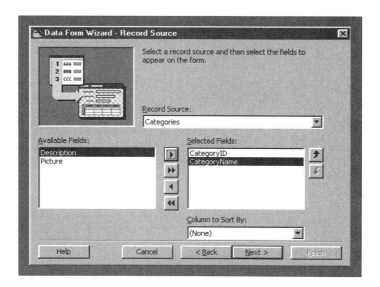

Figure B-13: Data Form Wizard—Record Source dialog

To complete the Record Source dialog, you select the table or query you want to use for the form in the Record Source list box. Once selected, the Available Fields list box displays the fields contained in the record source. The buttons located between the Available Fields list box and the Selected Fields list box allow you to select and deselect fields from the record source.

Next, the **Control Selection** dialog appears, as shown in Figure B-14.

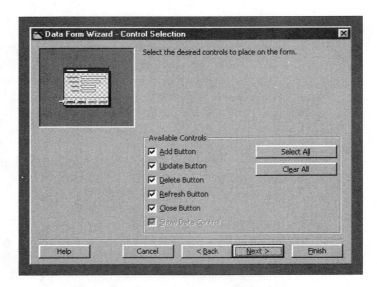

Figure B-14: Data Form Wizard—Control Selection dialog

This dialog allows you to define the buttons that appear on the form. These buttons enable the user to add, change, and delete records. You can also create buttons to refresh a recordset and close the form. Once you have specified all necessary information, the Data Form Wizard will create the form. You must, however, write the necessary statements to display the form. Earlier in this book, you displayed, hid, and unloaded forms using the Show and Hide methods and the Unload statement.

Templates

Although they are not expressly considered wizards, Visual Basic supplies several form templates that you can add to an existing program. Templates are form modules containing control instances and code to perform common tasks, such as displaying a splash screen. To add a form to a project with a template, you open the Add Form dialog, then select the New tab. The New tab lists the templates supported by Visual Basic. After selecting the New tab, click the desired template.

Visual Basic supports the following templates:

■ The **About Dialog** template contains predefined labels to display the application's title, version information, a textual description of the application, and any warning information related to copyright infringement.

■ The **Web Browser** template contains a toolbar to navigate the Web, a list box to select Web addresses, and an instance of the WebBrowser control to view information from the Web.

■ The **Dialog** template provides the OK and Cancel buttons supported by most modal dialogs.

■ The **Log in Dialog** template contains fields for the user to enter login and password information. Like most dialogs, it also contains OK and Cancel buttons.

- The **Splash Screen** template is used to implement a splash screen like the one you created in Chapter 6.
- The **Tip of the Day** template contains a picture box and text boxes intended to display ToolTips when the program first begins.
- The **Options Dialog** template is a tabbed dialog used to define options pertaining to the program.

S U M M A R Y

In this appendix, you saw how to create a new project using the Application Wizard.

To create a project with the Application Wizard:

- On the menu bar, click **File,** then click **New Project.** Double-click the **VB Application Wizard** icon.
- On the Introduction dialog, select a profile (if one is defined).
- From the Interface Type dialog, select the type of interface desired for the program.
- From the Menus dialog, select the menus that should appear on the form.
- From the Customize Toolbar dialog, select the toolbar buttons that should appear on the form.
- From the Resources dialog, select the desired option button to include or exclude a resource file from your program.
- From the Internet Connectivity dialog, select the Yes option button to enable Internet support from your application or click No to disable Internet support.
- From the Standard Forms dialog, select the form templates you want added to the program.
- If you want to generate forms based upon database tables, provide the necessary information in the Data Access Forms dialog.
- Click Finish on the Finished dialog to generate the application.

In addition to the Application Wizard, Visual Basic supports the Data Form Wizard. This wizard will create a new form with controls bound to a database table.

To create a form with the Data Form Wizard:

- Open a new or existing project.
- Click **Project,** then click **Add Form** to activate the Add form dialog. Click the **New** tab and select the **VB Data Form Wizard** icon.
- From the Introduction dialog, select a profile, if desired.
- From the Database Type dialog, select the desired type of database.
- From the Database dialog, select the name of the database.
- From the Form dialog, select the layout of the form.
- From the Record Source dialog, select the fields that should appear on the form.
- From the Control Selection dialog, select the buttons that should appear on the form.

To create a template:

- Click **Project,** then click **Add Form.** Select the **New** tab.
- Select the dialog icon or other template from the Add Form dialog.

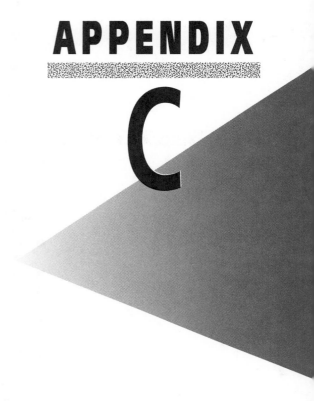

objectives

In this appendix you will:

■ Design a database
■ Create a new database
■ Create tables with fields
■ Define relationships to describe
   how different fields are associated
   with one another
■ Create queries based on a single
   table and many tables

Database Design

The Purpose of a Database

Before the advent of database technology, programs to manage large amounts of data were complex to create because traditional file-processing systems constituted the only means to process data files. In a **traditional file-processing system,** each computer application was designed with its own set of data files. Much of the data contained in these files likely existed in files for other applications as well. Furthermore, computer programmers had to sort data manually in several different physical files. If you wanted to create reports based on information in multiple files, then your program had to open each of the different files to obtain the necessary information, as well as examine and process each record (or entry) manually.

The same constraints applied if you wanted to change information in multiple files. The following list illustrates some of the disadvantages of traditional file processing:

- **Data redundancy**—In a traditional file-processing system, each application has its own files. This setup wastes disk space.
- **Inconsistent data**—When the same data is stored in different files, inconsistencies in the data can arise. For example, a person's name may be changed in one application's file but not in another.
- **Limited data sharing**—When each application uses its own files, few opportunities exist to share data between applications.
- **Low programmer productivity**—In a traditional file-processing system, programmers had to write statements to define each record and additional statements to control the input and output of data. As a result, programmers were not very efficient.

Using a database either minimizes or eliminates each of these problems. As a result, organizations now commonly take advantage of databases to manage their data.

Designing a Database

Before you create a database, you must design its structure. The structure of a database, known as the **schema**, describes each of the tables, the fields in those tables, and the relationships between the information contained in each table. Properly designing the database schema is an important step in creating a program.

The first task in designing a database is to identify each data item. A **data item** is the smallest unit of data that has meaning to the user. A data item is analogous to a field. Figure C-1 describes each data item stored in Atlantic Marketing's database, which you will create in this appendix.

Client ID	Salesperson ID
Last Name	Sales Date
First Name	Sales Amount
Telephone Number	Sales Description
Estimated Sales	
Notes	

Figure C-1: Atlantic Marketing data items

After identifying the data items, you should group them together such that data is stored only once. For example, the last name and first name of a client should exist only once in a single table. Data items are grouped together into data aggregates. A **data aggregate** is a collection of data items stored and referenced as a unit. A data aggregate is represented in a database as a table. Figure C-2 shows the various tables in Atlantic Marketing's database.

Clients Table	Sales Table
Client ID	Client ID
Last Name	Salesperson ID
First Name	Sales Date
Telephone Number	Sales Amount
Estimated Sales	Sales Description
Notes	

Figure C-2: Atlantic Marketing data aggregates

Each data aggregate or table can have a primary key, if necessary. A **primary key** uniquely identifies each record in a particular table. In Atlantic Marketing's database, a table named tblContact uses the Client ID field as the primary key. That is, each client ID stored in the table named tblContact uniquely identifies a particular record. Note that the Last Name field is not a primary key because a last name is not necessarily unique. For example, two or more people could have the last name of Smith. Multiple fields can, however, be combined as part of the primary key.

After creating each table, you can define the requisite associations. An **association**, or **query**, is a logical, meaningful connection between data items stored in one or more tables. In the database developed for Atlantic Marketing, client records are associated with sales records, as shown in Figure C-3.

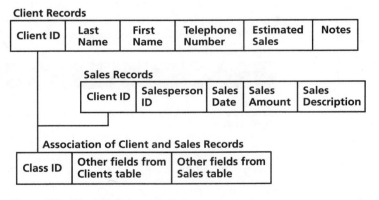

Figure C-3: Clients/Sales association

A common type of association is a **one-to-many association**. That is, for each data item stored in one table, there may be zero, one, or an arbitrary number of corresponding data items in another table. For example, the clients table includes one occurrence of the Client ID data item. In contrast, a sales table will have several occurrences of the Client ID data item, each identifying a sales record. When creating an association, each table must contain a common data item, such as the Client ID field.

Creating a Database

Microsoft Access offers the simplest way to create a new database for use with the Microsoft Jet database engine. With this type of database, all information is stored in a single file with the extension .mdb. This file contains all of the tables, fields, and other objects related to a particular database. The example in this appendix uses Access 97. If you are using another version of Access, your screens may differ slightly from those shown in the figures.

To create a new database:

1 Start **Microsoft Access**. The dialog shown in Figure C-4 will appear, allowing you to create a new database or open an existing database.

click to create a blank database

Figure C-4: Creating a database

2 Click the **Blank Database** option button, then click **OK**.

3 The File New Database dialog will appear, requesting the folder and file name of the database.

4 Select the folder named **Appendix.C**, enter the file name **AM_CMS.mdb**, then click the **Create** button. Set the drive designator as necessary. This choice will create an empty database.

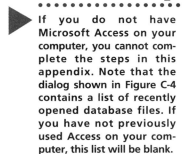

help

• • • • • • • • • • • • • • • •

If you do not have Microsoft Access on your computer, you cannot complete the steps in this appendix. Note that the dialog shown in Figure C-4 contains a list of recently opened database files. If you have not previously used Access on your computer, this list will be blank.

Although an empty database now exists, you have not defined the data items (fields), data aggregates (tables), or associations (queries) between the database tables. The next step in creating the database is to define the tables and the fields in those tables. You will then define how the tables are related to one another and specify how information in the different tables will be retrieved.

Creating a Table

Each table consists of one or more fields. Each field in a table must have a data type, just as a variable must have a data type. Figure C-5 lists the data types pertaining to the Microsoft Jet database engine.

Field Type	Description
Text	A Text field is a string containing letters, numbers, spaces, and special characters between 1 and 255 characters in length. Names and addresses, for example, are stored in Text fields.
AutoNumber	An AutoNumber field is most commonly used with primary keys. Microsoft Access will assign a new and unique number to each record created that can be used as the primary key to uniquely identify each record.
Currency	A Currency field is similar to the Number field in that it stores numeric data. A Currency field, however, eliminates the possibility of rounding errors when performing computations on very large or very small floating-point numbers.
Date/Time	A Date/Time field can store dates, times, or both, and is equivalent to the Date data type in Visual Basic. It is possible to perform calculations on date fields. For example, you can subtract one date from another to find out how many days have elapsed.
Memo	A Memo field is similar to a Text field in that it stores the same type of data, but Memo fields can store up to 64,000 characters.
Number	A Number field stores numbers like integers and floating-point numbers. Fields could be totals, amounts, accumulators, age, distance, weights, and size. As in Visual Basic, different types of numbers exist, such as integers and single.
OLE Object	An OLE Object is used for other applications that can be linked or embedded in a Microsoft Jet database.
Yes/No	A Yes/No field is equivalent to the Visual Basic Boolean data type. It stores True or False values.

Figure C-5: Data types supported by the Microsoft Jet database engine

Tables store information that does not repeat. For example, the Contact table for Atlantic Marketing contains fields for the Client ID, Last Name, First Name, Telephone Number, Estimated Sales, and Notes. Each of these fields is unique to a single client. Just as variable names must adhere to specific requirements, field names must also meet certain constraints:

- Field names can be up to 64 characters long.
- They can include letters, numbers, spaces, and characters, with three exceptions: the exclamation point (!), brackets ([or]), and apostrophe (').
- They cannot begin with a space.
- Each field should begin with the "fld" prefix followed by a descriptive name.
- Each table name should begin with the "tbl" prefix.

These naming conventions conform to the prefixes you have used for creating objects. Each field you create has properties because, in Access, fields are objects. The properties applicable to each field depend on the data type. The properties supported by a field include the following:

- The **Required** property allows you to specify whether a value is required in a field. If this property is set to Yes, you must enter a value in the field when entering a record.

- The **AllowZeroLength** property enables you to specify whether a zero-length string ("") is a valid entry in a field. This property applies only to Text and Memo fields.
- The **Indexed** property is used to set a single-field index. An index speeds up the processing on queries as well as sorting and grouping operations. For example, if you search for a specific employee name in a Last Name field, you can create an index for this field to significantly improve the performance of the search.

For Atlantic Marketing's database, you will now create the tables and the fields stored in those tables.

To create a table:

1 Click the **Tables** tab in the Database window, then click **New**. The New Table dialog will appear, as shown in Figure C-6.

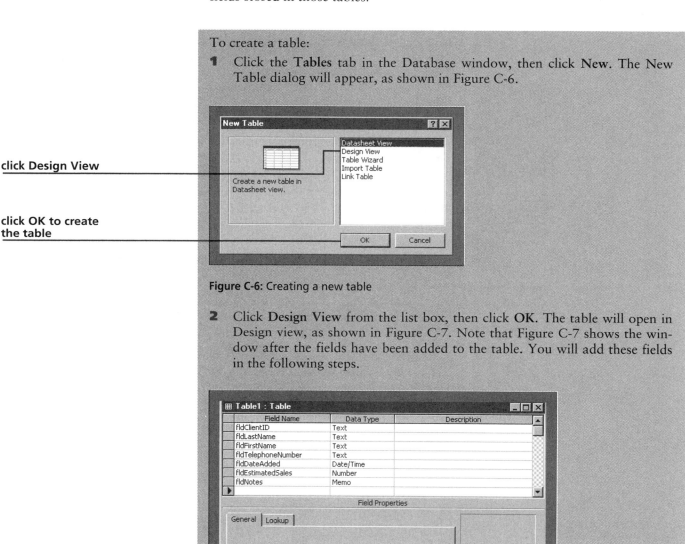

click Design View

click OK to create the table

Figure C-6: Creating a new table

2 Click **Design View** from the list box, then click **OK**. The table will open in Design view, as shown in Figure C-7. Note that Figure C-7 shows the window after the fields have been added to the table. You will add these fields in the following steps.

Figure C-7: Table Design view

The window is divided into two sections. In the first section, you define the field names, the data type for each of the fields, and the optional descriptions. In the second section, you define the properties of a particular field. The second section can be activated only when a field is selected. As shown in Figure C-7, five fields have been defined for the current table. Your screen will not contain these fields yet, because you have not defined them.

3   Enter the name **fldClientID** in the Field Name column, then press the **Tab** key to move to the Data Type column.

4   Select the **Text** data type from the list box. (The Text data type is the default option.) Because the field may store letters and numbers, this choice is the appropriate selection.

5   Click the **Primary Key** button 🔑 on the toolbar to make this field become a primary key. Thus each client ID must be unique. The Primary Key icon appears to the left of the field name.

6   Press the **Tab** key twice to make the cursor appear in the next row of the Field Name column. Create another field named **fldLastName** with a data type of **Text**. Set the Required property to **Yes**. Set the FieldSize property to **25**.

7   Set the field name to **fldFirstName** and set the data type to **Text**. Set the FieldSize property to **25**.

8   Create another field named **fldTelephoneNumber** with a data type of **Text**. Set the FieldSize property to **14**. Set the Required property to **No**. (This value is the default.) Set the AllowZeroLength property to **Yes**.

9   Create a field named **fldDateAdded** with a data type of **Date/Time**. Set the Required property to **No** (the default).

10   Create a field named **fldEstimatedSales** with a data type of **Number**. Set the Required property to **No**, then the FieldSize property to **Single**.

11   Create a field named **fldNotes** with a data type of **Memo**. Set the Required property to **No**, then the Allow Zero Length property to **Yes**.

Now that you have created each of the fields, you can save the table. Until the table is saved, no information about the table's characteristics is saved on the database.

To save the new table:

1   Click **File** on the menu bar, then click **Save**. The Save As dialog will appear, as shown in Figure C-8.

enter tblContact in the
Table Name text box

click OK to save table

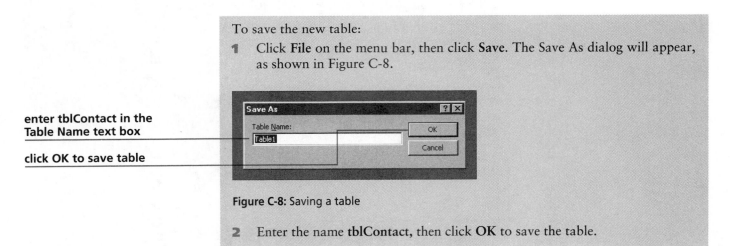

Figure C-8: Saving a table

2   Enter the name **tblContact**, then click **OK** to save the table.

3 Click the **File**, then click **Close** to close the Table Design window. The new table name now appears on the Tables tab in the Database window. Every table you create will appear on this tab.

In addition to the table for the contact information, you need a table to store the sales information. You must therefore create a second table named tblSales.

To create the second table named tblSales:

1 Click the **Tables** tab in the Database window, then click **New**. Click **Design View** from the list box, then click **OK**. The table will open in Design view.

2 Create the following fields:

Field Name	Data Type	Properties
fldClientID	Text	Required = Yes
fldSalespersonID	Number	FieldSize = Long Integer
fldSalesDate	Date/Time	Required = Yes
fldSalesAmount	Number	FieldSize = Single, Required = Yes
fldSalesDescription	Memo	Required = No

3 Click **File**, then click **Save** on the menu bar. Enter the name **tblSales**, then click **OK**. A message box appears indicating that there is no primary key defined. Click **No** in response to this dialog. Close the table.

Creating a Relationship

Microsoft Access is a **relational database**, which means that the data stored in multiple tables can be viewed as if it were stored in a single table. Furthermore, Access allows you to define the relationships between multiple tables. A relationship matches data between two tables using one or more fields from each table. For example, in the database for Atlantic Marketing, it does not make sense to create a sales record for a Client ID unless a corresponding Client ID exists in the Contact table. All relationships in Microsoft Access are created with the Relationships window.

To create a relationship:

1 Click **Tools**, then click **Relationships** to open the Relationships window.

2 Click the **Show Table** button on the toolbar, if necessary, to view the tables in the database. Figure C-9 depicts the Show Table dialog. Note that this dialog may be opened automatically when the Relationships window opens.

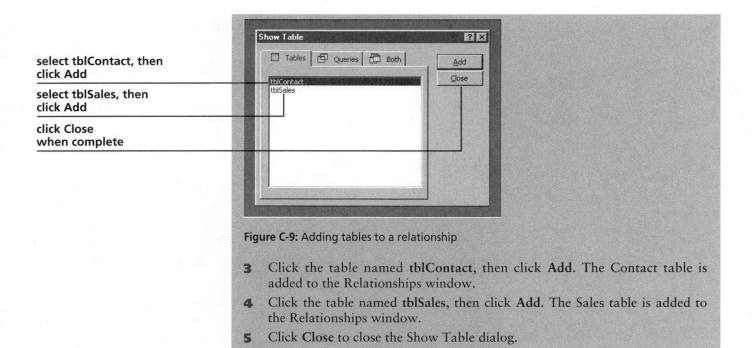

select tblContact, then click Add

select tblSales, then click Add

click Close when complete

Figure C-9: Adding tables to a relationship

3 Click the table named **tblContact**, then click **Add**. The Contact table is added to the Relationships window.

4 Click the table named **tblSales**, then click **Add**. The Sales table is added to the Relationships window.

5 Click **Close** to close the Show Table dialog.

Once you have added the tables that form the basis of the relationship, you need to create the relationship itself. In this case, you will create a one-to-many relationship between the tblContact and the tblSales tables. That is, for each Client ID in tblContact, many records with the same Client ID may exist in tblSales. A Client ID, however, cannot be created in tblSales unless a corresponding Client ID exists in tblContact. Once you specify this relationship, your program does not need to check that these rules are followed. Instead, if you try to add, change, or delete a record that would violate a relationship rule, the Microsoft Jet database engine will generate a run-time error. Your program can trap the run-time error with an error handler.

Now that you have defined the two tables involved in the relationship, you can create the relationship itself.

To create a relationship:

1 Click the field named **fldClientID** in the table named **tblContact** in the Relationships window.

2 Click and hold down the mouse, then drag the cursor to the field named **fldClientID** in the table named **tblSales**. The Relationships dialog will appear as shown in Figure C-10.

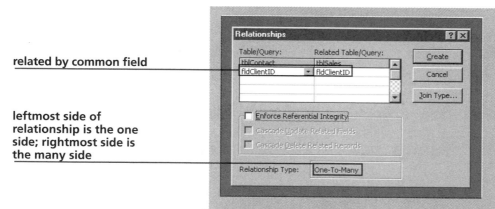

related by common field

leftmost side of relationship is the one side; rightmost side is the many side

Figure C-10: Relationships dialog

Notice that the tblContact table appears on the "one" side of the relationship and the tblSales table appears on the "many" side of the relationship. Also, note that the tables are related using the common field named fldClientID.

While creating a relationship, you can use a check box to enforce referential integrity. **Referential integrity** is the set of rules that are followed to preserve the defined relationships between tables as you add, change, or delete records. If you enforce referential integrity, the Microsoft Jet database engine prohibits the user from adding records to a related table when no corresponding record exists in a primary table. It also prohibits you from deleting a record in a primary table if such records exist in a related table.

In this relationship, the primary table is tblContact and the related table is tblSales. You want to ensure that a Client ID exists in the primary table for each record in the related table. Thus you should enforce referential integrity for this relationship.

Enforcing referential integrity on a relationship activates two other check boxes:

- If **Cascade Update Related Fields** is checked, then the content of the corresponding field in the related table will change automatically when the primary table is updated.
- If **Cascade Delete Related Records** is checked, then deleting a record from the primary table will delete all corresponding records in the related table as well.

The relationship for Atlantic Marketing should enforce referential integrity, and updates and deletions should be cascaded. That is, updating or deleting a record in the primary table should affect the corresponding records in the related table.

To enforce referential integrity on a relationship:

1 Click the **Enforce Referential Integrity** check box. Notice that the two check boxes below it are automatically enabled.

2 Click the **Cascade Update Related Fields** and **Cascade Delete Related Records** check boxes.

3 Click the **Create** button to finish creating the relationship. Your Relationships window should resemble Figure C-11.

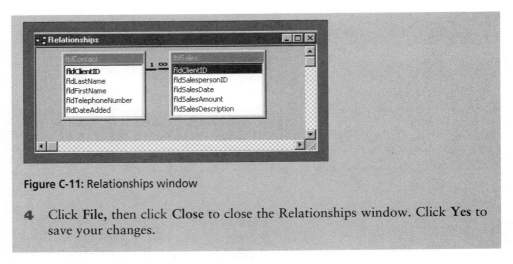

Figure C-11: Relationships window

4   Click **File,** then click **Close** to close the Relationships window. Click **Yes** to save your changes.

The database for Atlantic Marketing has a single relationship. If you create databases with many tables, however, you most likely will have several relationships.

Creating a Query

In addition to creating tables and relationships, you can create queries. A **query** is a formalized set of instructions to a database to return a set of records from one or more tables or perform an action on a set of records. A query enables you to ask a question about the data in your database.

In Microsoft Access, the most common way to create a query is to use Query by Example (QBE). The **QBE** user interface allows you to select the tables, the fields, and a method for sorting the records. You create a query using a procedure similar to the one you used to create a table. First, you activate the Queries tab in the Database window. Next, you click New to create a new query. Finally, you define the characteristics of the query and save the query.

To create a new query:

1   Click the **Queries** tab in the Database window, then click **New.** The New Query dialog will appear, as shown in Figure C-12.

click Design View

click OK to open the QBE window

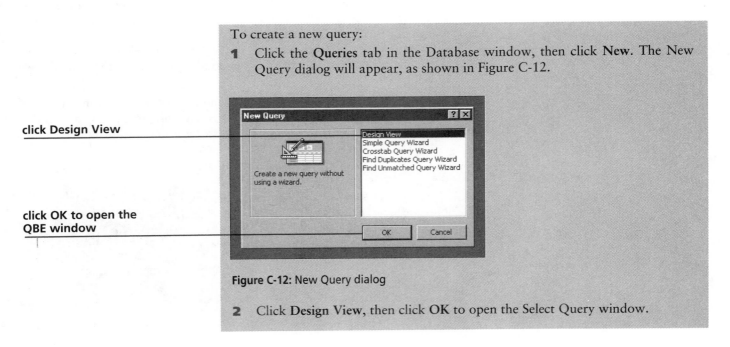

Figure C-12: New Query dialog

2   Click **Design View,** then click **OK** to open the Select Query window.

The next step in creating the query is to define which tables and fields it will use. The query you are creating will display each client record and corresponding sales records. You need to select both tblContact and tblSales. You can also create queries based on a single table or three or more tables.

To add the tables to the query:

1 Click **tblContact** in the Show Table dialog, then click **Add**.
2 Click **tblSales** in the Show Table dialog, then click **Add**.
3 Click **Close**. The two tables you added appear in the Query1: **Select Query** window, as shown in Figure C-13.

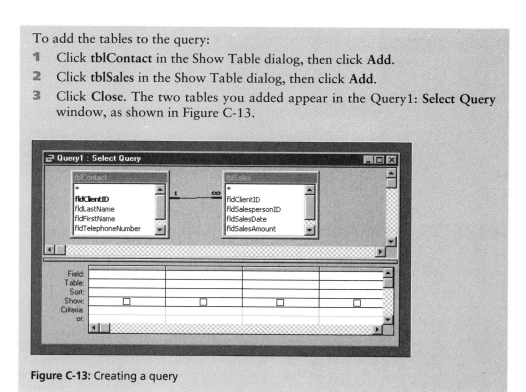

Figure C-13: Creating a query

Now that you have chosen the tables, you must select the fields. QBE allows you to select all of the fields in a table or just the fields required by the query. Your query will use all of the fields from both tables.

To add the fields to the query:

1 Double-click the field **fldClientID** in the **tblContact** table. The field will appear in the Query Design grid.
2 Repeat Step 1 for each field in **tblContact**. You may need to use the scroll bars.
3 Double-click the **fldClientID** field in the **tblSales** table.
4 Repeat Step 3 for each field in **tblSales**. You may need to use the scroll bars.

By default, each record in a query will appear in a random order. It is desirable to sort the records by a particular field. The Sort row in the Query Design grid allows you to control the order of the records. Atlantic Marketing's query should be sorted by last name. Two records with the same last name should be further sorted by the first name. You can sort records in ascending or descending order.

To sort the records in a query:

1 Click the **Sort** row in the **fldLastName** column in the Query Design grid.

2 Select **Ascending** using the list arrow.

3 Repeat Steps 1 and 2 for the field **fldFirstName.**

The query is now complete. You have selected the fields that make up the query and specified how the records will be sorted. Now you must save the query.

To save a query:

1 Click **File**, then click **Save** on the menu bar. The Save As dialog will appear.

2 Enter the name **qryContactSales**, then click **OK**.

S U M M A R Y

This appendix has introduced the process of creating a database, its tables, relationships, and queries. Although most databases you create will have more tables and relationships, the concepts here provide a template for creating more complex databases.

To create a new database:

- Start Microsoft Access. In the dialog that appears, click the **Blank Database** option button.
- When the New Database dialog appears, enter the folder and file name of a database.

To create a table:

- Make sure the database window is open and the Tables tab is active.
- Click **New** to begin creating a new table.
- Enter the desired field names, data types, and descriptions for each field in the table.
- Save the table.

To create a relationship:

- Click **Tools**, then click **Relationships** to open the Relationships window.
- Add the desired tables to the Relationships window.
- Use drag and drop to define the fields that make up a relationship. That is, select the desired field in the primary table and drag it to the field in the related table.
- When the Relationships dialog appears, specify whether referential integrity should be enforced and whether updates and deletes should be cascaded.

To create a query:

- Make sure the Database window is open and the Query tab is active.
- Select the tables that will be used in the query.
- Select the fields that will be used in the query.
- Save the query.

Index

& operator, 135
1stAirplanes_Click event procedure, 631, 646, 652, 654
3248.txt file, 720
3249.txt file, 720

A

ABC.ico file, 554
ABC_S.bas module, 565–566, 572–573, 583, 591, 593, 599
About Dialog template, A-26
about form, 268
About Microsoft Visual Basic command, 18
Access Help dialog, 474
accumulator, 278
accumulators
    adding to batch machine accumulators, 598
    batch machines, 569
    MDI child forms, 590
    testing grand total, 604
    updating, 576–577
    verifying update, 579–580
action query, 398–399, 406
Action variable, 250
Activate event, 191, 273, 275, 553
active control, 66
active object input focus, 73
ActiveX controls, 441, 680
    adding, 497–498
    adding to project, 442–443
    instance of, 443
    limiting, 444
    making available to project, 441–444
    memory, 444
    Microsoft Windows Common Controls, 497
    properties, 443
    Property Pages, 444
    setting design-time properties, 444
    types, 441–444

Add ActiveX control dialog, 443
Add Class Module command, 617
Add Class Module dialog, 617
Add Form dialog
    Existing tab, 268–269
    New tab, A-26
Add MDI Form command, 553–554
Add MDI Form dialog, 554
Add method, 498, 506, 623, 625
Add Procedure command, 150, 192, 634
Add Procedure dialog, 149–150, 192–193, 633, 634–635, 650
Add Record command, 278, 394
Add Watch command, A-13
Add Watch dialog, A-11–A-12
AddFuel method, 649–652
AddItem method, 316, 323–324, 330, 334, 346
addition (+) operator, 93
AddNew method, 220, 236–237
Advanced Optimizations dialog, 675, 677–679
AfterColInsert event, 467
AfterDelete event, 472
AfterInsert event, 465
AfterUpdate event, 465
Airplane class, 619–621, 632
Airplane class module, 618
Airplane object, 629–631
    adding to collection, 624
Airplane.cld module, 632
Airplane.cls class, 620, 648
Airplane.cls module, 618, 632, 634, 640, 643, 650, 655
AirplaneCurrent object, 650
AirplaneCurrent variable, 631
AirplaneID property, 619, 624–625, 632
    as default property, 646–648
    as write-once property, 648
AirplaneID variable, 620
AirplaneNew variable, 626
Airplanes collection, 622, 624, 628–629, 631–632
AirplaneType enumerated type, 640

AirplaneType property, 643–634
AirplaneType Property Let procedure, 641
Airsoft program
    computing total charges, 653
    declaring enumerated type, 640
    displaying arrival date and time, 636
    previewing, 614–615
    recording and displaying fuel charges, 651–652
    setting airplane type, 645–646
    testing, 626–627
    testing Click event procedure, 631
    testing Departure command button, 629
Align command, 71
Align property, 508–509
Alignment property, 456, 499
AllowAddNew property, 448, 464–465
AllowDelete property, 448, 464–465
AllowSizing property, 456
AllowUpdate property, 448, 464–465
AllowZeroLength property, A-33
alphabetizing properties, 16
AMCMS.mdb file, 228
amortization schedule
    detail lines, 299–301
    forcing new page, 302–303
    printing, 297–303
And logical operator, 133–134
annuities, future value of, 99–102
ANSI (American National Standards Institute), 397
App object, 666, 669–672, 709
    major and minor properties, 669–670
    reading properties, 671
    revision properties, 669–670
    setting properties, 670–671
Appearance property, 509
Append command, 458
Appendix.A\RunTime.vbp project, A-3

Application Wizard
    Application Created dialog, A-23
    Customize Toolbar dialog,
        A-20–A-21
    Data Access Forms dialog,
        A-22–A-23
    executing program created by,
        A-23–A-24
    Finished dialog, A-23
    Interface Type dialog, A-19–A-20
    Internet Connectivity dialog,
        A-21–A-22
    Introduction dialog, A-19
    MDI (Multiple Document
        Interface), A-20
    Menus dialog, A-20
    Resources dialog, A-21
    Standard Forms dialog, A-22
arguments, 44, 149
arithmetic operators, 93
Arrange Icons command, 587
Arrange method, 586
arrays, 326–335
    changing lower bound, 564–568
    dimensioned, 583
    elements, 326–327
    for storing from objects, 566
    locating element for form
        instances, 599
    management, 681
    memory, 327
    Private statement, 327
    redimensioning, 565
    referencing object variables, 564
    storing information in, 328–335
    subscripts, 326
    two-dimensional, 344–349
    variant, 349–352
Arrival dialog, 614
ArrivalDateTime property, 634–636
As keyword, 319
As type clause, 185, 590
Asc function, 139–140
ASC keyword, 426
ASCII-delimited files, 320–321, 352–353
assignment statements, 44–45
    converting numeric data to Boolean
        data, 121
    object variables, 231
    performing calculations, 93
associations, A-30
asType argument, 644

atAirplaneType variable, 644
AutoNumber fields, A-32
AutoShowChildren property, 553
AutoSize property, 499, 501–502
avoiding dead code, 682

B

BackColor property, 175, 553
.bas file extension, 709
Batch Machine Control command, 585
batch machines, 555–556, 559, 564
    accumulators, 598
    active number, 584
    adding accumulators to grand total
        accumulators, 598
    declaring first instance of form,
        566–567
    multiple concurrently, 582
    numbering, 564
    starting from forms, 584–585
    testing display of, 567
    verifying multiple instances, 585
BeforeColInsert event, 467
BeforeColUpdate event, 467–468
    arguments, 467
    verifying code, 469
BeforeDelete event, 472
BeforeInsert event, 465
BeforeUpdate event, 465
Beginning of File, 233–236
Bevel property, 499
binding, 561
bitmap files, 40
.bmp file extension, 40
BOF property, 223, 233–236
Bold property, 483
Bold.bmp file, 508
BoldStatus Private Sub procedure, 530
BoldStatus procedure, 532
Boolean data, 120–121
Boolean data type, 120
Boolean variables, 121, 233
BorderStyle property, 270, 448, 509,
    556–557
bound controls, 225–233, 449
    properties, 226
bound forms and databases, A-25
BoundColumn property, 444, 446
BoundText property, 444, 446, 460
break mode, 11, A-3

breakpoints, setting, A-9
Button collection, 504
Button objects, 504, 510, 538
    properties, 510–511
ButtonClick event, 503, 538
ButtonClick event procedure, 504, 511,
    538–539
ButtonHeight property, 509
buttons, 8–9
Buttons collection, 510, 512, 538
ButtonWidth property, 509
ByRef keyword, 149, 150
ByVal keyword, 149, 150

C

C++ programming language, 2–3
cab files, 686, 690
Cab Options dialog, 686
calculator program, 60–61
    Clear Values command button, 61,
        71, 102
    command buttons, 60
    Compute Future Value command
        button, 60–61, 102
    Create Future Value button, 70
    Exit command button, 61, 71
    Shape objects, 76
    testing, 101–102
    user interface design, 64–65
Call keyword, 152
Call statement, 154
    general procedure, 152
CallType property, 717
Cancel Edit command, 379, 394
CancelError property, 673
Caps Lock key, 496
Caption property, 27–28, 35, 96, 168,
    175–176, 220, 448, 455, 510,
    553–554, 564, 578, 584
CarrierName property, 624–625, 631
CarrierName variable, 620
Cascade command, 587
cascading events, A-14–A-15
CASE (Computer Aided Software
    Engineering), 62
Case Else clause, 130
Case Else statement, 644
Case statement, 578

cash register program, 166–167
    Clear command button, 167, 197
    computing delivery charge, 190–191
    computing output values, 167
    computing total, 192–197
    design criteria, 166
    event relationships, 195
    Exit command button, 167
    input validation requirements, 167
    option buttons, 167
    Print command button, 167, 196
    printing orders, 196–197
    resetting user interface, 197
    scroll bars, 167
    Shape control, 166
    visible and invisible objects, 183
Categorized tab, 31
categorizing properties, 16
cboProducts_Click event procedure, 351
CD command, 439
cdlCFBoth value, 484
cdlCFPrinterFonts value, 484
cdlCFScreenFonts value, 484
cdlPDNoPageNums flag, 520
cdlPDReturnDC flag, 520
cells, 448
    validating data, 467–472
Center in Form command, 72
Center.bmp file, 508
Change Colors dialog, 474
Change event, 73, 168, 172, 181–186,
    194–195, 516
Change Fonts dialog, 474
Chapter.01 folder, 10–11, 29
Chapter.01\Complete\Item1.bmp file, 11
Chapter.01\Complete\SPG_C.vbp file, 10
Chapter.02\Complete\IF_C.vbp file, 60
Chapter.03\Complete\DT_C.vbp
    project, 118
Chapter.03\Startup\DT_S.vbp
    project, 126
Chapter.04\Complete\MB_C project, 166
Chapter.04\Startup\MB_S.vbp
    project, 169
Chapter.05\Complete\AMCMS_C.vbp
    project, 206
Chapter.05\Startup\AMCMS.mdb file,
    221–222
Chapter.05\Startup\AMCMS_Svbp
    project, 209
Chapter.06\Complete\PB_Cvbp
    project, 266

Chapter.06\Startup\frmPrint.frm
    form, 269
Chapter.06\Startup\frmSplash.frm
    file, 269
Chapter.06\Startup\PB_S.vbp project, 268
Chapter.07\Complete\Start_C.vbp
    project, 312
Chapter.07\Startup\Product.txt file, 320
Chapter.07\Startup\Star_S.vbp project,
    314, 341
Chapter.08\Complete\Pay_C.vbp file, 378
Chapter.08\Startup\Pay_S.vbp
    project, 380
Chapter.09\Complete folder, 440
Chapter.09\Complete\Slight_C.vbp
    project, 439
Chapter.09\Startup folder, 438, 483
Chapter.09\Startup\Slight_S.vbp
    project, 442
Chapter.10\Complete\Demo.rtf file, 496
Chapter.10\Complete\PPS_C.vbp file, 496
Chapter.10\Startup\Cldsfold.ico file, 502
Chapter.10\Startup\Demo.rtf file, 525,
    527, 531, 540
Chapter.10\Startup\Demo1.rtf file, 525
Chapter.10\Startup\PPS_S.vbp
    project, 497
Chapter.11\Startup folder, 554
Chapter.11\Startup\ABC_S.vbp
    project, 554
Chapter.12\Complete\Air_C.vbp
    project, 615
Chapter.12\Startup folder, 618
Chapter.13\Complete\MT_C.vbp
    project, 667
Chapter.13\Startup folder, 676
Chapter.13\Startup\MT_S.vbp file,
    670, 686
check boxes, 168–171, 570
    selecting/unselecting, 181
    Visible property, 181–182
CheckBox control
    Caption property, 168, 170
    Click event, 169
    Name property, 170
    Value property, 169
CheckBoxConstants class, 181, 570
CheckBoxConstants enumerated
    type, 570
Checked property, 529
chkBurger_Click event procedure, 182

chkFrenchFries_Click event
    procedure, 182
chkSoftDrink_Click event procedure, 182
Chr function, 139–140
class instances, terminating, 655–657
class modules, 14, 614, 616–618
    creation of, 617–618
    customer service program, 717
    hiding data, 631–632
    methods, 717
    Name property, 66
    properties, 618–621, 717
    Public Sub procedure, 650
    Public variable, 618
    storing data, 563
classes, 4, 17, 558
    initialization, 632–633
    instances, 558, 616
    interface for, 616
    properties, 618–621
    viewing with Object Browser,
        620–621
classification functions, 121–122
Class_Initialize event procedure, 636, 654
Class_Terminate event, 655, 656
Clear All Breakpoints command, A-9
Clear method, 316, 340–342
Clear Values command button, 103
Click event, 538, 627
Click event procedure, 47, 70, 73, 100,
    103, 107, 126, 132, 135, 176, 183,
    195, 211, 400, 402, 408–409, 411,
    420, 461, 575, 630–631, 636, 651
    PrintFields function, 420
    PrintRecords function, 423
    Select Case statement, 169
Clng function, 96
Clnt function, 95
Close statement, 324–325
Close.ico file, 719
closing
    MDI child forms, 587–589
    MDI programs, 602–604
Clsdfold.ico file, 527
cmdAdd_Click event procedure, 330,
    333, 338, 346
cmdAddList_Click event procedure, A-13
cmdArray_Click event procedure, 678
cmdArrival_Click event procedure, 624,
    626, 645
cmdCalculate_Click event procedure,
    147, 152

cmdCancel_Click event procedure, 276, 285

cmdClear_Click event procedure, 197

cmdClearValues object, 103

cmdComputeFutureValue_Click event procedure, 102

cmdDeparture_Click event procedure, 628, 657

cmdDisplayImage object, 42–43

cmdDisplayImage_Click procedure, 43–44

cmdExit command button, 47

cmdExit object, 103

cmdExit_Click event procedure, 147, 324

cmdLookup_Click event procedure, 460

cmdMoveFirst_Click event procedure, 452

cmdNewQuotation_Click event procedure, 341

cmdOK_Click event procedure, 276, 284

cmdOverflow_Click event procedure, 678

cmdPrint_Click event procedure, 196, 275, 285, 291, 300, 303

cmdRandomize_Click event procedure, 667

cmdRecord object, 560

cmdRecord_Click event procedure, 575, 577, 593

cmdRemove_Click event procedure, 343

cmdSelect_Click event procedure, 414, 420–421, 424, 426, 428

cmdShell_Click event procedure, 673

cmdTrace_Click event procedure, A-15

cmdWriteQuotation_Click event procedure, 354

cnsgCol1 constant, 296

cnsgCol2 constant, 296

COBOL programming language, 2

code, 4

    assignment statements, 44

    comments, 46

    event procedure, 45–46

    functions, 44

    indenting, 44

    possible options for completing statement, 45

    printing copy of, 105–107

    program comments, 44

    whitespace, 92

Code window, 42–46, 92

    Close button, 46

    function procedures and sub-procedures, 149

    indenting continuation lines, 97

    Object list box, 42

    Procedure list box, 42

    Procedure View button, 81

    selecting object and event procedure, 42

    Toggle Breakpoint button, A-9

Collection object, 622, 630

    Count property, 623

collections, 288, 380

    adding items, 623–627

    creation of, 622–631

    default, 386

    examining individual objects in, 416–420

    finding item, 630–631

    Help page, 382

    Item method, 384

    names, 622

    numeric index, 382

    object references, 384

    one-based, 382

    referencing object in, 382–383

    removing items, 627–629

    storing references to like objects, 622

    string key, 382, 624, 630

    valid numeric index, 630

    zero-based, 382

color and control instances, 75

Color command, 540

Color dialog, 540

ColorConstants class, 83

colors

    for color palette, 474

    custom, 474

    RichTextBox control, 540

Column object, 455, 465

    Value property, 466

Column property, 448

columns

    aligning, 456

    defining layout, 456

    deleting, 458

    field, 455

    format, 455

    inserting, 458

    resizing, 458

    storing Event ID, 466

    title, 455

Columns collection, 455, 465

    fldEventID string key, 466

    numeric index, 465

    string key, 465–466

    Value property, 468

COM (component object modules), 441

combo boxes

    adding items to, 323–324

    creation, 316–317

    styles, 315–316

ComboBox control, 314–317, 442

    AddItem method, 316

    Clear method, 316

    ItemData property, 315

    ListCount property, 316

    ListIndex property, 316, 329–331

    NewIndex property, 315

    RemoveItem method, 316

    Sorted property, 315

    Style property, 315–316

    Text property, 316

COMDLG32.OCX file, 689

command buttons, 4, 39–40

    clicking, 70

    hot keys, 70

    properties, 69–71

    writing code, 42–46

CommandButton control, 4, 39–40, 69–71

    Caption property, 39, 70

    Default property, 70

    DisabledPicture property, 70

    DownPicture property, 70

    Enabled property, 70

    Height property, 39

    Left property, 39

    Name property, 39

    Picture property, 70

    properties, 107

    Style property, 70

    ToolTipText property, 70

    Top property, 39

    Width property, 39

commands, executing, 8

comments
    code, 46
    syntax rules, 80
    well-written, 80–81
    where to put, 82
    whitespace between, 92
Comments property, 669
common forms, A-22
CommonDialog control, 441, 443, 484,
    486, 496, 519–521, 524–525, 540,
    673, 680, 709
    applying formatting, 536
    CancelError property, 476, 478
    changing Visible property at run
        time, 482
    creating instance, 475
    FileName property, 479
    FilterIndex property, 476
    Flags property, 476, 484
    methods, 478
    model windows, 478
    Open dialog, 474–479
    Property Pages, 475
    setting design-time properties, 477
    setting properties at run-time, 475
Common\Tools\Vb\Controls folder, 438
Common\Tools\Vb\Regutils folder, 439
CompanyName property, 669
comparison operators, 95, 123–125
    precedence, 123
compilation, 673
compiling programs, 48
Complete folder, 10–11
completed examples, 29
component modules, 288
Component variable, 596–597
Component1 variable, 595
Component2 variable, 595
ComponentGravel variable, 595
Components command, 442, 498, 672
Components dialog, 441–442, 443,
    498, 672
ComponentSand variable, 595
Compute Payroll command, 408, 415
ComputeCharges method, 653–655
ComputeCharges Public Function
    procedure, 653
ComputeTotals general procedure,
    192–195, 336, 338
concatenating strings, 135, 402
configuration files, 684
Connect property, 220
Const statement, 185

constants, 83
    finding names of, 83–84
    intrinsic, 83–87
    message boxes, 146
    user-defined, 83, 185–188
contact management system, 206–207
    Edit menu, 210
    File and Edit menu items, 211–212
    File menu, 210
    Find menu, 210
    menu titles, 209–211
    submenus, 213–216
    viewing menu system, 214–216
containers, 176
Contents command, 18
continuation character, 97
control arrays, 177–180, 326
control boxes, 556
control instances, 17, 32–42, 480
    as active control, 66
    aligned on grid, 34
    alignment, 66
    balance, 66
    changing position and size, 281
    color, 66, 75
    consistency in size, 66
    Format menu, 71–72
    function grouping, 66
    Index property, 177, 190
    Locked property, 146
    modifying, 66–69
    moving, 35–36
    Name property, 177
    properties, 34–35
    redrawing, 283
    selecting multiple, 66–67
Control object, 480
ControlBox property, 556
controls, 3–4, 17, 179
    aligning borders, 71
    binding, 225–233
    centering on form, 72
    control arrays, 179
    copying and pasting multiple object
        instances, 178
    default properties, 384
    defining Click event, 190
    event procedures, 177
    grouping, 174
    Index local variable, 190
    Index property, 177

intrinsic, 32
making same size, 72
Name property, 177
option buttons, 178
output only, 146
program efficiency, 179
referencing specific element, 192
refreshing, 283
resizing at run time, 528
selection and use, 680
space between, 72
third-party add-in, 32
use with different languages, 441
user interface, 167
verifying visibility and invisibility,
    482–483
visibility, 480
Visible property, 480, 481
writing code for, 191–192
Controls collection, 480–483
coordinate systems, 289–290
copy buffer, 236
Copy command, 87
Copy (Ctrl+C) key combination,
    178–179, 182
copying and pasting
    multiple object instances, 178
    statements, 87
Count property, 623, 715
counters, 277
CPM (Critical Path Method), 62
Critical Message icon, 146
CSng function, 96
csngCol1 constant, 294
csngPl constant, 186
Currency fields, A-32
Currency format, 96
Current property, 715
CurrentAirplane class, 619
CurrentAirplane variable, 651
CurrentSummary property, 717
CurrentX property, 288
CurrentY property, 288
custom colors, 474
custom controls. See ActiveX controls
Custom property, 475
customer satisfaction program
    main form, 373–375
    questionnaire, 373
    splash screen, 373
    variant array, 375

customer service program
    call types, 716
    class module, 717
    input text file format, 716
    MDI child forms, 717–718
    MDI parent form, 718
    as MDI program, 717
    resolution codes, 716
    summary array, 717
    user-defined data types, 717
Customize dialog, 9
customizing toolbars, 9
Cut command, 458

D

DAO (Data Access Objects), 225
    DBEngine object, 381
    default methods and properties,
        383–384
    Default Workspace, 381
    hierarchy, 381–383
    opening databases programmatically,
        385–387
    programming the Recordset object,
        387–394
    referencing all other objects in, 381
    referencing another objects
        collection, 382
    referencing object in another
        collection, 382–383
    sessions, 381
    Workspaces collection, 381
DAO object library, 380–381
data aggregate, A-29
Data control
    buttons for navigating Recordset
        object, 225
    Caption property, 220–221
    Connect property, 220, 222
    connecting to Access database, 222
    DatabaseName property, 20,
        221–222
    EditMode property, 220
    First Record button, 229
    invisible, 236
    Last Record button, 229
    Name property, 221
    Next Record button, 229
    Previous Record button, 229

Recordset property, 223, 225, 230
RecordsetType property, 221, 237
RecordSource property, 220–221
retrieving query information, 224
Visible property, 235
Data controls, 444–445
    changing Visible property at run
        time, 482
    copy buffer, 464
    DatabaseName property, 446, 479
    Recordset property, 459
    RecordSource property, 446,
        459–460, 479
data files, 10
data flow diagrams, 62
Data Form Wizard, A-24–A-26
data hiding, 618–619, 631
data items, A-29
data lists, 314–317
data modeling, 62
data storage, 681
data types
    conversion, 187
    selection, 681
    user-defined, 589–602
    user-defined constants, 185
    variables, 87–88
data-aware controls, 225
Database object, 471, 560, 622
    db prefix, 386
    reference to collections and
        objects, 387
Database window
    Queries tab, A-38
    Tables tab, A-33
DatabaseName property, 220, 228,
    446, 479
databases
    adding records, 236–237, 240,
        465–466
    associations, A-30
    bound forms, A-25
    copy buffer, 236
    creation, A-31
    data aggregate, A-29
    data items, A-29
    deleting records, 241, 472–474
    designing, A-29–A-30
    displaying multiple rows and
        columns, 448–452
    dynasets, 221

inserting records, 398–404
locating records programmatically,
    452–453
manipulating records, 236–240
modifying records, 464
naming bound found, A-25
objects visible when opening, 482
one-to-many associations, A-30
open recordsets, 387
opening, 220–223
opening at run time, 479
opening programmatically, 385
preventing impossible operations,
    388–389
preventing user changes, 236
primary key, A-30
QBE (Query by Example), A-38
queries, 220, A-25–A-26, A-30,
    A-38–A-40
relational, 220
relationships, 220, A-35–A-38
removing records, 410–411
retrieving records, 413–429
searching for records, 243–247
selecting, A-25
selecting table and fields for
    form, A-25
table creation, A-31–A-35
tables, 219
types, 220
updating records, 237–241, 404–410
usage, 219–220
verifying correctness of data,
    247–251
viewing queries or tables, 222
Databases collection, 385–386, 471
DataField property, 226–228, 455,
    515–516
DataSource property, 226–228, 448, 450,
    515–516
datContact_Validate event
    procedure, 248
datCurrent variables, 141
date data, 140–143
Date data type, 88, 140
Date function, 140
Date variable mathematical
    operations, 141
DateDiff function, 141–142, 654

dates
    arithmetic operators, 141–142
    current, 140–141
    formatting, 96
    Date/Time fields, A-32
    Day function, 143
    dbEditAdd constant, 220
    dbEditInProgress constant, 220
    dbEditNone constant, 220
    DBMS (database management system), 219
    Debug object, A-10
    Print method, 277
datRegistration Data control, 459
db text intrinsic constant, 419
dbcEvents DBCombo box, 447
DBColumn control, 446
DBCombo control, 442–443, 444–447
    BoundText property, 460
    changing font, 486
    changing font and attributes, 484
    drop-down list of items, 444
    ListField property, 444
    properties, 445–447
    RowSource property, 444
    setting properties, 485
    storing Event ID, 447
    testing, 446
    visibility, 481
dbCurrent object variable, 559
DBEngine object, 381
dbgColumnNavigation constant, 451
dbgControlNavigation constant, 451
dbgGridNavigation constant, 451
dbgRegistration object, 457
dbgRegistration_BeforeColUpdate event procedure, 468, 470
dbgRegistration_BeforeDelete event procedure, 473
dbgRegistration_BeforeUpdate event procedure, 466
DBGrid control, 438, 442–443, 447, 448–452, 712
    active cell, 450
    aligning numeric data, 457
    Caption property, 455
    cells, 448
    changing font, 486
    changing Tab key behavior, 451
    Columns collection, 465
    copy buffer, 464
    creating instance, 449
    DataSource property, 449–450

deleting records, 472–474
events, 465–466
formatting columns, 453–461
locating first and last record, 452–453
losing focus, 450
making available, 438–439
making Event ID column invisible, 457
modifying data, 464–465
modifying row and column sizes, 458–459
navigating, 450
objects, 465–466
properties, 448, 464–465
Property Pages, 453–454, 465
setting general properties, 455
status information, 449
TabAction property, 451–452
testing, 450
testing formatting, 457–458
validating data, 467–472
visibility, 481
DBGrid32.ocx file, 439, 443
dbgrid.reg file, 439
dblBasicMatching constant, 445
dblExtendedMatching constant, 445
DBList control, 442–443, 479
    displaying item list, 444
    properties, 444–447
    reading and writing from database, 444
DBMS (database management systems), 397
dbText constant, 422
DDL (Data Definition Language) statements, 397
Debug toolbar
    Break button, A-8
    End button, A-8
    Step Into button, A-8
    Step Over button, A-8
    Toggle Breakpoint button, A-9
debugging, 62, A-1–A-16
    adding watch expressions, A-11–A-14
    break mode, A-3
    environment, A-2–A-4
    examining procedures, A-6–A-8
    Immediate window, A-10–A-11
    Locals window, A-15
    locating and fixing run-time errors, A-4–A-6

    setting breakpoints, A-9
    stepping into and over procedures, A-8
    tracing cascading events in programs, A-14–A-15
    tracing program execution, A-7–A-9
decision making
    comparison operators, 123–125
    If statement, 123–125
    multiway If statement, 128–129
    nested If statements, 126–129
decision trees, 62
default collection, 386
default form name, 27
default methods, 383–384
default objects, 386
default projects, 8
default properties, 383–384, 646–648
Default Workspace, 383
Default Workspace object, 386
DefaultValue property, 455
Delete command, 379, 394
Delete key, 37
Delete method, 241
Delete Old Payroll command, 411
DELETE statement, 410–411
deleting
    columns, 458
    objects, 37
    records, 241, 472–474
DepartureDateTime variable, 620
deploying applications, 684–695
deploying packages, 695
deployment, 684
Deployment Method dialog, 695, 697
Deployment Script dialog, 696
DESC keyword, 426
Description property, 253
design mode, 11–12
    forms, 34
    returning to, 13
designing databases, A-29–A-30
designing programs
    methodologies, 62–63
    user interface, 63–65
designing reports, 287–288
dialog, 119
Dialog template, A-26
dialogs
    controlling behavior, 476
    default filter, 476
    OK or Cancel button checked, 476
    opening and saving files, 441

Dim keyword, 90
Dim statement, 89–91, 323, 561, 572, 591, 625, 632
DisabledImageList property, 509
Display Image command button, 11, 44, 47
displaying/hiding toolbars, 9
division (/) operator, 93
.DLL extension, 441
DLLs (dynamic link libraries), 684
DML (Data Manipulation Language) statements, 397–398
Do loop, 276–278, 321–322, 420, 422, 521
    testing, 325
    Until keyword, 277
    While keyword, 277
docking, 13
    Double data type, 88
double-precision arithmetic, 681
DrawStyle property, 288, 304
DrawWidth property, 288, 304
Drive.ico file, 508
Duration property, 718
dynasets, 221

E

early binding, 561
eDaysOfTheWeek enumerated type, 571–572
Edit menu, 389
Edit method, 237, 239
Edit Record command, 378, 394
EditMode property, 220
eGravelSelected enumerated type, 576
eGravelSelected variable, 575–576, 578
eGravelType enumerated type, 573
Element not found message, 513
elements, 326–327
Else statement, 128
ElseIf statements, 128
Enabled property, 121, 274, 510
encapsulation, 568, 616
End command, 13
End Enum statement, 571
End Function statement, 150
End If statement, 123–124, 128
End of File, 233–236

End of Module (Ctrl+End) key combination, 154
End Property statement, 634
End property statement, 641
End Select statement, 130
End statement, 107
End Sub statement, 43, 150
End Type keyword, 590
EndDoc method, 289–290
EndTime property, 717
Enum statement, 570–580
enumerated types, 570–571, 639
    declaring, 573, 640
    declaring variables, 571–572, 574
    procedures returning, 571
    viewing in Object Browser, 573–574
enumerated variables, 574–575
enumeration, 569–580
environments, 13
EOF function, 321–323
EOF property, 223, 233–236
Err object, 253–254, 642
Error dialog, 119, 147
error handlers, 251–252, A-2
    run-time errors, A-4
error labels, 127
error-handling routines, A-2
errors
    logic, 104
    runtime, 104
    syntax, 103, 104
eSandSelected variable, 575–576, 578
eSandType enumerated type, 573
eToday variable, 572
Event Description combo box, 461
event descriptions, 438
event procedures, 42, 84, 148, 150
    control arrays, 177
    menu item creation, 216–217
Event Registration program, 438–440
event-driven programming language, 3
events, 12
    forms, 191–192
    regular time intervals, 273
    TextBox component, 81–83
.EXE extension, 441
executable files
    advanced optimizations, 677–679
    Allow Unrounded Floating Point Operations option, 678

Assume No Aliasing option, 677
native code, 674
P-Code, 674
Remove Array Bounds Checks option, 677–678
Remove Floating Point Error Checks option, 678
Remove Integer Overflow Checks option, 678
Remove Safe Pentium FDIV Checks option, 678
executable programs, 673–680
Execute method, 399, 402, 406, 408
executing commands, 8
executing programs, 672–673
EXEName property, 669
Exercise folder, 10
Exit command, 22, 439, 496
Exit command button, 147
    programming, 47
Exit For statement, 279, 417
Exit Function statement, 148, 252
Exit menu (Alt+X) hot key, 212
Exit Property statement, 634, 641
Exit Sub statement, 252, 254, 625
exiting Visual Basic, 22–23
ExitProgram general procedure, A-9
explicitly setting focus, 102–103
exponent (^) operator, 93
exposed data, 618
expressions, 93
    manipulating variables, 92–95
    precedence, 93–94
ExtraCases\Problem3\Survey.exe file, 376
ExtraCases\Project3\CompDemo.exe file, 375
ExtraCases\Project3\Comp.vbp project, 376
ExtraCases\Project3\frmMain.frm form, 375
ExtraCases\Project3\frmPage1.frm form, 376
ExtraCases\Project3\frmPage2.frm form, 376
ExtraCases\Project3\frmSplash.frm form, 375
ExtraCases\Project4 folder, 714
ExtraCases\Project5 folder, 719
ExtraCases\Project5\Credit.exe file, 720

F

False keyword, 120–121
Field object, 416, 422
   Name property, 419
   properties, 417
   Type property, 419
   Value property, 422
fields, 219, 417
   adding to queries, A-39
   AllowZeroLength property, A-33
   Indexed property, A-33
   names, A-32
   Required property, A-32
   selecting from table or query, 427–429
   types, A-32
Fields collection, 416–417
   Field object, 422
   printing column titles, 418
   printing each record in, 420
File menu, 22, 29
File Open dialog, 474
File Save As dialog, 474
Filename property, 476
files, 474
   beginning and end, 233–236
   dialogs for opening and saving, 441
   saving, 22–23
Filter property, 476, 525
FilterIndex property, 525
FindFirst method, 223, 243–246, 247, 397, 716
FindFirstSummary method, 716
finding item in collection, 630–631
FindLast method, 718
FindLastSummary method, 718
FindNext method, 243, 397, 718
FindNextSummary method, 718
FindPrevious method, 718
FindPreviousSummary method, 718
Finished dialog, 686, 694–695, 698
First command, 394
First to command, 378
First.bmp file, 719
Fixed format, 96
Flags property, 484, 520
floating-point arithmetic, 681
Floppy Drive dialog, 695, 697–698

focus, 73
   explicitly setting, 102–103
   folders, displaying contents, 15
Folder dialog, 695
Font dialog, 68, 440, 484, 496, 530, 535, 537
Font object
   properties, 483–484
FontBold property, 81–82, 85, 484
FontCount property, 483
FontItalic property, 484
FontName property, 288, 484
fonts, 474
   changing for visible object, 486
   monospace, 288
   panels, 500
   printer, 483–486
   printing reports, 290–291
   proportional, 288
   screen, 483–486
   setting properties, 484
Fonts command, 440, 486, 496, 536
Fonts property, 483
FontSize property, 289, 484
FontStrikethru property, 484
FontUnderline property, 484
For Each loop, 416–420, 422, 480–481
For loop, 279, 298, 337, 419, 423, 483, 667
   Step increment clause, 279
   terminating prematurely, 279
ForeColor property, 175
form instances
   creation of additional, 583–584
   locating array element for, 599
   multiple, 582–585
   removing from memory, 588
Form Load event procedure, 187
form module, 4, 14
Form object, 270
Form window, 16, 209
   activating, 15
   MDI mode, 28
   SDI mode, 28
Form1 form, 26–27
Form1 window, 26
Form_Activate event procedure, 273–274, 282–283, 671–672
Format function, 95–99, 331
Format menu control instances, 71

Format statement, 187, 194
   Fixed argument, 332, 334
FormatBold Private Sub procedure, 534
FormatItalic Private Sub procedure, 534
FormatTextBox sub procedure, 153–154
FormatUnderline Private Sub procedure, 534
formatting
   dates, 96
   numeric values, 96–99
Form_Load event procedure, 192, 291, 304, 312, 320, 322, 324–325, 345, 347, 351, 387, 390–391, 481–482, 526, 603, 671–672
Form_QueryUnload event procedure, 598
Form_Resize event procedure, 528
forms, 3
   adding, A-24–A-26
   adding pictures, 349–352
   adding scroll bars, 172–174
   appearance of objects, 16
   as classes, 558
   BorderStyle property, 270
   bound to tables or queries, A-23
   Caption property, 27–28
   centering controls, 72
   command buttons, 31, 39–40
   comments on purpose of, 92
   common, A-22
   control arrays, 179
   control instances, 32–42
   control limitations, 179
   default names, 27, 29
   defining buttons, A-26
   deleting objects, 37
   design mode, 34
   displaying, 272–273
   displaying labels, 33–38
   displaying Property window for, 26
   encapsulation, 568
   Error dialog, 119
   events, 191–192
   hiding, 275–276
   images or pictures, 40–41
   Label control, 33–38
   lines, 77–78
   making objects invisible, 482
   MDI programs, 552
   menu systems, 209

modal, 272
modeless, 272
moving objects, 35–36
multiple controls, 146
multiple instances, 552–559,
    582–585
multiple text boxes, 568
Name property, 27–29
naming, 28
printing, 196–197
properties, 556
property creation, 568–569
referencing current, 276
refreshing, 283
removing borders, 270
resizing, 528–538
Select Records command button, 420
setting font properties, 484
setting size and position, 31–32
setting startup position, 270
starting batch machines from,
    584–585
status bar, 498–503
storing accumulators in labels, 603
templates, 268
text boxes, 38
toolbar, 503–504
unloading, 272–273
user interface, 17
visual representation, 15
window state, 556
Frame control, 174
    BackColor property, 175
    Caption property, 175–176
    ForeColor property, 175
frames, 174–176
    copying and pasting objects into, 178
.frm file extension, 29
frmABCBatch class, 558, 562–563, 566
frmABCBatch form, 557, 559, 564–565,
    569, 574, 576, 584–586, 589, 593,
    596, 598, 600
frmABCBatch object variable, 562
frmABCBatch1 form instance, 563
frmABCBatch1 form module, 569
frmABCBatch1 object variable, 562
frmABCBatch1 variable, 588
frmABCBatch2 form instance, 563
frmABCBatch2 object variable, 562
frmABCBatch2 variable, 588

frmABCBatchRef1 object variable, 563
frmABCBatchRef2 object variable, 563
frmArrival form, 645
frmArrival module, 643
frmAtlanticContact form, 209
frmFuel form, 651
frmInstance1 object, 561
frmIslandCalculator form, 81
frmMain form, 268, 275, 285, 291, 295,
    300–302, 304, 614, 622, 624, 631,
    636, 644, 651, 657, 672–673
frmMB_S form, 169
frmPay form, 386, 389, 391–393,
    400, 402
frmPaymasterPayroll form, 415
frmPrint form, 275–276, 284–285, 296
frmSel form, 414, 418, 420–421, 424,
    426, 428
frmSettings form, 671
frmSPG file, 31
frmSPG form, 15
frmSPG_S.frm file, 30
frmSplash form, 270, 273–274,
    282–283, 671
frmStar.frm form, 314
frmStarlight Events form, 442
frmStarlightEvents form, 439, 453
frmTotals class, 558
frmTotals form, 565, 603
FROM clause, 414
FuelCharge property, 651–652
FuelCharge Public Property Get
    procedure, 650
Function keyword, 148
function methods, 649, 652–655
function procedures, 148, 150
    Call statement, 152
    creation, 149–151
    explicitly calling Call statements, 154
    Private keyword, 148
    Public keyword, 148
functions, 44, 148–149
    arguments, 44, 95
    calling, 44
    intrinsic, 44, 95
    type conversion, 95–96
    validating input, 140
FV (Future Value) function, 95, 99–102
    computing future value of
        investment, 100

G

Gantt charts, 62
gdbCurrent variable, 387, 415
general procedures, 148, 291, 299
    Call statement, 152
generic object variables, 560–561
gfrmABCBatchArray array, 566,
    584, 601
global variables, 89
GotFocus event, 553
GotFocus event procedure, 73, 81,
    85–85, 155, 273, 275
GoTo statement, 252, 254
graphical controls, 75–77
graphical objects, 303–304
graphical objects, printing, 303–304
graphics, 64
GravelHalt constant, 573
GravelQuarter constant, 573
GravelThreeQuarter constant, 573
grouping controls, 174

H

hDC property, 520–521
HeadLines property, 448
Height property, 31, 501, 509, 554
Help (F1) function key, 17, 22
Help library
    alphabetical list of Help topics,
        18–20
    available Help topics, 18, 21–22
    Close button, 22
    Contents tab, 18, 21–22
    differing topics in, 20
    hypertext, 17–22
    Index tab, 18–20
    Internet access, 18
    keyword search, 18
    navigation, 17
    pop-up menus, 22
    Print command, 22
    subsets, 18
Help menu, 17–18
    commands, 18
Help topics, printing, 22

Help window
   Contents, 21
   Controls Reference book, 21
   Display button, 19
   displaying information, 19
   Image Control topic, 21
   Index tab, 18
   Intrinsic Controls book, 21
   locating and selecting
      information, 19
   MSDN Library Visual Studio 6.0
      book, 21
   Reference book, 21
   visual Basic Documentation book, 21
Hide method, 275
hidden variables, 562–564, 632
hiding data, 631–632
hiding forms, 275–276
horizontal scroll bars, 171, 173
Horizontal Spacing command, 72
HotImageList property, 509
hot keys, 70–71, 209
Hour function, 143
HScrollBar control
   LargeChange property, 172
   Max property, 171
   Min property, 171
   SmallChange property, 172
   Value property, 172

I

.ico extension, 554
Icon property, 554, 557
icon sizes, 506
IDE (integrated development environment), 3, 13
If statement, 123–125, 151, 330, 346, 351, 419, 422, 426, 460, 482, 575, 629, 656
   different ways of writing, 125
   with logical operator, 135
   logical operators, 132
   multiway, 128–129
   nested, 126–129, 151
If...Then...Else statement, 124–125
Image control, 4, 40–41
Image object, 349
   appearance on form, 41
   displaying image in, 43

Height property, 41
Left property, 41
Name property, 41
Picture property, 45
Stretch property, 40
Top property, 41
Width property, 41
Image property, 510, 513–514
ImageCombo control, 497
ImageList control, 497, 504–508
ImageList property, 509
images, 4, 40–41, 504–508
   adding, 507
   describing purpose, 507
   height, 505
   setting properties, 505–506
ImageWidth properties, 505
Immediate window, A-10–A-11
Included Files dialog, 686
indenting continuation lines, 97
Index command, 18
Index property, 176, 499
Indexed property, A-33
infinite loop, 278
Information Message icon, 146
InitDir property, 525
Initialize event, 191, 272, 553, 632
Input # statement, 320–321, 351
input box, 244
input focus, 73
input validation program, 118–120
   Or logical operator, 134
InputBox function, 244–245, 354
Insert command, 458
Insert key, 496
INSERT statement, 398–404, 710
   building, 402–403
insertable objects, 441
Install Location dialog, 686
Install Locations dialog, 692–693
Installation Title dialog, 686, 690–691
InStr function, 138–139
Integer arithmetic, 681
Integer data type, 88
Integer data types, 681
integer division (\) operator, 93
Integer Variant data type, 349–350
IntelliSense technology, 45–46, 621
Interval property, 274
intrinsic constants, 83–87, 181
   strings, 137

intrinsic controls, 32
intrinsic functions, 44, 95
   strings, 136–140
IsDate function, 122, 250, 380–381
Island Financial program
   calculating interest rate, 98
   formatting initial investment, 97
   interest rate in month's, 99
   storing value as string, 97
IsNumeric function, 122, 151, 250, A-4–A-5
Italic property, 483
Italic.bmp file, 508
ItalicStatus Private Sub procedure, 530
Item method, 382–384, 623, 629–630
ItemData property, 315

J

Justify Private Sub procedure, 538

K

Kazmier, Leonard J., 63
Key property, 499, 502, 507–508, 510, 513–514, 538–539
KeyPress event, 73, 140
keywords, 43

L

Label control, 4, 33–38, 65–66, 72, 146
   Alignment property, 65
   Appearance property, 65
   BackColor property, 66
   BackStyle property, 65
   Caption property, 35, 66, 184, 341
   default name, 34
   Font property, 66
   ForceColor property, 66
   Height property, 37
   Left property, 37
   moving, 35–36
   Name property, 66

position indicator, 36
resizing, 36–37
resources, 146
Top property, 37
Width property, 37
Label object, 560
labels, 4, 33–38
properties, 65–66
Visible property, 179–180
LargeChange property, 172
Last command, 379, 394
Last.bmp file, 719
late binding, 561
lblDelivery_Change event procedure, 195–196
lblExtBurger_Change event procedure, 194
lblExtFrenchFries_change event procedure, 194
lblExtSoftDrink_Change event procedure, 194
lblPrompt object, 560
lblvsbQtyFrenchFries_Change event procedure, 187
lblvsbQtySoftDrint_Change event procedure, 187
LBound function, 583
Left property, 31
Left.bmp file, 508
LegalCopyright property, 669
LegalTrademark property, 669
Len function, 136
Line control
BorderColor property, 77–78
BorderStyle property, 77
BorderWidth property, 77–78
Line method, 289, 303–304
lines on forms, 77–78
list boxes
clearing contents, 340–342
looping through items, 335–338
removing item, 342–344
List property, 315, 335–336
ListBox control, 317–318
List property, 335–336
ListCount property, 316
ListField property, 444, 446
ListImage control, 505
ListImage object, 506
adding to ImageList control, 507–508
index value, 507
string key, 507

ListImages collection, 504, 506–507, 512
ListImages property, 504
ListIndex property, 316
lists of data, 314–317
ListView control, 497
Load event, 553
Load event procedure, 141, 186, 191, 272
Load Icon dialog, 554
Load method, 718
Load Picture dialog, 71
Load_Form event procedure, 328
LoadCurrentRecord private general procedure, 391
LoadFile method, 516, 521, 524
LoadPicture function, 44, 45, 351–352
loan amortization program, 266–267
adding form, 268–270
data entry form, 266
splash screen, 266
local variables, 126
displaying, A-15
Locals window, A-15
Locate menu, 389
Log in Dialog template, A-26
LogBOF property, 718
LogEOF property, 718
logic errors, 104, A-2
logical operators, 132–134
precedence, 133–134
login form, 268
Long Integer data type, 88
Lookup command, 471
looping through list box items, 335–338
loops
accumulator, 278
counters, 277
exiting, 278
infinite, 278
LostFocus event procedure, 73, 81, 85–86, 97, 138, 154, 376
Lyons.exe file, 720

M

MachineState array, 592–593, 595, 601
MachineState variable, 591
Major properties, 669
Make MT_S.exe command, 675
Make Project dialog, 48, 675
Make Same Size command, 72

Make SPG_S.exe command, 48
MatchEntry property, 445
MathError.exe file, 678
MathTek application, 666–668
MaxButton property, 556
mblnDirty variable, 524–525, 527
mblnRecordWritten variable, 656
mblnValid variable, 152
MDI (Multiple Document Interface), A-20
MDI child forms, 552, 601
accumulators, 590
arranging, 586–587
batch machines, 556
characteristics, 556–558
closing, 587–589
control box, 556
creation of, 557
customer service program, 717–718
differences from, 553
displaying, 557
Minimize button, 558
properties, 556
Restore button, 558
setting active and dirty state, 593
standard forms, 553
status information, 590
testing, 557–558
testing windows, 587
unloading, 588–589
window state, 556
MDI parent forms, 552, 554, 586
characteristics, 553–556
creation of, 554
customer service program, 718
displaying grand totals, 604
displaying MDI child forms, 556
menu system, 555
methods, 553
order entry system, 708
properties, 553
MDI parent window, 13
MDI programs
closing, 602–604
creation of, 552–558
forms, 552
MDI child forms, 552–553
MDI parent forms, 552–556
menu system, 554–555
standard forms, 552
mdiABC class, 557–558

mdiABC form, 555, 559, 565, 584–585, 604
mdiABC_S.frm form, 554
MDIChild property, 556–557
MDIForm_Load event procedure, 557, 566, 592–593
MDIForm_Unload event procedure, 604
MdtmArrivalDatetime variable, 632–633
mdtmArrivalDateTime variable, 635, 654
Me keyword, 276, 588–589
Me object, 592
Memo fields, A-32
memory
    ActiveX controls, 444
    removing form instances, 588
memory arrays, 327
menu bar, 8
Menu Editor, 209–210, 555
    Checked check box, 216
    Enabled check box, 216
menu item creation, 211
    Shortcut list box, 213
menu items
    Caption property, 209
    Click event as objects, 209
    creation, 211–213
    enabling and disabling, 212–213
    event procedure creation, 216–217
    followed by ellipsis (...), 211
    locating Click event procedure, 216
    Name property, 209
    needing name for duplicating names
        control array, 214
    not visible, 216
    separating, 213
    shortcut keys, 213
    submenus, 214
menu items, updating, 530–533
Menu objects, 482
menus
    adding to program, 208–217
    defining, A-20
    elements, 208
    hot key for menu title, 209
    hot keys, 209–210
    menu item creation, 211–213
    shortcut keys, 209
    titles, 209–211
    titles or menu item not visible, 216
    Windows look and feel, 211
menus, enabling/disabling menu items, 389–390

message boxes, 145–147
methodologies, 62–63
methods, 3, 102, 225, 616–617
    class module, 717
    CommonDialog control, 478
    creation of, 649–655
    default, 383–384
    MDI parent forms, 553
    naming conventions, 619
Microsoft Access, A-31
Microsoft DAO 3.51 Object Library, 381
Microsoft Data Bound List Controls, 443
Microsoft Jet database engine, 219, 245, A-31
    interface to, 381
    relational module, 397
Microsoft on the Web command, 18
Microsoft Windows, 2
microtasks, 63
Mid function, 138–139
MDI parent form, 714
MinButton property, 556
mintMonthTerm variable, 101
mintResult variable, 93
Minute function, 143
MinWidth property, 499
mnuBatch menu, 555
mnuBatchExit menu item, 555
mnuBatchExit_Click event procedure, 604
mnuBatchStart menu item, 555
mnuBatchStart_Click event procedure, 584–585
mnuBatchStop_Click event procedure, 589
mnuEditAdd_Click event procedure, 237, 393
mnuEditCancel_Click event procedure, 393
mnuEditDelete_Click event procedure, 241, 393
mnuEditRecord_Click event procedure, 238, 394
mnuEditRefresh_Click event procedure, 239
mnuEditUpdate_Click event procedure, 239, 253, 394
mnuFileExit_Click event procedure, 216
mnuFileNew_Click event procedure, 526
mnuFileOpen event procedure, 481

mnuFileOpen_Click event procedure, 478, 479, 482, 523
mnuFilePrint_Click event procedure, 217, 520
mnuFileSave_Click event procedure, 523
mnuFindLastName_Click event procedure, 245
mnuFindNavigateFirst_Click event procedure, 234
mnuFindNavigateLast_Click event procedure, 234
mnuFindNavigateNext_Click event procedure, 235
mnuFindNavigatePrevious_Click event procedure, 235
mnuFormatBold menu item, 529
mnuFormatBold_Click event procedure, 535
mnuFormatFonts_Click event procedure, 536
mnuFormatItalic_Click event procedure, 535
mnuFormatUnderline_Click event procedure, 535
mnuOptionsColor_Click event procedure, 540
mnuOptionsFonts_Click event procedure, 486
mnuPayrollComputePayroll menu item, 408–409
mnuPayrollDeleteOldPayroll menu item, 411
mnuPayrollReadASCIIFile menu item, 400, 402
mnuTabtoNewControl_Click event procedure, 451
mnuTabtoNextCellinGrid_Click event procedure, 451
mnuTabtoNextColumn_Click event procedure, 451
mnuWindowsArrangeIcons_Click event, 586
mnuWindwosCascade_Click event, 586
modal forms, 272
    displaying and hiding, 275–276
modeless forms, 272
modifying control instances, 66–69
modifying data, 464–465
modularization, 288

module-level variables, 89, 126
    declaring, 91–92
    Integer date type, 92
    Single date type, 92
modules, 14–15
    array changing default lower
        bound, 565
    general declarations section, 91
    organization, 681
    saving default names, 29
modulus (Mod) operator, 93
Monarch.exe file, 714
Monarch.mdb file, 714
monospace fonts, 288
Month function, 143
Move method, 281, 283
MoveFirst method, 229, 233, 240
MoveLast method, 229, 233
MoveNext method, 229, 230, 233, 423
MovePrevious method, 229, 233
moving Label object, 35–36
mrstContact object variable, 231
mrstCurrent variable, 390
MSComctl.ocx file, 498
MS-DOS prompt command, 439
MsgBox function, 145–147, 146, 152,
    248–249
msngCharges variable, 632
msngFuelCharge variable, 632, 651
msngGrossWages variable, A-13
msngInitialValue variable, 101
msngInterestRate variable, 90, 98
msngMonthRate variable, 93, 101
msngNumber array, 667
msngPrices array, 326, 345, 347
msngSquareFeet variable, 126
mstrAirplaneID variable, 649
MSVBVM50.DLL library, 674
MTNative.exe file, 676
MTPCode.exe file, 676
MT_S.exe file, 679, 689
MultiLine property, 516
multiple control instances, 67–69
multiple form instances, 582–585
multiplication (*) operator, 93
MVS (Multiple Virtual System), 2

N

name property, 27–28
Name property, 475, 484, 501, 505, 509,
    516, 554, 562, 568, 617
named formats, 96
naming forms and objects, 27–28
native code executable files, 674–675
NCR's ADS (Accurately Defined
    Systems), 62
nested If statements, 126–129, 151
nesting user-defined data types, 593–597
New command, 527
New keyword, 230, 231, 561–563, 565,
    567, 622
New Project command, A-18
New Project dialog, 7
New Project window, A-18
new projects, 25–29
New Query dialog, A-38
New Table dialog, A-33
NewIndex property, 315
NewPage method, 289, 302–303
Next statement, 417
Next.bmp file, 719
NoMatch property, 223
Not keyword, 482
Not logical operator, 133
Nothing keyword, 231, 562–563, 588
Now function, 140, 633
null string, 102
Num Lock key, 496
Number fields, A-32
Number property, 253
NumberFormat property, 455
numeric overflow, 104, A-2
numeric underflow, A-2
numeric values
    converting to string, 96
    formatting, 96–99

O

Object Browser, 83, 181, 570
    viewing classes, 620–623
    viewing enumerated types, 573–574
Object Brower command, 181

Object data type, 560
object library, 380
object references, 384, 558–561
    assigning, 415
object variables, 230–232, 559–564
object-oriented programming
    languages, 3
objects, 3
    copying and pasting multiple
        instances, 178
    DBGrid control, 465–466
    default, 386
    default methods, 383–384
    default properties, 383–384
    deleting, 37
    displaying properties, 27
    Enabled property, 233
    explicitly creating, 561–563
    insertable, 441
    methods, 3, 225, 616–617
    multiple references, 560
    name property, 27
    naming, 27–28
    properties, 3, 16, 616
    releasing when through with,
        587–588
    resizing, 36–37
    responding to events, 121
    series of statements acting on, 485
    setting properties, 44
    sizing handles, 34
    tab order, 73–74
    TabIndex property, 74
    templates for, 4, 616–618
    types, 480
    use with different languages, 441
    visibility, 121, 182
    visual representation, 15
    visually grouping, 75–76
    while program runs, 44–45
objGeneric object variable, 561
.OCX extension, 441
.ocx files, 684
.olb extension, 380
OLE Object fields, A-32
one-based collections, 382
OnError statement, 252, A-5
one-to-many associations, A-30

one-to-many relationship, A-36
Open command, 440, 483, 486, 496,
    525, 527
Open dialog, 268, 440, 474–479,
    524–525
    cldOFNoChangeDir flag, 471
    closing, 478
    displaying on-screen, 477–479
    valid flags, 476–477
Open Project command, 30
Open Project dialog, 11, 31, 686
Open statement, 319–320, 521
OpenDatabase method, 385–387, 471,
    559–560, 622
OpenFile general procedure, 524
OpenFile Private Sub procedure, 522
Openfold.ico file, 507
Open.ico file, 719
opening
    databases, 220–223
    files, 474
    projects, 10–11, 30
    operating systems, 2
    RTF (Rich Text Format) files,
        521–528
OpenRecordset method, 388, 399, 415,
    422, 471
    SELECT statement as argument, 413
    String variable, 413
operators, 93
    arithmetic, 93
    comparison, 95
    manipulating variables, 92–95
    nested parentheses, 94
    parentheses, 94–95
    precedence, 93–94
optAirplaneType_Click event
    procedure, 645
optDelivery_Click event procedure, 191
optGravelType option button, 574
optGravelType_Click event
    procedure, 576
optimizing programs, 680–682
Option Base statement, 564, 566
option buttons, 174, 176–177
    Click event procedure, 191
    clicking more than one, 175
    control arrays, 178
    copying and pasting multiple
        instances, 178
    not members of same group, 179
Option Explicit statement, 90–92, 620
option group, 174

OptionButton control, 174
OptionButton control instances, 176
Options command, 13, 620
Options dialog
    Advanced tap, 13
    Align Controls to Grid option, 34
    Background Compile check box, A-3
    Break in Class Module option
        button, A-3
    Break on All Errors option
        button, A-3
    Break on Unhandled Errors option
        button, A-3–A-4
    Compile on Demand check box,
        A-2–A-4
    Docking tab, 14
    Editor tab, 91
    General tab, 34, A-2–A-3
    handling errors, A-2–A-4
    run-time errors, A-3
    SDI Development Environment check
        box, 13
    syntax errors, A-2–A-3
Options Dialog template, A-27
optOrderBy control array, 426
optOrderBy option group, 427
optSandType option button, 574
optSandType_Click event procedure, 575
Or logical operator, 133–134
ORDER BY clause, 426–427, 460
order entry system, 706–714
output-only control, 146
overflow errors, A-4

P

Package and Deployment Wizard
    $(AppPath) macro, 693
    building package, 685, 687–688
    Cab Operations dialog, 690
    Cab Options dialog, 686
    $(CommonFiles) macro, 693
    Dependency File type, 688
    Deploy button, 685
    Deployment Method dialog, 697
    Deployment Script dialog, 696
    Finished dialog, 686, 694, 698
    Floppy Drive dialog, 697–698
    Included Files dialog, 686, 689
    Install Locations dialog, 686
    Installation Title dialog, 686,
        690–691

    listing project files, 689
    Manage Scripts option, 685
    Package button, 685
    Package Folder dialog, 685, 688–689
    Package to Deploy dialog, 696
    Package Type dialog, 685, 687–688
    Packaging Script dialog, 685, 687
    $(ProgramFiles) macro, 693
    Shared Files dialog, 693–694
    Standard Setup Package type, 688
    Start Menu Items dialog, 686,
        691–692
    $(WinPath) macro, 693
    $(WinSysPath) macro, 693
    $(WinSysPathSysFile) macro, 693
Package Folder dialog, 685, 688–689
Package to Deploy dialog, 696
Package Type dialog, 685, 687–688
packages, 684
    deploying, 695–699
    selecting, 686
Packaging Script dialog, 685, 687
Page property, 289
Panel object, 498, 500, 503
PanelClick event, 499
panels
    automatically updating, 502
    changing fonts, 500
    date and time, 502
    key status, 499, 502
    new, 500
    numeric index, 503
    properties, 499
    referencing, 503
    removing, 500
    string key, 503
Panels collection, 498, 501, 503
Panels property, 498
Paste command, 87
Paste (Ctrl+V) key combination,
    178–179, 182
Path property, 670
Paymast.mdb database, 378
Payroll Form command, 403, 408,
    411, 415
payroll program, 378–379, 405
    Do loop to read ASCII-delimited
        input file, 400
    opening database, 386–387
Payroll.txt file, 403–404
pbln variable, 530
pblnArg argument, 481
pblnDemo variable, 121

pblnFirst variable, 232–233
pblnFoundInactive variable, 600
pblnResult variable, 122
pblnValid variable, 123, 125
P-Code executable files, 674
pctlCurrent variable, 481–482
pdatEnd variable, 142
pdatMax argument, 149
pdatMin argument, 149
pdatStart variable, 142
Percent format, 96
PERT (Program Evaluation and Review Technique), 62
pfldCurrent variable, 419, 422
Philippakis, A.S., 63
picture boxes, 350–352
Picture property, 503
PictureBox object, 349–352
pictures, 40–41
    adding to forms, 349–352
pintCounter variable, 277–279
pintCurrentItem variable, 329, 337
pintElement variable, 600
pintIndex variable, 343
pintMachine variable, 600
pintMachineCount variable, 584
pintReturn variable, 248
pintSpaces variable, 419, 422–423
pintSquareFeet variable, 123, 125
planning programs, 9–10
Pmt function, 297–298
pnlText panel, 525, 527
Pointer tool, 67
precedence, 93
    comparison operators, 123
    logical operators, 133–134
Preserve keyword, 583
preventing user changes, 236
PrevInstance property, 669
Previous.bmp file, 719
price list creation, 317–318
primary key, A-30
Print (Alt+P) hot key, 211
Print command, 105, 521
Print dialog, 105–106, 474, 520–521
Print.bmp file, 508
Print method, 277, 289–293, A-10
Print object, 304
Print Options dialog, 267, 275, 287, 292
    page width, 292
    public variable, 284
Print statements, A-10
printCounter variable, 419

printer buffer, 290–292
    forcing information out of, 290
printer fonts, 483–486
Printer object, 483
    CurrentX property, 288, 293–294, 296
    CurrentY property, 288, 293, 296
    DrawStyle property, 288
    DrawWidth property, 288
    FontName property, 288
    FontSize property, 289
    Page property, 289
Printers collection, 288
PrintFields function, 420
PrintFields general procedure, 420
PrintFields Private Sub procedure, 418
PrintFile general procedure, 520
PrintForm method, 196, 216
PrintForm statement, 217
printing
    amortization schedule, 297–303
    each record in recordset, 420–423
    files, 474
    forms, 196–197
    graphical objects, 303–304
    Help topics, 22
    to Immediate window, 483
    lines, 303–304
    RTF (Rich Text Format) files, 519–521
printing reports, 288–292
    coordinate systems, 289–290
    detail lines, 299–301
    fonts, 290–291
    forcing new page, 302–303
    formatting page and column titles, 292–297
    relationship to page, 289–290
    report characteristics, 291–292
    ScaleMode property, 289, 292
    text width, 292
    title, 290–292
PrintIntField procedure, 301
PrintPageTitle procedure, 291, 295
PrintRecords function, 423
PrintRecords general procedure, 423
PrintRecords Private Sub procedure, 421
PrintSngField procedure, 301
PrintTitlePage general procedure, 304
Private keyword, 90, 148, 185, 571, 633
Private statement, 89–91, 561, 572, 591, 632
    arrays, 327

Private Sub keyword, 43
Private Sub procedure, 301
Private Sub statement, 43
Private variables, 618–619, 631–632
Procedure Attributes dialog, 647
procedure-level variables, 89
procedures
    adding, 150–151
    arguments, 149
    arguments passed by reference, 155–156
    arguments passed by value, 155–156
    beginning, 43
    ByRef keyword, 149
    ByVal keyword, 149
    ending, 43
    error handles, 251–252
    event, 148, 150
    examining, A-7–A-8
    explicitly calling, 148
    function, 148, 150
    general, 148
    naming, 150
    nested If statements, 151
    passing intrinsic data types, 155
    passing objects to, 155
    Private keyword, 150
    property, 150
    Public keyword, 150
    run-time errors, 251–252
    scope, 150
    stepping into and over, A-7–A-8
    sub, 148, 150, 153–156
processing text files, 319–326
Product2.txt file, 345
ProductName property, 669
profiles, A-19
program comments, 44
Program Design Concept, 63
program flowcharts, 62
programming errors, A-1
programming languages, 2–3
programming toolbars, 538–540
programs, 2
    accuracy, 62
    adding form, 268–270
    adding menus, 208–217
    common forms, A-22
    compiling, 48
    component modules, 288
    constant name, 84
    data storage, 681
    design mode, 12

designing, 62–65
designing user interface, 16
ease of understanding, 63
executable, 673–680
executing, 672–673
executing Application Wizard,
    A-23–A-24
execution efficiency, 63
form module, 4
forms, 3
improving efficiency, 179
Internet access, A-21–A-22
modification ease, 63
optimizing, 680–682
planning, 9–10
printing, 105–107
programmer efficiency, 63
project files, 4
readability, 186
resource files, A-21
run mode, 12
running, 12, 46–47
saving frequently, 5
setting edit state, 389
standard forms module, 4
startup form, 12
stopping, 13, 46
storing information, 87
terse, 188
testing, 5, 47
tracing execution, A-7–A-9
user interface statements, 5
user interface, 3
verbase, 188
well-written comments, 80–81
windows, 3
Windows-look-and feel, 3
writing code, 42–46
Programs command, 6
Programs submenu, 7
ProgressBar control, 497
Project Explorer, 439, 552
    activating, 14
    activating Form window, 15
    current project information, 26
    Form window, 16
    Form1 (Form 1), 26
    modules, 15
    Properties window, 16–17
    Toggle Folders button, 15
    View Code button, 15, 92
    View Object button, 15, 26, 67
Project Explorer button, 26
project files, 4

saving default names, 29
Project Properties dialog, 271, 554,
    670, 673
Project1 project, 620, 647
Project1 Properties command, 670, 675
projects
    adding ActiveX controls, 442–443,
        497–498
    adding forms, 268–270, A-24–A-26
    automatically making default, 8
    completed example files, 11
    defining menus, A-20
    form module, 14
    identifying modules, 15
    listing names and components, 14
    making ActiveX controls available
        to, 441–444
    modules, 14
    naming, A-20
    new, 25–29, A-18–A-24
    opening, 10–11, 30
    profiles, A-19
    recent, 31
    running, 12
    saving, 29–32
    single-form, 25
    startup files, 11
    templates, 25
    type of interface, A-20
    wizards, 25
properties, 3, 616
    alphabetizing, 16
    as arrays or fixed-length strings, 619
    Boolean values, 121
    categorizing, 16
    class module, 717
    command buttons, 69–71
    CommandButton object, 107
    control instances, 34–35
    creation of forms, 568–569
    default, 383–384, 646–648
    displaying, 27
    examining values, A-9–A-10
    fields, A-31–A-33
    forms, 556
    labels, 65–66
    MDI child forms, 556
    MDI parent forms, 553
    multiple control instances, 67–69
    name of, 17
    naming conventions, 619
    program runs, 44–45
    Public variables, 640

read-only, 635
read-write, 639–641
setting while, 44
storing values, 420
value of, 17
viewing and changing, 44
write once, 648–649
Properties command, 26, 444, 454, 465,
    501–502, 505
Properties window, 501, 504–505, 509
    activating, 16
    Alphabetic tab, 16–17, 28, 35
    Caption property, 28
    Categorized tab, 16–17, 26, 68
    current object information, 26
    DataField property, 227
    DataSource property, 227
    displaying, 26
    displaying object properties, 27
    Height property, 31
    Left property, 31
    modifying control instances, 66–69
    Name column, 17
    title bar, 27
    Top property, 32
    Value column, 17
    Width property, 31
Property Get ArrivalDateTime
    procedure, 635
Property Get procedure, 633–636,
    639–641, 643–644, 648–649
Property Let ArrivalDateTime
    procedure, 635
Property Let procedure, 633–636,
    639–641, 643–644, 648–649
Property Pages, 504–505, 538
    Buttons tab, 508, 511–514
    Fonts tab, 500
    General tab, 455, 506, 508–509
    Images list, 507
    Images tab, 507
    Insert Button command button,
        512–514
    Insert Picture command button, 507
    Layout tab, 456–457
    Open/Save As tab, 477
    Panels tab, 500–502
    Remove Button command button, 512
Property Pages dialog, 444, 454–455
Property procedures, 150, 639–640, 651
    read-only property, 635–637
    run-time errors, 641–646
    when to create, 640

proportional fonts, 288
prototyping, 62
prstArg variable, 422
prstCurrent recordset, 416–417
prstCurrent variable, 415
pseudocode, 62
psngExtPrice local variable, 332, 334, 346
psngHours Worked variable, 400
psngLastY variable, 296, 302
psngPrice variable, 322–323
psngSalesTax variable, 193
psngSubtotal variable, 193
psngTotal variable, 336–337
pstr string, 538
pstr2 variable, 135
pstrCounty variable, 130
pstrCurrent variable, 122
pstrData variable, 299
pstrEmployeeID variable, 400
pstrFROM variable, 415, 424
pstrIndex variable, 628–629
pstrInput variable, 151
pstrl variable, 135
pstrLastName variable, 245–246
pstrLine variable, 419, 422–423
pstrMessage variable, 248
pstrORDERBY variable, 427
pstrPicture variable, 346
pstrProduct variable, 322–323
pstrResult variable, 135
pstrSQL string, 409
pstrSQL variable, 401–402, 427, 460
pstrValue argument, 149
Public keyword, 90, 148, 185, 571, 633
Public statement, 89–91, 561, 572, 591
public variables, 283–285, 566, 591, 633, 639–640
  class module, 618
  form module, 568–569

Q

QBE (Query by Example), A-38
qryEmployeesPayroll query, 414–415
queries, 220, A-30
  adding fields, A-39
  adding tables, A-39
  displaying multiple records, 442
  QBE (Query by Example), A-38

retrieving records from, 413
saving, A-40
selecting all fields, 415
selecting fields from, 427–429
sorting records, A-40
viewing, 222
query analysis, 62
QueryUnload event, 596, 601–604
quotation program, 312–313
  Add Item command button, 329–330, 332
  adding pictures to forms, 349–352
  array for storing information, 326–335
  clearing contents of list box, 340–342
  combo box creation, 316–317
  discounted prices, 344–349
  looping through list box items, 335–338
  modifying, 340
  New Quotation command button, 341–342
  opening, 314
  price list creation, 317–318
  processing text files, 319–326
  Product combo box, 328–335
  quotation output, 354
  Remove Item command button, 342–344
  removing item from list box, 342–344
  two-dimensional array, 344–349
  writing to text files, 352–356
Quote.txt file, 356

R

radio buttons, 174
Raise method, 642
random number generator, 666
Randomize function, 666–667
range checking, 120
  And logical operator, 134
RDBMS (relational database management system), 220
Read ASCII File command, 403
reading text files, 320–323
read-write properties, 639–641
RecordCount property, 471

records, 219
  adding, 236–237, 240, 465–466
  deleting, 241, 472–474
  displaying multiple, 442, 444–447
  inserting, 398–404
  limiting retrieval by SELECT statement, 424–426
  locating programmatically, 452–453
  modifying, 464–465
  removing, 410–411
  retrieving, 413–429
  searching for, 243–247
  sorting, 426–427
  storing another field in property, 446
  updating, 237–241, 404–410
  validating data, 467–472
Recordset object, 414, 422, 444
  BOF property, 223
  calling methods of, 393–394
  current record pointer, 223
  Delete method, 241
  Edit method, 237
  EOF property, 223
  Fields collection, 416–417
  FindFirst method, 243
  first record, 224
  instance, 388, 471
  last record, 224
  MoveNext method, 230
  navigating methods, 225
  next record, 224
  NoMatch property, 223
  previous record, 224
  programming, 387–394
  properties and methods, 224
  referencing fields, 390–393
  Requery method, 237–238
  Update method, 237–238
Recordset variable, 470
recordsets
  copying data to unbound text box, 390
  field properties, 417
  numeric fields, 417
  open, 387
  opening, 415
  printing each record, 420–423
  refreshing, 479
  saving data to current record, 392–393

sorting records, 426–427
testing for fields displayed under correct titles, 423
text fields, 417
writing code to, 388
Recordsets collection, 387, 414
RecordsetType property, 221
RecordSource property, 220, 446, 459–460, 479
ReDim statement, 565, 582–584
redimensioning arrays, 565
References command, 380
References dialog box, 380–381
rreferential integrity, A-37–A-38
Refresh method, 283, 459–460, 479
relational database management system, 207
relational databases, 220, A-35
relationships, A-35–A-38
referential integrity, A-37–A-38
Relationships dialog, A-36–A-37
Relationships window, A-35–A-36
REM statements, 80
Remove method, 498, 623, 627–628
RemoveItem method, 316, 342–344, 629
removing panels, 500
removing records databases, 410–411
repetition statements, 276–283
accumulator, 278
counters, 277
For statement, 279–283
reports
characteristics, 291–292
designing, 287
forcing new page, 302–303
formatting page and column titles, 292–297
page width, 292
printing, 288–292
text width, 292
titles, 290–292
repositioning windows, 8
Requery method, 237–238, 240
Required property, A-32
reserved words, 92
Resize event, 528
resizing
columns, 458
controls at run time, 528
forms, 528–538

objects, 36–37
rows, 458
windows, 8
ResolutionCode property, 718
resource files, A-21
Resume Next statement, 252
Retrieve Fields command, 453
retrieving record from databases, 413–429
Revision properties, 669
rftText object, 531
RichTextBox control, 498, 515–517, 519, 521, 529
color, 540
creating instance, 516–517
formatting, 528–538
instance, 521
printing RTF file, 520
properties, 515–516
unsaved instances, 524
Richtxt32.ocx file, 498
Right.bmp file, 508
RightMargin property, 516, 538
Rnd function, 666–667
Row property, 448
RowDividerStyle property, 448
rows, resizing, 458
RowSource property, 444, 446
RTF (Rich Text Format) files, 515
new, 526–527
opening, 521–528
printing, 519–521
saving, 521–528
rtfCenter constant, 537
rtfLeft constant, 537
rtfRight constant, 537
rtfText_Change event procedure, 523
Run command, 675
Run menu, 13
run mode, 11–12
run-time errors, 251–252, 642–646, A-2
displaying message and continuing program, 253–254
error handlers, A-5
error numbers, A-5
fixing, 104–105
locating and fixing, A-4–A-6
numeric overflow, 104
Options dialog, A-3
type mismatch error, 104

S

Save Airplane As command, 618
Save As dialog, 476
Save command, 525
Save File As dialog, 29–30, 618
Save Project As dialog, 30
Save Project command, 29
SaveCurrentRecord private general procedure, 392
SaveFile method, 516, 521
SaveFile Private Sub procedure, 523
SaveFile procedure, 525
saving
default module names, 29
files, 22–23, 474
programs frequently, 5
projects, 29–32
queries, A-40
RTF (Rich Text Format) files, 521–528
tables, A-34–A-35
ScaleMode property, 289
scaling, 290
scope, 89
screen fonts, 483–486
Screen object
properties, 483
scroll bars
adding to form, 172–174
Change event, 184
Max property, 184
Min property, 184
regions, 172
Value property, 182–183
Visible property, 179–182
Scroll Lock key, 496
ScrollBar control, 172–174
ScrollBars property, 516–517
Search command, 18
searching for records, 243–247
Second function, 143
seed, 666–667
SelAlignment method, 538
SelAlignment property, 516, 537
SelBold property, 516, 528
SelChange event, 516, 529
SelChange event procedure, 531–532
SelColor property, 540

Select Case statement, 129–132, 191, 469, 538, 575, 578, 644
Select picture dialog, 502, 507
select query, 398–399, 413
Select Query window, A-39
Select Records command button, 423, 425
Select Records Form command, 379, 420, 423, 425, 427, 429
SELECT statement, 413–429, 459–560, 469–470
    FROM clause, 414–415
    LIKE clause, 709
    limiting records retrieved by, 424–426
    ORDER BY clause, 426–427, 460
    order entry system, 709
    selecting fields from table or query, 427–429
    WHERE clause, 424–426, 460
SelFontName property, 516
SelFontSize property, 516
SelItalic property, 516, 529
SelPrint method, 516, 519
SelStrikethru property, 529
SelUnderline property, 516, 529
Send to Back command, 76
separator bars for submenus, 213–216
sequential access, 319
sessions, 381
Set Next Statement command, A-7
Set statement, 231, 415, 561–562, 622
SetEditState private general procedure, 389
SetFocus method, 73, 102–103
Settings form, 372
SETUP.EXE file, 689
SETUP1.EXE file, 689
SetVisible general procedure, 481
Shape control
    BackColor property, 75
    BackStyle property, 75
    BorderColor property, 75–76
    BorderStyle property, 75
    BorderWidth property, 75
    cash register program, 166
    FillColor property, 75–76
    FillStyle property, 75–76
    positioning, 170
Shape property, 76
    Visible property, 76
Shared Files dialog, 693–694
Shell function, 66, 672–673

shortcut keys, 209, 213–216
Shortcut list box, 213
Show method, 272–273, 275, 557, 559, 584
Show Table dialog, A-35–A-36, A-39
Show Window List command, 587
ShowColor method, 478
ShowFont method, 478, 484, 486
ShowHelp method, 478
ShowOpen method, 477–479, 525
ShowPrinter method, 478
ShowSave method, 478, 525
ShowTips property, 509
SimpleText property, 498
Single data type, 88
Size property, 484
Slider control, 497
Slight.mdb file, 440, 483, 486
SmallChange property, 172
Sorted property, 315
sorting records, 426–427
Source property, 253
SPG (Southern Properties Group), 1
SPG_C.vbp file, 11
SPG_S.exe file, 48
SPG_S.vbp file, 30–31
splash screen, 7, 269–270
    animated, 266
    Timer control, 375
Splash Screen template, A-27
Split property, 456
sptrSQL variable, 415
SQL (Structured Query Language)
    DDL (Data Definition Language) statements, 397
    DML (Data Manipulation Language) statements, 397
    embedded spaces, 401
    extensions, 397
    inserting database records, 398–404
    keywords, 401
    naming conventions, 398
    String variable, 401
    updating database records, 404–410
    writing statements, 397
ST6UNST.EXT file, 689
standard dialogs, 474, 475
standard forms, 552–553
standard forms module, 4
standard module, 4, 14
standard modules storing data, 563
standard toolbar, 9

Starlight Events program
    adding new event registration, 471–472
    completed form, 440
    confirming deletion, 473
    displaying multiple records, 444–447
    selecting event registrations for current event, 460
    testing deletion code, 473–474
    testing Lookup command button, 461
    testing Member ID validation statements, 471–472
Start Batch Machine command, 585, 587
Start button, 6
Start Menu Group Properties dialog, 692
Start Menu Items dialog, 686, 691–692
StartBatchMachine general procedure, 589, 599
StartBatchMachine Public Sub procedure, 583
StartTime property, 717
Startup folder, 10
    saving files to, 29–30
startup form, 12, 266
startup object, 270–271
statements, 2
    breaking into multiple lines, 97
    copying and pasting, 87
    examining, A-6–A-7
    indenting, 125
    repeatedly executing, 276–278
    whitespace between, 92
Static keyword, 232, 633
Static statement, 233, 561
static variables, 232–233
status bar
    creation of, 501–502
    current time, 502
    manipulating contexts at startup, 503
    panel, 498
    panels, 499
    Properties window, 501
    text panel, 502
StatusBar control, 497–503
    automatically updating panels, 502
    properties, 498
Step increment clause, 279
Step Into button, A-7–A-8
Step Out button, A-7
Step Over button, A-8
Stop (Ctrl+Break) key combination, A-14

stopping programs, 46
StrConv function, 137–138
string data, 134–140
String data type, 88
    type conversion function, 95
string key, 382
    case-sensitivity, 507
String variable, 401, 408, 470
    storing SELECT statement, 414–415
String Variant data type, 349–350
strings, 88, 134, 245
    concatenating, 135, 402
    continuation lines, 401–402
    converting, 95
    converting ASCII character to
        numeric value, 139–140
    converting numeric value to, 96
    converting to upper-or lower case,
        137–138
    embedding Tab character, 137
    empty, 137
    extracting characters from, 138–139
    finding pattern in, 138–139
    having specific characteristics, 122
    intrinsic constants, 137
    intrinsic functions, 136–140
    length of, 136–137
    multiple assignment statements, 402
    operating on individual characters,
        139–140
    proper case, 138
    two-line character, 137
structure charts, 62
structured walkthroughs, 62
Style property, 315–316, 445, 498–499,
    501–502, 510–511, 513–514
Sub Main procedure, 708
sub methods, 649–652
Sub procedure, 420
Sub procedures, 148, 150, 153–156
    Call statement, 152
    creation, 149–151, 154–155
    Exit Sub statement, 153
    explicitly calling Call statements, 154
    Private keyword, 153
    Public keyword, 153
submenus
    menu items, 214
    separator bars, 213–216
    shortcut keys, 213–216
subscripts, 326
subtraction (-) operator, 93
summary array, 717

SummaryAverageDuration property, 718
SummaryCallBack property, 718
SummaryCallCount property, 718
SummaryCallType property, 718
SummaryProblemSolved property, 718
SummaryReferToSupervisor
    property, 718
syntax, 2
syntax errors, 103, A-1
    fixing, 104
    Options dialog, A-3–A-4

T

Tab Behavior command, 452
Tab to New Control command, 452
Tab to Next Cell in Grid command, 452
Tab to Next Column command, 452
TabAction property, 448, 451–452
TabIndex Property, 107
tables, 219
    adding to queries, 415
    creation, A-31–A-34
    displaying multiple records, 442
    fields, 219, A-31–A-33
    one-to-many relationship, A-36
    reading and writing data, 442
    records, 219
    relationships, A-35–A-38
    retrieving records from, 413
    saving, A-34–A-35
    selecting fields from, 427–429
    viewing, 222
TabStrip control, 497
Tag property, 566–567, 592
tblContact table, A-34
tblCustomers table, 706
tblEvents table, 438, 445
tblInventory table, 706–707
tblOrderDetail table, 706–707, 712
tblOrderMaster table, 706–707, 711
tblPayroll table, 400–401
tblPeople table, 438, 466, 470
tblRegistration table, 438, 449
tblSales table, A-35
tbrButtonGroup constant, 511
tbrCheck constant, 511
tbrDefault constant, 511
tbrDropdown constant, 511
tbrPlaceholder constant, 511
tbrPressed constant, 511
tbrSeparator constant, 511

tbrUnpressed constant, 511
Technical Support command, 18
templates, 25, 268, A-18, A-26–A-27
Terminate event, 655–656
terminating class instances, 655–657
terse programs, 188
text
    justifying, 538
    RTF (Rich Text Format), 515–517
text boxes, 4, 38
    changing color with focus, 83–87
    changing font, 81
    receiving focus, 81
text boxes, loading current record into,
    391–392
text fields, 417, A-32
text files
    closing, 324–325
    opening, 319–320
    processing, 319–326
    reading, 320–323
    sequential access, 319
    writing to, 352–356
text panel status bar, 502
Text property, 316, 444, 499,
    502–503, 517
TextBox class, 153, 568
TextBox control, 4, 38, 72–73, 146, 568
    Alignment property, 73
    Appearance property, 73
    BackColor property, 73
    BorderStyle property, 73
    events, 81–83
    Font property, 73
    ForeColor property, 73
    Height property, 38
    Left property, 38
    MultiLine property, 73
    Name property, 38, 73
    resources, 146
    ScrollBars property, 73
    setting properties, 226–228
    Tabindex property, 73
    Text property, 38, 73, 225
    Top property, 38
    Width property, 38
textboxes, 72–73
TextWidth method, 289, 292, 299
third-party add in controls, 32
time, 140–141
Time function, 140
Timer control, 273–274, 375
Tip of the Day template, 403

title bar
    Close button, 22
    operating modes, 11–13
Title property, 670
tlbRegistration table, 447
Toggle Breakpoint (F9) function key, A-9
toolbar, 8
    Add Standard EXE Project button, 9
    creation, A-20–A-21
    customizing, 9
    displaying/hiding, 9
    End button, 13, 46–47
    Menu Editor button, 209
    Object Browser button, 83
    Open Project button, 11
    Project Explorer button, 14, 268
    Properties Window button, 16, 68
    Save Project button, 32, 47
    Start button, 12, 46–47, 61
    ToolTips, 8
Toolbar control, 497, 503–504, 508–515
    properties, 508–509, 512
toolbars, 503–504, 508–515
    adding buttons, 511–513
    behavior of buttons, 511
    bold, italic, and underline formatting
      buttons, 513–514
    button as toggle switch, 504
    buttons, 510
    buttons and commands, 503
    buttons to justify text, 514
    default button behavior, 504
    deleting buttons, 512
    events and buttons, 503–504
    group of buttons, 504
    programming, 538–540
    setting general properties, 509–510
    submenus, 504
    updating buttons, 530–533
toolbox, 17
    CheckBox control, 170
    ComboBox control, 316
    CommandButton control, 39
    Data control, 221
    Frame control, 175
    Image control, 41
    Label control, 33
    ListBox control, 317
    OptionButton control, 176

TextBox control, 38
Timer control, 274
ToolTips, 17
VScrollBar control, 173
Tools menu, 13
ToolTips, 8–9, 17, 37
ToolTipText property, 510, 513–514
Top property, 31
Topics Found dialog, 19
Totals form, 602
tracing program execution, A-7–A-9
traditional file-processing system,
    A-28–A-29
TreeView control, 497
True keyword, 120–121
twips, 31
two-dimensional array, 344–349
    declaring, 345
    referencing, 345–346
two-way decision, 125
txtInitialValue text box, 81
txtInitialValue-GotFocus, 84
txtInterestRate object, 102
txtSQL Output text box, 420
type conversion functions, 95–96
Type keyword, 590
type library, 616
type mismatch errors, 104, A-5–A-6
Type statement, 590–591
TypeOf keyword, 480

U

UBound function, 582–585
UI (User Interface), 458
unbound text boxes, 390
Underline property, 484
UnderlineStatus Private Sub
    procedure, 530
Underln.bmp file, 508
underscore character (_), 97
UNIX operating system, 2
Unload event, 192, 596, 602, 604
Unload statement, 47, 273, 588, 601
unloading forms, 272–273
unloading MDI child form, 588–589
Until keyword, 277
Update method, 237–239, 241, 248, 250

Update Record command, 378, 394
UPDATE statement
    action query, 406
    computing gross pay, 408
    computing taxes withheld and net
      pay, 409
    expressions, 405
    verifying proper field update, 415
    verifying update, 408
    WHERE clause, 407
Update statement, 252–255
updating
    menu items, 530–533
    records databases, 404–410
updating records, 237–241
user input
    checking correctness, 95
    validating, 118–119
user interface, 2–23
    clarity, 63
    consistency, 63
    controlling program, 63
    controls, 167
    designing, 16, 63–65
    feedback, 63
    forms, 17
    graphical controls, 75–77
    graphics, 64
    input, 64
    intuitiveness, 63
    programs, 3
    user-friendliness, 63
user interface statements, 5
user-defined constants, 83, 185–188
user-defined data types
    customer service program, 717
    declaring variables, 592
    members, 590
    nesting, 593–597
    representing machine state, 591
    restrictions, 590
    sand and gravel grand totals,
      593–594
    With statement, 596–597

V

Val function, 95, 97, 193
Validate event, 247–251, 467
validating data, 467-472
validating user input, 120
ValidDate function, 149
ValidNumber function, 152
Value property, 169, 172, 176, 510
variables, 87–95
    Boolean data type, 120
    data types, 87–88
    declaring, 89–91
    declaring user-defined type, 592
    Dim statement, 89–91
    Dirty state, 591–592
    examining values, A-9–A-10
    explicitly declaring, 90
    global, 89
    grouping, 589–590
    hidden, 562–564
    implicit declaration, 90
    incorrectly spelled, 91
    manipulating, 92–95
    meaningful names, 619
    module-level, 89, 91–92
    names, 87–89
    Private keyword, 284
    Private statement, 89–91
    procedure-level, 89
    public, 283–285
    Public keyword, 284
    Public statement, 89–91
    scope, 89
    storing batch machine state, 591
    storing values, 420
    String data type, 134
    user-defined type, 591
variant arrays, 349–352
    customer satisfaction program, 375
    loading file names, 350–351
Variant data type, 349–350, 560, 681
vbArrangeIcons constant, 586
vbBlack constant, 85
vbBlue constant, 84
vbCascade constant, 586
vbChecked constant, 169, 570
vbCritical constant, 146
vbCrLf string, 137
vbDataActionCancel constant, 248, 250
vbDefaultButton1 constant, 146

VbDefaultButton2 constant, 146
vbDefaultButton3 constant, 146
vbDefaultButton4 constant, 146
vbExclamation constant, 146
vbGrayed constant, 169, 570
vbInformation constant, 146
vbLowerCase constant, 137
vbMaximized constant, 556
vbMinimized constant, 556
vbModal intrinsic constant, 272
vbMsgBoxStyle class, 145
vbNormal constant, 556
vbNormalFocus constant, 673
vbNullString constant, 102, 380
vbNullString string, 137
.vbp file extension, 29
vbProperCase constant, 137
vbQuestion constant, 146
vbTab string, 137
vbTileHorizontal constant, 586
vbTileVertical constant, 586
vbUnchecked constant, 169, 570
vbUpperCase constant, 137
vbYesNo constant, 146
verbose programs, 188
vertical and horizontal, 171
vertical scroll bars, 171, 173
Vertical Spacing command, 72
View Code command, 42
visible objects, 486
Visible property, 121, 456, 480, 482, 510
Visual Basic, 3
    components installed, 6
    displaying version, 18
    environments, 13–17
    executing other programs form,
      672–673
    exiting, 22
    IDE (integrated development
      environment), 3
    logic structure, 3–5
    starting, 6–8
    user interface, 2–23, 3
    visual designer window, 15
    Visual Studio, 20
Visual Basic Programming seminar
    Intermediate event, 469
Visual Basic programming Seminar-
    Beginning event, 440, 471
vsbBurger_Change event procedure,
    184, 187

vsbFrenchFries_Change event
    procedure, 184
vsbSoftDrink_Change event
    procedure, 184
VScrollBar control, 173
    LargeChange property, 172
    Max property, 171, 173
    Min property, 171, 173
    Name property, 173
    SmallChange property, 172
    Value property, 172

W

Warning Message icon, 146
Warning Query icon, 146
watch expressions
    adding, A-11–A-14
    setting, A-13
    testing, A-14
Watches window, A-12
Web Browser template, A-26
Web modules, 14
well-written comments, 80–81
WHERE clause, 424–426, 460
    expressions, 407
    selecting specific date paid, 424
While keyword, 277
whitespace, 92
Width property, 31, 456, 458, 499, 509,
    511, 554
WindowList property, 586
windows, 3
    appearance on-screen MDI parent
      docking, 13
    manipulating, 14
    repositioning, 8
    resizing, 8
Windows common controls, 497–498
    ImageList control, 504–508
    printing RTF file, 519–521
    RichTextBox control, 515–517
    StatusBar control, 498–503
    Toolbar control, 503–504, 508–515
Windows Help program, 474
Windowsfolder, 439, 443
WindowState property, 556
Winntfolder, 439, 443

With statement, 485–486
    user-defined data types, 596–597
wizards, 25, 393
    project creation, 25
Workspace object, 384, 471, 622
Workspaces collection, 383, 471
    Default Workspace object, 386
    Item method, 384
    relationship with DBEngine
        object, 381
Write # statement, 352–353
WriteAirplane Public Sub procedure, 657
write-once property, 648–649
writing to text files, 352–356

X

Xor logical operator, 133

Y

Year function, 143
Yes/No fields, A-32

Z

zero-based collections, 382